Bioinformatics

Chapman & Hall/CRC
Computational Biology Series

About the Series:

This series aims to capture new developments in computational biology, as well as high-quality work summarizing or contributing to more established topics. Publishing a broad range of reference works, textbooks, and handbooks, the series is designed to appeal to students, researchers, and professionals in all areas of computational biology, including genomics, proteomics, and cancer computational biology, as well as interdisciplinary researchers involved in associated fields, such as bioinformatics and systems biology.

Metabolomics: Practical Guide to Design and Analysis

Ron Wehrens, Reza Salek

An Introduction to Systems Biology: Design Principles of Biological Circuits

2nd Edition

Uri Alon

Computational Biology: A Statistical Mechanics Perspective

Second Edition

Ralf Blossey

Stochastic Modelling for Systems Biology

Third Edition

Darren J. Wilkinson

Computational Genomics with R

Altuna Akalin, Bora Uyar, Vedran Franke, Jonathan Ronen

An Introduction to Computational Systems Biology: Systems-level Modelling of Cellular Networks

Karthik Raman

Virus Bioinformatics

Dmitrij Frishman, Manuela Marz

Multivariate Data Integration Using R: Methods and Applications with the mixOmics Package

Kim-Anh LeCao, Zoe Marie Welham

Bioinformatics: A Practical Guide to NCBI Databases and Sequence Alignments

Hamid D. Ismail

For more information about this series please visit:
https://www.routledge.com/Chapman–HallCRC-Computational-Biology-Series/book-series/CRCCBS

Bioinformatics

A Practical Guide to NCBI Databases and Sequence Alignments

Hamid D. Ismail

CRC Press
Taylor & Francis Group
Boca Raton London New York

CRC Press is an imprint of the
Taylor & Francis Group, an **informa** business

First edition published 2022
by CRC Press
6000 Broken Sound Parkway NW, Suite 300, Boca Raton, FL 33487-2742

and by CRC Press
2 Park Square, Milton Park, Abingdon, Oxon, OX14 4RN

CRC Press is an imprint of Taylor & Francis Group, LLC

Library of Congress Cataloging-in-Publication Data
Names: Hamid, Ismail D., author. | National Center for Biotechnology Information (U.S.)
Title: Bioinformatics : a practical guide to NCBI databases and sequence alignments / Ismail D. Hamid.
Description: First edition. | Boca Raton : CRC Press, 2022. |
Series: Chapman & Hall/CRC computational biology series |
Includes bibliographical references and index.
Identifiers: LCCN 2021036517 | ISBN 9781032123691 (hardback) |
ISBN 9781032128740 (paperback) | ISBN 9781003226611 (ebook)
Subjects: LCSH: Bioinformatics.
Classification: LCC QH324.2 .H35 2022 | DDC 570.285–dc23
LC record available at https://lccn.loc.gov/2021036517

ISBN: 978-1-032-12369-1 (hbk)
ISBN: 978-1-032-12874-0 (pbk)
ISBN: 978-1-003-22661-1 (ebk)

DOI: 10.1201/9781003226611

Typeset in Minion
by Newgen Publishing UK

Access the companion website: http://hamiddi.com/

Contents

Preface, vii

Acknowledgments, ix

Author bio, xi

CHAPTER 1 ▪ The Origin of Genomic Information   1

CHAPTER 2 ▪ The Sources of Genomic Data   39

CHAPTER 3 ▪ The NCBI Entrez Databases   77

CHAPTER 4 ▪ NCBI Entrez E-Utilities and Applications   265

CHAPTER 5 ▪ The Entrez Direct   289

CHAPTER 6 ▪ R and Python Packages for the NCBI E-Utilities   343

CHAPTER 7 ▪ Pairwise Sequence Alignment   383

CHAPTER 8 ▪ Basic Local Alignment Search Tool   407

INDEX, 453

Preface

IT HAS BEEN A WHILE SINCE I BEGAN THINKING OF writing a bioinformatics book that introduces both theory and practice. I have been practicing bioinformatics for a decade and, during this time, I read tens of bioinformatics books of quality writing and contents. However, me as a reader, as many of my colleagues and students, were striving to find a comprehensive and self-contained book that adds both theory and application. The bioinformatics is a field of applied science where both theory and practice shall coexist side by side and therefore an ideal bioinformatics book should provide a good introduction and be clearly written with informative illustrations and provide sufficient depth and breadth to serve as a valuable reference for students and researchers. Thus, from the beginning I set a very clear goal to write a book that blends both components so it can serve as a quick reference for biologists.

The National Center for Biotechnology Information (NCBI) is a resource for molecular biology information worldwide. It sets its mission to develop new information technologies to aid in the understanding of fundamental molecular and genetic processes that control health and diseases. To achieve this mission, the NCBI has developed a variety of automated systems for storing and analyzing knowledge about molecular biology, biochemistry, and genetics. Thus, the NCBI's databases are the most comprehensive resources of biological data; they integrate the most major databases worldwide; and they are the most commonly used biological databases by biologists from around the globe.

Biological databases play a key role in the bioinformatics that modern biology relies on. They offer scientists the opportunity to access a wide variety of experimentally driven biological data and relevant information that can be used in genomic research and knowledge discovery in a wide range of applications in bioscience and biomedicine.

This book provides the basics of bioinformatics and in-depth coverage of NCBI databases, sequence alignment, and NCBI Sequence Local Alignment Search Tool (BLAST). As bioinformatics has become essential for life sciences, the book has been written specifically to address the need of a large audience, including undergraduates, graduates, researchers, healthcare professionals, and bioinformatics professors who need to use the NCBI databases, retrieve data from them, and use BLAST for finding evolutionarily related sequences, sequence annotation, construction of phylogenetic tree, finding conservative domain of a protein, just to name a few. Technical details of alignment algorithms are explained with a minimum use of mathematical formulas and with graphical illustrations. The uniqueness of this book is that it provides readers with the most used bioinformatics knowledge of bioinformatics databases and alignments, including both theory and application, via illustrations and worked examples. The book also discusses the use of Windows Command Prompt, Linux shell, R, and Python for both Entrez databases and BLAST.

The most important aspects of bioinformatics included in this book, and in-depth and up-to-date coverage of the NCBI databases and BLAST, make this book an ideal textbook for all bioinformatics courses taken by students of life sciences and for researchers wishing to develop their knowledge of bioinformatics to facilitate their own research. The chapters are organized to be progressive from basic to more complex but they are also linked and self-contained so that readers will find all the information they need to understand the content.

Chapter 1 discusses the basics of bioinformatics including eukaryote, prokaryote, and virus genome, composition and structures of DNA, RNA, genes, and protein, and the processes that are involved in biomolecule formation and structure, such as transcription, translation, and mutations. The purpose of this introductory chapter is to serve as a foundation for bioinformatics in general, but it also aims to provides the readers with the knowledge to understand the origin of the genomic data that are the major elements of the biological databases.

Chapter 2 continues setting the fundamental background knowledge for understanding the generation of genomic data from biological samples and the file formats used in bioinformatics and to store the sequence data on the genomics databases. It discusses the laboratory techniques that generate the experimentally driven genomic data, which are the very basic elements of genomics and genomics databases. The techniques discussed include polymerase chain reaction (PCR), first generation sequencing, next generation sequencing, and the file formats, including FASTA, FASTQ, SAM/BAM, VCF, and AGP.

Chapter 3 covers the NCBI's Entrez databases in detail. The discussion includes the use of the database, database indexed fields, construction of search queries, results pages, the content of record pages, and linked tools. This chapter aims to be practical, and readers can practice while reading to get the full benefit. The use of each database is illustrated with screenshots of the results pages and individual record pages accompanied with discussion of the content. This chapter also serves as introductory to Chapters 4, 5, and 6.

Chapter 4 also discusses the Entrez programming utilities (E-utils), which are programming application interfaces (APIs) to the NCBI Entrez databases and enables accessing the databases from computer programming languages. This chapters aims to provide readers with the basic programs of the E-utilities so programmers can use them and regular users will understand the concept for the applications from other programs.

Chapter 5 covers the Entrez Direct (EDirect), which is a set of command-line programs wrapping around the E-utils functions. The readers will learn how to install and use EDirect on Windows Linux and Mac OS environments. The chapter also discusses how to use Linux bash shell command and scripting language to extend the use of EDirect function for data retrieval and extraction.

Chapter 6 discusses the use of R packages (R Entrez) and Python (BioPython) for searching and retrieving data from the NCBI databases. Both R and Python are free and open-source and the most used programming scripting languages in the classroom and life science. Accessing Entrez databases from inside these two programming environments will help in developing desktop and web applications or in the advanced research works that require integration of different resources.

Chapter 7 discusses the basics and algorithms of the global and local alignments. It walks the reader through the steps of the dynamic programming for the sequence alignment. It also illustrates the algorithms of the regular BLAST and PSI-BLAST and demonstrates the steps of computing the position-specific scoring matrix (PSSM), which is used for motif discovery and detection of conserved regions in protein sequences. The aim of this chapter is to provide readers with the background knowledge on sequence scoring schemes, substitution matrices, and the sequence alignment algorithms.

Chapter 8 covers the uses of BLAST programs. In the first part, the chapter discusses the uses of web-based BLAST with worked examples of the most frequent scenarios, such as finding related sequences, construction of phylogenetic tree, finding conserved domain and structure in proteins, and sequence annotation. The second part of this chapter focuses on the stand-alone BLAST, which is essential for users who run searches exceeding the NCBI allowed limit. The chapter illustrates how to install and use the stand-alone BLAST and how to create a custom BLAST database.

Acknowledgments

I WOULD LIKE TO THANK DR AMANI BABEKIR FOR HER help in reviewing the chapter of this book several times and providing useful comments that add to the quality of the content. I would like also to thank Amna Ismail who helped me in drawing the figures of this books and designing the cover image. My thanks also extend to both Dr Cory Brouwer and Dr Roshonda Jones for reviewing the book proposal and their encouraging feedback.

Author bio

Hamid D. Ismail earned his Ph.D. and M.Sc. in computational science from North Carolina Agricultural and Technical State University, USA, and Doctor of Veterinary Medicine (DVM) and Applied Diploma in Statistics and Programming from the University of Khartoum, Sudan. He has worked as an adjunct professor, bioinformatics specialist, bioinformatics tool developer, senior scientist, statistician, and database consultant with several institutions. He is currently a Ph.D. Research Associate at North Carolina Agricultural and Technical State University. Dr. Ismail is a published author in bioinformatics, statistics, machine learning, and bio-science, and he has developed a number of bioinformatics desktop and web-based applications. He is also a reviewer for a number of academic journals.

## CHAPTER 1

The Origin of Genomic Information

INTRODUCTION

The diversity of life, from a simple organism like bacteria to the largest animals, and the diversity of individuals within a species, are guided by biomolecules inside the living cells called deoxyribonucleic acid (DNA). The DNA molecule is formed of only four basic monomeric units known as DNA nucleotides composing of a phosphate group, a sugar, and four different types of nucleobases or simply bases (adenine, cytosine, guanine, and thymine). In bioinformatics, those four units are given the letters: A, C, G, and T respectively. The DNA molecules in a living cell are represented as sequences of those four nucleotides forming the genome. Viruses usually have small genomes; *Bacteriophage spp* has a median total length of 8689 bases (8.689 kb). The smallest non-viral genome is that of a bacterium known as *Carsonella ruddii*, which has a genome of 164,376 bases (164.376 kb). The total length of the human genome is 3,272,090,000 bases (3,272.09 Mb). Segments of DNA known as genes control the different aspects of life of a living organism by instructing the cells to synthesize the proteins, which do most of the work in cells and are required for the structure, function, and regulation of the body tissues and organs. The instructions are transcribed into ribonucleic acid (RNA), which is translated into a specific protein. The two-step process (transcription and translation) by which the information in gene flows into proteins is known as the central dogma of molecular biology. The information in the DNA is also transmitted from one generation to another. The new generation of a living organism inherits characteristics due to DNA transmission from parents. The diversity in life is attributed to the ability of the DNA to change slowly in search of better traits to adapt with changes in nature. Such changes or mutations contribute to the diversity in life. Advancement in molecular biology and biotechnology made possible the capturing of the information carried by DNA, RNA, and proteins. Sequences and other biological information from diverse species and individuals within the species of organisms are now increasingly deposited by researchers and institutions onto bioinformatics databases to be available for retrieval and analysis for research purposes. The genomic information has revolutionized biology and made modern biologists dependent on bioinformatics, which uses computer science to store, organize, search, manipulate, and retrieve the genomic information. Institutions like the National Institute of Health (NIH), the European Molecular Biology Laboratory (EMBL), and the Japanese Institute of Genetics contributed largely to the progress made in bioinformatics. Together, those three institutes formed the International Nucleotide Sequence Database Collaboration (INSDC) [1], which is a joint effort to collect and disseminate databases containing DNA and RNA, and protein sequences. The INSDC includes GenBank (USA), the European Nucleotide Archive (UK), and DNA Data Bank of Japan (Japan). Those three partners capture, preserve, share, and exchange a comprehensive collection of nucleotide sequences and associated information on a daily basis. The INSDC policy allows public access to the global archives of nucleotide data generated in publicly funded experiments. The submission of this genomic data is instrumented by the fact that it is a pre-requisite for publication in scholarly journals. The database records are publicly available for scientists from all over the world to access, analyze, draw conclusion, and publish their findings.

DOI: 10.1201/9781003226611-1

Before digging deep, it is important to discuss some basics in genomics that will help readers to understand bioinformatics. The foundation of bioinformatics is built on the data that represents the flow of genomic information from the DNA, onto RNA, and proteins. Therefore, understanding the composition of these three kinds of biomolecules, gene structure, gene transcription and expression, mutation, and techniques used to obtain such genomic data is fundamental for understanding the biological databases and other bioinformatics applications.

GENETIC INFORMATION AND ITS TRANSMISSION

In the traditional Linnaean system of classification, living organisms are classified on the basis of cellular organization and methods of nutrition into five kingdoms: Monera (bacteria), Protista (protozoans and algae), Fungi (funguses), Plantae (plants), and Animalia (animals). A modern taxonomic classification has been made to extend the Linnaean system to consider genomic characteristics. Nowadays, biologists recognize only two vastly different cell types, prokaryote and eukaryote, based on the absence or presence of a membrane-bound nucleus containing the genetic material of the cell. Therefore, a living organism is either prokaryotic or eukaryotic [2, 3]. The prokaryote includes unicellular organisms that do not have a true nucleolus or membrane-bound organelles (Figure 1.1a). Prokaryote includes bacteria, which is the most abundant organism, and archaea, which are inhabitants of the most extreme environments on the planet, such as high temperature, alkaline, or acid waters. The eukaryote comprises all other living organisms (animals, plants, and fungi) whose cells possess clearly defined nucleus and organelles (Figure 1.1b).

The genetic information of any organism is carried by DNA, which is the hereditary material in living organisms. Nearly every cell of an organism has the same DNA molecules. Nuclear DNA molecules are known as chromosomes [4]. The most prokaryotic cells may possess a single circular chromosome, two circular chromosomes, one circular and one linear, or one linear chromosome free-floating in the cell cytoplasm. Circular chromosomes have no free ends. Some bacteria have small DNA molecules outside the chromatin body known as plasmids, which are independent from the chromosomal DNA. In eukaryotic cells, the DNA molecules or chromosomes are found inside a defined nucleus. Each somatic cell has the same number of chromosomes. In animal cells, a small amount of DNA is also found in the mitochondria (mitochondrial DNA or mtDNA). In plant cells, a small amount of DNA is found in the chloroplasts. Generally, each organism has a specific number of chromosomes (Table 1.1). The set of all DNA molecules in a single somatic cell of an organism (including mitochondrial DNA in animals and chloroplast DNA in plants and plasmids in bacteria) is called genome. The prokaryotic genome is haploid, which is formed of a single set of unpaired chromosomes (Figure 1.2a) while the chromosomes of eukaryotic cells are linear and diploid, which exist in pairs (Figure 1.2b); each one of the parents (father and mother) contributes one chromosome to each pair so that offspring will get half of their chromosomes from their mother and half from their father.

In complex eukaryotes, each organism has specific numbers of chromosomes, of which one pair is the sex chromosome (X and Y) and the remaining are non-sex chromosomes known as autosomes. For example,

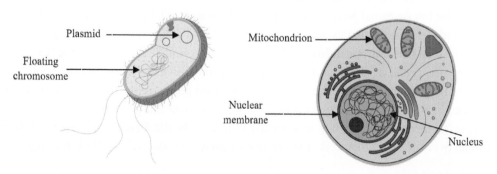

FIGURE 1.1 (a) Bacterial (prokaryotic) cell and (b) eukaryotic cell.

TABLE 1.1   Number of Chromosomes in the Somatic Cells of Some Organisms

Organism	Number of Chromosome Pairs
Human	23
Chimpanzee	24
Cow	30
Sheep	27
Goat	30
Horse	32
Dog	39
Cat	19
Rice	12
Bean	11
Tobacco	24

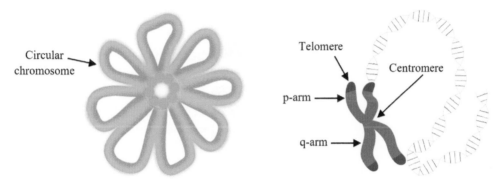

FIGURE 1.2   (a) A bacterial chromosome (b) eukaryotic chromosome.

a human somatic cell has 23 pairs of chromosomes, of which 22 pairs are autosomes, and one pair is the sex chromosome (X and Y). Each eukaryotic chromosome is made up of DNA tightly coiled many times around histones and it has a constriction point called the centromere, which divides the chromosome into two sections called arms. By convention, the shorter arm of the chromosome is known as the p-arm and the longer arm of the chromosome is known as the q-arm. The location of the centromere on each chromosome gives the chromosome its characteristic shape and can be used to describe the location of specific genes. The ends of chromosomes are protected by telomeres.

The DNA molecules in chromosomes wrap around complexes of histone proteins giving the chromosomes compact compressed shapes so that the DNA molecules can fit in the nucleus. Without such packaging, DNA molecules would be too long to fit inside cells.

There are different imaging techniques that can be used in studying the structure of chromosomes [5]. These techniques include light microscopy, fluorescence microscopy, electron microscopy, and coherent X-ray diffraction imaging. Staining is usually used to enhance the contrast between cellular components allowing the proper visualization of chromosomes with different imaging techniques. Differential staining along the length of a chromosome leads to the production of clearly visible bands (cytogenetic bands), which provide information about the chromosomes. Each chromosome has its own unique pattern bands. Therefore, they can be used to identify individual chromosomes, in cytogenetic location of a gene, and to study abnormalities in the chromosome due to deletions, insertions, or translocations.

The cytogenetic location consists of a chromosome number (in the human 1-23, X or Y), the arm of the chromosome (p or q), and the position of the gene on the p or q arm. The position is usually designated by two digits representing a region and a band. The two-digit region is sometimes followed by a decimal point and one or more additional digits representing sub bands within a light or dark area. For example, the cytogenetic location of BRCA1 gene in the human somatic cell is (17q21.31), which represents the address of BRCA1 gene

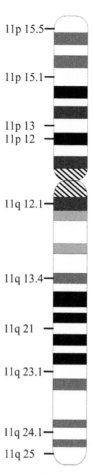

11p 15.5
11p 15.1
11p 13
11p 12
11q 12.1
11q 13.4
11q 21
11q 23.1
11q 24.1
11q 25

FIGURE 1.3   Human chromosome 11 showing banding patterns.

as position 21 and sub band 31 on the long arm of chromosome 17. Chromosomes are represented graphically by chromosome ideograms, which are used to show the relative size of the chromosomes of an organism and their characteristic banding patterns generated by staining (Figure 1.3).

In the most complex organisms, like the human, a copy of chromosome pair is inherited from the mother (ovum) and the other pair from the father (sperm). The offspring inherit some of their traits from their mother and others from their father. The pattern of inheritance is different for the circular mitochondrial DNA. Only ova keep their mitochondria during fertilization. Therefore, mitochondrial DNA is always inherited from the female parent.

In complex animals like the human, the ova in the female and sperms in the male are formed in specialized organs (ovaries in females and testes in males) by cell division called meiosis, which produces four different daughter cells from a single cell (Figure 1.4) [6]. Each daughter cell is haploid that contains only one copy of each chromosome pair. Generally, all male and female gametes, which are the products of meiosis cell division, are haploid.

Fertilization occurs when the nucleus of a male gamete (sperm) combines with the nucleus of a female gamete (ovum). In flowering plants, the male gamete is a cell in the pollen grain and the female gamete is an egg cell in the ovule. When the male and female gametes combine, the resulting cell is called a zygote (Figure 1.5) [7, 8].

Embryonic development, also known as embryogenesis, refers to the steps of development and formation of the embryo from a fertilized ovum to a mature embryo (Figure 1.6). Embryogenesis is characterized by the processes of mitosis cell division (after fertilization) and cellular differentiation of the embryo that occurs

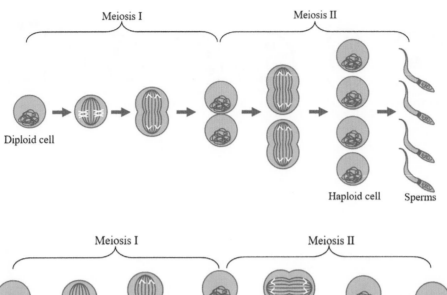

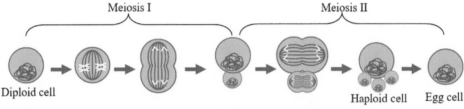

FIGURE 1.4   Cell division forming male sperms (top) and female egg (bottom).

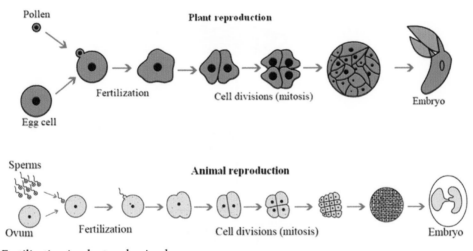

FIGURE 1.5   Fertilization in plant and animal.

during the early stages of development. Mitosis is a type of cell division that results in two daughter cells for tissue growth. Each daughter cell will have the same number and kind of diploid chromosomes as the parent cells [9].

After fertilization, the genetic material of the haploid sperm and haploid ovum then combine to form a single diploid cell called a zygote and the germinal stage of development kicks off. In the human, embryonic development covers the first eight weeks after fertilization. After nine weeks the embryo is turned into a fetus. The gestation or pregnancy period for human is around 40 weeks (nine months).

In the case of bacterial cells, reproduction takes place using binary fission, which is basically an asexual cell division where a single parent bacterial cell replicates its circular DNA and plasmids before splitting into two new identical daughter cells (Figure 1.7) [10].

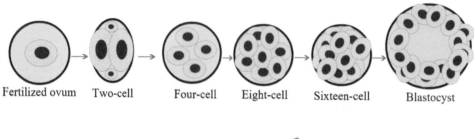

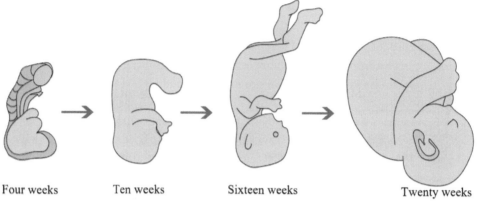

FIGURE 1.6   Embryonic and fetal development.

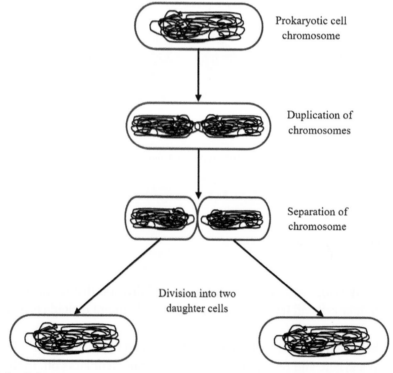

FIGURE 1.7   Bacterial cell division.

STRUCTURE OF DNA AND GENOME

In the previous section, we discussed how the genetic information of an organism is stored in DNA molecules or chromosomes and transformed from parents to offspring sexually in eukaryotes and asexually in prokaryotes. In this section, we will discuss the chemical structure of the genetic information and how it is transcribed and translated into functions that drive and characterize the life of an organism.

Deoxyribonucleic acid or DNA was first observed by the Swiss biochemist Friedrich Miescher in the late 1800s. The structure of DNA was resolved by James Watson and Francis Crick in 1953 [11]. DNA is made up of four molecules called nucleotides. Each nucleotide contains a phosphate group, a sugar group, and a nitrogenous base. The phosphate group and the sugar group called deoxyribose are the same for all four nucleotides (Figure 1.8). However, each nucleotide has a different nitrogenous base. Those four nitrogen bases that distinguish the four nucleotides are adenine (A), thymine (T), guanine (G), and cytosine (C). DNA consists of two strands that wind around each other like a twisted ladder. Each strand has a backbone made of alternating deoxyribose sugars and phosphate groups that form the phosphodiester bond.

The phosphodiester bond is the linkage between the 3` carbon atom of a deoxyribose molecule of one nucleotide and the 5` carbon atom of a deoxyribose molecule of another nucleotide (Figure 1.9).

The four nitrogenous bases give the four nucleotides their characteristics. Adenine (A) and guanine (G) are purine bases, which are structures that are composed of a five-sided and six-sided ring (Figure 1.10).

Cytosine (C) and thymine (T) are pyrimidines, which are structures composed of a single six-sided ring (Figure 1.11).

In DNA, any of the nitrogenous bases (A, C, G, and T) forms a glycosidic bond between its 1` nitrogen and the 1` -OH group of the deoxyribose forming a single DNA strand. The two DNA strands are formed

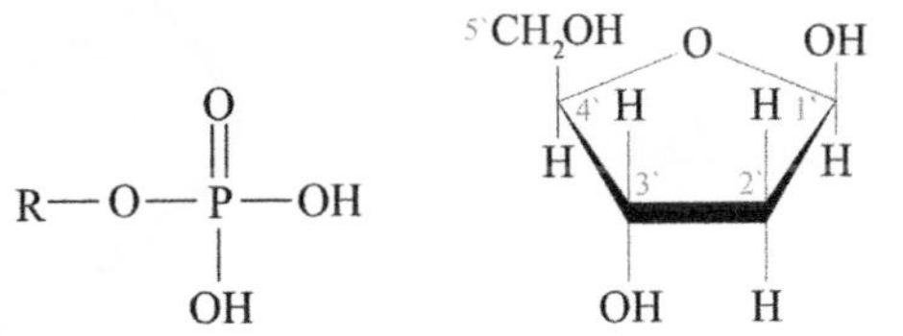

FIGURE 1.8   (a) Phosphate group and (b) deoxyribose sugar.

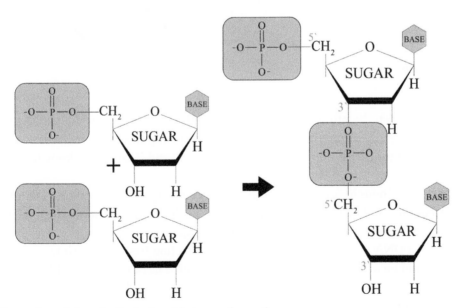

FIGURE 1.9   Formation of phosphodiester bond between deoxyribose sugars.

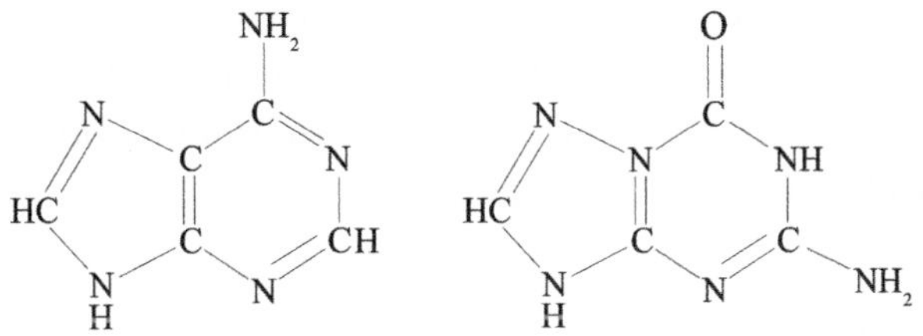

FIGURE 1.10   Purines adenine (left) and guanine (right).

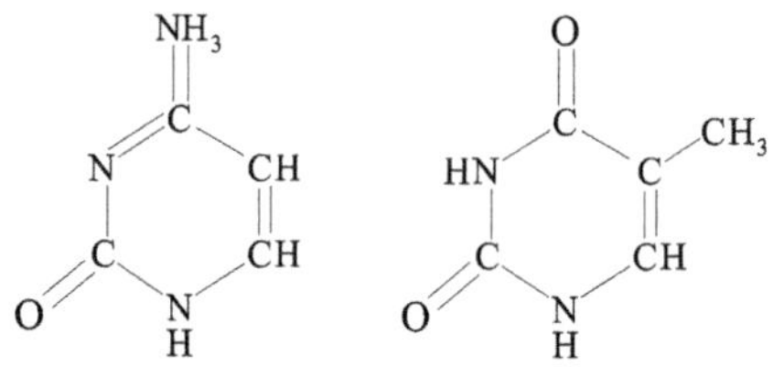

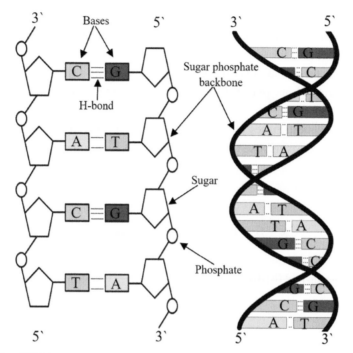

FIGURE 1.11   Pyrimidines cytosine (left) and thymine (right).

FIGURE 1.12   Duple helix of DNA.

by hydrogen bonds between the nitrogenous bases, where adenine (A) always binds to thymine (T), while cytosine (C) and guanine (G) always bind to one another forming the duple helix structure of the DNA (Figure 1.12). This relationship between any two bases (A and T) and (C and G) is known as complementary base pairing.

The order of the nitrogenous bases in the genome of a specific organism determines DNA instructions, or genetic codes, for building and maintaining the organism. The determined order of the four bases that make up the genome or a segment of the genome is called a DNA sequence.

The nucleotides in a DNA sequence are arranged in the direction from the 5-prime end, which has a free hydroxyl (or phosphate) on a 5` carbon to the 3-prime end, which has a free hydroxyl (or phosphate) on a 3` carbon. The DNA strand 5` → 3` is known as the plus "+" DNA strand and its complementary strand is known as the minus "-" DNA strand.

In bioinformatics, the nucleotide sequence of a piece of DNA is represented using the one-letter abbreviations of the four bases A, T, C, and G to identify the order of the nucleotides in the DNA molecule or a fragment of the DNA molecule. The DNA representation is usually for the plus DNA strand (from 5` end to 3` end). The complementary strand of a DNA sequence can be easily predicted from the other strand. For example, assume that the following is a representation of a DNA sequence:

CTCACTGA

Each letter represents a nucleotide base (A for adenine, C for cytosine, G for guanine, and T for thymine). As A will bind to T, and C will bind to G and vice versa, the complementary strand for the above DNA sequence will be:

GAGTGACT

The duple-stranded DNA can be represented as

Such representation of DNA sequence is the basis for the genomic data that the field of bioinformatics depends on.

Not all the genomic DNA sequence is functional; only small portion of it contains functional units called genes. A gene is the basic physical and functional unit of heredity in the genome. Genes vary in length from a few hundred DNA bases to millions of bases. Some genes carry the instructions to make proteins, which do most of the work in cells and are required for the structure, function, and regulation of the body tissues and organs. However, many genes do not code for proteins but may code for other biomolecules such as transfer RNA (tRNA), ribosomal RNA (rRNA), and microRNA, which are components of translation machinery and gene regulation. Scientists usually use sequence information to determine the genes and other sequence units of the genome and their functions and implication in traits and diseases. The Human Genome Project (HGP) estimated that humans have between 20,000 and 25,000 genes [12, 13]. Most genes are the same in individuals of the same organism, but a small number of genes may be slightly different among individuals due to mutations. In complex organisms, since chromosomes are in pairs, one pair is inherited from the mother and the other from the father, an individual will have two copies (versions) for each gene (a copy from the mother and another from the father). Those two copies for the same genes are called alleles. The two alleles of a specific gene may be identical and having the same sequence (homozygous) or may not be identical (heterozygous). The difference is usually due to mutation (substitution, deletion, or insertion), which contributes to variation among individuals within the same organism. A genotype is defined as all genes passed onto an individual by their parents. However, not all the genes passed to the offspring are translated into visible traits. The set of physical characteristics an individual has is called a phenotype. Any gene has two alleles (versions). An allele is either dominant, which shows its phenotypic effect, or recessive, which does not show its effect in the presence of a dominant allele. The dominant allele masks the effect of a recessive allele and it is denoted by a capital letter (A) versus small letter (a) for the recessive allele. In complex eukaryotes, since each parent provides one allele, the possible combinations are: (AA), (Aa), and (aa). The offspring whose genotype is either (AA) or (Aa) will have the dominant trait (A) expressed as a phenotype, while the individuals with (aa) will express the recessive trait. However, inheritance can also be codominance, which is a form of inheritance wherein the alleles of a gene pair in a heterozygote are fully expressed. As a result, the phenotype of the offspring is a combination of the phenotype of the parents. The AB blood type is an example of codominance in humans. A trait or phenotype may be influenced by multiple genes. Such trait is called polygenic trait.

Genes are given unique gene names and gene symbols following the guidelines published by the Gene Nomenclature Committee, which is the organization that sets the standards for gene nomenclature [14, 15]. For example, a gene on human chromosome 17 that has been associated with the suppression of breast tumor is known as *Breast cancer type 1 susceptibility gene* and its gene symbol is BRCA1.

The HGP completed the sequencing of the human genome for the first time in April 2003. The sequencing was followed by genome annotation, which is the process of identifying the locations of genes and the

TABLE 1.2   Genomes of Some Organisms (genome size in Mb= millions of base pairs)

Organism	Genome Size (Mb)	% Protein-Coding Sequence	Number of Protein-Coding Genes	Number of Proteins
Homo sapiens	2893.5	1.2%	19,593	121,425
Drosophila melanogaster	137.577	10%	13,719	30,717
Caenorhabditis elegans	102.915	25%	19,832	28,350
Saccharomyces cerevisiae	12.1571	70%	5,983	5,409
Escherichia coli	5.12122	88%	4,240	4,741
Haemophilus influenzae	1.8477	90%	1,713	1,716
Arabidopsis thaliana	1.86401	25%	27,442	27,334

protein-coding regions in a genome and determining what those genes do. The genome sequences of many organisms have been determined following the sequencing of the human genome. Their sequences provide interesting comparisons to that of the human genome and are proving useful in facilitating studies of different model organisms and in identifying a variety of different types of functional sequences, including regulatory elements that control gene expression. The genome sequences of humans and chimpanzees are about 99% identical. The genome of Neandertals, our closest evolutionary relative, has also been recently sequenced. It is estimated that Neandertals and modern humans diverged about 300,000–400,000 years ago [16]. The genomes of Neandertals and modern humans are more than 99.9% identical, significantly more closely related to each other than to chimpanzees. The number of genes in eukaryotic genomes is simply related to neither genome size nor biological complexity. The genome of the small plant Arabidopsis thaliana is only about 5% the size of the human genome, it contains approximately 26,000 protein-coding genes, compared with around 20,000 in the human genome. The discrepancies between the eukaryotic genome size and the number of protein-coding genes are because the genomes of most eukaryotic cells contain not only protein-coding sequences but also large amounts of DNA that does not code for proteins called non-coding sequence.

Table 1.2 shows the genome sizes, sizes of protein coding regions, and the number of proteins for some organisms. The data was obtained from the NCBI Genome database (last updated: January 27, 2020).

Generally, the genome of any organism can include two types of sequences: coding sequences or genes and non-coding sequences.

Gene Structure

The genes are genome sequences that contain genetic information or codes that can be transcribed into instruction or RNA (tRNA, rRNA, microRNA, and mRNA). RNAs are functional biomolecules that are expressed to carry out specific biological functions. Although the term gene is frequently used for only those DNA sequences that are transcribed into messenger RNA (mRNA) and translated into proteins, it can be used in a broader context to include any DNA sequences that contain code for performing biological functions in the cell. Thus, the gene can be defined as a genomic DNA sequence that represents a functional unit and can be either protein coding genes or non-protein-coding genes. Protein-coding genes are transcribed into mRNA molecules that carry the coding sequences or transcripts for protein synthesis. Non-protein-coding genes are transcribed into the other types of RNA.

Since the gene is a functional unit, it is different from non-genic DNA sequences. The gene structure determines when and where the gene will be expressed and the amount of gene expression and the products. The DNA sequence of a functional gene is divided into certain regions. The gene sequences of the eukaryotic organism have three types of regions – the regulatory region, introns (non-coding region), and exons (coding region) (Figure 1.13) [17, 18].

The gene structure of prokaryotic cells (bacteria and archaea) is simpler than that of eukaryotic cells as they lack introns.

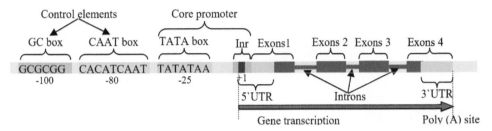

FIGURE 1.13   **Gene structure.**

Gene Regulatory Region

The regulatory region of a gene regulates the activation and suppression of a gene. Although the somatic cells of an organism have the same genome and the same set of genes, each type of cells (e.g., hepatocytes, neuron, white blood cells, etc.) may have its own gene expression patterns (some genes are on and some are off) to maintain their functions. Some genes are required in almost all cell types; therefore, they are expressed in all cells to perform essential biological activities such as DNA and protein synthesis, glycolysis, etc. These genes are called housekeeping genes and they require a regulatory network or machinery that keeps them on in almost every cell. Other kinds of genes are tissue-specific, and their expression is confined to cells of a specific tissue. Those genes are the ones that distinguish the cells of a tissue from others.

The genes are usually activated by special kinds of proteins called transcription factors (TFs), which are proteins that bind to the regulatory region of the genes to activate transcription of that gene into RNA. There are also some proteins called suppressors that can also bind to the regulatory region of the gene to suppress gene transcription and turn it off. The gene expression is usually regulated through complex pathways involving numerous factors.

The regulatory region of a gene is the DNA sequence of the gene where TFs, RNA polymerase, and suppressors can bind and interact to control the gene expression. The gene expression is regulated by activation or suppression of the gene transcription depending on the cell needs. In gene activation, a TF usually binds to the regulatory region of the gene. The TF binding then allows RNA polymerase to bind to the regulatory region to transcribe the gene into RNA. The process of RNA transcription is called gene expression. The regulatory region of the eukaryotic gene consists of enhancer, core promoter, and proximal control elements.

Enhancer   In some eukaryotic genes, the enhancer region enhances the transcription of the gene by assisting the core prompter to bind to a TF. The enhancer may be located upstream of a gene, within the coding region of the gene, downstream of a gene, or may be thousands of nucleotides away. The enhancer sequence is a binding site for transcription factors. The enhancing process is initiated when a DNA-bending protein binds to the enhancer sequence of the gene and bends it. This bending allows the interaction between the activators (bound to the enhancers) and the transcription factors (bound to the promoter region) and the RNA polymerase to occur (Figure 1.14) [19].

Core Promoter   The core promoter (Figure 1.15) is the region of the gene where the general TFs and RNA polymerase II (RNA Pol II) are assembled for the initiation of transcription of RNA. The core promoter sequence is about 25–40 base pairs upstream of the transcription start site (TSS) of the coding region. The core promoter may contain the following sequence elements, which act as recognition sites for the binding of the TFs.

(1) TATA box is a DNA sequence that indicates where a genic sequence can be read and decoded. The sequence of TATA box region is rich in thymine and adenine (T/A-rich sequence) with the consensus sequence, which is the most frequent nucleotide sequence, as 5`-TATAWAAR-3` (see Table 1.3 for

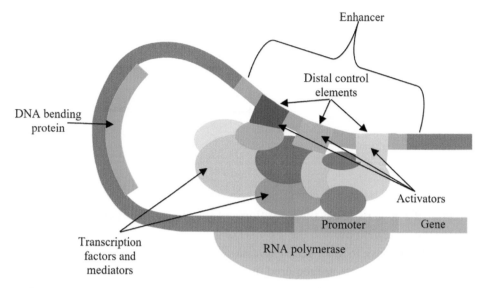

FIGURE 1.14   Enhancer.

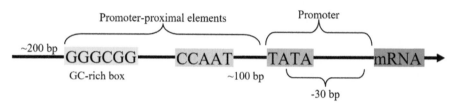

FIGURE 1.15   Promoter.

TABLE 1.3   IUPAC Degenerate Nucleotide Symbols [20]

Symbol	Description	Nucleotides
R	Purine	A or G
Y	Pyrimidine	C or T
W	Weak	A or T
S	Strong	C or G
M	Amino	A or C
K	Keto	G or T
H	Not G	A, C, or T
B	Not A	C, G, or T
V	Not T	A, C, or G
D	Not C	A, G, or T
N	Any	A, C, G, or T

the nucleotide symbols). The TATA box is usually located about 25-35 base pairs upstream of the TSSs (Figure 1.15). In bacteria, this region is called the Pribnow box, which has a shorter consensus sequence.

(2) Initiator (Inr) element is located from -2 to +4 overlapping the TSS. For example, the consensus sequence of Inr is 5`-YYANWYY-3` in humans and 5`-TCAKT in Drosophila (see Table 1.3 for the nucleotide symbols). The Inr works by enhancing binding affinity and strengthening the promoter.

(3) TFIIB recognition element (BRE), which is located at -32 to -37 and its consensus sequence is 5`-SSRCGCC-3` (see Table 1.3). It can have positive or negative effects on transcription in a promoter context-dependent manner.

(4) Motif ten element (MTE) is a conserved element with consensus sequence 5`-CSARCSSAACGS-3` (see Table 1.3). It promotes gene transcription by RNA polymerase II.

(5) Downstream promoter element (DPE) is located at +28 to +32. The DPE functions cooperatively with the Inr for the binding of TFIID in the transcription of core promoters in the absence of a TATA box.

Proximal Control Elements   The promoter proximal control element (PPE) is within around 100 nucleotides upstream from the core promoter. It stimulates transcription of the gene by interacting with TFs. The number, identity, and location of the proximal element vary from gene to gene. The PPE may contain a CAAT box, which is a distinct pattern with GGCCAATCT consensus sequence that occurs upstream by 60–100 bases to the TSS.

Introns

Introns are non-coding sections of eukaryotic genes. There are no introns in prokaryotic genes. They are transcribed in the mRNA, but they are removed before mRNA is translated into a protein. Introns can range in size from tens to thousands of base pairs and can be found in a wide variety of genes that generate RNA in most living organisms, including viruses. It is vital that introns be removed precisely, as any left-over intron nucleotides, or deletion of exon nucleotides, may result in a faulty protein being produced. This is because the amino acids that make up proteins are joined together based on codons, which consist of three nucleotides. An imprecise intron removal thus may result in a frame shift and the genetic code would be read incorrectly.

Exons

Exons are coding sections of a gene. In eukaryotic genes, after the removal of introns in the transcribed RNA, exons are spliced together to form gene transcripts, which include the codons that code for the amino acids of the proteins. The genetic code is the set of rules by which information encoded in RNA is translated into proteins (Table 1.4). The gene transcript is composed of tri-nucleotide units called codons, each coding for a single amino acid. The protein-coding gene transcript contains an open reading frame (ORF). The ORF is a continuous stretch of codons that begins with a start codon (usually ATG) and ends at a stop codon (usually TAA, TAG, or TGA) and the codons that are translated into amino acids are between the start codon and stop codon. In eukaryotic genes, following transcription, immature strands of messenger RNA, called pre-mRNA,

TABLE 1.4   Genetic Code for the Amino Acids Forming Proteins [21]

First Position	Second Position				Third Position
	T	C	A	G	
T	Phe	Ser	Tyr	Cys	T
	Phe	Ser	Tyr	Cys	C
	Leu	Ser	Stop	Stop	A
	Leu	Ser	Stop	Trp	G
C	Leu	Pro	His	Arg	T
	Leu	Pro	His	Arg	C
	Leu	Pro	Gln	Arg	A
	Leu	Pro	Gln	Arg	G
A	Ile	Thr	Asn	Ser	T
	Ile	Thr	Asn	Ser	C
	Ile	Thr	Lys	Arg	A
	Met	Thr	Lys	Arg	G
G	Val	Ala	Asp	Gly	T
	Val	Ala	Asp	Gly	C
	Val	Ala	Glu	Gly	A
	Val	Ala	Glu	Gly	G

may contain both introns and exons. These pre-mRNA molecules go through a modification process in the nucleus called splicing, during which the non-coding introns are cut out and only the coding exons remain. Splicing produces a mature messenger RNA or the transcript that is then translated into a protein.

The Non-Coding Genomic Sequences

A large portion of the genomes of a living organism has no known function. Around 98% of human genome does not code for protein. DNA that does not code for protein or has no known biological function is sometime called junk DNA even though some of those non-coding DNA was found to have a role in the regulation of some gene expression [22]. Generally, DNA without function is known as non-coding DNA. Most non-coding DNA lies between genes on the chromosome, and it includes repetitive sequences, pseudogenes, and telomeres.

Repetitive Sequences

Repetitive sequences are highly repeated non-coding DNA sequences that represent a large portion of eukaryotic genomes (hundreds of thousands of copies per genome). They are categorized into three major classes: simple repeated sequences, retrotransposons, and DNA transposons.

Simple Repeated Sequences   Simple repeated sequences, also known as short tandem repeats (STRs) or microsatellites, are a class of repeated sequences that consist of thousands of copies of short tandemly repeated DNA sequences of a repetitive unit of one to six base pair forming repetitive sequences of up to hundreds of nucleotides. For example, "AGGCT", which is a sequence of five nucleotides, is repeated tandemly six times.

AGGCT AGGCT AGGCT **AGGCT AGGCT** AGGCT

If the repeated sequence is short, it can be called a minisatellite. A longer tandemly repeated sequence is called a microsatellite. Such simple repeated sequences are widely found in prokaryotes and eukaryotes. They may account for about 5% of the total genomic DNA in humans and a varied percentage in the genomes of other organisms [23].

Retrotransposons   Retrotransposons are the transposable elements whose transposition in the genome is mediated by reverse transcription of RNA to DNA. Some RNA molecules are converted to complementary DNA (cDNA) by an enzyme called reverse transcriptase. The new DNA copy is integrated at a new site in the genome. This class of repetitive sequences is a major contributor to the genome size (45% of human genomic DNA). Retrotransposons are classified into short, interspersed elements (SINEs), long interspersed elements (LINEs), and retrovirus-like elements [24, 25]. SINEs and LINEs are examples of transposable elements that can move to different sites in genomic DNA. SINEs may have thousands of copies (850,000 in human genome). They range from 100 to 700 bp in length and make up around 21% of the genome. LINEs may have thousands of copies (1,500,000 in human genome), which make up around 13% of human genome. The retrovirus-like elements are DNA sequences that resemble retrovirus DNA sequences. A retrovirus is an RNA virus that uses RNA as its genetic material. It is characterized by inserting a copy of its genome into the genomes of infected cells. Analysis of genomic DNA reveals the presence of many thousands of retroviral-like elements, which suggests that some of the genomes of retrovirus integrated in animal genomes and that the reverse transcription of RNA to DNA played a major part in shaping the eukaryotic genome. The human retrovirus-like elements range from approximately 2,000 to 10,000 bp in length. There are approximately 450,000 retrovirus-like elements in the human genome (around 8% of human DNA) [26].

DNA Transposons   DNA transposons is a class of interspersed repetitive elements (DNA transposons) that moves through the genome by being copied and reinserted as DNA sequences, rather than moving by reverse

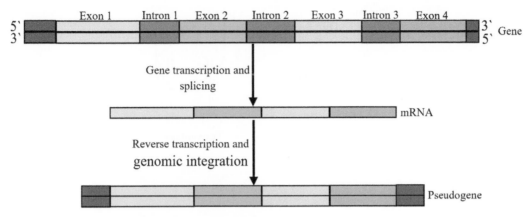

FIGURE 1.16   Formation of pseudogene by reverse transcription.

transcription. In the human genome, there are about 300,000 copies of DNA transposons, ranging from 80 to 3000 bp in length, and accounting for approximately 3% of human DNA [27].

Pseudogenes

A gene is a genomic DNA sequence with a coding region and regulatory regions. Sequencing and annotation of the human genome and the genomes of other organisms uncovered the presence of multiple copies of some known genes, but they lack some or their entire regulatory region. Therefore, they are not functional genes, and they are classified as non-coding sequence. These non-functional genes are called pseudogenes. In fact, some genes have multiple functional copies to produce more proteins when needed. Some of these copies may mutate and become pseudogenes. A pseudogene may also be formed when a functional gene is transcribed into mRNA but, instead of being transported to ribosome and translated into a protein molecule, it is converted into a piece of double-stranded complementary DNA (cDNA) by the enzymatic reverse transcription (Figure 1.16). This cDNA is then integrated into the genome and becomes part of it as nonfunctional pseudogene [28]. Studies have shown that there are around 11,000 pseudogenes in the human genome [29, 30].

Telomeres

A telomere (Figure 1.2b) is a repetitive nucleotide sequence of the genomic DNA found at each end of a eukaryotic chromosome and linear chromosome of several bacteria including Streptomyces, Borrelia, and Rhodococcus. Telomeres act as caps that protect the end of chromosomes from deterioration. They play critical roles in chromosome replication and maintenance during cell division. Studies showed that telomeres get shorter each time a cell copies itself. The repeated sequences of telomere consist of clusters of guanine residues (Gs). The sequence of telomere repeats in humans and other mammals is "TTAGGG", which is repeated hundreds or thousands of times and terminate with a 3` overhang of single-stranded DNA. Maintenance of telomeres appears to be an important factor in determining the life span and reproductive capacity of cells. Studies have shown that cancer cells have high levels of an enzyme called telomerase, which allow the cells to maintain the ends of their chromosomes through indefinite divisions [31, 32].

RIBONUCLEIC ACID

Ribonucleic acid or RNA, is a polymeric molecule produced from a gene by the process of gene transcription. RNA is essential in almost all biological activities for its roles in coding for proteins (mRNA), transferring of amino acids (tRNA), translating codons into amino acids (rRNA), and regulating expression of genes. An RNA molecule is a single-stranded polymer that is slightly different from the DNA. It contains the sugar ribose instead of deoxyribose that is found in the DNA molecule (Figure 1.17). The difference between ribose and

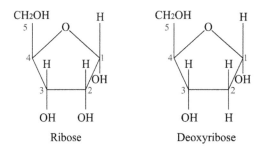

FIGURE 1.17   Ribose and deoxyribose.

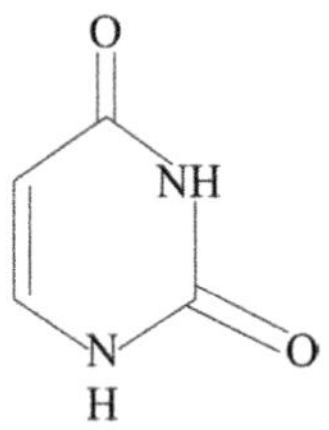

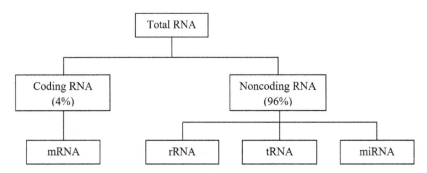

FIGURE 1.18   Uracil.

```
                          Total RNA
                   ┌──────────┴──────────┐
            Coding RNA              Noncoding RNA
              (4%)                     (96%)
                │             ┌──────────┼──────────┐
             mRNA          rRNA       tRNA       miRNA
```

FIGURE 1.19   RNA types.

deoxyribose is that ribose possesses the hydroxyl group binding to the second carbon atom while deoxyribose possesses only the hydrogen atom without oxygen [33].

Moreover, the RNA molecule is made up of the same nucleotides as DNA except that thymine is replaced by a similar nucleotide called uracil (U) (Figure 1.18). Thus, the RNA sequence is made up of A, C, G, and U.

The order of nucleotides in an RNA molecule or fragment is represented by a sequence that is composed of the letters A, C, G, and U for adenine, cytosine, guanine, and uracil nucleotide, respectively. An RNA sequence may look like:

CUCACUAAAGACAGAAUGAAUGUAGAAAAGGCUGAAUUCUGUAAU

RNA is always a product of a gene as a result of gene transcription that is regulated by regulatory factors and complex pathways to accommodate the biological activities in the cell. There are four types of RNA molecule in living cells (Figure 1.19): messenger RNA (mRNA), transfer RNA (tRNA), ribosomal RNA (rRNA), and MicroRNA (miRNA). Only mRNA is a protein-coding RNA (4%) while the others are protein non-coding RNAs (96%).

Ribosomal RNA

Ribosomal RNA (rRNA) molecules are one of the major components forming the protein-synthesizing organelle called ribosome in living cells. Growing mammalian cells may contain about ten million ribosomes. They are transcribed from genes in the nucleus in eukaryotes or chromatin body in prokaryotes and exported to the

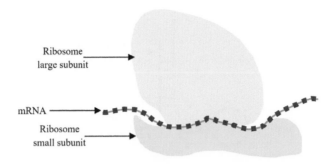

FIGURE 1.20   Ribosome.

cytoplasm to translate the genetic information carried by mRNA into proteins. There are several rRNA types depending on the molecule size measured on Svedberg coefficient (S). A Svedberg unit (S) is a non-metric unit for sedimentation rate in a test tube under the centrifugal force of an ultra-high-speed centrifuge. A Svedberg unit (S) is 10-13 seconds. The S value of an RNA molecule is determined by its mass, density, and shape. An rRNA molecule or ribosomal subunit may be given the name "nS", where "n" is the number of Svedberg units. Both prokaryotic and eukaryotic ribosomes are formed of a larger and smaller subunit (Figure 1.20). Prokaryotic ribosomes are composed of 50S and 30S while eukaryotic ribosomes are composed of 60S and 40S subunits. The two subunits come together during mRNA translation into a protein. Each ribosome subunit is made of both rRNA and proteins [34].

In bacteria, the larger ribosomal subunit (50S) contains 5S rRNA (≈120 nucleotides), 23S rRNA (≈3000 nucleotides), and 31 proteins. The smaller subunit (30S) contains 16S rRNA (≈1500 nucleotides) and 21 proteins. Each of these rRNA molecules (5S rRNA, 23S rRNA, and 16S rRNA) has its own gene called the 5S rRNA, 23S rRNA, and 16S rRNA gene, respectively. Ribosomal RNA genes are called ribosomal DNA (rDNA). The 16S rRNA gene is used in phylogeny and bacterial identification [35].

In eukaryotes, the 60S or large ribosomal subunit has three rRNA molecules, 28S rRNA (4,800 nucleotides), 5.8S rRNA (160 nucleotides), and 5S rRNA (120 nucleotides), and 50 proteins. The 40S small ribosomal subunit has only 18S rRNA (1,900 nucleotides) and 33 proteins. Each eukaryotic rRNA has its own coding gene. The rRNA gene or rDNA has been studied in detail for its biological importance and repeated nature [36, 37].

Transfer RNA

Transfer RNA (tRNA) plays an important role in the translation of protein synthesis in ribosomes. It translates the message coded in the nucleotide sequences of mRNA into specific amino acids, which are joined together to form a protein. Although tRNA is a single-stranded molecule, it can form double-stranded structures that are important to its function in protein synthesis. Single strands of tRNA can hybridize to form a double-stranded molecule and many secondary structures in which a single RNA molecule folds over and forms hairpin loops stabilized by hydrogen bonds between complementary nucleotides [38]. Such base-pairing of RNA is critical for tRNA. The tRNA molecule has two important regions: the amino acid binding site where a specific amino acid is binding to the tRNA molecule, and a hairpin-like trinucleotide region called the anticodon, which is complementary to a codon in mRNA in the time of translation (Figure 1.21). A codon consists of three nucleotides on an mRNA strand that encodes a specific amino acid. During translation (passing of mRNA between the two ribosome subunits), a codon on mRNA complements an anticodon on the tRNA and the corresponding amino acid is released from the tRNA and added to the growing polypeptide chain.

MicroRNA

MicroRNAs, or miRNAs, are small non-coding RNA molecules of about 22 nucleotides in length. They are encoded in the genomes; some of them are transcribed from within protein-coding units (exons) of a gene and others are transcribed from within non-coding regions of a gene (introns). The miRNAs generated from

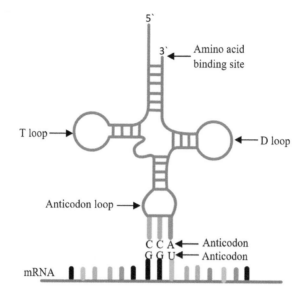

FIGURE 1.21   Transfer RNA.

exons are called canonical miRNAs, while the ones generated from introns are called non-canonical miRNAs. MiRNAs are produced by two ribonucleases (Drosha and Dicer). The precursors of the miRNAs may be long RNAs that fold to form hairpin secondary structures, which are then cleaved sequentially by the ribonucleases (Figure 1.22).

MiRNAs play important regulatory role in gene expression by halting translation of mRNA into protein with a process called RNA interference (RNAi) or gene silencing. A miRNA strand is incorporated into the RNA-induced silencing complex (RISC), which is a protein complex that uses the incorporated miRNA strand to complement the target mRNA and to stimulate its degradation by a protein in RISC.

The miRNA targeting sites are usually at 3`-untranslated regions (UTR) of the targeted mRNA. A single miRNA can target up to 100 different mRNAs. Therefore, miRNAs may regulate more than half of the protein-coding genes in eukaryotes. MiRNAs have also been linked to some types of cancers and translocation mutation in chromosomes [39, 40].

Messenger RNA

Messenger RNA (mRNA) is transcribed from a gene and synthesized in the nucleus using the nucleotide sequence of the gene as a template. The transcribed mRNA is complementary to the nucleotide sequence of one DNA strand of the gene. The process of mRNA transcription requires nucleotide triphosphates as substrates and the enzyme RNA polymerase II as a catalyst. The transcribed mRNA of prokaryotes is different from that of eukaryotes. The prokaryotic primary mRNA contains no introns, while the eukaryotic primary mRNA contains introns that will be spliced out to keep only the exons to form the final mRNA. The mRNA is formed in the nucleus and transported to the cytoplasm where it passes through the ribosome (between smaller and larger ribosome subunits) and interacts with the tRNA so the transcript will be translated into amino acids and the protein is assembled. In the following we will discuss both transcription and translation [41].

Messenger RNA transcription

In eukaryotes, genes can be transcribed into RNA molecules. There may be thousands of genes in the genome of an organism. For example, the human genome has around 30,000 genes. However, not all genes are transcribed; some of them are transcribed only when they are needed. The process and intensity of gene transcription into mRNA is known as gene expression. The set of all RNA transcripts, including coding and non-coding, in an individual or a population of cells is called transcriptome. In complex organisms, the genes expressed in the cells of each organ are different from others since each organ has different functions. The gene expression

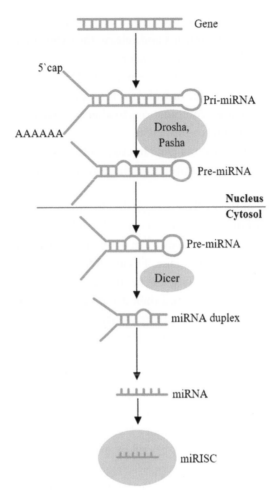

FIGURE 1.22   Formation of microRNA.

distinguishes cells of an organ from others even though all somatic cells have the same genome and the same set of genes. For example, the genes expressed in hepatocytes or liver cells are the genes that play pivotal roles in metabolism, detoxification, protein synthesis, and innate immunity against invading microorganisms. The set of gene expressed in liver cells will be different from the set of genes expressed in the cells of lungs, kidney, or brain. However, only housekeeping genes are expressed in all cells because they perform basic biochemical activities that occur in all cells. Housekeeping genes are typically required for the maintenance of basic cellular functions that are essential for the existence of a cell, regardless of its specific role in the tissue or organism. Thus, they are expressed in all cells of an organism under normal and pathophysiological conditions, irrespective of tissue type, developmental stage, cell cycle state, or external signal. Therefore, they are widely used as internal controls for experimental studies such as in polymerase chain reaction (PCR) experiments. The list of the housekeeping genes may vary from one organism to another. Some of the housekeeping genes of human and other animals may include beta-actin (ACTB), glyceraldehyde-3-phosphate dehydrogenase (GAPDH), phosphoglycerate kinase 1 (PGK1), peptidylprolyl isomerase A (PPIA), ribosomal protein P0 (PPLP0), acidic ribosomal phosphoprotein PO (ARBP), and others [42, 43].

Generally, the amounts and types of mRNA molecules in a cell reflect the biological activities of that cell. Thousands of different mRNAs are produced every second in every cell. The expression of any gene is regulated by a complex pathway to provide the adequate number of proteins. Since the gene expression in any kind of cells is affected by several factors, the level of expression of all genes called gene profiling in a cell in a specific time and in specific conditions always serves as a snapshot or check point for some genomic and cancer research and it is also used in diagnosis of some diseases.

RNA molecules are initially synthesized as precursors or pre-RNA, which must be processed by a process called splicing in order to remove the introns and release the exons that are spliced together to form the mature RNA. Splicing of pre-mRNA is therefore a major part of the process that results in synthesis of the protein-coding component of the transcriptome or the whole mRNA of the cell. Some eukaryotic genes have an ability to code for different protein variants or isoforms through so-called alternative splicing, which is the rearranging and joining of exons in varied combinations to alter the sequence of the coded proteins. The protein isoforms may have different functions or properties.

The steps of the mRNA transcription from a gene in eukaryotic cells include initialization of mRNA transcription, transcript elongation, transcript termination, and post-transcriptional modification [44].

Initialization Stage   Transcription of the mRNA is regulated by transcription factors, which are proteins that bind to the core promoter region of the gene. Most TFs have ligand binding domain (LBD) and DNA binding domain (DBD). LBD is the site that, when it binds to an activating substance, activates the DBD of the TF to bind to the DNA promoter region of the target gene. TFs are activated and deactivated by a complex pathway. Once a TF binds to the promoter region of a target gene, the RNA polymerase II will bind to the polymerase binding sequence of the core promoter region and then it separates the double-stranded gene providing two separate strands of DNA, one of which will be the template strand or anti-sense strand for the transcription of mRNA and the other is the non-template strand or coding strand or sense strand (Figure 1.23).

Elongation Stage   Once the two DNA strands of the gene are separated, only one strand (the template strand) will be the template for the RNA polymerase II. The enzyme will start to read one base at a time to build an RNA strand out of complementary nucleotides. The complementary RNA strand grows from 5` end to 3` end and will continue until all mRNA is transcribed (Figure 1.24). The RNA transcript will be identical to the non-template strand except that thymine (T) will be replaced by uracil (U).

Termination Stage   The mRNA strand will continue to grow in the above elongation stage until it reaches a transcribed sequence that bends to form a hairpin structure called a terminator, which terminates the transcription process (Figure 1.25). The pre-mRNA is then released from the RNA polymerase.

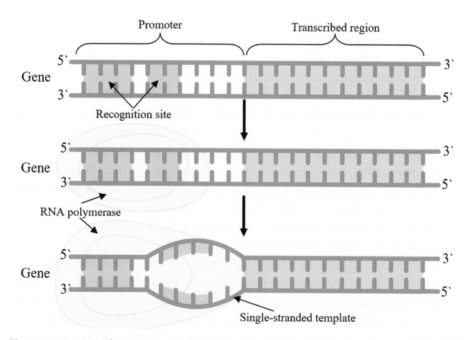

FIGURE 1.23   Transcription initialization.

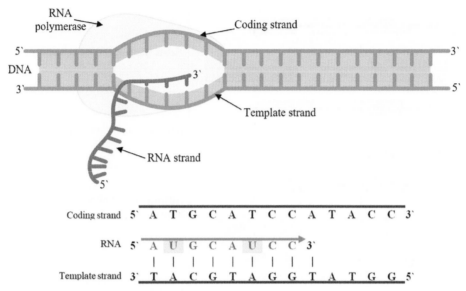

FIGURE 1.24   Transcription elongation stage.

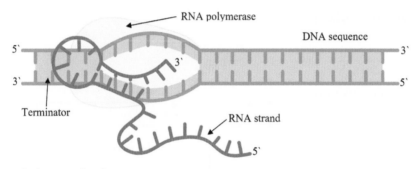

FIGURE 1.25   Transcription termination.

Posttranscriptional Modifications   After transcription, the pre-mRNA undergoes some essential modifications to be ready for the translation stage in ribosomes. The post-transcriptional modifications of the pre-mRNA include splicing and 5`-end and 3`-end modifications (addition of a cap to the 5`-end, and addition of a poly(A) tail to the 3`-end).

Gene Splicing   Gene splicing is a post-transcriptional modification in which a single gene can code for multiple protein variants or isoforms. There are several types of gene-splicing processes, which can take place simultaneously after the pre-mRNA is formed. Exon Skipping is the most common gene-splicing process in which an exon or exons are included or excluded from the final gene transcript leading to extended or shortened mRNA variants. Intron Retention (IR) is the splicing process in which an intron (non-coding region) is retained in the final transcript. The IR plays a role in gene expression regulation and associations with complex diseases. Alternative 3` Splice Site and alternative 5` Splice Site are the splicing mechanism in which an alternative gene splicing includes joining of different 5` and 3` splice site. Figure 1.26 shows the types of gene splicing [45].

The 5`-End and 3`-End Modifications   Both ends of the pre-mRNA are modified. A cap of 7-methylguanosine is attached at the 5`-end of the pre-mRNA. This cap is needed to help initiate translation of the mRNA into a protein in the ribosome.

A series of about 250 adenine nucleotides called poly(A) tail is attached to the 3`-end of the pre-mRNA. The poly(A) synthesis is catalyzed by poly(A) polymerase.

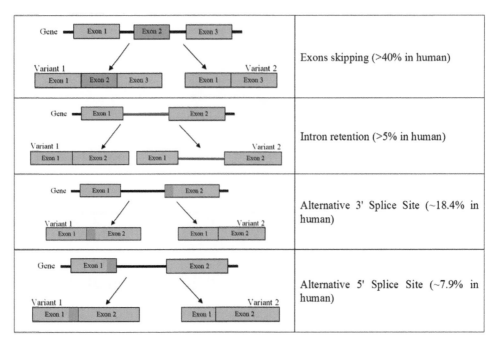

FIGURE 1.26   Gene alternative splicing.

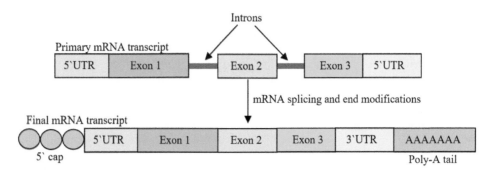

FIGURE 1.27   pre-mRNA modifications.

The structure of the mature functional mRNA consists of 5` cap, 5` untranslated region (5`UTR), coding region called open reading frame (ORF), 3` untranslated region (3`UTR), and poly-A tail (Figure 1.27).

Five Prime Untranslated Region   The 5`-untranslated region (5`-UTR) is the untranslated part of a mRNA strand that extends from its 5`-terminus (cap site) to the translational start codon (AUG). The 5`-UTR sequence length is about three to ten bases in prokaryotic mRNA and varies from hundreds to thousands bases in eukaryotic mRNA (150 bases in human).

Three Prime Untranslated Region   The 3`-untranslated region (3`-UTR) is the section of mRNA that immediately follows the translation termination codon (stop codon).

The Open Reading Frame   The protein-coding region is known as open reading frames (ORFs). It consists of a series of codons that specify the amino acid residues of the protein sequence that the gene codes for. A codon consists of three consecutive nucleotides that code for a specific amino acid. There are 64 possible codons but there are only 20 amino acids used for protein synthesis. Some amino acids can be coded by more than one codon.

TABLE 1.5 Genetic Code [21]

First Position	Second Position				Third Position
	U	C	A	G	
U	Phe	Ser	Tyr	Cys	U
	Phe	Ser	Tyr	Cys	C
	Leu	Ser	Stop	Stop	A
	Leu	Ser	Stop	Trp	G
C	Leu	Pro	His	Arg	U
	Leu	Pro	His	Arg	C
	Leu	Pro	Gln	Arg	A
	Leu	Pro	Gln	Arg	G
A	Ile	Thr	Asn	Ser	U
	Ile	Thr	Asn	Ser	C
	Ile	Thr	Lys	Arg	A
	Met	Thr	Lys	Arg	G
G	Val	Ala	Asp	Gly	U
	Val	Ala	Asp	Gly	C
	Val	Ala	Glu	Gly	A
	Val	Ala	Glu	Gly	G

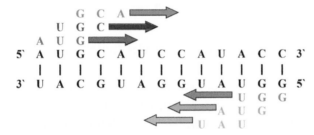

FIGURE 1.28   Possible open reading frames (ORFs)

Table 1.5 shows the codons and the amino acids. The first bases of the codon are in the first column, the second bases are in the first row, and the third bases are in the last column of the table. For example, UCU, UCC, UCA, and UCG are the codons for serine (Ser). The property, in which a single amino acid is coded by multiple codons, is called degeneracy of codons or the redundancy of the genetic code. The genetic code is degenerate mainly at the third codon position to reduce the effect of mutations.

The ORF usually (but not always) begins with the start codon AUG, and ends with a stop codon, which is any one of UAA, UAG, or UGA. ORF scanning or ab initio gene prediction programs predict genes by searching a DNA sequence for ORFs that begin with an ATG and end with a termination triplet. The gene scanning is complicated by the fact that each DNA sequence has six possible reading frames; three possible frames are in one direction and three frames are in the reverse direction on the complementary strand (Figure 1.28). Computers are quite capable of scanning all six reading frames for ORFs.

Given the coding region of a gene, we can use the above information to predict the mRNA sequence and the ORFs.

Messenger RNA Translation

Transcription and RNA processing are followed by translation and the synthesis of proteins as directed by the mRNA template. The mRNAs are read in the 5` to 3` direction, and polypeptide chains are synthesized by translating the ORF. Each amino acid is specified by three bases or a codon in the ORF, according to a nearly universal genetic code. Translation is carried out on ribosomes, with tRNA strands serving as adaptors between the mRNA template and the amino acids being incorporated into the protein. Protein synthesis thus

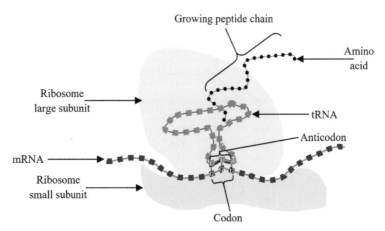

FIGURE 1.29   Translation in ribosome.

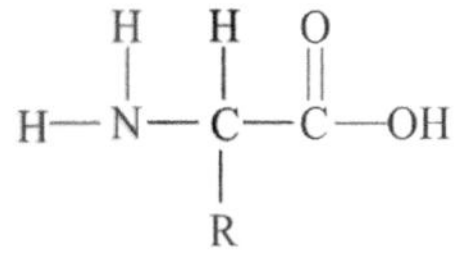

FIGURE 1.30   General chemical composition of amino acids.

involves interactions among three types of RNA molecules (mRNA, tRNA, and rRNA), as well as various proteins that are required for translation.

During the translation of a mRNA into a protein, the 20 amino acids are aligned with their corresponding codons on the mRNA template. A tRNA is approximately 75 nucleotides long and it forms complementary base pairing between different regions of the molecule and folds into an L-shape to fit onto ribosomes during the translation process (Figure 1.29). Each of the tRNA strand has the sequence CCA at its 3` terminus, where an amino acid is covalently attached to the ribose of the terminal adenosine (A). The codon on the mRNA template is recognized by the anticodon loop located at the other end of the folded tRNA, forming complementary base pairing. The attachment of each amino acid to its specific tRNA is mediated by a specific enzyme called aminoacyl tRNA synthetase. There is an enzyme for each amino acid. When a codon complements an anticodon, the amino acid attached to the tRNA will be released to bind to the growing protein sequence. The translation will continue until the entire ORF is translated and the stop codon is reached. The process of translation is carried out by millions of ribosomes in the cell simultaneously [46].

THE PROTEINS

Proteins are the biomolecules that are translated from gene transcript or mRNAs as discussed above. Any protein must be coded by a gene. However, a gene may code for multiple protein isoforms that differ in sequences and functions. A protein molecule is built of 20 amino acids, which are the building blocks of any proteins. Amino acids are small organic molecules that consist of an alpha (central) carbon atom linked to an amino group (NH2), a carboxyl group (COOH), a hydrogen atom (H), and a variable component called a side chain given the symbol (R) (Figure 1.30) [47].

In a protein molecule, multiple amino acids are linked together by peptide bonds, thereby forming a long chain or polypeptide. Peptide bonds are formed by a biochemical reaction that extracts a water molecule as it joins the amino group of one amino acid to the carboxyl group of a neighboring amino acid. The linear sequence of amino acids within a protein is considered the primary structure of the protein (Figure 1.31).

Each amino acid has a unique side chain (R), which has different chemistry from that of other amino acids. Most amino acids have non-polar side chains, which have pure hydrocarbon alkyl groups (alkane

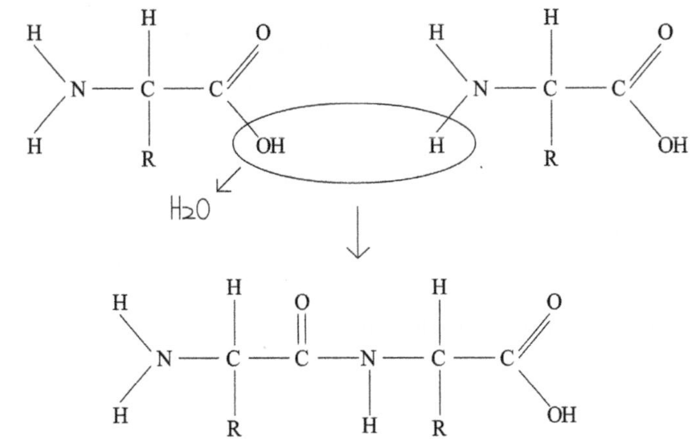

FIGURE 1.31   Formation of peptide bond between amino acids.

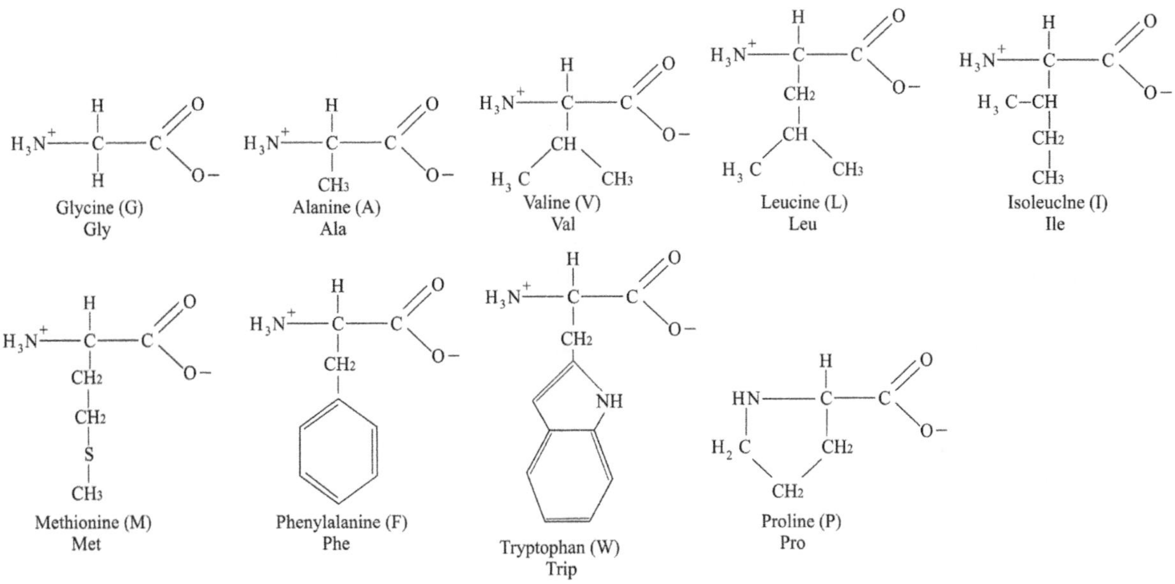

FIGURE 1.32   Non-polar side chains.

branches) or aromatic (benzene rings). Amino acids with non-polar side chains include glycine (G), alanine (A), valine (V), leucine (L), isopleucine (I), methionine (M), phenylalanine (F), tryptophan (W), and proline (P) (Figure 1.32).

Other amino acids have polar but uncharged side chains. These polar amino acids include serine (S), threonine (T), cysteine (C), tyrosine (Y), asparagine (N), and glutamine (Q) (Figure 1.33).

Other amino acids have side chains with positive (basic amino acids) or negative charges (acidic amino acids). Those amino acids that have electrically charged side chains include aspartate (D), glutamate (E), lysine (K), arginine (R), and histidine (H) (Figure 1.34).

The physicochemical properties of the side chains of amino acids are critical to protein structures because these side chains can bind with one another to fold the linear protein residues in a certain shape or conformation forming the so-called three-dimensional structure (3D) of protein. Any protein has a specific three-dimensional structure that determines its biological functions in the living cells. Charged amino acid side chains can form ionic bonds, and polar amino acids can form hydrogen bonds. Hydrophobic side chains interact with each other via weak Van der Waals interactions. Most bonds formed by these side chains are non-covalent. Only cysteines can form covalent bonds with their side chains that contain

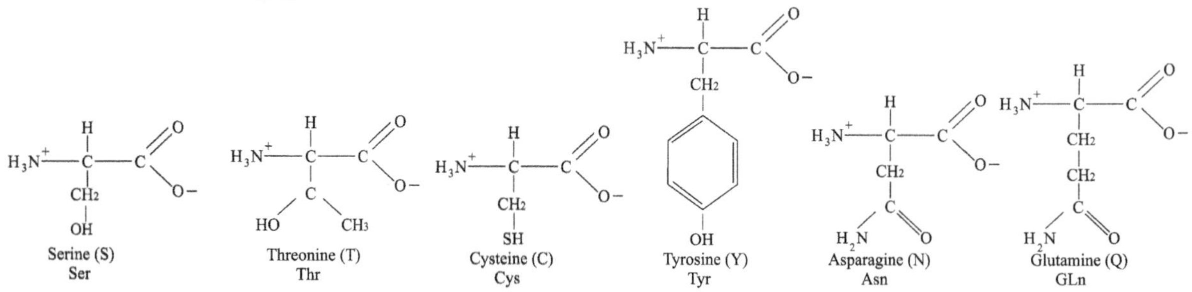

FIGURE 1.33 Amino acids with polar uncharged side chains.

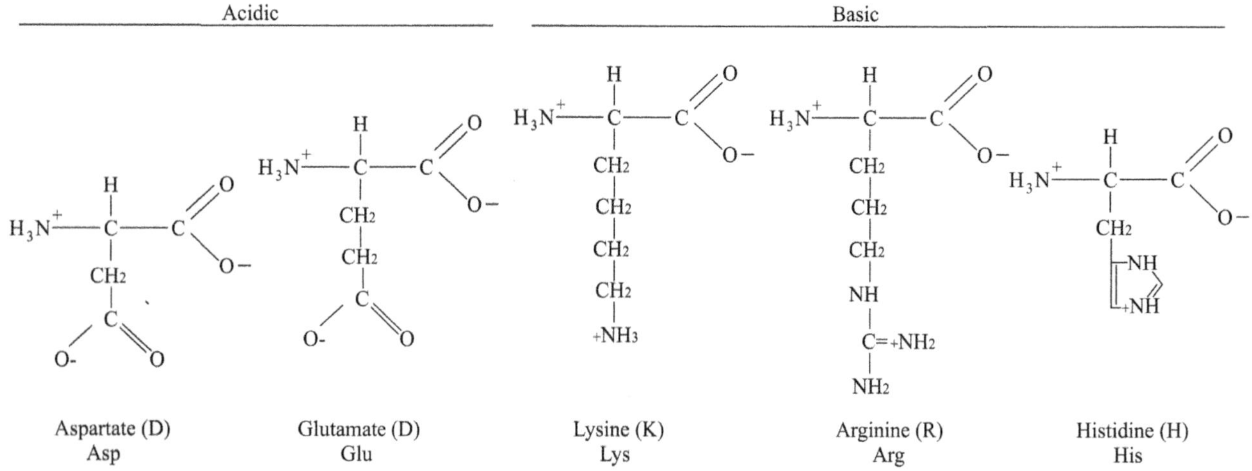

FIGURE 1.34 Amino acids with electrically charged side chains.

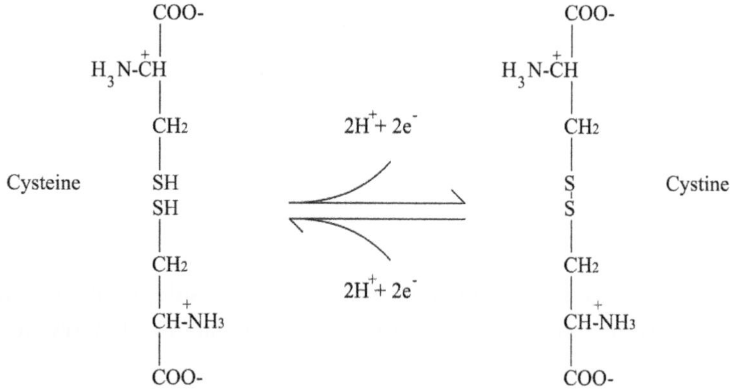

FIGURE 1.35 Disulfide bridges between two cysteine amino acids.

sulfur. If a sulfur atom is bonded to a sulfur atom of another cysteine, a covalent disulfide bridge is formed (Figure 1.35).

The order of amino acids in a protein or a polypeptide is represented by a sequence formed from single-letter abbreviations of the amino acid forming the molecule. Table 1.5 contains the names of the 20 amino acids and their three-letter and single-letter abbreviations.

In bioinformatics, the order of amino acids (linked to one another by peptide bonds) in protein molecules are represented by linear sequences made up of the single-letter symbols of the 20 amino acids as follows:

LTKDRMNVEKAEFCNKSKQPGLARSQHNRWAGSKETCNDRRTPSTEKKVDLNADPLCERKEWNKQK
LPCSENPRDTEDVPWITLNSSIQK

TABLE 1.5   Amino Acids and Their Symbols

#	Amino Acid	Three-Letter Symbol	Single-Letter Symbol
1	Alanine	Ala	A
2	Arginine	Arg	R
3	Asparagine	Asn	N
4	Aspartate	Asp	D
5	Cysteine	Cys	C
6	Glutamine	Gln	Q
7	Glutamate	Glu	E
8	Glycine	Gly	G
9	Histidine	His	H
10	Isoleucine	Iso	I
11	Leucine	Leu	L
12	Lysine	Lys	K
13	Methionine	Met	M
14	Phenylalanine	Phe	F
15	Proline	Pro	P
16	Serine	Ser	S
17	Threonine	Thr	T
18	Tryptophan	Try	W
19	Tyrosine	Tyr	Y
20	Valine	Val	V

Three-Dimensional Protein Structure

The order of the amino acids in a protein molecule in the sequence above represents a linear structure of a protein molecule, in which the amino acids are linked by peptide bonds. However, the side chains of the amino acids may link to one another forming the three-dimensional structure of a protein. Scientific studies found that the order of the amino acids in a protein sequence (the linear structure) determines the final three-dimensional shape of the protein or protein conformation. Even though a protein has an astronomical number of possible conformations (Levinthal's paradox), a specific conformation is adopted once the protein has been synthesized [48]. Research has shown that a protein can be denatured by treating with certain solvents, which destroy the non-covalent interactions (between the side chains) that hold the folded chain together. This treatment converts the protein into a polypeptide chain that has lost its natural three-dimensional shape. When the denaturing solvent is removed, the protein often refolds spontaneously, or re-natures, into its original conformation, proving that all the information needed for the specific conformation of a protein is contained in its linear amino acid sequence. There are four types of protein structure: primary, secondary, tertiary, and quaternary [44, 49].

Primary Structure   The primary structure in a protein molecule is the linear sequence of amino acids in a polypeptide chain. No links are presented between the amino acid residues but only the peptide bonds that create the chain (Figure 1.36). The sequence of a protein represents its primary structure.

Secondary Structure   The secondary structure of a protein molecule is that the amino acids in the molecules form hydrogen bonds with one another. Thus, regions of the polypeptide fold due to interactions between atoms of the backbone atoms. The arrangement and folding of the polypeptide chain may form two secondary shapes: alpha helix and beta strand.

The alpha-helix (α-helix) is a spiral configuration of the polypeptide chain for a helix structure, which has either a right direction (right-handed helix) or left direction (left-handed helix). In an alpha helix, the carbonyl (C=O) of one amino acid forms a hydrogen bond with the amino group (N-H) of another amino acid (e.g., the carbonyl of amino acid 1 would form a hydrogen bond to the N-H of amino acid 5). Such pattern of hydrogen

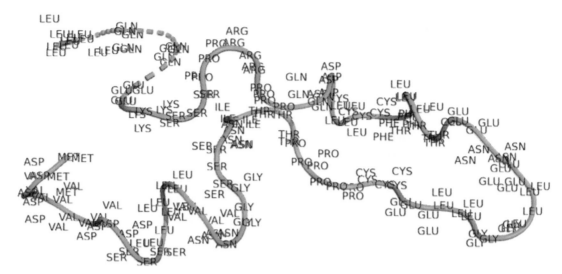

FIGURE 1.36   Primary structure of protein.

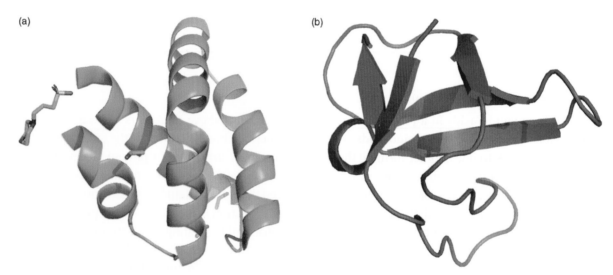

FIGURE 1.37   Secondary structures of protein (a) alpha helix and (b) beta sheet.

bonds shapes the polypeptide chain into a helical ribbon with each turn of the helix containing 3.6 amino acids. The side chains or R groups of the amino acids project outward forming the alpha helix (Figure 1.37a).

The Beta strand (β-sheet) is made of two or more adjacent segments of the same polypeptide chain, forming a sheet-like structure stabilized by hydrogen bonds (Figure 1.37b). The hydrogen bonds are formed between the carbonyl groups and amino groups of the backbone of the polypeptide, while the side chains extend above and below the plane of the sheet. The strands forming the beta sheet can be parallel, pointing to the same direction (N- and C-termini match), or anti-parallel, pointing in opposite directions (the N-terminus of one strand is positioned next to the C-terminus of the other).

Tertiary Structure   The tertiary structure of a protein molecule is the protein structure at which an entire polypeptide folds to form a three-dimensional shape. It is primarily due to interactions between the side chains (R groups) of the amino acids that make up the polypeptide. The side chain interactions that contribute to the tertiary structure may include hydrogen bonding, ionic bonding, dipole-dipole, and hydrophobic interactions. Moreover, the disulfide covalent bonds between the sulfur atoms in the side chain of cysteines in the polypeptide contribute as well to the tertiary structure of proteins (Figure 1.38).

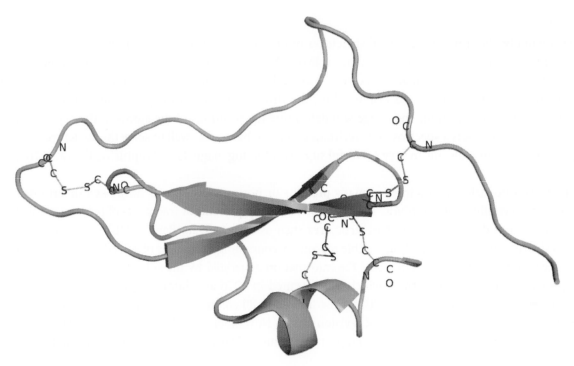

FIGURE 1.38   Tertiary structure of protein.

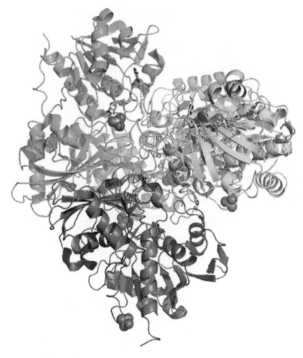

FIGURE 1.39   Quaternary structure of protein.

Quaternary Structure   Some proteins are formed of multiple polypeptide chains or subunits. The quaternary structure of a protein is formed by the association of several polypeptide chains or subunits into a closely packed protein arrangement. The subunits are held together by hydrogen bonds and van der Waals forces between non-polar side chains of the amino acids. Each of the subunits may have its own primary, secondary, or tertiary structure (Figure 1.39).

Protein Structure Representation and File Formats

Experimentally, the three-dimensional structures of proteins are solved by techniques such as X-ray crystallography and nuclear magnetic resonance (NMR). X-ray crystallography is a technique used for determining the atomic and molecular structure of a crystal by diffraction of X-rays and measuring the angles and intensities of these diffracted beams. Thus, the three-dimensional image of the density of electrons within the crystal is captured. The image will determine the positions of the atoms in the crystal and their chemical bonds. NMR is a spectroscopic technique that can be used as well to solve the structure of proteins by placing a protein molecule in very powerful superconducting magnets and capturing the radio frequency energy.

The three-dimensional structures of many proteins or portions of proteins have been determined using either X-ray crystallography or NMR. The solved structures of proteins or fragments of proteins are deposited by scientists into databases for protein structures such as Protein Data Bank (PDB), which is available at www.rcsb.org/. The PDB is a freely accessible repository containing thousands of solved structures of proteins and other biomolecules. The PDB stores the information generated by the solved three-dimensional shape of a protein in the PDB file format, which was invented in 1976 as a human-readable file to store protein coordinates. It has a fixed-column width format limited to 80 columns. The PDB file format has undergone several revisions over the years; the latest revision was on November 21, 2012. However, the PDB file format is no longer being modified or extended to support new content. Instead, the PDBx/mmCIF format is used [50].

PDB File Format

The PDB file for a protein contains detailed information about the protein structure, including the position of each atom in three-dimensional space and its connectivity [51]. Each line of information in the file is called a record. A PDB file may contain several different types of records, arranged in a specific order to describe a structure. The most used records include ATOM, HETATM, TER, HELIX, SHEET, and SSBOND. Each ATOM record describes the position of an amino acid in the protein molecule using atomic coordinates (XYZ coordinates). A HETATM record describes the position (XYZ coordinates) of a non-standard residue such as inhibitors, cofactors, ions, and solvent. A TER record indicates the end of a chain of residues. A HELIX record describes the location and type of helices. A helix has a single record. A SHEET record describes the location and direction of each sheet. A SSBOND record defines disulfide bond linkages between cysteine residues. More details about PDB file format are available at www.wwpdb.org/documentation/file-format. Figure 1.40 shows examples of ATOM and HETAM records that describe the positions of the atoms forming amino acids and ligands, respectively. The columns from left to right are the record type, atom number, atom identity, residue identity, residue number in the sequence, coordinates X, Y, and Z, occupancy, temperature factor, and element symbol.

X, Y, and Z coordinate

							X	Y	Z			
Atoms forming Amino acids	ATOM	1	N	PRO	A	206	1.575	18.395	22.186	1.00	62.03	N
	ATOM	2	CA	PRO	A	206	0.681	17.523	22.924	1.00	61.35	C
	ATOM	3	C	PRO	A	206	1.347	17.210	24.257	1.00	60.41	C
	ATOM	4	O	PRO	A	206	2.037	18.082	24.805	1.00	63.67	O
	ATOM	5	CB	PRO	A	206	0.619	16.271	22.027	1.00	60.19	C
	ATOM	6	CG	PRO	A	206	1.789	16.392	21.063	1.00	60.20	C
	ATOM	7	CD	PRO	A	206	2.563	17.608	21.434	1.00	61.71	C
Atoms forming ligands	HETATM	2340	O16	NSI	A	478	20.315	-11.837	5.030	1.00	25.36	O
	HETATM	2341	C13	NSI	A	478	22.562	-11.306	4.619	1.00	22.01	C
	HETATM	2342	N10	NSI	A	478	22.743	-10.394	5.612	1.00	20.77	N
	HETATM	2343	C12	NSI	A	478	21.653	-9.738	6.345	1.00	21.49	C
	END											

FIGURE 1.40   ATOM and HETATM records of a PDB file.

PDBx or mmCIF File Format

The PDBx/mmCIF format became the standard PDB archive and an alternative to the PDB format in 2014. It is now the default format used by the PDB. The name mmCIF stands for Macromolecular Crystallographic Information File. The PDBx/mmCIF format is closely related to the Crystallographic Information File (CIF), which is a standard text file format for representing crystallographic information [52]. It explicitly documents all relationships between common data items such as atom and residue identifiers. This permits software applications to evaluate and validate referential integrity with any PDB entry, and maps information between the residue sequences of the experimental sample and the model coordinates.

The same information in the PDB file format is now available in the PDBx/mmCIF format. All data items in the PDBx/mmCIF format are identified by a name that begins with the underscore character. Each data item may consist of a category name and an attribute name. The category name is separated from the attribute name by a period. This combination of category and attribute (e.g., _atom_site.id) is called an mmCIF token. Data categories are presented either in key-value or tabular. Figure 1.41 shows an example of the key-value style.

The tabular style is used when there are multiple values for each token. In the tabular style, a "loop_" token is followed by rows of data item names and then white-space delimited data values. Figure 1.42 shows an example for the tabular style.

Each data item name after "loop_" token and starting with "_atom_site" corresponds to the data value in the data line starting with ATOM. For example, the item names _atom_site.Cartn_x, _atom_site.Cartn_y, and _atom_site.Cartn_z correspond to the 11th, 12th, and 13th data items (atomic coordinates). The list of data items is then looped through for each line of data values.

Visualizing Protein Structure

Once a protein structure has been solved and the structure information has been stored in a file, the three-dimensional structure of that protein can be visualized using protein molecular graphic software. There are numerous computer graphics programs that have been developed for visualizing and manipulating complicated three-dimensional structures of biomolecules. Computer visualization programs allow users to visually manipulate the structural images through a graphical user interface (GUI). A user can move, rotate, and zoom in or out an atomic model on a computer screen in real time, or examine any portion of the structure in detail. Examples of molecular visualization programs include the VMD (Visual Molecular Dynamics) and PyMol. These programs are designed for modeling, visualization, and analysis of biomolecules. They can read the PDB and PDBx/mmCIF file formats and display the contained structure. They can also provide a wide variety of methods for rendering and coloring a protein molecule. The VMD is available at www.ks.uiuc.edu/Research/vmd/ as an open-source program. It requires registration for downloading and installation. PyMol is available at https://pymol.org and it has different licenses including free licenses for students and teachers. The PDB or PDBx/mmCIF file of a protein can be downloaded from the PDB website and visualized on any of these programs. Figure 1.43 shows PyMol visualizing the structure of the ligand binding domain of PPAR Gamma (PDB ID: 2HFP).

```
_cell.entry_id          4HHB
_cell.length_a          63.150
_cell.length_b          83.590
_cell.length_c          53.800
_cell.angle_alpha       90.00
_cell.angle_beta        99.34
_cell.angle_gamma       90.00
_cell.Z_PDB             4
```

FIGURE 1.41   Key-value style of PDBx/mmCIF format.

```
loop_
_atom_site.group_PDB
_atom_site.id
_atom_site.type_symbol
_atom_site.label_atom_id
_atom_site.label_alt_id
_atom_site.label_comp_id
_atom_site.label_asym_id
_atom_site.label_entity_id
_atom_site.label_seq_id
_atom_site.pdbx_PDB_ins_code
_atom_site.Cartn_x
_atom_site.Cartn_y
_atom_site.Cartn_z
_atom_site.occupancy
_atom_site.B_iso_or_equiv
_atom_site.pdbx_formal_charge
_atom_site.auth_seq_id
_atom_site.auth_comp_id
_atom_site.auth_asym_id
_atom_site.auth_atom_id
_atom_site.pdbx_PDB_model_num
ATOM  1   N N   . PRO A 1 11  ? 1.575  18.395  22.186  1.00 62.03 ? 206 PRO A N   1
ATOM  2   C CA  . PRO A 1 11  ? 0.681  17.523  22.924  1.00 61.35 ? 206 PRO A CA  1
ATOM  3   C C   . PRO A 1 11  ? 1.347  17.210  24.257  1.00 60.41 ? 206 PRO A C   1
ATOM  4   O O   . PRO A 1 11  ? 2.037  18.082  24.805  1.00 63.67 ? 206 PRO A O   1
ATOM  5   C CB  . PRO A 1 11  ? 0.619  16.271  22.027  1.00 60.19 ? 206 PRO A CB  1
#
```

FIGURE 1.42   Tabular style of PDBx/mmCIF format.

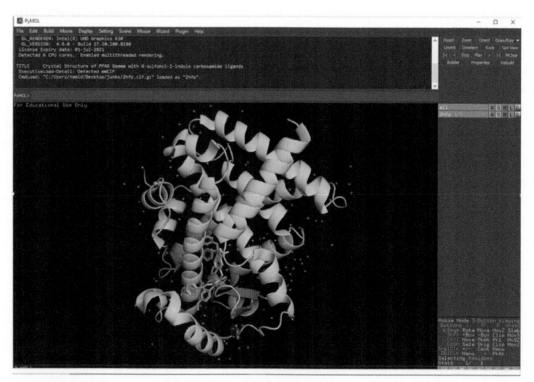

FIGURE 1.43   PyMol visualizing ligand binding domain of PPAR gamma.

GENE MUTATIONS

A gene mutation is the change that takes place in the sequence of a gene, and it contributes to diversity across organisms and may have widely differing consequences. For mutations to be heritable they must occur in cells that produce the next generation or germline cells. Such mutation is called germline mutations. On the other hand, somatic mutations (occur in the somatic cells) are not inheritable, and they only affect the present organism's body. The somatic mutations have no significance for the evolution. Evolutionary theory is mostly interested in germline mutations. Mutations may occur randomly, and the consequence may be harmful, useful, or have no effect at all. The beneficial gene changes may be conserved for a long term and passed to offspring. Generally, mutation rates are usually very low, and biological systems go to extraordinary lengths to keep them as low as possible, mostly because many mutational effects are harmful. Moreover, DNA repair or proofreading during DNA replication reduces the mutation rates. Mutations can also be due to the natural exposure of an organism to certain environmental factors, such as radiation or chemical carcinogens.

DNA mutations can occur in several ways. They have varying effects on the living organism, depending on where they occur and whether they alter the function of essential proteins. When the change involves only one nucleotide position in the DNA sequence it is called point mutation. DNA mutation can be caused by substitution, insertion, or deletion. In substitution mutation, a nucleotide will be replaced by one of the other three nucleotides. Substitution mutation that involves a single position is known as single nucleotide polymorphism (SNP). Substitution mutation can be silent, missense, or nonsense. In silent substitution mutation, the replacement does not change the coded amino acid (synonymous codon). For example, both codons GCA and GCC code for alanine amino acid (Ala), therefore replacing adenine (A) in GCA with cytosine (C) does not change the translated amino acid (Ala) and it has no effect on the protein. In missense substitution mutation, the nucleotide replacement will result in a codon that codes for a different amino acid (nonsynonymous codon). For example, the codon GGA codes for glycine (Gly), so substituting the first guanine (G) with adenine (A) will result in AGA codon, which codes for arginine amino acid (Arg). Therefore, it has a consequence in the protein translation. In a nonsense substitution mutation, the nucleotide substitution will result in a stop codon that terminates the protein translation before completion and the consequence will be a shorter protein that does not function properly. For example, the codon CAA codes for glutamine (Gln). If the cytosine (C) in CAA (in a protein coding region) is replaced by thymine (T), the resulting codon will be TAA (UAA), which is the stop codon. During translation in ribosome, the translation of protein will be terminated when UAA is reached. Figure 1.44 shows the three types of substitution.

In insertion mutation, a nucleotide or several nucleotides are inserted in the DNA sequence of a gene while in deletion mutation a nucleotide or several nucleotides are removed from the DNA sequence. Deletion and insertion mutation may cause frameshift, which occurs when mutation changes the open reading frame (ORF) of a gene. The resulting protein is usually nonfunctional.

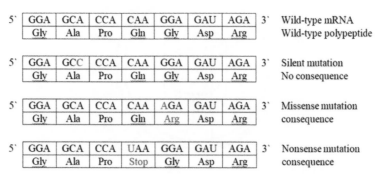

FIGURE 1.44   Substitution mutation and consequences.

VIRUS GENOME

Viruses are not living organisms; they lack the characteristics that living organisms have. Living organisms have definite cells that contain organelles and a metabolism system, and they can provide themselves with energy. Viruses do not have such ability; however, they can replicate but only inside living cells and can adapt to their environment and mutate. Since the virus is not a living organism it is defined as a small collection of genetic code, either DNA or RNA, surrounded by a protein coat called a capsid. The virus genome is surrounded by a nucleocapsid. Most viruses, but not all of them, are also surrounded by a membrane called the envelope surrounding the capsid. The virus envelope is usually acquired from the nuclear or cell membrane of the infected host cell (Figure 1.45) [33].

Viruses are classified based on the Baltimore classification system, which depends on the combination of their nucleic acid (DNA or RNA), nature of the strand (single-stranded or double-stranded), sense (positive-sense or negative-sense), and method of replication. The virus genome can be double-stranded DNA (dsDNA), single-stranded DNA (ssDNA), double-stranded RNA (dsRNA), or single-stranded RNA (ssRNA). The latter can either be positive-sense single-stranded RNA (+ssRNA), or negative-sense single-stranded RNA (-ssRNA). The positive-sense RNA strand if the RNA sequence of that strand is translated or translatable into protein and negative-sense RNA strand if the complementary RNA sequence of that strand, and not the original strand itself, is translated or translatable into protein [53]. The above criteria are used to classify viruses into several families such as Adenoviridae (dsDNA), Coronaviridae (ssRNA), Retroviridae (ssRNA), Parvoviridae (ssDNA), Poxviridae (dsDNA), etc.

Viruses proliferate by infecting cells and hijacking their protein synthesis machinery to replicate, producing multiple virions that are ready to infect new cells. A virion is a complete virus particle with all virus components. During infection, a virion first attaches to receptors on the membrane of a living cell. The receptors can be proteins, carbohydrates, or lipids. Once a virus is attached to a receptor it can enter the cell using one of two routes: endocytosis or non-endocytosis. In the endocytic route, the virus is coated with a clathrin protein and then transported in a vacuole into the cell. In non-endocytic route, the virus crosses the plasma membrane at neutral pH. Some viruses use both entry routes. Viruses such as retroviruses can also enter cells through cell-to-cell transmission [54].

Once the virus enters the host cell it will start to replicate. The replication depends on the viral genome (dsDNA, ssDNA, dsRNA, +ssRNA, -ssRNA, etc.). The transcription and translation are like the ones discussed above; however, viruses use their genomes, but they exploit the protein synthesis machinery to direct the host cell to synthesize their viral enzymes and capsid proteins and to assemble their new viral genomes. DNA

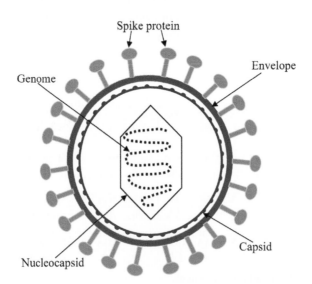

FIGURE 1.45 **Virus particle.**

viruses usually use the host cell proteins and enzymes to make additional DNA that is transcribed into mRNA translated into proteins. RNA viruses use the RNA strand as the template for mRNA, which is translated into proteins, and viral genomic RNA for assembling new virions. The RNA-virus Retroviruses, such as HIV, must be reverse-transcribed into DNA using reverse transcription process, which then is incorporated into the host cell genome. The process of reverse transcription is mediated by an enzyme known as reverse transcriptase. This enzyme is used at the laboratory to convert RNA into DNA called complementary DNA (cDNA) [55].

Following synthesis of viral proteins and viral genomes, the genomes are then encapsulated with capsid protein forming new virions, which are then released from the host cells. The number of virions released from a single infected cell is called the viral burst size. The virions can infect the adjacent cells and repeat the replication cycle. Some viruses are released after the death of the host cells, and some leave the infected cells by passing through the cell membrane without killing the infected cells.

Most viruses cause diseases; some of these diseases are severe, highly contagious and deadly. In past decades, the world has faced several viral disease outbreaks, such as the Ebola, SARS, and Zika viruses, which have had a massive death toll and impact on economies. Recently, the world has been struck by the outbreak of COVID-19, which is caused by a coronavirus called SARS-CoV-2. Up to this date, the world is trying to control its spread and to reduce its impact.

The COVID-19 infection starts with the attachment stage, in which the virus spike protein binds to the receptors on the cell membrane. Coronavirus uses the non-endocytic route to enter the host cell. The viral RNA is translated into large replicase polyproteins (pp1a and pp1ab), which subsequently cleave into viral NSPs (Nonstructural Proteins). The full anti-sense single-stranded RNA (-ssRNA) copies of the coronavirus genome are produced by the enzyme replicase using the full +ssRNA virus genome as a template strand. The spike protein, envelope protein, nucleocapsid protein, and capsid protein are translated from segments of the mRNA and are used in the assembly of new virions in Golgi body and endoplasmic reticulum of the host cell. Once virons have been assembled, they can be released by transporting them in vacuoles to the extracellular to infect new cells [56].

REFERENCES

1. Cochrane, G., et al., *The International Nucleotide Sequence Database Collaboration*. Nucleic Acids Res, 2011. **39** (Database issue): pp. D15–18.
2. Hetzer, M. and G. Cavalli, *Eukaryotic cells*. Curr Opin Cell Biol, 2011. **23**(3): pp. 255–257.
3. Souza, W., *Prokaryotic cells: structural organisation of the cytoskeleton and organelles*. Mem Inst Oswaldo Cruz, 2012. **107**(3): pp. 283–293.
4. Benbow, R.M., *Chromosome structures*. Sci Prog, 1992. **76**(301-302 Pt 3–4): pp. 425–450.
5. Schreck, R.R. and C.M. Disteche, *Chromosome banding techniques*. Curr Protoc Hum Genet, 2001. Chapter 4: Unit4 2.
6. Bolcun-Filas, E. and M.A. Handel, *Meiosis: the chromosomal foundation of reproduction*. Biol Reprod, 2018. **99**(1): pp. 112–126.
7. Garbers, D.L., *Molecular basis of fertilization*. Annu Rev Biochem, 1989. **58**: pp. 719–742.
8. Georgadaki, K., et al., *The molecular basis of fertilization (Review)*. Int J Mol Med, 2016. **38**(4): pp. 979–986.
9. Vaillancourt, C. and J. Lafond, *Human embryogenesis: overview*. Methods Mol Biol, 2009. **550**: pp. 3–7.
10. Margolin, W., *FtsZ and the division of prokaryotic cells and organelles*. Nat Rev Mol Cell Biol, 2005. **6**(11): pp. 862–871.
11. Watson, J.D. and F.H. Crick, *Molecular structure of nucleic acids: a structure for deoxyribose nucleic acid*. Clin Orthop Relat Res, 2007. **462**: pp. 3–5.
12. Green, E.D., J.D. Watson, and F.S. Collins, *Human Genome Project: Twenty-five years of big biology*. Nature, 2015. **526**(7571): pp. 29–31.
13. Salzberg, S.L., *Open questions: How many genes do we have?* BMC Biol, 2018. **16**(1): p. 94.
14. Bruford, E.A., et al., *Guidelines for human gene nomenclature*. Nat Genet, 2020. **52**(8): pp. 754–758.
15. Wojcik, F., *[Guidelines for human gene nomenclature]*. Ann Biol Clin (Paris), 2002. **60**(3): pp. 347–350.

16. Stringer, C., *The origin and evolution of Homo sapiens.* Philos Trans R Soc Lond B Biol Sci, 2016. **371**(1698).

17. Spieth, J. and D. Lawson, *Overview of gene structure.* WormBook, 2006: pp. 1–10.

18. Spieth, J., et al., *Overview of gene structure in C. elegans.* WormBook, 2014: pp. 1–18.

19. Haberle, V. and A. Stark, *Eukaryotic core promoters and the functional basis of transcription initiation.* Nat Rev Mol Cell Biol, 2018. **19**(10): pp. 621–637.

20. *IUPAC-IUB Commission on Biochemical Nomenclature (CBN). Abbreviations and symbols for nucleic acids, polynucleotides and their constituents. Recommendations 1970.* Eur J Biochem, 1970. **15**(2): pp. 203–208.

21. Shu, J.J., *A new integrated symmetrical table for genetic codes.* Biosystems, 2017. **151**: pp. 21–26.

22. Pennisi, E., *Genomics. ENCODE project writes eulogy for junk DNA.* Science, 2012. **337**(6099): pp. 1159, 1161.

23. Fan, H. and J.Y. Chu, *A brief review of short tandem repeat mutation.* Genomics Proteomics Bioinformatics, 2007. **5**(1): pp. 7–14.

24. Ponicsan, S.L., J.F. Kugel, and J.A. Goodrich, *Genomic gems: SINE RNAs regulate mRNA production.* Curr Opin Genet Dev, 2010. **20**(2): pp. 149–155.

25. Nelson, P.N., et al., *Human endogenous retroviruses: transposable elements with potential?* Clin Exp Immunol, 2004. **138**(1): pp. 1–9.

26. Cordaux, R. and M.A. Batzer, *The impact of retrotransposons on human genome evolution.* Nat Rev Genet, 2009. **10**(10): pp. 691–703.

27. Bourque, G., et al., *Ten things you should know about transposable elements.* Genome Biol, 2018. **19**(1): p. 199.

28. Zheng, D., et al., *Pseudogenes in the ENCODE regions: consensus annotation, analysis of transcription, and evolution.* Genome Res, 2007. **17**(6): pp. 839–851.

29. Torrents, D., et al., *A genome-wide survey of human pseudogenes.* Genome Res, 2003. **13**(12): pp. 2559–2567.

30. Bischof, J.M., et al., *Genome-wide identification of pseudogenes capable of disease-causing gene conversion.* Hum Mutat, 2006. **27**(6): pp. 545–552.

31. Turner, K.J., V. Vasu, and D.K. Griffin, *Telomere Biology and Human Phenotype.* Cells, 2019. **8**(1).

32. Aguado, J., F. d'Adda di Fagagna, and E. Wolvetang, *Telomere transcription in ageing.* Ageing Res Rev, 2020. **62**: pp. 101–115.

33. Lodish H.B.A., S.L. Zipursky, et al., *Molecular Cell Biology.* 4th ed. 2000. New York: Freeman.

34. Yusupov, M.M., et al., *Crystal structure of the ribosome at 5.5 A resolution.* Science, 2001. **292**(5518): pp. 883–896.

35. Torres-Machorro, A.L., et al., *Ribosomal RNA genes in eukaryotic microorganisms: witnesses of phylogeny?* FEMS Microbiol Rev, 2010. **34**(1): pp. 59–86.

36. Long, E.O. and I.B. Dawid, *Repeated genes in eukaryotes.* Annu Rev Biochem, 1980. **49**: pp. 727–764.

37. Sollner-Webb, B. and E.B. Mougey, *News from the nucleolus: rRNA gene expression.* Trends Biochem Sci, 1991. **16**(2): pp. 58–62.

38. Rich, A., *A Hybrid Helix Containing Both Deoxyribose and Ribose Polynucleotides and Its Relation to the Transfer of Information between the Nucleic Acids.* Proc Natl Acad Sci USA, 1960. **46**(8): pp. 1044–1053.

39. Bartel, D.P., *Metazoan MicroRNAs.* Cell, 2018. **173**(1): pp. 20–51.

40. Bartel, D.P., *MicroRNAs: target recognition and regulatory functions.* Cell, 2009. **136**(2): pp. 215–233.

41. Watson, J.D., *Molecular Biology of the Gene.* 7th ed. 2013. Pearson.

42. Eisenberg, E. and E.Y. Levanon, *Human housekeeping genes are compact.* Trends Genet, 2003. **19**(7): pp. 362–365.

43. Eisenberg, E. and E.Y. Levanon, *Human housekeeping genes, revisited.* Trends Genet, 2013. **29**(10): pp. 569–574.

44. Alberts B.J.A., J. Lewis, M. Raff, K. Roberts, and .P Walter, *Molecular Biology of the Cell.* 6th ed. 2008. New York: Garland Science.

45. Pan, Q., et al., *Deep surveying of alternative splicing complexity in the human transcriptome by high-throughput sequencing.* Nat Genet, 2008. **40**(12): pp. 1413–1415.

46. Cooper, G., *The Cell: A Molecular Approach.* 8th ed. 2018: Oxford: Oxford University Press.

47. Nelson, D.L., *Lehninger Principles of Biochemistry.* 7th ed. 2017: New York: W.H. Freeman.

48. Zwanzig, R., A. Szabo, and B. Bagchi, *Levinthal's paradox.* Proc Natl Acad Sci USA, 1992. **89**(1): pp. 20–22.

49. Pauling, L., R.B. Corey, and H.R. Branson, *The structure of proteins; two hydrogen-bonded helical configurations of the polypeptide chain.* Proc Natl Acad Sci USA, 1951. **37**(4): pp. 205–211.

50. Adams, P.D., et al., *Announcing mandatory submission of PDBx/mmCIF format files for crystallographic depositions to the Protein Data Bank (PDB).* Acta Crystallogr D Struct Biol, 2019. **75**(Pt 4): pp. 451–454.

51. Berman, H.M., *The Protein Data Bank: a historical perspective.* Acta Crystallogr A, 2008. **64**(Pt 1): pp. 88–95.

52. Brown, I.D., *CIF (Crystallographic Information File): A Standard for Crystallographic Data Interchange.* J Res Natl Inst Stand Technol, 1996. **101**(3): pp. 341–346.

53. Siegel, R.D. and C.G. Prober, *Classification of Viruses.* Principles and Practice of Pediatric Infectious Disease. 2008. 1001–1005. doi: 10.1016/B978-0-7020-3468-8.50207-8. Epub 2020 June 22.

54. Dimitrov, D.S., *Virus entry: molecular mechanisms and biomedical applications.* Nat Rev Microbiol, 2004. **2**(2): pp. 109–122.

55. Christopher J. Burrell, C.R.H.a.F.A.M., *Fenner and White's Medical Virology.* 5th ed. 2016: Cambridge, MA: Academic Press.

56. Yesudhas, D., A. Srivastava, and M.M. Gromiha, *COVID-19 outbreak: history, mechanism, transmission, structural studies and therapeutics.* Infection, 2021. **49**(2): pp. 199–213.

## CHAPTER 2

The Sources of Genomic Data

INTRODUCTION

In Chapter 1, we discussed the molecular aspects of the three major biomolecules DNA, RNA and proteins and gene transcription and translation, protein structures and mutations. In this chapter the focus will be on discussing the sources of the genomic data and how it will be generated from biological samples and represented digitally to serve as raw data for bioinformatics applications. The content of this chapter is a light introduction to some techniques in molecular biology and biotechnology laboratories. Those techniques are the sources of the genomics data; therefore, being familiar with these techniques and with data they generate will help in understanding bioinformatics databases. The chapter will begin with sample collection and extraction of DNA, RNA, and protein. Then we will discuss some essential techniques in biotechnology, such as polymerase chain reaction (PCR) sequencing of DNA and RNA. Those techniques are undertaken by biologists at the laboratories. They term this part the wet lab, distinguishing it from what happens next, the dry lab, or on the computer with the acquired raw data. This chapter will also briefly discuss some applications that generate intermediate data and file formats resulted from sequencing downstream data analysis. Therefore, this chapter is useful for readers who are not familiar with biotechnology techniques. But it is also a good refresher for readers with a biology background. In either case, it is strongly recommended to not skip this introductory chapter.

EXTRACTION OF DNA, RNA, AND PROTEINS

Scientists extract DNA, RNA, and proteins at the laboratories, where they can handle sample tissues or cells collected from organisms. Those three biomolecules are extracted using extraction kits and following certain protocols. Before DNA, RNA, or protein extraction a sample must be collected. Tissues or cells are collected from eukaryotic or prokaryotic organisms. Environmental samples are collected from water, food, vegetables, surfaces, etc. to extract the DNA, usually for bacterial identification purposes.

If the goal is DNA extraction, samples can be collected from a living or a dead organism, because the chemical composition of its double-stranded structure allows it to remain intact in dead cells for a long time. DNA can even be recovered from body fossils or fossilized remains including fossil bones and teeth. You may have already heard that the DNA of many extinct species, such as Neanderthal, have been sequenced from the samples of their remains that date back hundreds of thousands of years. In fact, the first Neanderthal DNA extracted was the mitochondrial DNA in 1997 [1]. A complete Neanderthal mitochondrial genome was sequenced in 2008 [2] and a complete Neanderthal nuclear genome was sequenced in 2014 [3]. Ancient DNA has been extracted from several extinct animals such as denisovans, mammoths, the passenger pigeon, and the zebra-like quagga. DNA was also extracted from Egyptian mummies.

RNA is extracted only from living tissues because gene transcription takes place only in living cells. Moreover, the chemical composition of RNA because of the presence of uracil (U) and its single-stranded

DOI: 10.1201/9781003226611-2

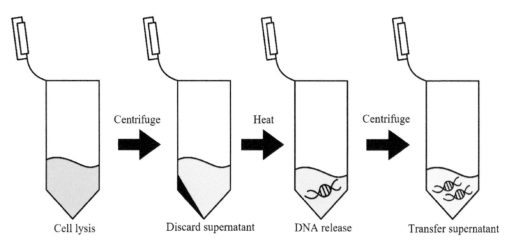

FIGURE 2.1   Example of DNA extraction steps.

structure makes it a target for several degrading factors such as ribonucleases (RNases), temperature, and others. Samples collected for RNA extraction are usually preserved using an RNA stabilizer that prevents degradation of RNA [4].

Proteins can be extracted from tissue collected from a living organism or recently died organism since, once an animal died, proteins may be denatured by enzymes, pH change, high temperature, or chemicals; therefore, samples need to be preserved and stored in the right conditions. There are several techniques for protein characterization including electron microscopy, NMR spectroscopy, chromatography, radioisotope labelling, protein identification and sequencing, UV spectroscopy, X-ray diffraction. Protein can also be sequenced using liquid chromatography tandem mass spectrometry [5–8].

Extracting any of these three biomolecules from samples is performed at the laboratories. Many life science companies provide extraction kits. A centrifuge is commonly used at the lab to separate those molecules following the kit protocol. Figure 2.1 shows the flow of one of the methods for DNA extraction.

DNA, RNA, AND PROTEIN QUALITY

After extracting DNA or RNA, the quality and concentration of DNA and RNA can be checked with a spectrophotometer (Nanodrop). The purity of DNA or RNA extractions is expressed as a 260/280 ratio, which is the ratio of light absorbance at 260 nm and 280 nm. A 260/280 ratio between 1.8 and 2.0 is generally accepted as "pure" DNA or RNA. On the other hand, the DNA or RNA concentration is given as nanogram per microliter (ng/µL) [9].

Although a Nanodrop spectrophotometer can be used to measure RNA purity and concentration, better results are achieved by using a Bioanalyzer, which, in addition to the purity and concentration, also provides a measure for RNA integrity (intact mRNA). Not like DNA, mRNA can be degraded easily by temperature and RNase or be broken down into nucleotides. RNA integrity is measured by the RNA integrity number (RIN), which ranges from 1 to 10. RNA with low RIN may not be suitable for RNA studies such as gene expression using PCR, microarray, or sequencing. The mRNA is only 1–3% of the total RNA and other RNA is around 97%. Direct measurement of mRNA integrity is not easy. Instead 28S rRNA:18S rRNA ratio (2:1) is used to assess the mRNA integrity. RIN has historically been assessed by electrophoresis of total RNA followed by staining with ethidium bromide and visual assessment of 28S:18S rRNA ratio on the image of agarose gels. These days that historical method has been replaced with the bioanalyzer, which uses capillary electrophoresis and fluorescence to evaluate both RNA concentration and RNA integrity [10].

The concentration of the extracted protein can be determined by protein assays. There are several kits for determining whole protein concentration, such as bicinchoninic acid assay (BCA assay) [11, 12], and for determining the concentration of a specific protein in a sample, such as enzyme-linked immunosorbent assay

(ELISA) [13]. All kits come with standard solutions with known concentrations to create a standard curve. Spectrophotometers (plate readers) are used to read the percentage of light absorbed by the solutions. The known concentrations of the standard solutions and the light absorbance of those solutions are used to obtain an equation by regression. The equation will then be used to obtain the concentration of the protein in the sample.

Using any of the three biomolecules in research depends on the objectives of the research. DNA is used for gene identification, whole genome sequencing, genotyping and variants identification (SNPs, InDels, and CNVs), and identification of bacterial and fungal population in environmental samples. RNA is used for studying gene expression, gene profiling, and whole exome sequencing (WES). Proteins are used in diagnostics and confirmatory research, profiling of certain protein panel, whole protein profiling, and pathways.

REVERSE TRANSCRIPTION

Since RNA is less stable and degradable, RNA is converted into complementary DNA (cDNA) before it is used in an experiment at the laboratory. The RNA is converted into cDNA by a process called reverse transcription, which uses reverse transcriptase enzyme to creates double-stranded DNA from an RNA template.

Reverse transcriptase is found in retroviruses that convert their RNA genome into double-stranded DNA. Reverse transcriptase first uses the mRNA strand as a template to transcribe a complementary strand of DNA making an RNA/DNA hybrid. Next, RNase degrades the RNA strand of the hybrid leaving the single-stranded DNA. The single-stranded DNA is then used as a template for synthesizing double-stranded complementary DNA (cDNA) as shown in Figure 2.2 [14].

POLYMERASE CHAIN REACTION

Polymerase chain reaction (PCR) is a technique used to amplify a specific target DNA sequence, allowing for the isolation, sequencing, or cloning of a single sequence of a gene, a region of a genome, a transcript, among many. The underlying principle of the PCR is taken from the process of DNA synthesis during gene transcription in living organisms using an enzyme called DNA polymerase. PCR was developed by Kary Mullis and colleagues at Cetus Corporation in the early 1980s. Later in 1993, Kary received a Nobel Prize in chemistry for his invention [15]. The PCR process involves adding all PCR reaction components in a PCR tube and heating to a high temperature and cooling several times. Historically, the challenge was the use of non-thermostable

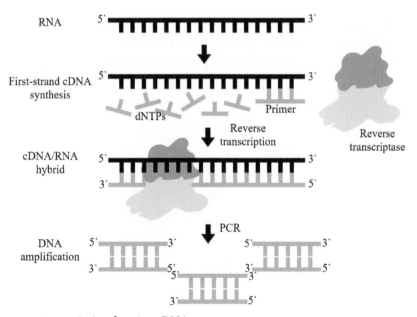

FIGURE 2.2 RNA reverse transcription forming cDNA.

DNA polymerase, which degraded every time the mixture was heated to a high temperature. Researcher used to add polymerase manually after every heating. The breakthrough in PCR came with the isolation and purification of thermostable DNA polymerases, or Taq polymerase, extracted from a thermophilic bacterium called *Thermus aquaticus* that can tolerate high temperatures [16]. This thermophilic species of bacteria resides in the outflows of thermal pools in Yellowstone National Park located in the western United States. This discovery allowed the evolution of PCR to the present automated and programmable PCR thermal cyclers. Since then, PCR has been elaborated in many ways and is now commonly used for a wide variety of applications including genotyping, cloning, mutation detection, sequencing, microarrays, forensics, and paternity testing.

At the present time, there are several PCR brands, but the underlying principle remains the same. The major components of a PCR reaction include (1) the DNA template, (2) forward and reverse primers, (3) Taq polymerase, and (4) the four DNA nucleotides called deoxynucleotide triphosphates or dNTP: deoxyadenosine triphosphate (dATP), deoxycytidine triphosphate (dCTP), deoxyguanosine triphosphate (dGTP), and deoxythymidine triphosphate (dTTP). There are other items that may be required by the PCR reaction, such as sterile, deionized water, PCR reaction buffer, magnesium chloride ($MgCl_2$), which provides Mg^{++} divalent cations required as a cofactor for the polymerase enzyme, and SYBR green, which is a dye used as a nucleic acid stain in real-time PCR. These days, the PCR reaction has been greatly simplified by PCR kit-manufacturing companies, which provide all the PCR components, except the template DNA and primers, as a single mixture called PCR supermix that includes polymerase, nucleotides, buffer, magnesium chloride, and SYBR green. At the wet lab, a researcher may need to provide only the DNA/cDNA samples (DNA template) and primers (primer designing is covered in Chapter 3 and 8). In a typical PCR reaction, all the above-mentioned PCR components are added in a tube, the PCR tube, and then the tube is put in a thermal cycler. In the following we will discuss the PCR components and what the thermocycler does.

DNA Template   The DNA template is either genomic DNA or cDNA obtained as a result of reverse transcription of mRNA. The purpose of PCR is to amplify a specific region of a DNA sequence (e.g., gene) or specific cDNA (e.g., gene transcript) by rapidly making millions to billions of copies of that specific DNA region, allowing trace and undetectable pieces of DNA to be larger and millions of copies enough to be studied and analyzed. All components of the PCR are mixed in a PCR tube. The first step in the PCR reaction is the denaturing of the double-stranded DNA creating two DNA strand from a single piece. The separation of DNA strands requires breaking the hydrogen bonds by heating the PCR reaction tube at ~98°C for one minute (Figure 2.3).

The purpose of PCR is to amplify a specific region of the DNA sequence. When we collect a DNA sample, it usually contains DNA fragments of the entire genome in the form of very small undetectable DNA fragments. However, the purpose of the PCR reaction is to amplify a specific sequence, which can be a gene or a segment

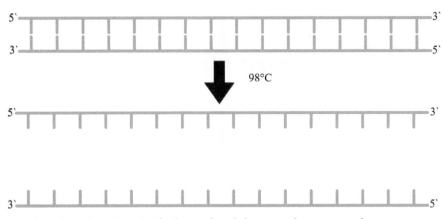

FIGURE 2.3   Denaturing of DNA by breaking hydrogen bonds between the two strands.

of a gene, intron, exon, gene transcript, etc. This specific region can be amplified specifically by using a small single-stranded DNA sequences called primers.

Primers A primer is a short single-stranded DNA or oligonucleotide that is usually between 18 and 25 bases and can bind (hybridize) to the target region of a template DNA. The PCR is inspired by the DNA synthesis in the cells of living organisms during gene transcription and primers are utilized by the cells for the initiation of DNA synthesis. For the same purpose, primers are used in the PCR reactions for the initiation of DNA elongation of the strand complementing the single template DNA strands separated by denaturing in the previous step. For a single target DNA region, two primers are required: the forward primer and the reverse primer. Each primer will anneal to a DNA strand at 3`end of the template strand so the synthesis of the complementary strand by Taq polymerase will move toward 5`end of the template strand. Following the separation of DNA strands at 98°C for a minute, the temperature can be reduced to a level known as the annealing temperature (~60°C for one minute) that allows the primers to form hydrogen bonds with their complementary regions of the targeted DNA region that is intended to amplify (Figure 2.4).

The primers must specifically bind to the targeted region, not to any other region in the genome; otherwise, the other regions will be amplified as well, leading to false results. For example, to show the importance of the specificity of the primers, assume that you wish to use PCR to study the gene expression of FAM83A, which encodes for the FAM83A protein isoform A. An elevated expression of this gene is associated with some tumors such as lung tumors, prostate cancers, and bladder carcinomas. To study FAM83A gene expression, you need to design specific forward and reverse primers to amplify this gene. Assume that the primers you designed are not specific for the FAM83A gene, but they can also anneal to regions of other genes. When you perform the PCR experiment, such non-specific primers will amplify other non-targeted regions and will lead to false gene expression results and false diagnosis. To avoid amplifying other genes, the primers used in the PCR must be specific for the target DNA region. Primer designing is covered in detail in Chapter 3 and 8. For the time being, it is enough to know that a primer is a small single-stranded DNA sequence that can hybridize specifically to a single strand of a targeted DNA region to initialize DNA synthesis by the polymerase enzyme.

Taq Polymerase The Taq polymerase is the thermostable polymerase enzyme that synthesizes the complementary strand of the template DNA strand. After the forward and reverse primers have annealed to template strands, the temperature can be adjusted to the temperature (~70°C for one minute) in which the polymerase will be activated and positioned at 3`end of the annealed primer sequences, and then it starts to add deoxynucleotides (dATP, dCTP, dGTP, or dTTP) to complement the template strand forming double-stranded DNA (Figure 2.5).

The order of denaturing, annealing, and elongation temperatures is called a cycle. The cycle is repeated several times (usually 40 cycles). After 40 cycles, if the target DNA segment is present, billions of copies will be created. For example, a single DNA is amplified 2^{40} (1,099,511,627,776) times. A DNA sample extracted from tissues may have thousands or millions of DNA pieces. After PCR completion, there will be an astronomical number of copies of the target DNA region if it is present in the sample. Otherwise, there will be no copy of the region of interest. The amplified DNA is known as PCR product or amplicon. The PCR product is either

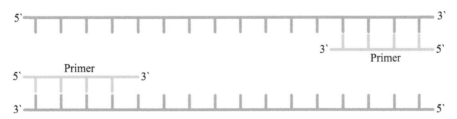

FIGURE 2.4   Forward and reverse primer forming hydrogen bonds with DNA strands.

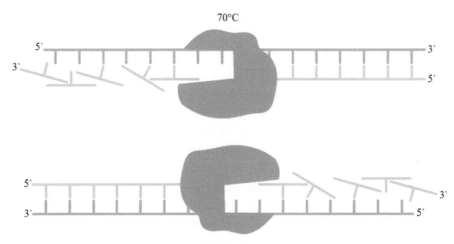

FIGURE 2.5   Complementary DNA strand synthesis by polymerase.

analyzed by using gel electrophoresis or using a real-time PCR technique. In the gel electrophoresis method, PCR is run in agarose gel electrophoresis and then stained with ethidium bromide, which is a fluorescent agent that binds only to the double-stranded DNA in the gel. An image of the stained gel can be taken using a UV illuminator or gel documentation system (Gel Doc). Bands of the PCR products can be analyzed.

Most labs nowadays use the real-time PCR technique, which enables them to view the PCR results in real time. A real-time PCR reaction uses fluorescent dyes such as SYBR green or TaqMan, which bind to the double-stranded DNA during the PCR process, and the fluorescence level emitted from these dyes increases every time the copies of the double-stranded DNA increase in number per cycle. The fluorescence levels and cycle numbers are graphed in an amplification plot on a computer screen and updated in real time until the last PCR cycle is reached. The PCR cycle in which fluorescence level of a sample starts to go up is known as the threshold cycle (Cq) or (Ct). The Cqs of samples are used for downstream analysis, especially in relative gene expression and absolute viral quantification.

Visualizing PCR results using either gel electrophoresis or real-time PCR amplification plot is followed by further analysis and investigation based on the research objectives. The PCR product can be sequenced using Sanger sequencing technique and the sequences can be submitted to the Nucleotide database.

FIRST-GENERATION SEQUENCING

DNA or RNA samples are extracted and purified at laboratories from tissues or cells of an organism. The genetic information carried by these biomolecules is represented by the orders of the nucleotides in these molecules. Sequencing is the determination of the orders of nucleotide bases, adenines (As), cytosines (Cs), guanines (Gs), and thymines (Ts), in the DNA or RNA molecules.

Bovine insulin was the first-ever protein to be sequenced [17]. That milestone was in 1952, when insulin was sequenced by Frederick Sanger, the British biochemist, who opened the door widely to the most amazing scientific progress in biology. The second milestone was the sequencing of alanine tRNA in 1965 after three years of continuous work with one gram of pure material extracted from 140 kg of yeast to determine a sequence of 76 nucleotides of the RNA [18]. The first sequencing of 12 bases of the DNA of bacteriophage lambda using the primer extension method was reported by Ray Wu at Cornell University in 1968 [19]. Two methods for sequencing were then developed in the 1970s: (1) Gilbert and Maxam developed chemical sequencing [20], which was based on nucleobase-specific partial chemical modification of DNA and subsequent cleavage of the DNA backbone at sites adjacent to the modified nucleotides and (2) Sanger and Coulson developed the chain-terminator method [21] based on the selective incorporation of chain-terminating dideoxynucleotides by DNA polymerase. These two methods were used in shotgun sequencing, which involved breaking genome into DNA fragments. These fragments were then sequenced individually and assembled based on the overlaps

[22]. A great stride forward was achieved by developing automated, fluorescence-based Sanger sequencing machines in 1987 by Smith, Hood and Applied Biosystems, which could generate around 1,000 bases per day.

The sequencing of genes and other parts of the genome of organisms have become essential for basic genomics research studying biological processes, diseases, the pathogenicity of diseases, diagnostic or forensic research, drug discovery, gene therapy, and more. The order of the nucleotide bases along DNA contains the complete set of genetic information and instructions that make up the genetic inheritance. Nowadays, there are several sequencing technologies [23].

Maxam-Gilbert Sequencing

The Maxam-Gilbert sequencing method is based on the chemical modification of DNA molecules and subsequent cleavage at specific bases. The various steps of Maxam-Gilbert sequencing include denaturing DNA, separation of single-stranded DNA (ssDNA) with gel electrophoresis, labeling the ssDNA with phosphorus radioactive isotope (in phosphate group), treating with chemicals for cutting the ssDNA into fragments, polyacrylamide gel electrophoresis, and autoradiography.

DNA Denaturing   The first step in Maxam-Gilbert sequencing is the denaturing of the double-stranded DNA (dsDNA) by heating or use of helicase enzyme to generate single-stranded DNA (ssDNA). A double-stranded DNA molecule will generate two complementary strands (Figure 2.6). Only one strand of the molecule can be used for sequencing.

Separation of ssDNA with Gel Electrophoresis   The ssDNA is run in a gel electrophoresis. The ssDNA with purine nucleotide bases (A and G) will be heavier than their complementary strands; therefore, they move slower in the gel electrophoresis than their complementary strands. This will give rise to two bands of ssDNA on the gel. Any of the bands can be cut and the DNA can be eluted to obtain the purified ssDNA in tubes.

Labeling With Radioactive Isotope (32P)   The 5` ends or 3` ends of the eluted ssDNA will be labeled by an isotope. The 5` ends are usually labeled by removing the phosphate group by using alkaline phosphatase and

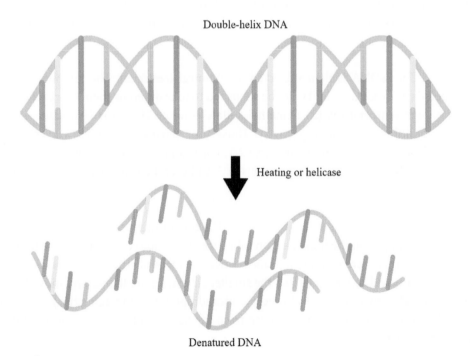

FIGURE 2.6   DNA denaturing.

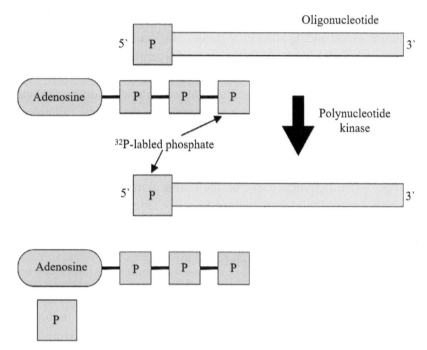

FIGURE 2.7 Labeling 5' ends of ssDNA molecules with 32P-labeled phosphate group.

TABLE 2.1 Chemical Treatments

Reaction Tube	1	2	3	4
Tube name	A+G	G	C+T	C
Chemical reactions	Dimethyl sulfate + NaOH + high temp	Dimethyl sulfate + dilute HCL	Hydrazine + piperidine	Hydrazine + piperidine + NaCl
Fragment positions	A or G	G	C or T	C

adding a ^{32}P-labeled phosphate group, which is transferred from adenosine triphosphate (ATP) by the enzyme called polynucleotide kinase that removes the gamma phosphate of the ATP and adds it to the 5` end of the ssDNA (Figure 2.7).

Chemical Treatment   The ssDNA is then subjected to chemical treatment. The sample is divided into four reaction tubes labeled (A+G, G, C+T, and C) to be subjected to four different chemical reactions: (1) Dimethyl sulfate + NaOH + high temperature, (2) Dimethyl sulfate + dilute HCL, (3) Hydrazine + piperidine, and (4) Hydrazine + piperidine + NaCl, respectively. Those four separate reactions will create breaks in the positions of the nucleotide bases, as shown in Table 2.1. For example, dimethyl sulfate + NaOH + high temperature will cut the ssDNA molecule in the positions of A and G and create breaks and the same for the other three reactions.

Polyacrylamide Gel Electrophoresis and Autoradiography   The 6% polyacrylamide gel is then used for running the four reactions. The samples in the four reaction tubes are loaded into different wells labeled A+G, G, C+T, and C so that, after running, there will be four lanes. Since the DNA synthesis takes place from 5` end to 3` end, the fragments or cuts will be sorted so that the smaller fragments are lighter and move faster in the polyacrylamide gel. The gel electrophoresis is followed by autoradiography for imaging the gel. The position order of the nucleotide bases A, C, G, and T can be solved from the bands on the gel. The order of the bases would be from the bottom to the top (Figure 2.8).

DNA sequence: ^{32}P-TGAGATCAGC

Cleavage the sequence at:

A+G	G	C	C+T
^{32}P-T	^{32}P-T	^{32}P-TGAGAT	^{32}P-TGAGA
^{32}P-TG	^{32}P-TGA	^{32}P-TGAGATCAG	^{32}P-TGAGAT
^{32}P-TGA	^{32}P-TGAGATCA		^{32}P-TGAGATCAG
^{32}P-TGAG			
^{32}P-TGAGATC			
^{32}P-TGAGATCA			

#	A+G	G	C	C+T	Base
10			■	■	C
9	■	■			G
8	■				A
7			■	■	C
6				■	T
5	■				A
4	■	■			G
3	■				A
2	■	■			G
1					T

FIGURE 2.8   Gel image and sequencing.

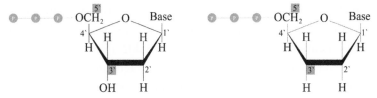

FIGURE 2.9   Normal nucleotide (dNTP) and radio-labeled nucleotide (ddNTP).

From the gel image, the order of nucleotide in the DNA molecule can be solved starting from the bottom to top. The sequence of the ten-nucleotide DNA is (5`-TGAGATCAGC-3`).

The downside of the Maxam-Gilbert sequencing method is that it is unsafe because of the toxic chemical and hazardous radioactive materials used and it also involves many steps that are difficult to automate.

Sanger Chain-Terminator Sequencing Method

The Sanger sequencing method, also called the chain-terminator method, is more efficient than Maxam-Gilbert and it uses fewer toxic chemicals and lower amounts of radioactivity. The key principle of the Sanger method is the use of PCR (ssDNA template, primer, polymerase, and normal nucleotide (dNTPs)) to sequence the template DNA. However, with the PCR reaction, radio-labeled dideoxynucleotide triphosphates (ddNTPs) are also added as DNA chain-terminators. The dNTPs have the hydroxyl group at the 3` position and hydrogen group at 2`position of the nucleotide sugar. On the other hand, the ddNTPs have hydrogen group at both the 2` and 3` position of the nucleotide sugar (Figure 2.9).

The four ddNTPs are ddATP, ddGTP, ddCTP, or ddTTP for the label A, G, C, and T respectively. Lack of a 3`-OH group in ddNTPs would prevent the formation of a phosphodiester bond between two nucleotides.

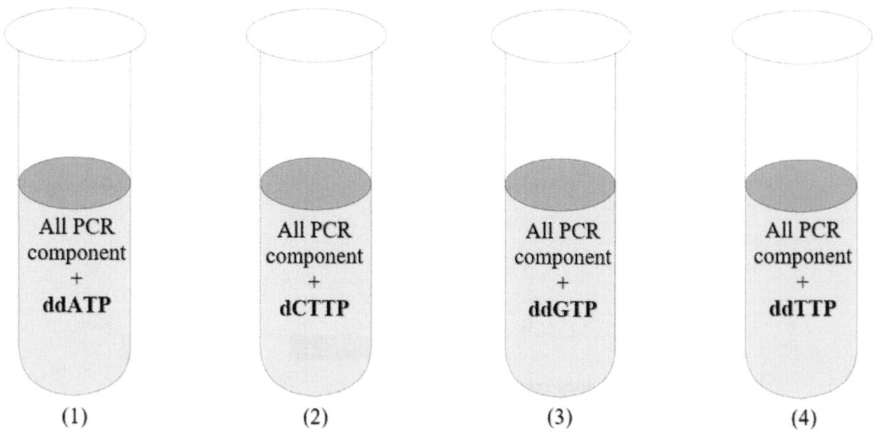

FIGURE 2.10   The four PCR reaction tubes for sanger sequencing method.

Thus, adding any of the ddNTPs instead of a normal nucleotide will terminate the DNA strand extension, resulting in DNA fragments of varying lengths.

The first steps in the Sanger method are like the PCR steps. However, for a single DNA sample there must be four different reactions in four separate PCR tubes labeled ddATP, ddGTP, ddCTP, and ddTTP. Each reaction tube will include the template DNA that we wish to sequence, primers, the polymerase enzyme, normal nucleotides (dATP, dCTP, dGTP, and dTTP), and only one type of ddNTPs (ddATP, ddGTP, ddCTP, or ddTTP) according to the labeled tube (e.g., for the tube labeled ddATP, ddATP will be added) (Figure 2.10).

The process will start by heating the reaction tube (denaturing temperature to ~98°C for one minute) to denature the DNA strands into ssDNA strands. The temperature is then reduced (annealing temperature at ~60°C for one minute) to allow primer annealing. Then the temperature is changed (enzyme activation temperature at 70°C for one minute) to allow the activation of polymerase and adding of nucleotides (A, C, G, or T) to elongate the complementary strand of the ssDNA. If a ddNTP is added instead, the elongation of the strand will be terminated at that position, forming a sequence fragment.

When this cycle is repeated many times, in the four tubes, there will be DNA fragments with different lengths ending with labeled ddNTPs at any position on the template DNA. For example, for any position in the DNA with G, there will be a fragment ending with ddGTP and the same for the other three nucleotides A, C, and T.

The newly synthesized DNA fragments with labeled ends are then separated by size using gel electrophoresis on a denaturing polyacrylamide-urea gel with each of the four reactions (ddATP, ddGTP, ddCTP, and ddTTP) running in a separate lane labeled A, T, G, and C respectively. The DNA fragments will be separated by lengths; the smaller fragments will move faster in the gel. The DNA bands are then visualized by autoradiography or UV light, and the order of the nucleotide bases on the DNA sequence can be directly read from the X-ray film or gel image. The relative positions of the different bands among the four lanes are then used to read the DNA sequence from bottom (5` end) to top (3` end) (Figure 2.11).

When all fragments are sorted by length and lined up, the last nucleotide, which is a labeled ddNTP, of each fragment is a complementary nucleotide at that position. For example, assume that we had the ssDNA strand with unknown sequence AGTTCACT; the fragments and their order from the bottom to the top after Sanger PCR method would be:

A
AG
AGT
AGTT

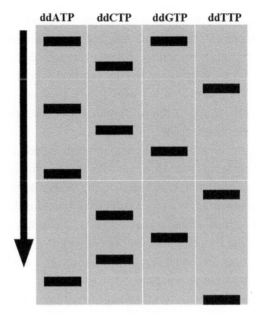

FIGURE 2.11   Gel image showing four lanes for sanger sequencing.

AGTTC
AGTTCA
AGTTCAC
AGTTCACT

The sequence would be the complement bases of the last labeled bases after sorting the fragments from the shortest to the longest. Each terminal nucleotide ddNTP has a different color so the solved sequence would be TCAAGTGA.

Sanger Dye-Terminator Sequencing Method

The key principle of the dye-terminator sequencing method is like the chain-terminator method, except that each of the chain-terminator ddNTPs are labeled with fluorescent dye with different wavelengths of fluorescence and emission. Moreover, there is no need for separate four reactions. The DNA template is combined in a tube with primers, DNA polymerase, normal DNA nucleotides (dATP, dTTP, dGTP, and dCTP), and the four dye-labeled dideoxynucleotides (ddATP, ddTTP, ddGTP, and ddCTP). The ddNTPs are added in a smaller amount. The mixture is first heated to denature the template DNA (denaturing temperature), then it is cooled so that the primer can bind to the single-stranded template (annealing temperature). Then the temperature is raised to allow the DNA polymerase to synthesize new DNA strands by adding nucleotides starting from the primer sequences. DNA polymerase will continue adding nucleotides to the chain until a ddNTP is added instead of a normal one. At that position, no further nucleotides will be added, so the strand synthesis will be terminated with the dye-labeled ddNTP. This process is repeated in several cycles. At the end, the dye-labeled ddNTPs would have been incorporated at every single position of the target DNA. Thus, the reaction tube will contain fragments of different lengths, ending at each of the nucleotide positions in the original DNA. The ends of each fragment will be labeled with a dye that indicates its final nucleotide. The fragments in the reaction tubes are run through a capillary gel electrophoresis tube. Short fragments move faster through the pores of the gel than long fragments. A detector using a laser illumination (camera) detects the attached dye when each fragment crosses a threshold line at the end of the tube. The smallest fragment, which crosses the line, is just a single nucleotide after the primer, followed by a fragment of two nucleotides, followed by a fragment of three nucleotides, and so on. The images or signals captured by the camera are converted to a readable form called an electropherogram, from which the sequence of the target DNA can then be determined. The electropherogram is a graphical representation of data received from a sequencing machine and is also known as a trace. In an electropherogram, each nucleotide base is represented by a different color and each line represents one of the four nucleotides. The peaks of the lines indicate the strength of the signal given off from the laser beam as it hits the DNA fragment. In other words, each peak corresponds to a fluorescently labeled nucleotide base, and the order of the peaks is the nucleotide sequence since the fragments have previously been ordered by the capillary gel electrophoresis.

Automation of the Sanger dye-terminator sequencing method is well established, and many companies provide sequencing service using this method. However, it is suitable for low-scale sequencing such as PCR products. The first automated sequencing machine based on the Sanger method was manufactured by Applied Biosystems in 1986. This machine was used by Craig Venter to initiate the Human Genome Project in October 1990 [24]. At that time, the sequencing machine was able to run 24 samples at a time and to yield 12,000 DNA letters per day. The Human Genome Project ended by sequencing the whole human genome in April 2003. Today's machines based on the Sanger method can typically handle 96 samples at a time and read around 750 to 1,000 base pairs of sequence from a single reaction.

Most automated sequencing machines based on the Sanger method provide the results of the DNA sequencing in three data files with file name extensions: ".ab1", ".seq", and ".phd.1".

The ab1 file (ABI sequencer data file), also known as the trace file, includes raw data that has been output from Applied Biosystems' Sequencing Analysis Software. The file can be opened using the right software. The file includes quality information for the base calls, the chromatogram (electropherogram), and the DNA sequence (Figure 2.12).

The data contained in the ab1 file represents the detection of the ordered fragments that were different by one base while they were passing by the detector. The line traces represent the florescence level of the dye-labeled ddNTP. The length of time that it takes to pass through the capillary gel matrix corresponds to the length of the amplified fragment. The peaks of the lines represent the quality of the base call at that location. The nucleotide bases are also shown at the top or bottom in ab1 file. Each base is given a color corresponding to the line color. The trace line of the good quality base call at a position call is steep, distinct, smooth, and with single peak. Such quality represents well-separated fragments as they pass through the florescence detector in the sequencing machine. If peaks of the lines are overlapped, jagged, or have broad shoulders the base calls are not reliable and should not be used. The poor quality may be due to contamination of the sample, multiple PCR products due to non-specific primers, or improper PCR process. The poor-quality base call at the beginning and the end of the read can be trimmed using software.

The phd.1 file (Phred file) is a simple text file containing two sections: comment section and base calling section. The comment section begins with "BEGIN_ COMMENT" and ends with "END_COMMENT" and includes technical information of the sequencing. The base calling section begins with "BEGIN_DNA" and ends with "END_DNA" and it includes three columns; base calls, and the associated Phred qualities and positions in the trace.

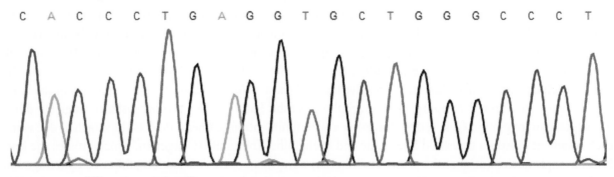

FIGURE 2.12   ABI sequencer data file.

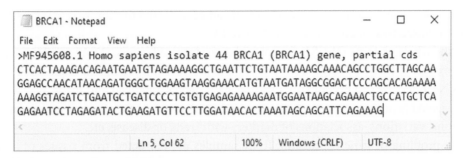

FIGURE 2.13   DNA sequence in FASTA format.

The Phred quality scores represent the likelihood of the corresponding base being called incorrectly and it is given by

$$Q = -10\log_{10} p \qquad (2.1)$$

where p is the probability that the base is called incorrectly.

$$p = 10^{-\frac{Q}{10}} \qquad (2.2)$$

For example, with a base call with Phred score of 10 (Q=10), there is a 10% (P=0.1) chance that the base at that position has been called incorrectly [25].

The seq file is a plain text file that contains the sequence of the nucleotide base of the sequenced DNA in FASTA format, which is a plain text file containing the sequence of the target DNA. The FASTA format file begins with a single-line description, followed by lines of sequence data. The description line is distinguished from the sequence data by a greater than (">") symbol in the first column. The word following the ">" symbol is the identifier of the sequence, and the rest of the line is the description (both are optional). There should be no space between the ">" and the first letter of the identifier (Figure 2.13) [26].

The FASTA file is the simplest data format for genomic data used in bioinformatics. The sequencing machines based on the Sanger method usually provide DNA sequences in FASTA format.

NEXT-GENERATION SEQUENCING

A few decades after first-generation sequencing invention, next-generation sequencing (NGS) was developed to revolutionize the collection of genomic data. NGS technologies are different from the first-generation sequencing method in that they provide massively parallel sequencing, extremely high throughput from multiple samples at much reduced cost. Millions to billions of DNA nucleotides can be sequenced in parallel, yielding substantially massive sequences.

NGS includes several high throughput methods that are able to sequence millions of DNA fragments simultaneously in a single experiment using a sequencing library rather than chain-termination sequencing, which is able to sequence only individual DNA fragments. NGS makes possible the sequencing of the genomes of many organisms in very short periods of time at far less cost and has revolutionized genomic research. Massive genomic data generated by NGS is deposited by researchers in databases on a daily basis. NGS is used in various applications such as sequencing the genome of an organism and investigation of genome diversity using whole genome sequencing, gene-expression profiling by RNA sequencing (RNA-seq), detecting variants in protein-coding region by sequencing the exome (whole-exome sequencing), studying specific panels of genes by targeted gene sequencing, identification of bacteria recovered from environmental samples using metagenomics sequencing, and studying genetic modifications that are not attributable to changes in the primary DNA sequence (e.g. methylation) by chromatin immunoprecipitation sequencing (ChIP-Seq). Such

NGS applications allow generation of massive data that can be analyzed to achieve several research objectives. NGS techniques are used to sequence either DNA or RNA.

To sequence the whole genome (WGS) of an organism or targeted genes, DNA samples are required. DNA samples can be extracted from tissues collected from a living or dead organism. Even DNA of some extinct animals such as Neanderthal and other extinct species have been sequenced and made available in databases. The WGS and targeted gene sequencing are usually used to identify genes, markers, and variants that help to study the functions, variations, associations of markers with traits or disease, etc.

To study gene profiling or gene expression, RNA samples are extracted from tissues of living organisms since, once an organism has died, the gene transcription will cease and RNAs will be degraded by enzymes and cannot be recovered. RNA is not sequenced as it is; instead, it is converted into complementary DNA (cDNA) before sequencing.

There are several NGS technologies with different underlying biochemistries and protocols [27]. Illumina sequencing technology is based on sequencing-by-synthesis [28], in which the base calling takes place while synthesizing a complementary strand of a DNA fragment. SOLiD (Sequencing by Oligonucleotide Ligation and Detection) uses a sequencing-by-ligation process. Oxford Nanopore Technologies uses nanopore sequencing, in which it sequences the DNA fragment through detecting differential electric field signal caused by different nucleotides when a strand of DNA passes through a nanopore structure. The workflow of an NGS experiment is similar for most of these technologies. However, we will discuss the sequencing-by-synthesis because it is the most used sequencing technology [29].

Library Preparation

Library preparation for NGS requires fragmentation of DNA and ligation of specific adaptor oligos to the fragments to be sequenced. First, DNA is fragmented to the optimal length determined by the NGS technology used for sequencing. Because DNA fragmentation does not result in homogeneous, blunt-ended fragments, end repair is needed to ensure that each DNA fragment is free of overhangs and contains 5` phosphate and 3` hydroxyl groups. In the following we will discuss DNA library preparation for whole genome sequencing, DNA preparation library for targeted genomic regions, and RNA library preparation. The library preparation is similar for most sequencing technologies. We will discuss two library preparation methods for Illumina, since these are the most used platform. The two methods are TruSeq-style and Nextera/Transposon.

TruSeq-style DNA Preparation
TruSeq DNA preparation involves several steps:

(1) Fragmentation. The DNA is fragmented mechanically by ultrasonication into DNA inserts (fragments) of optimal size (Figure 2.14). The most recent preparation kit provides either large fragments of 550 bp or small fragments of 350 bp insert.

(2) End repair. The fragmentation is followed by the repair or blunting of the fragment ends. After the fragmentation process, the ends of the DNA fragment may be left with unpaired, overhanging nucleotide bases.

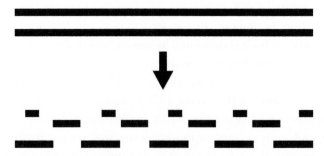

FIGURE 2.14   Fragmentation of DNA into inserts.

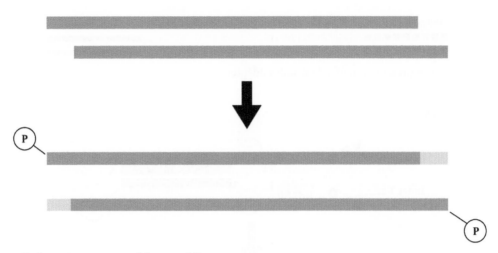

FIGURE 2.15   End repair to generate blunt-end fragments.

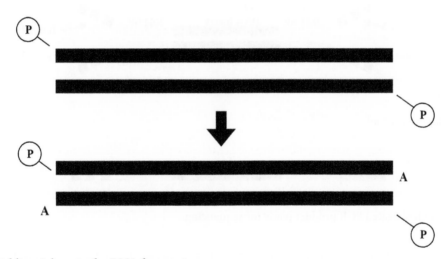

FIGURE 2.16   Adding A-base to the DNA fragments.

The blunting of fragments involves removal of unpaired bases by a combination of fill-in reactions and exonuclease activity (T4 polymerase, DNA polymerase I, and large (Klenow) fragment) (Figure 2.15).

(3) A-base. An adenosine or A-base is then added to the blunt ends of each strand so that each fragment will have a single A-base overhang, which allows the ligation of an adaptor sequence that has thymine (T) overhang by base pairing (Figure 2.16).

(4) Adaptor ligation. The adaptors are single-stranded DNA or oligonucleotide (oligo) sequences used in library preparation kits. Each adapter sequence contains a T-base overhang for ligating the adapter to the A-tailed fragmented DNA. These adapters contain the full complement of sequencing primer hybridization sites for single, paired-end, and indexed reads. Single or dual-index adapters are ligated to the fragments (Figure 2.17).

The Illumina dual-index adaptor consists of three sequence regions (Figure 2.18):

(1) The p5 and p7 are the single-stranded nucleotide sequences that have binding sites allowing the DNA library to bind to complementary short single-stranded oligonucleotides that decorated the flow cell. The flow cell is a glass slide where the sequencing chemistry occurs. It contains small fluidic channels, through which polymerases, nucleotides and buffers can be pumped to provide the attached DNA libraries with the reaction components. The flow cell oligos also act as primers to initiate the synthesis of strands complimentary to the library fragments.

FIGURE 2.17   Schematic representation of a dual-index adaptor.

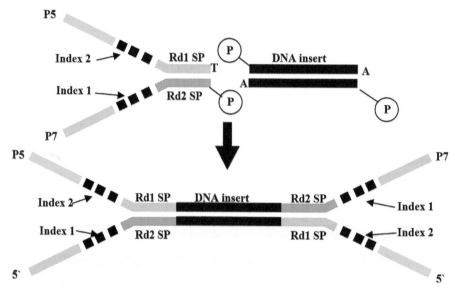

FIGURE 2.18   Adaptor ligation.

FIGURE 2.19   Amplified ligated PCR product ready for sequencing.

(2) Index sequences (Index 1 and Index 2 or i7 and i5 respectively), which are sample identifiers that allow multiplexing or pooling of multiple samples in a single sequencing run or flow cell lane (i.e., this sequence is specific for any sample).

(3) Two sequencing primer binding sites for read 1 and read 2 called Rd1 SP and Rd2 SP. These sites bind to the primer sequence of the cell flow oligo to initiate synthesis of the complementary strand during PCR clustering formation and sequencing.

(5) PCR amplification. PCR amplification is optional, and it is usually performed when there are little DNA fragments. PCR is used to obtain more copies of the DNA fragments (fragment clusters). Figure 2.19 shows a single DNA library after PCR.

Nextera DNA Preparation

Nextera DNA preparation takes advantage of transposase, which is an enzyme that binds to the end of a transposon and catalyzes its movement to another part of the genome by a cut and paste mechanism or a replicative transposition mechanism. The steps for Nextera are as follows (Figure 2.20):

(1) Tagmentation. In the tagmentation step both DNA fragmentation and adaptor ligation take place in a single step. The transposase binds to the end of the partial adaptors (oligonucleotide tags) forming transposomes. Transposases and oligo tags complexes bind to the sample DNA. Once they bind to the DNA (transposons), the complex cleaves the DNA leaving the oligo tags (tagging) with a universal overhang binding to the DNA fragment. The tagmentation generates DNA fragments with partial adaptors attached to their ends.

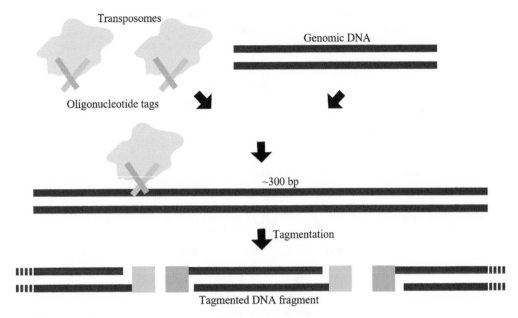

FIGURE 2.20   Tagmentation.

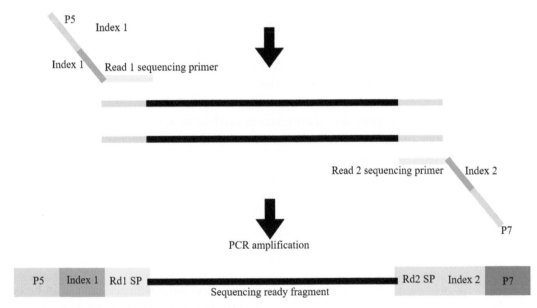

FIGURE 2.21   PCR to complete DNA library preparation.

(2) PCR amplification. PCR is used to amplify the tagmented DNA fragments using part of the partial adaptors as primers to complete the DNA library preparation by adding the rest of the adaptor sequences. The Nextera library preparation method is not PCR-free. After PCR, the DNA libraries are then ready for sequencing (Figure 2.21).

Enrichment Strategy

The isolation of specific DNA targets within genomes is critical for a variety of research. In many cases, we may not need to sequence whole genome of an organism but only specific regions of the genome such as the coding region of protein or a panel of genes we wish to study for their association with a specific disease or a trait. If this is the case, we need to target only those regions instead of the whole genome. To sequence such regions,

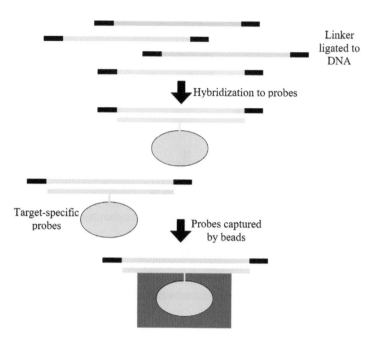

FIGURE 2.22   Capture-based method enrichment.

enrichment to the target regions must be performed. Hybridization-based enrichment is a useful strategy for analyzing the specific genomic region on a given sample. Target enrichment allows researchers to reliably sequence any part of genes. There are several enrichment strategies, but we will discuss only two methods: the capture-based method and the PCR amplification method.

Capture-Based Enrichment   The capture-based enrichment method is performed after DNA library preparation using the TruSeq-style or Nextera preparation method. Once we have prepared the DNA libraries, we will have a mixture of DNA fragments including both the regions of interest and other regions of no interest. For enrichment, we use biotinylated probes, which are DNA oligos designed to hybridize specifically to the region of interest. The probes are attached to biotin. Once the biotinylated probes bind to the targeted DNA regions, the fragments with the targeted regions are pulled down by beads. This is followed by washing to keep only the enriched regions, which are the DNA libraries of the region of interest and ready for sequencing (Figure 2.22).

Enrichment by PCR Amplification   Enrichment by PCR amplification starts with genomic DNA before library preparation. This method requires lots of primers for the targeted regions. The primers must have partial adaptors at their ends. After several PCR cycles, enrichment for the targeted region will be achieved. Another PCR is performed to add the final portions of the adaptors and to prepare the DNA libraries for sequencing.

RNA-Sequencing Library Preparation

RNA consists of nucleotides that are essential in the coding, decoding, regulation, and expression of genes. In the central dogma of molecular biology, the genetic information of DNA is transcribed into multiple copies of messenger RNA (mRNA), which is then translated into proteins. Thus, studying mRNA is essential for a variety of research (e.g., gene profiling or gene expression, transcriptome sequencing, etc.).

The mRNA accounts for only 1–4% of total RNA in the sample. The remainder (96–99% of RNA) is generally considered to be non-coding RNA, which may not be of interest for researchers. These types of RNA include ribosomal RNA (rRNA) and transfer RNA (tRNA). The mRNA sequencing (RNA-Seq) leverages the advantages of NGS to detect and quantify mRNA in a biological sample.

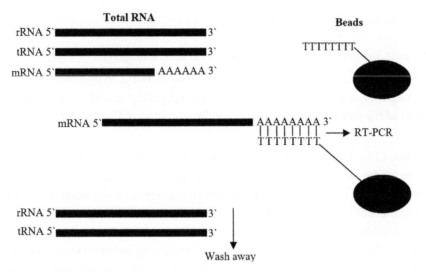

FIGURE 2.23   Enrichment with poly-A capture.

The mRNA is different from other non-coding RNA in that mRNA is polyadenylated or it has a tail of adenosine (Poly A).

Rather than DNA library preparation, there are extra steps are to be conducted before library preparation. These steps include enrichment/depletion and conversion of mRNA to cDNA.

RNA Enrichment   The mRNA can be enriched either by poly-A capture or rRNA depletion.

Enrichment with Poly A Capture   The mRNA, after being transcribed from protein coding genes, undergoes several post-transcriptional modifications before it becomes mature mRNA ready for translation into proteins. The mature mRNA has poly-A tail at its 3`end. The poly-A capture enrichment technique uses beads, which have oligo-dT (single-stranded sequence of deoxythymine) on their surface that can capture mRNA through interaction with ploy-A tails. Then the mixture is washed to remove rRNA and elute the poly-A mRNA from the beads. The eluted mRNA then is ready to go through the RNA library preparation step (Figure 2.23).

Enrichment by rRNA Depletion   This method focuses on removal of rRNA from the total RNA mixture leaving only mRNA. It uses a panel of biotin-linked DNA probes that can bind only to rRNA. The probes hybridize to the rRNA but not to the mRNA. Magnetic beads are used to pull these rRNA and probes complex out of the solution leaving only mRNA in the tube. The mRNA is then ready for library preparation.

RNA Library Preparation   The RNA library preparation is slightly different from DNA library preparation. We will discuss two common methods for RNA library preparation: TruSeq style and SMART-seq.

TruSeq-Style Library Preparation   TruSeq-style RNA preparation requires that the mRNA is to be enriched by one of the above methods. After enrichment, the mRNA can be converted into cDNA using reverse transcription. Once the cDNA is created, we can follow the same TruSeq-style method above for TruSeq library preparation.

SMART-seq   The SMART-seq method was developed by Ramskold et al. in 2012 for sequencing the transcriptomes of single cells [30]. It does not need RNA enrichment and it outperforms the existing methods in capturing sequences across the full length of mRNAs.

The following are the steps of SMART-seq:

(1) *Lysing of the cells.* The cells are lysed to extract RNA from a single cell or cells.

(2) *Synthesis of first strand of cDNA.* The mRNA with ploy-A tail is hybridized to an oligo-dT-containing primer. The oligo-dT is a sequence made of 20 deoxythymidylic acid (dT) residues that can hybridize to the poly(A) of the mRNA, and it will initiate the synthesis of the first strand of cDNA in the process of reverse transcription.

(3) *Template-switch (TS).* Use of reverse transcriptase that adds a few untemplated deoxycytosine (dC) nucleotides to the first strand of cDNA of the full-length transcripts forming poly(C) overhang. Then a template-switch oligo (TSO) is used to hybridize to untemplated dC nucleotides added by the reverse transcriptase. The TSO adds a common 5` sequence to the full-length cDNA that is used for down-stream cDNA amplification. The simple version of a TS oligo is a DNA oligo sequence that carries three riboguanosines (rGrGrG) at its 3` end. The complementarity between these consecutive rG bases and the 3` dC extension of the cDNA molecule empowers the subsequent template switching.

(4) *PCR amplification.* PCR is then used to amplify the full-length cDNA. The PCR products are purified prior library preparation.

(5) *DNA library preparation*: The PCR products, which are full-length cDNA, can be prepared for sequencing using any of the DNA library techniques (TruSeq or Nextera), which are discussed above.

Multiplexing and Use of Barcodes

NGS applications other than whole genome sequencing may require sequencing multiple samples. Sequencing samples separately is expensive and time consuming. Therefore, instead of sequencing individual samples separately, **multiplexing** or pooling of samples in a single reaction tube can be utilized. Multiplexing or multiplex sequencing allows large numbers of DNA libraries to be pooled and sequenced simultaneously during a single run. Multiplexing is useful in application such as study of gene expression or gene profiling in which several samples are used (e.g., treated sample and untreated, sample from cancer cells and sample from healthy cells, etc.). Multiplex sequencing is also useful when targeting specific genomic regions or working with smaller genomes. Pooling samples increases the number of samples analyzed in a single run, without drastically increasing cost or time.

Library preparation is done separately for each sample using any of the DNA or RNA library preparation techniques discussed above. Unique barcode sequences are ligated for each sample as discussed with adaptor ligation (Figure 2.24).

Specific barcode sequences are attached to DNA fragments to identify the sample reads and can be tracked after the downstream sequencing. Then the libraries of the samples are pooled and sequenced in parallel. Each new read contains both the fragment sequence and its sample identifying barcode. The Barcode sequences are used to **de-multiplex** or differentiate reads from each sample in the downstream sequence analysis (Figure 2.25).

For Illumina platform, Nextera library preparation uses an engineered transposome for tagging genomic DNA in a process that fragments DNA and then tags the DNA with adapter sequences in a single step. A limited-cycle PCR step uses the adapters to amplify the insert DNA. The PCR step adds index adapter sequences on both ends of the DNA, which enables dual-indexed sequencing of pooled libraries. These index

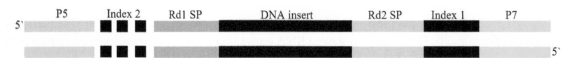

FIGURE 2.24   Barcodes attached to a DNA fragment.

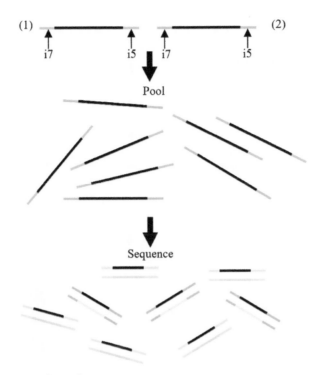

FIGURE 2.25 Multiplexing or sample pooling.

adapters cannot be used with other library preparations. On the other hand, the TruSeq library preparation uses adapter-embedded indexes to enable high throughput processing and application flexibility. The universal, *methylated adapter* design incorporates an index sequence at the initial ligation step. The same TruSeq kit can be used to prepare samples for **single-read**, **paired-end**, and multiplexed sequencing on all Illumina sequencing instruments. Both RNA and DNA preparation kits include adapters containing unique index sequences that are ligated to sample fragments at the beginning of the library construction process. This allows samples to be pooled and then individually identified during downstream analysis. These indexes can generally work with other library preparations.

The unique dual indexing uses unique identifiers on both ends of the sample. A single unique dual index plate enables 96 samples to be pooled together using 96 unique index 1 (i7) adapters and 96 unique index 2 (i5) adapters [28].

Sequencing by Synthesis

The sequencing will follow once the DNA or cDNA libraries have been prepared. The sequencing takes place in a flow cell, which is a glass slide containing microfluidic channels called lanes. The surface of each lane is covered with oligonucleotide sequences that are complementary to the anchor sequences (P5 and P7) in the adapters ligated to the ends of the DNA fragments. When the libraries are loaded into each of the lanes, DNA templates in the libraries bind to these oligonucleotide sequences and become immobilized onto the lane surface of the lanes. The fragments are washed, leaving behind fragment copies that are covalently bonded to the flow cell surface. The immobilized fragments bind by both ends forming bridge-like shapes. The flow cell is then placed on the sequencer. The DNA fragments are amplified in a process called **cluster generation**, resulting in thousands of copies of each DNA fragments called **clusters**. The P5 region is cleaved, resulting in clusters containing only fragments which are attached by the P7 region. This ensures that all copies are sequenced in the same direction. The sequencing primer anneals to the P5 end of the fragment and begins the sequencing by synthesis process. These clusters generate enough signal intensity for base calling during signal detection.

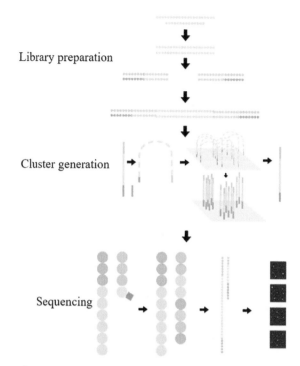

FIGURE 2.26   Sequencing by synthesis.

The sequencing by synthesis (SBS) uses four labeled deoxynucleotide triphosphates or dNTPs (dATP, dCTP, dTTP, and dGTP), which are chemically modified to contain a fluorescent tag and a reversible terminator that blocks incorporation of the next base. These dNTPs can bind to the DNA template strand through natural complementarity. During sequencing by synthesis, the labeled dNTPs, polymerase, and buffers are pumped through channels to the flow cell. A single labeled dNTP (dATP, dCTP, dTTP, or dGTP) will be added to each strand complementing the first nucleotide after primer. Since the added dNTP has a terminator, no new nucleotide will be added to the template strand. A fluorescent signal is immediately emitted by each dNTP added to a strand on the slide. The signal for each strand is received and converted to the corresponding letter (A, C, G, or T) and recorded for that strand. This process is performed in parallel for the millions of the fragments on the slide. Once the signal for each strand is recorded, the terminator is cleaved from the nucleotide in each strand to allow the next base to bind. The next labeled dNTP (dATP, dCTP, dTTP, or dGTP) with terminator is added to each strand. Again, the terminator does not allow the next nucleotide to be added. The signals are received by the detector and converted into the corresponding nucleotide base (A, C, G, or T). Then the terminator is cleaved to allow the next nucleotide to bind. The sequencing process will continue like this until all strands are sequenced. Figure 2.26 shows the steps of sequencing-by-synthesis [31].

Single-end read sequencing

In the single-end read sequencing, the sequencer reads a fragment from only one end and moves toward the other end, generating the complementary sequence of the template strand. Single-read sequencing is faster, cheaper and the single reads obtained are typically sufficient for profiling or counting studies such as RNA-Seq or ChIP-Seq. However, it is less accurate in other applications such as de novo assembly and variant calling [32].

Paired-end sequencing

The above sequencing by synthesis is a single-read sequencing approach since only a single fragment end is sequenced. The two ends of fragments can be sequenced, and such approach is called *paired end sequencing*. If

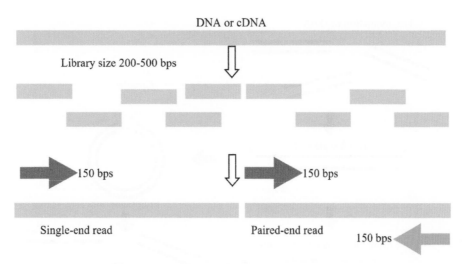

FIGURE 2.27   Single-end and paired-end sequencing.

the sequencing is **paired end**, when Read 1 is finished, everything from Read 1 is removed and an index primer is added, which anneals at the P7 end of the fragment. To sequence Read 2, DNA fragments are washed away leaving behind fragment copies that are covalently bonded to the flow cell surface in a mixture of orientations. This time, P7 is cut instead of P5, resulting in clusters containing only fragments which are attached by the P5 region. This ensures that all copies are sequenced in the same direction. The sequencing primer anneals to the P7 region and the sequencing process continues for Read 2 as before (Figure 2.27) [33].

The reads of 200–800 base pair obtained from short-insert paired-end are called SIPERs. Paired-end sequencing allows users to sequence both ends of a fragment and produce twice the number of reads for the same time and effort in library preparation. It generates high-quality reads that can be aligned easily to a reference genome and in de novo assembly and to detect insertion-deletion (INDEL) variants, which is not possible with single-end reads.

Mate Pair Sequencing

The mate-pair sequencing is like paired-end sequencing. However, the DNA fragments of the mate-pair reads are longer, and form longer reads than paired-end approach. The short-inserts paired-end reads or SIPERs are around 200 to 800 base pairs while the long-insert paired-end reads (LIPERs) or mate-pair reads are longer than that range. In library preparation step and after DNA fragmentation and end-repairing and biotinylation (adding of biotin), the DNA fragments are circularized, and the non-circularized fragments are removed by digestion. The circular DNA is cut into smaller fragments (400–600 bp). The biotinylated fragments are enriched (by biotin tag) and adapters are ligated. They are then ready for cluster generation and sequencing. The produced fragment contains the ends of the original long fragment. After sequencing, information about the original fragment is obtained.

The mate-pair sequencing is useful for several sequencing applications, including de novo sequencing, genome finishing, structural variant detection, identification of complex genomic rearrangements. Figure 2.28 shows the steps of mate pair sequencing.

Base Calling, Base Quality Score, and FASTQ File Format

Base calling is the process by which an order of nucleotides in a template is inferred during a sequencing reaction. The process of base calling is platform specific. The NGS platforms that use fluorescently labeled reversible terminators such as Illumina have a unique color for each nucleotide base (dNTP). These bases are incorporated into the complementary strand of the DNA template and then captured with a sensitive charge-coupled device (CCD) camera in each sequencing cycle. These images are then processed into signals

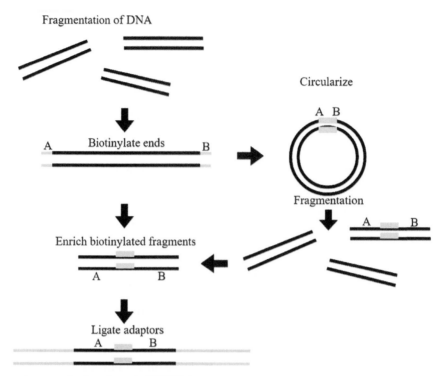

FIGURE 2.28   Long-insert paired-end reads (LIPERs).

which are used to infer the order of nucleotides also known as **base calling**. The sequencing platforms have integrated base calling software called **base caller**.

Base Calling and Base Quality Score

The Illumina sequencing technology depends on cluster image. A single cluster is made up of thousands of identical DNA template. During the sequencing process, in each step of synthesis, an image is taken for all clusters. The image is then analyzed by the base caller. Illumina uses integrated software with algorithm called **Bustard**, which analyzes the colors of the image, generates a base call and accompanying value of base for the quality of the base call in each sequencing cycle. During sequencing, when a dNTP is added to the template strand, for some reason, it may not terminate the synthesis of the strand and therefore, the next dNTP will be added before the color of the previous base call is included on the image of the cluster. Instead, different color masking the right color may be added to the image of cluster. Such errors will affect the confidence on the base call and therefore, a confidence score is required to show how likely a base was called incorrectly. The probability that a base is called incorrectly is calculated as the number of non-dominant lights divided by the total number of lights, which is basically the number of times that the base called incorrectly divided by the total number of calls for a single cluster. For example, assume that in a cluster of 1000 identical template fragments, in a single cycle of the sequencing after adding a dNTP, the image of that cluster included 990 yellow (for C base) spots and only 10 blue spots (for T base). The software will infer T as the base in that position with uncertainty of 10/1000 = 0.01, which is the probability that the T-base was called incorrectly or in other words; 10 incorrect calls in a cluster of 1000 DNA fragments in that sequencing cycle. The probability ranges between 0 and 1.0 and it is difficult to interpret. However, the probability is transformed to more interpretable value called **Phred quality score** (Q-score) [25, 34]. The sequencing platforms use Q-score to measure the quality of the base call. The Q-score is a common metric to assess the accuracy of a sequencing run and it is calculated as follows:

$$Q = -10 log_{10} P \qquad (2.1)$$

TABLE 2.2   Phred Quality Scores and Error Probability

Q	P	Base call accuracy
10	1 in 10	90%
20	1 in 100	99%
30	1 in 1000	99.90%
40	1 in 10,000	99.99%
50	1 in 100,000	99.999%
60	1 in 1,000,000	99.9999%

where P is the probability that the base was called incorrectly.

$$P = 10^{-\frac{Q}{10}} \tag{2.2}$$

For our above example, with P=0.01, Q-score=20.

Since the score is in minus log scale, the higher the score, the less likely that the base is called incorrectly. Table 2.2 shows some Q-score and their interpretation.

Binary Base Call (BCL) files are the binary raw data files generated by the Illumina sequencers. A BCL file contains a base call and a Phred quality score (Q-score) for each position. The BCL file generated by the sequencer is converted into FASTQ file, which is a text-based sequence file format that stores both raw sequence data and quality scores. FASTQ files have become the standard format for storing NGS data from sequencing systems and can be used in the downstream data analysis.

FASTQ File Format

FASTQ format was developed by Wellcome Trust Sanger Institute to meet the need of sequencing process and to report the nucleotide sequence and quality of each base call [35]. The name FASTQ was derived from FASTA and Quality. By convention, a file of the FASTQ format can have a name with an extension ".fq" or ".fastq". At the present time, FASTQ format became the *de facto* standard for the massive sequences generated by the NGS technologies. A single FASTQ file may contain entries of multiple reads. Each entry in a FASTQ files consists of 4 lines. Those 4 lines are called spot (Figure 2.42). There may be thousands of spots in a single file.

Line 1: The first line begins with a '@' character and is followed by a sequence identifier and an optional description. This line may vary based on the sequencing technology and it usually contains specific information for the technology.

Line 2: The second line contains a sequence generated by the sequencer for the read. The sequence will be made up of the four bases (A, C, T, and G). The letter N may be included when the base is ambiguous and the base caller was unable to identify it because of the noise.

Line 3: The third line begins with a '+' character; it marks the end of sequence and is optionally followed by the same sequence identifier again in line

Line 4: The fourth line contains the quality per base call expressed in Phred quality score (Q-score) encoded as ASCII characters.

Figure 2.29 shows FASTQ format of three sequence reads.

In FASTQ files, Phred quality scores (Q) are encoded into a compact form, which uses only 1 byte per quality value. In this encoding, a quality score is represented as a character with an ASCII code equal to its value + 33. Table 2.3 shows the relationship between the encoding character, its ASCII code, and the value of the quality scores (between 0 and 79). Programs which use FASTQ files usually convert the ASCII codes into numeric Phred scores.

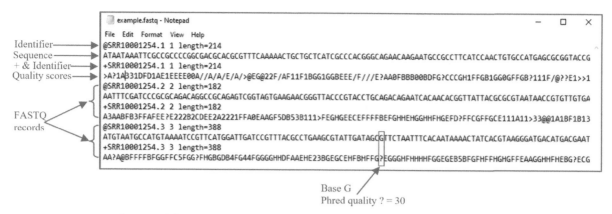

FIGURE 2.29   FASTQ format of three sequence reads.

TABLE 2.3   Part of the ASCII Table

Dec	Sym	Q	Dec	Sym	Q	Dec	Sym	Q	Dec	Sym	Q
33	!	0	53	5	20	73	I	40	93	]	60
34	"	1	54	6	21	74	J	41	94	^	61
35	#	2	55	7	22	75	K	42	95	_	62
36	$	3	56	8	23	76	L	43	96	`	63
37	%	4	57	9	24	77	M	44	97	a	64
38	&	5	58	:	25	78	N	45	98	b	65
39	'	6	59	;	26	79	O	46	99	c	66
40	(	7	60	<	27	80	P	47	100	d	67
41	)	8	61	=	28	81	Q	48	101	e	68
42	*	9	62	>	29	82	R	49	102	f	69
43	+	10	63	?	30	83	S	50	103	g	70
44	,	11	64	@	31	84	T	51	104	h	71
45	-	12	65	A	32	85	U	52	105	i	72
46	.	13	66	B	33	86	V	53	106	j	73
47	/	14	67	C	34	87	W	54	107	k	74
48	0	15	68	D	35	88	X	55	108	l	75
49	1	16	69	E	36	89	Y	56	109	m	76
50	2	17	70	F	37	90	Z	57	110	n	77
51	3	18	71	G	38	91	[	58	111	o	78
52	4	19	72	H	39	92	\	59	112	p	79

A FASTQ file generated by a NGS sequencer may contain thousands or millions of read entries and may reach to several gigabytes in size. They can be compressed with compression software like GZIP, which adds ".gz" to the FASTQ file name. When FASTQ files are compressed with GZIP their sizes are reduced to more than 10 times.

As the sequences generated by a Sanger sequencer are provided in FASTA file format, the short sequences or short reads generated by NGS are provided in FASTQ files. Genomic data in these two formats are the basic raw data for the most of the downstream genomic data analyses. Researchers usually submit their raw sequence data in FASTQ format to the databases such as NCBI databases as evidence for their research findings and as supplementary materials to their research papers.

Downstream NGS Data Analysis

Getting FASTQ files from the sequencer is just the beginning. What to do next with the reads in the FASTQ depends on your goal. The NGS data analysis is easy if it is done under Linux platform since the software used are command-line, Linux-based, open-source programs but there are several commercial programs as well. The FASTQ files and resulting files require large storage space and the processing requires sufficient computer memory and a number of processors. Most of institutions have their own servers that can provide a platform for NGS data analysis. In addition, nowadays, finding a computational resource for NGS analysis, even for individuals, is not challenging any more since cloud computing has become an affordable option and available from several providers like Amazon Web Services (AWS), Microsoft Azure, Google cloud computing, and others. Most programs used for NGS are open source but enhanced commercial ones are also available. Installation of the open-source programs in Linux and using Linux is straightforward but needs some Linux knowledge. We will not delve into the NGS data analysis since this is not in the scope of this book, but we will discuss some steps and file formats generated by some downstream analyses that you may encounter when we discuss the bioinformatics databases, which are one of the topics of this book. In the following, we will discuss the general NGS analysis pipeline and generated file formats. As Figure 2.30 shows, the quality of reads in the FASTQ file is assessed based on several criteria. A decision can be made on filtering or trimming or both if the reads require cleaning. Read **demultiplexing** is performed to generate a FASTQ file for each sample when multiple samples were sequenced in a single run. The adaptor sequences specific for the technology must be trimmed before the downstream analysis. The reads in the cleaned FASTQ file are aligned to a reference genome or used to perform *de novo assembly* if no reference genome is found. In both cases SAM/BAM files are generated. From this point, the analysis pipeline depends on the type of applications, which include variant calling, RNA-Seq quantification, ChIP-Seq peak call, Methyl-Seq calling, and more [36].

Quality Control After generating FASTQ files, several pipelines for downstream analysis lie ahead. Before analysis, the reads in a FASTQ file may be inspected using software like *fastqc*, which assesses the quality per base, quality per read, and provides other quality metrics for detecting any potential problem. Usually, the FASTQ files require cleaning by trimming the reads, filtering reads based on their quality, masking the bases with poor quality, or removing the adaptor sequences using software like *Fastx-toolkit* and FASTQ Processing Utilities. The cleaned FASTQ file can then be used for the downstream analysis, which depends on the sequencing application [37].

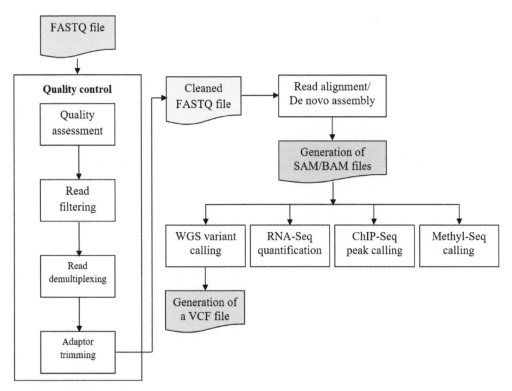

FIGURE 2.30   General NGS pipeline.

Alignment   After cleaning the FASTQ files, the next step for most applications is the alignment of the reads in FASTQ file to a **reference genome** of an organism of interest. A reference genome sequence is stored in a FASTA file. A reference genome is assembled and curated as a representative example sequence of one idealized individual organism of a species. These days, most organisms have reference genomes available in the genome database. The reference genome is usually downloaded to a local drive and indexed and then one of the mapping programs called *mappers* is used to align short reads in the FASTQ file or files to the sequence of the reference genome (Figure 2.31). Several mapping programs exist such as *BWA* [38], *Bowtie2* [39], *Maq* [40], *Stampy* [41], and *NovoAlign* [42]. These programs use certain algorithms to handle the computational burden for aligning huge number of reads to a substantially long genome sequence. The aim of sequence alignment is to find the genomic location where a read originates from and to determine how many reads aligned to that position.

When short reads are aligned to a reference genome, we may need to understand some terminologies such as sequencing coverage, breadth coverage, contigs, scaffolds, and the file format for the mapped reads (SAM/BAM file format).

a. Per-base depth   The per-base depth of coverage is the average number of times a base of a genome is sequenced. This coverage is shown when unique reads are aligned to a reference genome. The number of bases aligned to a specific position in the reference genome is the per-base coverage or depth at that position. Thus, the aligned reads can be tiled in level of times (e.g., 1x, 2x, 3x, etc.,). Figure 2.31 shows reads of length 13 bp aligned to a reference genome and the depth at each position [43].

b. Coverage depth of a genome   The coverage depth or sequencing coverage of a genome is the average number of reads aligned to or covered specific bases of the reference genome. It denotes the expected coverage based on the number and the length of high-quality reads before or after alignment to the reference. The coverage depth of a genome is calculated as the number of bases of all short reads that match a genome divided by the length of this genome [44].

$$\text{Average coverage of a genome} = \frac{read\,size \times number\,of\,reads}{genome\,size} \tag{2.1}$$

It is often expressed as 1x, 2x, 3x, etc., which means 1-, 2-, or 3-times coverage.

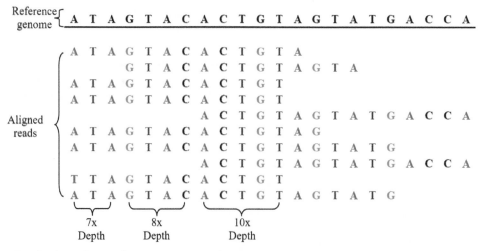

FIGURE 2.31   Reads aligned to a reference genome.

TABLE 2.4   Depth Coverage Recommended for Some Applications

Application	Recommended Coverage
Whole genome sequencing	30× to 50×
Whole-exome sequencing	100×
RNA sequencing	Numbers of millions of reads to be sampled
ChIP-Seq	100×

For example, if the size of a reference genome is 100 mega base pairs (Mbp) and there are 10,000,000 reads of 100 bp size, then the depth coverage at genome level would be calculated as

$$\text{Average coverage depth} = \frac{100 \times 10,000,000}{100,000,000} = 10\text{x}$$

The depth of coverage often determines whether variant discovery can be made with a certain degree of confidence at specific base positions. Depth coverage requirements vary by application. In some experiments, high depth coverage is needed to be confident about the results. This is especially important for heterogeneous samples such as tumor samples in which we may find mixture of normal cells (with no mutations) and cancer cells (with mutations). Deep sequencing or high depth is required in variant calling such SNP, insertions and deletions (INDEL). Generally, High depth is important in research and diagnostics as it gives more confident results that researcher can rely on. Table 2.4 shows the recommended depth coverage for some NGS applications [45].

One of the problems of the alignment is that short reads can sometimes align equally well to multiple locations in the genome. Therefore, the longer the read the easier it is to find its right position. However, paired end sequencing strategy may overcome this problem.

c. Breadth of coverage   Breadth of coverage is the percentage of target bases that are sequenced a given number of times. It is calculated as the percentage of bases of a reference genome that are covered with a certain depth. For example, we can say 95% of a genome is covered at 1X depth; and 90% is covered at 2X depth and so on [44].

d. Contigs and scaffolds   A contig, which comes from *contiguous*, is a set of overlapping short reads that together represent a *consensus region* of DNA sequence when the short reads are aligned to a reference genome. While a scaffold is a segment of the DNA sequence composed of contigs and gaps [46]. Figure 2.32 shows sequence reads, contigs, and scaffolds.

The aligned reads create a longer contigs, by tiling of the short reads. A good quality titling is the one with significant read overlaps. The more depth of coverage we get, the more significant overlaps we must correctly align our sequence.

e. SAM/BAM file format   All alignment programs require FASTQ files, a reference genome, and the index file for that reference genome as input. The output of the mapping program is a file containing the aligned reads; this file is called the SAM (Sequence Alignment/Map) file or BAM file, which is the binary version of SAM file [47].

SAM file is a TAB-delimited text format consisting of two sections: a header section (optional) and an alignment section. The header section contains information about the entire file and additional information for alignments. The alignments then associate themselves with specific header information. All header lines must start with '@'. Each alignment line has 11 mandatory fields (from 1 to 11) for essential alignment information, and variable number of optional fields for flexible or aligner specific information. The order and names of the alignment columns are as follows (Table 2.5):

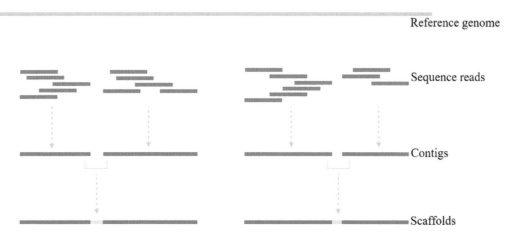

FIGURE 2.32   Contigs and scaffolds.

TABLE 2.5   Column Names of the SAM Alignment Section

Order	Column name	Description
1	QNAME	Read name.
2	FLAG	SAM flag.
3	RNAME	Contig name or * for unmapped.
4	POS	Mapped position of first base of a read on the reference sequence.
5	MAPQ	Mapping quality in Phred quality score.
6	CIGAR	A string describing insertions and deletions and matches
7	RNEXT	Name of mate.
8	PNEXT	Position of mate.
9	TLEN	Template length.
10	SEQ	Read sequence.
11	QUAL	Read quality
12	TAGS	Additional information in TAG:TYPE:VALUE format.

In the following, we will describe POS, CIGAR, QUAL, and TAG column of SAM/BAM format while the other columns are clear from the descriptions in Table 2.5:

POS: POS is an integer that shows the position of the first base of the aligned read on the reference sequence.
CIGAR: CIGAR string is a sequence of base lengths. It is used to indicate which bases in the aligned read match and which ones do not match (mismatch) with the reference, deleted from the reference, or insertions that are not in the reference. The aligned read may have additional bases that are not in the reference or may be missing bases that are in the reference.

For example, assume that we wish to align the short read "ACTAGAATGGCT" to the reference sequence "CCATACTGAACTGACTAAC".
Also assume that Figure 2.33 shows the read aligned to the reference sequence.
Considering the above alignment, we can write POS and the CIGAR string of the read alignment as follows:

POS: 5
CIGAR: 3M1I3M1D5M

The alignment shows that it starts at the position POS=5 on the reference sequence. The CIGAR indicates that the first 3 bases in the read sequence match with the reference (3M). The next base in the read does not

Ref POS	1	2	3	4	5	6	7		8	9	10	11	12	13	14	15	16	17	18	19
Reference	C	C	A	T	A	C	T		G	A	A	C	T	G	A	C	T	A	A	C
Read					A	C	T	A	G	A	A		T	G	G	C	T			

FIGURE 2.33   A read aligned to a reference sequence.

exist in the reference; therefore, a single base is inserted in the read sequence (1I). Then 3 bases match (align) with the reference (3M). The next reference base does not exist in the read sequence; therefore, a base is deleted (1D) from the read sequence. Finally, 5 bases match with the reference (5M). Note that at position 14, the base in the read is different from the reference, but it still counts as an M since it aligns to that position.

QUAL: QUAL is an indicator for how accurate each base in the query sequence (SEQ) is and it is described as Phred Quality score.

TAGs: The TAG is the 12th column of the alignment section. It contains optional fields. A TAG is comprised of a two-character TAG key, the value type, and the value. The field can be in the following form:

$$\left[A-Za-z\right]\left[A-za-z\right]:\left[AifZH\right]:.^{*}$$

The TAG key can be any two valid characters from A to Z, uppercase or lowercase. The type is used to indicate the type of value stored in the tag. It can be a character (A), an integer (i), a float (f), a string (Z), or a hex string (H).

De novo genome assembly   In the last section, we discussed alignment of reads to a reference genome using one of the mapping programs called mappers or aligners. However, sometimes, there might be no sequence of a reference genome available for some organisms. Therefore, we can not avail of aligning the reads in FASTQ file to a reference genome. In this case, the **de novo** genome assembly is used to assemble the sequence of the genome from the short reads obtained from NGS. There are several programs available for performing de novo genome assembly such as ABySS [48] and SOAPdenovo [49]. The de novo programs align short reads against others to obtain sequence overlap between them to build larger contiguous sequences or (contigs). A contig is a set of overlapping DNA reads or segments that together represent a **consensus sequence** of DNA nucleotide bases. Two or more contigs can form a scaffold, which consists of sequences separated by gaps of known length. A group of scaffolds can form a **chromosome**, which represent a DNA molecule (Figure 2.34).

The goal of de novo approach is to build a single contig that encompasses the entire genome of the organism. However, this is usually not an easy task. The paired end reads are beneficial in de novo assembly, as they can potentially link two smaller contigs together that are separated by a region that is impossible to sequence. Mate-pair reads are also linked together, which would help in the same manner as paired-end reads, linking contigs separated by regions of thousands of base pairs that cannot be aligned.

Variant Calling   The variant calling is the process of identifying variants from the reads aligned to a reference genome in SAM/BAM file format. The variants are usually called from the reads obtained from whole genome sequencing or whole exome sequencing. After reads have been aligned to a reference genome and processed, the next step in the variant calling pipeline is to identify the differences observed between the bases of the selected reference genome and the bases of the newly sequenced reads. The aim of variant calling is to identify polymorphic sites where nucleotides are different from the ones on the reference genome. However, before read alignments, there are additional post-alignment processing steps that must be performed to ensure that only the highest quality reads are retained in the SAM/BAM file. Those steps may include removal of duplicate reads that originated from the same DNA fragments during the DNA library preparation and recalibration

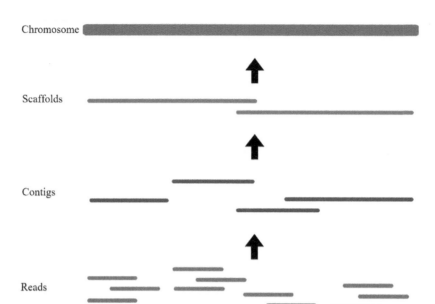

FIGURE 2.34   De novo assembly.

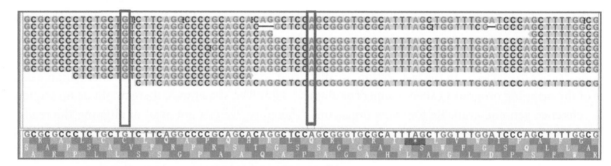

FIGURE 2.35   Visualizing reads aligned to a reference genome.

of the base quality score. Figure 2.35 shows reads aligned to a reference genome sequence after duplicate read removal and the consensus sequence is shown at the bottom.

BAM files can be opened in a genome browser (as we will discuss later when we cover the genome database) to view the short reads aligned against a reference sequence. If a variant is observed in only a small percentage of the reads, then it can be assumed that it is likely a false positive. Algorithms using statistical methods are used to evaluate if the observed polymorphism is a true variant or due to chance. Therefore, variant calling is performed by programs that utilize such statistical methods to call variants at specific positions and provide a quality score for variant calling. There are some standard variant calling programs, such as SAMtools [47] and GATK [50], which use SAM/BAM file as input and generate VCF file format as output. The single nucleotide polymorphisms (SNPs) and small Insertion-Deletions (InDels) of length less than 50 bp require different algorithms compared to a pipeline for detecting large InDels and structural variations such as copy number variations (CNVs).

Variant Call Format File   The variant call file (VCF) is the standard file format for storing variation data [51]. It is the standard output of variant calling software such as SAMtools and GATK and the standard input for variant analysis tools. Millions of variants can be stored in a single VCF file. The VCF file as shown in Figure 2.36 contains meta-information lines included after ##, a header line for the column names, and data lines, each of which contains information about a position in the genome. The VCF file can also contain genotype information on samples for each position.

```
##fileformat=VCFv4.2
##fileDate=20090805
##source=myImputationProgramV3.1
##reference=file:///seq/references/1000GenomesPilot-NCBI36.fasta
##contig=<ID=20,length=62435964,assembly=B36,md5=f126cdf8a6e0c7f379d618ff66beb2da,species="Homo sapiens",taxonomy=x>
##phasing=partial
##INFO=<ID=NS,Number=1,Type=Integer,Description="Number of Samples With Data">
##INFO=<ID=DP,Number=1,Type=Integer,Description="Total Depth">
##INFO=<ID=AF,Number=A,Type=Float,Description="Allele Frequency">
##INFO=<ID=AA,Number=1,Type=String,Description="Ancestral Allele">
##INFO=<ID=DB,Number=0,Type=Flag,Description="dbSNP membership, build 129">
##INFO=<ID=H2,Number=0,Type=Flag,Description="HapMap2 membership">
##FILTER=<ID=q10,Description="Quality below 10">
##FILTER=<ID=s50,Description="Less than 50% of samples have data">
##FORMAT=<ID=GT,Number=1,Type=String,Description="Genotype">
##FORMAT=<ID=GQ,Number=1,Type=Integer,Description="Genotype Quality">
##FORMAT=<ID=DP,Number=1,Type=Integer,Description="Read Depth">
##FORMAT=<ID=HQ,Number=2,Type=Integer,Description="Haplotype Quality">
#CHROM POS     ID         REF  ALT   QUAL FILTER INFO                          FORMAT        NA00001         NA00002         NA00003
20     14370   rs6054257  G    A     29   PASS   NS=3;DP=14;AF=0.5;DB;H2       GT:GQ:DP:HQ   0|0:48:1:51,51  1|0:48:8:51,51  1/1:43:5:.,.
20     17330   .          T    A     3    q10    NS=3;DP=11;AF=0.017           GT:GQ:DP:HQ   0|0:49:3:58,50  0|1:3:5:65,3    0/0:41:3
20     1110696 rs6040355  A    G,T   67   PASS   NS=2;DP=10;AF=0.333,0.667;AA=T;DB GT:GQ:DP:HQ 1|2:21:6:23,27 2|1:2:0:18,2   2/2:35:4
20     1230237 .          T    .     47   PASS   NS=3;DP=13;AA=T               GT:GQ:DP:HQ   0|0:54:7:56,60  0|0:48:4:51,51  0/0:61:2
20     1234567 microsat1  GTC  G,GTCT 50  PASS   NS=3;DP=9;AA=G                GT:GQ:DP      0/1:35:4        0/2:17:2        1/1:40:3
```

Header
Body

FIGURE 2.36   VCF format.

A meta-information is included after the ## string and must be key=value pairs. The meta-information lines describe the INFO, FILTER, and FORMAT entries used in the body of the VCF file and can be included in the meta-information section.

The VCF header line includes the name of eight fixed, mandatory columns. These columns are #CHROM, POS, ID, REF, ALT, QUAL, FILTER, and INFO. All data lines are tab delimited. Missing values are specified with a dot ('.'). Optional columns can be added to provide more information such as FORMAT and SAMPLE #.

The following are descriptions of the VCF columns:

(1) *CHROM*. An identifier from the reference genome for the chromosome number.

(2) *POS*. The reference position, with the first base having position 1.

(3) *ID*. A semi-colon separated list of unique identifiers when available such as rs numbers of dbSNP variants.

(4) *REF*. Reference base(s). Each base must be one of A, C, G, T, and N.

(5) *ALT*. Alternate base(s): Comma separated list of alternate non-reference alleles. The options are base strings made up of the bases A, C, G, T, N, and *. The '*' allele is reserved to indicate that the allele is missing due to an upstream deletion.

(6) *QUAL*. This represents Phred-scaled quality score for the assertion made in ALT.

(7) *FILTER*. Filter status. PASS if this position has passed all filters, i.e., a call is made at this position. Otherwise, if the site has not passed all filters, a semicolon-separated list of codes for filters that fail. e.g. "q10;s50" might indicate that at this site the quality is below 10 and the number of samples with data is below 50% of the total number of samples. "0" is reserved and should not be used as a filter String. If filters have not been applied, then this field should be set to the missing value. (String, no whitespace or semi-colons permitted.)

(8) *INFO*. Additional information. No white space is used. Semi-colons or equals-signs are permitted. The INFO fields are encoded as a semicolon-separated series of short keys with optional values in the format: <key>=<data>[,data].

For more information about the VCF file, check the Variant Call Format (VCF) Version 4.2 Specification at https://samtools.github.io/hts-specs/VCFv4.2.pdf.

Variant Annotation   Most of the phenotypic variations among individuals are resulted from genotypic variations that are due to variants such as SNPs, InDels, or CNVs. Variant annotation refers to the process of predicting the biological effect or function of genetic variants after variant calling [52]. There are several annotation tools available. They use the

VCF files generated by variant calling as input and output a report of annotated variants and their biological effect. A VCF file may contain thousands of variants. The variants on a VCF file are usually filtered to keep only high-quality variants. The common variants in a population can also be removed when looking for a rare variant that is associated with a specific disease or phenotype. The variant annotation tools use information from databases, which contain variants that have previously been described such as dbSNP and ClinVar. Some annotation tools use algorithms for the prediction of protein function such as SnpEff [53], SnpSift[53], and PolyPhen [54], which categorize each variant based on its relationship to coding sequences in the genome and how it may change the coding sequence and affect the gene product. These functional annotation tools depend on the set of transcripts used as the basis for annotation. The widely used annotation databases and browsers such as ENSEMBL, RefSeq, and UCSC contain sets of transcripts that can be used for variant annotation. For example, SnpEff takes information from the provided annotation database and populates the input VCF file by adding it into the INFO field name ANN. Data fields are encoded separated by the pipe sign "|" (Figure 2.37).

Variant Interpretation Variant interpretation is the association of the genotypic variation to a phenotypic variation, and it is done by researchers who use scientific methodology for reaching reliable conclusions. The genotype-phenotype association requires collection of sufficient genetic information and tremendous efforts. However, to standardize variant interpretation about human diseases, guidelines have been developed for Mendelian disease diagnosis [55]. The guidelines use a set of standard questions that are applied to each case, alongside phenotypic information to rank variants based on several demographic factors. The conclusion made in the interpretation process will determine the classification of the variants, whether it is pathogenic, benign, malignant, or of unknown significance (VUS) when there is currently not enough evidence available to classify the variant.

AGP File Scientists usually submit the sequences obtained from their research onto NCBI databases. The contigs, scaffolds, or chromosomes forming a genome are described using the AGP file format (Figure 2.38). Each line of the file describes a different piece of the object. The entries in a line are organized into tab-delimited columns as follows:

#CHROM	POS	ID	REF	ALT	QUAL	FILTER	INFO
Chr11	2456221	.	A	G,T	.	.	ANN=G|... , T|...
Chr11	2556221	.	C	A	.	.	ANN=A|...

FIGURE 2.37   SnpEff annotation.

```
##agp-version    2.0
# ORGANISM: Homo sapiens
# TAX_ID: 9606
# ASSEMBLY NAME: EG1
# ASSEMBLY DATE: 09-November-2011
# GENOME CENTER: NCBI
# DESCRIPTION: Example AGP specifying the assembly of scaffolds from WGS contigs
EG1_scaffold1    1       3043    1    W    AADB02037551.1  1       3043    +
EG1_scaffold2    1       40448   1    W    AADB02037552.1  1       40448   +
EG1_scaffold2    40449   40661   2    N    213     scaffold        yes     paired-ends
EG1_scaffold2    40662   117642  3    W    AADB02037553.1  1       76981   +
EG1_scaffold2    117643  117718  4    N    76      scaffold        yes     paired-ends
EG1_scaffold2    117719  145387  5    W    AADB02037554.1  1       27669   +
EG1_scaffold2    145388  145485  6    N    98      scaffold        yes     paired-ends
EG1_scaffold2    145486  148437  7    W    AADB02037555.1  1       2952    +
EG1_scaffold2    148438  148560  8    N    123     scaffold        yes     paired-ends
```

FIGURE 2.38   Scaffold formed from sequences.

(1) The name that identifies the object, such as a contig, scaffold, or chromosome.

(2) Starting coordinates of the component sequence on the object.

(3) Ending coordinates of the component sequence on the object.

(4) The line count for the sequence that makes up the object.

(5) Sequence type, which can be "A" for an active finishing, "D" for draft High Throughput Genomic (HTG), "F" for finished HTG, "G" for Whole Genome Finishing, "O" for other sequence, "P" for pre-draft, "W" for WGS contig, "N" for a gap with specified size, "U" for gap of unknown size.

(6) Sequence identifier if the component type is not "N" or "U". Otherwise, the value will be the gap length.

(7) The beginning of the sequence if the component type is not "N" or "U". Otherwise, the value will be the gap type (scaffold, contig, centromere, telomere, repeat, or contamination).

(8) The end of the sequence if the component type is "N" or "U". Otherwise, a linkage (yes/no) is used.

(9) Orientation of the sequence, which can be plus (+), minus (-), unknown (?), irrelevant (na), if it is not "N" or "U". Otherwise, it will be linkage evidence (e.g., paired-end, pcr, etc.).

Refer to the AGP format specifications at www.ncbi.nlm.nih.gov/assembly/agp/ for more information about AGP file format.

REFERENCES

1. Krings, M., et al., *Neandertal DNA sequences and the origin of modern humans.* Cell, 1997. **90**(1): pp. 19–30.

2. Green, R.E., et al., *A complete Neandertal mitochondrial genome sequence determined by high-throughput sequencing.* Cell, 2008. **134**(3): pp. 416–426.

3. Prufer, K., et al., *The complete genome sequence of a Neanderthal from the Altai Mountains.* Nature, 2014. **505**(7481): pp. 43–49.

4. Kap, M., et al., *Histological assessment of PAXgene tissue fixation and stabilization reagents.* PLoS One, 2011. **6**(11): p. e27704.

5. Deissler, H., et al., *Rapid protein sequencing by tandem mass spectrometry and cDNA cloning of p20-CGGBP. A novel protein that binds to the unstable triplet repeat 5'-d(CGG)n-3' in the human FMR1 gene.* J Biol Chem, 1997. **272**(27): pp. 16761–16768.

6. Hunt, D.F., et al., *Protein sequencing by tandem mass spectrometry.* Proc Natl Acad Sci USA, 1986. **83**(17): pp. 6233–7.

7. Nardiello, D., et al., *Strategies in protein sequencing and characterization: multi-enzyme digestion coupled with alternate CID/ETD tandem mass spectrometry.* Anal Chim Acta, 2015. **854**: pp. 106–117.

8. Ziady, A.G. and M. Kinter, *Protein sequencing with tandem mass spectrometry.* Methods Mol Biol, 2009. **544**: pp. 325–341.

9. Desjardins, P. and D. Conklin, *NanoDrop microvolume quantitation of nucleic acids.* J Vis Exp, 2010(45).

10. Schroeder, A., et al., *The RIN: an RNA integrity number for assigning integrity values to RNA measurements.* BMC Mol Biol, 2006. 7: p. 3.

11. Smith, P.K., et al., *Measurement of protein using bicinchoninic acid.* Anal Biochem, 1985. **150**(1): pp. 76–85.

12. Olson, B.J. and J. Markwell, *Assays for determination of protein concentration.* Curr Protoc Protein Sci, 2007. Chapter 3: Unit 3 4.

13. Engvall, E., *The ELISA, enzyme-linked immunosorbent assay.* Clin Chem, 2010. **56**(2): pp. 319–320.

14. Temin, H.M. and S. Mizutani, *RNA-dependent DNA polymerase in virions of Rous sarcoma virus. 1970.* Biotechnology, 1992. **24**: pp. 51–56.

15. Kary, B., F.F. Mullis, and Richard A. Gibbs, *The Polymerase Chain Reaction.* 1996: Boston: Birkhäuser.

16. Chien, A., D.B. Edgar, and J.M. Trela, *Deoxyribonucleic acid polymerase from the extreme thermophile Thermus aquaticus.* J Bacteriol, 1976. **127**(3): pp. 1550–1557.

17. Stretton, A.O., *The first sequence. Fred Sanger and insulin.* Genetics, 2002. **162**(2): pp. 527–532.

18. Holley, R.W., et al., *Structure of a Ribonucleic Acid.* Science, 1965. **147**(3664): pp. 1462–1465.

19. Xue, Y., Y. Wang, and H. Shen, *Ray Wu, fifth business or father of DNA sequencing?* Protein Cell, 2016. **7**(7): pp. 467–470.

20. Maxam, A.M. and W. Gilbert, *A new method for sequencing DNA.* Proc Natl Acad Sci USA, 1977. **74**(2): pp. 560–564.

21. Sanger, F. and A.R. Coulson, *A rapid method for determining sequences in DNA by primed synthesis with DNA polymerase.* J Mol Biol, 1975. **94**(3): pp. 441–448.

22. Staden, R., *A strategy of DNA sequencing employing computer programs.* Nucleic Acids Res, 1979. **6**(7): pp. 2601–2610.

23. Pareek, C.S., R. Smoczynski, and A. Tretyn, *Sequencing technologies and genome sequencing.* J Appl Genet, 2011. **52**(4): pp. 413–435.

24. Shampo, M.A. and R.A. Kyle, *J. Craig Venter—The Human Genome Project.* Mayo Clin Proc, 2011. **86**(4): pp. e26–27.

25. Ewing, B., et al., *Base-calling of automated sequencer traces using phred. I. Accuracy assessment.* Genome Res, 1998. **8**(3): pp. 175–185.

26. Zhang, H., *Overview of Sequence Data Formats.* Methods Mol Biol, 2016. **1418**: pp. 3–17.

27. Behjati, S. and P.S. Tarpey, *What is next-generation sequencing?* Arch Dis Child Educ Pract Ed, 2013. **98**(6): pp. 236–238.

28. Meyer, M. and M. Kircher, *Illumina sequencing library preparation for highly multiplexed target capture and sequencing.* Cold Spring Harb Protoc, 2010. (6): pdb prot5448.

29. Mardis, E.R., *DNA sequencing technologies: 2006–2016.* Nat Protoc, 2017. **12**(2): pp. 213–218.

30. Ramskold, D., et al., *Full-length mRNA-Seq from single-cell levels of RNA and individual circulating tumor cells.* Nat Biotechnol, 2012. **30**(8): pp. 777–782.

31. Ravi, R.K., K. Walton, and M. Khosroheidari, *MiSeq: A Next-generation sequencing Platform for Genomic Analysis.* Methods Mol Biol, 2018. **1706**: pp. 223–232.

32. Mohideen, A., S.D. Johansen, and I. Babiak, *High-Throughput Identification of Adapters in Single-Read Sequencing Data.* Biomolecules, 2020. **10**(6).

33. Campbell, P.J., et al., *Identification of somatically acquired rearrangements in cancer using genome-wide massively parallel paired-end sequencing.* Nat Genet, 2008. **40**(6): pp. 722–729.

34. Ewing, B. and P. Green, *Base-calling of automated sequencer traces using phred. II. Error probabilities.* Genome Res, 1998. **8**(3): pp. 186–194.

35. Cock, P.J., et al., *The Sanger FASTQ file format for sequences with quality scores, and the Solexa/Illumina FASTQ variants.* Nucleic Acids Res, 2010. **38**(6): pp. 1767–1771.

36. Torri, F., et al., *Next generation sequence analysis and computational genomics using graphical pipeline workflows.* Genes (Basel), 2012. **3**(3): pp. 545–575.

37. Andrews, S., *FASTQC a quality control tool for high throughput sequence data.* www.bioinformatics. babraham.ac.uk/projects/fastqc. 2019.

38. Li, H. and R. Durbin, *Fast and accurate short read alignment with Burrows-Wheeler transform.* Bioinformatics, 2009. **25**(14): pp. 1754–1760.

39. Langmead, B. and S.L. Salzberg, *Fast gapped-read alignment with Bowtie 2.* Nat Methods, 2012. **9**(4): pp. 357–359.

40. Li, H., J. Ruan, and R. Durbin, *Mapping short DNA sequencing reads and calling variants using mapping quality scores.* Genome Res, 2008. **18**(11): pp. 1851–1858.

41. Lunter, G. and M. Goodson, *Stampy: a statistical algorithm for sensitive and fast mapping of Illumina sequence reads.* Genome Res, 2011. **21**(6): pp. 936–939.

42. Yu, X., et al., *How do alignment programs perform on sequencing data with varying qualities and from repetitive regions?* BioData Min, 2012. **5**(1): p. 6.

43. Pedersen, B.S. and A.R. Quinlan, *Mosdepth: quick coverage calculation for genomes and exomes.* Bioinformatics, 2018. **34**(5): pp. 867–868.

44. Sims, D., et al., *Sequencing depth and coverage: key considerations in genomic analyses.* Nat Rev Genet, 2014. **15**(2): pp. 121–132.

45. Illumina. *Coverage depth recommendations.* www.illumina.com/science/technology/next-generation-sequencing/plan-experiments/coverage.html. 2021.

46. Schatz, M.C., A.L. Delcher, and S.L. Salzberg, *Assembly of large genomes using second-generation sequencing.* Genome Res, 2010. **20**(9): pp. 1165–1173.

47. Li, H., et al., *The Sequence Alignment/Map format and SAMtools.* Bioinformatics, 2009. **25**(16): pp. 2078–2079.

48. Simpson, J.T., et al., *ABySS: a parallel assembler for short read sequence data.* Genome Res, 2009. **19**(6): pp. 1117–1123.

49. Xie, Y., et al., *SOAPdenovo-Trans: de novo transcriptome assembly with short RNA-Seq reads.* Bioinformatics, 2014. **30**(12): pp. 1660–1666.

50. McKenna, A., et al., *The Genome Analysis Toolkit: a MapReduce framework for analyzing next-generation DNA sequencing data.* Genome Res, 2010. **20**(9): pp. 1297–1303.

51. Danecek, P., et al., *The variant call format and VCFtools.* Bioinformatics, 2011. **27**(15): pp. 2156–2158.

52. Yang, H. and K. Wang, *Genomic variant annotation and prioritization with ANNOVAR and wANNOVAR.* Nat Protoc, 2015. **10**(10): pp. 1556–1566.

53. Cingolani, P., et al., *A program for annotating and predicting the effects of single nucleotide polymorphisms, SnpEff: SNPs in the genome of Drosophila melanogaster strain w1118; iso-2; iso-3.* Fly (Austin), 2012. **6**(2): pp. 80–92.

54. Adzhubei, I., D.M. Jordan, and S.R. Sunyaev, *Predicting functional effect of human missense mutations using PolyPhen-2.* Curr Protoc Hum Genet, 2013. Chapter 7: Unit7 20.

55. Richards, S., et al., *Standards and guidelines for the interpretation of sequence variants: a joint consensus recommendation of the American College of Medical Genetics and Genomics and the Association for Molecular Pathology.* Genet Med, 2015. **17**(5): pp. 405–424.

## CHAPTER 3

The NCBI Entrez Databases

INTRODUCTION

The genomic databases store and organize the genomic data in a way that can be searched and retrieved using the Internet. Generally, a bioinformatics database is formed of well-organized records that can be updated, searched, and retrieved. Even though there are several genomic databases, the National Center for Biotechnology Information (NCBI) databases are the central databases that integrate almost all other major databases, including the European Molecular Biology Laboratory (EMBL), the DNA Data Bank of Japan (DDBJ), and several other major databases such as the Protein Data Bank, PIR, and more. The NCBI, EMBL, and DDBJ together form the International Nucleotide Sequence Database Collaboration (INSDC), which unifies the collaborative efforts to share genomic data acquired by continuous submission and curation on a daily basis.

The NCBI provides a variety of online resources for biological information and data. It introduces its database services through the NCBI Entrez, which is a molecular biology database system that provides integrated access to nucleotide and protein sequence data, genomic mapping information, protein structure data, life science literature, and more. The NCBI databases play a central role in genomics research. They offer scientists the opportunity to access a wide variety of biologically relevant data, including genomic sequences and related information of a large number of organisms. Enormous amounts of experimentally driven raw sequence data are generated daily and deposited to the NCBI databases. This raw data are the hallmarks of modern genomic research and are used by researchers from around the world for further understanding of the different aspects of biology. Through NIH generous funding, the NCBI's databases are well equipped with tools and software that facilitate database searching, data retrieval, and data analysis.

In this chapter, we will discuss the web-based Entrez system to learn how to use the NCBI's website to submit, search, and retrieve data. This chapter is intended to be practical so learners can follow with practicing while reading. You may need a computer and an Internet connection to access the NCBI's Entrez databases.

There are over 40 NCBI's databases that can be accessed through the Entrez retrieval system. Those databases are categorized into overlapping groups, including (1) DNA and RNA, (2) genes and gene expression, (3) proteins, (4) protein domains and structures, (5) genomes and maps, (6) homology, (7) variation, (8) taxonomy, (9) literature, and others. Table 3.1 lists some of the Entrez databases, descriptions of biological materials used, and the number of records on each database as of May 2021.

Most of the entries of the NCBI databases are submitted by institutions and researchers, while the others are curated by the NCBI staff or collaborating institutions. The NCBI provides several tools that researchers can use to submit their experimentally driven data. Data is submitted to the NCBI databases based on the type of the data. Sequence data obtained from sequencing can be submitted to GenBank, SRA, dbSNP, dbVar, and GEO. The data obtained from microarray experiments can be submitted to the dbGaP if it includes clinical information that requires controlled access; otherwise, it can be submitted to GEO database. Data obtained from human clinical studies or genetic tests are submitted to the dbGaP or GTR database. Peer-reviewed

TABLE 3.1   Entrez Databases and Number of Records (as of May 2021)

#	Entrez Database	Description of Biological Materials Used	Number of Entries
1	Assembly	Assembled genomes	934,215
2	Biocollections	Collection of historical samples	8,154
3	BioProject	Genomic and genetic studies	480,436
4	BioSample	Description of biological materials used in assay	15,671,142
5	BioSystems	Biological relationship	983,968
6	Books	Biomedical books	990,206
7	ClinVar	Human variations and observed health status	855,642
8	CDD	sequence alignments and profiles of protein domains	59,951
9	dbVar	Large-scale genomic variation	6,064,701
10	dbGaP	Studies which investigate the genotype and phenotype	363,665
11	dbSNP	SNPs and small-scale insertions and deletions	720,643,623
12	Nucleotide Database	Nucleotide sequences from GenBank, RefSeq, etc.	437,701,698
13	Gene	Genes and gene-specific data	47,519,524
14	GEO Datasets	Curated datasets of gene expression and abundance	4,263,019
15	GEO Profiles	Individual gene expression and molecular abundance	128,414,055
16	Genome	Whole genomes and annotation	72,921
17	GTR	Genetic information	77,238
18	HomoloGene	An automated system for homology groups from gene sets	141,268
19	Identical Protein Groups	Consolidated records of proteins in annotated coding regions	350,922,167
20	MeSH	Vocabulary for indexing articles for MEDLINE/PubMed.	348,031
21	OMIM	Human genes and genetic disorders	26,993
22	PopSet	Related DNA sequences from phylogenetic studies	355,597
23	Protein Clusters	Related protein sequences (clusters)	1,137,329
24	Protein Database	Protein sequences from GenPept, RefSeq, Swiss-Prot, etc.	893,858,484
25	PubMed	Citations and abstracts for biomedical literature	31,922,204
26	PMC	Full-text biomedical and life sciences journal literature	6,760,696
27	RefSeqGene	Human gene-specific reference genomic sequences	6,850
28	RefSeq	Curated, non-redundant DNA, RNA, and protein sequences	71,199,522
29	SRA	Sequence Read Archive (SRA) for data from the NGS	12,722,487
30	Structure	3D structures derived from the Protein Data Bank	169,336
31	Taxonomy	Names and phylogenetic lineages of organisms	2,425,420

journal manuscripts of research funded by NIH should be submitted to PubMed Central database (PMC). The submission of any type of data will be discussed in the relevant database section.

Each Entrez database organizes the data into records. A database has its own identification system that assigns a unique identifier (UID) to any new record created. The sequence data (DNA, RNA, or protein) submitted to GenBank database is given a unique identifier called GenInfo identifier (gi), which is a series of digits assigned consecutively to each sequence record processed by the NCBI. The NCBI database records are also assigned an additional unique identifier called the accession number, which is formed of a prefix, unique digits, a dot, and a digit for version (PRxxxxxx.x), where "PR" is for the prefix, "xxxxxx" are for the accession number, and ".x" for the version number. The assignment of accession numbers occurs at the time when the record is made available by the NCBI. Submitters are allowed to update the record data that they have submitted. A new *gi* will be issued to the record if the sequence is changed; however, only the version part will be incremented in the accession number to track the sequence update.

The records of a database are indexed by indexed fields that are used in searching the database.

ENTREZ RETRIEVAL WEB INTERFACE

The NCBI's databases are accessed through the Entrez retrieval system, which is available at www.ncbi.nlm.nih.gov/. The main page, as shown in Figure 3.1, contains links to important tools for data submission, downloading, learning resources, analysis tools, and links to application programming interfaces (APIs) for developers [1]. The page also contains three important sections: (1) the resource list (A–Z), (2) a search bar, and (3) a list of popular resources.

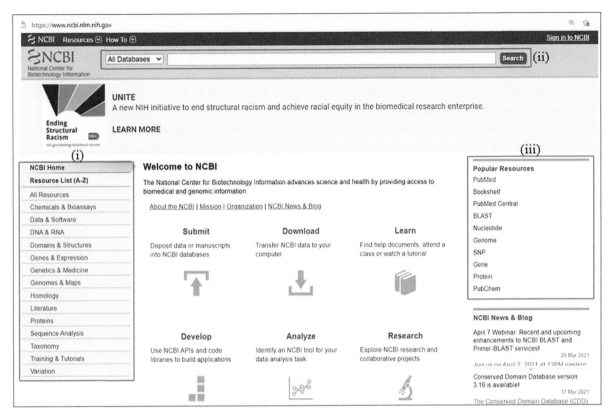

FIGURE 3.1   The web page of the NCBI resources.

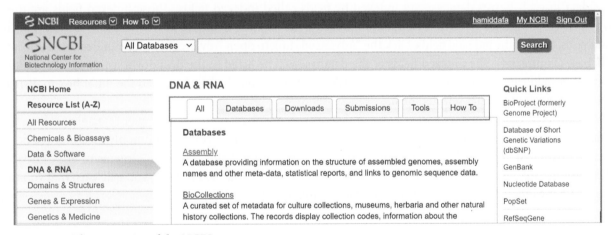

FIGURE 3.2   The categories of the NCBI resources.

(i) The resource list. The resource list, on the right side, categorizes the databases into several groups. Clicking the group name in the list will open a page with several tabs. For example, for DNA & RNA group there are six tabs: "All", "Databases", "Downloads", "Submission", "Tools", and "How To" as shown in Figure 3.2. The "All" tab includes the names and descriptions of all resources in that group. The "Databases" tab includes only the database names and descriptions. The "Downloads" tab contains links to download data of the databases in that group. The "Submission" tab contains links to the pages, where information or wizards are provided to submit data onto one of the databases in that group. The "Tools" tab includes the bioinformatics tools that can be used with the databases in the group. The "How To" tab includes the links that help the users to do the major tasks related to the database in the group.

(ii) Entrez search bar. The search bar, on the top of the page, consists of a dropdown list, a search box, and a search button. The dropdown list contains the list of all Entrez databases that can be accessed through the web page. The Entrez databases are searched by selecting the target database from the dropdown list, entering search terms into the search box, and then clicking the "Search" button.

(iii) Popular resources. The list of the popular resources, on the right side of the page, includes the list of the most commonly used NCBI databases.

Before using the NCBI Entrez web page for searching, it is recommended to create your own MY NCBI account using the link on the top right corner on the main Entrez web page. Creating an account and logging on when using the NCBI Entrez databases will allow you to save searches and results, manage filters, customize your viewing setting (NCBI site preferences) for major NCBI databases, set up alerts, create a bibliography, and to create an NCBI API key that you can use later in Chapters 4, 5, and 6 with the programs that use the NCBI's API to retrieve the Entrez databases.

Entrez Database Web Page

From the main Entrez web page, you can open any database web page by choosing a database from the database dropdown list and then click the "Search" button while the search box is empty.

Each Entrez database web page is provided with the links and tools used with the database. The top part of an Entrez database web page (Figure 3.3) remains the same for almost all database pages. The top common part of the page includes a blue menu bar, the search bar, and "Advanced" and "Help" links. The menu bar contains the NCBI logo, "Resources" dropdown menu, "How To" dropdown menu, and "Sign in to NCBI" link. Clicking the NCBI logo, at any time, will take you back to the main NCBI page. The "Advanced" link below the search box will open an advanced search query builder that is used to build complex search queries.

Entrez Database Indexed Fields

The data in each Entrez database are indexed by fields called indexed fields. Those indexed fields are used to build search queries. We will discuss the indexed fields of each database in the database section. For all databases, to view the indexed fields, click the "Advanced" link to open Advanced Search Builder of the selected database (Figure 3.4). The indexed fields of the database will be listed in the dropdown list under the Builder section. A field can be selected from the list. Click the "Show index list" link next to the input box to display the indexed values for that selected field.

Any indexed field may have a long name and short name. For example, most sequence databases have the indexed fields: Accession (long field name) and ACCN (short field name). Other commonly used indexed fields include "All Field" and "ALL", "Author" and "AUTH", "Gene Name" and "GENE", "Organism" and "ORGN", "Properties" and "PROP", "Publication Date" and "PDAT", "Title" and "TITL". Later you will learn that you can use either the long name or short name to create a search query.

Searching Entrez Databases

Most Entrez databases contains thousands of entries for several organisms (see Table 3.1). However, some databases such as OMIM and dbGaP store human data only. Any Entrez database is searched by selecting the database name from the database dropdown list, entering a search term into the search box, and then clicking the "Search" button. The search results will be displayed on the search results page. If you select "All

FIGURE 3.3   Search box and "Advanced" link.

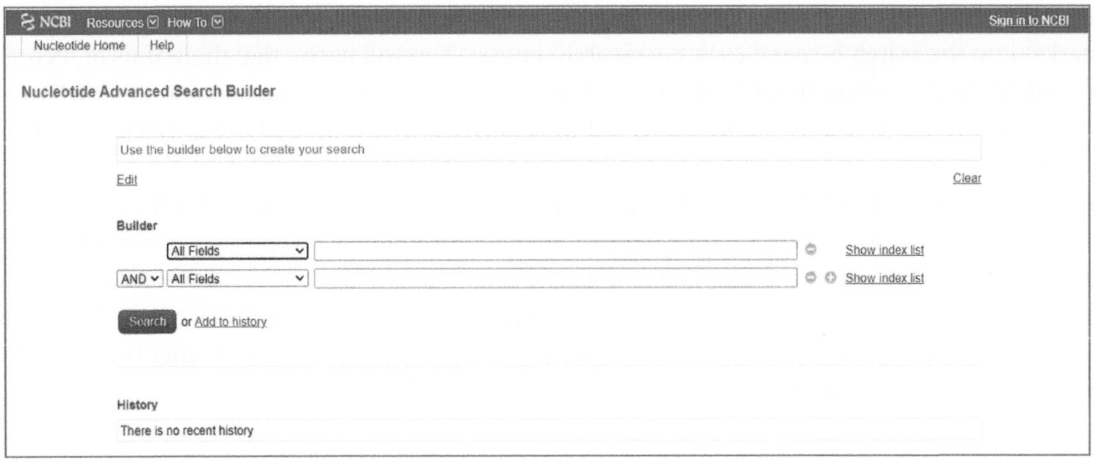

FIGURE 3.4   Advanced Search Builder.

Databases" from the database dropdown menu, the term you enter in the search box will be searched on all Entrez databases and the results will show the number of records matching your search terms on each database. This feature is called global query searching and you can use it to know the availability of records matching a specific search term on all Entrez databases. Try to select "All Databases" from the dropdown menu, enter any search term (e.g., PPARG) into the search box, and click the "Search" button. The results will be the counts of the records matching the search query on all databases.

Usually, before searching, you may have a clear plan of what data you need and which target database to search. The results of a database search may include thousands of irrelevant records; therefore, having a prior plan will help you to formulate your search query to return more specific search results. The keywords entered into the search box is called a search query. A search query can be a simple query made up of a single term or an advanced query including multiple search terms linked with Boolean operators (AND, OR, and NOT), as we will discuss very soon.

Simple Query Using Unique Identifiers   You can retrieve a database record directly by entering its UID into the search box if you have the UID of the record. The UID can either be a gi or an accession number. Searching by a single UID will display the record page while searching by multiple UIDs (comma-separated) will open the database results page that displays the summary info and links to the record pages.

For example, you can retrieve the PPARG nucleotide record with the "1823752908" UID by selecting Nucleotide database, entering the UID, and then clicking the "Search" button. PPARG is the gene symbol for the Peroxisome proliferator-activated receptor gamma, which is a gene that codes for several transcriptional factors (TFs). For multiple UIDs, you can enter 1823752908, 1743235135, 1823691621 into the search box and click the "Search" button. A results page containing the summaries of the three records of PPARG mRNA variants will be displayed.

Searching by UIDs is not common as it requires that you have the UIDs of records you wish to display.

Simple Search by Free Text   A free text term is any text entered into the search box. When searching by free text, the database system would search on all indexed fields of the database and the results would not be specific. The database searching engine would search the indexed data of all fields; any record that contains a match for the search term will be included in the results. Searching by free text usually returns many records. For example, select Nucleotide from the database dropdown list, enter "pparg" as a keyword and click the "Search" button. The results would be thousands of nucleotide records.

Free text can also be a phrase of multiple words. When multiple words are used as free text, the system may create different sets of the words as search terms, which would be searched as well returning many irrelevant records in the results. For example, enter "Peroxisome proliferator-activated receptor gamma" (without quotation marks) into the search box and click the "Search" button. You will notice that thousands of records have been found. To let the system to deal with a phrase as a single search term, use quotation marks around the phrase. Repeat the above search, but this time use the quotation marks around the gene name and you will notice that the number of the records has been greatly reduced.

The quotation marks should be used only if you intend to force the system to consider the phrase as a single search term; otherwise, you may miss some relevant records. For example, the phrase "women breast cancer" with the quotation marks will force the system to search only for the whole phrase. The records that contain a match for "breast cancer" only and not "women breast cancer" may be missing in the results. Therefore, you need to be careful when you use quotation marks as the phrase may be in a different order (e.g., breast cancer in women) or the word "women" may be separate in a different field.

Simple Search by an Indexed Field   Using free text only as a search term will allow the free text to be searched on all indexed fields "All fields" of the target database and many irrelevant records may be included in the results. You can use the indexed fields to limit the search to a specific field or fields and only the records matching the search terms on that indexed fields will be reported in the results. This will reduce the number of irrelevant records. Searching by an indexed field requires adding the tagged name of the field. For example, to restrict the search results to a specific organism use "organism name"[ORGN], where the organism name can be an organism's common name or scientific name (e.g., human[ORGN]). Other commonly used tagged fields include [TITL], [AUTH], [PDAT], [GENE], [PROP], [FILTER], etc. You can also use the Advanced Search Query Builder to display the indexed field names of a database and to create search terms with tagged indexed fields. The indexed fields of the databases will be listed in their relevant sections.

Advanced Search Queries   An advanced search query is the query that consists of several search terms. The advanced query makes the search results more specific. It is built of a combination of free text and tagged indexed fields linked by Boolean operators (AND, OR, and NOT) as shown in Table 3.2. The Boolean operators must be in uppercase. When AND is used between two terms, the search will return only the records that include both the search terms (term1 AND term2). When OR is used, records that contain any of the two terms will be reported (term1 OR term2). If NOT is used, the system will search for both terms and then it removes any record with the second term from the results (term1 NOT term2).

For example, assume that you intend to find the Nucleotide records for the human PPARG gene. The pieces of information that you have, in this case, are the database name (Nucleotide), organism (human), and gene symbol (PPARG). The search will be performed by selecting Nucleotide from the database dropdown list and entering the following advanced query into the search box:

pparg[GENE] AND human[ORGN]

Notice that for the field name, you can use either the long name or short name. The above query will request the database system to search for "PPARG" in the GENE field only and to search for "human" in the ORGN field only and report only the records that contain matches for both terms and not only one of them.

TABLE 3.2   Boolean Operators

Boolean Operator	Condition	Example
AND	term1 AND term2	Both term1 and term2 must be found
OR	term1 OR term2	At least one of the two terms must be found
NOT	term1 NOT term2	Term1 and not term2 must be found

Using indexed fields and Boolean operators will make the search more specific. Assume that, this time, you intend to search for PPARG nucleotide records for all mammals except human. You can build your search query as follows:

pparg[GENE] AND mammals[ORGN] NOT human[ORGN]

The database searching system usually processes the query from left to right. In some cases, you may need to change that order to obtain the search results you need. The order of the search process is changed by using parentheses "()". Search terms in parentheses will be processed first from left to right. Assume that this time, you wish to find the mammalian nucleotide pparg records, but you want to exclude human and mouse records from the results. If you enter the following query, you may obtain millions of irrelevant records and that is not what you intend to find.

pparg[GENE] AND mammals[ORGN] NOT human[ORGN] OR mouse[ORGN]

However, when entering the following query, the results would be more specific as only few records would be returned:

pparg[GENE] AND mammals[ORGN] NOT (human[ORGN] OR mouse[ORGN])

For getting search results that meet your goal, you need to think of the pieces of information that help you to build an efficient query. The following are some points that you can consider when searching any NCBI database:

1 Determine the type of data that you need to search for. This is important for selecting the target database. For DNA or RNA records you may select the Nucleotide database; for protein records you may select the Protein database; for articles you may select PubMed, etc. It is important to know the type of data stored in each NCBI database.

2 Determine the pieces of information that are needed to make the search results more specific.

3 Create search terms from the pieces of information. Put a phrase in quotation marks if you need the system to process it as a single unit.

4 Determine the indexed fields of the terms. You may have several terms from the same field or from different fields, such as ORGN, TITL, PDAT, etc.

5 Link the search terms using Boolean operators and parentheses according to the logic of the search.

6 Review the query to make sure that all pieces of information are included in the query and they are in the right order and tagged with their right indexed fields.

Using the indexed fields will help you to make the search results more specific and relevant. Most of the NCBI databases share the commonly used indexed fields as shown in Table 3.3.

TABLE 3.3   Commonly Used Database Indexed Fields

Indexed Field	Description
[Author] or [AUTH]	For searching by author
[Filter] or [FILT]	For filtering the results
[Gene Name] or [GENE]	For searching by gene symbol
[Organism] or [ORGN]	To limit the search to the records of a certain organism
[Properties] or [PROP]	To limit the search to a certain property
[Publication Date] or [PDAT]	To limit the search to a date or a range of dates
[Title] or [TITL]	For searching a term in the title

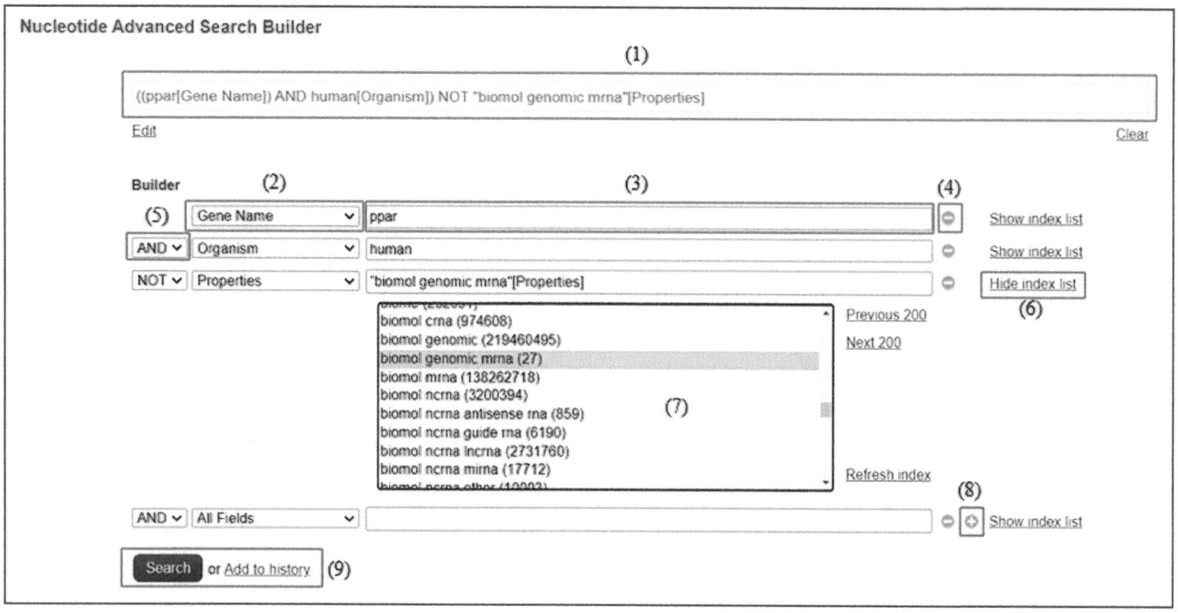

FIGURE 3.5   Nucleotide Advanced Search Builder.

For example, to search the Nucleotide database for a genomic DNA record of the human PPARG, you can use the following query:

pparg[GENE] AND human[ORGN] AND biomol_genomic[PROP]

To search for nucleotide PPARG records for all biomolecules except mRNA, you can enter the following query:

pparg[GENE] AND human[ORGN] NOT biomol_mrna[PROP]

Instead of composing a query manually, you can create a search query using the Advanced Search Builder shown in Figure 3.4.

With the Advanced Search Builder you can build an advanced query using indexed field names and Boolean operators (AND, OR, and NOT). The indexed fields for the database are in the dropdown list. For example, to build the above query, use the Advanced Search Query Builder as illustrated in Figure 3.5:

- Select "Gene Name" from the dropdown list (2) and enter "pparg" onto the next input box (3).
- Use the dropdown list of the Boolean operators (5) to choose AND.
- Choose "Organism" from the next dropdown list and enter human onto the next input box.
- Choose NOT from the Boolean operator dropdown list.
- Choose "Properties" from the field dropdown list and instead of entering a string on the next input box, click "Show/Hide index list" link (6) to show the list of indexed values (7) for the Properties field, scroll down, and choose "biomol genomic mrna".
- Any time you add a complete field, it will be added to the Query box (1).
- To delete any field, use the minus sign "-" (4) next to the field and to add a new field click the plus sign "+" (8).
- Once you have finished building the query, you can either click the "Search" button to start the search or you can click "Add to history" (9) to add the query to the history list for later use.

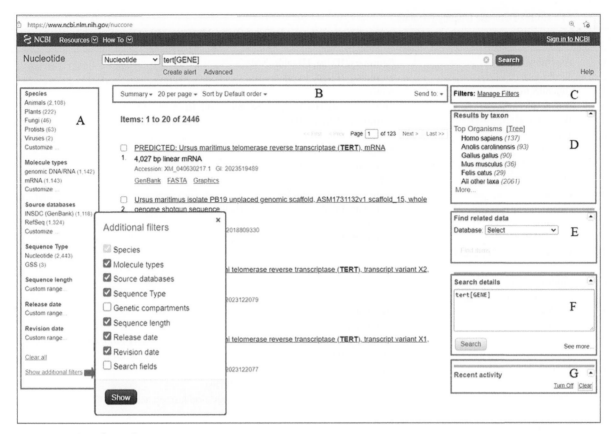

FIGURE 3.6   **Search results page.**

Entrez Search Results

Searching a database will display the records matching the search query on the search results page. The summaries of the returned records are usually displayed on the page. Generally, the layout of the results page is similar for almost all Entrez databases. The layout of the page is shown in Figure 3.6 and described below:

Filter List   A filter list may be found on the left side of the results pages of most databases. It is populated by the active filters available for the database. The number of records filtered by each filter is shown between parentheses. Clicking any filter will activate the filter and the filtered records will be displayed on the results page. When a filter is activated, a warning will be displayed at the top of the results. An activated filter can be cleared using the "Clear All" link. The filters can be controlled by clicking the "Show additional filters" link at the bottom of the filter list.

Menu Items   The menu items include "Format", "Items per page", "Sort by", and "Send To" dropdown menus. For some results pages, those items may be found on a single menu or one of them may be missing. The "Format" dropdown menu lists format options for displaying the results. The display format for each Entrez database is shown in Table 3.4. The "Item per page dropdown" menu is used to limit the number of records displayed on the results page. The "Sort by" dropdown menu lists the options to sort the results on the page. "Send To" dropdown menu is used to send the results to a destination, which can be a file, collections, or the clipboard. Consider "Send To" menu when you need to retrieve record data.

Managed Filters   The filters on the top right of the search results page are managed only when a user logs onto My NCBI. Click the "Manage Filters" link to open the Filters window. The system may ask you to log on. The Filters window (Figure 3.7) will allow you to choose the preferred filters or to create custom filters so they

TABLE 3.4   Entrez Database Display Formats

#	Entrez Database	Format
1	Assembly	Summary, ID list, ID table, XML
2	BioProject	Summary, ID list, accession list
3	Biocollections	Summary
4	BioSample	Summary, full, HapMap, ID list, accession list
5	BioSystems	Summary, abstract, ID list
6	Book	Summary
7	Clinvar	Summary, tabular, ID list
8	Conserved Domains	Summary, abstract, ID list
9	dbGaP	Tabular
10	dbVar	Summary, ID list, tabular
11	Gene	Summary, tabular, ASN.1, XML, ID list
12	Genome	Summary
13	Geo DataSets	Summary, ID list
14	Geo Profiles	Summary, ID list
15	GTR	Tabular
16	HomoloGene	Summary
17	Identical Protein Groups	Summary
18	MedGen	Summary, ID list, XML
19	MeSH	Summary, full
20	Nucleotide	Summary, GenBank, FASTA, ASN.1, revision history, accession, GI
21	OMIM	Summary, ID list
22	PMC	Summary, MEDLINE, PMCID list
23	PopSet	Summary, ASN.1, revision history, ID list
24	Protein	Summary, GenPept, FASTA, ASN.1, revision history, accession, GI
25	Protein Clusters	Summary
26	Protein Family Models	Summary, ID list
27	PubChem BioAssays	Summary, abstract, ID map ID list
28	PubChem Compounds	Summary, properties, synonyms, ID list
29	PubChem Substances	Summary, properties, synonyms, ID map, ID list
30	PubMed	Summary, abstract, PMID, PubMed
31	SNP	Summary
32	SRA	Summary
33	Structure	Summary, ID list
34	Taxonomy	Summary, taxon name, tax ID, info, common tree

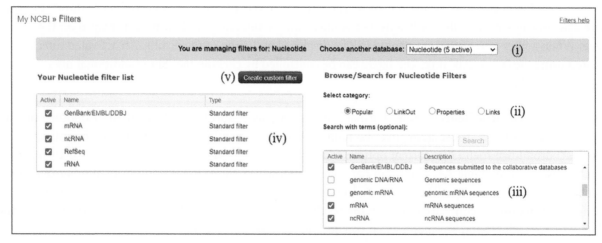

FIGURE 3.7   **Managed filters.**

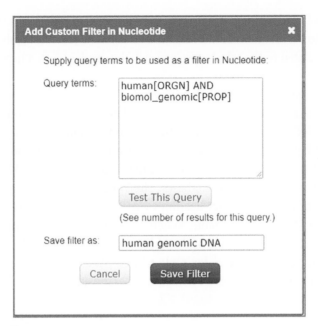

FIGURE 3.8   Adding custom filter.

can be active every time you search a database. Only five filters are allowed for all Entrez databases, except for PubMed, where the maximum number of allowed filters is 15. You can choose your preferred filters for a database as follows:

(i)   Choose a database from the database dropdown list.

(ii)   Select a category. There are three filter categories: "Popular", "LinkOut", "Properties", and "Links". The "Popular" option lists the most popular filters for the database. The "LinkOut" option lists the external resources that link to the database. The "Properties" option lists specific criteria that group the database records. The "Links" option lists the links to other Entrez databases.

(iii)   Select filters from the list (15 filters for PubMed and five filters for others are allowed).

(vi)   The selected filters will be displayed on the active filter list and will be active every time you search the database.

(v)   You can also create a custom filter by clicking "Create custom filter" button to open "Add Custom Filter" dialog window (Figure 3.8), enter query terms onto the Query box, click the "Test This Query" button to test your query, enter a name for the filter, and then save the filter. The filter will be shown on the filter list. You need to select it to be active. The custom filter can be edited or deleted from the filter list. The query terms are created following the query rules discussed above.

Once you have selected your preferred filters, they will be saved for that database so every time you search the database, they will be active and shown on the top right of the search results page.

Results by Taxon   This section organizes the records in the search records by taxon or organism. The number of records in each taxon is shown between parentheses. Clicking a taxon will open the results page for the records of that taxon.

Find Related Data   This section helps users to find the related data from other Entrez databases for any records in the results page. For example, if your results are Nucleotide records you may think to find the related records from other databases such as the Gene or Protein databases. Most commonly, users may prefer to find the related articles from the PubMed or PMC databases. To find the related data, select a record from the results page, then from the dropdown menu on "Find related data" section select a database, and finally click "Find item" button. The records related to the selected records will be displayed on a new results page.

Search Details   The "Search details" box displays the terms of the search query that has generated the results. The search terms entered into the search box of an Entrez database may be modified if no quotation marks and no indexed fields are used. The modification of the search terms may include adding an indexed field for a term without an indexed field or creating multiple terms from a phrase without quotation marks. Entering a term without an indexed field, will enable a process called Automatic Term Mapping (ATM) to add "[All Fields]" after the term for most of the Entrez databases. The PubMed database has an advanced ATM that uses three indexing tables built of medical subject headings (MeSH) to add "[MeSH Terms]" after a term if that term is found on any of the MeSH indexed table. When a search phrase is entered without quotation marks, the database system will search first, in a table of the indexed phrases and words, the phrases and words from the search phrase. The term found in the index table will be used as search terms linked with "AND". For example, assume that you intend to search SRA database for archived data with the following phrase:

breast cancer in women

Select SRA from the database dropdown list, enter the above search phrase and click on the "Search" button. Scroll down to the "Search details" box. Notice that the query has been modified to become:

breast cancer[All Fields] AND women[All Fields]

Two terms "breast cancer[All Fields]" and "women[All Fields]" have been created and linked with "AND". However, if the above phrase is used with the quotation marks and indexed fields, the query would remain unchanged, but you may miss some relevant records or you may find no records at all. Therefore, do not use quotation marks unless you intend to find records with the exact phrase.

Recent Activity   The "Recent activity" box is where the recent searches are stored while your session is on. This activity can be turned off and on and can be cleared using the buttons on the top of the activity list. Use "clear" to clear the searches on the list. Choose Protein from the database dropdown list and search the Protein database with the following four separate queries in the same order:

pparg[GENE]
pparg[GENE] AND human[ORGN]
pparg[GENE] AND human[ORGN] AND refseq[Filter]
pparg[GENE] AND human[ORGN] AND refseq[Filter] AND "isoform 1"[Title]

You will notice that each time you run a search, the search query and the number of records in parentheses will be displayed on the activity list.

Clicking any of the searches will open the results of that search.

These searches on the recent activity list are also found in the history list on the Advanced Search Builder. The history table has five columns: "Search", "Add to builder", "Query", "Item found", and "Time". The Search column contains the serial numbers of the searches. An action menu will pop up when you click the number of the search. This menu will allow you to add AND/OR/NOT and the search query to the builder. The action menu also allows you to delete a search from the history, to show search results, to show search details, and to save a search to MyNCBI for future use.

The above was a general introduction to the Entrez web page and the general rules used to search the Entrez databases. In the following sections, we will discuss most of the Entrez databases in more detail and we will try different worked examples to demonstrate the uses of the databases.

NUCLEOTIDE DATABASE

The NCBI Nucleotide database is a comprehensive DNA and RNA database that includes sequences from three major resources: the NCBI GenBank, the EMBL Nucleotide Sequence Database (EMBL), and the DNA Data Bank of Japan (DDBJ). Those three databases are collectively known as the International Nucleotide Sequence Database Collaboration (INSDC). The NCBI database was founded by the Los Alamos National Laboratory in 1979 and then its ownership was transferred to the National Library of Medicine (NLM), on the campus of the US National Institutes of Health (NIH) in Bethesda, MD, as one of the NCBI databases in early 1990s. The EMBL Nucleotide Sequence database was founded in 1981 and then transferred to the European Bioinformatics Institute (EBI), located at Hinxton, near Cambridge, UK, in 1993. DDBJ was founded in 1986 by the National Institutes of Genetics at Mishima, Japan. Sequences submitted to these three databases are synchronized on a daily basis and made available to the public through the NCBI Entrez retrieval system. Each record includes a description of the sequence, the source organism, and bibliographic references. The sequence may be an individual gene or a segment of a gene, whole genome shotgun (WGS), RNA (mRNA, tRNA, or rRNA) as cDNA, or environmental sequences of unknown source organisms.

Submission of Sequence Data to GenBank

A sequence can be submitted to the GenBank database by clicking "Submit to GenBank" link under Nucleotide Tools on the main Nucleotide database web page or by accessing the submission page at www.ncbi.nlm.nih.gov/genbank/submit/. The nucleotide sequence submitted to GenBank will be in FASTA format. The submission web page provides several tools for submitting a sequence record to the GenBank database as follows:

BankIT. BankIT is a web-based wizard that guides the submitter step-by-step until the submission is completed successfully. Several types of sequences can be submitted using this tool including (1) SARS-Cov2, (2) rRNA, (3) multicellular animal, (4) influenza virus, (5) norovirus, (6) dengue virus, (7) eukaryote and prokaryote genomes (WGS or complete), (8) transcriptome shotgun assembly (TSA), (9) raw sequence read (fastq), and (10) mRNA, genomic DNA, organelle, ncRNA, plasmid, other viruses, phages, and synthetic sequences. The submission wizard starts by selecting one of the above options. The wizard then will guide you through each step to provide the metadata and the sequence and finalize the submission.

Submission portal. The submission portal is a unified system for multiple submission types, and it is available at https://submit.ncbi.nlm.nih.gov/, where you can submit several types of sequence data.

Tbl2asn. tbl2asn is a command-line program that can be downloaded from the NCBI FTP server for the different platforms and installed on your computer. Once it has been installed, it can be used from the command line (Command Prompt on Windows or terminal on Linux). tbl2asn is used to automate the creation of sequence records for submission to GenBank. The command syntax and the description of the options used with the command are available at the NCBI web page www.ncbi.nlm.nih.gov/genbank/tbl2asn2/.

Genome Workbench. NCBI's Genome Workbench is an open-source desktop graphical user interface (GUI) application for Windows, Linux, and Mac OS. It consists of integrated tools for studying and analyzing genetic data. Workbench is provided with a submission wizard that allows you to prepare submissions of single eukaryotic or prokaryotic genomes.

The sequences can be submitted to GenBank before or after publication. An accession number will be assigned for the submitted sequence to serve as a unique identifier for the new data and to allow the community to retrieve the sequence upon reading the publication. There are two types of sequence identifiers assigned to the new sequences; a GI number (GenInfo identifier), which is a serial number assigned to each record processed by NCBI and the accession number, which consists of a base Accession number, a dot, and a

TABLE 3.5   GenBank Divisions

No.	Abbreviation	Division Name	Basis
1	PRI	Primate sequences	Taxonomy
2	ROD	Rodent sequences	Taxonomy
3	MAM	Other mammalian sequences	Taxonomy
4	VRT	Other vertebrate sequences	Taxonomy
5	INV	Invertebrate sequences	Taxonomy
6	PLN	Plant, fungal, and algal sequences	Taxonomy
7	BCT	Bacterial sequences	Taxonomy
8	VRL	Viral sequences	Taxonomy
9	PHG	Bacteriophage sequences	Taxonomy
10	SYN	Synthetic sequences	Taxonomy
11	UNA	Unannotated sequences	Taxonomy
12	EST	EST sequences (expressed sequence tags)	Strategy
13	STS	STS sequences (sequence tagged sites)	Strategy
14	GSS	GSS sequences (genome survey sequences)	Strategy
15	HTG	HTG sequences	high-throughput genomic
16	HTC	Unfinished high-throughput cDNA sequencing	high-throughput
17	ENV	Environmental sampling sequences	high-throughput
18	PAT	Patent sequences	high-throughput
19	WGS	Whole genome sequencing projects	high-throughput

version suffix that starts with 1. The two identification systems run in parallel to each other. When a change is made to a record, it receives a new GI number while the version part of the accession number is incremented by 1. Since 1982, the number of sequences in GenBank has been growing exponentially.

The Nucleotide records include nucleotide sequences obtained from different species including animals, plants, fungi, protists, bacteria, archaea, and viruses. The nucleotide sequences are also for different molecule types (genomic DNA/RNA, mRNA, cRNA, ncRNA, rRNA, tRNA, and transcribed RNA). The cRNA (complementary RNA) is the viral RNA, from which mRNA is synthesized by the viral enzyme RNA-dependent RNA polymerase. The ncRNA is the non-coding RNA that is not translated into proteins. The nucleotide sequences may also be from different genetic compartments including chloroplast in plants, mitochondrion in animal and bacteria, plasmid in bacteria, or plastid, which is a membrane-bound organelle found in the cells of plants, algae, and some other eukaryotic organisms.

The sequence records, submitted to the GenBank database, are grouped into several divisions based either on the taxonomical group of the source organism or the sequencing strategy used to generate the sequencing data (Table 3.5).

GenBank Format

The GenBank records are displayed in the GenBank format, which is plain text that includes three regions: (1) header, (2) feature table, and (3) sequence (Figure 3.9). The header and feature table are the metadata for the sequence or annotation section. The start of the annotation section is marked by a line beginning with the word "LOCUS". The start of sequence section is marked by a line beginning with the word "ORIGIN" and the end of the section is marked by a line with only "//".

The header includes the following lines:

- *LOCUS.* The LOCUS line includes accession, sequence length in base pair (bp), nature of the sequence (linear, or circular), division type which is denoted by the division abbreviation, and the submission date.
- *DEFINITION.* The definition line includes sequence description, which may include the organism and name of the gene, and whether the sequence is complete or partial.
- *ACCESSION.* the record accession number.

```
     ⎡ LOCUS       U93453                    109 bp    DNA    linear  (VRT) 24-JUL-2016
     │ DEFINITION  Scyliorhinus canicula PPARG gene, partial cds.
     │ ACCESSION   U93453
     │ VERSION     U93453.1
     │ KEYWORDS    .
     │ SOURCE      Scyliorhinus canicula (smaller spotted catshark)
     │   ORGANISM  Scyliorhinus canicula
     │             Eukaryota; Metazoa; Chordata; Craniata; Vertebrata; Chondrichthyes;
     │             Elasmobranchii; Galeomorphii; Galeoidea; Carcharhiniformes;
     │             Scyliorhinidae; Scyliorhinus.
     │ REFERENCE   1  (bases 1 to 109)
     │   AUTHORS   Escriva,H., Safi,R., Hanni,C., Langlois,M.C., Saumitou-Laprade,P.,
①  ⎨             Stehelin,D., Capron,A., Pierce,R. and Laudet,V.
     │   TITLE     Ligand binding was acquired during evolution of nuclear receptors
     │   JOURNAL   Proc. Natl. Acad. Sci. U.S.A. 94 (13), 6803-6808 (1997)
     │   PUBMED    9192646
     │ REFERENCE   2  (bases 1 to 109)
     │   AUTHORS   Escriva,H., Safi,R., Hanni,C., Langlois,M.C., Saumitou-Laprade,P.,
     │             Stehelin,D., Capron,A., Pierce,R. and Laudet,V.
     │   TITLE     Direct Submission
     ⎣   JOURNAL   Submitted (14-MAR-1997) INSERM U167, Institut Pasteur de Lille, 1
                   Rue du Prof. A. Calmette, Lille 59019, France
     ⎡ FEATURES             Location/Qualifiers
     │    source           1..109
     │                     /organism="Scyliorhinus canicula"
     │                     /mol_type="genomic DNA"
     │                     /db_xref="taxon:7830"
     │    CDS              <1..>109
②  ⎨                     /note="nuclear receptor C domain"
     │                     /codon_start=3
     │                     /product="PPARG"
     │                     /protein_id="AAB68730.1"
     ⎣                     /translation="VKLDYDQCERNCKIQKKNRNKCQSCRFQKCFPVGMS"
     ⎡ ORIGIN
     │        1 gggtgaagct ggattatgat cagtgtgaac gcaattgtaa gattcaaaaa aaaaaccgca
③  ⎨       61 acaagtgcca gtcctgtcgt tttcagaagt gcttccccgt cggcatgtc
     ⎣ //
```

FIGURE 3.9   GenBank format of a sequence record.

- *VERSION*. Accession number and version number of the sequence record.
- *KEYWORDS*. The keywords that help to identify the sequence records. It is used to identify reference sequences.
- *SOURCE*. This indicates the source organism and its taxonomy classification.
- *REFERENCE*. This lists the bibliographic references that cited the records. This section includes the authors, title, journal, and PubMed identifier (PMID) for each reference.

The feature table section may include the feature names and feature entries in the form of key-value pairs:

- *Source*. The source feature may include organism, molecule type (mol-type), taxonomy database number (db_xref).
- *CDS*. The coding sequence feature may include the CDS description (Note), codon_start (the base number at which the CDS starts), the name of the CDS product (protein), the protein id (for the protein record in the Protein database), and the translation (the sequence of amino acids).

- *Gene.* This feature may include the gene name.
- Other features may also be found.

The sequence data section starts with "ORIGIN" and ends with "//".

Nucleotide Sub Databases

In addition to the DNA/RNA sequences mentioned above, the GenBank database now includes nucleotide sequences that were in separate databases. These sequences include Expressed Sequence Tags (EST), Genome Survey Sequences (GSS), Sequence-Tagged Sites (STS), Reference Sequence (RefSeq), and Reference Gene Sequence (RefSeqGene). Those types of sequences can be searched from the Nucleotide database. In the following subsections we will discuss each of these kinds of nucleotide records.

Expressed Sequence Tags

The Expressed Sequence Tags (EST) was a separate database, but it became a division of the GenBank database in 2019. The dbEST was a collection of ESTs, which are short sequence reads (less than 1000 bp) from mRNA (cDNA). ESTs are important in research because they represent a snapshot of genes expressed in a specific tissue or at a specific condition. The dbEST provides ESTs obtained from different organisms except bacteria and viruses. The GenBank formatted EST record has "EST" on the KEYWORDS section as shown in Figure 3.10. This keyword will help in the Nucleotide database searching for EST sequence. The term "EST[KEYWORD]" is used to restrict the results to EST records. The word "EST" is also found on the LOCUS line indicating the GenBank division.

Genome Survey Sequences

The Genome Survey Sequences (GSS) is a GenBank division and archive for sequences similar to ESTs but they are genomic in origin not cDNA. The GSS sequences may include random "single pass read" genome survey sequences (sequences generated along single pass read by random selection), cosmid/BAC/YAC end sequences (genomic end-side sequences generated by cosmid/bacterial artificial chromosome/yeast artificial chromosome), exon trapped genomic sequences (sequences containing exons), Alu PCR sequences (repetitive element in mammalian genome), transposon-tagged sequences (sequences generated from transposon tagging), etc. The word "GSS" is added to the KEYWORDS line on the GenBank formatted GSS record (Figure 3.11) and used in the Nucleotide database search query as "GSS[KEYWORD]" to restrict the results to GSS records.

Sequence-Tagged Sites

Sequence-Tagged Sites (STS) is a relatively short sequence, usually around 200 to 500 bp in length. It is produced from a polymerase chain reaction (PCR) product. The PCR product is then sequenced to obtain the STS sequence. This method is very helpful in identifying microsatellites markers such as Simple Sequence Repeats (SSRs), Sequence-Tagged Microsatellite Sites (STMS), or Simple Sequence Repeats Polymorphisms

```
LOCUS       AU098869                 300 bp    mRNA    linear    EST 29-JAN-2011
DEFINITION  AU098869 Sugano Homo sapiens cDNA library Homo sapiens cDNA clone
            HEP03909 5' similar to Human breast and ovarian cancer
            susceptibility (BRCA1) mRNA, mRNA sequence.
ACCESSION   AU098869
VERSION     AU098869.1
DBLINK      BioSample: SAMN00163320
KEYWORDS    EST.
```

FIGURE 3.10 The header section of an EST GenBank record.

```
LOCUS       AY410046                444 bp    DNA      linear   GSS 02-OCT-2013
DEFINITION  Homo sapiens HBB gene, VIRTUAL TRANSCRIPT, partial sequence,
            genomic survey sequence.
ACCESSION   AY410046
VERSION     AY410046.1
DBLINK      BioProject: PRJNA13698
KEYWORDS    GSS.
```

FIGURE 3.11   The header section of a GSS GenBank record.

```
LOCUS       HUMUT6410               222 bp    DNA      linear   STS 07-AUG-1996
DEFINITION  Human STS UT6410, sequence tagged site.
ACCESSION   L18196
VERSION     L18196.1
KEYWORDS    STS; PCR primer; STS sequence; microsatellite marker;
            microsatellite repeat; repeat polymorphism; sequence tagged site.
SOURCE      Homo sapiens (human)
```

FIGURE 3.12   The header section of a STS GenBank record.

(SSRPs). The STS sequences can also be markers such as Sequence Characterized Amplified Region (SCARs), Cleaved Amplified Polymorphic Sequences (CAPs), and Inter-simple Sequence Repeats (ISSRs).

The word "STS" will be on the KEYWORDS line of the Nucleotide STS record and LOCUS (Figure 3.12). The term "STS[KEYWORD]" is added to the search query to restrict the search results to STS records.

Reference Sequence

The Reference Sequences (RefSeqs) are a collection of highly standard, non-redundant sequences selected from the sequences, submitted to INSDC databases (GenBank, EMBL, and DDBJ), to be as references to the sequences of the organisms they are representing. The RefSeqs collection includes a variety of genomic entities such as chromosomes, complete genomic assemblies of organisms, contigs, curated genomic functional regions and their products such as mRNAs, tRNA, rRNA, and proteins. The RefSeqs of nucleotides and proteins are generated either by manual curation from annotations copied from GenBank genomic sequence records, curated annotations provided by model organisms databases such (e.g., FlyBase), or computationally by processing the genomes through the Eukaryotic Genome Annotation Pipeline and the Prokaryotic Genome Annotation Pipeline. The curated RefSeq sequences generated from experiments are called known RefSeqs while those computationally predicted through automated pipelines are called model RefSeqs. The RefSeqs are assigned a unique accession number consisting of a prefix of two letters, underscore '_', and six digits. The prefix of a RefSeq may indicate the type of the molecule and method of generation (the model mRNAs are given prefix 'XR_' and model proteins are given prefix 'XP_'. Table 3.6 lists the prefixes of reference sequences and their descriptions.

On the KEYWORDS line of the GenBank RefSeq record, the word "RefSeq" will be found as shown in Figure 3.13 to indicate that the record is for a RefSeq sequence.

In addition to the RefSeq keyword, the COMMENT" section of the GenBank RefSeq record indicates the RefSeq status, which will be either, MODEL, INFERRED, PREDICTED, PROVISIONAL, REVIEWED, VALIDATED, or WGS. The COMMENTS section may also include the source accession used to generate the RefSeq sequence (if applicable) and the collaborating team if found (Figure 3.14).

Table 3.7 contains the RefSeq status codes that may be found in COMMENT sections and their description.

In the search query, you can use either "refseq[KEYWORD]" or "srcdb_refseq[PROP]" to restrict the results to the Nucleotide RefSeq records only.

TABLE 3.6   RefSeq Accession Prefixes

Accession prefix	Molecule type	Description
AC_	Genomic	Complete genomic molecule (alternate assembly)
NC_	Genomic	Complete genomic molecule (reference assembly)
NG_	Genomic	Incomplete genomic region
NT_	Genomic	Contig or scaffold (clone based or WGS)
NW_	Genomic	Contig or scaffold (primarily WGS)
NZ_	Genomic	Complete genomes and unfinished WGS data
NM_	RNA	Protein-coding transcripts (usually curated)
NR_	RNA	Non-protein-coding transcripts
XM_	mRNA	Predicted model protein-coding transcript
XR_	RNA	Predicted model non-protein-coding transcript
AP_	Protein	Annotated on AC_ alternate assembly
NP_	Protein	Associated with an NM_ or NC_ accession
YP_	Protein	Annotated on genomic molecules without an instantiated transcript record
XP_	Protein	Predicted model, associated with an XM_ accession
WP_	Protein	Non-redundant across multiple strains and species

```
LOCUS       NM_007294              7088 bp    mRNA    linear   PRI 11-JUL-2020
DEFINITION  Homo sapiens BRCA1 DNA repair associated (BRCA1), transcript
            variant 1, mRNA.
ACCESSION   NM_007294
VERSION     NM_007294.4
KEYWORDS    RefSeq; MANE Select.
SOURCE      Homo sapiens (human)
  ORGANISM  Homo sapiens
            Eukaryota; Metazoa; Chordata; Craniata; Vertebrata; Euteleostomi;
            Mammalia; Eutheria; Euarchontoglires; Primates; Haplorrhini;
            Catarrhini; Hominidae; Homo.
```

FIGURE 3.13   Header section of a RefSeq GenBank record showing KEYWORDS.

```
REFERENCE   11 (bases 1 to 7088)
  AUTHORS   Petrucelli,N., Daly,M.B. and Pal,T.
    TITLE   BRCA1- and BRCA2-Associated Hereditary Breast and Ovarian Cancer
  JOURNAL   (in) Adam MP, Ardinger HH, Pagon RA, Wallace SE, Bean LJH, Stephens
            K and Amemiya A (Eds.);
            GENEREVIEWS((R));
            (1993)
   PUBMED   20301425
COMMENT     REVIEWED REFSEQ: This record has been curated by NCBI staff. The
            reference sequence was derived from AL701927.1, U14680.1,
            BC072418.1, BU617173.1 and BU679389.1.
            On Aug 31, 2019 this sequence version replaced NM_007294.3.
```

FIGURE 3.14   COMMENT of a RefSeq GenBank record.

RefSeqGene

The RefSeqGene genes are genomic sequences and a subset of the RefSeqs that are part of reference genome and well-defined, complete genes used as stable reference genes for defining the coordinates of all gene regions (such as promoter, introns, exons, and flanking regions) and gene mutations and biological significant variants such as SNPs CNV, etc. Rather than RefSeq, RefSeqGene provides gene-specific sequence for each recognized gene including all and complete set of regions. The RefSeqGene sequences are aligned to reference chromosomes and are considered as standard, normal allele, and baseline reference that gene sequences can

TABLE 3.7   RefSeq Status Codes

Code	Description
MODEL	The record is provided by the Genome Annotation pipeline.
INFERRED	The record has been predicted by genome sequence analysis and it is not yet supported by experimental evidence.
PREDICTED	The record has not yet been subject to individual review.
PROVISIONAL	The record has not yet been subject to individual review.
REVIEWED	The record has been reviewed by NCBI staff or by a collaborator.
VALIDATED	The record has undergone an initial review to provide the preferred sequence standard. The record has not yet been subject to final review.
WGS	The record is provided to represent a collection of whole genome shotgun sequences.

TABLE 3.8   GenBank Indexed Fields

Full Field Name	Short Field Name	Full Field Name	Short Field Name
Accession	ACCN	Organism	ORGN
All Fields	ALL	Page Number	PAGE
Author	AUTH	Primary Accession	PACC
EC/RN Number	ECNO	Primary Organism	PORGN
Feature Key	FKEY	Properties	PROP
Filter	FILT / SB	Protein Name	PROT
Gene Name	GENE	Publication Date	PDAT
Genome Project	-	SeqID String	SQID
Issue	ISS	Sequence Length	SLEN
Journal	JOUR	Substance Name	SUBS
Keyword	KYWD	Text Word	WORD
Modification Date	MDAT	Title	TITL
Molecular Weight	MOLWT	Volume	VOL

```
LOCUS       NG_005905              193689 bp    DNA     linear   PRI 27-JUL-2020
DEFINITION  Homo sapiens BRCA1 DNA repair associated (BRCA1), RefSeqGene
            (LRG_292) on chromosome 17.
ACCESSION   NG_005905
VERSION     NG_005905.2
KEYWORDS    RefSeq; RefSeqGene.
SOURCE      Homo sapiens (human)
```

FIGURE 3.15   KEYWORDS of a RefSeqGene GenBank record.

compare to for reporting variants such as dbSNP and dbVar. The RefSeqGene sequences are also annotated with reference standard transcripts and non-standard transcript. NCBI provides an interface for comparing sequences to the RefSeqGene sequences. The GenBank records of RefSeqGene sequences have "RefSeq" and "RefSeqGene" as KEYWORDS as shown in Figure 3.15. The Nucleotide search results can be restricted to RefSeqGene records by adding "RefSeqGene[KEYWORD]" to the search query.

Searching Nucleotide Database

The GenBank Nucleotide database can be chosen from the database dropdown list on the main Entrez website or using www.ncbi.nlm.nih.gov/nuccore/. Refer to the section "Searching Entrez Databases" above for Entrez search and query building. Table 3.8 shows the indexed field names that can be used to build advanced search queries.

Since the GenBank Nucleotide database includes diverse nucleotide sequences including complete genes, partial genes, transcripts, subsets of nucleotide sequences (EST, GSS, STS, etc.) for more than 400,000 species [2], the search results may include a large number of records. An advanced query can be used to find relevant records. Any of the indexed fields, listed in Table 3.8, can be used for building the search query but [FILT],

[GENE], [KYWD], [ORGN], [PROP], [PDATE], [PROT[, [SLEN], and [TITL] are the most commonly used tagged indexed fields.

General Nucleotide Searching Strategy

One of the common scenarios is to search for nucleotide record by a gene name or a phenotype. However, if you search by free text, thousands of records may be reported. Therefore, you can include other information in your search query to narrow the results as follows:

- Review the "Searching Entrez Databases" section above.
- Use [TITL] to search the term on DEFINITION section of the GenBank records. This will cut numerous irrelevant records as a gene name, or a phenotype is usually included in the definition line.
- Use [ORGN] if you are searching for records of a specific organism. This will remove the records of other species. Either the common name or the scientific name of the organism can be used (e.g., human[ORGN] or "homo sapiens"[ORGN]).
- Use refseq[KYWD] or srcdb_refseq[PROP] if you are searching for non-redundant reference sequence record. This will narrow the results only to the reference records.
- Use EST[KYWD], GSS[KYWD], or STS[KYWD] to narrow the results to EST, GSS, or STS, respectively.
- Use [PDAT] to restrict the results to a specific year or range of dates. This is useful, for example, if you are targeting recent records (e.g., 2015:2021[PDAT]).
- Use [FILTER] to filter the results based on species such as animal, plants, fungi, bacteria, archaea, viruses, etc. (e.g. bacteria[FILTER]) or based on genetic compartment such as chloroplast, mitochondrion, plasmid, plastid (e.g. mitochondrion[FILTER]).
- Use [PROP] to narrow the results to a specific biomolecular type. The most commonly used biomolecular types are shown in Table 3.9.

You can use the Advanced Search Builder as explained in the introduction to build an efficient Nucleotide search query.

Worked Examples

The following are worked examples for some common Nucleotide searches:

Example 1 One of the main uses is to search Nucleotide database for nucleotide sequences of a gene across different organisms (orthologs). Such search may be used to obtain orthologous sequence for comparative homology purposes such as performing multiple sequence alignment, constructing phylogenetic tree, etc. We will use breast cancer 1 (BRCA1) as an example. The breast cancer type 1 (BRCA1) gene codes for BRCA1 protein that acts as a tumor suppressor, which helps prevent the uncontrolled and growing and rapid division of cells and it is also involved in repairing damaged DNA.

From the NCBI all resources web page, choose Nucleotide from the database dropdown list, enter "BRCA1" into the search box and click on the search button. You will notice that thousands of records have been found.

TABLE 3.9 Common Biomolecular Types

Tagged Property	Sequence Biomolecular Type
biomol_crna[PROP]	Complementary RNA OF viruses
biomol_genomic[PROP]	Genomic DNA that may include both coding and non-coding sequence
biomol_mrna[PROP]	Gene transcript or cDNA that includes only coding region of a gene
biomol_rrna[PROP]	Ribosomal RNA
biomol_trna[PROP]	Transfer RNA

The Nucleotide results page is a typical Entrez database results page as discussed in the "Searching Entrez Databases" section above. The results may include numerous irrelevant records. Since BRCA1 is a gene name, you can use the tagged field [GENE] as follows:

BRCA1[GENE]

We will notice that the number of records has been greatly reduced. This is because the database system would search only on the gene name indexed field. However, the results may include diverse sequence types such as genomic DNA, transcript, and other Nucleotide subsets. Assume that you are interested in the gene transcript or mRNA only. Thus, you can repeat the search with the following query:

BRCA1 [GENE] AND biomol_mrna[PROP]

The results will include only BRCA1 transcripts. You can also notice that the number of records has become fewer. However, the results may include redundant sequences (multiple sequences for the same organism). To restrict the results to only non-redundant BRCA1 transcripts, you can add the reference sequence term as follows:

BRCA1[GENE] AND biomol_mrna[PROP] AND srcdb_refseq[PROP]

The search would report only RefSeq BRCA1 transcripts. Remember that some of the reference transcripts may be models or computationally predicted sequences rather than obtained from experiments. You may decide to exclude the model reference sequences from the results as follows:

BRCA1[GENE] AND biomol_mrna[PROP] AND srcdb_refseq[PROP] NOT model[Filter]

You will notice that the number of records has become very few as shown in Figure 3.16. You can also notice that there are multiple transcript variants for the same gene. The transcript variation is due to the alternative splicing. A transcript variant codes for a different protein. Since there are a few records, you can download the sequences of all records or selected records by using the "Send To" dropdown menu as shown in Figure 3.16. The records can be saved in different formats including Summary, GenBank, FASTA, ASN.1, XML, feature table, accession list, GI list, and GFF3.

If you click a record title on the results page, a GenBank formatted record will open. The GenBank format was discussed in the "GenBank Format" section above.

Example 2   For polymerase chain reaction (PCR), primers are needed to amplify a specific gene (see the section "Polymerase Chain Reaction" in Chapter 2). Researchers usually design primers using a computer program such as Primer-BLAST and they send the primer sequences to a laboratory for the primer (oligo-nucleotide) synthesis. However, before designing primers, a sequence of the gene or gene transcript must be retrieved from the Nucleotide database. The type of sequence depends on whether your sample is DNA or RNA and on the targeted region of the gene. In the case of a DNA sample, primers are usually retrieved from a genomic sequence of the gene, while in the case of an RNA sample primers are retrieved from a gene transcript. In this example, we will assume that we have a human DNA sample, and we wish to amplify the BRCA1 gene. For this purpose, the reference sequence of the human BRCA1 gene must be retrieved from Nucleotide database using the following query:

brca1[GENE] AND human[ORGN] AND RefSeqGene[KEYWORD] AND biomol_genomic[PROP]

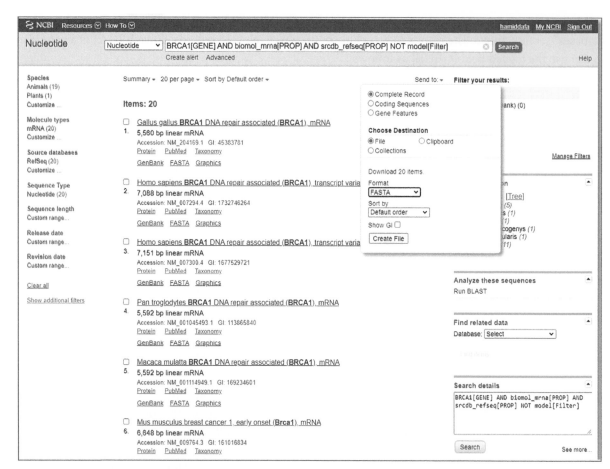

FIGURE 3.16   Nucleotide search results page.

This may open the GenBank record of the human reference BRCA1 gene. The complete FASTA formatted sequence of the gene can be downloaded using the "Send To" dropdown menu. The sequence then can be used with a primer-designing program to design the primers. Moreover, the primers can be designed using "Pick Primers" link under the "Analyze this sequence" section on the right site of the Nucleotide record page. Primer-BLAST and primer designing will be discussed later in this chapter and in Chapter 8.

Other than the "Pick Primers" link, the Nucleotide record page is also provided with other tools for sequence analysis including "Run BLAST" for searching similar sequences, "Highlight Sequence Features" for highlighting the feature region on the sequence data, "Find in the Sequence" for finding a pattern on the sequence, and "Show in Genome Data Viewer, for viewing the sequence in the genomic context. BLAST will be discussed in detail in Chapters 7 and 8 and the Genome Data Viewer will be discussed later in this chapter.

GENE DATABASE

Genes are the functional genomics regions in the genome of a living organism. The functional genes code for proteins and a few genes codes for functional RNA (rRNA, tRNA, microRNA). An organism may have thousands of genes (e.g., the human has around 25,000 genes). A gene, as described in Chapter 1, consists of different regions including promoter, coding region, and non-coding region. The sequence of a complete eukaryotic gene includes promoter, upstream and downstream flanking regions, introns, and exons. When transcribing mRNA from a gene, only exons are spliced together to form the transcript (mRNA). Prokaryotic genes are missing the introns. The region of the mRNA that comprises the codons that are translated into amino acids is known as the coding sequence (CDS). Due to alternative splicing, a single eukaryotic gene may have several transcripts called transcript variants, which encode for different proteins called isoforms or protein variants. The regions of genes that have biological significance, such as exons, CDS, etc., are known as gene features. A functional gene may have a non-functional copy in a different part of the genome (e.g., different chromosome). The non-functional gene, the pseudogene, is a gene missing a promoter region and cannot be activated and, therefore, cannot be transcribed into mRNA and translated into a protein. Generally, a complete gene is annotated at specific regions of a reference genome. The gene annotated region is called the gene locus, which includes the sequence of the gene (promoter, coding, and non-coding region) described by coordinates that are formatted as (chromosome:start-end). For example, the position of human BRCA1 on the current reference genome is chr17:43044295-43125364, which indicates that the gene is located on chromosome 17, the first base position is 43044295, and the end base position is 43125364. The gene region may also include other annotations such as markers (e.g., SNPs, CNVs, etc.).

The NCBI Gene database is a database for storing information of genes identified in a completely sequenced reference genome. The data includes the name of the gene, the position of complete sequence of the gene in a reference genome, gene features (introns, exons, CDS, protein products, etc.), associated markers (dbSNP, dbVar, etc.), phenotypes (traits, functions, condition, etc.), citations, homologs (related genes), and links to several external databases.

Information of a new gene entry is provided only by a recognized genomic database or by the NCBI Genome Annotation Pipeline [3] to the Gene database. However, scientists can enrich the functional annotation of genes included in the Gene database. They can use the GeneRIF (Gene Reference into Function) submission form, which is available on the Gene database web page, to submit a concise statement of a function or functions along with the PMID (PubMed identifier) of the peer-reviewed published paper that describes that function.

The Gene database includes both the experimentally confirmed genes (known genes), which were confirmed through laboratory experiments, and predicted genes (model genes), which were predicted using automated annotation and computational methods. A verified gene is assigned a unique integer and species-specific identifier called GeneID. The established gene is also assigned a category, which may be a functional protein-coding gene, pseudogene, ribosomal RNA (rRNA), or unknown. A gene will be labeled as unknown when it is under review. The NCBI staff will update a gene record if they receive new information about the gene [4].

The Gene database website can either be opened by choosing "Gene" from the database dropdown list on the Entrez database website or accessed directly by opening www.ncbi.nlm.nih.gov/gene/.

For searching the Gene database and building a search query, refer to the sections above where we discussed the searching of the Entrez databases, the search terms, and the layout of the search results page. The indexed fields of the Gene database are listed in Table 3.10.

We can find a specific gene record by using a geneID, gene symbol, or we can find multiple Gene records by using a general search term. The Advanced Search Builder is useful in building an advanced search query.

The simplest Gene searching is the searching by a gene name or a gene symbol. Each known gene has a name and a symbol (abbreviation) designated by the HUGO Gene Nomenclature Committee (HGNC). For example, "BRCA1 DNA repair associated" gene has the gene symbol "BRCA1". To search a gene by a full gene name, use the tagged indexed field [GFN]:

BRCA1 DNA repair associated[GFN]

To search a gene by a gene abbreviation, you can either use [GENE] or [SYM]:

BRCA1[SYM]

However, when you use the gene name or abbreviation only, the results page may show multiple gene records for different species.

TABLE 3.10   Gene Indexed Fields

Field Description	Short Field Name	Field Description	Short Field Name
Assembly Accession	AACC	Modification Date	MDAT
Nucleotide/Protein Accession	ACCN	MIM ID	MIM
All Fields	ALL	Default Map Location	MV
Assembly Name	ASM	Nucleotide Accession	NCAC
Creation Date	CDAT	Nucleotide UID	NUID
Chromosome	CHR	Organism	ORGN
Base Position	CPOS	Protein Accession	PACC
Date Discontinued	DDAT	Protein Full Name	PFN
Disease/Phenotype	DIS	PubMed ID	PMID
Domain Name	DOM	Preferred Symbol	PREF
EC/RN Number	ECNO	Properties	PROP
Expression/Tissues	EXPR	Protein UID	PUID
Filter	FILT	Taxonomy ID	TID
Gene Name / symbol	GENE or SYM	Gene/Protein Name	TITL
Gene Full Name	GFN	UniGene Cluster Number	UGEN
Gene Length	GL	UID	UID
Gene Ontology	GO	Text Word	WORD
Group	GRP	Exon Count	XC

The Gene results page is a typical Entrez results page as discussed above, but the default display format is tabular.

To make the search specific, use both the gene abbreviation and organism name as follows:

BRCA1[GENE] AND human[ORGN]

The above search query will open the human Gene BRCA1 records page

A typical Gene record page is displayed in "Full Report" format. A Gene record page begins with a line including the gene symbol, full gene name, and the organism's scientific name. The second line includes the GeneID and the record update date. The Download Datasets button on the right is used to download the gene sequence, transcript sequences, and protein sequences as shown in Figure 3.17. The downloaded datasets will be in a zipped folder including the FASTA formatted sequence file and detailed data report in both TSV and JSONL formats. The TSV report file contains important information of transcript variants transcribed from the gene and the protein variants (isoforms) translated from the transcripts. Such information includes transcript accessions, transcript names, protein accessions, isoform names, and more. A gene may have several transcripts due to alternative splicing and each transcript is translated into an isoform.

In the following, we will discuss the other sections of the Gene record page.

Summary   The summary section contains the basic information about the gene as shown in Figure 3.17. The summary information includes official symbol and full name as provided by HGNC, gene type, status, organism, lineage, synonyms, abstract (summary), the organ where it is expressed, and orthologs. The summary includes important information about the gene biological functions and phenotypes, or conditions associated with it.

The *orthologs* provide links to evolutionarily related genes in the (1) mouse (a model animal) and (2) all organisms. The orthologs "All" link opens a page that shows the list of non-redundant orthologous genes and links for downloading their genomic sequences and protein sequences and link to tools for multiple sequence alignment and phylogenetic tree visualization. The orthologous sequences can be used for different research purposes, such as multiple sequence alignment, phylogenetic tree construction, and other comparative homology uses.

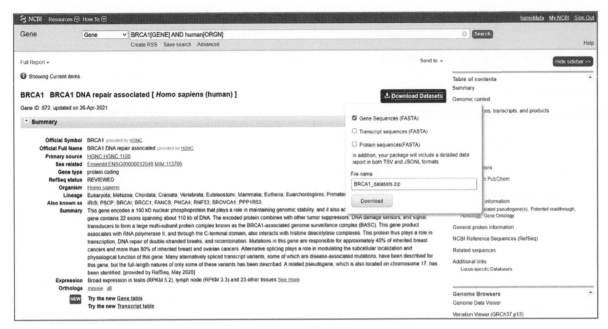

FIGURE 3.17   Gene record's summary.

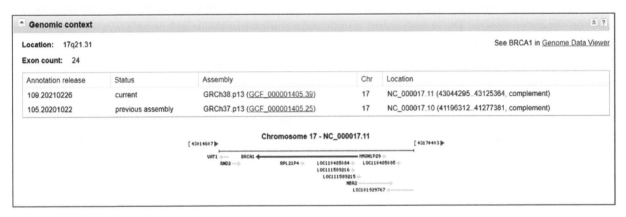

FIGURE 3.18   Genomic context.

Genomic Context   The genomic context section (Figure 3.18) contains information about the location of the region of the gene on the reference genome. At the top left, "Location" shows the cytogenetic location of the gene in the chromosome and "Exon count" shows the number of exons in the gene. The location of BRCA1, which is expressed as cytogenetic location, is 17q21.31, indicates that the gene locus is on the long arm (q) of chromosome #17, region #2, band #1, and sub-band #31. The BRCA1 gene has 24 exons comprising the coding sequence for the BRCA1 proteins (BRCA1 gene codes for multiple isoforms by alternative splicing).

At the right corner of the genomic context section there is a link for displaying the gene and its annotated features in the Genome Data Viewer (GDV). The GDV will be discussed in detail in the Genome database section.

The genomic context table contains annotation release, status, assembly, chromosome number, and location of the current and previous assembly. The positions of the gene sequence in the current and previous genome (location of gene in genomic context) are described by the genome coordinates, which are formed of the chromosome accession number, position of the first base of the gene, and position of the last base of the gene. The BRCA1 gene in the current genome assembly is found on the chromosome #17 (accession # NC_000017.11. The first base of BRCA1 gene is at position 43044295 and the last base is at position 43125364.

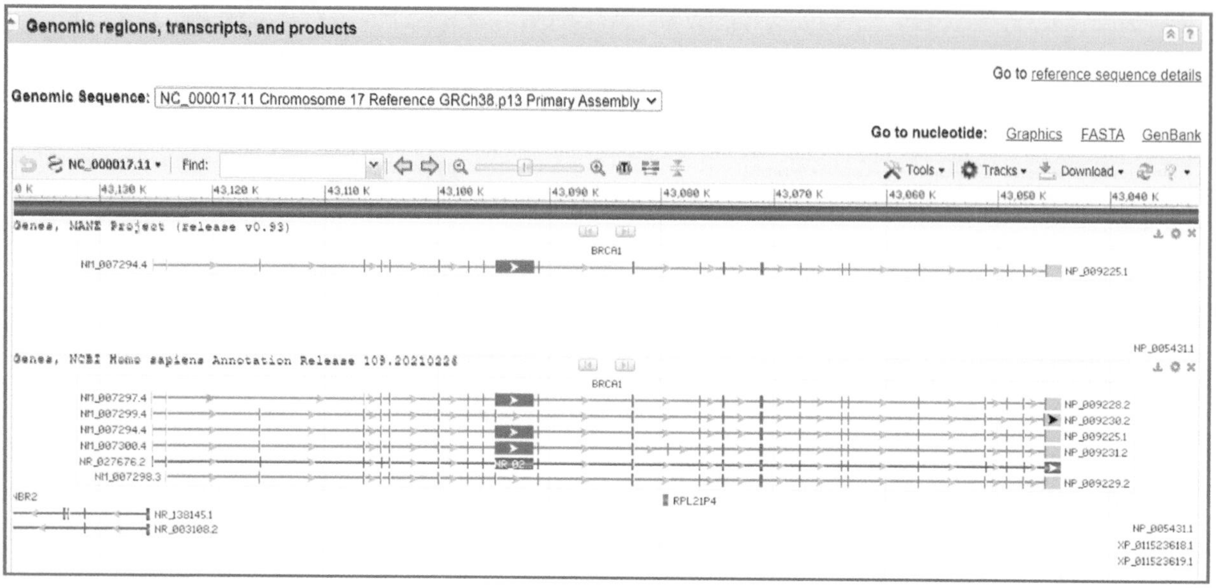

FIGURE 3.19   Sequence viewer displaying BRCA1 annotation.

The diagram at the bottom of the genomic context is shown only if the gene annotation is available in the current reference genome. The diagram sketches the positions and orientations of the gene and neighboring genes on the chromosome. The gene diagram is in maroon color while the neighboring genes are in gray color. Clicking on any of neighboring gene diagram or label will open that gene page. Instead of chromosome, the diagram may show a reference contig, reference genomic region, alternate assembly chromosome, or alternate assembly contig.

Genomic Regions, Transcripts, and Products Section This section (Figure 3.19) provides a graphic sequence viewer displaying the reference sequence or chromosome (the solid blue bar), and tracks for displaying annotation. Tracks can be added and removed using "Tracks" menu. You can display a track for annotated gene transcripts and gene products. The sequence viewer will be discussed in detail in the Genome database section.

Expression   The expression section provides a graphical description of the gene expression in different organs or tissues of the organisms. The bar chart is generated from normalized data computed from RNA-seq reads aligned to the most recent RefSeq gene models on the reference genome. The data are usually produced by different RNA-seq projects; therefore, the data are binned by specific BioProject to reduce the variability emerged from methodologies.

Gene expression quantification by RNA-seq is performed by counting the number of reads that map/align to the gene using programs such as HTSeq-count [5]. Read counts are affected by transcript length (longer transcripts have higher read counts) and total number of reads. Thus, to compare expression levels between samples, the raw read counts are normalized. The read counts are normalized with RPKM (reads per kilobase of exon model per million reads) and its derivative FPKM (fragments per kilobase of exon model per million reads mapped). Correcting for gene length is not necessary when comparing changes in gene expression within the same gene across samples. However, it is necessary for correctly ranking gene expression levels within the sample to account for the fact that longer genes accumulate more reads (at the same expression level).

The bar chart of the BRCA1 gene expression shows that the gene is expressed normally in most human organs, but it is expressed significantly higher in testis, lymph nodes, appendix, bone marrow, thyroid, and colon (Figure 3.20). The level of gene expression reflects the level of biological activity (functions) that the gene is performing in that organ. You can use the dropdown menu on the top left to choose a different project. Some

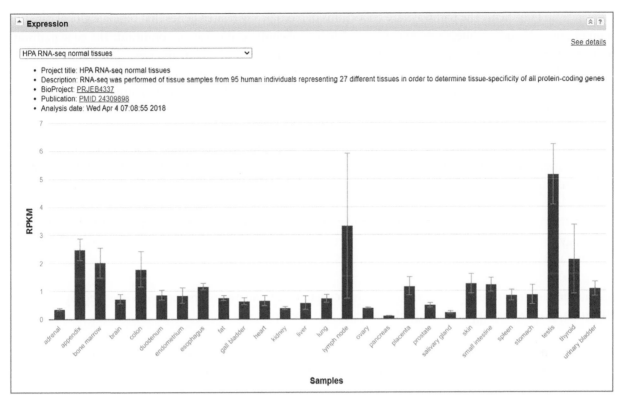

FIGURE 3.20   BRCA1's gene expression.

projects may present the gene expression in a specific condition or a disease. Project description, BioProject identifier, publication PubMed identifier (PMID), and analysis date are listed on the top left.

Clicking on the 'See details' link on the top right corner of this section will open a page where you can find the details of the samples, BioSample, RPKM, count, and links to the sample data. The data of the bar chart can be downloaded by clicking on the "Download" button to download the gene expression data in a text file.

Bibliography   The bibliography section displays the supporting citations in PubMed and GeneRIFs. The latter is a concise phrase describing functions of the gene added by scientists.

Phenotypes   The phenotype section provides information about the impact of the gene on a specific phenotype (trait or disease). Several sub-sections may be found. The associated conditions sub-section lists the diseases or conditions linked to the gene dysfunction. Notice that BRCA1 is associated with breast-ovarian cancer, Fanconi anemia, and pancreatic cancer.

Variation   The variation section provides a quick link to the gene-specific variant records in other NCBI's variant databases, such as dbSNP, dbVar, and ClinVar. This section also provides links to view the gene-specific variants in genomic context on the Variation Viewer.

HIV-1 Interactions   The HIV-1 section was added to track protein interactions with HIV-1. Some proteins may increase the virulence and the speed of replication of the HIV-1 virus. The data in this section is provided with a review by the NCBI Gene database staff from the Southern Research Institute, which collects data based on whole genome screening using small interfering RNAs (siRNAs) to knock down the gene and to observe the impact on HIV-1 interactions and replication. You can notice that the knockdown of BRCA1 by siRNA inhibits HIV-1 replication.

Pathway from PubChem The pathways are collections of biologically related genes that regulate global function of an organ or tissue or collectively may have a role in a phenotype, disease, or condition. The gene pathways are important in the study of physiological functions and genetically complex diseases.

The pathways in this section are generated from the BioSystems database. This section provides information about pathways including products of the gene and the products of all genes in the pathway. Clicking on the title of a pathway will open the PubChem pathway page.

Interactions The interactions section provides unreviewed information about genes, gene products, and complex interacted with the specific gene. It also provides links to the database records of the interactant and the related PubMed articles.

General Gene Information This section provides general information about the gene, including markers, homology (orthologous genes from different sources), Gene Ontology (GO) (function, process, cellular component), and genotypes (links to reports from dbSNP about allele frequencies).

General Protein Information This section provides names and aliases of the proteins encoded by this gene. Therefore, this section applies only to the genes that encode proteins.

NCBI Reference Sequences (RefSeqs) This section describes the reference sequences (RefSeqs) specified by NCBI to this gene. It may also provide description of each RefSeq transcript variant, links to other NCBI databases, lists of domains in the sequence, etc.

Related Sequences The related sequences section provides a list of sequence accessions related to the gene and it also provides links to the sequence records in other NCBI databases. This sequence list in this section is not intended to be comprehensive.

Additional Links Additional links to other external resources (LinkOuts) and locus-specific databases are listed in this section.

BIOCOLLECTIONS

The NCBI Biocollections is a database of curated dataset of metadata for samples collected from natural history collections, culture collections, museums, herbaria and other natural resources [6, 7].

Historical collections of living organisms are the specimens that have been collected over broad geographic ranges and over many years by specialized institutions and museums. Multiple samples of individual species collected from different habitats are preserved for documenting the variations among individuals and studying and linking them to ecological factors or evolutionary factors. A specimen voucher is a term used for a representative sample of an identified organism deposited and stored at a facility from which researchers may later obtain the specimen for examination and study. Herbarium and museum collections [8] are the basic materials for obtaining information about biodiversity. Herbarium specimens also provide materials for research on variation at the DNA level, genome structure, and gene expression. The historical collections are the primary data sources of dried and labeled specimens that are arranged to allow for easy retrieval access and archival storage.

The specimens of Biocollections are grouped into the following categories and each category has its own unique identifier to facilitate classification and retrieval:

(1) *Specimen voucher.* [9] A specimen voucher is the specimen of physical remains of an organism that is preserved to be a permanent record of wildlife at a museum or an institution. Any specimen with this description is identified in the database as "specimen_voucher". This category includes museum, herbarium, and frozen tissue collection.

(2) *Culture collection.* [10] The culture collection includes microbial culture collection and cell lines, which are valuable resources for the sustainable use of microbial diversity and conservation. The identifier of culture collection is "culture_collection".

(3) *Biomaterial.* Biomaterial is any material that is not specimen voucher or culture collection, including biological material from zoos, aquariums, arboretums, botanical gardens, DNA banks, stock centers, germplasm repositories, and seed banks. This group is isdentified as "bio_material".

The NCBI Biocollections database stores curated datasets of metadata of historical collection including specimen vouchers, specimen collections, or biomaterials connected to sequence records in the GenBank databases. The Biocollections database provides links to NCBI database records and the information about institutions where the historical specimens are preserved. The database website can be accessed by choosing Biocollections from the dropdown list on the common Entrez database page or at www.ncbi.nlm.nih.gov/biocollections/.

Table 3.11 includes the indexed fields of the NCBI Biocollections database.

Assume that we wish to search for the biocollections related to the University of Alaska (UAM) museum. We can use the institution code "UAM" to search for all entries related to the University of Alaska (e.g., uam[uicode]).

In another scenario, assume that we wish to find mammal biocollections. We can use mammal[cname] as a search term. The results page will display all the institutes and museums that have preserved mammal samples as biocollections as shown in Figure 3.21.

TABLE 3.11   Biocollections Indexed Fields

Long Field	Short Field	Long Field	Short Field
ALL fields	ALL	Modification Date	MDAT
Collection code	CCDE	Institution name	NAME
Collections for given institution	CDRN	All names	NAMES
Collection name	CNAME	Institution for given collection	PRNT
Institution code	CODE	Properties	PROP
all codes	CODES	Unique institution code	UICOD
Country name	CTRY	UID	UID
Filter	FILT	Text Word	WORD

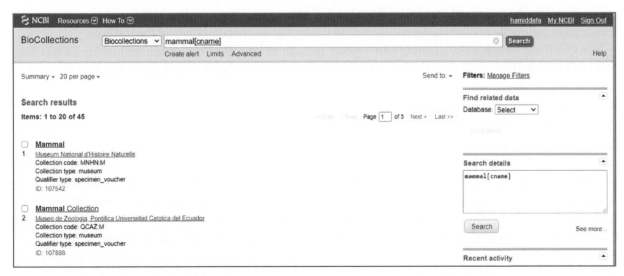

FIGURE 3.21   Biocollections search results.

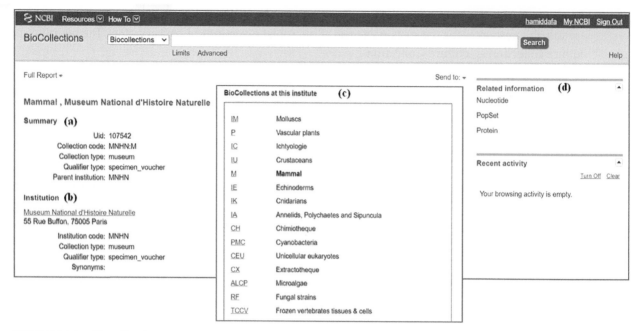

FIGURE 3.22   Biocollections summary.

When you click on the title of any entry, the biocollections record page for that institute will open. Click on the title of the first entry. The page of the Museum National d'Histoire Naturelle will open. The biocollections record page, as shown in Figure 3.22, contains (a) a summary of the biocollections selected from the Biocollection at this institute, (b) institution information, (c) biocollections at the institute, and (d) related information.

The list of biocollections at this institute includes all biocollections preserved at Museum National d'Histoire Naturelle. Clicking on the code of any biocollection in the list (e.g., M̲ Mammal) will display the summary information of that collection on the summary section top (a). The summary shows the name of the specimen, the unique identifier (UID), the collection code, the collection type (museum), the qualifier type, and the parent institution (MNHN) (Figure 3.22).

A biocollections record is usually linked to records from other NCBI databases. The linked databases will be listed in the Related information section (d) on the top right. For example, the mammals biocollections of this institute are linked to Nucleotide, PopSet, and Protein records. Clicking on any of these databases will open a page that lists the records of that NCBI database. For example, clicking on Nucleotide will open Nucleotide results page listing the nucleotide records linked to the mammals biocollections of the institute.

The GenBank format of Nucleotide and Protein records of biocollections origin and under FEATURES, there will be a qualifier indicating the type of biocollections (e.g., specimen_voucher) as shown in Figure 3.23.

PROTEIN DATABASES

Proteins are the products of genes. Compared to nucleotide sequences, protein sequences contain more information because they are built up of 20 amino acids represented by 20 single-letter abbreviations in bioinformatics. A protein is translated from a coding sequence of a gene (CDS). A gene may have multiple CDSs due to alternative splicing. Each three bases or codon of the CDS is translated into one of the 20 amino acids. A single gene may produce multiple proteins or isoforms. The linear sequence of a protein defines its 3D structure that includes conserved functional domains. The protein conserved domain determines the protein functions, which mange the biological activities in a living organism and manifest themselves in phenotypes. the dysfunction of a protein may be associated with some diseases and disorders. Therefore, proteins provide a wide range of information for biomedical and bioscience research and NCBI created several databases

```
   TITLE         Mitochondrial and Nuclear Genes-Based Phylogeography of Arvicanthis
                 niloticus (Murinae) and Sub-Saharan Open Habitats Pleistocene
                 History
   JOURNAL       PLoS ONE 8 (11), E77815 (2013)
   PUBMED        24223730
   REMARK        Publication Status: Online-Only
REFERENCE       2  (bases 1 to 1113)
   AUTHORS       Dobigny,G., Tatard,C., Gauthier,P., Ba,K., Duplantier,J.-M.,
                 Granjon,L. and Kergoat,G.J.
   TITLE         Direct Submission
   JOURNAL       Submitted (26-JUL-2013) INRA - CBGP, Campus international de
                 Baillarguet, Montferrier/Lez, Herault 34988, France
COMMENT         ##Assembly-Data-START##
                 Sequencing Technology :: Sanger dideoxy sequencing
                 ##Assembly-Data-END##
FEATURES             Location/Qualifiers
     source          1..1113
                     /organism="Arvicanthis niloticus"
                     /organelle="mitochondrion"
                     /mol_type="genomic DNA"
                     /specimen_voucher="MNHN:M:VV1995-041"
                     /db_xref="taxon:61156"
     gene            <1..>1113
                     /gene="cytb"
     CDS             <1..>1113
                     /gene="cytb"
```

FIGURE 3.23   A nucleotide record related to a biocollections record.

to store protein information. Those databases include the Protein database, the Protein Reference Sequence (Protein RefSeq), the Conserved Domain Database (CDD), Identical Protein Groups (IPG), Protein Clusters, and Protein Family Model.

Protein Database

The Protein database stores protein sequences obtained from several sources. Rather than nucleotides, protein sequences are made up of amino acids. Protein database records are stored in the same format as GenBank Nucleotide records. Most of the protein sequence records in the Protein database were translated from annotated coding regions (CDS) in GenBank, RefSeq and Third-Party Annotation (TPA) sequences. Other Protein database records are obtained from other protein databases including SwissProt, the Protein Information Resource (PIR), the Protein Research Foundation (PRF), and the Protein Data Bank (PDB) [11]. The following are some details of the resources that contribute to the NCBI Protein database:

- *GenBank Nucleotide translation.* GenBank maintains a database for protein sequences translated form CDS of the GenBank genes collected for each GenBank release. This database of CDs is called the GenPept database. GenPept is not an official release from the NCBI but is thoroughly maintained and synchronized with each new release of GenBank. The GenPept are available on the Protein databases.

- *RefSeq translation.* Some protein records are products of RefSeq transcripts. Protein sequences translated from RefSeq transcripts are RefSeq proteins (reference proteins), which have the accession numbers with a prefix 'NP_' for the protein sequences generated from known experimentally generated transcripts and a prefix 'XP_' for protein sequences generated from model transcripts predicted by an automated pipeline. The RefSeq protein sequences are non-redundant and well supported by NCBI.

- *Swiss-Prot.* SwissProt contributes significantly to the NCBI Protein database. It is a curated protein sequence database and a collaborative effort of the European Molecular Biology Laboratory (EMBL) and the Swiss Institute of Bioinformatics (SIB). The protein sequences of SWISS-PROT database are well annotated, less redundant, and well-integrated with other databases.

- *The Protein Information Resource (PIR).* PIR is also one of the NCBI Protein database contributors. PIR is an integrated public resource of protein sequences and information for supporting genomic and proteomic research. PIR manages the Protein Sequence Database (PSD), which is an annotated protein database that contains thousands of sequences covering the entire taxonomic range.

- *The Peptide Institute (PRF).* PRF is one of the NCBI Protein database contributors stationed in Japan. It represents a major source for the predicted protein sequences reported in literature.

- *Protein Data Bank (PDB).* PDB is the largest database for protein sequences and their three-dimensional structures obtained by X-ray crystallography, NMR spectroscopy, cryo-electron microscopy, and submitted by biologists and biochemists from around the world.

The Protein database can be accessed by choosing Protein from the database dropdown menu or using the URL www.ncbi.nlm.nih.gov/protein/. Refer to the sections on "Searching Entrez Databases" and "Entrez Search Results" above for building simple and advanced search queries and Entrez database searching. Table 3.12 includes some indexed fields of the Protein database.

In the Gene database section, we searched for BRCA1 gene. In this section, we can search for BRCA1 protein records in the Protein database. We can always use the Advanced Search Builder to build an advanced search query. To search for BRCA1 protein records by gene name or gene symbol, choose Protein from the database dropdown menu, enter the following term, and click on the Search button:

BRCA1[GENE]

The results of that search term will be general, including all BRCA1 protein sequence records in the Protein database (i.e., redundant BRCA1 proteins and BRCA1 RefSeq proteins of all species in the database). If you add human[ORGN] to the above term, the results will include only the human BRCA1 protein redundant records and BRCA RefSeq protein records.

BRCA1[GENE] AND human[ORGN]

We can also notice that the results from thousands of BRCA1 protein records have dropped to hundreds. To make searching more specific, you can add the term refseq[KEYWORD] to restrict the results to only nonredundant BRCA1 RefSeq protein records.

TABLE 3.12   Protein Indexed Fields

Description	Short Field	Description	Short Field
Accession	ACCN	Publication date	PDAT
All fields	ALL	Primary organism	PORG
Assembly	ASSM	Properties	PROP
Author	AUTH	Protein name	PROT
Division	DIV	Sequence length	SLEN
Filter	FILT	SeqID string	SQID
Gene name	GENE	Strain	STRN
BioProject	GPRJ	Title	TITL
Keyword	KYWD	UID	UID
Organism	ORGN	Text word	WORD

BRCA1[GENE] AND human[ORGN] AND refseq[KEYWORD]

The results of the above search query will include only BRCA1 RefSeq protein records. There are five BRCA1 protein isoforms coded by the same BRCA1 gene, but they have different amino acid sequences and different sequence lengths due to the alternative splicing and they have also different biological functions.

The Protein database results page is a typical Entrez database results page as discussed in detail above. On the right side on the page, there are protein analysis tools, including Run BLAST, align sequence with COBALT, and Identify Conserved Domain with CD-Search. The first two tools are used for finding similar protein sequences while the latter is used to identify conserved domains on a protein sequence. BLAST and COBALT will be discussed in Chapter 8 and CD-Search will be discussed later in this chapter.

The protein sequence data of the search results can be downloaded using the "Send To" menu. Downloadable data is available in several formats including Summary, GenPept, FASTA, ASN.1, XML, feature table, accession list, GI list, and GFF3.

Protein Clusters

Two or more sequences of DNA may be homologous or they have a shared ancestry because of either a speciation event (orthologs) or a duplication event (paralogs) [12]. Both these events take place slowly in the evolutionary path due to accumulative mutations. Homology among proteins or DNA is often detected based on sequence similarity. High sequence similarity might occur because of convergent evolution, which is defined as the sequence similarity that occurred by chance and that the sequences have no common ancestral sequence. Convergent evolution is more likely to be found in short sequences. In some protein sequences, only segments of these sequences may have a high similarity while the remaining regions of the sequences are variables. Those similar segments of the multiple protein sequences are called conserved domains (CD). The similar regions in a group of proteins are usually conserved because of their role in a biological function. Proteins with similar structures may have similar functions. Protein sequences in the same species and with significant similarity are called paralogs. While similar protein sequences in different species are called orthologs. Homologous proteins (paralogs or orthologs) are more similar than others and can be aligned together obtaining a higher optimal multiple alignment score (sequence alignment will be covered in a later chapter). Therefore, similar proteins can be grouped together by means of a clustering technique, which is an unsupervised machine learning method that does not require prior knowledge of the class of genes but it clusters genes sequences based on their scoring distances from one another. The protein sequences from protein clusters can be used for constructing a phylogenetic tree. To serve various research purposes, NCBI created the Protein Clusters database [13], which clusters protein sequences obtained from viruses, bacteria, archaea, fungi, plants, and protozoans. Protein clustering is used to construct meaningful groups of similar proteins to serve as targets for efficient searching for numerous research purposes.

The NCBI Protein Clusters database contains protein sequences grouped by their similarity and evolutionary relatedness using a machine learning clustering technique. The similarity of sequences is measured by maximum alignment between the sequences aligned by BLAST. A Protein Clusters dataset consists of proteins encoded by genes from the RefSeq protein sequences of microorganisms (prokaryotes, viruses, fungi, protozoans) and curated protein clusters from RefSeq sequences of complete genomes of plants, chloroplasts and mitochondria. Each cluster is given a unique accession prefix followed by five numbers (Table 3.13).

TABLE 3.13   Protein Cluster ID Prefixes

Cluster ID Prefix	Cluster Description
PRK	Prokaryotes (Curated Protein Clusters)
CLS	Prokaryotes (Uncurated Protein Clusters)
CHL	Chloroplasts
CLSC	Chloroplasts (Uncurated Chloroplast Clusters)

The Protein Clusters database contains two types of protein clusters: curated and non-curated sets. The curated protein clusters have consistent nomenclature and protein function descriptions, while the non-curated protein clusters are automatically generated and have not yet been manually annotated. The non-curated clusters may contain both orthologs and paralogs. Therefore, researchers are advised to manually remove the redundant sequences.

The Protein Clusters database is chosen from the Entrez database dropdown list or by using the link www.ncbi.nlm.nih.gov/proteinclusters/. Table 3.14 contains some of the Protein Clusters database indexed fields that can be used to build a search query.

Assume that we are looking for protein clusters for bacteria including *Salmonella enterica* based on the Porin protein, which is a bacterial cellular membrane protein that acts as a pore, through which chemical molecules can diffuse. The purpose is to find how *Salmonella enterica* is related evolutionarily to other bacteria based on the Porin protein. We can search the Protein Clusters database using the following query:

("salmonella enterica"[organism]) AND porin[protein name] AND 25:100[Size]

This query is to find clusters that include *Salmonella* (in addition to other bacteria) and the clustering is based on the Porin protein. The query is limiting the results to only those clusters that consist of 25 to 100 proteins. So, any clusters with number of proteins less than 25 or more than 100 will be excluded from the results.

The Protein Clusters results page looks like any other Entrez database results page. Clicking on a cluster title will open the page of the cluster record. Click on the cluster (PCLA_910324), which has 42 protein sequences. The cluster page displays two sections: Statistics and Protein Table. The Statistics section shows the number of proteins in the clusters, conserved protein domain, number of organisms, and HMM accessions. The Protein Table contains the cluster members' sequence information including organism, protein name, protein accession, protein length, and a link to BLAST. Clicking on any of the anchor items of these columns will open a relevant page. Clicking on the "Organism" item will open the Taxonomy page of that organism, clicking on "Protein" item or "Accession number" will open the Identical Protein database record page, which includes the list of protein identical to that protein. Clicking on the "BLAST" item will open the BLAST page for that protein.

TABLE 3.14   Protein Clusters Indexed Fields

Description	Short Field	Description	Short Field
Accession	ACCN	Locus Tag identifier	LTAG
All Fields	ALL	Modification Date	MDAT
Average Length of proteins	AVGL	Organism	ORGN
Creation Date of the record	CDAT	Protein Accession	PACC
Clusters of Orthologous Groups	COG	Number of paralogs in the cluster	PARA
COG group	COGG	PubMed ID	PMID
Conserved In	CONS	Properties based on DNA source	PROP
Protein domain Name	DOM	Protein Name	PROT
Number of domains in the cluster	DOMS	Protein GI	PUID
EC/RN Number assigned by CAS	ECNO	Size	SIZE
Filter	FILT	Sequence Length	SLEN
Gene Name	GENE	SwissProt Accession	SPCN
Gene Synonym	GSYN	Title of protein cluster	TITL
Number assigned to a protein family	HMAP	Total Publications	TPUB
HMM Accession	HMM	Taxonomy ID	TXID
Number assigned to orthologous genes	KO	UID	UID

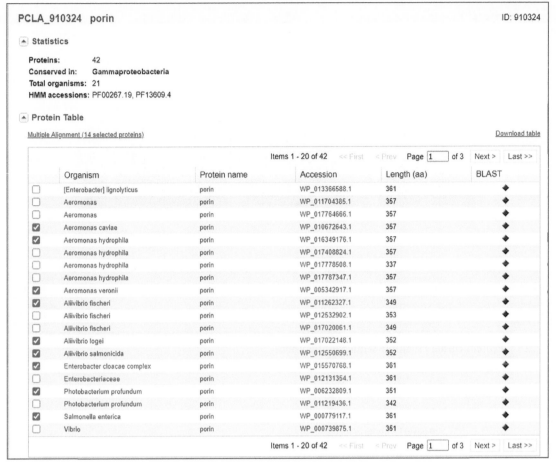

FIGURE 3.24   Protein clusters record page.

The protein cluster may include multiple protein sequences for the same organism. For our purpose, we can use the check box before each organism name to select cluster members we wish to include. Try to select a single entry for each organism. You can select the following bacteria as shown in Figure 3.24:

Aeromonas caviae, Aeromonas hydrophila, Aeromonas veronii, Aliivibrio fischeri, Aliivibrio logei, Aliivibrio salmonicida, Enterobacter cloacae complex, Photobacterium profundum, Salmonella enterica, Vibrio alginolyticus, Vibrio campbellii, Vibrio cholerae, Vibrio parahaemolyticus, Vibrio vulnificus.

Use the "Next" button to move to the next page. After selecting the above clusters members, click on the "Multiple Alignment" link at the top of the list to open the page of the multiple sequence alignment of the selected member sequences. The page of multiple sequence alignment includes the Graphical Overview, Description, and Alignments sections (Figure 3.25). We will discuss the alignment in a later chapter. For now, we will focus on the evolutionary relatedness of these bacteria including *Salmonella enterica* based on the Porin protein sequences. Click on the "Phylogenetic tree" link on the top left corner of the page of the multiple sequence alignment to visualize the phylogenetic tree of the selected cluster member sequences as shown in Figure 3.25. You can also download the protein sequences to align them using any other multiple sequence alignment software or use them to build a phylogenetic tree.

The phylogenetic tree can be downloaded in different formats using the Tools menu on the tree view. Figure 3.26 shows the phylogenetic tree of the Porin protein sequences. Study the relationship between bacterial species. We can notice that the Porin protein of *Salmonella enterica* is close to that of *Enterobacter spp.* and the Porin sequences of both species are close to that of *Aeromonas spp.*

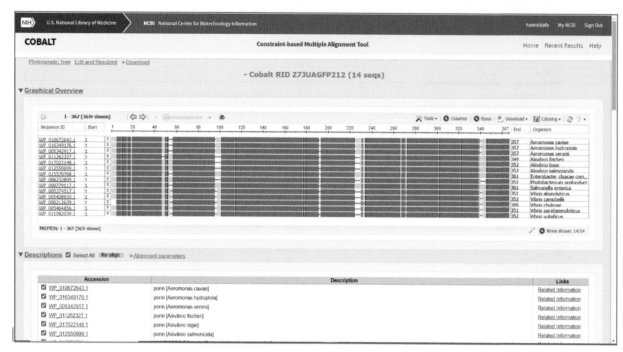

FIGURE 3.25   Protein clusters multiple sequence alignment.

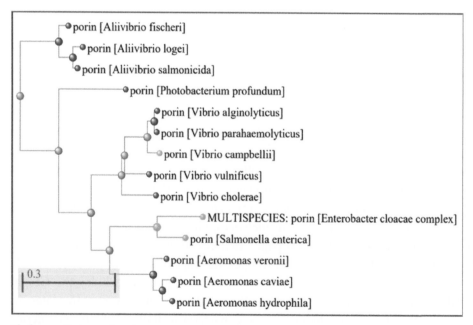

FIGURE 3.26   Phylogenetic tree of porin sequences.

The phylogenetic tree presents a visual description for the hierarchy of the relatedness between the members. We can notice that the members of each bacterial genus are grouped together.

Identical Protein Groups

Searching the NCBI Protein database by a protein name or a protein symbol may report many redundant protein records for different organisms. To deal with this, NCBI created the Identical Protein Groups (IPG) database to group identical proteins together to make searching easier to find information about proteins

TABLE 3.15 Identical Protein Groups Indexed Fields

Description	Short Field	Description	Short Field
Accession	ACCN	Organism	ORGN
All Fields	ALL	Primary Accession	PACC
Assembly	ASSM	Properties	PROP
Creation Date	CDAT	Protein Name	PROT
Division	DIV	Protein Count	ProtCount
Filter	FILT	Sequence Length	SLEN
BioProject	GPRJ	Title	TITL
Modification Date	MDAT	Update Date	UDAT
Molecular Weight	MLWT	Unique identifier	UID
Organism Count	OCNT	Text Word	WORD

rather than exploring an overwhelming list of records returned by the search of the Protein database. The IPG database contains a single entry for each protein translation found at the sources of NCBI. The members of IPG groups can come from several sources including GenBank, RefSeq, INSDC, SwissProt, PDB, and others. The IPG database provides records representing any unique protein sequence in the NCBI databases, coding regions, and nucleotide coordinate mapping for each coding region. The database also offers search filtering options including the source database, taxonomy, and the size of the group. Since each IPG record represents a unique protein sequence, this makes getting information of a specific protein sequence straight forward. The IPG database is available at www.ncbi.nlm.nih.gov/ipg or can be chosen from the dropdown list of the search bar on the common Entrez database website.

Table 3.15 includes the IPG indexed fields that can be used to create advanced search queries. An advanced search query can also be created using the Advanced Search Builder.

When a non-specific search term is used for searching the Protein database, thousands of records may be found. In contrast, if you use the same term in the IPG database you may get fewer records. When a single IPG record is returned, it will be displayed.

Assume that we wish to find an IPG record for a viral spike protein also called S protein. The spike protein plays a crucial role in penetrating host cells and initiating infection. The length of the S protein ranges from around 1,160 amino acids for avian infectious bronchitis virus (IBV) to 1,400 amino acids for feline coronavirus (FCoV) [14]. To search for the S protein on the IPG, use the following term:

"S protein" [PROT]

This search term may return thousands of IPG records. The IPG results page is the same as that of Protein results. To make the search more specific, you add more specific pieces of information to the search query. Assume that you wish to find the S protein of SARS-CoV-2, which is the causing agent of Covid-19 viral infection. You can use the following query:

"S protein" [PROT] AND SARS-coV-2[ORGN]

Since the search is specific, the IPG record page of the S protein of SARS-CoV-2 will be displayed as shown in Figure 3.27. The IPG record page includes summary, taxonomic groups, and the list of the members of the protein group.

The summary includes the name of the protein, accession of the protein RefSeq sequence and the length of protein, taxonomic group, assembly accessions, protein accessions, number of CDS regions, and the total number of sequences (total rows). Thus, you can notice that the name of the spike protein is a surface protein; the Spike protein RefSeq accession is YP_009724390.1 and it has 1,273 amino acid; the taxonomic group is viruses; there are 82 genome assemblies, 3,540 reference sequences, and 3,524 coding sequences (CDS); and

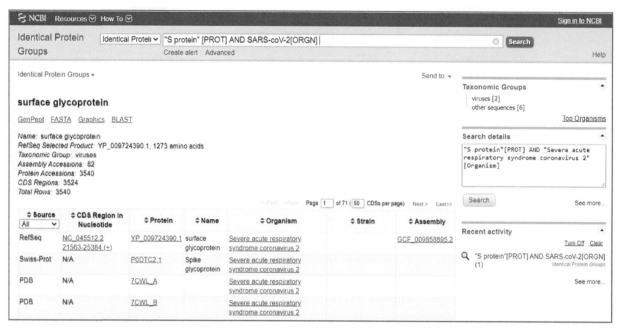

FIGURE 3.27   IPG record page.

the total number of protein sequences in the group is 3,540. On the top, the GenPept link displays the GenPept format of the protein RefSeq and FASTA displays the FASTA format of the protein RefSeq sequence. Graphics links open the Sequence Viewer that displays the protein RefSeq and other features. The Sequence Viewer will be discussed in the Genome section. The BLAST link opens the BLAST tool, which will be discussed in Chapters 7 and 8.

The taxonomic groups are shown on the top right corner of page. They act as filters that group the member sequences of the IPG group.

The members of the IPG are listed in a table showing the source database (Source) of the sequence, the transcript accession (CDS region in Nucleotide) if applicable, Protein accession, protein name, organism, strain, and genome assembly. You can notice that the accession of the current genome assembly for SARS-CoV-2 is GCF_009858895.2, which is the UID that you can use to retrieve information of the genome of the virus.

Conserved Domain Database

Protein functions are protected by conservation in the gene sequence. The bases of the gene sequences that encode the functional domains in a protein are more conserved than other bases to preserve the biological functions of the translated proteins. Similar conserved domain sequences of different proteins may have similar functions and the sequence similarity itself also suggests a common ancestor of sequences. Classification of proteins into families depends on the sequence similarity of domains. Members of the same protein family usually share similar conserved domains and similar functions. Thus, a database for the conserved domains in proteins is crucial for proteomic research.

NCBI developed the Conserved Domain Database (CDD) to provide researchers with the information about conservation and divergence in protein sequences related to their biological functions [15]. The CDD includes records for conserved protein domains, secondary structures of homologous protein sequences, and multiple sequences alignment for sequence profiling. Researchers use the NCBI CDD for protein classification, identification of protein functions, and identification of the function of a specific amino acid in a protein sequence.

The CDD web page is accessible at www.ncbi.nlm.nih.gov/cdd/ or by choosing "Conserved Domains" from the database dropdown list on Entrez common web page.

TABLE 3.16   CDD Indexed Fields

Description	Short Field Name	Description	Short Field Name
Alternative Accession	AACN	Publication Date	PDAT
Accession	ACCN	PSSM Length	PLEN
All Fields	ALL	The description of sites	SD
Database	DB	Structure Representative	STRP
Filter	FILT	Subtitle	STTL
Modification Date	MDAT	Title	TITL
Number of Sites	NS	UID	UID
Organism	ORGN	Text Word	WORD

The CDD web page contains important links to resources and tools used for conserved domains in proteins. The following are the CDD tools on the Conserved Domains page:

- *CD-Search* is used to search for conserved sites in a sequence using a FASTA formatted or bare protein or nucleotide sequence or a valid NCBI sequence identifier.
- *Patch CD-Search* is used to search for conserved domain sequence in a patch of sequences in a file. The number of sequences should not be more than 4,000 per request.
- *Conserved Domain Architecture Retrieval Tool (CDART)* is used to retrieve all proteins with similar domain architectures by entering the FASTA sequence, bare protein sequence, set of conserved domain sequences, or a protein sequence identifier into the CDART search box.
- *SPARCLE (protein labeling engine)* stands for Subfamily Protein Architecture Labeling Engine, is a resource used for the functional characterization and labeling of protein sequences grouped by their characteristic conserved domain architecture. The domain architecture of a protein is the sequential order of conserved domains in its sequence.
- *BLAST* links to BLAST, which is a tool that is used to align a nucleotide or protein sequence to sequences in a target database.

Table 3.16 shows the CDD indexed fields that can be used to construct advanced search queries.

Finding Conserved Domain of Proteins

One of the uses of CDD is the search for a specific conserved domain in a group of protein sequences. Assume that we wish to search for conserved domains in peroxisome proliferator-activated receptors (PPAR). PPARs are protein members of a subgroup of the nuclear receptor superfamily (NR) that acts as transcriptional factors (TFs) regulating expression of genes. PPARs regulates the expression of gene-controlling metabolism and their dysfunction is associated with metabolic disorder such as obesity, hyper pressure, diabetes type II, and high cholesterol [16]. It is known that PPAR proteins have two highly conserved domains; ligand binding domain (NR_LBD_Ppar) and DNA binding domain (NR_DBD_Ppar). Those two domains are essential for the transcriptional functions of PPARs, and any protein that has these two domains will be classified as NR protein. To search for a specific conserved domain on CDD, you can enter the domain name. For example, to search for PPAR Ligand binding Domain, you can enter the terms:

"ligand binding domain" AND PPAR

However, if you know the name of the conserved domain you can enter it to get specific results. For example, the name of the PPAR ligand domain is "NR_LBD_Ppar". When you use this domain name in the search you will get exactly two records: the first record is for the conserved domain of PPAR family and the second is for the conserved domain of the nuclear receptor superfamily as shown in Figure 3.28.

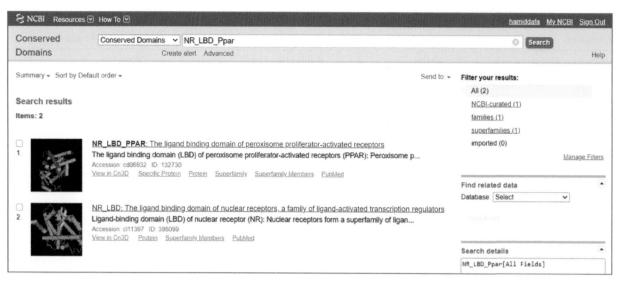

FIGURE 3.28   CDD results page for nuclear receptor ligand binding domain.

The CDD results page is displayed in summary format by default. The summary includes a thumbnail of the conserved domain, the title, description, and links to other databases and tool. The following are the links and their descriptions:

- *View in Cn3D* link is used to visualize the domain in the Cn3D visualization program if it is installed.
- *Specific Protein* link opens the Protein results page displaying the sequences of the family protein members for all organisms.
- *Protein* link opens the Protein results page displaying the protein records that have similar domains.
- *Superfamily* link opens the CDD page for the protein superfamily.
- *Superfamily Members* link opens the CDD results page showing the protein members of the superfamily.
- *PubMed* link opens the PubMed citations linked to the conserved domain records.

Clicking on the title or the thumbnail will open the CDD record page of the conserved domain.

The CDD record page begins with the conserved domain name and a menu bar for the links of the current records to other NCBI databases. The CDD record page has the following sections as displayed in Figure 3.29:

1 *Summary section.* The summary is shown at the top of a CDD record page. It was written by the NCBI curators to provide an outline of the domain's biological function. The summary is generated from the representative conserved domain in the family.

2 *Links box.* This section provides the links to retrieve additional data associated with the conserved domain, including taxonomy, PubMed citation and literature, protein representatives, structure, and other related data.

3 *Statistics box.* The statistic box contains information such as position-specific scoring matrix (PSSM) id, link to view the PSSM, which is created from the multiple sequence alignment, the number of aligned protein domain sequences, the threshold used for convergence, and the created and update date. PSSM is discussed in Chapter 7.

4 *Structure box.* The structure box provides a link to visualize or download the 3D structure of the conserved domain. To view the 3D structure, Cn3D software must be installed on the computer. It

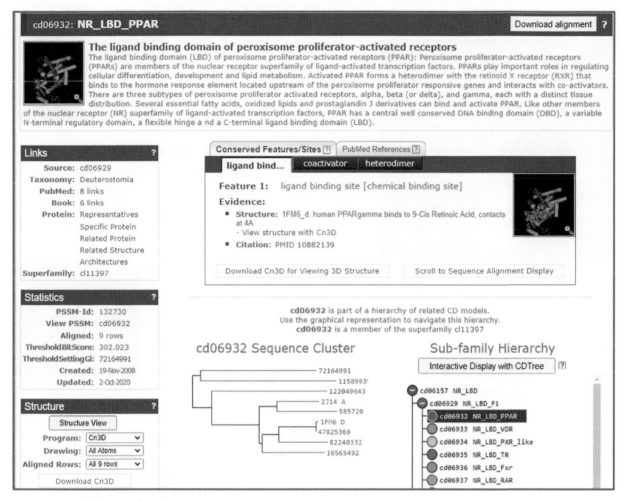

FIGURE 3.29   CDD results page.

is available at www.ncbi.nlm.nih.gov/Structure/CN3D/cn3dinstall.shtml. Once the software has been installed, click on the "Structure View" button to view the structure of the domain with Cn3D.

5   *Conserved features/sites tab.* If conserved features or sites were annotated on the conserved domain, each feature or site will be described in a separate sub tab in the conserved features/sites tab. The details of a feature are displayed by clicking on the tab. Each feature within the conserved domain is given a serial number and feature name, which reflects the function of the conserved feature or site, and evidence, which may be a comment, structural evidence that can be visualized in a solved 3D structure, or literature citations indicated by PubMed identifiers. The thumbnail image of the solved 3D structure is displayed if it is available. The conserved amino acids that characterize the feature are highlighted in both the thumbnail image and in the interactive view of the structure when the thumbnail is clicked to launch the structure in the Cn3D program. In the example CDD record page, when you click the thumbnail image, the PPAR ligand binding domain is viewed in the Cn3D program. You can notice that the PPAR ligand binding domain has three features: the ligand domain, coactivator, and heterodimer. The Cn3D viewing program has a structure viewer, sequence/alignment viewer, and panels for controlling the display of features (Figure 3.30). Use the annotation panel to show the different features within the domain. The sequence/alignment viewer shows the aligned sequences of the member proteins in the family. The identifiers are shown on the left side of the viewer.

6   *PubMed references.* This tab includes the list of PubMed references that have been identified by curators as citations for the conserved domain.

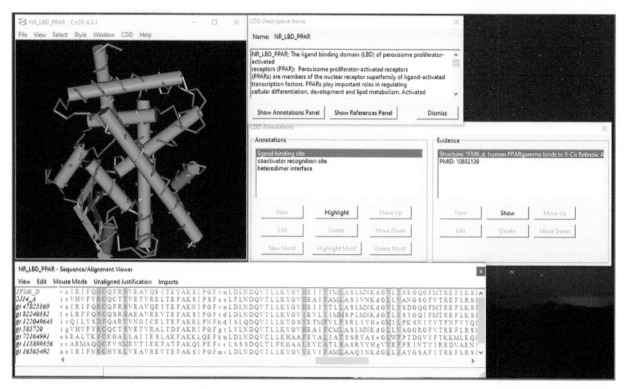

FIGURE 3.30   Viewing PPAR ligand domain features with Cn3D.

7   *Domain sub-family hierarchy.* This hierarchy serves as a table of contents for the CDD and it is available only for NCBI-curated domains. Clicking on any color (node) will display the corresponding sequence cluster (phylogenetic tree) with the same color. A node may have a sub-node, which represents a sub-cluster. The sequence cluster is a phylogenetic tree built from the aligned sequences. Colors used in the sequence cluster correspond to color of the node selected in the domain sub-family or family hierarchy. The phylogenetic tree can also be viewed using the CDTree program, which is a free NCBI phylogenetic tree visualization program that can be downloaded from www.ncbi.nlm.nih.gov/Structure/cdtree/cdtreeInstall.shtml. Once the program has been installed, you can click on the "Interactive Display with CDTree" button to view the phylogenetic tree interactively in detail.

8   *Sequence alignment.* This section shows the multiple sequence alignment for the ten most diverse members from the cluster of the sequences that formed the domain model.

Finding Protein Conserved Domains
Using CD-Search

In another scenario, assume that we have a protein sequence, and we wish to find the conserved domain in that sequence. In such case we can use CD-search (Figure 3.31), which is a tool for finding conserved domains in protein sequences by providing the protein sequence as an input. The CD-search is found under Tools on the main CDD webpage. On the query input box of the CD-search, you can enter a protein or nucleotide accession, GenBank identifier (gi), or a sequence in FASTA format in the query box of CD-search and then click on Submit button. For multiple sequences, you can use Batch CD-search instead. There are some options including a target database, which you can choose from the database dropdown menu, and expect value (E-value), which is the number of expected hits of similar alignment score that could be found just by chance. The default E-value (0.01) allows very rare false positive results. CD-search provides a list of targets databases that you can choose from based on your goal. These databases include the following:

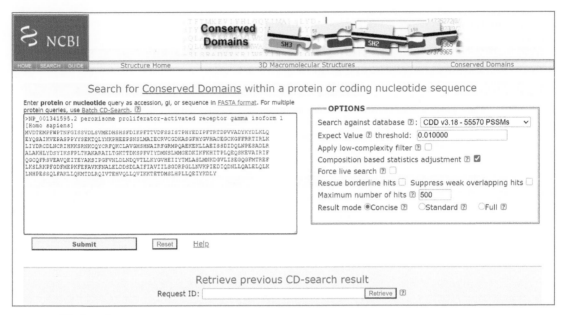

FIGURE 3.31   CD-Search.

- *CDD.* The NCBI-curated domains and domains from other databases.
- *Pfam.* A database of protein families that includes their annotations and multiple sequence alignments.
- *SMART.* It stands for Simple Modular Architecture Research Tool. It is a database used in the identification and analysis of protein domains within protein sequences.
- *PRK.* Curated prokaryotic protein clusters.
- *TIGRFAMs.* Curated multiple sequence alignments.
- *COG.* Orthologous protein families focusing on prokaryotes.
- *KOG.* Orthologous protein families focusing on eukaryotes.

For example, assume that you wish to search for the domains in the protein sequence with accession "NP_001341595.2", which is PPAR gamma isoform1. You can retrieve the FASTA sequence from the Protein database and enter it in the query box or you can enter the accession number, choose CDD database from the database dropdown menu, leave the default settings of the other options, and click on the Submit button.

The results displayed by CD-search are either pre-calculated search results or live search results. The pre-calculated results are displayed if the default CDD database is used, and the query is an accession number or GI of a sequence already in the Entrez Protein database. The live search results are displayed if the defaults CDD database is used, and the query is a FASTA-formatted sequence and the FASTA definition line (defline) does not include a GenBank identifier or one of the other databases (not CDD) is selected. If you select the default CDD database, you can force the live search by checking the checkbox next to "Force live search".

The CD-search results page shows three major sections: protein classification, graphical summary, and list of domain hits, as shown in Figure 3.32.

1   *Protein classification.* This section is available only if there is a curated label for the protein family. It provides a functional characterization of the architecture of the conserved domain found in the query protein sequence. For the PPAR gamma isoform sequence that we used as a query sequence, the search found two conserved domains as shown in Figure 3.32: "NR_DBD_PPAR and NR_LBD_PPAR domain-containing protein" (domain architecture ID 10576352). Those two domains are the

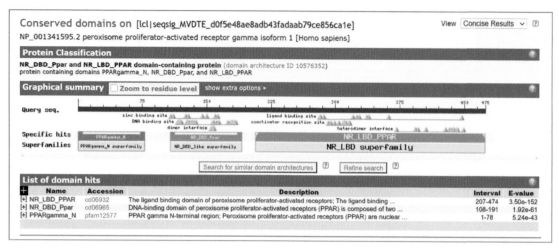

FIGURE 3.32   CD-Search results.

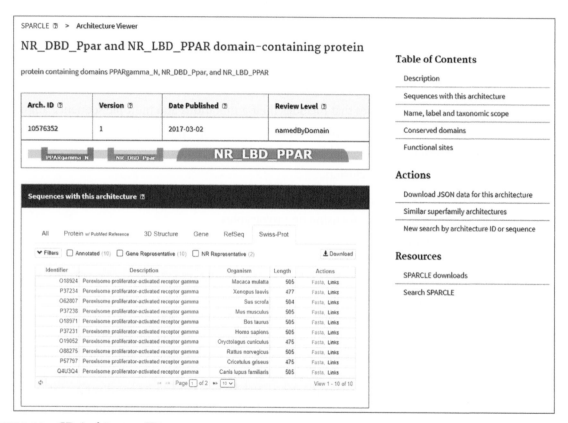

FIGURE 3.33   CD Architecture Viewer.

PPAR DNA Binding Domain (NC_DBD_PPAR) and the PPAR Ligand Binding Domain (NR_LBD_ PPAR) that characterize the proteins in the nuclear receptor superfamily. The link of the anchor domain architecture ID will open the Architecture Viewer as shown in Figure 3.33. The Architecture Viewer is used to visualize the structure of the conserved domain and to provide information of the domain architecture, descriptions and links to the protein, genes, reference genes, and Swiss-Prot record of the protein sequences sharing the architecture. You can also download a comma-separated value (CSV) file containing geninfo identifier (gi), ID, defline, and sequence length.

2 *The graphical summary.* The graphical summary (Figure 3.32) shows a solid dark bar representing the query sequence, annotations of the sequence (the small triangles indicate the amino acids that comprise the conserved site), and three bars with different colors representing the identified conserved domains in the query sequence. There are three conserved domains where identified: PPARgamma_N, NR_DBD_Ppar, and NR_LBD_PPAR. The former one is specific for PPAR gamma proteins while the other two domains are shared by the nuclear receptor superfamily members.

3 *The list of domain hits.* The list of domain hits, shown in Figure 3.32, includes the domains identified for the query sequence and their associated information and statistics. The list shows domain name, domain accession, domain description, domain position (interval) within the query sequence, and E-value that measure the uncertainty of the domain identification.

Finding Proteins with Similar Domain Architectures

We may also wish to find all protein sequences on the database that have conserved domains similar to domains of a query protein sequence. This is particularly useful for the classification of a newly found protein, identification of a protein, or inferring functions of a protein. For this purpose, we will use CDART (Conserved Domain Architecture Retrieval Tool). On the CDD main page under Tools, click on CDART to open the page of the Conserved Domain Architecture Retrieval Tool as shown in Figure 3.34. Enter the example FASTA-formatted sequence of NP_001341595.2 (you can retrieve the FASTA sequence from Protein database) into the query box or you can enter the accession and then click on the Submit button.

On the page of the CDART search results (Figure 3.35), the query sequences and hit sequences found by the search are represented graphically. At the top of the CDART search results, the query you entered is displayed with a yellow background. The length of the protein in amino acids is shown at the end of each graphic representation of a sequence. The domain architectures similar to the domain architecture of the query sequence are listed below the query sequence. The proteins, which have at least one conserved domain similar to a domain in the query sequence, will be considered similar protein. The similarity score of the domain architecture indicates the number of sequences in the architecture that match the domain in the query protein sequence. Only the first protein sequence in the group is displayed. You can display all protein sequences by clicking on (+) to expand the list.

The "Filter your results" bar at the top of a CDART search results page allows you to refine the search results by including or excluding proteins from specific taxonomic groups or architectures.

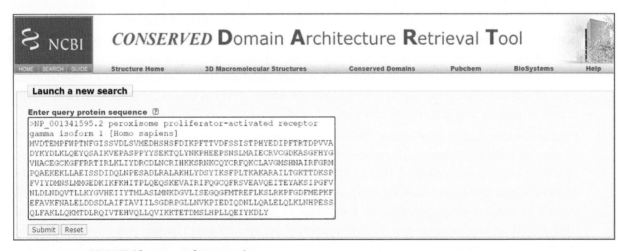

FIGURE 3.34 **CDART (domain architectures).**

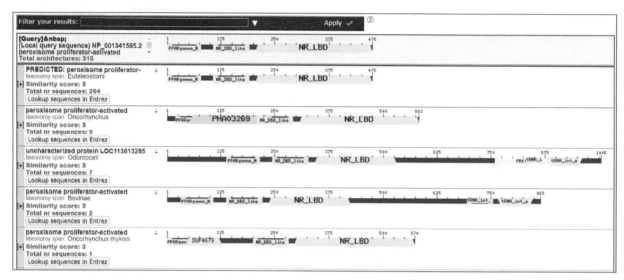

FIGURE 3.35 Graphical summary of similar domain architectures.

Protein Family Models

Introduction to Protein Classification

Proteins are classified into superfamilies and families based on their structures and functions. Classification of proteins into families provides valuable clues to protein structure, activity, and biological role. Protein members of the same family will have similar structure and functions. High-throughput sequencing technologies have resulted in a rapid accumulation of genome sequences for thousands of organisms. Thus, it has become crucial to identify the genes in these genomes and the proteins coded by those genes and to understand how these proteins function. The experimentally verified information on protein structures and functions helped to set methods and rules for genome annotation and classification and identification of proteins. The acceleration of accumulation of experimentally verified genomic data has been coupled with the development of algorithms and computational methods that have become the concrete foundation for advanced bioinformatics infrastructure for reliable and automatic genome annotation, protein identification and classification. Several curated and automatic protein classification systems have been developed to classify proteins into families. Those systems include the following:

1 *Superfamily/family protein classification system.* This classification system was developed by Protein Information Resource (PIR) [17, 18]. It depends on the protein domain architecture to provide comprehensive, non-overlapping, and hierarchical clustering (phylogenetic tree) of sequences to reflect their evolutionary relationships. Thousands of protein superfamilies have been manually curated based on the PIR system and managed by the Protein Sequence Database (PIR-PSD), which is a public domain. Each superfamily is represented by a seed sequence, which serves as a basis for automatic classification of new sequences into existing superfamilies.

2 *Protein domain classification system.* This system organizes protein sequences into families based on sequence similarity. The protein members of a family are sharing significant sequence similarity detected by a suite of programs called HMMER3 [19], which is a free software package used for identification of homologous protein or nucleotide sequences by comparing a profile hidden Markov (profile-HMM) models to either a single sequence or a database of sequences. The profile-HMMs are probabilistic models that capture position-specific information about evolutionary changes that have occurred in a set of homologous sequences aligned using multiple sequence alignment. This homology-based protein classification is used by the pfam [20] protein database, which contains several thousands of manually curated protein families.

3   *Sequence motifs classification system.* This protein classification system is based on sequence motifs and conserved regions in a protein sequence. It is used by the PROSITE protein database [21, 22], which created a set of rules, called ProRule[23], that enhances the discriminatory efficiency of motifs by providing additional information about the structurally and functionally important amino acid residues in a protein sequence.

4   *Structural classification of protein.* This protein classification is based on the similarities of protein structures and sequences (homology of protein sequences). The basic rule of classification is that protein sequences with similar structures but with low sequence similarity will be put in the same superfamily while the sequences that have similar structures and sequences are placed in the same family. This classification method is used in the SCOP (Structural Classification of Protein) database [24].

5   *Integration of all classification systems.* Some protein classification databases integrated all known classification systems to classify proteins into families. The iProClass database [25] is an example of an integrated database that includes family relationships, structural classification, functional classifications, and features.

Protein Family Models Database

The NCBI Protein Family Models are a collection of curated protein families organized hierarchically based on the Hidden Markov Model (HMM) and protein families identified by BLAST (BlastRules) and Conserved Domain Database architectures for assigning names, gene symbols, publications and EC (Enzyme Commission) numbers to the prokaryotic RefSeq proteins that meet the criteria for inclusion in a protein family [26]. The Protein Family Models database is an Entrez database that provides a way to search across NCBI database. It uses the NCBI annotation pipelines for protein identification and classification by using three types of evidence: Hidden Markov Models (HMMs), BlastRules, and domain architectures:

1   *Hidden Markov Models (HMMs).* HMMs [27] are a probabilistic model used to determine the protein family. The model building is based on multiple sequence alignments of the sequences of proteins with known functions. A position-specific scoring matrix (PSSM) is generated from the multiple sequence alignments of the related seed sequences to create an HMM-profile. Amino acids at each position on the alignment are given a score measuring their frequency. A threshold is used to classify a protein as a member of the HMM-based family.

    The PSSM is discussed in Chapter 7. The profile-HMMs are obtained from several sources including NCBI protein clusters (PRKs), TIGRFAMS, pfam, and other sources.

2   *BlastRules.* BlastRules [28] are types of evidence for functional classification of proteins based on BLAST. They consist of protein models with known biological functions such as proteins that have significant roles in pathogenicity, evolution, antibiotic resistance, or virulence of a prokaryote. BLAST uses a threshold to identify a protein sequence as a BlastRule hit.

3   *Domain architectures.* Proteins can be classified into groups based on their domain architecture [29] and the signature of their conserved domain. This is usually manually curated and associated with a specific function. Domain architectures supported by sufficient evidence are given names. The protein sequences that are put on a cluster based on their conserved domains are named by PGAP using SPARCLE (Subfamily Protein Architecture Labeling Engine).

A protein family model classification is determined by evidence hierarchy from the highest to the lowest precedence.

The Protein Family Models database can be chosen from the database dropdown list or by accessing it from www.ncbi.nlm.nih.gov/protfam/.

TABLE 3.17   Protein Family Models Database Indexed Fields

Description	Short Field Name	Description	Short Field Name
All Fields	ALL	Gene Description	GD
CDD Description	CDDDesc	Gene Symbol	GS
CDD Title	CDDTL	Method	METH
Description	DESC	Publication Date	PDAT
EC Number	EC	PDB Title	PDBTL
EC Title	ECTL	PubMed ID	PMID
Family Accession	FamAcc	Product Name	PN
Family Accession Orig	FamAcc Orig	Product Name Orig	PNO
Family Type	FamType	Review Level	RL
Filter	FILT	Shortname	SN

The Protein Family Model database can be searched the same way as any Entrez database. The search term can be a protein family model name, a full protein name or symbol, a publication, or a type of model (SPARCLE or Conserved Domain architecture, BlastRule, or HMM). An advanced query can be constructed using the Advanced Search Builder or using the database indexed fields listed in Table 3.17.

Assume that you wish to search the Protein Family Models database for the family models that have DNA binding domain (DBD), which is a domain that characterizes the transcriptional factor proteins, and binds to the promoter region of a gene upon gene regulation. You can use the following term to search the database:

"DNA binding domain"

The search results page will show hundreds of protein family models. The filters on the top right organize the results based on method into HMM, BLAST rules, Curated Domain Architecture, Domain Architecture, and Unreviewed Domain Architecture. Clicking on any one of these filters will limit the results accordingly.

The summary format of the results displays the title, summary description, gene symbol, date, family accession, and the method. However, the contents of the record page of HMM or BLAST Rules are different from that of the Domain Architecture method. To explore the results page, click on each filter type to limit the results to that method and then click on a title of a record to display the record page for that method. Figure 3.36 shows the contents of the record page of a family model based on the HMM method or BLAST rules method. The record page consists of the Protein Family Model description, Details, References, and Protein hits, which constitute the family.

The record page of a Domain Architecture based family model consists of several sections including (1) description, (2) sequences with this architecture, (3) name, label, and taxonomic scope, (4) conserved domains, and (5) functional sites. Those sections are listed in the table of contents on the right side of the record page for easy navigation. Try to study the record page and understand the content of each section and the provided links.

In another example, assume that you wish to find the protein family models that have SH3 domain and specific for phosphatidylinositol 3-kinases. The SH3 domains (Src homology 3) are around 50 amino acid residues, and they have characteristic 3D structure. To search the database for family models by SH3 and phosphatidylinositol 3-kinases, you can use the following query:

SH3 AND "phosphatidylinositol 3-kinases"

The search will return protein family models with SH3 and phosphatidylinositol 3-kinases. Click the first entry on the results page to open the record page that displays the domain architecture of the family model (Figure 3.37). If you click on the SH3 diagram, it will open the Conserved Protein Domain Family page that displays information.

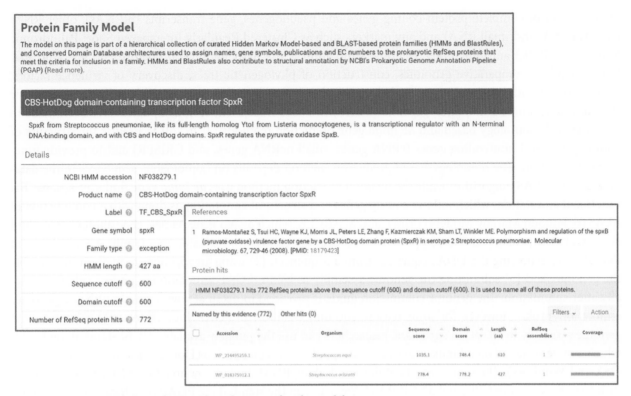

FIGURE 3.36 Record page of HMM-based protein family models.

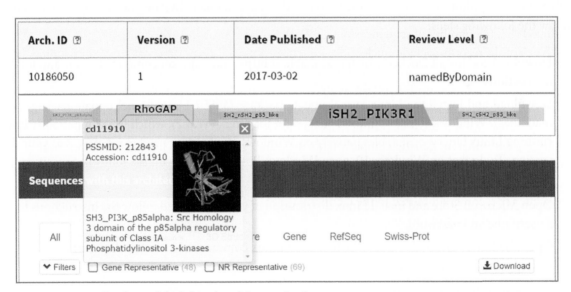

FIGURE 3.37 Protein family model of phosphatidylinositol 3-kinases.

On the main web page of the Protein Family Models, there are several tools. CD-search has already been discussed in the previous section and BLAST will be discussed in Chapters 7 and 8. We will discuss the Prokaryotic Genome Annotation Pipeline (PGAP) because it uses some of the methods used by the Protein Family Models database.

Annotation of Prokaryotic Genome
Researchers may wish to annotate bacteria or archaeal genome sequences such as chromosomes or plasmids obtained from NGS projects. The annotation may include the identification of gene features such as the

identification of complete protein-coding genes and pseudogenes, gene transcripts (mRNAs), other RNAs (tRNA, rRNA, and small RNA) and any markers such as Clustered Regularly Interspaced Short Palindromic Repeats (CRISPR) and mutations. Genome annotation is the basis for several downstream genomic analyses, including comparative genomics, construction of phylogenetic trees, discovery of virulence factors, exploration of pathways, and more. To help researchers to achieve that goal, NCBI launched an automatic Prokaryotic Genome Annotation Pipeline (PGAP) in 2001. Since then, various updates have been made to combine both homology based and *ab initio* gene prediction methods [3, 26, 28] to predict the structure of coding genes and non-coding genes (rRNA genes, small ncRNA genes, and CRISPR) and to provide functional annotation. The homology-based prediction method depends on homologous sequences in the database using a BLAST algorithm while the *ab initio* prediction method uses *ab initio* gene finder programs. The functional annotation, which follows coding genes and structural annotation, is done with a combination of BLASTp, Hidden Markov Model (HMM), and SPARCLE, which assign gene names, gene abbreviations, and citations to the prokaryotic RefSeq proteins that meet the criteria for inclusion in a family. A typical flow of PGAP is (1) acquiring the DNA sequences from a sequencer, (2) using an appropriate method to assemble the genome, and (3) submitting the genome assembly to NCBI. PGAP annotation is performed automatically after submission. The genome submission guide is provided in detail at www.ncbi.nlm.nih.gov/genome/annotation_prok/. However, for some reason, you may wish to run PGAP yourself to avoid submitting the genome assembly to NCBI. In such case, researchers can use the publicly available NCBI stand-alone PGAP, which can be installed on a Linux system or a compatible container such as Docker for other platforms (Max OSX and Windows). The requirements of the stand-alone PGAP include Python 3.6 or later version, 100GB disk free space, 8-core CPU, and 32 GB RAM. You can run the stand-alone PGAP on a local computer or on the cloud. First you need to choose on which platform you need to install the program. Follow the instructions available at https://github.com/ncbi/pgap/wiki to install a stand-alone PGAP on your machine. For Windows 10 follow the following steps:

1   Download and install Docker, which is available at https://docs.docker.com/get-docker/ and follow the instructions.

2   Download and install the Linux kernel update package (WSL2 Linux kernel update package for x64 machines). Windows 10 has Windows Subsystem for Linux (WSL2), which is a compatibility layer for running Linux binary executables natively on Windows 10. You may need to set WSL 2 as your default version. To do that on Windows 10, open Windows PowerShell and run the following command:

wsl --set-default-version 2

3   Open Microsoft Store and install Linux distribution of your choice and follow the instructions to create a username and password.

4   Open the Linux terminal and run the following Linux commands to create a directory:

$ mkdir pgap #create a directory

$ cd pgap #change to the directory

5   Download the PGAP Python script file and make it executable (Figure 3.38).

$ curl -OL https://github.com/ncbi/pgap/raw/prod/scripts/pgap.py

$ chmod +x pgap.py

6   Update the pgap required files. Figure 3.39 shows the files were downloaded.

$ ./pgap.py --update

Once the files have been downloaded and extracted, you can notice the reference data and example genomes as shown in Figure 3.40. The example genomes are provided for quickly testing and practicing.

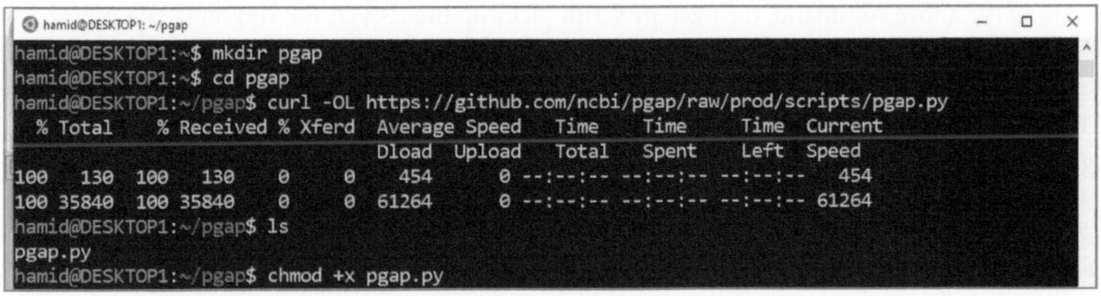

FIGURE 3.38   Downloading the stand-alone PGAP Python script.

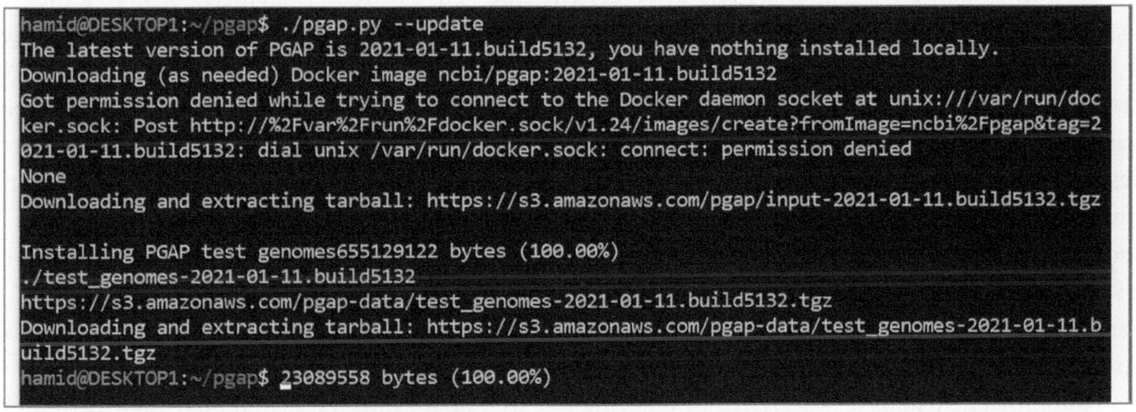

FIGURE 3.39   Downloading PGAP required files.

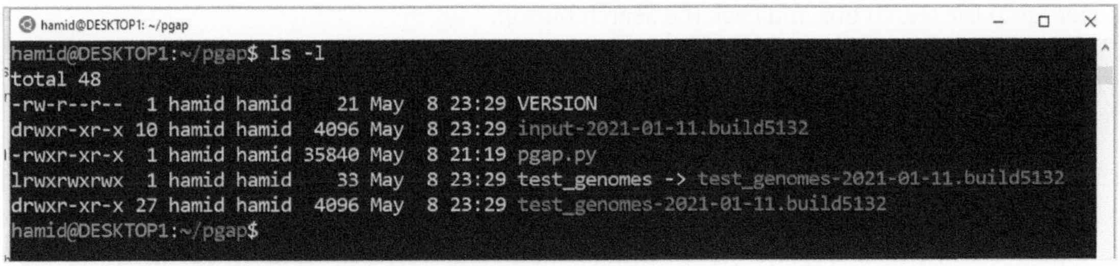

FIGURE 3.40   PGAP input reference data and test genome directories.

You can check the genomes in the test_genomes directory, which includes several sub-directories. In each example genome directory, you will find the YAML input file, the YAML metadata file, and the genome FASTA file.

7   You can use an example genome for testing the stand-alone PGAP program. For example, you can annotate the genome of *Mycoplasma genitalium*. To do that you will use YAML formatted file as an input file. YAML file format is a human-readable data-serialization format commonly used for configuration files and in applications where data is being stored or transmitted. The PGAP YAML input file points to two files: (a) the FASTA file of the genome assembly and (b) the metadata file that includes the topology of the sequence (linear or circular), organism, contact info and authors, etc. The PGAP program is executed as follows:

$ ./pgap.py -r -o mg37_results test_genomes/MG37/input.yaml

The option "-r" is to report to NCBI whenever the pipeline is run, "-o" for the output directory to be created. Visit "https://github.com/ncbi/pgap/wiki/Quick-Start" for the other options and uses.

After running the above command, the pgap.py script picks up the FASTA file and metadata file, provided by the YAML file, and Docker image reference data and creates an instance of the Docker container, where execution of the pipeline and task distribution take place. The output files will include annot.faa (annotated protein in FASTA format), annot.sqn (annotated genomic sequence in ASN format (for submission to NCBI if needed), annot.gff (annotated genome in GFF3 format), and annot.gbk (annotated genomic sequence in GenBank file format). Open the GenBank annotation file and study how the FASTA sequence has been annotated.

HomoloGene

HomoloGene [1, 30] is a system for automated detection of homologs in the NCBI databases and provides sets of eukaryotic homologous genes and their transcripts (mRNA) and genomic and protein sequences that can be used in comparative homology and phylogenetic tree construction. The entries of the HomoloGene database are generated automatically from the records of other NCBI databases. The process of generating HomoloGene entries begins first by building sets of protein sequences of organisms; then the protein sequences are aligned using BLASTp and grouped by similarity. The BLASTp is a sequence alignment tool for protein sequences and will be discussed in Chapter 8. A tree for a specific protein is built of the similar protein sequences. The proteins are then mapped to their genomic DNA sequences. Distance matrices are computed and the sequences from the same species are filtered so only similar sequences from different species will be in the sequence set. The building process ends up by constructing a set of homologous genes that includes similar gene sequences from different organisms.

The HomoloGene web page is opened by selecting HomoloGene from the dropdown menu on the Entrez web page or by using the link www.ncbi.nlm.nih.gov/homologene/.

The HomoloGene database is searched by entering a search query into the search box. Table 3.18 includes the database indexed fields.

Assume that you wish to find the gene homologs for human PPARG gene. You can enter the following search query into the search box and click the Search button.

PPARG AND "Homo sapiens"[ORGN]

The HomoloGene record page can be displayed in several formats including summary, HomoloGene, alignment scores, multiple sequence alignment, and FASTA format. The default display is HomoloGene format (Figure 3.41), which displays (1) the lists of homologous genes (Genes), (2) their corresponding proteins (Proteins) and diagrams representing the protein domains, (3) links to protein multiple alignment and pairwise similarity score and evolutionary distance between sequences (Protein Alignment), (4) the protein conserved domains (Conserved Domains), (5) the health conditions and diseases associated with the homologs (Phenotypes), (6) Related Homology Resources, and (7) associated articles (Publications).

TABLE 3.18   HomoloGene Indexed Fields

Complete Field	Short Field	Complete Field	Short Field
All Fields	ALL	Organism	ORGN
Ancestor	ANCS	Protein Accession	PRAC
Domain Name	DOM	Properties	PROP
Filter	FILT	Protein UID	PUID
Gene Description	GDSC	Title	TITL
Gene Name	GENE	UniGene ID	UGID
Gene ID	GNID	UID	UID
Nucleotide Accession	NCAC	Text Word	WORD
Nucleotide UID	NUID		

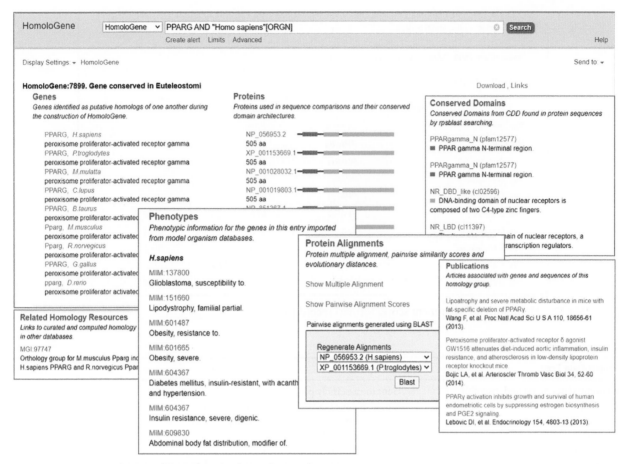

FIGURE 3.41   HomoloGene (HomoloGene format) record page.

Use Display Setting on the top of the page to switch to the different display formats. The summary format displays only the full name of the gene, gene symbols, and HomoloGene identifier (hgid).

The alignment Scores format, shown in Figure 3.42, displays the pairwise alignment identity scores of the protein and DNA sequences for each gene in the HomoloGene group against the other group members. For example, the PPARG protein of the human (*H. sapiens*) is 99.8% identical to that of chimpanzee (*P. troglodytes*) and the human PPARG gene is 99.5% identical to that of chimpanzee. The BLAST link opens the BLAST pairwise alignment of the two protein sequences and the dot matrix view, which will be discussed in Chapter 7.

The Multiple Sequence Alignment format displays the multiple alignments of the protein sequences of the HomoloGene group and the FASTA format displays the multiple FASTA formatted protein sequences.

The "Download" link on the top right opens a page that you can select and download HomoloGene data (protein, mRNA, and genomic). The data then can be downloaded using the "Send to" dropdown menu.

BIOPROJECT

The NCBI BioProject database is a collection of metadata of projects conducted by researchers or research institutions. It was established by NCBI to assist in organization and classification of project data submitted to any of the International Nucleotide Sequence Database Collaboration members (NCBI, EBI, and DDBJ databases) [31]. A BioProject record contains precise descriptive information about the research project's scope, material, and objectives and provides a framework for accessing metadata about research projects and a mechanism to access specific datasets. It serves as a container for the sample metadata (BioSample).

Creation of a BioProject is recommended for projects that generate a large volume of data submissions and submission from several team members. Moreover, a BioProject is required for submission of data to some NCBI

Display Settings: ▾ Alignment Scores

HomoloGene:7899. Gene conserved in Euteleostomi

Pairwise Alignment Scores

Gene		Identity (%)		
Species	Symbol	Protein	DNA	
H.sapiens	**PPARG**			
vs. P.troglodytes	PPARG	99.8	99.5	Blast
vs. M.mulatta	PPARG	99.2	98.5	Blast
vs. C.lupus	PPARG	98.2	92.3	Blast
vs. B.taurus	PPARG	95.8	91.0	Blast
vs. M.musculus	Pparg	96.2	90.1	Blast
vs. R.norvegicus	Pparg	95.8	89.8	Blast
vs. G.gallus	PPARG	92.8	82.2	Blast
vs. D.rerio	pparg	69.3	67.0	Blast

FIGURE 3.42   HomoloGene (alignment scores format) record page.

TABLE 3.19   Project Data Type

Project Data Type	Description
Genome sequencing and assembly	Genome assembly project
Raw sequence reads	Raw sequence reads (FASQ or BAM/SAM)
Genome sequencing	Whole, or partial, genome sequencing project
Assembly	Genome assembly
Clone ends	Clone-end sequencing project
Epigenomics	DNA methylation, histone modification, chromatin accessibility datasets
Exome	Exome resequencing project
Map	Non-sequence map data (e.g., genetic map, cytogenetic map, etc.)
Metagenome	Sequence analysis of environmental samples
Metagenome assembly	A genome assembly generated from sequenced environmental samples
Phenotype or Genotype	Project correlating phenotype and genotype
Proteome	Large-scale proteomics experiment
Random Survey	Sequence generated from a random sampling of the collected sample
Targeted locus (loci)	Project to sequence specific loci, such as a 16S rRNA sequencing
Transcriptome or Gene expression	Large-scale RNA sequencing or expression analysis
Variation	Project for identifying sequence variation across populations
Other	A free text description is provided to indicate other data type

databases such as SRA, dbVar, and GenBank microbial and eukaryotic genomes. Before submitting data to those databases, you may be asked to provide a BioProject accession if you have already created a BioProject or to create a new BioProject to continue submitting your data. To submit a BioProject metadata, you need to log onto your MyNCBI account and access the new submission web page, which is available at https://submit.ncbi.nlm.nih.gov/subs/bioproject/. Click the New Submission button to open the submission portal, which issues a temporary accession number that begins with "SUB". The submission wizard will take you through seven tabs (steps) named (1) Submitter for submitter information, (2) Project Type, as shown in Table 3.19, to select one or more of the project types that describe your project and sample scope, (3) Target for the target organism information such as species, strain, cultivar, and others, (4) General Info such as release date, project title, public description, relevance, external links, grant info, (5) BioSample to enter a BioSample accession if you have already created one (leave it blank as BioSample will be discussed in the next section), (6) Publication to add the PubMed identifiers (PMIDs) if a publication for this project has been published (otherwise leave the field blank), and (7) Review & submit for reviewing the entries and submit the submission form.

TABLE 3.20   BioProject Database Indexed Fields

Long Field	Short Field	Long Field	Short Field
Assembly Accession	AACC	Organism	ORGN
Replicon accession	ACCN	ProjectID	PID
All Fields	ALL	PMID	PMID
Assembly name	ANME	Project Accession	PRJA
Attribute Name	ATNM	Properties	PROP
Attribute	ATTR	Relevance	RELV
BioProject ID	BPRJ	Replicon name	RNME
Submitter Organization	CEN	Replicon type	RTYP
Registration Date	DATE	Project Subtype	STPE
DOI	DOID	Title	TITL
Project Data Type*	DTPE	Top BioProject	TPRJ
Filter	FILT	Project Type	TYPE
Funding Agency	FUND	UID	UID
Grant ID	GRNT	WGS Accession	WGSA
Keyword	KWRD	Description	WORD

After submission it will be reviewed by curators and, if it is accepted, a permanent BioProject accession, which begins with "PRJN", will be issued, and emailed to you. The BioProject accession then can be used when creating BioSample records, as it will be discussed in the next section.

Since a BioProject is the container for samples (BioSample) and data associated with the samples in the project, it can be used to access all datasets or some of the datasets in the project. The BioProject database is searched as any Entrez database. The BioProject can be chosen from the database dropdown menu or via www.ncbi.nlm.nih.gov/bioproject/. Table 3.20 contains the indexed fields that can be used to search the BioProject database.

The project types in Table 3.19 can be used as search term with [DTPE] or [Project Data Type]. For example, to search the BioProject database for projects about gene expression, we can use the following search term:

"gene expression"[DTPE]

Assume that you wish to find the projects (BioProject) that studied human breast cancer and were focused on variation (SNPs). You can use the following query:

variation[DTPE] AND human[ORGN] AND "breast cancer"

The BioProject results page is displayed in summary format by default. The summary includes the title, organism, taxonomy group, project data type, scope, and BioProject accession. You can notice that using [DTPE] tagged field narrows the results to the specified data type, which is useful when searching for a project linked to a specific data type.

Clicking on the title of any search results item will open the BioProject record page of that hit as shown in Figure 3.43.

The BioProject record page provides information about the project and links to the data on the project. The Project Data table shows the Resource Name and Number of Links.

BIOSAMPLE

The NCBI BioSample is a database for storing metadata of the samples in a BioProject. The metadata is descriptive information about the samples used in the studies to generate the data. A BioSample entry can be a sample from any species and any form of biological specimen. One goal of BioSample is to standardize the terms used

FIGURE 3.43   BioProject record page.

in sample description by using consistent attribute names and values that provide precise descriptions to the samples [31].

The BioSample records are linked with the related BioProject records by the BioProject accessions. Multiple BioSample records can be linked to a BioProject. The objectives of the NCBI BioSample database are to link sample metadata to the related data records across the NCBI databases and to promote the use of specific descriptive fields and values for samples, which help in cross-database search queries.

Upon BioSample submission, you need to specify a sample type. A sample type is represented by a BioSample package that specifies the list of attributes of the sample. There are two categories of BioSample packages that were developed to be used by submitters: (1) the NCBI standard packages and (2) Minimum Information (MIxS) packages, which include attributes defined by the Genome Standards Consortium (GSC) [32]. The following are the list of the BioSample packages:

- *Standard packages.* The standard BioSample packages are the most commonly used, and they describe the attributes of samples associated with a family of organisms. The current standard packages include SARS-CoV-2, microbe, model organisms or animal, metagenome or environmental, invertebrate, human, plant, virus, and beta-lactamase.

- *Pathogen.* The pathogen BioSample packages describe the attributes of samples collected for pathogens. The pathogen packages include clinical or host-associated and environmental.

- *MIGS.ba.* The packages of Minimum Information about a Genome Sequence (MIGS) [33] of bacteria are used for cultured bacterial or archaeal genomic sequences.

- *MIGS.eu.* The packages of MIGS of eukaryotes are used for eukaryotic genomic sequences.

- *MIGS.vi.* The packages of MIGS of viruses are used for virus genomic sequences.

- *MIMAG.* The packages of Minimum Information about a Metagenome-Assembled Genome (MIMAG) [34] are used for metagenome-assembled genome sequences generated with tools that group sequences into individual organism genome assemblies starting from metagenomic datasets.

- *MIMARKS.specimen.* The packages of Minimum Information about a Marker Gene Sequence (MIMARKS) [35] are used for any type of marker gene sequences (e.g., 16S rRNA) obtained from cultured or voucher specimens.

- *MIMARKS.survey.* Those MIMARKS packages are used for any type of marker gene sequences obtained directly from the environment, without culturing or identification of the organisms.
- *MIMS.me.* The packages of MIMS Metagenome/Environmental are used for environmental and metagenome sequences.
- *MISAG (Single Amplified Genome).* The packages of Minimum Information about a Single Amplified Genome (MISAG) [34] are used for single amplified genome sequences produced by isolating individual cells.
- *MIUVIG.* The packages of Minimum Information about Uncultivated Virus Genome (MIUVIG) [36] are used for uncultivated virus genome identified in metagenome and metatranscriptome datasets.

As with the BioProject database, it is required to submit BioSample for submitting SRA, dbVar, and GenBank microbial and eukaryotic genome data. To submit single or multiple BioSample records, you can use https://submit.ncbi.nlm.nih.gov/subs/biosample/ for new submissions. The submittal portal provides a temporary accession beginning with "SUB". The BioSample information is provided on seven tabs (steps): (1) Submitter for submitter's information, (2) General Info to enter release date and to specify whether you are submitting a single sample or a file containing multiple samples, (3) Sample Type to select one of the NCBI packages that organize the sample types into certain groups, (4) Attributes to enter sample information (name, organism, strain, sex, tissue, etc.), (5) BioProject to specify the accession of the BioProject that you have created in the above section or there is a link to create a new BioProject, (6) Description to enter a sample title and public description, and (7) Review & Submit to review the information you entered and submit. After submission, the application will be reviewed by curators and then permanent accession will be emailed for each BioSample. The BioSample accessions can then be used upon data submission as required by some databases, such as those mentioned above.

While a BioProject can be used to search for the entire data in that project, a BioSample is used to search for the sample data. The BioSample can be chosen from the NCBI database dropdown menu or via www.ncbi.nlm.nih.gov/biosample/. The BioSample indexed fields shown in Table 3.21 can be used to build an advanced search query.

For example, assume that you wish to find the BioSample records associated with the human for bacteria of genus *Salmonella*, for which sequence read archive (SRA) data is available. You can use the following query:

"Salmonella"[ORGN] AND biosample sra[FILT] AND "human associated"[FILT]

Clicking on a BioSample title will open the page of that record as shown in Figure 3.44.

The BioSample record page may show the BioSample title, BioSample identifier and linked database record identifier, the package used to describe the BioSample, the BioSample attributes, the BioProject accession and description, submission information, and links to the BioProject database and the database on which the data is found.

TABLE 3.21   BioSample Indexed Fields

Long Field	Short Field	Long Field	Short Field
Accession	ACCN	Modification Date	MDAT
All Fields	ALL	Organism	ORGN
Attribute Name	ATNM	Publication Date	PDAT
Attribute	ATTR	Properties	PROP
Author	AUTH	Title	TITL
Submitter Organization	CEN	UID	UID
Filter	FILT	Text Word	WORD

Full ▾   Send to: ▾

WGS of Salmonella enterica subsp. enterica serovar Typhi strain 160011TY

Identifiers   BioSample: SAMD00061310; SRA: DRS058005

Organism   Salmonella enterica subsp. enterica serovar Typhi
cellular organisms; Bacteria; Proteobacteria; Gammaproteobacteria; Enterobacterales; Enterobacteriaceae; Salmonella; Salmonella enterica; Salmonella
enterica subsp. enterica

Package   MIGS: cultured bacteria/archaea; human-associated; version 5.0

Attributes
sample name	Salmonella enterica subsp. enterica serovar Typhi **strain** 160011TY	
collection date	2016	
broad-scale environmental context	not applicable	
local-scale environmental context	not applicable	
environmental medium	not applicable	
geographic location	Japan	
host	not applicable	
isolation and growth condition	not collected	
latitude and longitude	not collected	
number of replicons	not collected	
project name	WGS of Salmonella Typhi	
reference for biomaterial	not collected	
strain	160011TY	
serovar	Typhi	
sub species	enterica	

Description   Keywords: GSC:MIxS;MIGS:5.0

BioProject   PRJDB5169 Salmonella enterica subsp. enterica serovar Typhi
Retrieve all samples from this project

Submission   Department of Bacteriology I, National Institute of Infectious Diseases; 2018-01-25

Accession: SAMD00061310 ID: 8392751
BioProject   SRA

Related information
BioProject

SRA

Taxonomy

Recent activity
Turn Off Clear

Your browsing activity is empty.

FIGURE 3.44   BioSample record page.

DbSNP

The dbSNP database [11, 37] or the database of Short Genetic Variations was established in 1999 by NCBI for submittal and retrieval of simple genetic variants including SNPs, small variants (less than 50 bp of length), small-scale multi-base deletions and insertions (INDELs), and microsatellite repeat variations or short tandem repeats (STRs), which are short sequences known for their high mutability and are implicated in several diseases. The dbSNP database includes variants for all species and for any part of the genome. However, since September 1, 2017, the dbSNP database stopped accepting submissions of non-human organism data. The information in dbSNP records includes physical mapping, functional analysis, pharmacogenomics, phenotype-genotype association studies, and evolutionary studies.

Genetic variation is due to mutation, which is the change that takes place in a genomic DNA sequence. This change is either germline mutation (inherited change) that occurs in the germ cells or somatic mutation (non-inherited mutation) that occurs in the somatic cells during the lifetime of an organism. A eukaryotic gene exists in two copies called alleles; each allele is inherited from a parent. Identical alleles of a gene in an organism are called homozygous alleles. Non identical alleles (when one allele is different due to a mutation) are called heterozygous alleles. The genetic mutation can be substitution, deletion, or insertion. In the substitution mutation, a particular base is substituted by one of the other three bases (e.g., cytosine (C) may be replaced by thymine (T)). When such substitution takes place in a single nucleotide, we call that a point mutation. A particular nucleotide in a gene may be replaced by one of the other nucleotides (polymorphic nucleotide). We call such point mutation single nucleotide polymorphism (SNP) or single nucleotide variation (SNV). A SNP may have either molecular consequence or may not. If a substitution of a nucleotide does not affect the codon that codes for the amino acid in a protein sequence, we call this codon a synonymous codon and we call the mutation a silent mutation. On the other hand, if a point mutation affects an amino acid, we describe the affected codon as nonsynonymous. The mutation that causes nonsynonymous codon will have one of two consequences; either it may produce a stop codon, which will result in a truncated, incomplete protein, or the new codon codes for a different amino acid, which changes the protein sequence. The former mutation, which results in an incomplete protein, is known as nonsense mutation, and the latter, which produces new amino acid, is called missense mutation.

A deletion mutation is the removal of one base pair or more from a gene sequence, which will result in a shifting of the coding frame (frame shift). Deletion of only one or two base pairs from the gene coding region will alter the translational frame and garble the mRNA, which will be translated into nonfunctional protein. If three nucleotides are deleted, there will be no shift in the codon reading frame; however, there will be a missing amino acid in the final protein and that may affect the function of the protein.

The insertion mutation is the addition of base pairs to a gene coding region, which may shift the coding frame depending on whether multiples of three base pairs are inserted. Combinations of insertions and deletions (INDEL) may lead to a variety of consequences. The term "variant" is a general term used for any kind of mutation (substitution, insertion, or deletion).

A mutation may be significant if it alters a biological function or a phenotype. Some mutations in certain genes are known by experimentation to have biological significance, such as the association of a specific mutation with a trait or disease (e.g., breast cancer in women is associated with known SNPs in BRCA1 and BRCA2 genes and sickle cell anemia is associated with known SNPs in HHB gene). Thus, the dbSNP database is important for biomedical research as the dbSNP records are cross-annotated within other NCBI resources such as GenBank records, genome sequences, PubMed, and others. Moreover, the link of dbSNP records to supporting publications provided at submission time makes the dbSNP database part of the NCBI discovery space [38].

The dbSNP variant, which is any variant less than 50 bp of length, is used as a positional marker and mapped to a unique location in a reference genome. The position of a variant is defined by its unique flanking sequence; therefore, it serves as a stable landmark in the genome. The flanking sequence of a dbSNP is either assayed (verified experimentally) for variation or adopted from a published sequence, or a combination of the two. For an adequate mapping to the right position in a reference genome, the length of the flanking sequence of a dbSNP entry is restricted to a minimum length of 25 bp in both 5` and 3` flanks and 100 bp overall flanking sequence. However, SNPs with flanks less than that criterion can also be submitted, but they may not map to the correct position.

The dbSNP Submission

The NCBI database does not accept the submission of non-human variants. Researchers can still submit their data to the European Variation Archive available at www.ebi.ac.uk/eva/. For a submission to dbSNP be accepted, the variant must be a simple variation (< 50 bp), a single-base nucleotide substitution, a small-scale multi-base deletion or insertion, a microsatellite repeat, variation genotype data, or variation allele frequency data. The dbSNP does not accept submission containing patient-sensitive information or when the individuals where the variants were observed did not sign a consent form for displaying their genetic information on a public website. Such variants can be submitted to NCBI's Database of Genotypes and Phenotypes (dbGaP). The variants identified in individuals with a phenotype that has not yet been interpreted for functional or clinical significance and meet the above dbSNP criteria can be submitted to dbSNP [39].

The submission of genetic variations requires logging in your MyNCBI account. For submitting variation data to dbSNP, you will begin with the dbSNP Pre-Submission Process, which consists of the following steps:

(1) Deposit your sequence data in the right NCBI database. For example, for a variation on a nucleotide sequence, deposit the sequence in GenBank. If the variation is described in mapped short sequence read (e.g., SAM/BAM), you can deposit the mapped reads in the SRA database or dbGaP, etc.

(2) Submit a BioProject (project metadata) and obtain a BioProject accession as described above.

(3) Submit a BioSample (sample metadata) and obtain a BioSample accession as described above.

(4) Request a Submission Handle, which is used to trace data origin over time. A handle is requested by filling out and submit the submission handle form prior to submission. The form is available at www.ncbi.nlm.nih.gov/projects/SNP/handle.html. The form includes the contact information of the submitter and handle information. The handle identifier can be a short abbreviation or acronym to identify the laboratory. Once the form has been submitted, a confirmation email will be sent to the contact email address in the form.

(5) Prepare the submission metadata files. There are two kinds of metadata files required: (a) the required metadata file that includes handle, publication, method, population, and other information associated with the submission as described by the dbSNP Metadata File Specifications; and (b) the dbSNP VCF file that described the variation. The VCF file format is discussed in Chapter 2. You can also follow the guide posted on the dbSNP web page to create the VCF submission file or Excel flat submission using a template.

(6) Send the submission files to snp-sub@ncbi.nlm.nih.gov.

The major elements of a submission to dbSNP may include the following [40]:

- *Sequence context.* The sequence context of the variation being submitted must be precisely defined. The context is based on asserted positions and the flanking sequence. Submission of variations to dbSNP requires that a variant location must be as an asserted position on RefSeq or INSDC sequences. The asserted position is a statement based on experimental evidence that a variant is located at a specific position on an INSDC or RefSeq sequence or on a sequence that is part of one of the NCBI genome assemblies. The flanking sequence is used only to report the sequence context for the variants whose location could be described as assertion positions. The dbSNP variants based on the flanking sequence only will not be displayed on maps or graphic representations of the assembly. Only dbSNP variants are displayed on graphic representations such as the Sequence Viewer and Genome Viewer. The variant submitted to dbSNP with flanking sequence only must be with a minimum length of 25 bp on either side of the variation to facilitate its mapping. The accepted variations with asserted positions mapped to a reference sequence are assigned an accession prefixed with "rs" as reference variants (RefSNP) while the ones submitted with flanking sequence will be assigned a number prefixed with "ss".

- *Alleles.* Alleles define the variation classes which include (1) the Single Nucleotide Variation (SNV), (2) deletion/insertion variations, (3) heterozygous alleles, (4) microsatellite or short tandem repeat (STR), etc.

- *Method.* The method used to generate the variations and the tools used to estimate the allele frequencies are to be defined.

- *Asserted allele origin.* The assertion with supporting experimental evidence of allelic origin is to be provided in the submission.

- *Population.* The population from which the variations have been identified is to be described in the submission.

- *Sample size.* There are two sample sizes to be defined in the submission: the number of chromosomes used to ascertain the variation (SNPASSAY SAMPLE SIZE), and the number of chromosomes used as the denominator in computing the estimates of allele frequencies (SNPPOPUSE SAMPLE SIZE).

- *Population-specific allele frequencies.* The alleles that exist at different frequencies in different populations are to be described. Allele Frequency Aggregator (ALFA) [41] is data pooled from dbSNP and the dbGaP to compute allele frequency for different populations. The ALFA dataset includes aggregated and microarray chip genotyping, exome, and genome sequencing data. The NCBI Allele Frequency Aggregator (ALFA) is data pooled from dbSNP and the dbGaP to compute allele frequencies for different ancestry populations and to facilitate the comparison of allele frequency across populations and filter common and rare variants, and variant interpretation. The populations included millions of subjects and covered millions of variants and trillions of genotypes. ALFA is fully integrated with dbSNP annotation. The Minor Allele Frequency (MAF) is the frequency of an allele with frequency more than 5%. An allele with frequency less than 5% is called a rare allele [42], which may have a clinical significance. MAF provides information that differentiates between common and rare variants in a population.

- *Individual genotypes.* Those are the genotype from individuals that have signed a consent that their DNA sequences are to be in a public database (e.g., the 1000 Genomes project).
- *Validation information.* Variations with "ss" identifiers can be validated. Assays can be validated by the submitter through the VALIDATION section by showing the type of evidence used to confirm the variation.

After a successful SNP submission and processing, a SNP with a unique flanking sequence will be mapped physically to a reference genome and used as a physical marker to serve as a landmark in the reference genome and can be viewed in a graphic representation such as Genome Viewer.

Searching the dbSNP Database

The dbSNP can be searched using Entrez common web interface or can be accessed directly from www.ncbi.nlm.nih.gov/snp/. The dbSNP database is searched by entering search terms into the dbSNP search box as for other Entrez databases. Table 3.22 shows the indexed fields of dbSNP database.

The following are only some examples of dbSNP searching:

Searching dbSNP by Function Class and Clinical Significance   The dbSNP function class field (FXN) defines the position of a polymorphism with respect to identifiable features of a specific transcript of a gene. The function classes in gene features may be defined by the location of the variation with respect to transcript exon boundaries. Therefore, the function class indexed field provides a way to refine the dbSNP search results. Table 3.23 contains the function classes that can be used with [FXN] or [FUNCTION_CLASS]. When using function class, the searching can be more refined by using the indexed field of clinical significance [CLIN] of the variation in the search query. For example, assume that you wish to find the records in dbSNP database for missense variants in BRCA1 gene. You can use the following query:

brca1[GENE] AND "Missense variant"[FXN]

TABLE 3.22   dbSNP Indexed Fields

Description	Short Field	Description	Short Field
Accession	ACCN	Gene Name	GENE
ALFA African population MAF	ALFA_AFR	Gene ID	GENE_ID
ALFA Asian population MAF	ALFA_ASN	Global Minor Allele Frequency	GMAF
ALFA European population MAF	ALFA_EUR	Genotype	GTYP
ALFA Latin American 1 population MAF	ALFA_LAC	Submitter Handle	HAN
ALFA Latin American 2 population MAF	ALFA_LEN	Organism	ORGN
ALFA Other population MAF	ALFA_OTR	Reference SNP ID	RS
ALFA South Asian population MAF	ALFA_SAS	SNP Class	SCLS
All Fields	ALL	SNP Index	SIDX
Chromosome	CHR	Submitter SNP ID	SS
Clinical Significance	CLIN	UID	UID
Base Position	CPOS	Validation Status	VALI
Base Position Previous	CPOS_GRCH37	Allele	VARI
Filter	FILT	Text Word	WORD
Function Class	FXN		

TABLE 3.23 Function Classes of dbSNP [FUNCTION_CLASS]

Function Class	Description
"3 prime utr"	3` untranslated regions of the gene
"5 prime utr"	5` untranslated regions of the gene
"coding sequence"	Protein coding sequence of the gene
"downstream transcript"	The direction of transcription of the gene
"frame shift"	The SNP results in frame shift and alters the protein sequence
"genic downstream transcript"	The downstream direction of transcription of the gene
"genic upstream transcript"	The upstream direction of transcription of the gene
"inframe deletion"	SNP results in a deletion of an amino acid from a protein sequence
"inframe indel"	SNP results in an insertion or deletion of an amino acid in a protein sequence
"inframe insertion"	SNP results in insertion of deletion of an amino acid in a protein sequence
"initiator codon variant"	Insertion of an amino acid in a protein sequence
"Introns"	non-coding region of a gene
"Missense variant"	SNP results in a different amino acid in a protein sequence
"non coding transcript variant"	SNP in non-coding region of a gene
"Nonsense variant"	SNP results in a premature stop codon that truncate a protein sequence
"splice acceptor"	The site at the 3' end of an intron of a gene
"splice donor"	The site at the 5' end of an intron of a gene
"stop gained"	SNP results in a new stop codon that alters the protein sequence
"stop lost"	SNP results in abnormal extension of a protein that alters the protein
"Synonymous"	SNP in an exon but protein is not modified (synonymous substitution)
"terminator codon variant"	Stop codon variant
"upstream transcript"	The upstream direction of the transcription

TABLE 3.24 Variation Classes of dbSNP [SNPCLASS]

Variation Class	Description
Del	Deletion
Delins	Deletion and insertion
Ins	Insertion
Mnv	two or more nearby variants
SNV	Single nucleotide variant

The dbSNP results page for the above query may show thousands of missense variants reported in BRCA1 gene. The results page is a typical Entrez results page. The filters on the right side of the page provide an efficient way to narrow the results to a specific filter. Moreover, you can use the dbSNP Advanced Search Builder to build an advanced query using indexed fields and their indexed values. In case of the BRCA1 gene, it is known that some of the missense variants in this gene lead to translated proteins that do not perform their tumor suppression function; therefore, those missense variations may be responsible for tumorigenesis and they are considered as driver mutations of breast cancers [43]. You can narrow the results of the above search query by adding the clinical significance indexed field [CLIN] to narrow the results to a clinical significance (e.g., benign) by using the following query:

brca1[GENE] AND "Missense variant"[FXN] AND benign[CLIN]

The dbSNP results will show the dbSNP records of missense variants in the BRCA1 gene that are associated with benign breast cancer.

Searching dbSNP by SNP Class   The SNP class defines the type of sequence mutation. Table 3.24 contains the SNP classes that can be used as search terms with [SNPCLASS] or [SCLS] to refine dbSNP search results.

Assume that you wish to find the dbSNP records of deletion variants in BRCA1 that have benign clinical significance. You can use the following query:

brca1[GENE] AND del[SCLS] AND benign[CLIN]

The dbSNP results will include only the deletion variants in BRCA1 that are associated with benign breast cancer.

Searching dbSNP by ALFA and MAF   You can filter the dbSNP search results with ALFA (Allele Frequency Aggregator) frequency by adding the "alfa[VALI]" term to the search query. The dbSNP records that are validated by ALFA will have a filter "by-ALFA" added under Validation Status. You can also filter the dbSNP records with a range of GMAF (Global Minor Allele Frequency) by using the tagged term [GMAF].

Assume that you wish to find the dbSNP records of missense variants in the BRCA1 gene that have benign clinical significance and were validated by ALFA and identified as rare alleles with GMAF ranging between 1 and 5% (GMAF 1–5%) based on ALFA. To find such records you can use the following search query:

brca1[GENE] AND "Missense variant"[FXN] AND benign[CLIN] AND by alfa[VALI] AND 0.01:0.05[GMAF]

The dbSNP search results page shows that there are 21 records that meet the criteria set by the above search query. Notice that MAF frequencies were computed based on several projects.

The dbSNP results page displays the dbSNP accession, variant type, alleles and flanking region, chromosome (chromosome number, variant position, and reference genome), canonical SPDI, gene symbol, functional consequence, clinical significance, validation, MAF, and HGVS of each record as described below.

- The dbSNP id is the accession of the reference variant.
- Variant type indicates the variant types, which can be one of the types shown in Table 3.24.
- Alleles indicate the alleles in the human subject. The alleles for the record shown in Figure 3.45 is heterzygous C (Cytosine) and T (Thymine) in the position 43094464 on chromosome 17. The base in the same position in the reference genome is T. The alleles are presented as T>C (i.e. T was substituted by C in the human subject). The SNV flanks are viewed showing the affected position in red.
- Chromosome shows the chromosome number and position of the variant in the current and previous reference human genome assembly. In the example, the exact position of the SNV is in the chromosome 17, position 43094464 of GRCh38 genome assembly (the current reference human genome) and in the chromosome 17, position 41246481 of GRCh37 genome assembly (the previous reference human genome).
- Canonical SPDI [44] also describes the position of the variant. SPDI, which is pronounced "speedy", defines a variant as a sequence of four operations: start at the boundary before the first position in the sequence S, advance P positions, delete D positions, and then insert the sequence in the string I. The position of the example SNV is described by the canonical SPDI as NC_000017.11:43094463:T:C.
- The gene shows the gene symbol and a link to display the variants on the Variation Viewer (Figure 3.46). The position of the dbSNP variant (rs1799950) is indicated by the blue marker.
- Functional consequence shows the consequence of the variant on the translated protein.
- Clinical significance indicates the clinical significance of the variant.
- Validated shows the method used to validate the variant (validated by MAF or by cluster).

FIGURE 3.45   Part of dbSNP research page.

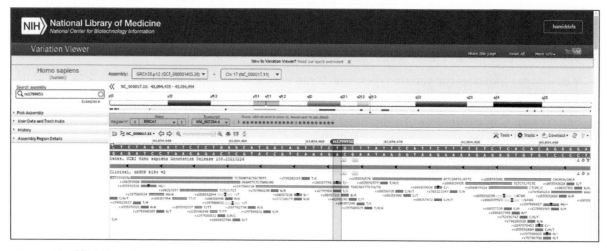

FIGURE 3.46   Variation viewer.

- The MAF section shows MAFs calculated by different projects. MAF (ALFA) is based on data aggregated from dbGaP database and MAF(1000Genomes) is based on data aggregated from 1000Genomes and so on. MAF (ALFA) of C=0.064611/9452 means that the minor allele is C for that particular locus; 0.064611 is the frequency of the C allele (MAF), i.e., 6.4611% within the ALFA dataset; and 9452 is the number of times this SNP has been observed in the population covered by ALFA. For MAF based on 1000Genomes project, C=0.021765/109 (1000Genomes); the MAF is 2.1765%; this minor allele has been observed only 109 times in the 1000Genomes population. The same for MAF based on other populations. MAF reflects the risk in a population.

- The HGVS (Human Genome Variation Society) field shows the variant according to the HGVS nomenclature (e.g., NC_000017.11:g.43094464T>C); where "NC_000017.11" is the chromosome accession

TABLE 3.25   Reference Sequence Types and Prefixes

Type	Abbreviation	Prefix Description
DNA	g.	Linear genomic RefSeq sequence
	c.	Coding RefSeq sequence
	m.	Mitochondrial RefSeq sequence
	n.	Non-coding DNA RefSeq sequence
	o.	Circular genomic RefSeq sequence
RNA	r.	RNA RefSeq sequence
Protein	p.	Protein RefSeq sequence

number; "g" for indicating that reference sequence is genomic; 43094464 is the variant position; "T" is the major allele, and "C" is the minor allele.

HGVS [45] is the society that developed the standards for describing the mutations in the sequences to avoid confusion. The general format of HGVS expression is "accession:sequence_type:variant_description". The accession is the accession of the reference sequence, the colon ":" is used as a separator, the sequence type is represented by a single letter and a dot "." as shown in Table 3.25, and the variant_description is the expression that describes the position and the change (mutation) in the sequence. Table 3.25 shows the reference sequence types and their abbreviations.

The genomic reference DNA abbreviation (g.) can be a linear DNA molecule based on a recent genome build (e.g., NC_000011.10), gene-based genomic reference sequence (NG_) that includes all known exons and covers all gene transcript, or coding DNA reference sequence if the complete gene reference sequence is not available. The coding DNA reference sequence (c.) includes the coding DNA sequence (CDS) and the 5` and 3` UTR regions of the gene and does include intron or 5` and 3` gene flanking sequences. It is important to pay attention that the location of a variant may be different based on the orientation of a genomic or a coding DNA reference sequence (minus or plus strand). The circular genomic reference DNA sequences (o.) include chloroplast sequences, plasmid sequence, and viral sequences. The mitochondrial reference DNA sequences (m.) are a special type of circular genomic reference sequences. The non-coding DNA reference sequences (n.) include non-coding reference sequences, which should be complete sequences that cover the major parts. The RNA reference sequences (r.) must include the entire transcript excluding the poly A-tail. The protein reference sequence (p.) should correspond exactly to the associated DNA and RNA reference sequence used. The reference sequence must represent the primary translation product of a gene not a final mature protein. The sequence also should include the starting Methionine and any other signal peptide sequences.

dbSNP Record Page

These elements are on the dbSNP results page that contains multiple records displayed in summary format. Click on a dbSNP accession to open a dbSNP record page. The dbSNP record page includes the same information we discussed above but with more details. It consists of three main sections as shown in Figure 3.47: (a) summary section, (b) report tabs, and (c) Variation Viewer.

dbSNP Summary Section   The dbSNP summary section includes the same information we discussed above. It includes the dbSNP accession of the variant, organism, variant position, alleles, variant type, frequency of minor allele based on several projects, clinical significance, gene and consequences, publications cited the variant, and a link to the Genomic Viewer displaying the variant.

Report Section   The report is divided into eight vertical tabs as shown in Figure 3.48: Variants Details, Clinical Significance, Frequency, HGVS, Submissions, History, Publications, and Flanks. These tabs as follows:

FIGURE 3.47   dbSNP record page (rs1799950).

Variant Details   The variant details tab as shown in Figure 3.48 provides detailed information about the variant. First, on the top, it provides the Genomic Placements table, which displays the reference sequence name and the subject sequence change described with HGVS nomenclature [45] as explained above. Secondly, it provides a table that contains all the gene transcripts and proteins and the change occurred on these gene products due to the dbSNP variant.

You can notice that the BRCA1 gene has six transcript variants due to the alternative splicing that produce six BRCA1 protein isoforms. However, the dbSNP variant (rs1799950) occurred in the protein coding sequences (exon) of the BRCA1 transcript variant 1, 2, and 3 while it occurred in the non-protein region (intron) of the BRCA1 transcript 4, 5, and 6. Therefore, this variant (SNV) had impact only on BRCA1 protein isoform 1, 2, and 3. The change is described with HGVS nomenclature. For example, NM_007294.4:c.1067A>G describes that in the position "1067" in the reference transcript with the accession NM_007294.4, which represents a coding sequence (c), the base is A (Adenine) but in the transcript sequence of the subject individual is G (Guanine). Notice that "g" in the HGVS nomenclature indicates "genomic sequence", "c" indicates "coding sequence", "n" indicates "non-coding sequence", and "p" indicates protein sequences", where the change took place. That change had consequence in the translated amino acid, which described as Q [CAG] > R [CGG], which indicates that the codon in the reference transcript sequence is CAG that codes for Q (Glutamine) while the codon in the transcript sequence of the subject individual is CGG, which codes for R (Arginine). The SO term column is used to sort the contents.

Variant Details	Genomic Placements		❓
Clinical Significance	**Sequence name** ▲	**Change**	
Frequency	BRCA1 RefSeqGene (LRG_292)	NG_005905.2:g.123520A>G	
HGVS	GRCh37.p13 chr 17	NC_000017.10:g.41246481T>C	
Submissions	GRCh38.p12 chr 17	NC_000017.11:g.43094464T>C	

Gene: BRCA1, BRCA1 DNA repair associated (minus strand)

Molecule type ▲	Change	Amino acid[Codon]	SO Term
BRCA1 transcript variant 1	NM_007294.4:c.1067A>G	Q [CAG] > R [CGG]	Coding Sequence Variant
BRCA1 transcript variant 2	NM_007300.4:c.1067A>G	Q [CAG] > R [CGG]	Coding Sequence Variant
BRCA1 transcript variant 3	NM_007297.4:c.926A>G	Q [CAG] > R [CGG]	Coding Sequence Variant
BRCA1 transcript variant 4	NM_007298.3:c.787+280A>G	N/A	Intron Variant
BRCA1 transcript variant 5	NM_007299.4:c.787+280A>G	N/A	Intron Variant
BRCA1 transcript variant 6	NR_027676.2:n.1244A>G	N/A	Non Coding Transcript Variant
breast cancer type 1 susceptibility protein isoform 1	NP_009225.1:p.Gln356Arg	Q (Gln) > R (Arg)	Missense Variant
breast cancer type 1 susceptibility protein isoform 2	NP_009231.2:p.Gln356Arg	Q (Gln) > R (Arg)	Missense Variant
breast cancer type 1 susceptibility protein isoform 3	NP_009228.2:p.Gln309Arg	Q (Gln) > R (Arg)	Missense Variant

FIGURE 3.48   Variant details of dbSNP record (rs1799950).

Allele: C (allele ID: 50242)

ClinVar Accession ▲	Disease Names	Clinical Significance
RCV000034725.6	not provided	Benign
RCV000047326.9	Hereditary breast and ovarian cancer syndrome	Benign-Likely-Benign
RCV000111539.8	Breast-ovarian cancer, familial 1	Benign
RCV000120281.12	not specified	Benign
RCV000132455.4	Hereditary cancer-predisposing syndrome	Benign
RCV000207264.1	Ductal breast carcinoma	Uncertain-Significance
RCV000462965.1	Familial cancer of breast	Benign

Variant Details
Clinical Significance
Frequency
HGVS
Submissions
History
Publications
Flanks

FIGURE 3.49   Clinical significance of the dbSNP variant (rs1799950).

Clinical Significance   The clinical significance tab as shown in Figure 3.49 provides a table that lists the ClinVar accession, disease names, and clinical significance associated with the dbSNP variant. The ClinVar is an NCBI database for the genetic variation associated with clinical condition, and will be discussed in the next section. The current dbSNP SNV in BRCA1 is associated with benign hereditary breast and ovarian cancer, breast ovarian cancer, and ductal breast carcinoma.

Variant Details	**ALFA Allele Frequency (New)**				

Variant Details

Clinical Significance

Frequency

HGVS

Submissions

History

Publications

Flanks

ALFA Allele Frequency (New)

The ALFA project provide aggregate allele frequency from dbGaP. More information is available on the project page including descriptions, data access, and terms of use.

Release Version: 20201027095038

Search: [   ]

Population	Group	Sample Size	Ref Allele	Alt Allele
Total	Global	319072	T=0.936575	C=0.063425
European	Sub	273012	T=0.931699	C=0.068301
African	Sub	8662	T=0.9857	C=0.0143
African Others	Sub	304	T=0.997	C=0.003
African American	Sub	8358	T=0.9853	C=0.0147
Asian	Sub	6908	T=1.0000	C=0.0000
East Asian	Sub	4954	T=1.0000	C=0.0000
Other Asian	Sub	1954	T=1.0000	C=0.0000
Latin American 1	Sub	1396	T=0.9527	C=0.0473
Latin American 2	Sub	6666	T=0.9656	C=0.0344
South Asian	Sub	368	T=0.981	C=0.019
Other	Sub	22060	T=0.94723	C=0.05277

FIGURE 3.50   Allele frequency of a dbSNP record (rs1799950).

Frequency   The frequency tab as shown in Figure 3.50 provides a report about the major and minor allele frequencies of global and regional populations based on the ALFA project. Such information is used to obtain a clear picture of the major and minor allele frequencies in a specific regional population such as Africans, Asian, European, etc., and in the overall population. When a variant is associated with a disease or a health condition, the minor allele frequency describes the risk factor. Several projects conducted this kind of genomic study, other than ALFA projects, that computed the minor allele frequency of certain populations. Those projects include 1000Genomes [46], GnomAD [47], ExAC [48], TopMed [49], and others.

The table contains Population (ancestry group), Group (global/sub), Sample size (the number of human subjects in the study), Reference Allele (the allele and the major allele frequency), and Alt Allele (the alternative allele and the minor allele frequency). A large sample size usually provides more confidence on the frequency. The minor allele (C) of dbSNP SNV (rs1799950) is more prevalent in European (C=0.068301) than other populations. Therefore, we can expect that presence of this SNV on the BRCA1 gene of a European woman is more likely to have a role in benign breast cancer. However, there was no evidence that this variant exists in Asian woman (C=0.0000).

HGVS   The HGVS tab as shown in Figure 3.51 describes the dbSNP variant placements and allele changes on genomic, transcript and protein sequences using HGVS nomenclature as discussed above. The Placement column shows the name of the sequence (RefSeqGene or Transcript variants), the second column shows the position of the reference allele, and the third column shows the position and change (alternative change). Notice that the (A>G) is the same as (T>C) because of the complementary nature of the DNA strands.

Submission   The submissions tab includes information about the variant data submitted to the dbSNP. The information includes submitter handle, submission identifier, and date and Build number.

Placement	T=	C
BRCA1 RefSeqGene (LRG_292)	NG_005905.2:g.123520=	NG_005905.2:g.123520A>G
BRCA1 transcript variant 1	NM_007294.4:c.1067=	NM_007294.4:c.1067A>G
BRCA1 transcript variant 1	NM_007294.3:c.1067=	NM_007294.3:c.1067A>G
BRCA1 transcript variant 2	NM_007300.4:c.1067=	NM_007300.4:c.1067A>G
BRCA1 transcript variant 2	NM_007300.3:c.1067=	NM_007300.3:c.1067A>G
BRCA1 transcript variant 3	NM_007297.4:c.926=	NM_007297.4:c.926A>G
BRCA1 transcript variant 3	NM_007297.3:c.926=	NM_007297.3:c.926A>G
BRCA1 transcript variant 4	NM_007298.3:c.787+280=	NM_007298.3:c.787+280A>G
BRCA1 transcript variant 5	NM_007299.3:c.787+280=	NM_007299.3:c.787+280A>G
BRCA1 transcript variant 5	NM_007299.4:c.787+280=	NM_007299.4:c.787+280A>G
BRCA1 transcript variant 6	NR_027676.2:n.1244=	NR_027676.2:n.1244A>G
BRCA1 transcript variant 6	NR_027676.1:n.1203=	NR_027676.1:n.1203A>G

FIGURE 3.51   HGVS names of the dbSNP variant (rs1799950).

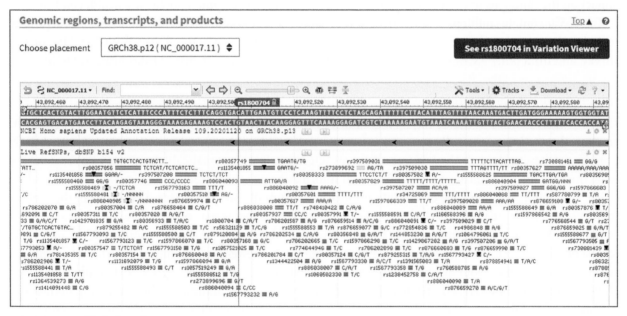

FIGURE 3.52   Variation viewer.

History   The history tab displays RefSNPs from previous builds (Build) that now support the current RefSNP, and the dates in which the history was updated for each associated ID.

Publications   The publications tab displays PubMed articles citing the variation. The information displayed include PMID, Title, Author, Year, and Journal.

Flanks   The Flanks tab provides retrieving flanking sequences of a dbSNP on all molecules that have placements.

Genome Viewer   The Genome Viewer (Figure 3.52) at the bottom of the dbSNP record page displays the genomic regions, transcript, and proteins and the variant position on each of those sequences. The type of the reference sequences is chosen from the Choose Placement dropdown menu. The position of the selected variant is indicated by a blue marker.

DBVAR DATABASE

The Database of Genomic Structural Variation (dbVar) [50] is similar to dbSNP but it is for human genomic variations that are larger than 50 bp. Such variations may include Insertion/Deletion (INDEL), deletion, duplication, copy number variation (CNV), translocations, or inversions.

Insertion and deletion cause shift of the protein coding frame and result in garbled mRNA. The genomic DNA duplication is another source of variation in genomic sequences. A region of a chromosome may be copied several times and added to the genome sequence. A region of the chromosome may also be inverted or translocated to a different region. The duplicate or the affected region may encompass thousands to hundreds of thousands of bases. Such alteration of genome may cause variation in length of the genes and genome among individuals; therefore it is known as copy number variation (CNV). Sometimes, the copy number variants include a duplicate gene or several genes, which may affect the level of gene expression and consequently the phenotype and may cause diseases. A duplicate adjacent to the original region is known as a tandem duplicate. A duplicate sequence may also be a displaced sequence separated by non-duplicated nucleotides from the original sequence. CNVs are also known as structural variation (SV).

Such large-scale genomic variants have more significance than the dbSNP variants as they may have more impact on the functions of the affected proteins, disrupt normal development or cause a health condition.

The dbVar contains millions of such structural variants from thousands of human subjects. Several projects contributed to this database, including the 1000 Genomes Project, gnomAD, and the CNV Global Population Survey, and from other NCBI databases such as ClinVar as well as variants shared from EBI and DDBJ.

Submission to dbVar Database

The variants submitted to the dbVar database must be human variants of length greater than 50 bp and with no clinical assertion or clinically sensitive information. Variants with clinical assertion are submitted to the ClinVar database and the dbVar will import the structural variants automatically from the ClinVar database. Also, the variants with sensitive personal clinical information are submitted to the dbGaP database and the dbVar will import the aggregate of variants automatically from dbGaP. The asserted positions of the variants submitted to dbVar are preferable to be on a reference sequence that is part of one of the NCBI assemblies to be remapped to the most recent assembly versions and distributed with the dbVar monthly release and will be represented graphically in the Genomic Viewer and Variation Viewer. The submitted structural variant with asserted position on an assembly not housed by NCBI will not be mapped or represented graphically on any of the NCBI graphic viewers. For detailed guidelines visit: www.ncbi.nlm.nih.gov/dbvar/content/submission/.

Three forms of data are submitted to dbVar: (1) variants as part of studies (STD), (2) variant regions (SV), and (3) variant calls (SSV):

(1) *STD*. Structural variants that have been submitted as part of a coherent study and performed by the same author around the same time will be prefixed with "nstd", "estd", and "dstd" if they are submitted to NCBI, EBI, and DDBJ, respectively.

(2) *SV*. The variant region is a region of a genome identified by the submitter as a structural variant. The SV identifiers are prefixed with "nsv", "rsv", and "dsv" if they are submitted to NCBI, EBI, and DDBJ, respectively.

(3) *SSV*. The variant calls are the structural variants that were observed in a study based on output of raw data analysis. They include several types of structural variations such as duplication, INDEL, inversion, translocation sequence alteration, tandem repeat, etc. The identifiers of variant calls will be prefixed as "nssv", "essv", and "dssv" if they are submitted to NCBI, EBI, and DDBJ, respectively.

To submit structural variations to the dbVar database, follow the same steps discussed for dbSNP. However, you need to email the files to dbvar@ncbi.nlm.nih.gov.

Structural Variant Representation

Since the structural variants are large variants, their representation is complex because of their length and breakpoints, which are approximated most of the time. Such approximation may raise uncertainty. Thus, the graphical representation of the dbVar structural variants reflects that approximation uncertainty, which is described using a set of coordinates and color keys. The dbVar variant graphical representation is used in graphic viewers, such as Variation Viewer and Genome Viewer. The keys to understand the graphic representation are also provided with the viewer.

The following are some visual representations of the variants:

- When the breakpoints of a variant are known, the variant is represented graphically as a solid bar.
- When the actual breakpoints of a variant are unknown, but the region affected by the variation is known, the variant is represented graphically as a dark solid bar defining the affected region and lighter region outside the dark region defining the breakpoints.
- When the breakpoints are undefined, but the inner bounds are known, the variant is represented by a solid bar with triangles pointing away.
- When the breakpoints are undefined, but the outer bounds are known, the variant will be represented graphically as a solid bar with triangles pointing inward.

For more details of graphical representation of dbVar structural variants, visit the web page at www.ncbi.nlm.nih.gov/dbvar/content/overview/.

Searching dbVar

The dbVar web page is available at www.ncbi.nlm.nih.gov/dbvar/ or the dbVar can be chosen from the drop-down list on main Entrez database website. Table 3.26 contains the dbVar indexed fields. Refer to the dbVar Advanced Search Builder to display the indexed values for some of the indexed fields.

Continuing searching for variants in the BRCA1 gene, assume that you wish to find the dbVar structural variants reported in BRCA1 that have clinical interpretation. You can use the indexed fields to build an advanced query that includes those pieces of information (gene name and whether the SV has clinical interpretation) or you can use the dbVar Advanced Search Builder to do the same. To find the dbVar structural variants as described above, you can use the following search query:

BRCA1[GENE_NAME] AND 1[HASCLIN]

The search results will include hundreds of records of dbVar variants that have clinical interpretation. The dbVar search results page is a typical search results page of an Entrez database. You can use the "Send To" menu to download the summary or the identifier list of the dbVar hits. Remember that filters are provided on the most Entrez results pages to help searchers to narrow the results to a specific category.

When searching dbVar, you should remember that there are three types of records (STD, SV, and SSV) as explained above. You may think to retrieve the dbVar records that are associated with study records. Assume that you are interested in finding the dbVar study variants in the BRCA1 gene and those variants have clinical interpretation. You can use the following query for that:

BRCA1[GENE] AND 1[HASCLIN] AND "STUDY"[OT]

TABLE 3.26   dbVar Indexed Fields

Long Field Name	Short Field Name	Long Field Name	Short Field Name
Accession	ACC	MeSH ID	MHID
Allele Frequency in Africans	AFR	OMIM	MIM
Age of Subject	AGE	Organism	ORG
All Fields	ALL	Object Type	OT
Origin	ALLELE_ORIGIN	Allele Frequency in Others	OTH
Allele Frequency in Americans	AMR	Pathogenic Overlap Range	PATHO_RNG
Assembly	ASSM	Publication Date	PDAT
Author	AUTH	Population	POP
ChrPos	BASE	BioProject	PROJ
Chr	CH	Publication	PUBMED_ID
ChrEnd	CHR_END	Allele Frequency in S. Asians	SAS
Clinical Interpretation	CLIN	Sample Count	SC
Clinical Phenotype	DISEASE	Sample	SMPL
Allele Frequency in East Asians	EAS	Study	STDY
Allele Frequency in Europeans	EUR	Study Type	STYPE
Filter	FILT	Subject Phenotype status	SUBPSTAT
Global Allele Frequency	FREQ	Taxonomy ID	TAX
Sex of Subject	GENDER	UID	UID
Gene	GENE_NAME	Variant Size	VLEN
Has Clinical Interpretation (0,1)	HASCLIN	Variant Type	VT
Method Type	METH	Zygosity	ZYG
MeSH	MH		

FIGURE 3.53   dbVar search results page.

The search results returned only five studies as shown in Figure 3.53. The tabular view of the search results page displays a table listing the dbVar identifiers, organism, study types, number of variants in the study, and cited publication.

A dbVar study variant page will include detailed information of the study (variant summary, sample sets, experimental details, and validations) as well as remapping summary.

More often, you may wish to search for dbVar variants that are associated with a specific disease. For example, it is known that the autism spectrum disorders have associations with some structural variants in

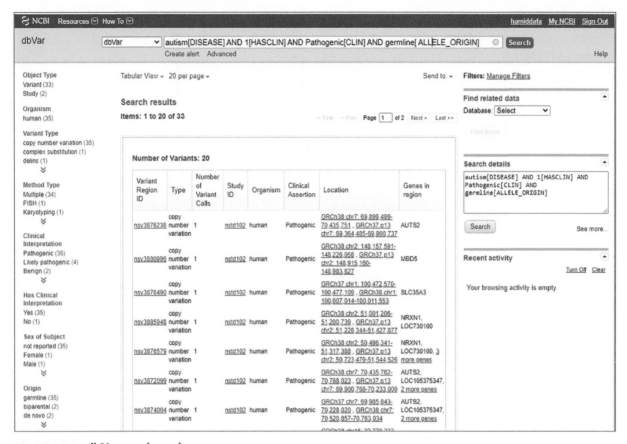

FIGURE 3.54   dbVar search results page.

some genes [51]. Assume that you are looking for dbVar structural variants that are associated with autism and known for their pathogenic clinical interpretation and allelic origin; you can use the following query:

autism[DISEASE] AND 1[HASCLIN] AND Pathogenic[CLIN] AND germline[ALLELE_ORIGIN]

The above search query is useful when your goal is to find variants that are associated with a specific disease without specifying a gene name. The results will include the variants in all affected genes as shown in Figure 3.54, which displays the variants records associated with autism in the dbVar database. The tabular view of the results page displays a table listing the variant region id, type of variant, number of variant calls, study id, location, and the affected genes. Notice that a structural variant may extend to multiple genes.

The dbVar Record Page

Clicking on "variant region id" of any record will open the dbVar page of that record. Click on the id of the first item to open the record page. The dbVar record page (Figure 3.55) shows detailed information about the variant region. At the top of the page, you will find summary information about the structural variant, chromosome ideograms highlighting the chromosome and the position on the chromosome where the variant is located, and links to other NCBI resources.

At the bottom of the dbVar record page, there are detailed reports divided into five horizontal tabs: Genome View, Variant Region Details and Evidence, Validation Information, Clinical Assertions, and Genotype Information.

The Genome View tab displays, on Sequence Viewer, the location of the current variant and other variants mapped to that part of the reference genome. The Assembly dropdown menu provides options to select other

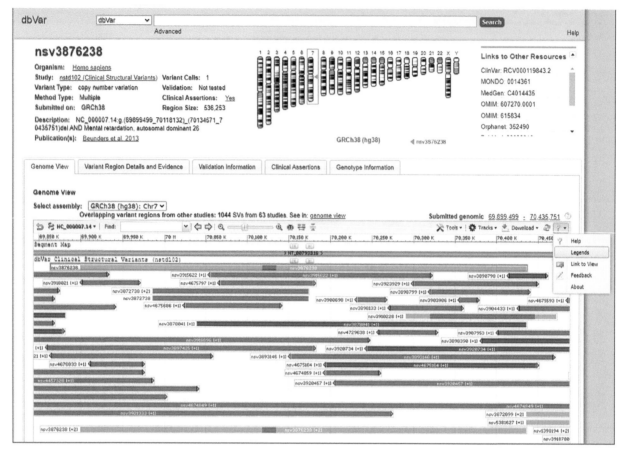

FIGURE 3.55   A dbVar record page.

available assemblies. The solid blue bar on the top represents the segment of the assembly sequence to which variants are mapped. The others graphical parts of the Sequence Viewer are manageable tracks that represent annotations, and they can be added or removed, and they can also be moved up and down by holding the mouse on the track and drag it up or down.

The dbVar (Clinical Structural Variants) track that displays the structural variants is mapped to this segment of the reference sequence. However, the first bar in the dbVar track is representing the variant reported on the current dbVar record page. Notice that the current page is for "nsv3876238", which is represented by first light red bar with a dark red region in the middle indicating the affected region as explained above. The dbVar id is presented next to the bar. You can also use the help menu on the top right corner (as shown in Figure 3.55) of the Genome Viewer and click on Legends to display the legends that will help you interpret the graphical presentations of the mapped structural variants.

The Variant Regional Details and Evidence tab (Figure 3.56) contains three tables as follows:

1   Variant Region Placement Information includes detailed information about the variant mapping and placement on the current and previous genome assembly (e.g., chromosome, start position and end position of the variant, inner and outer bound of the affected region, etc.).

2   The Variant Call Information table displays the information of supporting variant calls that were merged to define the variant region. It also displays the subject phenotype, clinical interpretation, source of interpretation, and link to the ClinVar database if available.

3   The Variant Call Placement Information table displays the variant placement information (coordinates) on the current and previous genome assemblies. Notice that the placement of the variants is also described by HGVS nomenclature.

Genome View | Variant Region Details and Evidence | Validation Information | Clinical Assertions | Genotype Information

Variant Region Placement Information

Variant Region ID	Placement Type	Score	Assembly	Assembly Unit	Reciprocity	Sequence ID	Chr	Outer Start	Inner Start	Inner Stop	Outer Stop
nsv3876238	Submitted genomic		GRCh38 (hg38)	Primary Assembly		NC_000007.14	Chr7	69,899,499	70,118,132	70,134,571	70,435,751
nsv3876238	Remapped	Perfect	GRCh37.p13	Primary Assembly	First Pass	NC_000007.13	Chr7	69,364,485	69,583,118	69,599,557	69,900,737

Variant Call Information

Variant Call ID	Type	Method	Analysis	Subject Phenotype	Clinical Interpretation	Source of Interpretation	ClinVar ID
nssv15119417	deletion	Multiple	Multiple	Autism spectrum disorder due to AUTS2 deficiency; MENTAL RETARDATION, AUTOSOMAL DOMINANT 26; MRD26; Mental retardation, autosomal dominant 26	Pathogenic	ClinVar	RCV000119843.2

Variant Call Placement Information

Variant Call ID	Placement Type	Score	HGVS	Assembly	Reciprocity	Sequence ID	Chr	Outer Start	Inner Start	Inner Stop	Outer Stop
nssv15119417	Submitted genomic		NC_000007.14:g.(69899499_70118132)_(70134571_70435751)del	GRCh38 (hg38)		NC_000007.14	Chr7	69,899,499	70,118,132	70,134,571	70,435,751
nssv15119417	Remapped	Perfect	NC_000007.13:g.(69364485_69583118)_(69599557_69900737)del	GRCh37.p13	First Pass	NC_000007.13	Chr7	69,364,485	69,583,118	69,599,557	69,900,737

FIGURE 3.56 Variant region details and evidence tab.

Genome View | Variant Region Details and Evidence | Validation Information | Clinical Assertions | Genotype Information

Clinical Assertions

Variant Call ID	HGVS	Type	Allele Origin	Subject Phenotype	Clinical Interpretation	Source of Interpretation	ClinVar ID
nssv15119417	GRCh38: NC_000007.14:g.(69899499_70118132)_(70134571_70435751)del	deletion	germline	Autism spectrum disorder due to AUTS2 deficiency; MENTAL RETARDATION, AUTOSOMAL DOMINANT 26; MRD26; Mental retardation, autosomal dominant 26	Pathogenic	ClinVar	RCV000119843.2

FIGURE 3.57 Clinical assertions.

The Validation Information tab provides the details of the methods and analyses used to validate the structural variant if another validation method was used.

The Clinical Assertions tab (Figure 3.57) includes the details of the established association between a variant call and a phenotype observed in the subject. If during a study an association was established between a variant call and a phenotype observed in a subject, details will be provided in this table. The information includes variant call ID, HGVS coordinates, variant type, allele origin (germline or somatic), phenotype, clinical interpretation, and ClinVar ID.

The Genotype Information tab provides information about the genotype related to the variant if it is present.

CLINVAR DATABASE

ClinVar is a public and free accessible NCBI database for the storing and retrieving of reports of the relationships among human genotypic variations and phenotypes with supporting evidence [52].

Protein-coding genes are transcribed into transcripts (mRNA), which are translated into proteins that do most of the work in cells and are required for the structure, function, and regulation of the body's tissues and organs. The level of an expression of a gene is regulated by complex processes and factors collectively known as the regulatory pathway of a gene. There are thousands of genes in a living organism. The Human Genome Project has estimated that humans have between 20,000 and 25,000 genes. The same set of genes is present in the genomes of all somatic cells of an organism except red blood cells in complex organisms like mammals. However, only subsets of genes will be on in a cell or cells of tissues or an organ to accommodate the biological functions of the cells. The gene expression is regulated by turning genes off and on to produce the required level of protein amounts. The dysfunction of a gene due to mutations may cause a cascade effect that leads to a health disorder or a disease (phenotype). Numerous projects and studies focus on finding the association between genetic variations and phenotypes and several databases are focused on disease-causing mutations and resulting diseases or phenotypic abnormalities. Several disorders such as autism, cancer, sickle cells, and many other diseases have been reported to be associated with mutations of certain genes. The databases that store such associations play a crucial role in biomedical and life science research, as they provide assistance in assigning pathogenicity to genetic variants [53].

The ClinVar database was created to contain information about the relationship between genotypic variants and phenotypes among human with evidence including the significance of a disease symptom. The goal of ClinVar is to facilitate computational re-evaluation and to support ongoing methods that depend on extracting knowledge from variant-condition association.

Submitting Data to ClinVar

Information on the genotype–phenotype relationship is submitted by concerned organizations to the ClinVar database. The submitted information includes genetic variants found in patient samples, the significance of clinical symptoms associated with those variants, and supporting evidence. For submitting data to ClinVar, your organization must be registered in the Submission Portal. ClinVar only accepts submissions from organizations such as clinics, research labs, and genomic databases. Data submitted to ClinVar will be available to the public without restriction. The data submitted to ClinVar are variant-level interpretations of the clinical or functional significance of a variant along with their supporting evidence. The supporting evidence can be aggregate data resulted from affected subjects versus unaffected subjects or case data of each anonymous individual with the variant to abide by NCBI guidelines. Upon submission, you will be asked for submitter information, a valid description of the variant (HGVS expression, chromosome coordinate and change, cytogenetic description), conditions, interpretations (clinical or functional), data collection method, allele origin (germline or somatic), and the status of the subject (affected or not affected). The submitted data can be prepared in spreadsheet, csv, or XML file format. Submission template files and detailed guidelines are available at www.ncbi.nlm.nih.gov/clinvar/docs/submit/. Once you have prepared your submission files, use the submission wizard and follow the instructions.

ClinVar will analyze the content of submission and will validate the variants with either a manual check by the staff or with automated checks using NCBI Variation Services available at https://api.ncbi.nlm.nih.gov/variation/v0. Variants are validated with locations described by either an HGVS expression or chromosome coordinates. The NCBI Variation Services are based on the SPDI data model for variants [54], which defines variants as a sequence of four attributes – sequence, position, deletion, and insertion – and can be applied to nucleotide and protein variants. Only variants that pass the validation will be processed. The result of the analysis and validation is either acceptance or rejection of the submission or returning to the submitter for reviewing. The passed submission will be given an accession number with the format SCV000000000.0. Similar submissions with similar variation/condition (genotype/phenotype) pairs are clustered within ClinVar's data flow and given a reference accession with the format RCV000000000.0. It is possible for a single record to be included in multiple RCV reference accessions. The variants described in the submission are mapped to a reference sequence and reported according to HGVS standards [55].

Searching ClinVar Database

The ClinVar webpage is available at www.ncbi.nlm.nih.gov/clinvar/ or the database can be accessed by selecting ClinVar from the database dropdown menu on the main Entrez database web page. The database is searched as other Entrez database by entering a simple or an advanced search query into the search box. Details of building search queries have been described above. Table 3.27 contains the indexed fields that can be used to build advanced search queries.

The following are some examples for ClinVar searching:

TABLE 3.27 ClinVar Indexed Fields

Long Field Name	Short Field Name	Long Field Name	Short Field Name
ClinVar accession	ACCN	Modification Date	MDAT
Nucleotide/Protein Accession	ACCN	MIM	MIM
AlleleID	ALID	Organism	ORGN
All Fields	ALL	Origin	ORIG
Base Position for Assembly GRCh38	C38	PubMed ID	PMID
Creation Date	CDAT	Properties	PROP
Chromosome	CHR	Replaced Variation ID	RPLD
Date of last change	CLINSIG	Review status	RVST
Complexity	CMPL	Submitter	SBM
Combination Variation ID	COMB	Submitter Batch	SID
Base Position	CPOS	Study Name	STNM
Canonical SPDI	CSPDI	Taxonomy ID	TID
Cytogenetic band	CYT	Name of the ClinVar record	TITL
Disease/Phenotype	DIS	Trait identifier	TRID
Filter	FILT	UID	UID
Gene Name	GENE	Variant Accession	VACC
Gene Full Name	GFN	Variation ID	VID
Gene ID	GID	Length of the variant	VLEN
Accession for a test registered in GTR	GTRT	External allele ID	VRID
HGNC identifier for human gene	HGNC	Variant name	VRNM
Last interpreted	IMOD	Type of variation	VRTP
Molecular consequence	MCNS	Text Word	WORD

Searching for ClinVar Records in a Specified Region Often a researcher may be interested in finding the clinical conditions associated with genetic variations in a chromosome or a region of a chromosome. To do that you can use [CHR] and [C38] to specify a chromosome and a segment of the chromosome sequence, respectively. For example, assume that you wish to find the ClinVar records for the variants in the region between 43000000 and 44000000 on the human chromosome 17. You can use the following as a search query:

17 [CHR] AND 43000000:44000000[C38]

The search results for this query will include all variation/condition records submitted to the ClinVar database for the specified region of the chromosome.

Searching for ClinVar Records by a Disease The names of the clinical conditions and diseases (phenotypes) are indexed. The popular names of diseases can be used with [DIS] tagged field on a search query to limit search results to a specific disease or condition. Often, searchers may wish to find a locus, gene, or genetic variations that are associated with a specific disease. Assume that you wish to find all the genes whose variations are associated with the autism spectrum disorder and the clinical significance of the variations is confirmed as pathogenic. You can use the following search query:

"autism"[DIS] AND "clinsig pathogenic" [PROP]

The results will include all ClinVar records of the pathogenic variations associated with autism disorder. The ClinVar results page is displayed in the tabular view format by default. The table includes variation locations, genes, protein changes, conditions, clinical significance, review status, and ClinVar accessions.

Use the Download dropdown menu on the top of the results page to download a tab-delimited file containing gene names, protein changes, conditions, clinical significance, review status, accessions, chromosomes, locations, variation IDs, allele IDs, dbSNP IDs, and Canonical SPDI. The file can be opened on Excel and used for further analysis.

How you search the ClinVar database depends on what you are searching for. That would be formulated by your research goal. The above are just some examples; however, you can use the indexed fields and the ClinVar Advanced Search Builder to construct the search query to find the ClinVar records that meet your goal.

ClinVar Record Page

Clicking on the title or ClinVar accession of a record on the ClinVar search results page will open the ClinVar record page of that record. A ClinVar record page includes the following sections as illustrated in Figure 3.58:

1   *Summary section.* The summary section includes the HGVS expression that describes the variant on the reference sequence, interpretation, review status, submissions, last evaluated, variant accession, variant ID, and description. Review status provides a graphical representation of the review status (four stars: practice guideline assertion, three stars: reviewed by expert panel, two stars: criteria provided from multiple submitters, one star: criteria provided from a single submitter, and none: no assertion provided). Submission indicates the number of submission and the most recent submission date.

2   *Report tabs.* Variant reports are divided into three tabs: Variant Detail, Conditions, and Genes. The Variant Details tab provides detailed information about the variant including allele ID, variant type, variant length, cytogenetic location (location in the chromosome), location in the current and previous

FIGURE 3.58   ClinVar record page.

reference genome, HGVS expression (on current and previous chromosome sequence, current NM/NPs and RefSeqGene), canonical SPDI, functional consequence, allele frequencies, and link to other databases (e.g., dbSNP, dbVar).

The Conditions tab provides information about each condition and its aggregate interpretation, number of submissions that supported the interpretation, review status, last evaluated date, and ClinVar accession of the variation/condition.

The Genes tab provides information about the genes affected by the variants. The variants in the gene can be viewed in the Variation Viewer as discussed with dbSNP and dbVar. There is a link for the current and previous genome assembly. In the "Within gene" column, the number of variants within the gene and all variants affecting the gene are shown. Clicking on any of these numbers will open the ClinVar page that lists the variants. Most variants are SNPs, which are found within the gene, but copy number variants (CNVs) might affect more than a gene.

3 *Submitted interpretations and evidence*: This section provides a summary from the submitted records for the variant and supporting evidence. The data included in this section is not aggregated by ClinVar and it reflects the individual submitter's interpretation. The overall interpretation depends on the aggregation of interpretations in this section.

4 *Functional evidence*. The functional evidence section includes information about the supporting evidence.

5 *Citations for this variant*: The citations section displays the list of publications provided by the variant submitter and supporting the variant.

Generally, the clinical significance of a variant on the ClinVar database is evaluated by the number of submitters per condition, their aggregate interpretation, review status, evidence provided, and the number of citations. The aggregated interpretation of this ClinVar record (VCV000224713.4) is pathogenic/likely pathogenic as shown by the interpretation in the summary section.

GENE EXPRESSION OMNIBUS (GEO) DATABASE

Studying the expression level of a specific gene depends on quantifying the mRNA transcribed from that gene before the mRNA is translated into a protein. Thousands of genes are expressed to drive the various aspects of the biological activities of a living organism. Some genes are essential for basic biological activities; therefore, they are expressed in all cells of an organism. These genes are known as house-keeping genes. The expression of other genes is regulated by the need of the cells. In comparative gene expression studies, a gene expression may be described as over-expressed, under-expressed, or normally expressed depending on certain conditions. The change in the level of an expression is regulated by other genes and factors. Gene expression profiling of cells is a snapshot of gene expression at that moment in which the sample is taken. Gene expression profiling is used to study diseases and factors affecting an organism. In a study of diseases like cancers, the gene expression of the affected tissues may be compared to the gene expression of healthy tissues. Specific pattern may be discovered in gene expression under specific conditions, which may help in knowledge discovery and identification of the molecular signature of a disease or a condition. That signature is used to understand pathogenicity of a disease, drug discovery, and correlation of pharmacodynamic marker with the dose-dependent responses to a drug.

Gene expression is quantified using microarray, real-time polymerase chain reaction (RT-PCR), Serial Analysis of Gene Expression (SAGE), or high-throughput sequencing technologies (e.g., RNA-Seq). The quantification of gene expression varies depending on the technology used in the study. Microarray quantifies gene expression by capturing spot color intensity [56]. Real-time-PCR quantifies the gene expression either by absolute counting of cDNA strands or relatively by the number of fold change compared to a control sample

[57]. High-throughput sequencing and SAGE quantify the gene expression by counting the number of short reads mapped to a reference genome [58].

The Gene Expression Omnibus (GEO) [59] database is a public repository for submitting and retrieving gene expression data. Researchers submit the gene expression data to the database as supporting evidence to their publications. Most journals require that datasets of gene expression study to be submitted to a public repository before publishing. The GEO database is fully integrated with other NCBI databases and tools and the datasets can be downloaded, visualized, and analyzed.

Submitting Gene Expression Data to GEO

Three types of gene expression data are accepted by GEO. These data types include microarray data, high-throughput sequencing data, and other kinds of gene expression data such as NanoString, RT-PCR, and the traditional SAGE. You can follow the guidelines available at www.ncbi.nlm.nih.gov/geo/info/submission.html to submit any of these three types of gene expression data. The submitted data is reviewed by the NCBI curators. The accepted data will be given an accession number. There are three types of records that may be provided by submitters: Platforms, Samples, and Series. The NCBI adds a curated record type called a GEO dataset. The following are the description of each of these four types of GEO records:

- *Platform records.* Platform records are used to define the data table template for the gene list depending on the platform. Each Platform record is assigned a unique identifier called the GEO accession with the prefix "GPL". Any Geo Sample used that platform can be linked to the Platform record.
- *Sample records.* A Sample record describes the gene expression of an individual Sample. Each Sample record is assigned a unique identifier or GEO accession with prefix "GSM". A Sample record must reference only a single Platform record, but it may be included in multiple Series records.
- *Series records:* A Series record describes a set of related GEO Samples, which are usually part of a group. Each Series record is assigned a unique identifier or accession with a prefix "GSE".
- *GEO DataSet* records are curated sets of GEO Sample data. They are given an accession with the prefix "GDS". A GEO DataSet represents a collection of biologically and statistically comparable Samples referencing the same platform and sharing the same probe elements.

Those four types of record are organized into two GEO databases: (1) the GEO DataSets database for a curated collection of biologically and statistically comparable GEO Samples and (2) the GEO Profiles database for providing expression of individual genes across all samples in a dataset.

GEO DataSets

The GEO DataSets database provides the above four kinds of records (Series, Samples Platforms, and Curated). The datasets include a variety of gene expression data including data generated by microarray, high-throughput sequencing, high-throughput RT-PCR, genome variation profiling, SNP arrays, serial Analysis of Gene Expression (SAGE), and protein arrays.

The GEO DataSets web page is available at www.ncbi.nlm.nih.gov/gds/ or can be chosen from the database dropdown menu on the main Entrez database web page. Table 3.28 contains some of the GEO DataSets indexed fields that can be used in an advanced search. The fields (GTYP, FILT, PTYP, STYP, and VTYP) require keywords from fixed lists. Use the GEO DataSets Advanced Search Builder to obtain the keywords used with those fields or to build an advanced search query.

GEO DataSets Searching Examples

Example 1   Assume that you wish to find gene expression studies using high-throughput sequencing for metastatic breast cancer in human. Here you have pieces of information that you can use to build your search

TABLE 3.28   GEO DataSets Indexed Fields

Long Field Name	Short Field	Long Field Name	Short Field Name
Attribute Name	ATNM	Publication Date	PDAT
Attribute	ATTR	Project	PROJ
Description	DESC	Properties	PROP
Entry	ETYP	Platform Technology Type	PTYP
Filter	FILT	Related Platform	RGPL
DataSet Type	GTYP	Related Series	RGSE
Submitter Institute	INST	Sample Source	SRC
MeSH Terms	MESH	Sample Type	STYP
Number of Samples	NSAM	Title	TITL
Organism	ORGN	Sample Value Type	VTYP

query. These pieces of information are: "human" as an organism, "breast cancer" and "metastasis" as parts of the title, and "high-throughput sequencing" as a platform type. Moreover, you can filter the results by GEO Series records since a series includes multiple samples. When you put the above pieces of information together with their tagged field, you can build the following search query:

human[ORGN] AND "breast cancer"[TITL] AND metastasis[TITL] AND "high-throughput sequencing"[PTYP] AND gse[FILT]

The GEO DataSets search results page will show several GEO Series of human metastatic breast cancer. The studies used high-throughput sequencing. A Series record includes several GEO Samples. The summary view format of the search results page displays summary information about the Series record that includes the number of samples. Your dataset choice may depend on your goal. Click on the title of a record to open the GEO Series record page as shown in Figure 3.59.

The Series record page includes:

(1) The record information, which consists of Series accession, status, title, organism, experiment type, summary, overall design, contributors, and citations.

(2) Submission information, which includes submission dates, contact and address of the submitter.

(3) Accessions of GEO DataSets records and related database, which include the Platform accession (GOL), the list of GEO Sample accessions, BioProject accession, and SRA accession. Both BioProject and SRA are other NCBI databases. Those accessions can be used to download the Sequence Read Archive (SRA) data as we will discuss in the SRA database section.

(4) The download family and supplementary file section includes the data files that can be downloaded. However, the raw data are available in SRA, which requires special tools for downloading.

Example 2   In this example, you will search for data generated by microarray. We will notice that the record page for such GEO records will provide a tool for gene expression data analysis that is not available on the record page of data generated by sequencing.

For example, assume that you wish to find gene expression datasets for metastatic breast cancer in humans and that the data was generated using microarray. You can use the following search query:

human[ORGN] AND "breast cancer"[TITL] AND metastasis[TITL] AND gse[FILT] AND "Expression profiling by array"[FILT]

The search query returned around 65 Series records whose data were generated using microarray platform type. The results page displays the same information as the page for the dataset generated with sequencing.

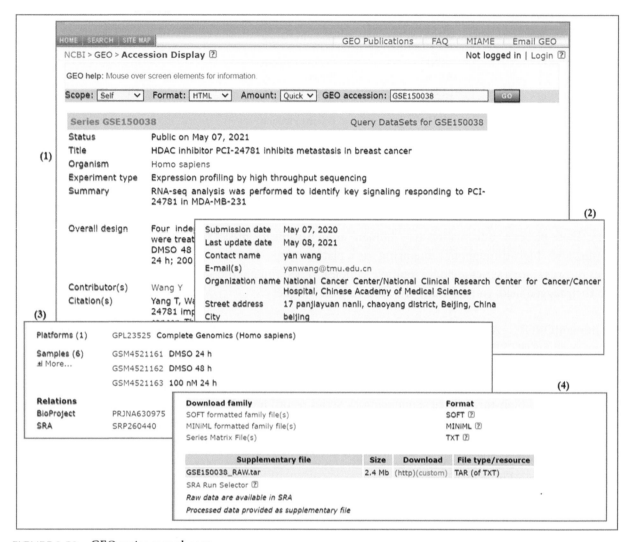

FIGURE 3.59   GEO series record page.

The number of samples is shown for each record. Scroll down and click on the title of the record with Series accession (GSE125989) to open the Series record page. This series has 32 Samples for a study designed for matching primary breast cancers and brain metastases from 16 patients. The microarray experiments were conducted on 16 samples with primary breast cancers and 16 samples with breast cancer and brain metastases. If you click on Platform, you can see the gene list (22277 genes). The microarray Series record is like that Series record page of the dataset generated by sequencing. However, if you scroll down to the bottom of the page you will notice a blue button "Analyze with GEO2R".

GEO2R [60] is an R-based analysis tool that is used to analyze the gene expression data generated by a microarray platform. You can use this tool to compare between two or more groups of GEO Samples to identify genes that are differentially expressed across experimental conditions. The results of the analysis are presented as a table of genes ordered by significance, in which the top differentially expressed genes are displayed. Several graphs depicting the expression of the genes of the selected GEO Samples in the groups may also be displayed. Click on the "Analyze with GEO2R" button to open the GEO2R page for the selected GEO Series record. The GEO2R page displays the list of 32 GEO Samples (16 from primary origin and 16 from brain origin) as indicated in the origin column. Assume that you wish to compare between the gene expressions of the two groups of GEO Samples. To do that use the "Define Group" button to define two groups (Primary and Brain). Each time, type the group name and press the Enter key (Figure 3.60). To add a sample to each group, use the

GEO accession	GSE125989		Set	Primary breast cancers and brain metastasis		

▾ **Samples**   ▾ Define groups

Enter a group name: List

Primary	GSM3587388		reast cancer	primary breast cancer	breast cancer
Primary	GSM3587389	✕ Cancel selection	reast cancer	primary breast cancer	breast cancer
Primary	GSM3587390	☐ Primary (16 samples) ⊠	reast cancer	primary breast cancer	breast cancer
Primary	GSM3587391	☐ Brain (16 samples) ⊠	reast cancer	primary breast cancer	breast cancer
Primary	GSM3587392	EA1690_12: primary breast cancer		primary breast cancer	breast cancer
Primary	GSM3587393	EA1690_13: primary breast cancer		primary breast cancer	breast cancer
Primary	GSM3587394	EA1690_14: primary breast cancer		primary breast cancer	breast cancer
Primary	GSM3587395	EA1690_15: primary breast cancer		primary breast cancer	breast cancer
Primary	GSM3587396	EA1690_16: primary breast cancer		primary breast cancer	breast cancer
Brain	GSM3587397	EA1690_17: brain metastases		brain metastases	breast cancer
Brain	GSM3587398	EA1690_18: brain metastases		brain metastases	breast cancer
Brain	GSM3587399	EA1690_19: brain metastases		brain metastases	breast cancer
Brain	GSM3587400	EA1690_20: brain metastases		brain metastases	breast cancer
Brain	GSM3587401	EA1690_21: brain metastases		brain metastases	breast cancer

FIGURE 3.60   GEO2R page.

mouse to select the sample and then click on the group to which you want to add the sample. To add multiple samples to a group, press the Ctrl key and use the mouth to select multiple samples and then click on the group to add the selected samples. In Primary group add the 16 samples with "primary" origin and in Brain group add the 16 samples with "brain" origin.

You can notice that there are four tabs (GEO2R, Options, Profile graph, and R script) at the bottom of the GEO2R page. The Option tab includes the analysis parameters that you can adjust, or you can leave the default selections. The Profile graph tab is used to view a specific gene expression profile by entering the gene ID from the table of gene list on the Platform record. R script displays the generated R script for the analysis. In the GEO2R tab click on the "Analyze" button to begin analyzing the selected groups.

The analysis results will be displayed as shown in Figure 3.61. The results include several graphs and a table of genes ordered by significance (p-value). The top differentially expressed genes are displayed first.

The volcano graph is a scatterplot that shows the statistical significance in P-value versus magnitude of change described as fold change. The volcano plot enables quick visual identification of genes with large fold changes that are also statistically significant. These may be the most biologically significant genes. Click on the volcano graph to enlarge it. As shown on the graph, the red spots represent up-regulated genes while the blue spots represent the down-regulated genes. Both up and down regulated genes are significant genes. On the enlarged volcano plot, you can click on the "Explore and download" button to visualize the volcano plot page, where you can also download the significant genes by clicking on the "Download significant gene" button.

You can click on any of the graphs to visualize the data in different graphical presentations, which may provide insight about the difference between the compared groups.

To view the expression profile of any gene listed in the table, click on the row of that gene; a bar chart for the gene expression level of that gene in each sample will be displayed. For example, clicking on the row of the COL1A1 gene will display a bar chart showing the COL1A1 gene expression level in the samples of the two

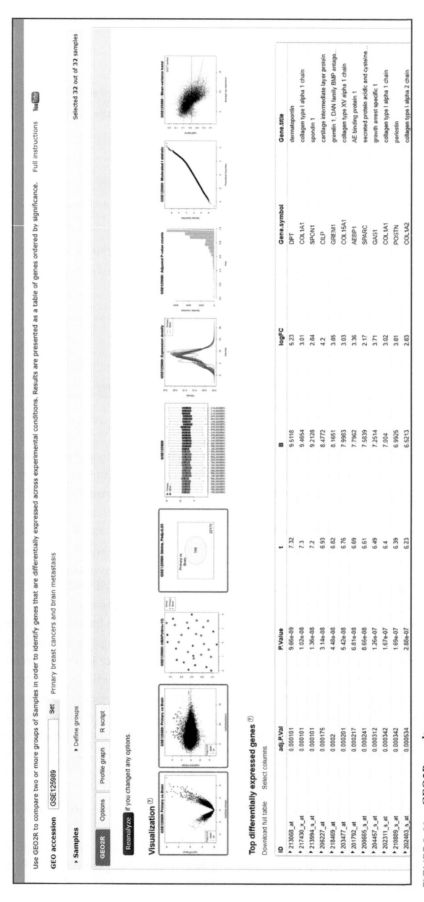

FIGURE 3.61   GEO2R results page.

groups (Figure 3.62). You can notice that the COL1A1 gene expression in the samples of the Brain group is lower than that of the Primary group. The graph will disappear by clicking on the row.

You can also use the "Profile Graph" tab and use the search box to enter the ID of the gene of interest to display its gene expression profile.

The "Download full table" link on the top of the table is used to download the data of the full table and the "Select columns" link is used to remove or add columns to the table.

Example 3   The GEO curated dataset (GDS) is curated by NCBI staff from submitted GEO datasets. A GDS is curated from single studies that have a Series and Samples that use the same Platform to allow easy comparison of gene expression in the study. The big advantage of having curated dataset is the possibility to link the GDS to other resources, which are found under "Related information" and to visualize the pathways of genes. You can filter the search results of the GEO DataSets by using "gds[FILTER]" to limit the search results to the curated GEO DataSets only. Enter the following query into the search box and click on "Search" button.

human[ORGN] AND "breast cancer"[TITL] AND gds[FILT]

Notice that the results page of the curated records is slightly different from others as each GDS summary will have a thumbnail cluster image and the accession of the records prefixed with "GDS" (Figure 3.63). You can click on Platform accession to open the Platform record and learn about the Platform description, number of genes, and gene list.

Click on the title of the GDS record with the accession (GDS5621) to open the GDS Dataset Browser page (Figure 3.64). This GDS Dataset is linked to a Platform record with 48,107 genes.
On the bar on the top of the GDS Data Browser page (Figure 3.64), there are three buttons:

(1) *Expression Profiles.* This button will open the GEO Profiles search results page for the GEO Profiles records of all genes in the Platform record. There are 48,107 genes for the example dataset. The GEO Profiles database will be discussed next.

(2) *Data Analysis Tools.* As illustrated in Figure 3.65, (A) "Find genes" is used to identify genes that are differentially expressed according to experimental subsets of the samples. The subsets will be displayed so you can select or deselect a subset. (B) "Compare 2 sets of samples" is used to compare two sets of samples. You can use either the t-test or value means difference test. (C) "Cluster heatmaps" is used to display the heatmap of the cluster. (D) "Experiment design and value distribution" is used to display a box plot depicting the distribution of expression values of each sample within a dataset.

(3) *Sample Subsets.* This shows the groups of the samples. Clicking on the "Sample Subsets" button for the example record will display the following table in Figure 3.66, which shows the samples and the subsets of the samples based on two factors (genotype/variation and agent). The highlight colors indicate these subsets.

On the top of the page there is a description section including Title, Summary, Organism, GEO Platform accession and description, Citation, Reference Series accession (GSE), Value type of the gene expression, thumbnail image and Download box.

Clicking the thumbnail cluster image on the right will open the DataSets record page that contains several data analysis tools, including clusters heatmaps.

The Download box below the thumbnail provides download links to the following files:

(1) *DataSets full SOFT file.* This is a tab-delimited text file that contains DataSets information, experiment variable subsets, expression value measurements and comprehensive up-to-date gene annotation for the DataSets Platform.

Top differentially expressed genes ⑦
Download full table   Select columns

ID	adj.P.Val	P.Value	t	B	logFC	Gene.symbol	Gene.title
► 213068_at	0.000101	9.66e-09	7.32	9.5118	5.23	DPT	dermatopontin
▼ 217430_x_at	0.000101	1.02e-08	7.3	9.4654	3.01	COL1A1	collagen type I alpha 1 chain

GSE12599@217430_x_at/COL1A1

■ expression value

Sample values

► 213994_s_at	0.000101	1.36e-08	7.2	9.2128	2.84	SPON1	spondin 1
► 206227_at	0.000175	3.14e-08	6.93	8.4772	4.2	CILP	cartilage intermediate layer protein
► 218469_at	0.0002	4.48e-08	6.82	8.1651	3.85	GREM1	gremlin 1, DAN family BMP antago…
► 203477_at	0.000201	5.42e-08	6.76	7.9983	3.03	COL15A1	collagen type XV alpha 1 chain
► 201792_at	0.000217	6.81e-08	6.69	7.7962	3.36	AEBP1	AE binding protein 1
► 200665_s_at	0.000241	8.66e-08	6.61	7.5839	2.17	SPARC	secreted protein acidic and cysteine…
► 204457_s_at	0.000312	1.26e-07	6.49	7.2514	3.71	GAS1	growth arrest specific 1

FIGURE 3.62   Gene expression profile.

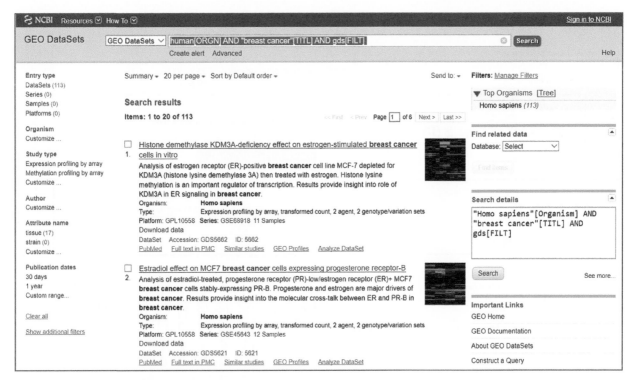

FIGURE 3.63   Curated GEO DataSets results page.

FIGURE 3.64   GDS dataset browser.

(2) *DataSets SOFT file.* This is a tab-delimited text file that contains DataSets information, experiment variable subsets, expression value measurements and gene symbols.

(3) *Series family SOFT file.* This is a tab-delimited text file that contains the complete, original, submitter-supplied records that form the basis of these DataSets.

(4) *Series family MINiML file.* This is an XML file that contains the complete, original, submitter-supplied records that form the basis of these DataSets.

(5) *Annotation SOFT file.* This is a plain-text annotation SOFT file that contains comprehensive up-to-date gene annotation for the DataSets Platform.

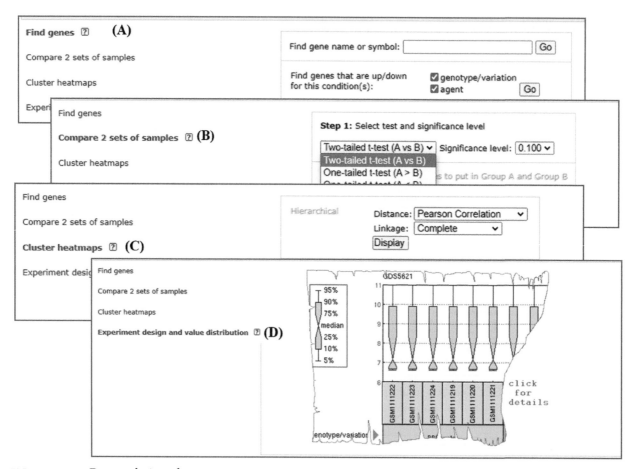

FIGURE 3.65   Data analysis tools.

Samples	Factors		
	genotype/variation	agent	
GSM1111222	PRB vector	estradiol	MCF7_PRB_E2_6h, rep1
GSM1111223	PRB vector	estradiol	MCF7_PRB_E2_6h, rep2
GSM1111224	PRB vector	estradiol	MCF7_PRB_E2_6h, rep3
GSM1111219	PRB vector	control	MCF7_PRB_vehicle_6h, rep1
GSM1111220	PRB vector	control	MCF7_PRB_vehicle_6h, rep2
GSM1111221	PRB vector	control	MCF7_PRB_vehicle_6h, rep3
GSM1111216	empty vector	estradiol	MCF7_vector_E2_6h, rep1
GSM1111217	empty vector	estradiol	MCF7_vector_E2_6h, rep2
GSM1111218	empty vector	estradiol	MCF7_vector_E2_6h, rep3
GSM1111213	empty vector	control	MCF7_vector_vehicle_6h, rep1
GSM1111214	empty vector	control	MCF7_vector_vehicle_6h, rep2
GSM1111215	empty vector	control	MCF7_vector_vehicle_6h, rep3

FIGURE 3.66   GDS dataset browser.

GEO Profiles

GEO Profiles [59] is a database for storing gene expression profiles of individual genes across all GEO Samples with the GEO DataSets. The GEO Profiles records are generated from curated GEO DataSets. The gene expression profile of a single gene across all GEO Samples within the GEO dataset is presented as a chart. A Profile may have links to other related records in NCBI databases. The dataset type of the gene expression profile of a gene is either produced by microarray (array) or by Massively Parallel Signature Sequencing (MPSS) [61], which is a platform that analyses the level of gene expression in a sample by counting the number of individual mRNA molecules produced by each gene.

The gene expression profile of a specific gene across samples gives a clear picture about the role of that gene in the studied conditions. For example, a profile of a gene across samples of two groups (diseased and healthy) will give an insight of the role of the gene in the disease.

Searching GEO Profiles

The GEO Profiles web page is available at www.ncbi.nlm.nih.gov/geoprofiles/ or GEO Profiles can be chosen from the dropdown menu on the main Entrez database web page. Building a search query was discussed earlier. Table 3.29 contains the indexed fields of GEO Profiles.

Example 1   Researchers are usually interested in checking gene profile across samples in a specific condition such as a disease. For example, assume that we wish to find the GEO Profiles records of BRCA1 in samples collected from healthy and diseased human breast. We can use the following query:

BRCA1[SYMB] AND human[ORGN]

The search results page of GEO Profiles (Figure 3.67) is like the search pages of other Entrez databases. The filters in the left-hand side can be used to narrow the search results. The search results can be displayed as summary or as unique identifiers using the Format dropdown menu at the top left. The summary results display information of each profile including the title, Annotation, Organism, Reporter, Dataset type, ID, internal and external links, and a thumbnail chart.

The links in the last line of the summary of each record include a link to the GEO DataSets record from which the profile is derived (GEO DataSets), link to the Gene record of the gene profiled (Gene), link to first 200 GEO profiles of the other genes in the same GEO DataSets (Profile neighbors), link to GEO profiles of the first 20 neighbor genes of the selected gene in the chromosome (Chromosome neighbors), and link to the first 200 neighbor homologous gene in the HomoloGene database (HomoloGene neighbors).

TABLE 3.29   GEO Profiles Indexed Fields

Long Field Name	Short Field Name	Long Field Name	Short Field Name
GEO Accession	ACCN	Dataset Type	GTYP
All Fields	ALL	ID_REF	ID
Annotation Type	ATYP	Reporter Identifier	NAME
Chromosome	CHR	Number of Samples	NSAM
Base Position	CPOS	Organism	ORGN
Filter	FILT	Max Value Rank	RMAX
Flag Information	FINF	Min Value Rank	RMIN
Flag Type	FTYP	Ranked Standard Deviation	RSTD
Gene Description	GDSC	Platform Reporter Type	RTYP
GDS Text	GDST	Sample Source	SRC
GEO Description/Title Text	GEOT	Gene Symbol	SYMB
GI	GI	UID	UID
Gene Ontology	GO	Sample Value Type	VTYP

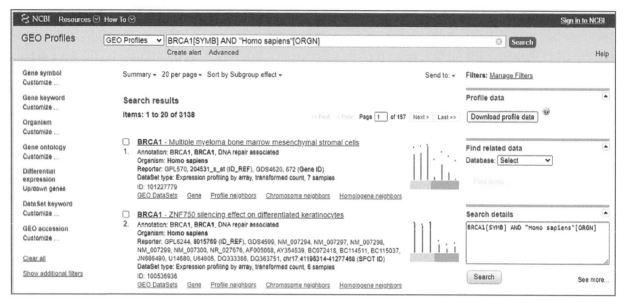

FIGURE 3.67   GEO profiles search results.

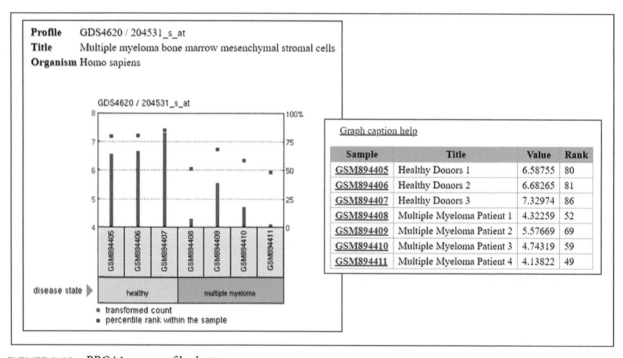

FIGURE 3.68   BRCA1 gene profile chart.

The thumbnail chart of each profile displays the expression level of the gene across all GEO Samples within a GEO DataSet. The thumbnail charts enable rapid visual scanning and comparison of the groups of samples. Clicking on the thumbnail chart will display the full profile chart. Figure 3.68 shows the BRCA1 (GDS4620/ 204531_s_at) Profile across the seven samples. You can notice that the BRCA1 expression level is higher in healthy samples than in multiple myeloma patients.

In the chart, the GEO Sample identifiers are in the X-axis while the gene expression measurements are in the Y-axis. There are two gene expression scales: the expression values, which are represented by red columns (left Y-axis), and expression ranks, which are represented by blue squares and are in scale of 1–100% (right Y-axis). The GEO Samples of the example were divided into healthy samples and patient samples. The profile chart

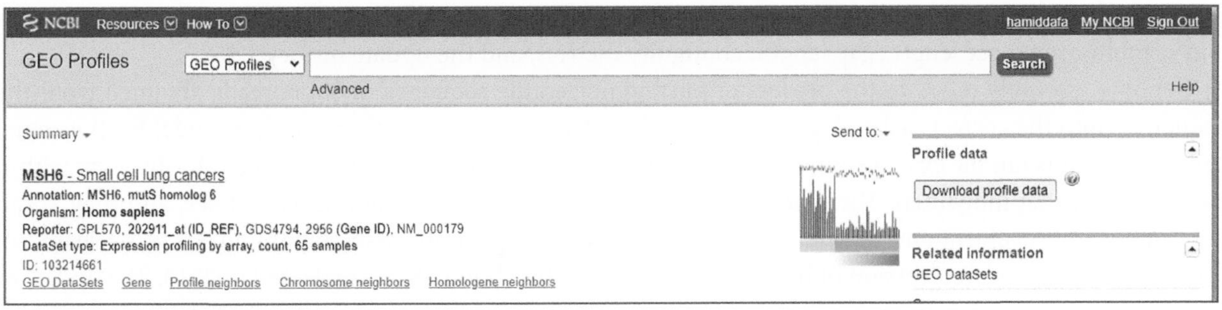

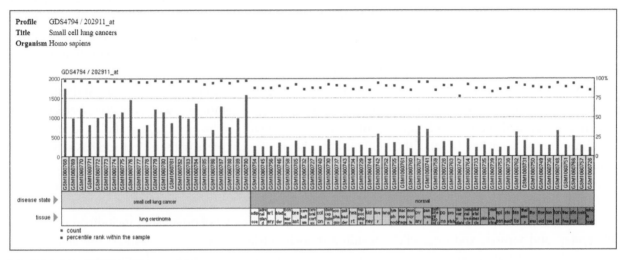

FIGURE 3.69   GEO profiles record.

FIGURE 3.70   GEO profiles record.

shows that the BRCA1 gene is over-expressed in healthy subjects and under-expressed in patient subjects. The profile may suggest the role of low-level gene expression of the BRCA1 gene in multiple myeloma.

Example 2   In this example, we wish to find the GEO Profiles records for MSH6 gene, which codes for a protein that plays an essential role in repairing DNA. MSH6 has been found to be involved in colon cancer. The following search query will try to find MSH6 Profiles records with samples extracted from colon tissue.

> MSH6[SYMB] human[ORGN] AND colon[SRC]

The GEO Profiles will display tens of records. Scroll down to the dataset with an ID (103214661) as shown in Figure 3.69. This dataset consists of 65 samples divided into two groups: Samples from individuals affected by lung carcinoma and healthy individuals.

Click on the chart thumbnail to display the full profile chart of HSH6 (Figure 3.70). The chart shows that the HSH6 gene is over-expressed in samples with lung carcinoma.

ASSEMBLY

The NCBI Assembly database provides access to the reference genome assemblies that researchers often use for mapping sequence reads and annotations. The sources of the Assembly database records are the RefSeq assemblies curated by the Genome Reference Consortium and the assemblies submitted by specialized institutions and laboratories. The assembly structures housed by the Assembly database include sets of unordered contigs or scaffold sequences, bacterial genomes, and complex structures of genomes with allelic variations. The

Assembly database also provides information of assembly metadata and statistics such as number of contigs and scaffolds, sequence length, gap length, contiguity metrics, and the update history.

Genome assembly refers to the process of putting nucleotide sequence or short reads obtained from the sequencer into the correct order. A genomic assembly of an organism represents only a model for the actual genome, and it is not the exact genome. An assembly of an individual cannot represent all the diversity within the species of that individual. Therefore, there are multiple versions of genomic assemblies, and they are in continuous improvement and update. For example, the human genomic assembly (build 37) was released in 2009 and a new improved version of human genomic assembly (build 38) was released in 2013. The update of assembly is a continuous process and a new version with better resolution can be released at any time.

A Genome assembly is made by aligning many short DNA sequences or reads. The contigs of an assembly are the consensus sequences of the overlapped reads. The assembly scaffolds are created from the merged contigs. Then the scaffolds are used to build up the so-called "A Golden Path" or **AGP** either by positioning the scaffolds along the physical map of a chromosome or using the best guess [62]. The AGP approximates what the real genome looks like. It is the best estimate of the genome, and it may include gaps that make the assembly longer than the typical base pair length of a genome.

The file format that is used to describe the structure of a genome assembly is known as AGP file format (see Chapter 2 "Downstream NGS Data Analysis"). In a AGP file a genome assembly is described as a large sequence object made up of small sequence objects. A large object can be a contig, a scaffold (super-contig), or a chromosome. Each line (row) of the AGP file describes a different piece of the object and has a number of column entries and extended comments. For more information on GAP files refer to the latest AGP specification (as of this date the latest is AGP Specification v2.1), which is available at www.ncbi.nlm.nih.gov/assembly/agp/AGP_Specification/.

The NCBI Assembly database includes assemblies from a wide range of organisms, including prokaryotes, eukaryotes, and viruses, and organelles including mitochondria, plasmid, and plastids. The genomes are sequenced using whole genome shotgun (WGS), cloning, or completely sequenced genome, and assembled using computational assembling algorithms.

The assembled genomes in the Assembly database are found in the form of (1) complete genome assemblies, (2) assemblies that include chromosomes, scaffolds, and contigs, (3) assemblies that include scaffolds and contigs, and (4) assemblies that include only contigs.

Assembly Submission

Genome assemblies are either simple or complex. A simple genome assembly is the one that does not build an entire genomic molecule such as a complete replicon that is gapless sequence and WGS contigs only. A complex assembly is one with a high structure such as scaffolds and chromosomes. A complex assembly can be one of the following:

(1) *Haploid only*, which consists of unplaced scaffolds and chromosomes, in which any locus may not be represented more than once. Such genome assembly collapses the two sequences of loci into a single haploid consensus sequence. Therefore, it fails to capture the diploid nature of the genome of an organism.

(2) *Haploid + alternatives*, which are a collection of chromosome assemblies plus alternative loci of an organism's genome. A locus may be not existing at all (0) or may exist once (1), or more than once (>1). However, a chromosome will be either missing (0) or represented once (1). An example of this kind of assembly is GRCh37 assembly for *Homo sapiens*.

(3) *Diploid/Polyploid* genome assembly is the assembly that has all sets of chromosomes. This kind of assembly represents the full genome of the individual and it captures the diploid nature of the genome of an organism.

Submitting a genome assembly may require some of the following files:

(1) *FASTA file.* A multiple FASTA file for the sequences of the components forming the genome. Each sequence has a definition line beginning with ">" and a unique sequence identifier (e.g., contig0001, contig0002, etc.) and the genomic sequence.

(2) *SQN file.* The sqn file is required only if annotations are included in the submission. The sqn file is prepared using tbl2asn, which is an NCBI program that reads a template file along with the FASTA sequence and annotation table files, and outputs an ASN (.sqn) file for submission to GenBank.

(3) *AGP file.* This file describes how contigs, scaffolds, and chromosomes are assembled. Refer to Chapter 2 "Downstream NGS Data Analysis."

(4) *Pseudo-autosomal definition file.* The Pseudo-Autosomal Region (PAR) file describes the location of the pseudo-autosomal regions (PAR1 and PAR2) in mammals. The pseudo-autosomal regions (PAR1 and PAR2) are short regions between the mammalian X and Y chromosomes. The description includes chromosome name (chr-name:), name of PAR region (par-name:), the base where PAR starts on the chromosome (start:), and the base where PAR ends on the chromosome (stop:).

(5) *Alternate locus alignment file.* This is an optional file that contains the alignment of alternate locus scaffolds to a chromosome sequence. The alternative loci are used to describe the highly divergent regions in chromosome context.

(6) *Genomic Region Definition file.* This is an optional and tab-delimited file that defines the genomic region if the assembly has alternate locus scaffolds that have been put into a chromosome context. If this is not provided, the Genomic Regions will be created based on the placements provided.

(7) *Alternate locus assignment to Genomic Region.* This is an optional file that associates alternative locus scaffold with a specific region.

(8) *Annotation file.* This file contains the annotations mapped to the genome assembly based on the NCBI guidelines.

To submit a genome assembly to GenBank you need to follow the guidelines available at www.ncbi.nlm.nih.gov/assembly/docs/submission/, which provide instructions for each type of assembly. The submission requires creating a BioProject as discussed in the BioProject database section. NCBI also provides a command-line program called tbl2asn, which automates the creation of sequence records for submission to GenBank.

Once you have your submission files prepared, you can use the Submission Portal, which is available at https://submit.ncbi.nlm.nih.gov/ to submit a single genome or a batch of genomes using the genome submission wizard.

The genome submission can also be via the NCBI Genome Workbench, which is an open-source desktop application that can be downloaded from the NCBI web page at www.ncbi.nlm.nih.gov/tools/gbench/downloads/. The NCBI Genome Workbench can be installed on Windows, Linux, and Mac OS. After installation, you need to enable the editing package by clicking the "Tools" menu and then click "Package" to open the Configure Packages dialog box. From the packages choose "Sequence editing" and then select the "Enable" checkbox as illustrated in Figure 3.71.

Click "OK" and the change will take effect after you close and reopen the program. The Submission menu will appear after enabling the sequence editing package. Use the Genome Submission Wizard to submit your genome sequence (FASTA or ASN.1). The wizard will guide you through the submission steps to enter submitter info, general info, genome info, organism info, molecule info, annotation, reference, and validation.

The genomes submitted to the Genome database may include both completely sequenced genomes and those in progress.

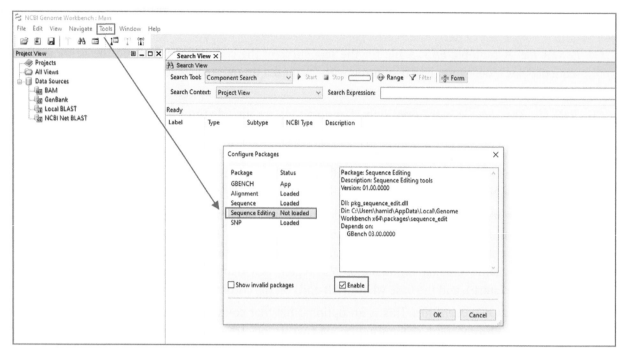

FIGURE 3.71   NCBI Genome Workbench (enabling sequence editing package).

The assemblies submitted to the GenBank are given unique identifiers or accession numbers that start with "GCA_", while the curated reference assemblies are given accessions start with "GCF_". The complete identifier of an assembly is in the format "ACCESSION.VERION". The first instance of an assembly provided by a submitter receives an accession and version 1.

Searching the Assembly Database

The Assembly web page is accessed by choosing "Assembly" from the dropdown menu on the Entrez database web page or you can use the direct link www.ncbi.nlm.nih.gov/assembly/. Refer to the "Searching Entrez Databases" section above for building search queries and searching an Entrez database.

Table 3.30 lists the indexed fields that can be used in building advanced search queries for the Assembly database.

The following are some examples for searching the Assembly database:

Example 1   In this example, you will search the Assembly database for the latest human genome assemblies that have annotation. To build a search query you can either use the indexed fields listed in Table 3.30 or you can use the Assembly Advanced Search Builder, which is a powerful tool for constructing search queries. To find the latest human genome assemblies that have annotations, use the following query:

"Homo sapiens"[ORGN] AND ("latest genbank"[FILT] AND "has annotation"[PROP])

The search query will return the assemblies that match the search query. The first hit will be the current human reference genome.

The Assembly search results page is a typical Entrez database search results page. The Assembly search results page also provides links to download the assemblies. Clicking the "Download Assemblies" button will open a dropdown menu that allows you to select the source database, which is either GenBank or RefSeq, and a file type from the dropdown list, which includes a wide range of file formats for the genomic sequence, annotations, features, and products (transcripts and proteins) as shown in Figure 3.72.

TABLE 3.30   Assembly Indexed Fields

Long Field Name	Short Field Name	Long Field Name	Short Field Name
Accession	ACCN	BioProject IDs and Accessions	PROJ
All Fields	ALL	Properties	PROP
All Names	ALLN	RefSeq Category	RCAT
Assembly Accession	ASAC	Chromosome Count	REPL
Assembly Level	ASLV	Reference Guided Assembly	RGAS
Assembly Method	ASMM	Total Sequence Length	RLEN
Contig L50	CL50	Date – RefSeq Assembly Release	RRLS
Contig N50	CN50	Release Type	RTYP
Contig Count	CNTG	RefSeq ID	RUID
Coverage	COV	BioSample	SAMP
Description	DESC	Single Cell Amplification	SCAM
Expected Final Version	EXFV	Sex	SEX
Filter	FILT	Scaffold L50	SL50
From Type Material	FTYP	Scaffold N50	SN50
Genome Coverage	GCOV	Date – Sequences Release	SRDT
GenBank ID	GUID	Sequencing Technology	TECH
Infraspecific Name	INFR	Taxonomy ID	TXID
Isolate	ISOL	Assembly Type	TYPE
Total Sequence Length in Mbp	LEN	UID	UID
Linked Assembly	LINK	All UIDs	UIDS
Assembly Name	NAME	Ungapped Length in Mbp	UNGL
Excluded from RefSeq	NFRS	Unlocalized Scaffolds Count	UNLO
Organism	ORGN	Unplaced Scaffolds Count	UNPL

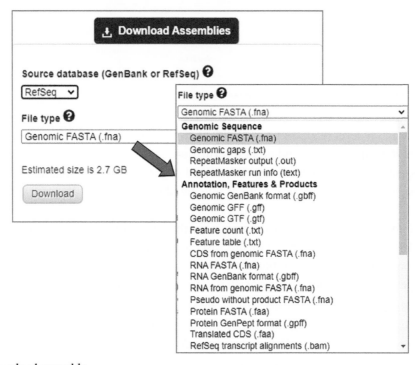

FIGURE 3.72   Download assembly.

Selecting RefSeq source database allows you to download the latest reference sequence in FASTA format, which is essential for mapping of the sequence reads generated by the high-throughput sequencing.

The search results are displayed in summary format by default. Summary information of a search hit includes information about the assembly, such as organism, submitter, date of submission, assembly type (e.g.,

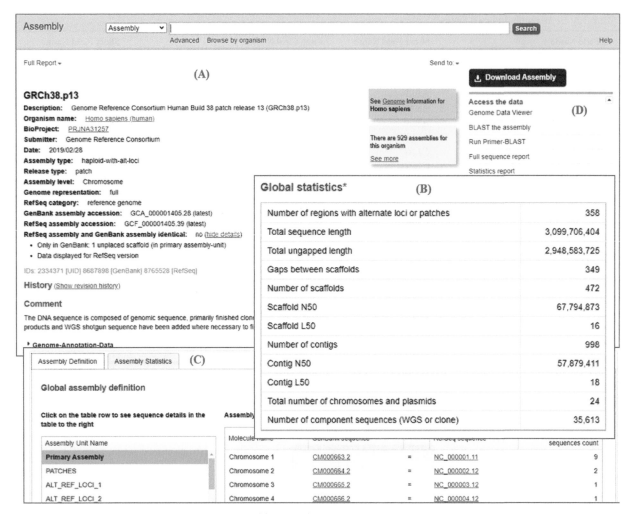

FIGURE 3.73   Reference human genome assembly record page.

haploid, diploid), assembly level (e.g., contig, scaffold, or chromosome), gene representation (full or partial), GenBank accession, RefSeq accession, and other information.

Click the first assembly title to open the Assembly record page of the current human reference genome. The Assembly record page consists of several sections as illustrated in Figure 3.73. They are as follows:

(A) *Summary information.* The summary section is like the information on the search results page. Clicking "Show revision history" will expand the list displaying the previous versions. The comment provides a description of the genome assembly. Clicking "Genome-Annotation-Data" will display information about the genome annotation data associated with the Assembly record.

(B) *Global statistics.* The global statistics section provides statistics about the assembly as shown in the figure. Notice that the length of the current human reference genome is 3,099,706,404 bp including 349 gaps between the scaffolds. The genome is made up of 24 chromosomes.

Both N50 and L50 are measures that describe the quality of an assembled genome that contains contigs and scaffolds of different lengths. Contig N50 is the shortest contig length needed to cover 50% of the genome and scaffold 50 is the shortest scaffold length needed to cover 50% of the genome. Contig L50 and scaffold L50 are defined as the smallest number of contigs and scaffolds respectively whose length sum makes up half of genome size. For the reference human genome, contig N50 is 57,879,411 bp and contig L50 is 18 contigs, and scaffold N50 is 67,794,873bp and scaffold L50 is 16 scaffolds. Long contig N50 and scaffold N50 and small contig L50 and scaffold L50 indicate the good quality of the assembled human genome.

(C) *Assembly Definition and Assembly Statistics tabs.* The Assembly Definition tab includes two lists (Assembly Unit Name and Region) that can be used for navigation. Clicking any item of these two lists will display the detailed genomic components of the assembly unit or region. The Assembly Statistics tab includes four sub-tabs (Primary Assembly, Non-nuclear, Information by region, and Information by alt assembly-unit). The Primary Assembly sub-tab displays the list of chromosomes and their statistics (total length, scaffold count, ungapped length, scaffold N50, spanned gaps, and unspanned gaps). The Non-nuclear sub-tab shows the total length of non-nuclear component of the genome. The Information by region sub-tab shows a table containing region name, location, scaffold count, total length, ungapped length, scaffold N50, and spanned gaps of each region forming the genome assembly. The Information by alt assembly-unit tab displays a table containing unit name, scaffold count, total length, ungapped length, scaffold N50, and spanned gaps of the alternative loci of the genome assembly.

(D) *Access the data tools.* This section displays tools and links where the genome assembly data can be searched, visualized, or downloaded. Those tools and links include:

- Genome Data Viewer for viewing the genome assembly and annotations.
- RefSeq Annotation Report for providing information about the annotation release and gene and feature statistics.
- BLAST the assembly for searching for a sequence in the genome assembly.
- Run Primer-BLAST for searching for PCR primers for a region in the genome assembly sequence.
- Full sequence report, which is a flat text report about the full sequence of the genome assembly.
- Statistics report, which is flat text statistics report about the units forming the genome assembly.
- FTP directory for RefSeq and GenBank assemblies are links for downloading the RefSeq and GenBank assembly sequences.
- NCBI Datasets is a new project developed to make finding NCBI sequence data easy and fast. It is also available as command-line tools that can be installed and used on Linux, Windows, and MAC OS. However, it is still in alpha version and will become stable after fixing the bugs and adding new features.

Example 2   This example will show you how to find the latest reference genome assembly of an organism. To find a reference genome assembly, use the organism scientific or common name with [ORGN] and "reference genome"[FILT] in the search query. Assume that you wish to find the reference genome assembly of *Salmonella enterica*. You can use the following query:

"salmonella enterica"[ORGN] AND "reference genome"[FILT]

This search query will open the page of the Assembly record page of the *Salmonella enterica* reference genome (Figure 3.74), where you will be able to download the reference genome sequences, annotation data, and find information and statistics about the assembly as discussed in the above example.

Example 3   COVID-19 is caused by a coronavirus called severe acute respiratory syndrome coronavirus 2 or short as SARS-CoV-2. Older adults and people with severe underlying medical conditions, such as heart or lung disease or diabetes, seem to be at higher risk of developing more serious complications from the COVID-19 illness than younger people and people without such medical conditions. Assume that you wish

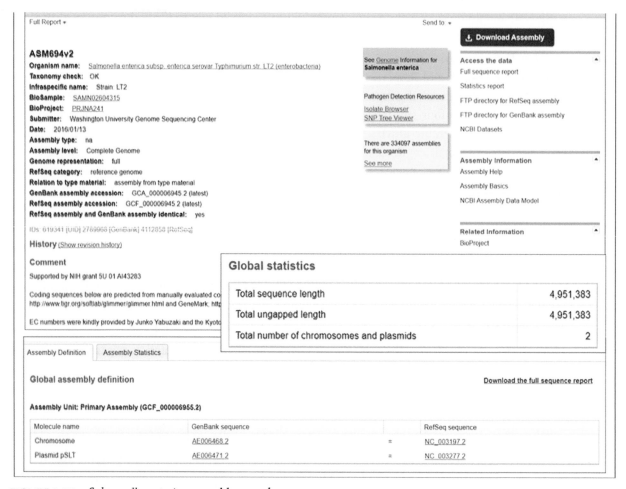

FIGURE 3.74   *Salmonella enterica* assembly record page.

to download the latest genome assembly of the severe acute syndrome coronavirus 2 (SARS-CoV-2) from the NCBI Assembly database. You can use the following query to find the latest SARS-CoV-2 reference genome assembly:

"Severe acute respiratory syndrome coronavirus 2"[ORGN] AND "latest refseq"[FILT]

This will display the latest reference genome assembly record. To download the sequence, use the "Download Assembly" dropdown menu to select the sequence format you need, as explained above.

GENOME DATABASE

The NCBI Genome database is the database that stores the information of large-scale genomics projects of different organisms from prokaryotes, eukaryotes, viruses, and organelles. The genomic information includes genome sequences and assemblies, and mapped annotations such as variations, markers, and data from epigenomics studies.

Searching Genome Database

The Entrez Genome web page is available at www.ncbi.nlm.nih.gov/genome or it can be accessed by choosing "Genome" from the dropdown menu on the main Entrez database website. Table 3.31 contains the indexed fields for Genome database.

TABLE 3.31   Genome Indexed Fields

Long Field Name	Short Field Name	Long Field Name	Short Field Name
Assembly Accession	AACC	Organism	ORGN
Replicon accession	ACCN	Protein Accession	PACC
Assembly ID	AID	ProtClust ID	PCID
All Fields	ALL	Protein GI	PGI
Assembly Name	ANAM	ProjectID	PID
biological properties	BIOP	PubMed ID	PMID
Create Date	CDT	Project Accession	PRJA
Title	DFLN	Project Type	PRJT
Genome description	DSCR	Properties	PROP
Filter	FILT	Protein Name	PROT
Gene Name	GENE	Replicon name	RNAM
Replicon GI	GI	Status	STAT
GeneID	GNID	Strain	STRN
Host	HOST	UID	UID
Locus Tag	LTAG	WGS prefix	WGSP

The simplest way to search for a genome of any organism is to use either the organism's common name or scientific name as a search term with [ORGN]. An advanced search query can also be built from the indexed fields or by using the Advanced Search Builder. In the following, we will discuss an example for eukaryotes, prokaryotes, and viruses.

Example 1   As an example, for eukaryotes, you will search for the human genome using the following search query:

Human[ORGN]

The human genome record page will open as shown in Figure 3.75 and described as follows:

A   This section provides a link to the current reference assembly record, links to download the reference genome, transcript, and protein, links to download annotations in GFF, GenBank, and tabular formats, links to find a sequence in the genome sequence database, the transcript sequence database, and the protein sequence database. This section also provides a link to list all genomes for the species in the genome browser.

B   The Organism Overview provides information and links to the genome Assembly and Annotation report and organelle annotation report in the genome browser, the organism's name, lineage, and summary about the genome project, transcripts per gene and exons per transcript statistics, BUSCO analysis of gene annotation, and references. BUSCO is a validation tool that is used to assess completeness of a genome assembly, gene set and transcriptome [63].

C   The Summary provides summary information about the sequence data (number of assemblies for the species and number of reads), statistics (median total genome length, median protein count, and median GC %), and a link to NCBI annotation release, where you can find all information about the annotation of the current genome, such as assemblies, gene and feature statistics, and detailed reports about the feature lengths. You can notice that the number of genome assemblies used to generate the reference genome is 916, the median total length of the human genome is 2,860,190,000 bases (2,860.19 MB), the median protein count is 122,962, and GC % is 40.4.

D   References include the most recent 20 publications.

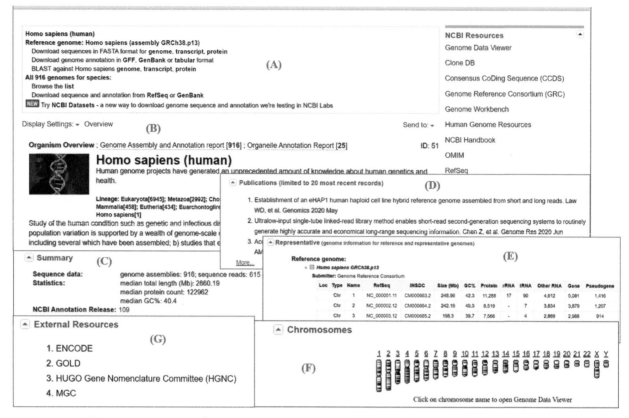

FIGURE 3.75   Human genome record.

E   Representative (genome information for reference and representative genomes): this section includes the table listing the chromosomes, their RefSeq and INSDC accession, sizes, GC%, number of proteins, rRNA, tRNA, and other RNA, and number of genes and pseudogenes. For example, the length of the human chromosome 1 is 248,960,000 bp (248.96 Mb), its GC% is 42.3, and it encodes 11,288 proteins, 17 rRNA, 90 tRNA, 4,612 other RNA, and it has 5,091 genes and 1,416 pseudogenes.

F   The Chromosomes section displays the chromosome ideograms representing the chromosomes of the organisms. In the human, there are 23 pairs of chromosomes (22 pairs of autosomal chromosomes and one pair of sex chromosome). Each autosomal pair is represented by a single ideogram, but the sex pairs are represented by an X-ideogram and Y-ideogram. Those ideograms act as navigation tools so that clicking on any ideogram will open the Genome Data Viewer displaying that chromosome and the default annotation tracks.

G   The External Resources section provides links to external resources and databases.

Example 2   As an example, for prokaryotes, you can search for *Escherichia coli* (*E. coli*) using the following search query:

"Escherichia coli"[ORGN]

The *Escherichia coli* genome record page will open as shown in Figure 3.76. The sections of the genome records of prokaryotes are the same as those of the eukaryotes except that section (6) may display dendrogram (phylogenetic tree) based on BLAST. The *Escherichia coli* bacterium (*Escherichia coli* O157:H7 strain Sakai) has a single circular chromosome and two plasmids. Not all *E. coli* strains have plasmids. Plasmids usually have genes that code for enzymes that play roles in the bacterial antibiotic resistance.

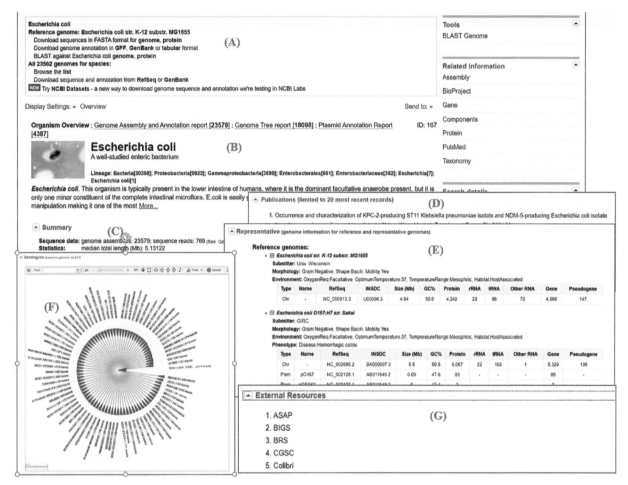

FIGURE 3.76 *Escherichia coli* genome record.

Example 3   In this example, you will search the Genome database for the genome of the COVID-19 virus (severe acute respiratory syndrome coronavirus 2 or SARS-CoV-2) using the following search query:

"severe acute respiratory syndrome coronavirus 2"[ORGN]

As shown in Figure 3.77, you can notice that the length of the SARS-CoV-2 genome is 29,882 bases (29.9 Kb) and it has 11 genes that code for 12 proteins.

Several tools and resources are available on the main web page of the Genome database. In the following sections, we will discuss some of these tools.

Browse by Organism

Browse by Organism is a browser that enables you to find the genome of an organism by entering either the scientific or common name of the organism, accession, or an assembly or BioProject. It is available at www.ncbi.nlm.nih.gov/genome/browse#!/overview/ or it can be accessed from the link on the Genome web page. By default, the browser categorizes all genomes into overview, eukaryotes, prokaryotes, viruses, plasmids, and organelles. Clicking each of these subsets will limit the list to the individuals of that subset. The browser is also provided with a Filter menu and download button on the top right.

To find a subset of genomes, enter an organism name into the search box and then click on the "Search by organism" button. A search term can be an organism name or any of the taxonomic groups such as kingdom, phylum, class, order, family, genus, and species. For example, you can enter "Primates" to display the list of

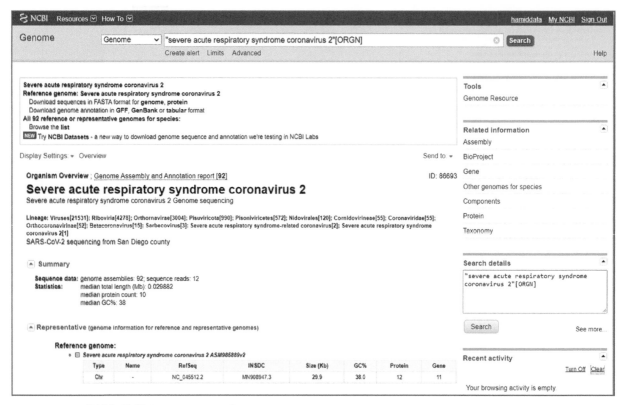

FIGURE 3.77   SARS-CoV-2 genome record.

the genomes of primates or you can enter "Salmonella" to display the genomes of the *Salmonella* species available in the Genome database. Clicking a genome in the browser list will open the Genome record page of that organism.

Human Genome

Human Genome Resources at NCBI [11] can be accessed from the Genome main web page or via www.ncbi.nlm.nih.gov/genome/guide/human/. The Human Genome is maintained by the Genome Reference Consortium (GRC) whose collaborators include a number of institutes such as the National Center for Biotechnology Information (NCBI), the Genome Center at Washington University, the Wellcome Trust Sanger Institute, the European Bioinformatics Institute (EBI), and more [64]. The Human Genome web page provides several resources including (1) human chromosome ideograms that act as navigation tools directing users to the Genome Viewer, (2) the Download section for downloading reference sequences and annotations of the current and previous genome assemblies, (3) the Browse section that provides links to the NCBI databases and resources, (4) the View section that includes the links to the Genome Data Viewer, 1000 Genomes, and the Variation Viewer, and (5) the Learn section that includes featured webinars and fact sheets in PDF format about the NCBI databases and resources used with the human genome.

The "Search for Human Genes" search box, on the top, is used to search the Gene database for human genes. You can use either free text or the indexed fields of the Gene database to build a search query. However, the "human[organism]" tagged field will be added automatically to the query.

Genome Data Viewer

The NCBI Genome Data Viewer (GDV) allows users to visualize molecular data in a genomic context. The genomic data mapped to the reference genome are represented graphically in tracks that can be added to the GDV or removed. The NCBI has several tracks for various types of genomic data such as gene annotations, markers, dbSNP variants, dbVar variants, phenotypes, gene expression, etc. However, there are some tracks developed by other institutions and stored in registries to be accessed and visualized on GDV. User data can be visualized and analyzed on GDV as well. The GDV replaced the previous NCBI Map Viewer. GDV supports exploring and analysis of hundreds of NCBI-annotated and a selection of non-NCBI annotated eukaryotic genome assemblies. It can be accessed from the main NCBI Genome web page or via www.ncbi.nlm.nih.gov/genome/gdv/.

Genome Data Viewer Front Page

The default GDV page has several components as illustrated in Figure 3.78 and described below:

A   *Switch View.* Clicking Switch View will switch the display view of the page from tree view to tabular view and vice versa.

B   *Search Organisms search box.* This search box is used to search for an organism by entering either the scientific name or common name of the organism. Enter the organism's name that you wish to view or search its genome. Once you have entered the name, the organism will be selected, and changes will be reflected in all other fields on the page.

C   *Navigation tree.* This tree is used to select an organism. The root of the tree is Eukaryota and then it branches out from the root to the leaves, which represents all eukaryotic organisms that have genome assemblies. Click the nodes that have plus sign (+) to view more organisms. Use this tree to select the organism that you wish to view or search its genome. The tree will be replaced by a table if Switch View is clicked.

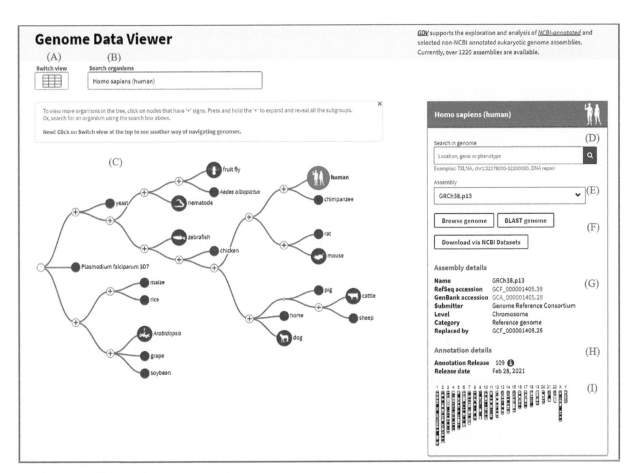

FIGURE 3.78   Genome data viewer main page.

D   *Search in Genome.* This search box provides a way to search the selected genome using a location, gene symbol, or a phenotype. For the location you can use format "Chromosome_number: start_position-end_position" coordinates format, which consists of the chromosome number, colon ":" position of the first base, dash "-", and the position of last base if you intend to find a range of a sequence. For example, to view BRCA1 in the GDV, enter "chr17:43044295-43125364" (without quotations) into the search box and click the search icon. The GDV page displaying that region will open. Instead of a location, you can enter a gene symbol (e.g., BRCA1), or a phenotype (e.g., breast cancer).

E   *Assembly dropdown list.* This list provides the list of the available assemblies for the selected organism. There may be several assemblies; however, you must pay attention as annotations and coordinates vary from an assembly to another and some annotations in one assembly may not be available in another.

F   *Tools.* This section provides the tools that can be used with genome assemblies. These tools include "Browse genome", "BLAST genome", and "Download via NCBI Datasets". Clicking Browse genome will open the GDV. Clicking BLAST genome will open the BLAST page, where you can search a sequence in the genome assembly. Clicking Download via NCBI Datasets will open the NCBI datasets to download the genome sequence in different structures.

G   *Assembly details.* This section displays the information of the selected assembly. The information of the current assembly of the selected organism is usually displayed by default. The information will change when another assembly is selected from the Assembly dropdown list.

H   *Annotation details.* This section displays the number and the link of the assembly release and the date of the release.

I   *Ideograms.* The chromosome ideograms represent the genome units of the selected organism. In the case of the human, they represent 22 chromosomes, the X-chromosome, and the Y-chromosome. Those ideograms act as navigation tools. Clicking any ideogram will open GDV displaying the chromosome represented by that ideogram.

Components of Genome Data Viewer

Enter "human" into the "Search Organisms" search box (A) or choose human from the tree (B) to select human. On the "Search in genome" search box, enter "chr17:43044295-43125364", without quotations, make sure the Assembly is GRCh38.013 and click the search icon. The GDV will display the region of BRCA1 in the genome assembly. The components of GDV are illustrated in Figure 3.79:

(1) *Assembly bar.* This is the top bar that displays the organism's name, Assembly dropdown list, and the selected chromosome (chromosome number and RefSeq accession). The assembly dropdown list shows the current genome assembly of the organism, but you can choose a different assembly from the list.

(2) *The current location.* The location of the current genome region is shown by coordinates consisting of the accession of the chromosome, a colon ":", the start-position, a dash "-", and the end-position of the region. The location coordinates of the current region displayed in the GDV is "NC_000017.11:43,044,295 – 43,125,364".

(3) *Chromosome ideogram.* The chromosome ideogram represents the current chromosome graphically. It shows the chromosome's relative size and banding pattern. Any chromosome is formed of a short arm (p) and a long arm (q). The bands on the ideogram represent the distinct pattern of bands on a chromosome when it is stained with Giemsa solution and viewed under the microscope. The labels indicate the gene's cytogenetic location, which describes the position of a particular band on the chromosome and can be used as addresses for genes. The letter "p" or "q" indicates the short or long arm respectively, the first number before the dot "." represents a region and the number after the dot represents a band. The cytogenetic location of BRAC1 is indicated by the tiny vertical blue line indicated by the red arrow

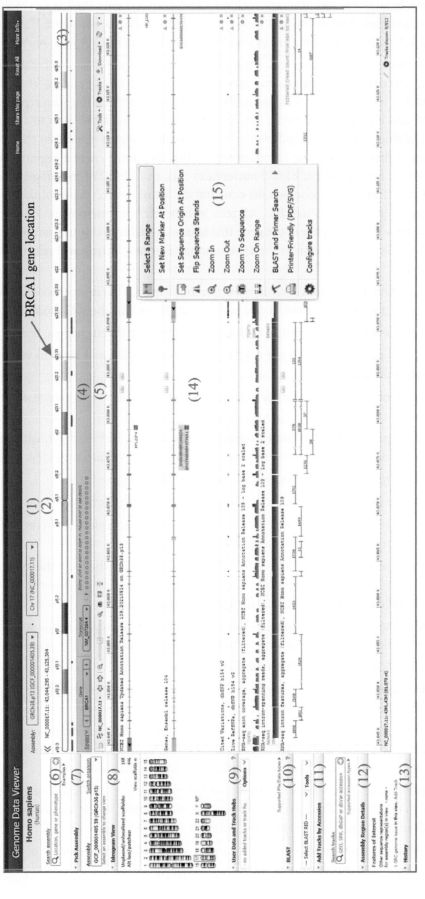

FIGURE 3.79   Genome data viewer.

in the right-hand of the ideogram on the long arm region and described as 17q21.31. This cytogenetic location is interpreted as that BRCA1 gene is on the long arm of chromosome 17, region 21, band 3, and sub-band 1. Compare this with the cytogenetic location in the BRCA1 gene record.

(4) *Gene and transcript navigation tools.* The tools include the Region dropdown list, the Gene dropdown list, the Transcript dropdown list, and exons represented by empty circles. The number of circles is corresponding to the number of exons. A filled circled indicates that the exon represented by that circle is selected and it is the current one. The Region dropdown list allows you to select a region with or without padding. The Gene dropdown list allows you to choose a gene from the list if there are multiple genes in that region of the chromosome. In the case of the current region, there are two genes: BRCA1, which has a length of 81,070 nucleotides (nt), and RPL21P4 pseudogene, which has a length of 556 nt. The Transcript dropdown list contains the list of the accessions of the reference transcripts of the selected gene. The human BRCA1 gene has six reference transcripts. You can select any of the transcripts to select the region of the gene that is transcribed into this transcript. Hovering the mouse pointer over the circle will display the exon number. Clicking a circle will select the exon represented by that circle.

(5) *Tool bar.* The tool bar includes several tools. The following are the descriptions of those tools from left to right. Hovering the pointer over a tool icon will display a hint about the tool:

- The *curved arrow* is used to return to the previous position if you changed the coordinates.
- *Pan left* and *pan right* arrows are used to pan the screen left and right to view the upstream and downstream regions.
- Zooming tools: The zooming tools include the *magnifying glass* or *zooming slider* are used to zoom in and out.
- *Zoom to sequence* (ATG) is used to zoom to the sequence level so you can see the bases of the sequence. You can use the *curved arrow* to return to the previous screen view.
- *Switch On/Off* (the colored bars) will display all or hide the gene tracks.
- *Switch to the slim mode* switches to the compact mode of the sequence viewer.
- The *Tools* menu is used for navigation, searching the selected region, changing the orientation of the strand, set an origin, viewing features, and setup preferences.
- The *Tracks* menu is used to add, remove, or configure tracks, which are the major part on the GDV and they are the graphical representation of the annotations mapped to the genome. Examples of tracks include gene, dbSNP, dbVar, ClinVar, gene expression, etc.
- The *Download* menu is used to download the sequence of the region of the specific range in FASTA and GenBank format and to download track data and printing.
- The *Refresh* icon is used to refresh the GDV display.
- The *Help* menu provides help about the GDV elements and legends for the graphical shapes that represent annotation on the tracks.

(6) *Search Assembly.* This search box is used to search the assembly by a location, gene symbol, a phenotype, dbSNP accession, dbVar accession, etc. For the location you can use format "chromosome_number: start_position-end_position" coordinates format as discussed above.

(7) *Pick Assembly.* The Pick Assembly dropdown list provides the available assemblies for the selected organism to select from. The current assembly is the default one. When you choose a different assembly, the coordinates of genes and markers and annotations may change.

(8) *Ideogram view.* Ideogram view represents the genome units of the selected organism. In case of the human, they are 22 chromosomes, the X-chromosome, and the Y-chromosome. Those ideograms act

as navigation tools. Clicking any ideogram will open GDV displaying the chromosome represented by that ideogram. The current chromosome is indicated by a green rectangle.

(9) *User Data and Track Hub*. The "Option" button allows user to add a track of user data as it will be demonstrated in a coming example.

(10) *BLAST*. BLAST allows user to search the selected genome assembly by using a query sequence and then adding the BLAST hits as a track to GDV, as it will be demonstrated in a coming example.

(11) *Add Tracks by accession*. This allows user to add tracks to GDV by entering a supported accession of an NCBI database. The supported accessions include GEO accessions (GSE25249 for GRCh37 and GSM1541970 for GRCm38 of the house mouse), SRA accession (SRR834589 for GRCh37), dbGaP accession (pha000001 for GRCh38) and dbVar accession (nstd82 for GRCh38).

(12) *Assembly Region Details*. This section provides more information about GRC assembly regions.

(13) *History*. The search history will be listed in a dropdown list.

(14) *Sequence Viewer*. The Sequence Viewer is the main part of the GDV, where the genomic data are viewed in genomic context in the forms of graphical representations in tracks. The solid blue bar on the top represents a region of the reference genome assembly. Tracks of genomic data mapped to the genome sequence are displayed below the blue bar. Tracks can be added to the Sequence Viewer, removed, or configured using the "Tracks" menu. Several tracks representing different kinds of annotations such as genes, dbSNP, dbVar, ClinVar, gene expression and more are available. Tracks displayed on the Sequence Viewer can be rearranged by dragging and dropping using the mouse. A track can also be removed by clicking on the red cross "x" button at the right end of each track. The display settings of a track are accessed by clicking the gear icon on the right side of the tracks. The download icon on the right side of a track may allow users to access the download option for that track.

(15) *The pop-up menu*. The pop-up menu is invoked by placing the mouse pointer on any spot of the Sequence Viewer and clicking the right mouse button. The pop-up menu includes all menu items for all the operations performed by the tools and menus on the tool bar.

Using Tools Menu

After selecting a region of a gene or a region of the genome assembly on the Sequence Viewer, several operations can be done using the tools and menus provided on the tool bar and pop-up menu. The following are some examples of those operations:

Navigation to a Specific Position   To go to a specific position or to display a range of sequences of the genome assembly, click the "Tools" menu and then select "Go To". A dialog box will pop up allowing you to enter a position or a range of positions. The position or range can be entered in any of the shown formats: 10k-20k, -20--10, -10k:-5, 5 to 515, -1m..1m. For example, while you are selecting chromosome 17, you can enter 43082403 on the "Go to position/range" dialog box to go to the beginning of exon 12 of BRAC1 gene or you can enter 43082403-43082576 to display exon 12 of BRCA1.

Finding on Genome Sequence   To find a sequence by entering a range of coordinates, a sequence, or a pattern, or to find a variant by entering an accession number, click the "Tools" menu and select "Search". The "Find on Sequence" dialog box will pop up prompting you to enter a search term. You can use any of the position formats you used with "Go To" above or you can use an HGVS expression (e.g. NC_000017.11:g.43082403). To find a dbSNP enter a dbSNP accession. You can also enter a sequence or a pattern using a regular expression [65].

Downloading an Exon Sequence   You can use this feature to find a sequence of a specific region of a gene such as an exon. For example, to find the sequence of exon 12 of BRCA1 gene and then to download it, enter the range of coordinates

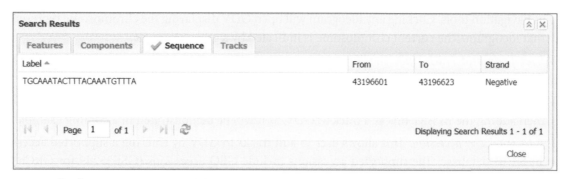

FIGURE 3.80   Finding a sequence on BRCA1 gene.

"43082403-43082576" into the "Find on Sequence" dialog box and then click the "Download" menu and select "FASTA (Visible range)" to download the file.

Finding a Sequence in a Gene Sequence   You can also use this feature to find a sequence in a sequence of a chromosome or a gene. You can use the curved arrow to go back to the previous view any time. Click the "Tools" menu and select the "Search" menu item and enter "tgcaaatactttacaaatgttta" into the "Find on Sequence" dialog box and click the "OK" button. The "Search Results" box will be displayed. If the sequence has been found, a green check sign will mark the "Sequence" tab on that box. Click on the "Sequence" tab to display the results as shown in Figure 3.80. The start and end positions of the sequence and the orientation of the strand are shown.

Using Regular Expression for Finding a Sequence   The regular expression [65] is a sequence of characters that specifies a search pattern. You can use this feature to find a sequence of codons that are translated into a specific sequence of amino acids. For example, assume that you wish to search for the codons that code for the "tyr-lys-cys-leu" amino acid sequence. You know that multiple codons may code for a single amino acid. Tyrosine (tyr) is coded by TAC or TAT, lysine by AAA, cysteine (cys) by TTA or TTG, and leucine (leu) by TTA and TTG. You can use regular expressions to specify a pattern for that sequence of amino acids by clicking the "Tools" menu and select the "Search" menu item and then enter "ta[c/T]a{3}tg[t/c]tt[a/g]" and click the "Ok" button. The results will be displayed in the "Search Results" box as in Figure 3.81 (234 hits). The results show the sequences, start and end positions of the sequences, and orientations of the strands.

Flipping the Strand   The orientation of the DNA strand is either positive or negative based on the transcript of a gene. The positive DNA strand is the one whose sequence contains the instructions for building a protein, while the negative strand contains the complementary sequence. To reverse the orientation of a DNA strand, click the "Tools" menu and select the "Flip strand" menu item or you can use "Flip Sequence Strands" from the pop-up menu. You can confirm the orientation by the direction of the coordinates on the ruler.

Creating a Marker   A marker is a line or a highlighted region with a label on a specific position or a range of position on the Sequence Viewer created by the user to mark a position or a region such as a starting sequence of an exon, a SNP, etc. To create a marker, click the "Tools" menu and select the "Markers" menu item to invoke the "Set New Marker" dialog box. Enter a label for the marker and the position on which you intend to create the marker. You can select a color as well and then click the "OK" button to create the marker. It is easier to use the pop-up menu to create a marker at a specific position. Use the zooming tools and pan left and pan right icons to adjust the position or the range on which you intend to create a marker. Fix the mouse pointer on the position (or hold and drag the mouse on the ruler to select a range) and then click the right button of the mouse to invoke the pop-up menu and select "Set New Marker at Position" or select "Set New Marker on Selected Range" if you selected a range of positions. A pink marker on a range is shown in Figure 3.82.

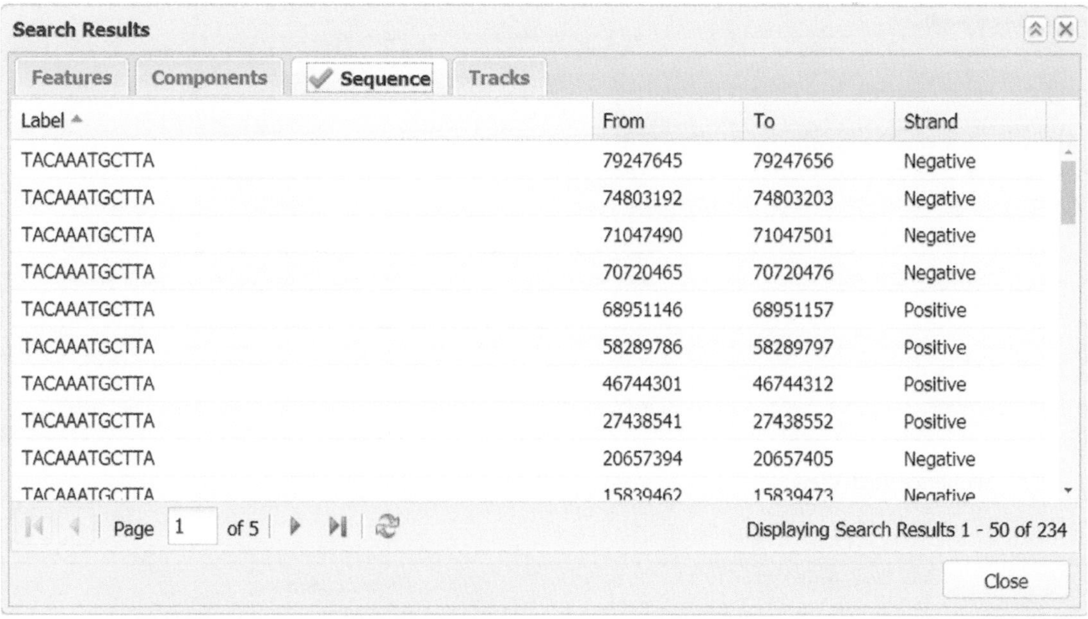
Search Results

Features | Components | Sequence | Tracks

Label	From	To	Strand
TACAAATGCTTA	79247645	79247656	Negative
TACAAATGCTTA	74803192	74803203	Negative
TACAAATGCTTA	71047490	71047501	Negative
TACAAATGCTTA	70720465	70720476	Negative
TACAAATGCTTA	68951146	68951157	Positive
TACAAATGCTTA	58289786	58289797	Positive
TACAAATGCTTA	46744301	46744312	Positive
TACAAATGCTTA	27438541	27438552	Positive
TACAAATGCTTA	20657394	20657405	Negative
TACAAATGCTTA	15839462	15839473	Negative

Page 1 of 5 Displaying Search Results 1 - 50 of 234

Close

FIGURE 3.81 Finding a pattern using regular expression.

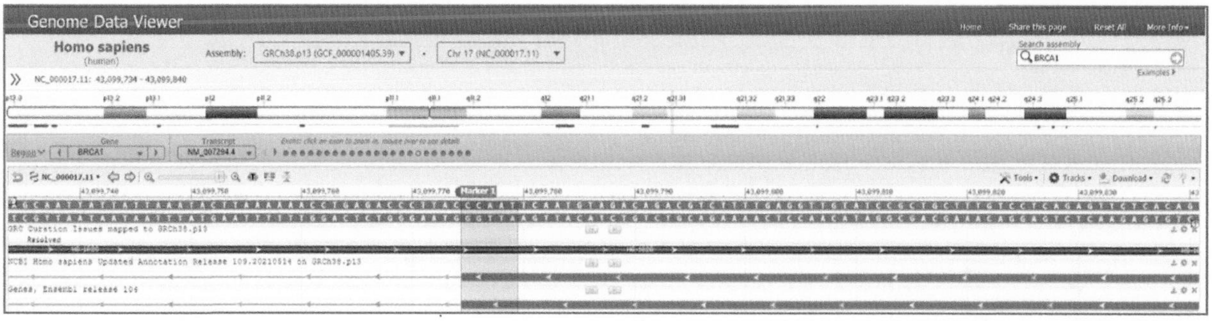

FIGURE 3.82 Creating a marker.

Viewing Gene, CDS and Protein Sequences The Sequence Text View is used to view sequence features and proteins of a selected region. The sequence types are distinguished by different highlighting colors (the protein coding regions (CDS) with amino acid translation are pink/white, RNA in purple, and gene in green. To view the sequence, CDS, and proteins of the BRCA1 gene, click the "Tools" menu and select the "Sequence Text View" menu item. The Sequence View is displayed as shown in Figure 3.83. The accessions of the transcripts/proteins are listed in the dropdown list. You can select an item from the list to view the transcript and the amino acids translated from that script.

Searching Primers for PCR Primers are used in PCR to amplify a specific region of a genomic or transcript sequence. They are specific sequences of a length between 18 to 25 bases. Since a DNA molecule has two strands, two primers are required for each strand (forward and reverse primer). Primers for a specific gene or a region of a gene are searched using BLAST (Basic Local Alignment Search Tool), which we will discuss in Chapters 7 and 8. To find primers for a region of gene, first select the region that you wish to amplify. If your sample is genomic DNA, you can select a region that includes both introns and exons of the gene. But if your sample is cDNA (mRNA), then you must select a region that includes exons only. Assume that you wish to design primers for the exon 21 of the BRCA1 gene. Click the circle that represents exon 21 on the Gene and Transcript navigation bar, use the mouse to select the region, and then either use the "Tools" menu or pop-up menu to select "Primer BLAST (Selection)". That will forward you to the Primer-BLAST page shown in Figure 3.84.

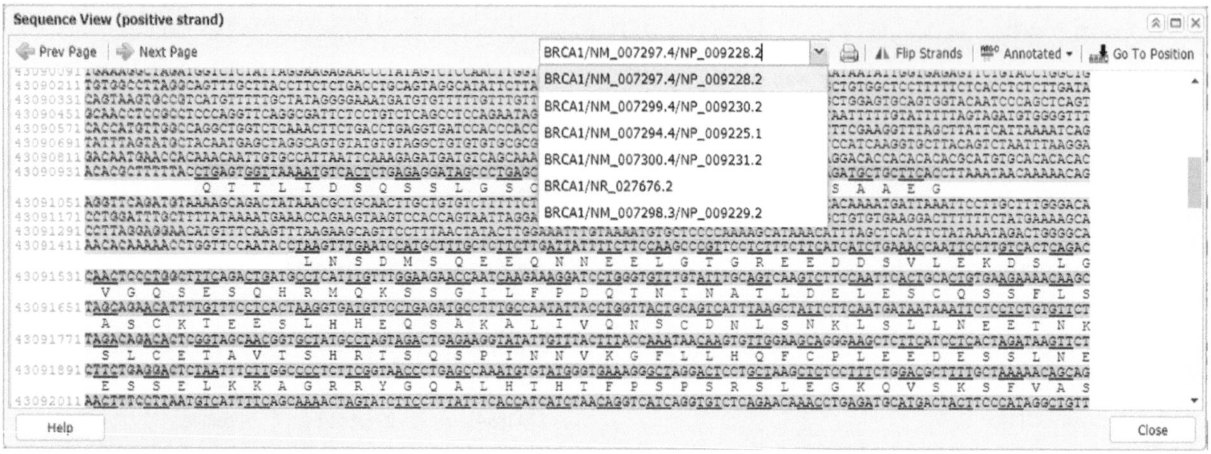

FIGURE 3.83 Sequence Text View.

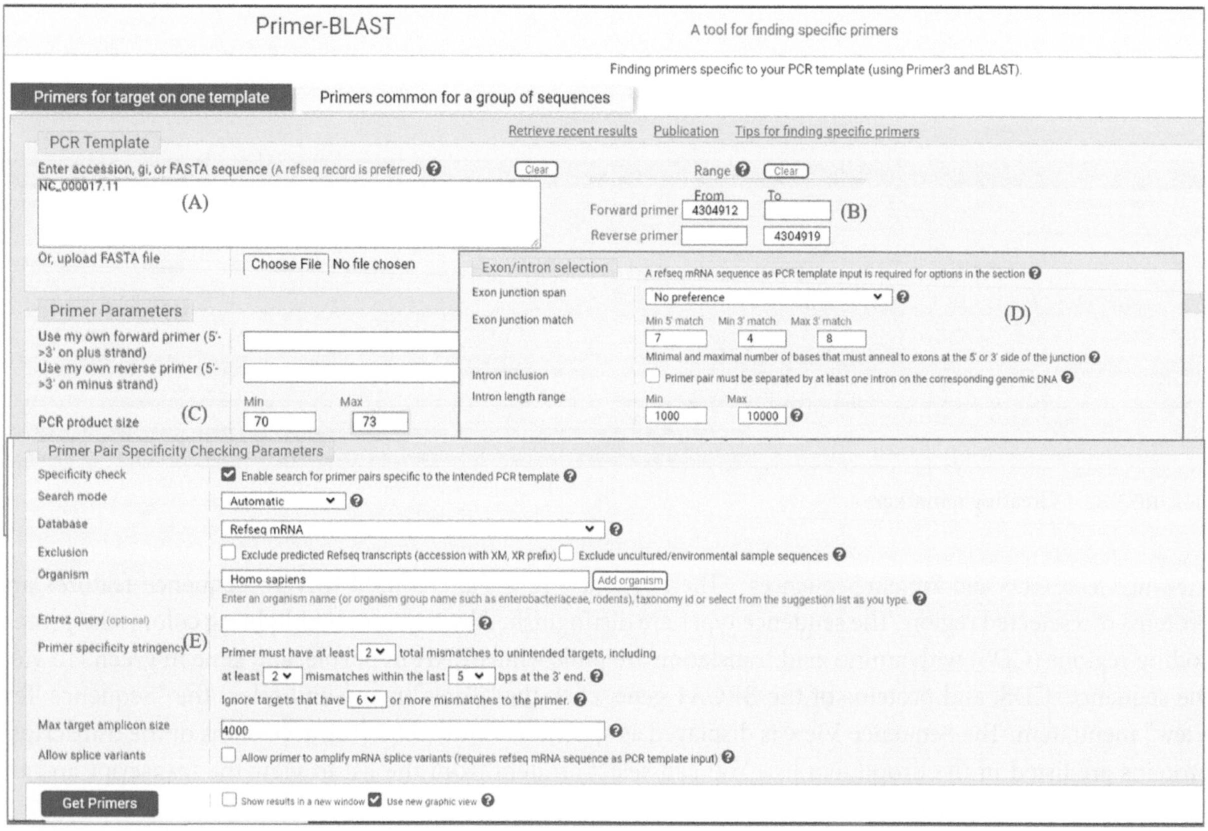

FIGURE 3.84 Primer-BLAST.

The RefSeq of the chromosome has been copied to the Query box (A). The sequence range is determined by "From" and "To" input fields (B). The options in section (C) are used to set the length of the PCR product, number of primers, and primer melting temperatures. You can accept the default values for the fields in section (E) and click "Get Primers". Since the BRCA1 gene has multiple transcript variants, Primer-BLAST will display the list of variants to select all or some of them. Assume that you are interested in variant 1; select the checkbox of BRCA1 transcript 1 and click the "Submit" button. Several primers will be displayed. Choose the primers that are suitable for your PCR experiment as shown in Figure 3.85.

Primer pair 1										
	Sequence (5'->3')	Template strand	Length	Start	Stop	Tm	GC%	Self complementarity		Self 3' complementarity
Forward primer	TGTGCCAAGGGTGAATGATGA	Plus	21	43049121	43049141	59.92	47.62	3.00		2.00
Reverse primer	CAACTGGAATGGATGGTACAGC	Minus	22	43049192	43049171	59.32	50.00	4.00		2.00
Product length	72									
Products on intended targets										
>NM_007294.4 Homo sapiens BRCA1 DNA repair associated (BRCA1), transcript variant 1, mRNA										

FIGURE 3.85 **Primer sequences.**

For researchers who design such PCR primers to amplify a gene region, the next step would be to synthesize oligonucleotides (DNA) that can be used as PCR primers.

There are other operations that you can do using the "Tools" menus such as set an origin, references, and other options to search for PCR primers. Try to explore that by yourself.

Using Tracks Menu

Tracks contain graphical representation for the genomic data in genomic context. Tracks are categorized into two main groups: NCBI tracks and custom tracks:

(1) *NCBI tracks.* NCBI tracks are the tracks that are provided with the GDV, and they are divided into several categories based on types of genomic data, including (a) Sequence, (b) Genes/Products, (c) Variation, (d) Phenotype and Disease, (e) Alignments, (f) Genomic clones, (g), Expression, (h) Epigenomics, and (i) Comparative genomics. Those categories may vary with organisms and assemblies.

(2) *Custom data*: Custom data are used by users to create custom tracks or can be user data or data imported from other resources. The sources of custom data may include (1) BLAST results, (b) Data file, (c) Remote files, (d) Alignment MUSCLE/FASTA, (e) URL, and (f) Text.

NCBI tracks and tracks for custom data are added, removed, and configured using the Configure Page menu item under the "Tracks" menu. NCBI tracks and custom data are in separate horizontal tabs as shown in Figure 3.86.

NCBI tracks are categorized into vertical tabs. The "Active Tracks" tab lists the tracks that have been selected and they are currently displayed on the GDV. From the NCBI tracks, select the tracks that serve your needs.

In the following you will use some NCBI tracks and tracks from custom data. You will continue using BRCA1 as an example. If the GDV is not displaying the region of the BRCA1 gene, enter "chr17:43044295-43125364" into the "Search assembly" box and click the arrow to display the gene region. You will also need to delete all tracks except the "Sequence" track. To do that click the "Track" menu and then select the "Configure Tracks" menu item to open the "Configure Page" dialog box. Click "Active Tracks", unselect all tracks except "Sequence", and click the "Configure" button. The Sequence Viewer will display only the blue Sequence track as shown in Figure 3.87.

Adding NCBI Tracks   The Sequence Viewer in Figure 3.87 does not include any annotation. You may need to add a gene annotation track so as to be able to view the BRCA1 gene structure (intron and exons). To add a gene annotation track, use the "Configure Tracks" menu item to open the "Configure Page" dialog box and from the "Gene/Product" vertical tab select the "NCBI Homo sapiens Updated Annotation Release 109.20210514 on GRCh38.p13" track and click the "Configure" button to display the gene annotation track on the Sequence Viewer as shown in Figure 3.88.

You can notice that the gene annotation track shows the BRCA1 gene structure (introns and 23 exons). However, we may need to display the transcripts and proteins as well. BRCA1 has several transcripts and each transcript codes a protein. To display the transcripts and proteins, open the "Configure Page" dialog

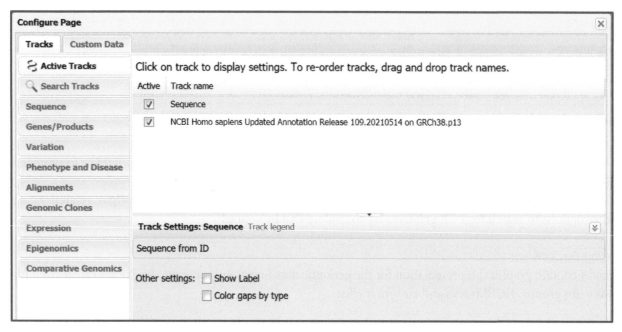

FIGURE 3.86   Track Configure Page.

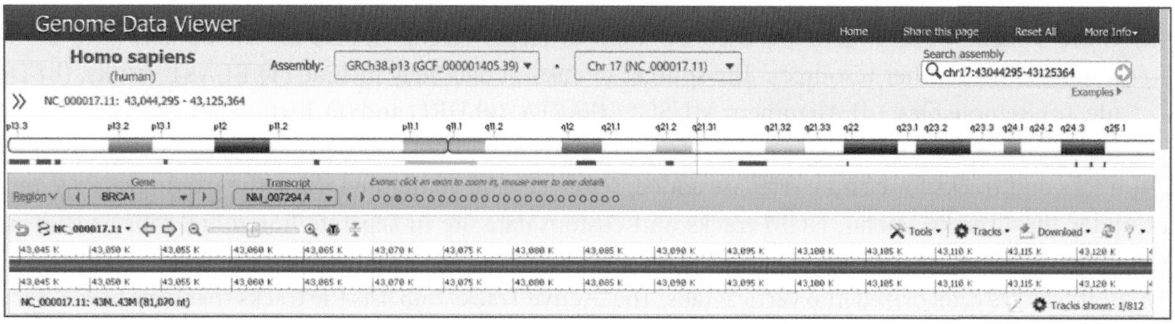

FIGURE 3.87   Sequence viewer without annotation tracks.

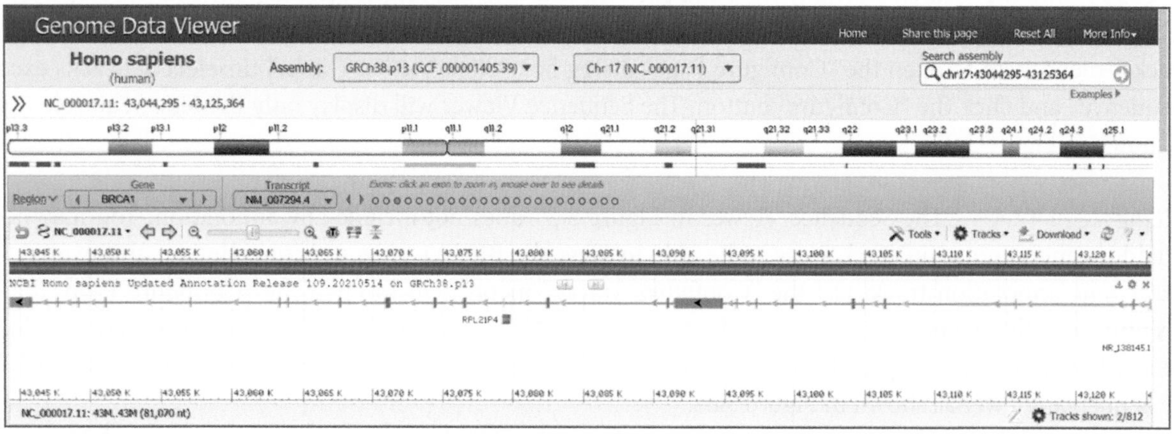

FIGURE 3.88   Sequence viewer gene annotation tracks.

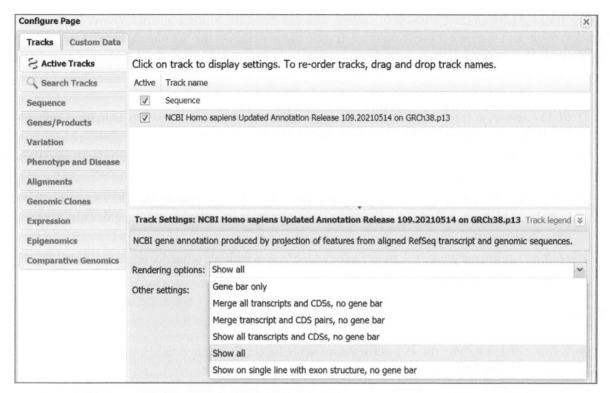

FIGURE 3.89   Sequence viewer gene annotation tracks.

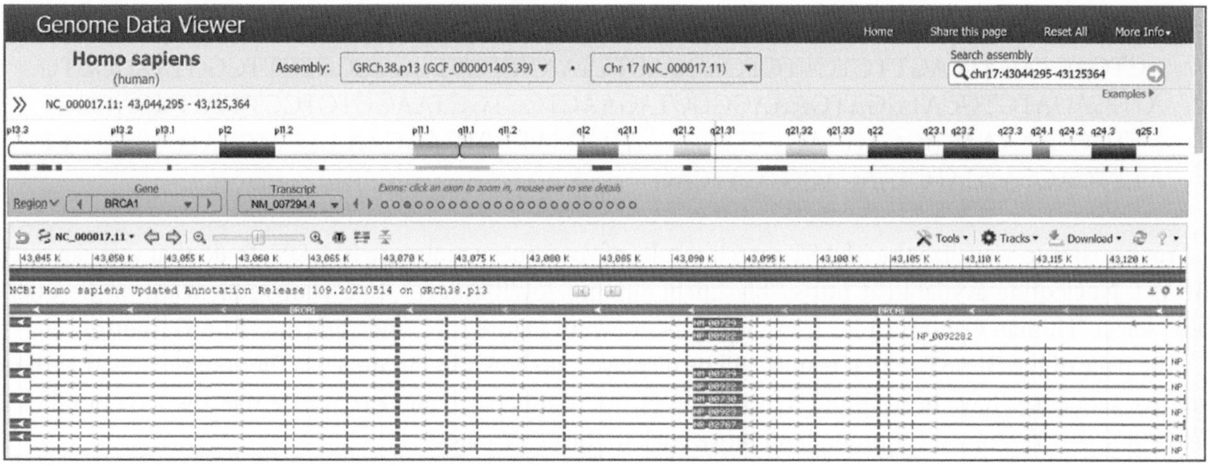

FIGURE 3.90   Sequence viewer showing gene structure, transcripts, and proteins.

box", and click the "Active Tracks" vertical tab, then select "NCBI Homo sapiens Updated Annotation Release 109.20210514 on GRCh38.p13". From the "Rendering options" dropdown list, select "Show all" as shown in Figure 3.89 and click the "Configure" button.

The gene annotation track will be configured to display the BRCA1 gene in green, BRCA1 transcripts in purple and BRCA1 protein isoforms in red (Figure 3.90).

Adding a gene annotation track and configuring it is just an example. You can add the tracks that meet your goal. For example, you can add tracks from the Variation group to visualize dbSNP and dbVar or you can add a disease track from the Phenotypes and Disease category and so on.

Adding Tracks of Custom Data   Tracks of custom data can be added to the Sequence Viewer by clicking the "Tracks" menu and then select the "Configure Tracks" menu item. On the "Configure Page" dialog box, click the "Custom Data" horizontal tab. Several options are available in the "Custom Track" tab to add tracks from custom data, including:

(1) *BLAST results.* A track of BLAST results is added to the Sequence Viewer by entering a request ID (RID) after performing the BLAST search on the BLAST web page.

(2) *Data file.* A track can be added from a variety of local data files including ASN.1, BED, aligned FASTA, GFF2, GFF3, GTF, VCF, WIG, and XML.

(3) *Remote file.* A track of data file can be added from the URL of a remote file. The remote file formats include BAM, BigBed, BigWig, VCFTabix. Those files must be indexed, and the index files are to be at the same location.

(4) *Multiple sequence alignment.* A track can be added from a multiple sequence alignment in MUSCLE file format or FASTA file format.

The following are some examples for adding track from custom data.

Adding Tracks of BLAST Results   BLAST will be discussed in Chapters 7 and 8 in detail. However, you will use BLAST to learn how to add a track from the BLAST results.

Assume that you have obtained the following sequence from a PCR product of a certain region in BRCA1 gene:

>Seq1
CCTCACTAGATAAGTTCTCTTCTGAGGACTCTAATTTCTTGGCCCCTCTTCGGTAACCCTG
ATCCAGATGTGCATGGATGAAAGGGCTAGAACTCCTGCTAAGCTCTCCTTTCTGGACGCT
TTTGCTAAAAACAGCAGAACTTTCCTTAATGTCATTTTCAGCAAAACTAGTATCTTCCTTT
ATTTCACCATCATCTAACAGGTCATCAG

Your goal is to visualize the BLAST search results of your query sequence in GDV. To do that you can open BLAST Nucleotide available at https://blast.ncbi.nlm.nih.gov/Blast.cgi, paste your sequence into the query box, select "Human Genomic plus transcripts" as shown in Figure 3.91, and click the "BLAST" button.

The page of the BLAST search results will be displayed as shown in Figure 3.92. The results show that there are five sequences have been found. On the top of the results page, you can notice that the RID number is "ANP0C1SS013". Copy this number and move back to the GDV page.

On the GDV, click the "Track" menu and select the "Configure Tracks" menu item to open the "Configure Page" dialog box. Click the "Custom Data" tab and select "BLAST results", paste the RID number, and click the "Upload" button to upload the track. After the track has been uploaded, click the "Configure" button. The track of the BLAST results will be displayed in the Sequence Viewer as shown in Figure 3.93.

Adding Tracks of Local VCF Files   The VCF or variant call file contains variants that may be called from a SAM/BAM file using variant calling programs such as VCFtools. The VCF file contains variants from an individual sample. Visualizing such variants in the GDV will enable you to visualize the significant variants and markers such dbSNP and dbVar variations in the sample sequence or to identify the links of genotypes to phenotypes. The GDV supports variants in several file formats including VCF, BED, GFF3, GTF, GVF, HGVS, and ASN.1.

For this example, you can download one of the NCBI VCF files from the NCBI's ftp server https://ftp.ncbi.nlm.nih.gov/pub/dbVar/data/Homo_sapiens/by_assembly/GRCh38/vcf/GRCh38.variant_call.all.vcf.gz to a local drive and then click the "Tracks" menu and select the "Configure tracks" menu item

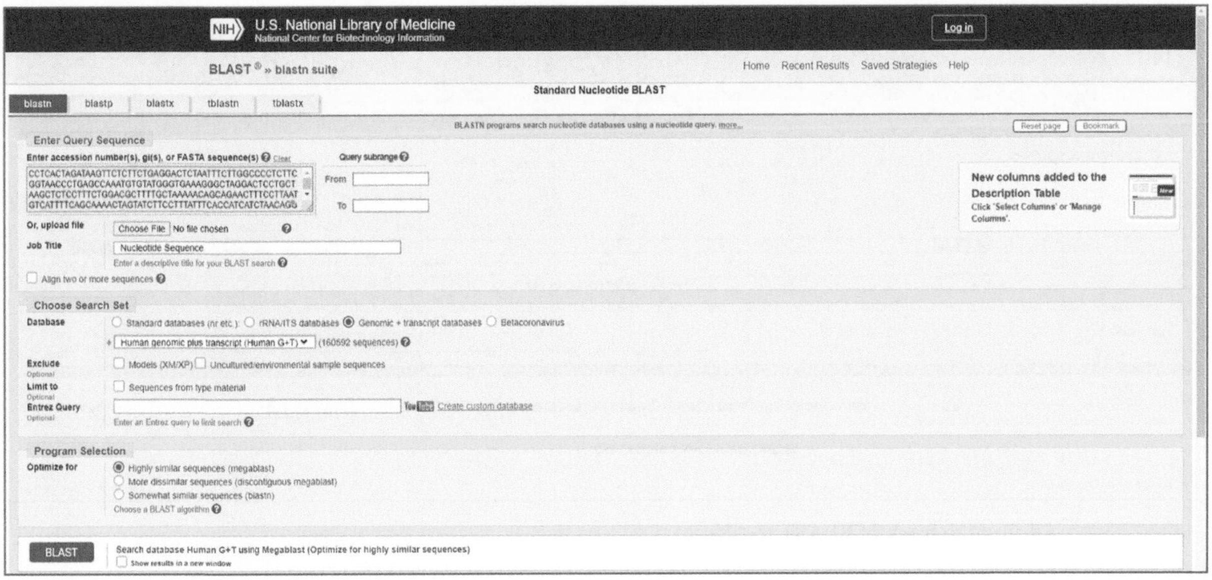

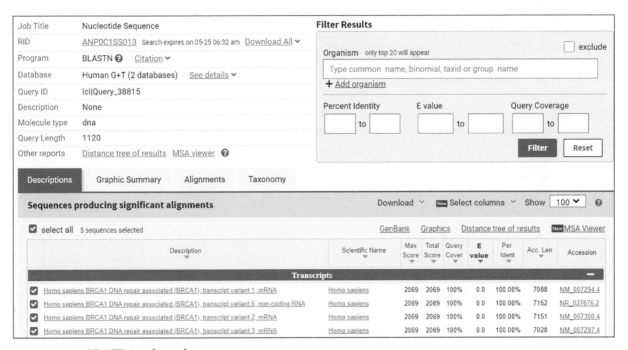

FIGURE 3.91   **BLAST nucleotide page.**

FIGURE 3.92   **BLAST search results.**

and from the "Custom Data" horizontal tab select "Data File", browse to the file, and select it, click "Upload" to upload the file. After the upload has been completed, click the "Configure" button to add the track. After the track has been added, you can use the zooming tools to zoom in to the base level to visualize small variations such as dbSNP. You may need to add an NCBI dbSNP, dbVar, or ClinVar track, etc. for annotation.

Adding Tracks of Remote VCF Files   Instead of using a local file you can also upload a remote file by entering the file web address in the URL field in the "Custom Data" tab and click the "Upload" button to begin uploading the file. Uploading may take a long time depending on the size of the file. After the file has been uploaded, click the "Configure" button to add the track to the Sequence Viewer.

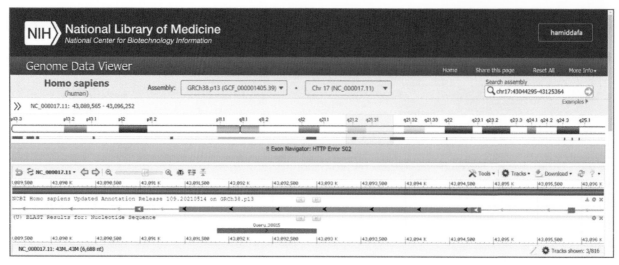

FIGURE 3.93   Adding the track of BLAST results.

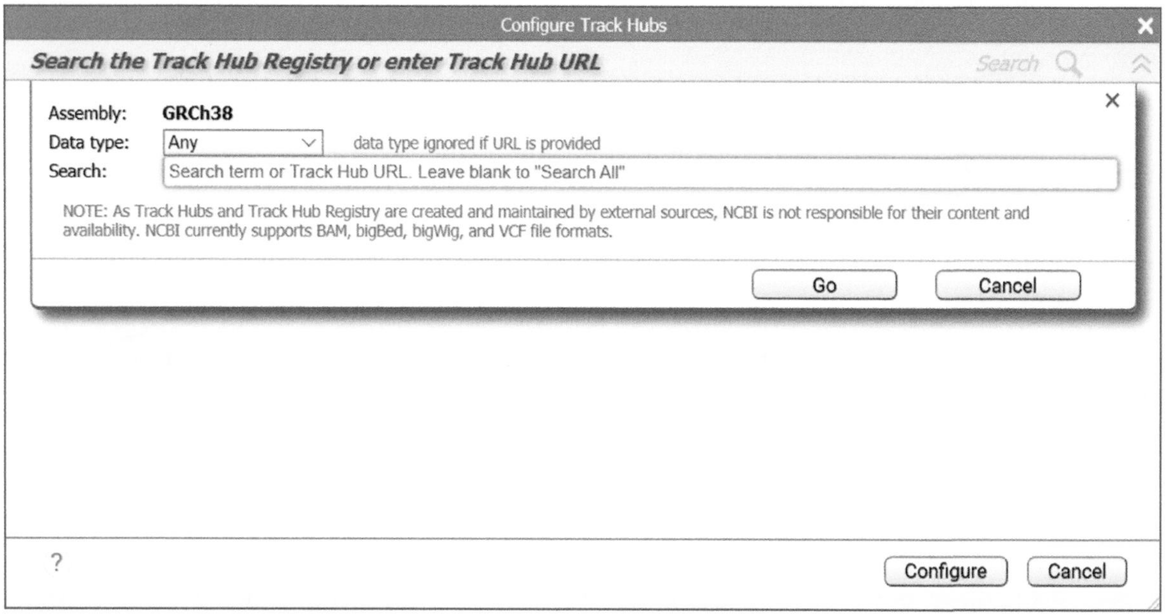

FIGURE 3.94   Configure track hubs.

Adding Track from Track Hub   The Track Hubs are web-based directories of a variety of genomic data including transcriptomic, proteomic, and epigenomics data that can be viewed on the genome viewers such as GDV and the UCSC Genome Browser. The Track Hubs Registry are created and maintained by external sources rather than NCBI. The data may be stored in the hubs registries in large files; however, importing tracks from Track Hubs is faster because only the track will be displayed on the Sequence Viewer while the underlying data is stored in the provider' server. The NCBI GDV currently supports BAM, bigBed, bigWig, and VCF file formats. The Track Hub Registry at https://trackhubregistry.org is a global collection of publicly accessible track hubs supported by funding from the BBSRC, the Wellcome Trust and the European Molecular Biology Laboratory. Track hubs are also available at https://genome.ucsc.edu/cgi-bin/hgHubConnect, which are curated by UCSC (University of California Santa Cruz). To add a track from track hubs, click the "Tracks" menu and select the "Configure Track Hubs" menu item. The "Configure Track Hubs" dialog box will pop up, as shown in Figure 3.94, to allow you either to search the track hub registry or to enter a track hub URL. The "Configure Track Hubs" dialog box displays the assembly release, a dropdown list for data types (genomics, transcriptomics, or proteomics), and search box for entering a search term or a URL. The data type is

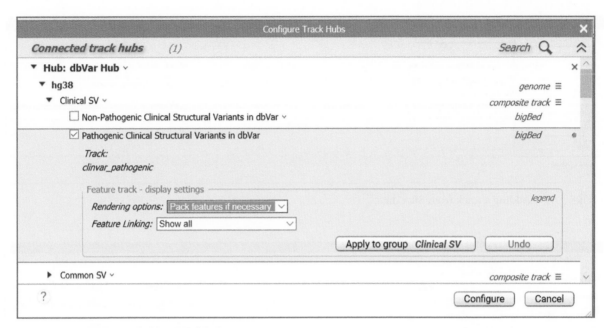

FIGURE 3.95   Adding track from track hubs.

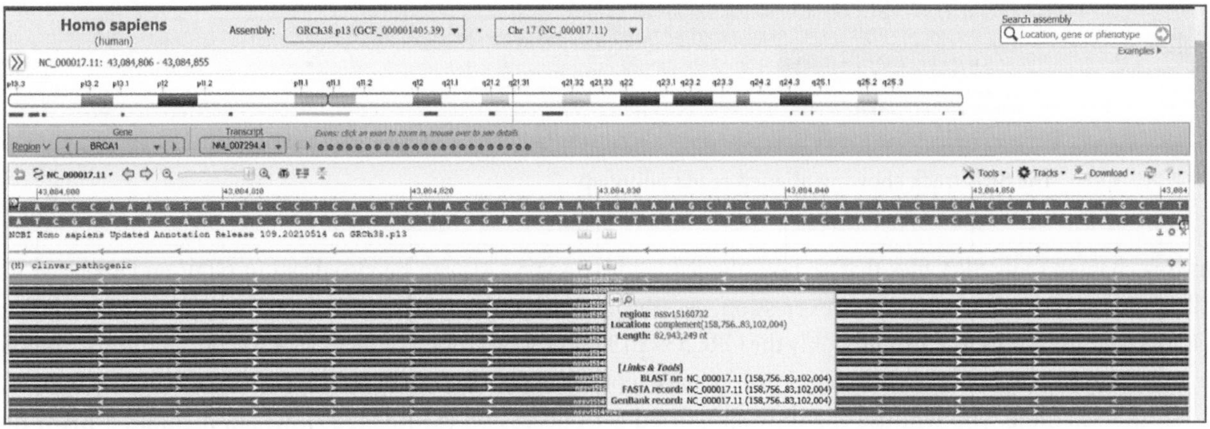

FIGURE 3.96   GDV displaying a track from track hubs.

ignored if a URL is used. The tracks are added by connecting to the track hubs, uploading files, or streaming data from remotely hosted files.

The GDV has numerous built-in tracks added by NCBI. Those built-in tracks are the most commonly used. Assume that we wish to find a dbVar track from track hubs. Leave the search box empty and click the "Go" button to begin searching for the available hub tracks. When the results are displayed, scroll down to "dbVar Hub", select "Clinical SV", and check "Pathogenic Clinical Structural Variants in dbVar" as shown in Figure 3.95. You can configure the track to meet your goal and click the "Configure" button; the track will be viewed on the Sequence Viewer.

You can use the zooming tools to zoom in and out and to the base level to view the variants and you can click a variant to read about it as shown in Figure 3.96.

Analyzing SRA Files from NCBI Dataset   The raw sequencing data such as FASTQ files and alignment information (SAM/BAM) files are obtained from high-throughput sequencing technologies and submitted by researchers to the NCBI Sequence Read Archive (SRA) database as supporting data for their published publications. Such massive data are compressed and stored in SRA files to be available for researchers. The SRA database will be discussed later

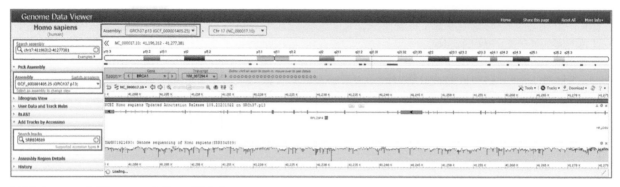

FIGURE 3.97   Adding a track from SRA data.

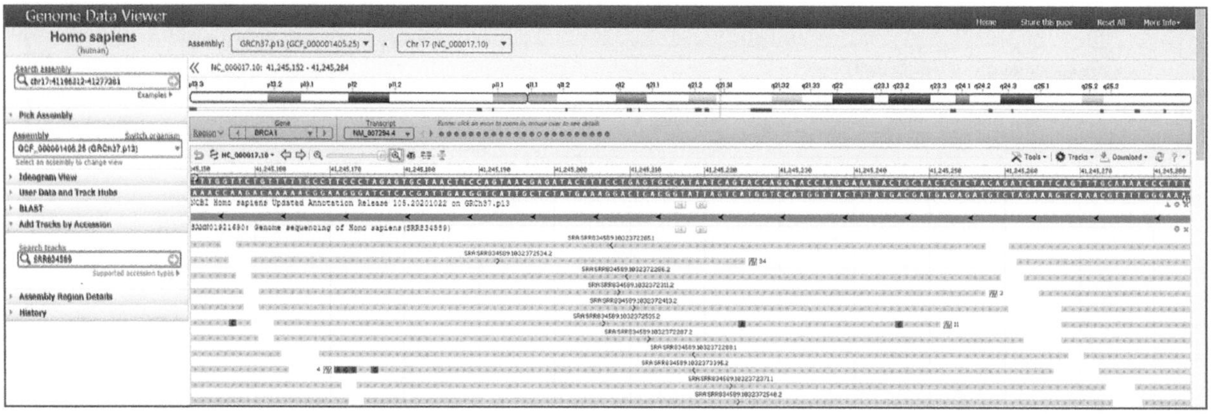

FIGURE 3.98   The SRA track showing aligned reads piling up.

in this chapter. Only SRA files that archive aligned reads (BAM/SAM) can be visualized in GDV and analyzed for allelic and mutational analysis, gene expression, etc. The mapped reads in archived BAM/SAM must be aligned to an NCBI's genome assembly. Currently, only the GRCh37.p13 genome assembly supports SRA data for the human. Before importing data of SRA to the GDV, select the right assembly from the "Assembly" dropdown menu.

In this example, you will use the only supported SRA accession (SRR834589), which includes a BAM file of aligned reads of a human whole genome sequencing project. You can open this SRA record by entering the accession into the search box of the SRA database to read more about this SRA archive. Remember that the GDV support only this SRA accession. However, if you wish to view your BAM file using GDV, you can view it only using the remote URL feature.

The sequence reads in the SRA file of this accession are mapped to GRCh37.p13 assembly. To add the track of this SRA data to the Sequence Viewer of the GDV, first select GRCh37.p13 from the "Assembly" dropdown list. Remember that the BRCA1 gene will be in a different position in this assembly. You can obtain this information from the Gene database. The BRCA1 gene is in "chr17:41196312-41277381" region in GRCh37.p13 assembly. Enter these coordinates into the "Search assembly" search box and click the arrow to display the BRCA1 region on the Sequence Viewer as shown in Figure 3.97. The highlight fields are the fields that you use to enter the above information.

The SRA track has been added to the sequence viewer as shown in Figure 3.98. It is shown that there are reads mapped along the BRCA1 gene (completely covered BRCA1 gene region). You can zoom in to view these reads. It will be better if you zoom in on an exon region.

In Figure 3.98, the SRA track shows that the reads aligned to the BRCA1 gene are piled up. Several kinds of analyses and visualizations can be performed with the SRA track. If the mapped reads are of mRNA (e.g.,

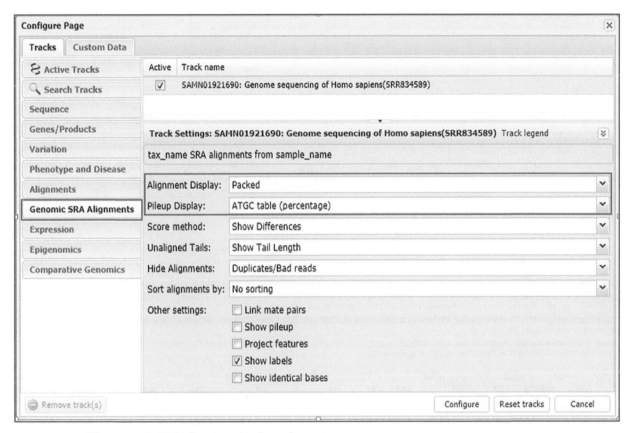

FIGURE 3.99   The genomic SRA alignment track configuration.

RNA-seq), the gene expression can be evaluated based on the coverage depth of the reads. If the reads are of genomic DNA origin, they can be used for genotyping and variation discovery. Anyway, the research objective usually determines the kind of analysis.

We have already known that this SRA is the mapped reads of whole genome sequencing of an individual human. What you can do with this data is: (1) SNP genotyping, (2) variation discovery (dbSNP and dbVar), and (3) checking whether any of the variations, if present, are associated with a pathogenic condition or a disease such as breast cancer, since some of the BRCA1 gene mutations are associated with breast-ovarian cancer.

To perform SNP genotyping, you must configure the SRA track by clicking the "Track" menu and select the "Configure Tracks" menu item to open the "Configure Page" dialog box. You will notice that a vertical tab named "Genomic SRA Alignment" has been added. Click that tab to open the track settings. Change the "Alignment Display" to "Packed" and change "Pileup Display" to "ATGC Table (percentage)" as displayed in Figure 3.99 and click the "Configure" button

After the configuration, the SRA alignment track will be packed as shown in Figure 3.100 and the percentage of each nucleotide (A, T, G, and T) is calculated across the aligned reads for each position.

To view the nucleotide percentage in each position, you need to zoom in the sequence to the base level using "Zoom to sequence" or the ATG icon as shown in Figure 3.101. You can notice that at the bottom of the Sequence Viewer, five lines were added. Those lines are (Intron%, Gap%, C%, G%, T%, and A%) for the percentage of intron, gap, C, T, G, and T in each position. You can use the pan left and pan right to scroll left and right to explore the SNP genotype of the positions of interest. The following conclusions can be drawn from the percentage of each nucleotide in each position:

- If the percentage is very small, it may be due to sequencing error and that nucleotide cannot considered as an allele in that position.

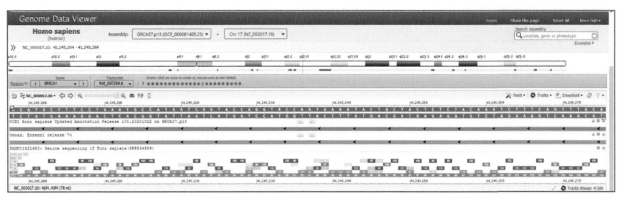

FIGURE 3.100   Packed SRA alignment track with match and mismatch counts.

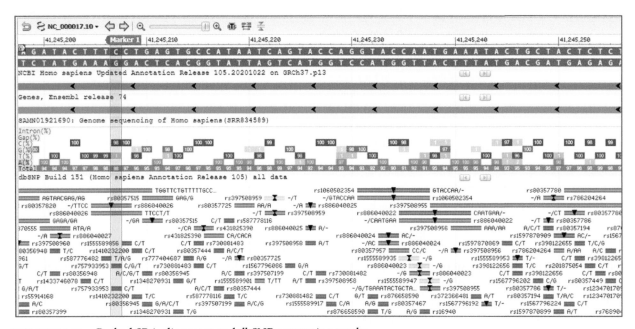

FIGURE 3.101   Packed SRA alignment and dbSNP annotation tracks.

- If a nucleotide has more than 90% or 100% in that position that means the allele at that position is homozygous.
- If the two nucleotides have percentage around 50% each, the allele at that position will be heterozygous.

Use the "Tracks" menu to add a track for dbSNP annotation to view the dbSNP variants as shown in Figure 3.101. That will help you to identify dbSNP accessions and their phenotypic associations. For example, the position marked by the pink marker has 98% C and 1% T. Thus, this T in this position is due to error and this position has only a single nucleotide in both gene allele; therefore, the position is homozygous. You can also notice that there are two visible dbSNP variants reported at this position of the genome assembly (rs757933953 (C/G/T) and rs757933953 (C/T)). You can read the detailed information of these two dbSNP variants and their association to any phenotype. However, this example SRA data has neither of these two dbSNP variants since the allele at that position is C.

100 Genome Browser

The 100 Genome project was launched in 2008 and continued for seven years until 2015 as an international collaboration effort among several international research groups to develop an archive for genomic variation, genotype, and regions of the genome associated with common human diseases for supporting future medical research. The project goal was to benefit from the development in sequencing technology to find most genetic variants with allelic frequencies of at least 1% in the populations studied. The variants cataloged by the project were from genome-wide association studies comparing genomes from large cohorts of people to identify variants that are associated with diseases or other phenotypes. Because sequencing was still expensive, the project decided to sequence each sample to only 4x genome coverage to achieve that goal although at that coverage sequencing cannot discover all genetic variants in the sample. The project combined data from 2,504 samples to accurately determine the variant sites in each sample. The project included samples of anonymous participants from 26 populations across five continental regions – Africa, America, East Asia, South Asia, and Europe. The datasets and analyses produced by the 1000 Genomes Project have been openly released and used in thousands of publications [66]. Since the project ended in 2015, funding is being received by EMBL-EBI to maintain the data of the 1000 Genome Project to ensure future access, incorporate additional published genomic data, and to expand data collection via the International Genome Sample Resource (IGSR) [67]. However, the original sequence data of the 1000 Genome Project was carried out in phases. The data of the third phase represents the finalized dataset, and it was released in 2013. The current analyses of variation and phenotype were based on Phase 3, which has datasets from 2,504 samples from 26 populations across five continental regions. The exomes of all samples were sequenced at low coverage and 24 samples were sequenced at high coverage for validation.

The 1000 Genome Browser [46] is the 1000 Genome Browser project tool that allows users to search for variants and genotypes and to view the supporting sequence read alignments. You can use the browser to display the global and regional allelic frequencies of variants and their record details. This project allows researchers to discover that some variants associated with diseases or traits are more prevalent in certain regional populations than others.

Links to the 1000 Genome Browser are available at the human genome web page, dbVar web page, and at www.ncbi.nlm.nih.gov/variation/tools/1000genomes/. The browser supports the Phase 3 datasets, and it uses dbSNP build 144.

The 1000 Genome Browser is like the GDV, but it has an additional table called phenotype table, as shown in Figure 3.102. The phenotype table displays phenotypes, variants, and allows users to view the supporting sequence read alignments of a sample. The column headers of the phenotype table are labeled by the coordinates of the variants and variant accessions. In a single coordinate you may find a single variant or more. The cells of each column in the phenotype table represent allelic frequencies of the variant or variants. The first row of the phenotype table is for the global allelic frequency while other rows are for regional allelic frequencies of the variants. Most of the components of the 1000 Genome Browser have been discussed with GDV. The following are the descriptions for the illustrated parts in Figure 3.102:

(A) Search box is to search the dataset. The search term can be a phenotype, a dbSNP accession, a coordinate, etc. Examples are shown when you put the mouse over "Search examples" below the search box. For example, you can enter the "rs713040" dbSNP and click the arrow to begin the search.

(B) The dbSNP will be displayed in the Sequence Viewer as indicated by the marker.

(C) The yellow column is the column of the dbSNP. The header cell carries the coordinate of that dbSNP and its accession number. The first cell after the header, which is in "Population/Sample" row, contains the global frequency (A=0.2857 and G=0.7143). The global frequency of A is 0.2857 and the global frequency of G is 0.7132 at that position. The other rows represent the regional frequencies of these alleles as indicated by the row titles.

(D) The alignment of the sequences of the samples of each region can be viewed by clicking on the triangle icon before the row title and then checking the sample whose sequence read alignment you intend to view on the Sequence Viewer.

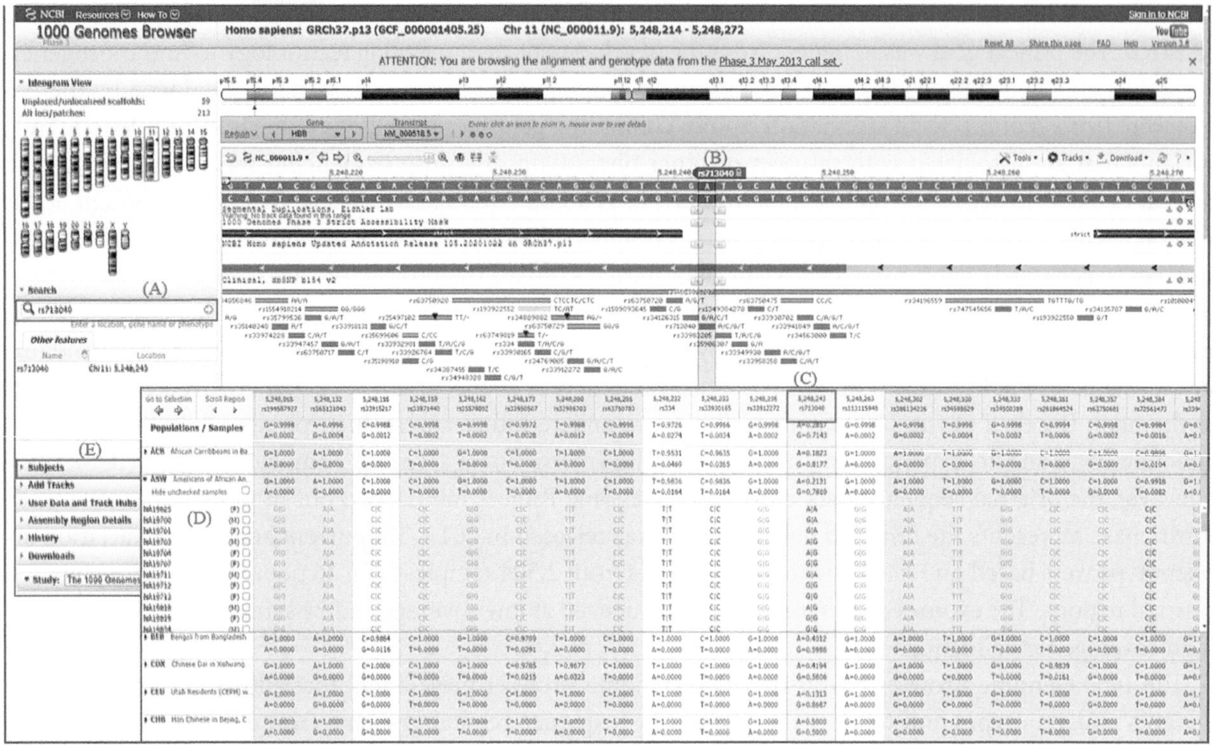

FIGURE 3.102   100 genome browser.

(E)   Subjects include track filters (phenotype, population, and sample) to control the tracks that you intend to view on the Sequence Viewer.

ONLINE MENDELIAN INHERITANCE IN MAN

Online Mendelian Inheritance in Man (OMIM) [68] is a public database for human genes (genotypes), diseases or disorders (phenotypes), and relationships between them. It was first published in 1966 by Dr Victor A. McKusick as a catalog of Mendelian traits and disorders and went online in 1985. NCBI began to maintain its content and support its searching and integration with other NCBI databases in 1995. OMIM stores curated genes, phenotypes, and the relationships between them and it also contains information on all known Mendelian disorders. OMIM is an important resource for supporting human genetics research and education and the practice of clinical genetics as an authoritative source of information for genes and genetic phenotypes.

OMIM records are either OMIM gene records or OMIM phenotype records. A gene record includes gene information and may or may not have allelic variants. A phenotype record includes phenotype information with clinical synopsis. A genotype record is always mapped to a genetic map while a phenotype may be mapped to a gene map or may not. A genetic map is a chromosome map that shows the relative locations of genes and other important features. Similar phenotypes may be associated with several genes across the genome. The set of these phenotypes is called phenotypic series. Figure 3.103 illustrates the relationship between a genotype record and a phenotype record [69].

The OMIM interface provides an interactive access to the available data including genomic coordinates of the gene map, views of genetic heterogeneity of phenotypes in phenotypic series, and side-by-side comparisons of clinical synopses. The relationships between phenotype and genotype are tabulated in a "Phenotype-Gene Relationships" table also called OMIM's Gene/Morbid Map of the Human Genome. Only OMIM entries, for which cytogenetic locations have been published in the cited references, are represented in the phenotype–gene relationships table. Each OMIM record (gene or phenotype) is given a unique identifier called an MIM

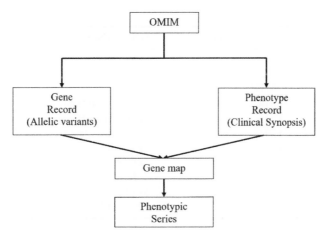

FIGURE 3.103   A diagram shows the structure of OMIM.

TABLE 3.32   OMIM ID Symbols

Symbol	Indication
*	A gene
#	A descriptive entry (of a phenotype) and it does not represent a unique locus
+	A gene of known sequence and a phenotype
%	Confirmed mendelian phenotype or genotype, molecular basis is not known
^	The entry was removed or moved to another entry and no longer exists

number. The OMIM record contains description for the OMIM record and structured summaries of related information collected by experts who review biomedical literature. A MIM number is a unique six-digit number preceded by a symbol for distinguishing the content of the phenotype or genotype records as shown in Table 3.32.

Searching OMIM

The OMIM database can be searched either by using the search box of the common Entrez database interface at www.ncbi.nlm.nih.gov/omim or by using the direct OMIM main web page available at https://omim.org/.

Searching OMIM from Entrez Interface

When you search OMIM using the Entrez interface, search queries will be built as discussed above. Advanced search queries can be built by using a combination of indexed fields and Boolean operators or with the help of the Advanced Search Builder. Table 3.33 contains the indexed fields of the Entrez OMIM database.

Since OMIM entries are either gene entries or phenotype entries, it can be searched from both a gene and clinical features perspective.

For example, assume that you wish to use "breast cancer" to find the OMIM records associated with this clinical condition. You can simply use the following query:

"breast cancer"[TITL]

The search results page displays several OMIM records as shown in Figure 3.104 in summary display format. The summary of each hit includes the title, cytogenetic locations, OMIM number, and links to related data. Notice that the OMIM identifier in the title is preceded by the symbol that identifies the content of the OMIM entry. Refer to Table 3.32 for the record symbols. The cytogenetic location indicates the location of the gene on the chromosome. For example, record 22 is for a gene on chromosome 17, region 22 (17q22).

TABLE 3.33   Entrez OMIM Indexed Fields

Full Field Name	Short Field Name	Full Field Name	Short Field Name
All Fields	ALL	Filter	FILT
Allelic Variant	ALVR	Gene Name	GENE
Contributor	AUTH	Gene Map	GMAP
Chromosome	CHR	Modification Date	MDAT
Clinical Synopsis	CLIN	Modification History	MDHS
Clinical Synopsis Date	CSDT	Publication Date	PDAT
Clinical Synopsis Editor	CSED	Properties	PROP
Clinical Synopsis Key	CSK	Reference	REFR
Gene Map Disorder	DSDR	Title	TITL
EC/RN Number	ECNO	MIM ID	UID
Editor	EDTR	Text Word	WORD

FIGURE 3.104   Entrez OMIM results page.

OMIM can also be searched using a gene symbol or a name. However, in this case, the search may return a single record. For example, try the following search term to find the BRCA1 gene record:

brca1[GENE]

When you use the Entrez interface, you can compose a search query that is built up of any of the indexed fields listed in Table 3.33. For example, to find all OMIM records associated with chromosome 17, you can use:

17[CHR]

Searching OMIM from Original OMIM Interface

If you use the original OMIM web page, which is available at https://omim.org/, to search the database, you will use different search rules. The search will be performed by entering a search query into the OMIM search box. You must pay attention that the search is case-sensitive.

TABLE 3.34   OMIM Search Rule and Examples

Syntax	Example	Description
Free text	women breast cancer	The terms are searched in any order
+ (plus) before a term	women +breast +cancer	Entries with terms preceded by "+" are returned
- (plus) before a term	-women +breast +cancer	Entries without the term preceded by "-" are returned
"terms"	"women breast cancer"	Only entries contained the phrase are returned
?	Wom?n breast cancer	? is a wild card for a single character
*	*breast*	* is a wild card for multiple characters
title:term	title: "+breast +cancer -ovarian"	Search terms only within the "title" field
AND, OR, NOT	breast AND cancer NOT ovarian	Boolean operator
(terms)	(breast cancer) OR (ovarian cancer)	Search grouping to indicate precedence
"terms"~ integer	"breast cancer"~5	limit the distance in words between two terms to 5
Term^integer	women breast cancer^10	Boost the weight of the term cancer' by a factor of 10
date_updated:date	date_updated:2015/1/1-*	Date from 2015/1/1 and to up to date
Cytogenetic location	17q14	Search the band 14 on the long arm of chromosome 17
Genomic coordinates	1:12,000,000-48,000,000	Search chr 1 between 12,000,000 and 48,000,000

Table 3.34 shows syntaxes and examples of OMIM search queries. You can refer to the OMIM Help for more detailed examples and search fields.

For example, to find OMIM records whose titles include "breast cancer" and the BRCA1 gene, you can enter the following query:

title:+"Breast cancer" AND +BRCA1

Tens of OMIM records will be found. The displayed summary for each entry will show the OMIM identifier, cytogenetic locations, matching items, and links to Phenotype-Gene-Relationships, Phenotypic Series, etc. Notice the symbol before the OMIM identifier. That symbol indicates the content of the OMIM records as shown in Table 3.32.

OMIM Gene Record Page

Click the title of the first OMIM entry on the results page to open the BRCA1 OMIM record page. The record has the "* 113705" OMIM identifier, which indicates that it is a gene record page as illustrated in Figure 3.105 and described below.

(A) Both OMIM gene and phenotype record pages have a table of content on the left-hand side that lists the sections of the page and can be used to move from a section to another.

(B) This includes the title section and gene–phenotype relationship section. The title section includes the OMIM identifier, full gene name, and gene symbol.

(C) The gene–phenotype section includes the cytogenetic location of the gene, the coordinates of the gene on the current genome assembly, and the gene–phenotype relationships table. The BRCA1 gene is found in the long arm of chromosome 17 (17q21.31) between 43,044,294 and 43,125,363 in the current human assembly (GRCh38). Clicking the cytogenetic location will open the Gene Map and Morbid Map as shown in Figure 3.106. The OMIM Gene Map presents the cytogenetic locations of the genes, genes/loci, and gene MIM numbers. On the other hand, the Morbid Map presents the phenotypes (disorders), phenotype MIM numbers, Phenotype map key, and comments. Only cytogenetic locations published in cited references are represented in the Gene Map and Morbid Map. The OMIM Gene Map is provided with a search bar on the top of the page. The OMIM Gene Map can be searched by a gene symbol (e.g., "BRCA1"), chromosomal location (e.g., "17", "1pter", "Xq"), or by disorder keyword (e.g., "breast cancer").

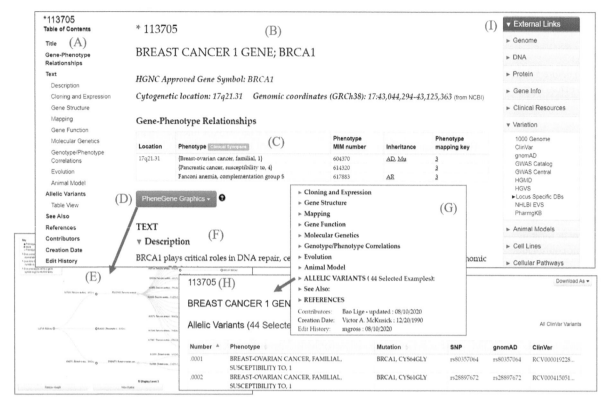

FIGURE 3.105   OMIM gene record page.

FIGURE 3.106   OMIM Gene Map and Morbid Map page.

The gene–phenotype relationships table has five columns – location (cytogenetic location of the gene), phenotype (list of diseases), phenotype MIM number (OMIM ID for each listed phenotype), inheritance (mode of inheritance), and phenotype mapping key. The inheritance can be classified as Autosomal Dominant (AD), Autosomal Recessive, or Multifactorial (Mu). The phenotype mapping key takes a number from 1 to 4 ("1" indicates that the disorder was positioned by mapping of the gene;

"2" indicates that the disorder itself was mapped; "3" indicates the molecular basis of the disorder is known; and "4" indicates the disorder is a chromosome deletion or duplication syndrome). The gene–phenotype relationships table shows that variants in the BRCA1 gene are implicated in three clinical conditions (phenotypes), each has its own OMIM phenotype record as shown by the phenotype MIM numbers. For example, the {breast-ovarian cancer, familial 1} is inherited as autosomal dominant (AD) and multifactorial (Mu) and the molecular basis of the disorder is known. Clicking on a phenotype MIM number will open the OMIM phenotype page of that phenotype.

(D) The PheneGene Graphics button is also provided with a dropdown list (click the white triangle) including two options: linear and radial. Selecting any of these options will forward you to the PheneGene Graphics page.

(E) The PheneGene Graphics tree is a hierarchal graphical representation that depicts the relationships between the gene and phenotypes, and each phenotype and the phenotypic series of genes that are implicated in the phenotype. As shown in the linear tree in Figure 3.107, the root of the tree begins by the gene and then the OMIM phenotypes associated with the gene are branched out. Branches from each phenotype also come out to represent the genes in the Series that are implicated in that phenotype.

(F) The Description section of the OMIM record page provides an abstract for the OMIM entry (gene or phenotype) and link to the supporting publication.

(G) This lists the other sections included in the table of contents of the OMIM record page. Each section can be expanded or collapsed by clicking the triangle icon. The descriptions of these sections are as follows:

- The Cloning and expression section provides summaries and links to publications that studied the cloning and expression of the gene.

- The Gene expression section provides summaries and links to publications that studied the expression of the gene.

- The Mapping section provides summaries and links to studies that mapped the gene and its pseudogenes to their cytogenetic locations in the human and model animal genomes.

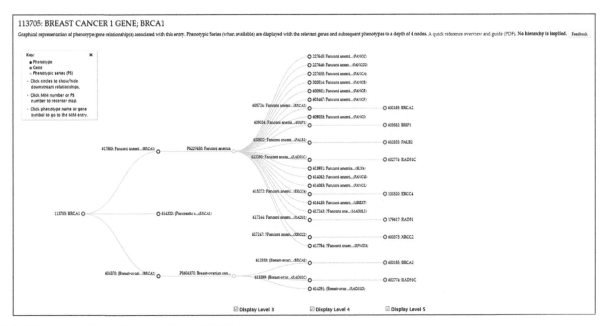

FIGURE 3.107   PheneGene graphics of BRCA1 gene.

- The Gene function section provides summaries and links to publications that studied the functions of the gene.
- The Molecular Genetics section provides summaries and links to publications that studied the mutations in the gene.
- The Genotype/Phenotype correlations section provides summaries and links to publications that studied the associations between the gene and the phenotype.
- The Evolution section provides summaries and links to publications that studied comparative evolutionary relatedness across species.
- The Animal Models section provides summaries and links to publications that studied the gene using model animals.
- The Allelic variants section provides summaries and links to publications that studied the allelic variants associated with the gene. Those variants may be dbSNP or dbVar variants. Links to the variants are provided as well as a link to a table (Table View) to display the dbSNP variants as shown in Figure 3.105 (H) and a link to the ClinVar records associated with the variants of the gene.
- The "See also" section provides links to other studies about the gene.
- The References section provides a list and links to other references supporting the OMIM entry.

(H) This is the allelic variant table that is displayed when the "Table View" button in the Allelic variants section is clicked. The table contains the allelic variants that were reported to be in the gene. The table shows the number of variants in the gene and then it lists the phenotypes, mutations, dbSNP accessions, Genome Aggregation Database (gnomAD) identifiers, and ClinVar accessions for the ClinVar records that detail the association between the variants and the phenotypes.

(I) External links on the right side of the OMIM record page provide the links to external database and resources in genome, DNA, protein, gene info, clinical resources, variation, animal models, cell lines, and cellular pathways.

OMIM Phenotype Record Page

Previously we have discussed the structure and content of the OMIM gene record page. The OMIM phenotype record page has the same layout and similar content to that of OMIM gene record page except the record-specific topics. Allelic Variants is a gene-specific topic, so it is not present on the phenotype page. Inheritance, Clinical Management, Pathogenesis, and Population Genetics are phenotype-specific topics, so they are present in the OMIM phenotype page to provide summaries and links to publications supporting those topics. Generally, the topics relevant to an OMIM record may vary. However, the phenotype record page is provided with the Phenotype–Gene Relationships table, which is like the Gene–Phenotype Relationships table in the OMIM gene record. Below the Phenotype–Gene Relationships table there are three buttons: Clinical Synopsis, Phenotypic Series, and PheneGene Graphics buttons.

While you are at BRCA1 gene record ("* 113705), click the "604370" phenotype MIM number to open the OMIM phenotype record page of "Breast-ovarian cancer, familial, 1" as shown in Figure 3.108.

Clicking the "Clinical Synopsis" button will open the clinical synopsis for the phenotype entry. The clinical synopsis provides an outline that summarizes the information about the phenotype. Clicking "Phenotypic Series" will open the Phenotypic Series associated with the phenotype. The phenotypic series is a group of clinically similar phenotypes associated with different genes. For example, the "Breast-ovarian cancer, familial" phenotype is like other four phenotypes associated with four different genes – BRCA2, RAD51D, BRCA1, and RAD51C. Those four phenotypes represent a phenotypic series.

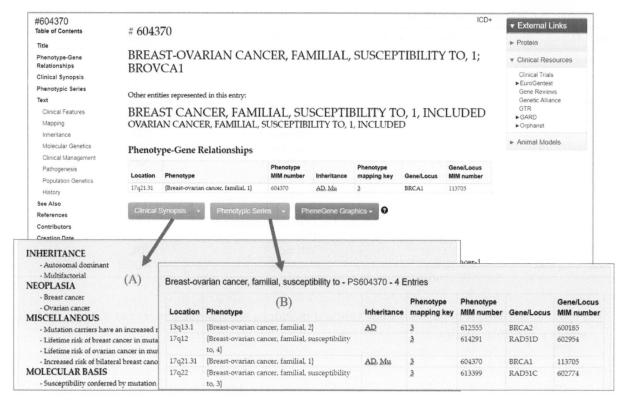

FIGURE 3.108   OMIM phenotype record page.

POPSET

PopSet [70] is an NCBI database for collecting sequences to serve as datasets for evolutionary and phylogenetic studies and comparative genomics research. The records of PopSet include sequences from samples collected from populations. A population is identified by the researcher, and it may include individuals, species, or any other taxonomic groups. The sequences of a dataset are usually nucleotide or protein sequences from two or more samples. The dataset may include sequences from the same species or from different species of all kinds of organisms. For example, a PopSet record may be made of the sequences of a specific gene or protein across several species or strains to study the evolutionary relatedness of those species or strains based on that gene or protein. Researchers usually submit such kinds of sequences to the PopSet database to be available for other researchers. The submitted sequences can be in the form of a multiple FASTA file (multiple FASTA sequences in a single file) or can be sequences aligned using any of the multiple sequence alignment programs such as ClustalW [71], MUSCLE [72], T-COFFEE [73], etc. Sequences can be submitted to PopSet via the GenBank submission tools. The PopSet datasets may be categorized into several types of studies, including environmental or ecological study, mutational study, phylogenetic study, and population study. The dataset can also be for barcode sequences, which are canonical barcode sequences from vouchered specimens, to be used for species identification. The following are descriptions of these types of studies:

- *Ecological study.* An ecological study (ecoset) includes sequences from environmental samples as direct molecular isolates from the environment and not from identified specimens or cultured microbes.

- *Mutational study.* A mutational study (muset) includes a set of sequences representing mutations within a particular species.

- *Phylogenetic study.* A phylogenetic study (physet) includes a set of sequences representing phylogenetic research in an organism or across a group of organisms.

TABLE 3.35   PopSet Database Indexed Fields

Long Field Name	Short Field Name	Long Field Name	Short Field Name
Accession	ACCN	Nucleotide Count	NCNT
All Fields	ALL	Organism	ORGN
Author	AUTH	Primary Accession	PACC
Breed	BRD	Page Number	PAGE
Cultivar	CULT	Protein Count	PCNT
EC/RN Number	ECNO	Publication Date	PDAT
Filter	FILT	Properties	PROP
Feature key	FKEY	Protein Name	PROT
Gene Name	GENE	SeqID String	SQID
BioProject	GPRJ	Strain	STRN
Isolate	ISOL	Substance Name	SUBS
Issue	ISS	Title	TITL
Journal	JOUR	UID	UID
Keyword	KYWD	Volume	VOL
Modification Date	MDAT	Text Word	WORD

- *Populational study.* A population study (popset) includes a set of sequences representing a population within a particular species.

Searching PopSet Database

The same Entrez searching conventions (see "Searching Entrez Databases" above) are used to search the PopSet database. Advanced search queries can be built with indexed fields or by using the Advanced Search Builder.

PopSet can be chosen from the database dropdown menu of the main Entrez database, or it can be accessed directly from www.ncbi.nlm.nih.gov/popset.

Table 3.35 includes the list of the indexed fields for the PopSet database that can be used in searching the database.

You can use free text, an organism name, a gene name or any a term with any of the above indexed fields. For example, assume that you wish to find PopSet entries about toxoplasma; you can enter the following:

toxoplasma[ORGN]

The results shown in Figure 3.109 indicate that there are 221 toxoplasma PopSet datasets. On the top right, the filters show that there are 42 alignment datasets, nine mutational studies, 57 phylogenetic studies, and 148 population studies. Clicking on any of these categories will limit the results to the records of the clicked category.

The summary format of the PopSet search results page shows the titles, types of study and numbers of sequences in the datasets, PopSet identifiers, and links to related data from other NCBI databases. Clicking the title of a record will open the page of that record. The PopSet record page may include the title and PopSet ID on the top, Study Details, and the sequence list in the dataset. The sequences can either be displayed by clicking the FASTA link on the top left or using the "Send To" dropdown menu to download the sequences in a single file.

When searching PopSet by a non-specific search term, there may be several records that you can explore manually; you should choose the one that meets your goal. Most times, you may have a specific goal about what you are searching for. You can use either the indexed fields or the Advanced Search Builder to compose the query that may help you to make the search results more specific. One of the best strategies for searching the PopSet database is by filtering the results by the type of study. You can limit the results to population studies if you are interested in datasets that represents a specific population. For example, assume that you

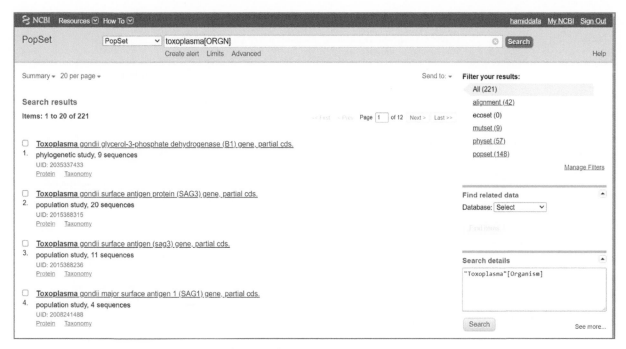

FIGURE 3.109   PopSet search results page for toxoplasma.

wish to find datasets of population studies on human breast cancer and associated with the BRCA1 gene only. To find records with that specification, use the following query:

"breast cancer"[TITLE] AND brca1[GENE] AND "population study"[FILT]

Once you find the dataset that meets your goal, you can then download it as described above. The datasets of population studies are usually used in investigation research of the population represented by the sampled sequences. On the other hand, the datasets of mutational studies are used to study mutations, and the datasets of phylogenetic studies are used for phylogeny.

Assume that you wish to find the available PopSet datasets of phylogenetic studies on primates including the human and that the study used TMF-regulated nuclear protein 1 (TRNP1). The TRNP1 gene is known for the crucial role that it plays in cellular proliferation and brain development. To find such phylogenetic studies you can enter the following query:

"primate"[ORGN] AND human[ORGN] "phylogenetic study"[FILT] AND trnp1[GENE]

Figure 3.110 shows that only three phylogenetic studies with that description have been returned.

For the sake of simplicity, click the title of the entry #3 (Catarrhini TMF-regulated nuclear protein 1 (TRNP1) gene, complete CDS.) to open the record page. The dataset of this phylogenetic study has six TRNP1 gene sequences. You can download the sequences as described above or you can create a phylogenetic tree using "Run BLAST Alignment" on the top right of the record page.

Figure 3.111 is illustrated with the steps of creating a phylogenetic tree or distance tree from the six TRNP1 gene sequences included in the phylogenetic studies. (A) Clicking the "Run BLAST Alignment" link will forward the sequences in the dataset to the BLAST, which runs sequence alignment. (B) Clicking "Distance tree of results" on the top of the alignment graphic summary will allows an algorithm to compute the distance among the aligned sequences and to construct a distance tree or phylogenetic tree (C) that presents the relationships among the sequences graphically. The tree shows that human is in a separate branch and other

FIGURE 3.110   PopSet search results page for primates.

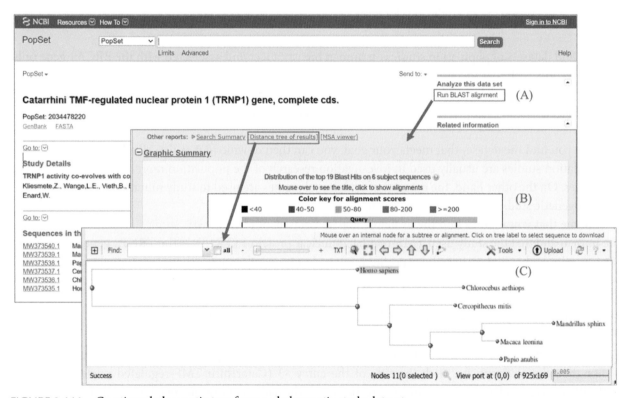

FIGURE 3.111   Creating phylogenetic tree from a phylogenetic study dataset.

primates in different branches based on the evolutionary distances among the sequences of TRNP1 gene across the species in the study.

The PopSet database also includes aligned sequences. The aligned sequences were usually aligned using one of the multiple sequence alignment programs such ClustalW, MUSCLE, T-COFFEE, etc. The aligned sequences can be downloaded and used by other comparative genomics software for other purposes such as motif finding, conserved sequence discovery, phylogenetic tree construction, homology modeling, etc.

The not aligned FASTA sequences of PopSet datasets can also be downloaded and aligned using multiple sequence alignment programs to be used for any of the above-mentioned purposes.

BIOSYSTEMS

The dynamic functioning of a living cell is governed by a complex process involving the interactions of several elements such as DNA, proteins, molecular complexes, molecular architectures, and small molecules. Each process is governed by a complex process. At the molecular level, the regulation of a gene involves the interaction of numerous other genes and biomolecules. Any trait or disease is also governed by a complex series of interacting elements such as proteins, small molecules, variants, etc. Generally, a biological system is a complex network of biologically relevant processes. The BioSystems entries are the biological pathways, which are a series of actions among molecules in living cells that lead to a certain product or a change in the cells. Generally, there are three types of pathways:

- *Metabolic pathways.* The metabolic pathway is a series of interconnected biochemical reactions that convert a substrate molecule or molecules yielding a final product or products. The metabolic pathway is either an anabolic pathway (building molecules) or a catabolic pathway (breaking down molecules). For example, one catabolic pathway for carbohydrates breaks starch down into glucose while the anabolic pathway of carbohydrates may synthesize glycogen from glucose for storage [74].

- *Gene regulation pathways.* Gene regulation pathways are the series of processes of controlling a gene in a cell. A gene may be turned on or off or may be over-expressed or under-expressed based on controlling factors including transcription factors, cofactors, and other elements. Different genes may have different gene regulation pathways [75].

- *Signal transduction pathways.* Signal transduction pathways involve the binding of extracellular molecules and ligands to receptors located on the cell surface or inside the cell that trigger events inside the cell, to invoke a response that may alter the biological activities in the cell [76].

Biologist have spent a tremendous amount of time and effort in discovering new components of pathways and connections among those components. Without databases gathering these pathways it would be very difficult to use such scientific knowledge. The databases of pathways collect such information from publications and provide interfaces for accessing the database entries. Several databases were developed to store pathways. These databases include KEGG [77], BioCarta [78], BioCyc [79], Protein ANalysis THrough Evolutionary Relationship (PANTHER) [80], the Pathway Interaction Database (PID) [81], and Reactome [82].

The NCBI BioSystems database focuses on collecting information of biological systems and pathways from the studies conducted by researchers and it also integrates records from other NCBI databases such as Gene, Protein, and others as well as records from external resources including KEGG, BioCyc, Reactome, the National Cancer Institute's Pathway Interaction Database (PID), WikiPathways [83], and Gene Ontology (GO) [84]. The entries of the BioSystems database include biologically related list of gene, protein, and small molecule identifiers, along with the characterization of interactions, citations, and other annotations [85]. Each BioSystems record has a stable, unique identifier called BSID.

The NCBI BioSystems database allows users to categorize genes, protein, and other biomolecules by the types of biological systems and functions pathways such as metabolic pathway, immune-response pathway, disease state, or any other types. The BioSystems database helps researchers to gather such information of pathways from integrated resources without wasting time on inferring biological relationships from literature or experimental datasets. Some examples for the use of the BioSystems database include (1) listing gene, proteins, and small molecules involved in a biological pathway, (2) finding the pathways in which a specified gene, protein, or a small molecule is involved, (3) retrieving 3D structures of proteins involved in a pathway, (4) finding related pathways that are linked to one another because they shared a common biomolecules or

TABLE 3.36   BioSystems Indexed Fields

Complete Field	Short Field	Complete Field	Short Field
All Fields	ALL	ProteinCount	PCT
CIDCount	CCT	CreateDate	PDAT
CID	CID	ProteinID	PID
ChemicalName	CN	ProteinName	PN
Comments	COM	SourceAccession	SACC
Description	DESC	SIDCount	SCT
Filter	FILT	SidExternalID	SEID
GeneCount	GCT	SID	SID
GeneExternalID	GEID	SourceName	SRC
GeneID	GID	SourceID	SRID
GeneName	GN	Title	TITL
ModifyDate	MDAT	BioSystemType	TYPE
Organism	ORGN	UID	UID

other elements, (5) retrieving ranked list of pathways for a list of proteins as input, and (6) retrieving a ranked list of pathways in which upregulated genes and downregulated genes are involved [86].

The NCBI BioSystems database is available at www.ncbi.nlm.nih.gov/biosystems/ or can be selected from the database dropdown menu on the Entrez main web page. Table 3.36 contains the indexed fields of the BioSystems database.

Searching BioSystems

As other Entrez databases, BioSystems can be searched using free text, indexed fields, or a combination of free text and indexed fields linked with Boolean operators. The Advanced Search Builder can be used as well. In the following we will discuss some examples of the use of the BioSystems database.

Finding Genes and Proteins Involved in a Pathway

Finding genes and proteins involved in a pathway is one of the most common uses of BioSystems. Assume that you wish to find BioSystems records for the pathways of Alzheimer's disease in the human and that your preference source is the KEGG database. You can use free text or a phrase such as "Alzheimer's disease" as a research term. However, non-specific search terms may return numerous results. Using the indexed fields will limit the results to the records your need. To find records that satisfy the above specifications, enter the following search query into BioSystems search box and click the "Search" button.

"Alzheimer's disease" AND human[ORGN] AND pathway[FILT] AND KEGG[SRC]

Three pathway records from the KEGG database for Alzheimer's disease in the human have been returned. The results page displays a summary for each search hit. The summary includes (1) the title, (2) entry description, (3) the BioSystems type, taxonomic scope, organism-specific biosystem, and organism, (4) the entry identifiers, and (5) links to other NCBI databases.

Click the title of the first record to open the BioSystems record page for that pathway as illustrated in Figure 3.112.

(A) *BioSystems description.* The description provides the definition of the pathway and describes the biomolecules and processes that play roles in its prevalence.

(B) *KEGG pathway.* KEGG stands for Kyoto Encyclopedia of Gene and Genomes. KEGG organizes data into overlapped groups including KEGG Pathway, KEG BRITE (functional hierarchies), KEG

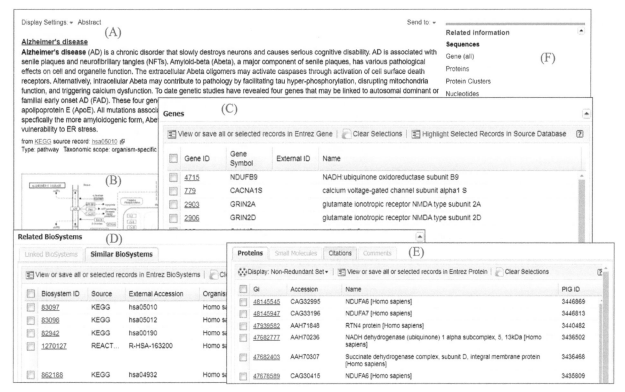

FIGURE 3.112   BioSystems record page.

Modules, KEGG Diseases, KEGG Drugs, KEGG Orthology, KEG Genomes, KEG Genes, KEGG Compounds, and KEGG Reactions. However, the BioSystems record page, as shown in Figure 3.112(B), integrates only KEGG Pathways, which are divided into seven categories including (1) Metabolism, (2) Genetic information processing, (3) Environmental information processing, (4) Cellular processes, (5) Organismal systems, (6) Human diseases, and (7) Drug development. Each of these categories is organized into hierarchical structure. The KEGG pathway is represented graphically by pathway maps that consist of manually drawn shapes representing the pathway components and components interactions. The shapes include rectangles, which represent gene products such as enzymes, small circles, which represent chemical compounds, and upstream and downstream interactions including protein–protein interactions, gene expression regulation, and enzyme–enzyme relations.

Clicking on the KEGG diagram will open the page of the KEGG Pathways maps for Alzheimer's disease as shown in Figure 3.113. The KEGG Pathways maps are formed from manually drawn shapes as explained above. The legends of these shapes are also illustrated in Figure 3.114. You can use these legends to understand the components of the pathways and also to track the steps of the pathway processes. The protein complex is represented by four rectangles. On the left side, the KEGG Pathways map page is provided with a hierarchical list of networks that can be selected to highlight the selected path and components of the pathway. There is a search box to search for a pathway component. On the top of the KEGG pathway map; the following links may be found as illustrated in Figure 3.113:

- *Pathway menu.* The menu provides a navigation menu to KEGG pathways.

- *Pathway entry.* This includes name, description, class, pathway map, networks, disease, drug (list of drugs), organism, gene (list of gene and products), compound (list of compounds), and references.

- *Download KGML.* This allows you to download the KEGG pathway entry in KEGG markup language (KGML) format.

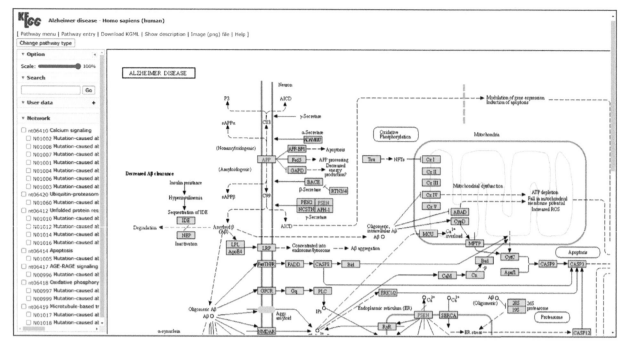

FIGURE 3.113 KEGG pathway map.

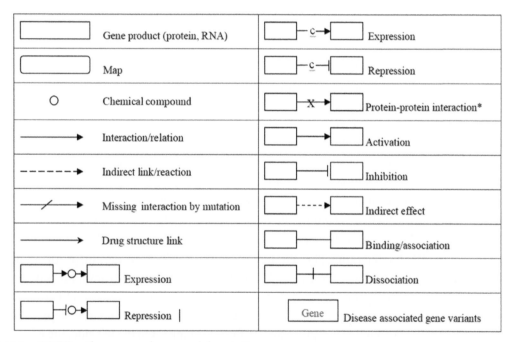

FIGURE 3.114 KEGG pathway map shapes and descriptions.
Keys: X can be any of: +p: phosphorylation, -p: dephosphorylation, +u: ubiquitination, -u: de-ubiquitination, +g: glycosylation, +m: methylation.

- *Image (png)*. This link allows you to download the KEGG Pathway map image in png image format. Figure 3.114 can be used to understand the shapes of the KEGG pathway map.

(C) *Genes*. The gene table in the BioSystems record page (Figure 3.112 (C)) lists the genes involved in the BioSystems. The table shows the Gene ID, gene symbol, and gene name. Clicking the Gene ID of a gene will direct you to its Gene record page. Moreover, if you wish to view or save the gene involved in the BioSystems, click "View or Save all or selected records in Entrez Gene" on the top left of the gene table, which will direct you to the Gene results page that includes the list of the genes involved in the BioSystems. To save those records, use the "Send To" menu as discussed before.

(D) *Similar BioSystems.* This table (Figure 3.112 (D)) includes the list of similar BioSystems. The table displays the BioSystems ID, source database, external accession, organism, and name of the BioSystems. To view or save the BioSystems list, click "View or Save All or selected records in Entrez BioSystems" and then on BioSystems results page use the "Send To" menu to save the summary or the identifier list.

(E) *Proteins.* This table (Figure 3.112 (E)) provides the list of proteins that play roles in the BioSystems record. The table includes, the GI (GenBank identifier), protein accession, protein name, and PIG ID (Protein Identical Group identifier). To save the protein list click "View or Save all or selected records in Entrez Protein" and then use the "Send To" menu to save the protein in different formats.

(F) *Related Information.* This section (Figure 3.112 (F)) provides the links to the related records on other databases and resources that are categorized into Sequences, Small molecules, Literature, Related BioSystems, and other links.

Finding a Pathway by a Gene

Sometimes, researchers may need to find the pathways in which a specific gene is involved or may need to find the role of that gene in a specific pathway. For example, assume that we wish to find the pathways in which the PPARG gene is involved. PPARG gene codes for several nuclear receptor protein isoforms that act as ligand-activated transcriptional factor, and it has roles in several pathways. To find the pathways in which PPARG is involved, you can enter the following search query:

pparg[GN]

The results of this search may include all BioSystems entries in which PPARG is involved in all organisms including the human and model animals. The current search results are 1,073 BioSystems records and they may increase in the future. The entries also will come from all integrated databases; therefore, some of the entries may have no KEGG Pathway map. This generic search is especially good if you intend to include the findings of studies in model animals. Most pathways of diseases are studied in model animals.

Assume that you wish to restrict the results to the human pathways in which PPARG is involved:

pparg[GN] AND human[ORGN]

The current search results of this search query are 22 BioSystems in which PPARG plays a role. However, not all of the returned records are provided with a KEGG Pathway map, which most researchers prefer because it helps in understanding the pathways. To restrict the search results to only those that have KEGG Pathway maps, use the following query:

pparg[GN] AND human[ORGN] AND KEGG[SRC]

This search returned only eight KEGG pathways in which PPARG is involved in the human.

Generally, searching the BioSystems database by a gene [GN], a protein name [PN], or a chemical name [CN], will return the pathways in which that element is involved.

DBGAP

The main goal of the Human Genome Project (HGP) was to determine the order of base pairs that make up the human DNA, and to identify and map the genes of the human genome from both a physical and a functional standpoint. The association between genotypes and phenotypes has been revolutionized by high-throughput sequencing technology, algorithms and programs for genotyping and analysis of complex association between genomic variants and diseases. Researchers are continuously collecting rich sets of phenotype data associated with genotypic findings in clinical studies. The NCBI developed the dbGaP database [87] for depositing of genomic data associated with clinical and non-clinical phenotypes collected from human subjects. The collected data includes genomic studies, medical sequence data, and molecular diagnostic assays. These records of dbGaP are built from several sequencing sources including whole exome sequencing, whole transcriptome sequencing, whole genome sequencing, custom targeted RNA sequencing, and targeted exome sequencing.

The dbGaP database is a rich resource of data and results from studies that have investigated the association of genotype and phenotype in humans. The main goal of the dbGaP database is to be a permanent archive for studies with phenotype and genotype data in the human so such data is accessible to researchers on public web pages with summary level data and controlled access for individual level data that include sensitive personal information. A dbGaP entry represents a study that consists of the following types of data:

- *Phenotype variables.* Phenotype variables are the attributes describing phenotypes or traits and they can be demographic, clinical, biomarker, or exposure variables. Each value in the variable is mapped to an individual. A variable has a variable name and a data type (numeric, string, date, etc.). Phenotype variables are organized in a phenotype or trait table (rectangular files), where a column represents a phenotype, and a row represents an individual. A phenotype table is given a unique identifier prefixed by "pht" and each variable (column) in the table is given a unique identifier prefixed by "phv". Summaries of phenotypes are accessible to the public without restriction.

- *Molecular data.* The molecular data of dbGaP include a variety of molecular data such as gene expression (RNA-Seq), gene expression (microarray), SNP/CNV genotypes, imputed genotypes (statistically inferred genotypes), methylation (ChIP-Seq), miRNA-Sequin different formats, etc. The study raw data are generated using several platforms (Sanger sequencing, high-throughput sequencing, PCR, microarray). The datasets are also available in different formats depending on the technology used. The sequences generated by sequencing are usually archived as Sequence Read Archive (SRA). The microarray data are probe intensity tables listing the gene names and their intensities. For each row (individual) in the phenotype table there will be molecular data (SRA file or microarray table). The unique identifier of the genotype is prefixed by "phg". Because molecular data is in longitudinal files limited summaries may be available on public pages.

- *Analysis data.* The analysis data of a dbGaP study are the values resulted from the phenotype–genotype association analysis.

- *Study documents.* The study documents are the documents related to the study such as study descriptions, protocol documents, and data collection instruments as questionnaires. The unique identifier of a study document is prefixed by "phd".

For each study there is a dictionary file (key: value) that matches the different datasets in the study record of the dbGaP database.

Submitting Data to dbGaP

Since the data submitted to the dbGaP database include sensitive information about individuals from which the samples were collected, the submitters require following the NCBI guidelines. Submitters must be NIH funded or non-NIH funded principal investigators (PIs). The data submission to the dbGaP database passes through three stages: study registration, data submission, and study release. In addition to the study phenotype file, molecular data files, and study document files, submitters also need to prepare four types of core files:

- *Subject/sample listing file.* This file describes how data of individuals can be used later. It includes codes for consent groups, a master list of the participants in the study, and reference to other subjects.

- *Subject sample mapping table file.* This file maps participants to their molecular samples. An individual may have multiple samples in some studies. This file also maps genotypes of individuals to their molecular data.
- *Sample attributes file.* This file includes sample level variables.
- *Pedigree file.* This file is required when there are genetically related individuals within the study. The pedigree file defines the family and the relationship of the family members.

After a submitter has prepared the phenotype file, molecular data files, document files, and core files, those files can be transferred using the dbGaP Submission Portal. For the complete submission guidelines, follow the "How to submit" link on the dbGaP database web page. The submission guides are also available at www.ncbi.nlm.nih.gov/gap/docs/submissionguide/.

A submitted study is assigned a unique identifier with the "phs" prefix. The dbGaP identifier is in "phsxxxxxx.v#.p#" format, where "x" is any digit and "#" is any integer, ".v#" indicates the version of the study and ".p#" indicates the version of the participant set. The study version is incremented when the study is altered and the participant set version is incremented when the number of individuals in the study has been changed. The change in participant set may be because of alterations in the consent status [88].

Accessing dbGaP Data

To obtain access to controlled data available in the dbGaP database, PIs must first obtain an NIH eRA Commons account and then obtain authorization to access the controlled data. The eRA Commons portal is an online interface where grant applicants can access and share administrative information relating to research grants. An institution will need to register at NIH eRA Commons before its IPs can apply for an eRA Commons account that is necessary to access dbGaP. Once the institution registration is complete, the eRA Commons account administrator of the institution can assist individual IPs under the institution to set up their own eRA Commons account. A PI with an eRA Commons account can then access the dbGaP database and grant access to lab members. The PI can also assign a downloader to download the controlled datasets.

Submitting a request for accessing controlled dbGaP data is performed after logging into the dbGaP controlled-access portal. The NCBI staff will study the request and then may approve it if the request meets the requirement. However, a summary of the studies of the controlled dbGaP datasets are available for the public.

The controlled data files distributed through the dbGaP database are either SRA files or non-SRA files. The dbGaP SRA files are the raw sequence data generated by sequencing technology for genotyping while the non-SRA files are the files that include gene expression data generated by microarray or PCR for gene profiling and the file that contain phenotypes. Both types of dbGaP files will be encrypted by NCBI and they can be decrypted only by using decryption tools with a key emailed by the NCBI to the authorized users. The decryption tools, called the SRA toolkit, are NCBI programs that can be downloaded from the NCBI server and installed on the computer. The SRA toolkit will be discussed in the next SRA database section. The decryption of the dbGaP files with the SRA tools requires a dbGaP repository key, which is a dbGaP project-wide security token that can be obtained after logging into the dbGaP study page. The key is generated by clicking on the "get dbGaP repository key" link of the project on Authorized tab as shown in Figure 3.115.

The key is provided in a file with suffix ".ngc". The key file can be downloaded and saved in a directory to be used with the SRA toolkit to download and decrypt the controlled dbGaP SRA and non-SRA. Downloading dbGaP data using the SRA toolkit will be discussed in the next SRA database section. Since you may not have access to a dbGaP project and you need to practice downloading and decrypting the controlled dbGaP data files, the NCBI made one project available for those who need to practice. You can download a test dbGaP repository key file from:

https://ftp.ncbi.nlm.nih.gov/sra/examples/decrypt_examples/prj_phs710EA_test.ngc

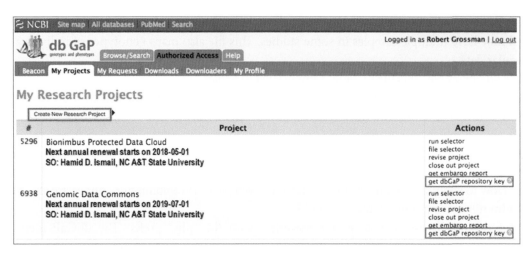

FIGURE 3.115   Generating dbGaP repository key file.

This is an example dbGaP repository key file that can be used to download and decrypt test dbGaP files from the NCBI 1000 Genomes data. You can download that file into a directory for the later use.

Searching dbGaP

The dbGaP database is accessed by selecting dbGaP from the database dropdown menu on the Entrez main web page or can be accessed from www.ncbi.nlm.nih.gov/gap/. The dbGaP database is searched using the same Entrez conventions. Table 3.37 contains the indexed fields that can be used to search the dbGaP database.

You can use the same search strategies you used with the other Entrez databases. You can either use indexed fields to build an advanced search query or you can use the Advanced Search Builder. The advanced search query will help you to find more specific search results.

Assume that you are looking for raw sequence data generated by whole genome sequencing (WGS) for patients with breast cancer in a case control study. You can use the following query:

("breast cancer"[DIS] AND "breast cancer"[STNM]) AND "true"[SRA] AND "wgs"[MOLE] AND "case control"[DESN]

The above search query requests that the dbGaP studies in the results to be for breast cancer and "breast cancer" also is to be in the name of the studies. The returned studies will also have SRA and used the whole genome sequencing for generating the sequences.

The dbGaP search results, as shown in Figure 3.116, are found in six tabs: Studies, Phenotype Datasets, Variables, Molecular Datasets, Analyses, and Documents. The results page contains several filters on the left side. You can use these filters to restrict the results to more specific records. The summary of each results item provides information about the items. Assume you intend to filter the search studies by breast cancer only. Thus, while the Study tab is active, click the "Study Disease/Focus" button and then scroll down and select the "Breast Neoplasms" checkbox. You may also need to limit the studies to only those that have a specific type of molecular data. Assume that you are looking for SNP Genotype data generated from next-generation sequencing. Thus, click the "Study Molecular Data Type" button and select the "SNP Genotypes (NGS)" checkbox. There are more filters you can use to find exactly what you are looking for.

In addition to the summary descriptive information, a study item on the dbGaP search results page may include links to other related databases, resources, and tools including "FileSelector", "RunSelector", "MeSH", "BioProject", "BioSample", and "SRA", which allow users to access the study-related information and data on other databases. The "FileSelector", "RunSelector", and "SRA" links are used to access and download the study datasets. Those tools will be discussed with SRA database in the next section.

TABLE 3.37   dbGaP Indexed Fields

Long Field Name	Short Field Name	Long Field Name	Short Field Name
All Fields	ALL	Genotype Platform	GENO
Ancestor	ANCE	Has Analysis	HASA
Analysis ID	ANID	Has Document	HASD
Analysis	ANLS	Has PhenX Mapping	HASP
Analysis Name	ANNM	Has Dataset	HAST
Study Archive	ARCH	Has Variable	HASV
Attribution	ATTR	Molecular Data Type	MOLE
Belongs To	BELO	Project	PROJ
Common Data Element Resource	CDER	Primary Phenotype in Study	PRPH
Common Data Element Term	CDET	PhenX	PX
Data Access Committee	DAC	Is Root Study	RTST
Document ID	DCID	Study Has SRA Components	SRA
Document Name	DCNM	Study ID	STID
Study Design	DESN	Study Name	STNM
Disease	DIS	Study	STUD
Discriminator	DISC	Is Top-Level Study	TLST
Document	DOC	UID	UID
Document Part	DOCP	Variable	VAR
Dataset	DS	Variable Description	VRDS
Dataset ID	DSID	Variable ID	VRID
Dataset Name	DSNM	Variable Name	VRNM
Filter	FILT		

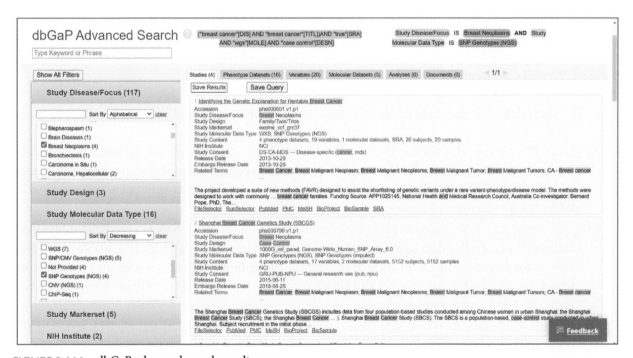

FIGURE 3.116   dbGaP advanced search results page.

After applying the two filters, only four studies have been found to meet the specifications. The first study, on the results page, is with "phs000601.v1.p1" accession and it focused on breast cancer as a disease. The study used the whole exome sequencing to perform genotyping on the SNPs called from the sequence reads. This study also has four phenotype datasets, 19 variables, one molecular dataset as SRA, 20 subjects, and 20 samples.

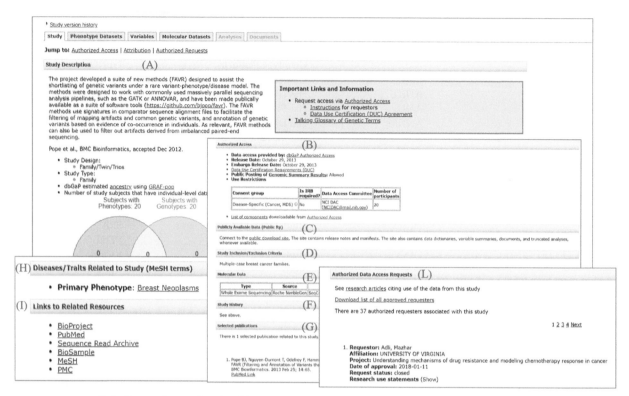

FIGURE 3.117   dbGaP record page (study tab).

Clicking the title of that study will open the study page, where you can find detailed information about the contents of the study and ways to access the data. The dbGaP record page includes six tabs: Study, Phenotype Datasets, Variables, Molecular Datasets, Analyses, and Documents.

Study Tab   The sections of the Study tab are illustrated as shown in Figure 3.117 and described below.

(A) *Study Description.* This section provides description of the study including the study design, study type, number of subjects studied (number of samples), and contribution. This section may also include a Venn diagram showing the intersection among numbers of subjects with phenotype, number of subjects with genotypes, and number of subjects in the pedigree file.

(B) *Authorized Access.* This section provides information and links about how to access the study information. The controlled data requires dbGaP authorized access while the publicly available data can be downloaded from the ftp server without restriction. The Authorized Access section also contains consent group, the answer for whether IRB (Institutional Review Boards) is required or not, data access committee, and number of participants.

(C) *Publicly Available Data (Public ftp).* This section includes the information and the FTP server link to the publicly available data if found.

(D) *Study Inclusion/Exclusion Criteria.* This section describes the criteria used to conduct the study. It may include any criteria used for including or excluding subjects from the study and the experimental groups.

(E) *Molecular Data.* This section shows the type of data, source of data, platform, number of Oligos or SNPs, SNP batch id, and comment.

(F) *Study History.* This section shows the history of the study if changes were made.

(G) *Selected publications.* This section lists the publications related to the study if found.

(H) *Disease / Traits related to the study (MeSH terms).* This section lists the primary MeSH terms of the phenotypes or diseases.

(I) *Links to related resources.* This section lists the links to related databases or resources.

(L) *Authorized data access requests.* This section lists the requestors that were authorized to access the data of the study, their affiliation, projects, date of approval, request status, and research use statement.

The last section on the study tab is the Study Attribution, which lists the principal investigators and funding sources and the acknowledgment statement.

Phenotype Datasets   On the top of Phenotype Datasets, there are two links. The first link will forward you to the phenotype datasets in the dbGaP search results page within the study and the second will forward you to the list of the phenotype datasets within the study. The Phenotype Datasets tab also includes the following sections as illustrated in Figure 3.118.

(A) *Dataset Name and Accession.* This section lists the dataset name and dataset accessions.

(B *Dataset Description.* This section provides a brief description of the datasets and dataset type whether it is simple (contains only one row per subject ID) or multiple (contains multiple rows per subjects ID). Some datasets have multiple rows for a single subject. For example, a cancer study may take multiple samples from a single subject (e.g., healthy tissue and diseased tissue).

(C) *Dataset Summary.* This section includes links to download the study variable report and study data dictionary and a table listing the variable accessions, variable names, and variable descriptions.

Variable Tab   The Variable tab, as illustrated in Figure 3.119, contains three sections:

(A) *Variable Name and Accession.* This section lists the variable name, variable accession, and the dataset that the variable belongs to.

(B) *Variable Description.* This section provides a description to the variable.

(C) *Statistical Summary.* A graph that shows the distribution of values of the variable.

Molecular Datasets Tab   This tab (Figure 3.120) contains a summary of molecular data. The summary includes a table that shows the Study (accession), Molecular Data Type, and sample and subject counts organized by Consent Group and Molecular Data Types. The legend is to define the groups.

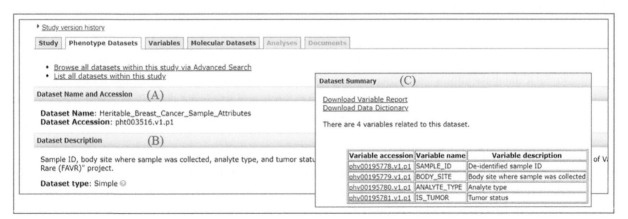

FIGURE 3.118   Phenotype datasets tab.

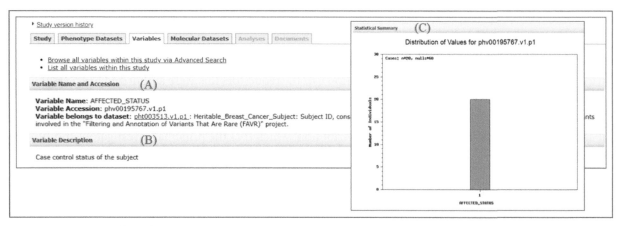

FIGURE 3.119 Variables tab.

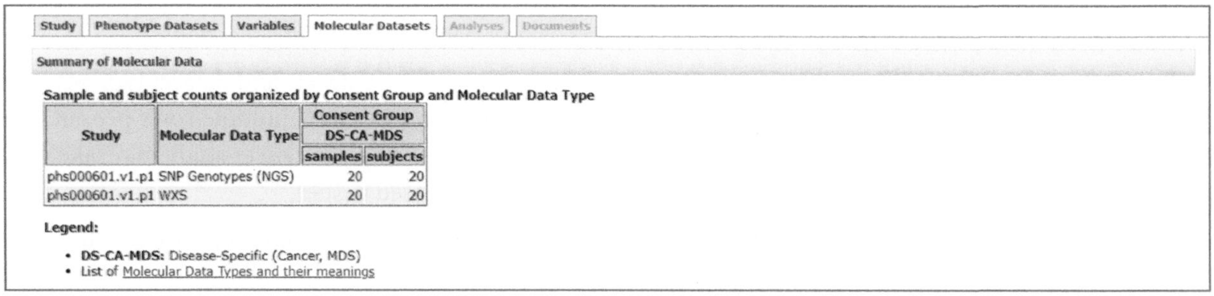

FIGURE 3.120 Molecular datasets tab.

SRA DATABASE

The Sequence Read Archive (SRA) is an Entrez database, established in 2007, as a repository for genomic sequencing data generated by high-throughput sequencing. The genomic data cover studies using a variety of sequencing strategies, including whole genome sequencing (WGS), whole exome sequencing (WXS), targeted gene sequencing, targeted exome sequencing, epigenomic sequencing, metagenomic sequencing, and microbiome sequencing. The SRA database is also part of the International Nucleotide Sequence Database Collaboration (INSDC). The sequencing raw data archived in the SRA database are generated using sequencing platforms including Roche 454 GS System, Illumina Genome Analyzer, Life Technologies AB SOLiD System, Helicos Biosciences Heliscope, Complete Genomics, and Pacific Biosciences SMRT. The genomic raw sequences generated with NGS are massive in number and size; therefore, they require a certain way of archiving. The SRA allows users to compress the sequencing data up to three-fold and also to establish columnar database search for aligned and unaligned sequences to grab data regions and to perform fast BLAST search for query sequences.

The raw sequencing data consists of sequence reads and per-base quality, usually in FASTQ format, and the aligned sequence reads are the reads that are aligned to a reference genome and stored in SAM/BAM file format. The SRA database allows researchers to deposit their massive research raw data and it makes that data available so other researchers can use it in their own research project. Some dbGaP database data are also archived as SRA. NCBI provides tools to download and dump the data archived on the SRA database.

Submitting Data to SRA Database

Researchers submit their research raw sequencing data generated with NGS to the SRA as supporting evidence for their publications. Most journals require that the raw sequence data be submitted to a public domain before publication. Researchers who conducted a research project funded by NIH may submit their raw data to abide by the NIH policies.

The data submitted to the SRA database is the genetic data that are stored in file formats with quality scores produced by next-generation sequencing technologies. The accepted formats include FASTQ, SAM/BAM, CRAM, HDF5, and many other files of sequence and per base quality. SAM files must be converted into BAM files before submission.

Submitting data to SRA is performed via the SRA Submission Portal Wizard. You must log into your MYNCBI account. You need BioProject accession and BioSample as discussed earlier. If you do not have one, the Submission Wizard will allow you to create a BioProject and BioSample at the beginning of the submission process. Upon submission, you will be asked to provide some metadata. The SRA metadata describes the technical aspects of the sequencing experiments (sequencing libraries, preparation techniques, and data files). The SRA metadata that you will be asked to enter includes experiment (unique library_ID) and sequence data files (file type and name). After providing the metadata and data releasing date, the wizard will prompt you to upload your sequence file. If the data submission is successful, the submission will be reviewed by the NCBI staff and the accession number for your data will be emailed to you.

The SRA accession number is a reference number representing five distinct data types. The SRA accession consists of a prefix and six digits. The first letter of the prefix indicates which INSDC archive the data originated from (S =NCBI-SRA, E = EMBL-SRA, and D = DDBJ-SRA). Table 3.38 lists the prefixes of the records originated from NCBI, EMBL, and DDBJ and the accession types.

Searching for SRA Data

The SRA database web page is accessed by choosing SRA from the Entrez database dropdown menu on the Entrez main page or by using www.ncbi.nlm.nih.gov/sra. You can follow Entrez conventions to search the SRA database. The indexed fields listed in Table 3.39 will help you to build advanced search queries together with Boolean operators (AND, OR, and NOT). You can also use the Advanced Search builder as well.

Some of the indexed fields in Table 3.39 are used with specific terms. These fields include [LAY], [PLAT], [SRC], and [STRA]. For example, with [LAY] you can use either "paired" or "single" (e.g., paired [LAY]). For other fields use the Advanced Search Builder to find the indexed values.

TABLE 3.38 SRA Prefix of INSDC Archives

Ncbi Prefix	Embl Prefix	Ddbj Prefix	Description
SRA	ERA	DRA	SRA Submission accession
SRP	ERP	DRP	SRA Study may include multiple SRA Experiments
SRX	ERX	DRX	SRA Experiment may include multiple SRA Runs
SRR	ERR	DRR	SRA Run (a single run has a single SRA file)
SRS	ERS	DRS	Sample accession
SRZ	ERZ	DRZ	Analysis accession

TABLE 3.39 SRA Indexed Fields

Long Field Name	Short Field Name	Long Field Name	Short Field Name
Accession	ACCN	Organism	ORGN
Access	ACS	Publication Date	PDAT
All Fields	ALL	Platform	PLAT
Aligned	ALN	Properties	PROP
Author	AUTH	ReadLength	RLEN
BioSample	BSPL	Selection	SEL
Filter	FILT	Source	SRC
BioProject	GPRJ	Strategy	STRA
Layout	LAY	Title	TITL
Mbases	MBS	UID	UID
Modification Date	MDAT	Text Word	WORD

One of the common search scenarios for searching the SRA database is to search by an accession number to find a specific Study, Sample, Experiment, or Run if you already have the accessions. Use Table 3.38 to identify the type of accession numbers. For example, you can enter "SRX10825493" to display the record page of an experiment with that accession number.

The Center for Food Safety and Applied Nutrition (CFSAN) is one of the product-oriented centers that carry out the mission of the US Food and Drug Administration (FDA). The CFSAN conducted an umbrella project that holds a set of data BioProject, each representing a laboratory sequencing of *Salmonella enterica* in collaboration with GenomeTrakr's open genomic epidemiology surveillance effort for the real-time monitoring of foodborne pathogens. The purpose of the GenomeTrakr project is to assist researchers and public health officials to speed food-borne illness outbreak investigations and to reduce food-borne illnesses and deaths. The sequence data were deposited to the public NCBI SRA databases to be accessed by researchers. Assume that you wish to use the sequence data of the GenomeTrakr in your project. You can find the data of *Salmonella enterica* of the GenomeTrakr by using the following search query:

"Salmonella enterica"[ORGN] AND "GenomeTrakr"

This search query returned thousands of records as shown in Figure 3.121.

The SRA search results page is a typical Entrez database search results page. The results are displayed as a summary that includes the title, sequencing platform used in sequencing and run information, and experiment accession.

The filters on the left side of the page can be used to make the search results more specific. For example, assume that you are interested in the paired library layout; click "paired" under the "Library Layout" filter. You may also prefer FASTQ data so select "fastq" under "File Type". Those two filters will limit the SRA data to the paired-end, FASTQ *Salmonella enterica* data generated by GenomeTrakr.

On the right side, the "Search in related databases" table classifies the data by database (BioSample, BioProject, dbGaP, Geo Datasets) and access (public or controlled). BioSample database contains sample descriptions and BioProject database contains project description. The dbGaP and GEO datasets may have data archived in SRA. Access to dbGaP data that contain personal clinical information is controlled. The table shows that 48 SRA-archived data were submitted by GenomeTrakr. Click the BioProject number and you will be forwarded to the BioProject search results page as shown in Figure 3.122.

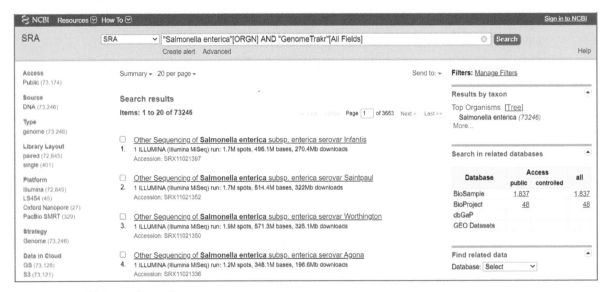

FIGURE 3.121   SRA search results page.

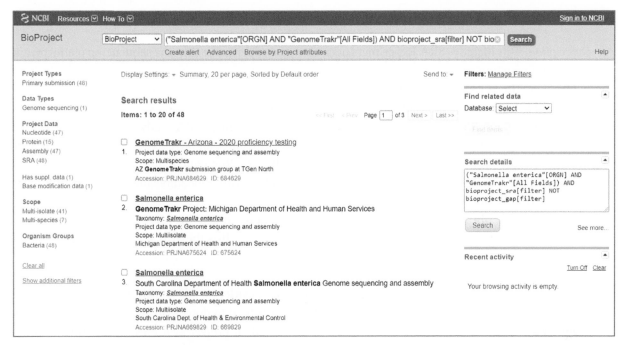

FIGURE 3.122   BioProject search results page.

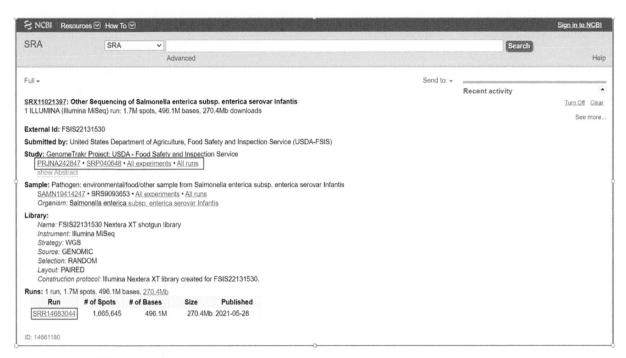

FIGURE 3.123   SRA record page.

The BioProject results page displays the GenomeTrakr's projects that have SRA archived data. The BioProject database was discussed earlier. Later in this chapter, you will learn how to use the accession number of those BioProject to download SRA data. If you click a title of a BioProject you will open that BioProject record page, which includes the details of the samples and data in the project.

Use the back arrow to return to the SRA search results page as shown in Figure 3.121. Click the title of the first item to open the SRA record page (Figure 3.123).

The SRA record page includes the following:

- *Description.* This includes SRA Experiment accession, the experiment title, the sequencing platform, and the run information.
- *External id.* This is a sample identifier defined by the submitter when submitting a BioSample.
- *Submitted by.* The name of the submitter who submitted the data to SRA database.
- *Study.* This includes the project name, BioProject accession number, SRA Study accession number, "All Experiments link", which opens the SRA Study page that includes all SRA Experiments, and "All Run", which opens SRA Run Selector, which is used to select the SRA Run data to download.
- *Sample,* This shows the sample title as defined in BioSample record, BioSample identifier that links to the SRA Experiment, and SRA Sample accession.
- *Library.* This describes the library used in the next-generation sequencing.
- *Run.* This shows the number of run (SRA files) and sizes. It also lists the SRA Run accession, number of spots, number of bases, size, and published date for each run.

To download the SRA Run file, you can use the run accession (SRR14683044) with the SRA toolkit as you will soon learn. However, instead of only a single run you may intend to download all SRA files (runs) of the SRA Study or a selection of SRA files. If you intend to download all project SRA files, then you will use the BioProject accession (PRJNA242847) with the SRA toolkit as you will soon learn. All files of an SRA Study may require large storage space; for example, the BioProject (PRJNA242847) has 23,570 runs (SRA files) that require 10.83 T (terabyte) of storage. So, you may need to download only some SRA files. To select some runs to download you can use one of two options:

(1) Use the "All Experiments" link under Study, which will open the search results page of SRA Study (SRP040648) that includes all the experiments in the project. Select the experiments for which you intend to download their SRA data, then click the "Send To" dropdown menu, and finally select "Run Selector", as shown in Figure 3.124, to open the SRA Run Selector with the selected runs.

(2) Use the "All run" link under Study to open the SRA Run Selector, which will display a list of all runs in the project. The SRA Run Selector allows you to select the runs that you need to download their SRA files. The SRA Run Selector is shown in Figure 3.125.

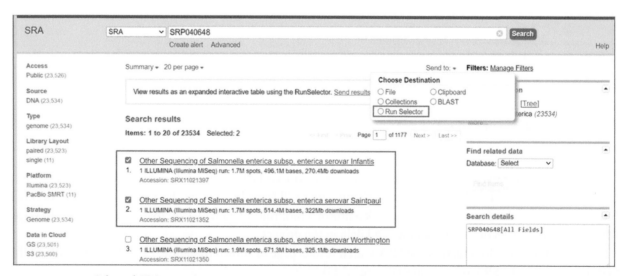

FIGURE 3.124 Selected SRA experiments.

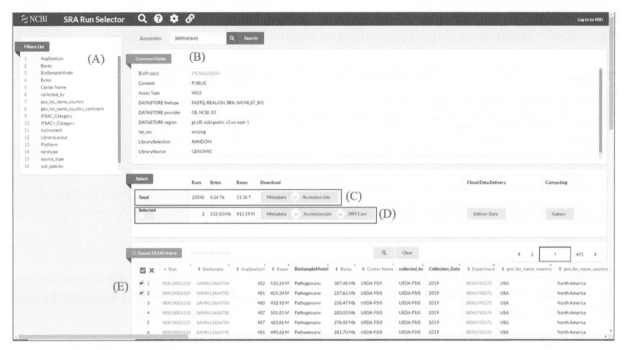

FIGURE 3.125   **SRA run selector.**

The SRA Run Selector is the tool that you can use to select files to download. The dbGaP also uses this tool as well. It consists of the following section as illustrated in Figure 3.125:

(A)   *Filters.* The filters are used to filter the data.

(B)   *Study description.* This includes the BioProject description.

(C)   *Total.* This shows the total number of runs, the storage size required for all run files, the total number of bases, a link to download the metadeta, and a link to download the accession list of all runs. The accession list can be used to download all SRA run files.

(D)   *Selected.* This shows the number of selected runs, the storage size of the selected run files, the total number of bases of the selected runs, a link to download the metadeta, a link to download the accession list of the selected runs, and JWT (JSON Web Token) cart respectively. Both accession list file or JWT cart file are used with the SRA toolkit to download and dump the SRA files.

(E)   *Run list.* This lists all runs on the BioProject. You can scroll down and up and move to the next page to select the runs that you need to download. Once you finish selecting the run, then click the "Accession list" button (D) to download the accession of the selected runs.

Installing SRA Toolkit

SRA files are archive files that contain compressed files for aligned or not aligned sequence reads with per base quality. There are usually large files as well. Therefore, downloading SRA files requires special tools to guarantee that the archived files are downloaded successfully. The tools that are used to download and extract SRA files are called the SRA toolkit, which are command-line programs developed by the NCBI to download and extract SRA archived data into the original data types. Remember that dbGaP and the GEO Dataset may have data archived as SRA files. When we discussed dbGaP we pointed out that the dbGaP SRA data and non-SRA data are downloaded and decrypted using the SRA toolkit with a "ngc" file containing the "dbGaP repository key".

The NCBI SRA toolkit is available to download for all computer platforms (Linux, Windows, and MacOS) from https://trace.ncbi.nlm.nih.gov/Traces/sra/sra.cgi?view=software. You can follow the guides on the website to download and install the latest SRA toolkit that works on the computer platform that you are using. The following are the steps to install the SRA toolkit on Linux and Windows. Make sure that your computer meets the installation requirement. You can follow the same steps for Mac OS and other platforms.

Installing SRA Toolkit on Linux   The following steps are for downloading and installing the SRA toolkit on a Linux computer:

- Open the web page https://trace.ncbi.nlm.nih.gov/Traces/sra/sra.cgi?view=software.
- Use the right mouse button on "Ubuntu Linux 64-bit architecture" and copy the link address as shown in Figure 3.126.
- Open the Linux terminal and type on the command line "wget" Linux command, paste the link address, and then press the "Enter" key to download the tarball file in the default directory as shown in Figure 3.127.
- Extract the tarball file using:

  $ tar xvzf sratoolkit.2.10.8-ubuntu64.tar.gz

  Pay attention that the file name may be changed in a new version. The SRA toolkit files will be extracted in the "sratoolkit.2.10.8-ubuntu64" directory. You can rename this directory to a shorter name "sratoolkit" by using:

  $ mv sratoolkit.2.10.8-ubuntu64 sratoolkit

- The SRA toolkit commands will be saved on the "sratoolkit/bin/" directory. You must add this directory to the Linux path so that SRA toolkit programs are to be used from any directory on the computer. Change to the "sratoolkit/bin/" directory using:

  $ cd sratoolkit/bin

  and then use the "pwd" Linux command to display the absolute path of the SRA toolkit programs. And copy the path (Figure 3.128).

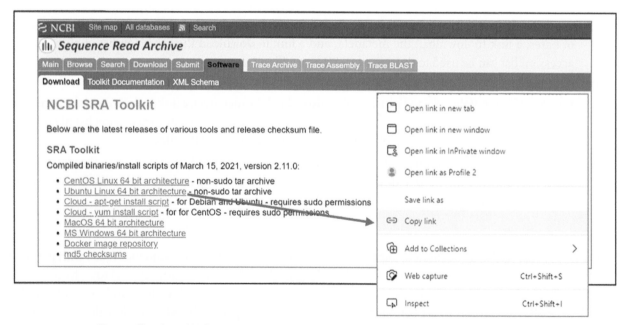

FIGURE 3.126   SRA toolkit download page.

```
hamiddafa@dax:~$ wget https://ftp-trace.ncbi.nlm.nih.gov/sra/sdk/2.10.8/sratoolkit.2.10.8-ubuntu64.tar.gz
```

FIGURE 3.127   Using "wget" Linux command to download SRA toolkit.

```
hamiddafa@dax:~$ cd sratoolkit/bin/
hamiddafa@dax:~/sratoolkit/bin$ pwd
/home/hamiddafa/sratoolkit/bin
hamiddafa@dax:~/sratoolkit/bin$
```

FIGURE 3.128 Copying SRA toolkit absolute path.

```
# enable programmable completion features (you don't need to enable
# this, if it's already enabled in /etc/bash.bashrc and /etc/profile
# sources /etc/bash.bashrc).
if ! shopt -oq posix; then
  if [ -f /usr/share/bash-completion/bash_completion ]; then
    . /usr/share/bash-completion/bash_completion
  elif [ -f /etc/bash_completion ]; then
    . /etc/bash_completion
  fi
fi

export PATH="/home/hamiddafa/sratoolkit/bin:$PATH"
```

FIGURE 3.129 Adding the path of SRA toolkit programs to the path.

```
hamiddafa@dax:~$ which prefetch
/home/hamiddafa/sratoolkit/bin/prefetch
hamiddafa@dax:~$
```

FIGURE 3.130 Checking the SRA toolkit setup.

- Change to the home directory by using "cd ~".
- Open the ".bashrc" file in a text editor such as vim or nano text editor (e.g. vim .bashrc).
- Add

  export PATH="/home/hamiddafa/sratoolkit/bin:$PATH"

  to the last line of the file as shown in Figure 3.129.
- Save the ".bashrc" file, exit the file, and restart your terminal. After restarting the terminal, you can run "which prefetch"; if the setup is successful that command will display the path and the program name as shown in Figure 3.130.
- After the successful installation and path setup, you can configure the directory where the SRA files will be downloaded. We will use the "vdb-config" command to configure the SRA download path.

  $ vdb-config -i

  The command will open the SRA Configuration window (Figure 3.131). Use the Alt+C key combination to move to the CACHE tab. The path under "location of user-repository" is where the SRA files will be dumped. The download directory on my computer is "/home/hamiddafa/ncbi/public". You can use "vdb-config" to change the download location to the directory of your choice.
- Press Alt+S to save and then Alt+X to exit the SRA Configuration. Thus, the SRA toolkit utilities are ready to use.

A final remark about the SRA toolkit installation on Linux, we can simply use the "sudo apt-get install sra-toolkit" to install it but the version of the installed SRA toolkit may not be the latest.

Installing SRA Toolkit on Windows 10

* Open the web page https://trace.ncbi.nlm.nih.gov/Traces/sra/sra.cgi?view=software.

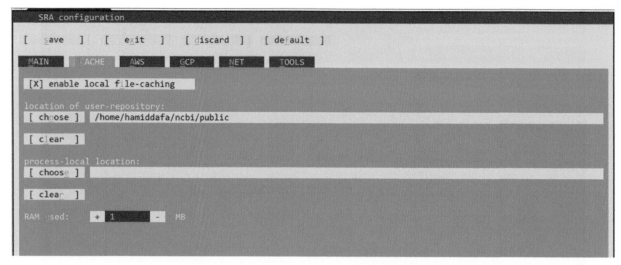

FIGURE 3.131   SRA Configuration window.

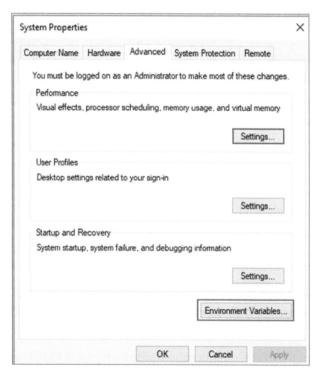

FIGURE 3.132   Windows system properties.

- Click on "MS Windows 64bit architecture" to download the compressed file on your computer.
- Extract the zipped archive and copy the folder inside the extracted folder to any location you prefer and rename the folder to a shorter name. In this installation we will copy the folder to "c:\" and rename the folder that contains the SRA toolkit subfolders and files, to "sratoolkit". So, the absolute path of the SRA toolkit executable files would be "c:\sratoolkit\bin".
- In the Windows Search, search for "environment".
- Click on the "Edit the system environment variables". The System Properties dialog box will pop up as shown in Figure 3.132.
- On the advanced tab, click on the "Environment Variables" button. The Environment Variables dialog box will pop up.

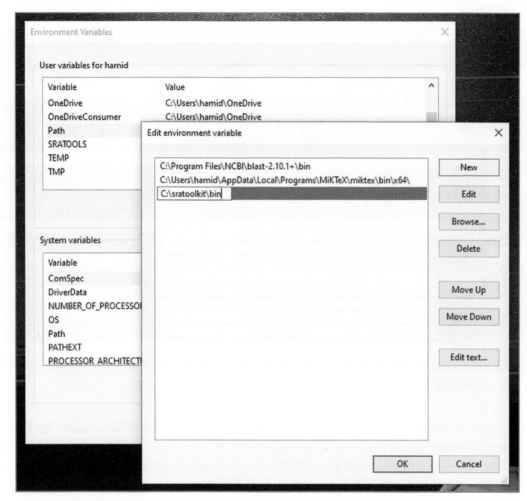

FIGURE 3.133   Adding the path of SRA toolkit to the Windows path variable.

FIGURE 3.134   Command prompt window.

- On the user variable list look for the "Path" variable and double-click it or select it and click the "Edit" button. The "Edit environment variable" dialog box will pop up.
- Click on the "New" button and specify or browse to the directory where the SRA toolkit executable files are saved. In our case, the path is "c:\sratoolkit\bin". Click the "OK" button (Figure 3.133).
- Close all remaining windows by clicking "OK".
- Use the Windows search bar to search for "Command Prompt" and open the command prompt window.
- In the command prompt type "vdb-config -i" and press the "Enter" key as shown in Figure 3.134.

If the SRA toolkit has been installed and its path has been added to the Windows path successfully, the SRA Configuration window will pop up as shown in Figure 3.135.

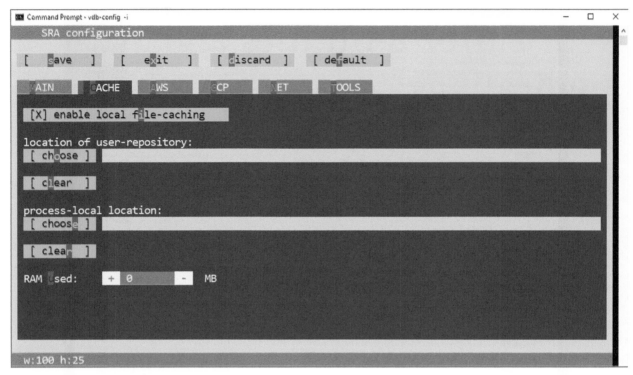

FIGURE 3.135   SRA Configuration window.

Use SRA Configuration to configure the SRA download path by using Alt+C to move to the CACHE tab. You can then use "choose" under "location of user-repository" to browse to a folder or to create a folder where the SRA archive files will be downloaded and extracted. In this installation example, the SRA archive files will be downloaded and extracted in the "c:\Users\hamid\ncbi\SRA" directory as shown in Figure 3.136.

Using SRA Toolkit Executables

The SRA toolkit has several executable programs. Table 3.40 contains the most commonly used SRA tools and their descriptions. The complete list of SRA programs will be found in the SRA toolkit bin folder (in Windows) or directory (in Linux).

Downloading SRA Files with Prefetch

The SRA database archives only the sequence files with per-base quality scores such as FASTQ, BAM, CRAM, and HDF5. The FASTQ and BAM are the most common SRA archived files. The library layout of the sequence reads in the SRA archived FASTQ may be single or paired. For the paired layout there may be two FASTQ files. Although it is possible to encounter paired-end reads merged in a single FASTQ file, two separate files for the paired library (R1.fastq and R2.fastq) are the most common. For other formats such as BAM there is only one file that includes the mapped sequence reads for pair-end reads. The SRA data can be downloaded with the "prefetch" SRA toolkit program, which uses HTTP to contact the SRA database, resolves the accessions that you provide, and then downloads the data. You can either provide the path of an SRA file or an SRA accession to the "prefetch" utility. Notice that the "$" dollar sign is just to show the symbol of the command line prompt and not part of the command. The command syntaxes are the same for all computer platforms (Linux, Windows, and MacOS). The SRA Toolkit requires Internet connectivity to download SRA data. The syntax of prefetch command is as follows:

$ prefetch [options] [accessions(s)…]

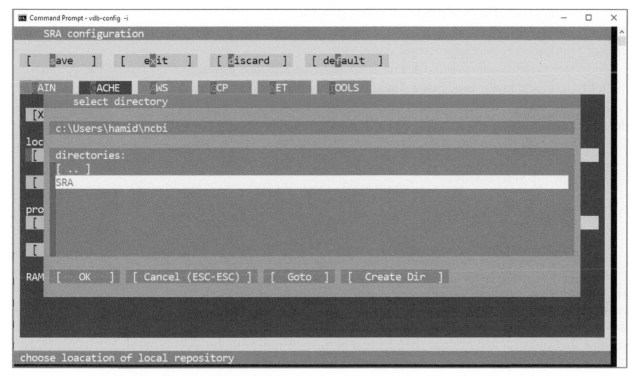

FIGURE 3.136   Configuring the SRA download path.

TABLE 3.40   SRA Toolkit Commands

SRA Tool	Description
Prefetch	allows command-line downloading of SRA, dbGaP, and ADSP data
fastq-dump	converts SRA data into FASTQ format
sam-dump	convert SRA data to SAM format
sra-pileup	generates pileup statistics on aligned SRA data
vdb-config	displays and modifies VDB configuration information
vdb-decrypt	decrypts non-SRA dbGaP data ("phenotype data")
abi-dump	converts SRA data into ABI format (csfasta / qual)
illumina-dump	converts SRA data into Illumina native formats (qseq, etc.)
sff-dump	converts SRA data to sff format
sra-stat	generates statistics about SRA data (quality distribution, etc.)
vdb-dump	outputs the native VDB format of SRA data.
vdb-encrypt	encrypts non-SRA dbGaP data ("phenotype data")
vdb-validate	validates the integrity of downloaded SRA data

The possible options of prefetch command can be listed with their descriptions by running:

    $ prefetch -h

Use the above command every time to explore the options used with the prefetch command.

A single accession or a list of accessions can be used with prefetch as indicated by [accession(s)…]. The accessions used with prefetch command can be a single or a list of run accessions. For example, to download all the SRA in the BioProject with accession PRJNA24284 (Figure 3.123), you can save all run accessions in a text file (e.g allrun.txt) and use prefetch command as follows:

    $ prefetch $(<allrun.txt)

The "-p" option is used to show the downloading progress.

However, you are not advised to download the SRA files of the entire BioProject unless you have to. All SRA files of a BioProject require large storage space.

The above prefetch command is used on Linux only; for Windows platform use "--option-file" option with prefetch command as discussed below. The run accession numbers in the text file must be each in a single line. The complete accession list of the SRA runs in a BioProject can be obtained by using Run Selector to download the total accession list as discussed below and shown in Figure 3.140. However, for a single SRA run, use the following prefetch command:

$ prefetch -p SRR14683044

You can provide a list of accessions to download the SRA files of multiple SRA runs as follows

$ prefetch -p SRR10005228 SRR10005229

This will create two directories, one for each run.

Instead of typing the accession list to the command line, you can save the list in a flat text file and provide it to the prefetch command as an argument, but you must also provide the "--option-file" option. For example, assume that you wish to download the SRA files of the SRA runs with the SRR14683044, SRR10005228, and SRR10005229 accessions. You can save these accession numbers in a flat text file. Use the text editor of your choice (e.g., Notepad on Windows and vim or nano on Linux). The accessions must be saved in a text file as shown in Figure 3.137.

Then you can run the following command to download the SRA files for those accession numbers.

$ prefetch -p --option-file idlist.txt

Three SRA files will be downloaded in separate directories.

The accession list is usually prepared by selecting SRA runs using SRA Run Selector as shown in Figure 3.125. First find the right SRA Study and then use SRA Run Selector to select the runs, download the accession list file to your current directory, and then use the prefetch command as shown above to download the SRA files.

You can also use prefetch to download access-controlled dbGaP SRA files and non-SRA files. See above to review the dbGaP database. The dbGaP files are usually encrypted because they contain human personal information. Accessing the controlled dbGaP data requires request approval as discussed in the dbGaP section. Access tokens come either in the form of the old NGC file, or a newer JWT version. Each has its application. The NGC, which contains a "dbGaP repository key", is used with the prefetch option "--ngc <path-to-ngc-file>" while the JWT file is used to provide permission only on commercial clouds. When a JWT file is used on the cloud instead of an NGC file, it is used with the option "--perm <path-to-jwt-file>". Since students may

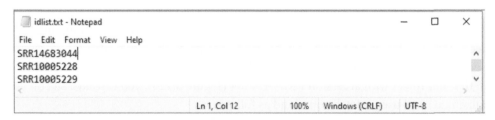

FIGURE 3.137   SRA Run accession saved in a text file.

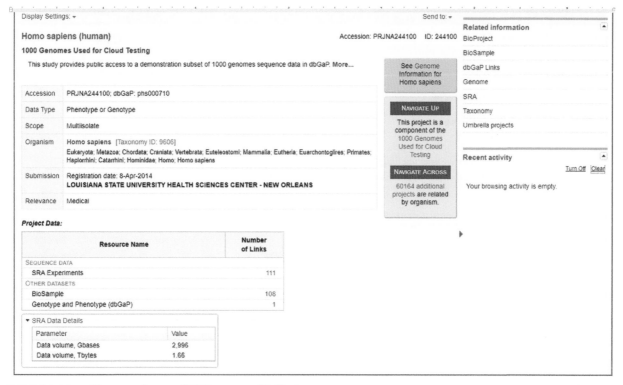

FIGURE 3.138   The record page of 1000 genome BioProject.

not have access to dbGaP, the NCBI provides a file for a dbGaP repository key for accessing the dbGaP project: 1000 Genomes Used for Cloud Testing. The "1000 Genomes Used for Cloud Testing" dbGaP project has the BioProject accession (PRJNA244100).

From the database dropdown menu of the Entrez web page choose BioProject, enter "PRJNA244100" BioProject accession, and click the "Search" button to open the BioProject record page of that project to read more about that BioProject.

We can notice that, as shown in Figure 3.138, this testing BioProject has 111 SRA Experiments. Click that number in the "Number of Links" column to open the SRA search results page containing the 111 SRA Experiments of that BioProject. Use the filters on the left side to select "paired" under the Library Layout filter and also select "fastq" under File Type filter to limit the SRA experiments to those that have paired-end library layout and SRA-archived FASTQ files.

After applying the two filters, the number of SRA experiments has become only six as shown in Figure 3.139. To download the SRA files of these records, take the following steps:

(1) Click the "Send To" dropdown menu, select "Run Selector", and click the "Go" button as shown in Figure 3.140 to open the SRA Run Selector.

(2) Select the three SRA Runs as shown in Figure 3.140 (those three have the smallest size for practicing). The total size 5.04 GB.

(3) Click the "Accession List" button of the selected run to download the list file. Save the file to the directory in which you run the SRA toolkit commands. The file is "SRR_Acc_List.txt".

(4) Use prefetch to download the SRA files of the accession number in the file. Since those SRA files are controlled dbGaP SRA data, you cannot download them as you did with SRA files above. Anyway, you can try this:

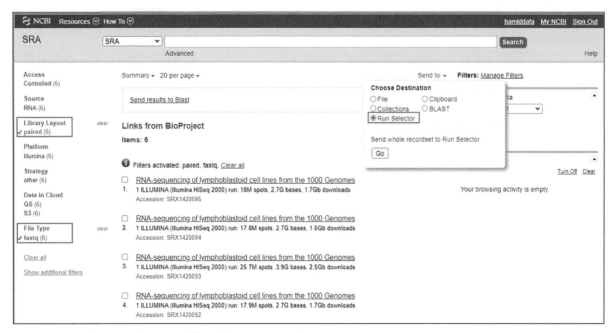

FIGURE 3.139   SRA search page of filtered 1000 genome SRA experiments.

FIGURE 3.140   dbGaP SRA Run Selector.

```
$ prefetch -p --option-file SRR_Acc_List.txt
```

You will get an error as shown in Figure 3.141.

Access has been denied because downloading dbGaP data requires an "ngc" file that contains the dbGaP repository key for that project. This NCG file for this testing project can be downloaded from:

https://ftp.ncbi.nlm.nih.gov/sra/examples/decrypt_examples/prj_phs710EA_test.ngc

You may need to save the file in the same directory where you saved the accession list file. Then use the following command:

```
$ prefetch -p --ngc prj_phs710EA_test.ngc --option-file SRR_Acc_List.txt
```

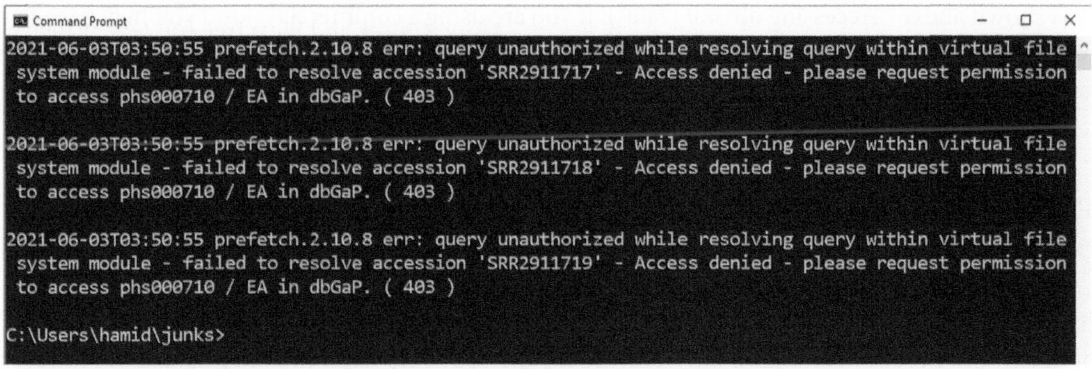

FIGURE 3.141   Access denied for controlled dbGaP SRA data.

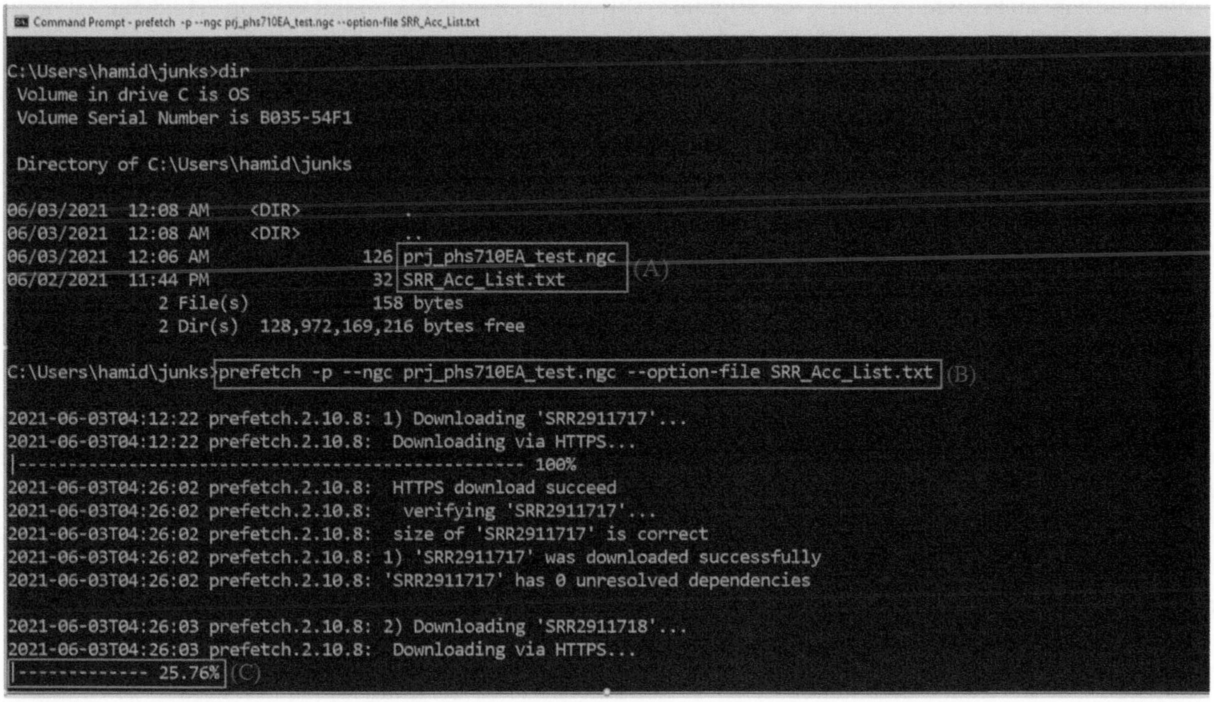

FIGURE 3.142   Downloading in progress after providing NGC file.

Figure 3.142 shows that the downloading is in progress after providing the NGC file as an argument to prefetch. As illustrated in Figure 3.142:

(A) This indicates that the file containing the accessions of dbGaP SRA files, and the NGC file are present in the same working directory where the prefetch command is executed. However, the files can be in a different directory or separate directories, but you must provide the complete path for each file.

(B) The complete prefetch command with the options as written above.

(C) This shows that one SRA file has been downloaded successfully and the download is still in progress.

You must provide the NGC file to download and decrypt the controlled dbGaP files. If you have a dbGaP account and have access to a controlled dbGaP dataset, you can generate a dbGaP repository key for that dataset as shown above ("Accessing dbGaP Data"). If you are using a commercial cloud you may need to download JWT file by clicking on the "JWT cart" button on the SRA Run Selector and then use the JWT file with the prefetch command as shown by the following two syntaxes – the first if you provide an SRA Run accession number directly to prefetch and the second if you provide an accession list in a plain text file.

    $ prefetch --perm <path-to-jwt-file> SRRxxxxxxxxx
    $ prefetch --perm <path-to-jwt-file> --option-file Acc_List.txt

Extracting Data from SRA Files

The "prefetch" SRA toolkit command only downloads the SRA files from the SRA database. However, after downloading, you will need to extract the archived files from the downloaded SRA files. The process of extracting archived files from the SRA files is called dumping. The SRA Toolkit includes several dumping programs that can be used to extract the original archived files. As of SRA toolkit version 2.10.8, the list of the dumping programs or dumpers includes:

(1) *fastq-dump*. This extracts FASTQ and FASTA file formats from the SRA files.

(2) *fasterq-dump*. The same as fastq-dump but it is faster and use multithreading.

(3) *sam-dump*. This extracts BAM file format from SRA files.

(4) *sff-dump*. This extracts sff file format from SRA files.

(5) *abi-dump*. This extracts csfasta/csqual format from SRA files.

(6) *illumina-dump*. This extracts Illumina native and qseq formats from SRA files.

In the following section we will discuss "fastq-dump" and "fasterq-dump" and "sam-dump", that are used to extract FASTQ files and SAM/BAM respectively. The other dumpers are used in the same way to extract other file formats.

The dumpers can either extract files from the SRA files downloaded by the "prefetch" program or can do both the downloading and extraction at the same time. In other words, dumpers can do the prefetch job as well.

fastq-dump   The fastq-dump command extracts FASTQ files from an SRA file previously downloaded by the "prefetch" command or can do both downloading and extraction. The SRA file may contain a single file for the sequence reads generated with the single-end sequencing or may contain two files for the sequence reads generated with paired-end sequencing. The following are the fastq-dump syntaxes:

    $ fastq-dump [options] <path/file> [<path/file> …]
    $ fastq-dump [options] <accession>

The first syntax is to extract the FAST file/files from an SRA file that has already been downloaded by the "prefetch" command (e.g., $ fastq-dump SRR10001254). The second syntax requires an SRA Run accession so the "fastq-dump" will download the SRA file and extract the FAST file/files from it at the same time.

To display the different options used with "fastq-dump" command run the following:

    $ fastq-dump -h

In the following, we will discuss two examples of FASTQ-archived SRA file: single-end and paired-end FASTQ-archived SRA file.

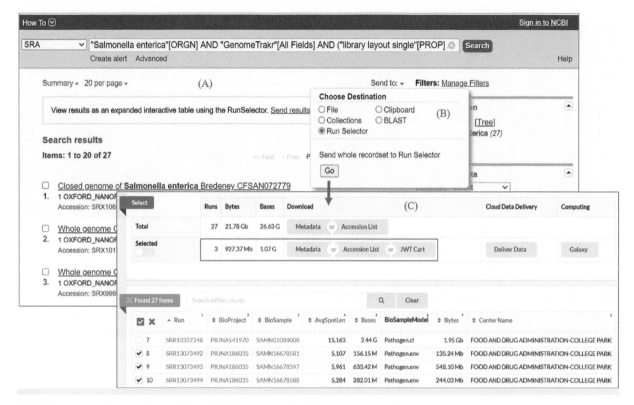

FIGURE 3.143   The steps for making SRA Run accession list.

Extracting Single-End FASTQ Files from SRA Files   This example will show you how to extract a FASTQ file from a single-end FAST-archived SRA file. In this case the SRA file will contain a single FASTQ file for the sequence reads generated by a single-end sequencing. For this example, first you need to obtain an accession of an SRA file with a single-end FASTQ file. The steps for getting SRA Run accession list of SRA files that contain single-end FASTQ files are illustrated in Figure 3.143 and described as follows:

(A) Find SRA files archived single-end FASTQ files for *Salmonella enterica* from GenomeTrakr project by searching the SRA database using the following query:

"Salmonella enterica"[ORGN] AND "GenomeTrakr"[All Fields] AND ("library layout single"[PROP] AND "filetype fastq"[PROP])

The SRA search results page of this query will include the SRA entries from GenomeTrakr that have single-end FASTQ files as shown in Figure 3.143 (A).

(B) Click the "Send To" dropdown menu, select "Run Selector", and then click the "Go" button to open the SRA Run Selector.

If you wish to download and extract a FASTQ file from a single run as an example, copy the SRA run accession (SRR13073492) of the item # 8, which has only 135.24 Mb, and use it with "fastq-dump" command to download "SRR13073492.sra" file and convert it into "SRR13073492.fastq" file as follows:

$ fastq-dump SRR13073492

Figure 3.144 shows (A) the execution of the "fastq-dump" program followed by reading from the server and writing into the destination directory and (B) the FASTQ file after being extracted successfully.

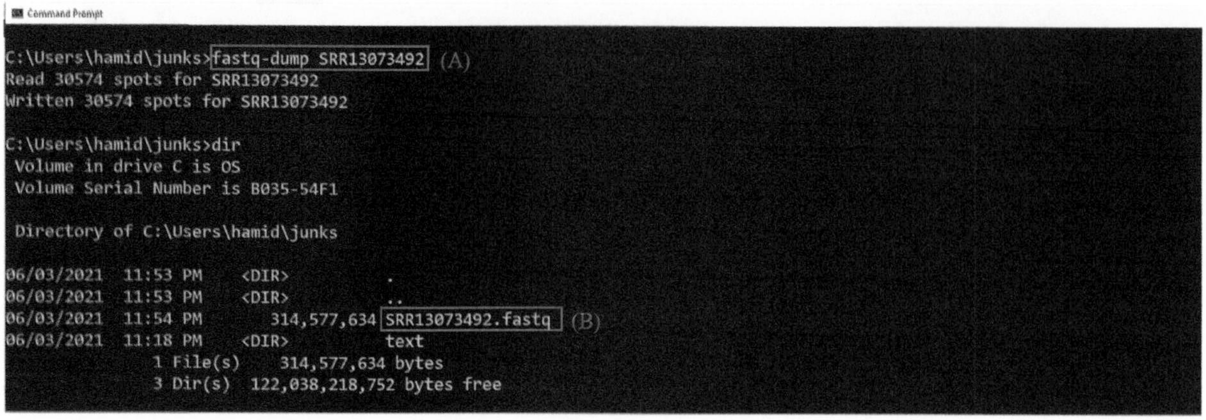

FIGURE 3.144   Downloading and extracting single-end FASTQ file.

However, instead of only a single file, you may wish to download a list of SRA files and extract them at the same time. This time, select any number of SRA runs (three runs are enough for the demonstration) as shown in Figure 3.143 (C). The selected three runs in the example have 927.37 Mb. After selecting the runs click the "Accession list" button to download the file to your local drive. Copy the file to your working directory and you can rename it (e.g., SRR_Acc_List2.txt). Since "fastq-dump" command does not read accession from a file, if you are using Windows you may need to provide the accession list to the "fastq-dump" as follows:

> fastq-dump SRR13073492 SRR13073493 SRR13073494

But if you are using Linux or MacOS, you can import the accessions from the file by using the pipe symbol "|" with shell "cat" and "xargs" Linux command as follows.

$ cat SRR_Acc_List2.txt | xargs fastq-dump

Those steps work the same for dbGaP SRA datasets, but since the dbGaP SRA files are encrypted you need to use the "--ngc" option and the NGC file as follows:

$ fastq-dump --ngc the_ngc_file.ngc <accession … .>

On Linux and MacOS you can also import the list of accession numbers from a file as follows:

$ cat SRR_Acc_List2.txt | xargs fastq-dump --ngc the_ngc_file.ngc

Displaying the First Spots on a FASTQ Archived in SRA   The "fastq-dump" command can also be used to display the first number of spots (X) of the FASTQ file before downloading or converting the SRA file. For example, to display the first 1 spot of the SRA run (SRR13073492), you can execute the following command (Figure 3.145):

$ fastq-dump -X 1 -Z SRR13073492

Extracting FASTA from a Single-End FASTQ File Archived in SRA   You can also use the "fastq-dump" command to extract the spots in the FASTQ file in FASTA format by using "-I" and "--fasta" options with "fastq-dump" command:

$ fastq-dump -I --fasta 60 SRR13073492

```
C:\Users\hamid\junks>fastq-dump -X 1 -Z SRR13073492
Read 1 spots for SRR13073492
Written 1 spots for SRR13073492
@SRR13073492.1 1 length=333
AGCAACGCTCTGGCAATCAGCCGCTGTTTTGCCCACCCGATAACAGCGCCCGTTCGCCTACCTGCGTGTCGTAGCCTGAGAGCAACAGAGATATCCTCATGTAC
GCTGGCTAAACGCGCCGCCTGTTCAATCCTCACCTGAGTCGCACTCAGGGCGTCCGAGGCGCAAATATTATTGGCAATAGAGGTCCGAGAACAAAAACGGCGTC
TGGCTGACGACCGCCAGTCGGCTACGCCAGCTATCCAGTTGCGAATGCGTCAACAGCATGTCATGGAATCGGATCTCACCCCTGCGTCACATCAAATAGCTGGA
TAAATGATGGAATTGTGCTTT
+SRR13073492.1 1 length=333
5,,/%9=<@D@G>9:.*;)(''-8>A>G@3/33/%+1&62-'#$#)$$++'(%:6/347/*('($(''&0$%&%12.')&$/22(()&+$).0//24A:53/$1
+?;B@@CGD8460:67%))**))*('%')&/$&&'*'8::(-')/9&+665://=*$'+'&((&%.5587=?AE?C76794&2$$;23:B6340).'&&%-,-4
(.5:<@><?7799>;47/;7?;<8A=KG;405,+,<+<.7,++,10.(,(@6)$%,./0049045:-191)1-05)1'++*%$$377>96406*(0//289A28
1/)$#$##$&$$$&&(($$%%
```

FIGURE 3.145   Displaying the first spot in the SRA file.

```
Command Prompt

C:\Users\hamid\junks>fastq-dump -I --split-files SRR10005228 SRR10005229
Read 1056826 spots for SRR10005228
Written 1056826 spots for SRR10005228
Read 842285 spots for SRR10005229
Written 842285 spots for SRR10005229

C:\Users\hamid\junks>dir
 Volume in drive C is OS
 Volume Serial Number is B035-54F1

 Directory of C:\Users\hamid\junks

06/04/2021  02:12 AM    <DIR>          .
06/04/2021  02:12 AM    <DIR>          ..
06/04/2021  02:12 AM       596,567,392 SRR10005228_1.fastq
06/04/2021  02:12 AM       596,735,182 SRR10005228_2.fastq
06/04/2021  02:15 AM       473,864,422 SRR10005229_1.fastq
06/04/2021  02:15 AM       474,002,418 SRR10005229_2.fastq
06/03/2021  11:18 PM    <DIR>          text
               4 File(s)  2,141,169,414 bytes
               3 Dir(s)  119,781,683,200 bytes free
```

FIGURE 3.146   Extracting paired-end SRA file.

The "-I" option adds a sequence read ID and sequence length as a definition in the defline of the FASTA sequences.

Extracting FASTQ Files and FASTA Files from a Paired-End SRA   The sequence reads generated with paired-end sequencing are usually stored in two FASTQ files (R1.fastq and R2.fastq). Those two files are archived together in a single SRA file in the SRA database. The "fastq-dump" can be used to extract the two files by using the "--split-files" option. As examples, you can use the SRA Run accessions: SRR10005228 and SRR10005229, which were used above. When you extract these SRA runs, two FASTQ files will be extracted from each SRA run as shown in Figure 3.146:

    $ fastq-dump -I --split-files SRR10005228 SRR10005229

To extract FASTA files from the SRA runs of paired-end sequencing, you can use the following command:

    $ fastq-dump -I --split-files --fasta 80 SRR10005228 SRR10005229

Two FASTA files will be extracted for each run.

fasterq-dump   The "fasterq-dump" program is a streamlined alternative to the "fastq-dump" program that can be used to download and convert SRA fastq files. It is faster since it uses temporary files and multi-threading to speed up the downloading and conversion of SRA files. Fasterq-dump has the following syntax:

$ fasterq-dump [options] [<accession>…]

To list the options used with "fasterq-dump" command run the following:

$ fasterq-dump –h

Downloading FASTQ Files for Paired-End Library   You can provide only the accession of the paired-end SRA run:

$ fasterq-dump --progress SRR10005228

This will download the two FASTQ files: SRR10005228_1.fastq and SRR10005228_2.fastq. "fasterq-dump" will create a temporary directory if it needs it to extract the temporary files and then deletes it when it finishes. When "fasterq-dump" is used without split option as above, the default option is "--split 3", which splits the paired-end library SRA into two FASTQ files as shown above.

For a large SRA file downloading, you can use the multi-threading feature of fasterq-dump by adding the "--thread n" option, where "n" is number of processors to be used in the process. For example, to use four processors to download the above files, you can use the following:

$ fasterq-dump --threads 4 --progress SRR10005228

The "--progress" option is to show the progress as shown in Figure 3.147.

If you wish to write all read spots of the paired-end SRA into a single FASTQ file, use the following:

$ fasterq-dump --split-spot --progress SRR10005228

This will create a single FASTQ file containing all spots. A FASTQ spot has four lines as described in Chapter 2.

However, if you need to separate the spots of paired-end library reads into different FASTQ files as above use "--split-files" as follows:

$ fasterq-dump --split-files --progress SRR10005228

This will create two FASTQ files.

Remember that for dbGaP SRA datasets, you need to add the "--ngc" and use the dbGaP repository key as shown above.

```
hamiddafa@dax:~/junks$ fasterq-dump --threads 4 --progress SRR10005228
join    :|--------------------------------------------------- 100%
concat  :|--------------------------------------------------- 100%
spots read      : 1,056,826
reads read      : 2,113,652
reads written   : 2,113,652
hamiddafa@dax:~/junks$ ls
SRR10005228_1.fastq  SRR10005228_2.fastq
hamiddafa@dax:~/junks$
```

FIGURE 3.147   Extracting paired-end FASTQ files using fasterq-dump.

sam-dump   The "sam-dump" program is the dumper for the BAM archived on the SRA database. The SRA file can either be downloaded first using "prefetch" and then converted with the "sam-dump" program or it can be downloaded and converted into a BAM file in a single step with the "sam-dump" program. The following is the syntax of the "sam-dump" SRA toolkit command.

$ sam-dump [options] <path/file> [<path/file> …]

$ sam-dump [options] <accession>

To display the options used with the "sam-dump" command you can run the following command:

$ sam-dump -h

Extracting BAM Using sam-dump   To demonstrate how the archived BAM files are downloaded from the SRA database and extracted, we will search the SRA database for SRA entries with BAM data. For this example, we will search for aligned reads in the BAM files for the lung cancer study conducted on the mouse (*Mus musculus*) as a model animal. Open the SRA database web interface, enter the following search query, and click the "Search" button.

"Mus musculus"[ORGN] AND "lung cancer"[TITL] AND "filetype bam"[PROP]

The SRA search results page, as shown in Figure 3.148, shows that only six SRA entries have been found. Click the "Send To" dropdown menu, select "Run Selector", and then click the "Go" button to open the SRA Run Selector as illustrated in Figure 3.148. From the run list, select the runs with the smallest size for the sake of downloading speed. In this example, the selected runs are SRR4252571 and SRR4252573 with a total size of 1.11 Gb. Those two runs are aligned sequence reads generated from the ChIP-Seq experiment. You can open

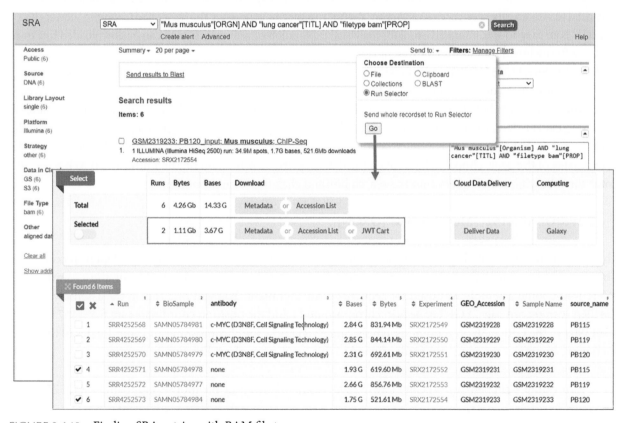

FIGURE 3.148   Finding SRA entries with BAM file type.

the records of these two SRA runs and BioSample records to read more about the nature of the experiments. Click "Accession List" to download the accession list file. The following command will extract the BAM file from "SRR4252571" accession:

```
$ sam-dump --output-file SRR4252571.bam SRR4252571
```

This will extract the two BAM files from the SRA databases.

Remember that for dbGaP SRA datasets, you need to add the "--ngc" and use the dbGaP repository key as shown above.

Extracting Reads Aligned to a Chromosome   In some cases, instead of extracting the whole BAM file, you may wish to extract the sequence reads that aligned to a specific chromosome or to a region in a chromosome. This is especially useful if your goal is to focus on a specific chromosome or a specific locus. By using this feature, you will consume little computer storage and memory. Assume that you are interested in the sequence reads of SRR4252571 SRA file that are aligned to the mouse chromosome 11 (the mouse has 19 pairs of chromosomes, plus X and Y chromosome). To extract only the sequence reads aligned to chromosome 11, you can run the following:

```
$ sam-dump --aligned-region chr11 --output-file mouse_chr11.bam SRR4252571
```

This will extract all reads aligned to the mouse chromosome 11 and then write them into a file named "mouse_chr11.bam"

Remember that for dbGaP SRA datasets, you need to add the "--ngc" and use the dbGaP repository key as shown above.

Extracting Reads Aligned to a Locus   The BAM file contains reads aligned to a specific reference genome. Researchers may need to visualize the sequence reads that are aligned to a specific gene using the Integrated Genomic Viewer (IGV). The IGV is an easy-to-use, interactive tool for the visual exploration of genomics data. It can be downloaded free from https://software.broadinstitute.org/software/igv/.

Since the SRR4252571 SRA run accession is for aligned sequences (BAM) of a sample from a study on lung cancer, assume that you are interested in the sequence reads mapped to "epidermal growth factor receptor" gene whose gene symbol is "Egfr". This gene is known to undergo genetic changes (mutations) in patients with lung cancer. To extract the reads that aligned to this gene in the reference genome, you need to know the coordinates of that gene in the reference genome assembly used to align the reads in the BAM file. To find the coordinates of the gene, choose "Gene" from the database dropdown menu on the Entrez main web page, and enter the following search query into the search box and click the "Search" button:

EGFR[GENE] AND "Mus musculus"[ORGN]

The Gene search page will display the mouse RefSeq EGFR gene. Click the title to open that Gene record page. The chromosome and the coordinate of the gene will be in the Genomic context table. You must know which reference genome assembly was used for sequence read alignment. You will find this in the assembly link on the SRA Run record page. EGFR gene is in chromosome 11 and the position coordinates are from 16752203 to 16913907 in the GRCm38.p6 genome assembly. Since you know the chromosome and coordinates of the gene, then you can extract the sequence reads aligned to this locus using the following command:

```
$ sam-dump --aligned-region Chr11:16752203-16913907 --output-file mouse_egfr.bam SRR4252571
```

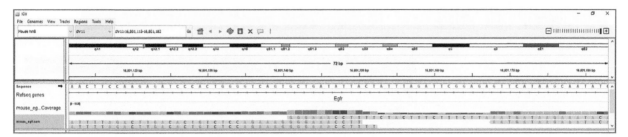

FIGURE 3.149   IGV viewing reads aligned to EGFR gene.

This command will extract all sequence reads from SRR4252571 SRA run and write them into a file name "mouse_egfr.bam". To visualize the sequence reads saved in the separate BAM file, open the IGV. From the drop-down menu on the top left corner choose the right genome assembly. If you did not find the genome, choose "More" to display all the list of available reference genomes. The right genome for this BAM file is "mouse mm8". From the "File" menu, choose "Load from File" and browse to the directory where you saved "mouse_egfr. bam" and open it. From the chromosome list on the top left, choose chromosome 11, enter "chr11: 16752203-16913907" into the coordinate box and click the "Go" button to move the view to the gene region in the chromosome. Then you can zoom in and move to visualize the reads mapped to the EGFR gene (Figure 3.149).

Compressing Extracted BAM File   The extracted BAM file may have a large size. Using the "--gzip" with "sam-dump" will compress the BAM file.

```
$ sam-dump -r --gzip --output-file SRR4252571.bam.gz SRR4252571
```

The "-r" option is for reconstructing the header.

Extracting Data from dbGaP Non-SRA Files

You already know that there are two kinds of dbGaP datasets: dbGaP SRA files for genotype datasets and dbGaP non-SRA files for phenotype datasets. Both kinds of datasets are downloaded and decrypted using the SRA toolkit and an NGC file containing the dbGaP repository key for the datasets. Generation of the NGC file was discussed earlier. Since the dbGaP database may not be accessible to all users, NCBI provides the "1000 Genomes Used for Cloud Testing" project for testing and practicing. The NGC file for the datasets of this testing project can be downloaded from:

https://ftp.ncbi.nlm.nih.gov/sra/examples/decrypt_examples/prj_phs710EA_test.ngc

Some examples of dbGaP phenotype datasets are made available by NCBI at www.ncbi.nlm.nih.gov/Traces/study/. Use that link to open SRA Run, select "Base Files", and click the "1000 Genomes Used for Cloud Testing" link to open the dbGaP File Selector as shown in Figure 3.150. Select any phenotype files (e.g., 6, 7, and 9) and click the "Cart file" button to download the cart file, which contains information of the selected phenotypes for downloading and decryption.

Make sure that both NGC file and cart file are in the working directory; otherwise, you may need to provide the complete path to the SRA toolkit program for each file. You can also rename the cart file to make the name shorter (e.g., cart_prj0.krt).

The dbGaP non-SRA files are downloaded from the dbGaP database with the "prefetch" SRA toolkit program with the "--ngc" option and NGC file and the cart file. You can download the three dbGaP files selected above as follows:

```
$ prefetch --ngc prj_phs710EA_test.ngc cart_prj0.krt
```

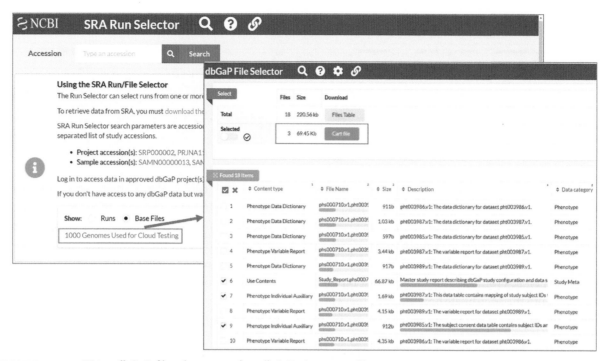

FIGURE 3.150 Using dbGaP file selector to select dbGaP phenotype files.

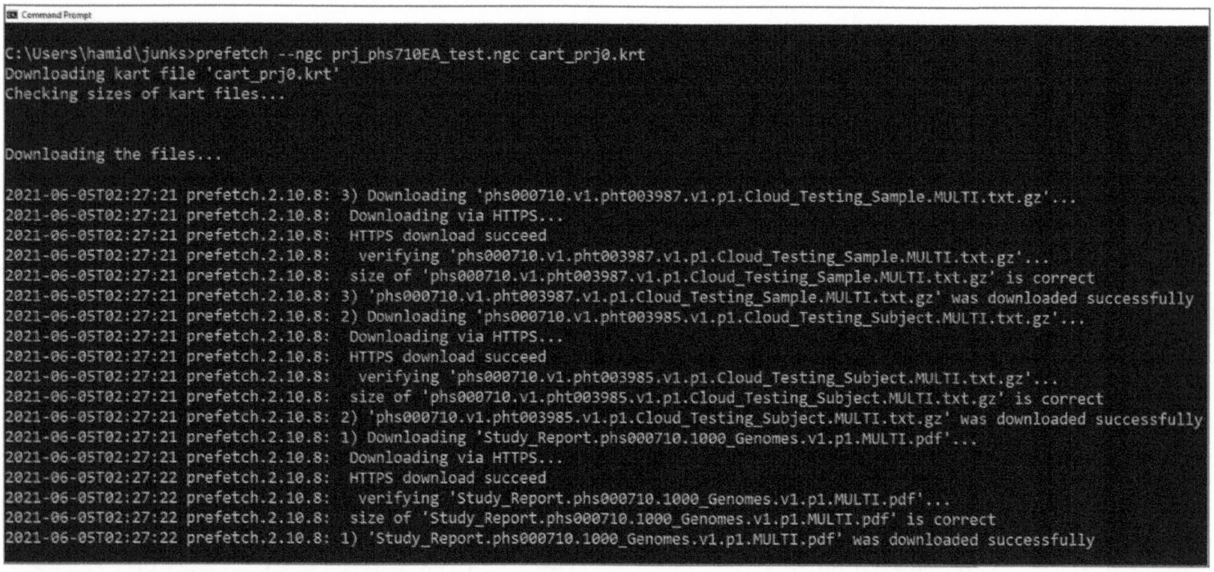

FIGURE 3.151 Downloading encrypted dbGaP non-SRA files.

This command created a subdirectory named "dbGaP-0" and then it downloaded the three encrypted dbGaP files into that subdirectory. Figure 3.151 shows that the files were downloaded successfully. The names of the downloaded files are:

phs000710.v1.pht003985.v1.p1.Cloud_Testing_Subject.MULTI.txt.gz.ncbi_enc
phs000710.v1.pht003987.v1.p1.Cloud_Testing_Sample.MULTI.txt.gz.ncbi_enc
Study_Report.phs000710.1000_Genomes.v1.p1.MULTI.pdf.ncbi_enc

The dbGaP phenotype files are encrypted with ".ncbi_enc" extension indicating that the files are encrypted by the NCBI. The names of those files are long so you can rename them with short names for easy handling. For example, you can leave only the phenotype table accession numbers and the extensions. So, you can rename them as follows:

pht003985.txt.gz.ncbi_enc
pht003987.txt.gz.ncbi_enc
Study_Report.pdf.ncbi_enc

Those three files are still encrypted as indicated by their extensions ".ncbi_enc". So, you cannot view their content. The first two files are encrypted, compressed phenotype test files, and the third file is an encrypted pdf file. The NCBI-encrypted dbGaP files are decrypted with the "vdb-decypt" SRA toolkit program whose syntax is as follows:

$ vdb-decrypt --ngc your_file.ngc enc_file.ncbi_enc

Since the encrypted files are in "dbGaP-0" subdirectory, you need to change into that directory first by using "cd" command. Then from inside "dbGaP-0" subdirectory, you can run the following commands to decrypt the three files:

$ vdb-decrypt --ngc ..\prj_phs710EA_test.ngc pht003985.txt.gz.ncbi_enc
$ vdb-decrypt --ngc ..\prj_phs710EA_test.ngc pht003987.txt.gz.ncbi_enc
$ vdb-decrypt --ngc ..\prj_phs710EA_test.ngc Study_Report.pdf.ncbi_enc

Pay attention to use "../" instead of "..\" in the above commands if you are using Linux or MacOS.

Figure 3.152 shows the decryption of the three files was successful. However, the two text files are compressed so they must be decompressed first before they are used. The third file is a pdf file and can be opened.

```
C:\Users\hamid\junks\dbGaP-0>dir
 Volume in drive C is OS
 Volume Serial Number is B035-54F1

 Directory of C:\Users\hamid\junks\dbGaP-0

06/04/2021  11:28 PM    <DIR>          .
06/04/2021  11:28 PM    <DIR>          ..
06/04/2021  11:26 PM            32,864 pht003985.txt.gz.ncbi_enc
06/04/2021  11:26 PM            32,864 pht003987.txt.gz.ncbi_enc
06/04/2021  11:26 PM            98,528 Study_Report.pdf.ncbi_enc
               3 File(s)        164,256 bytes
               2 Dir(s)  112,443,277,312 bytes free

C:\Users\hamid\junks\dbGaP-0>vdb-decrypt --ngc ..\prj_phs710EA_test.ngc pht003985.txt.gz.ncbi_enc
2021-06-05T03:29:47 vdb-decrypt.2.10.8: Decrypting file in place pht003985.txt.gz.ncbi_enc
2021-06-05T03:29:49 vdb-decrypt.2.10.8: copying pht003985.txt.gz.ncbi_enc to .pht003985.txt.gz.ncbi_enc.vdb-decrypt-tmp
2021-06-05T03:29:49 vdb-decrypt.2.10.8: renaming .pht003985.txt.gz.ncbi_enc.vdb-decrypt-tmp to pht003985.txt.gz
2021-06-05T03:29:49 vdb-decrypt.2.10.8: exiting: success

C:\Users\hamid\junks\dbGaP-0>vdb-decrypt --ngc ..\prj_phs710EA_test.ngc pht003987.txt.gz.ncbi_enc
2021-06-05T03:30:05 vdb-decrypt.2.10.8: Decrypting file in place pht003987.txt.gz.ncbi_enc
2021-06-05T03:30:07 vdb-decrypt.2.10.8: copying pht003987.txt.gz.ncbi_enc to .pht003987.txt.gz.ncbi_enc.vdb-decrypt-tmp
2021-06-05T03:30:07 vdb-decrypt.2.10.8: renaming .pht003987.txt.gz.ncbi_enc.vdb-decrypt-tmp to pht003987.txt.gz
2021-06-05T03:30:07 vdb-decrypt.2.10.8: exiting: success

C:\Users\hamid\junks\dbGaP-0>vdb-decrypt --ngc ..\prj_phs710EA_test.ngc Study_Report.pdf.ncbi_enc
2021-06-05T03:30:23 vdb-decrypt.2.10.8: Decrypting file in place Study_Report.pdf.ncbi_enc
2021-06-05T03:30:25 vdb-decrypt.2.10.8: copying Study_Report.pdf.ncbi_enc to .Study_Report.pdf.ncbi_enc.vdb-decrypt-tmp
2021-06-05T03:30:25 vdb-decrypt.2.10.8: renaming .Study_Report.pdf.ncbi_enc.vdb-decrypt-tmp to Study_Report.pdf
2021-06-05T03:30:26 vdb-decrypt.2.10.8: exiting: success
```

FIGURE 3.152   dbGaP file decryption.

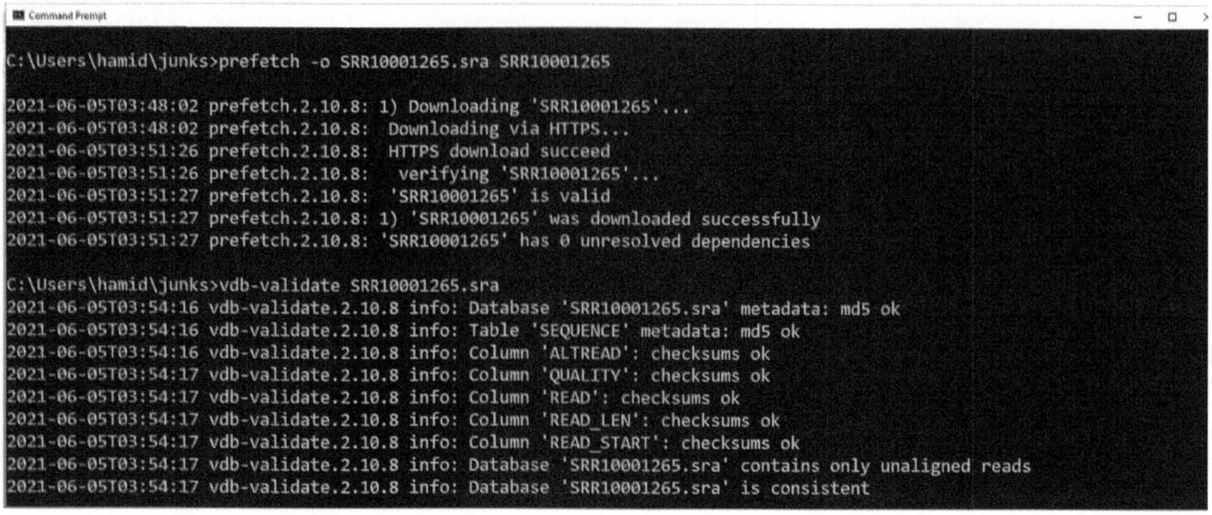

FIGURE 3.153   SRA file download validation.

Validation of Downloaded SRA Data Integrity

If you have downloaded SRA files using "prefetch", you may need to check the integrity and checksum of the file to make sure that the download was successful. For validating the SRA data, you will use the "vdb-validate" program. The downloaded SRA file must be in the working directory. The output must report "ok" and "consistent" for all parameters as shown in Figure 3.153; otherwise, the download and conversion were not successful. For example, you can download SRR10001265 SRA file using prefetch and then validate the download with vdb-validate as follows:

```
$ prefetch -o SRR10001265.sra SRR10001265
$ vdb-validate SRR10001265.sra
```

TAXONOMY

Taxonomy is the branch of biology that names, describes, and classifies organisms including all plants, animals, and microorganisms. Basically, taxonomy bases the identification, description, and classification of species on morphology, behavioral, genetics, and biochemical observations. Around 1.2 million of species have been identified and classified but still millions of species remain unidentified [89]. Taxonomy was developed by the Swedish botanist Carl Linnaeus in the 18th century. Linnaeus invented the binomial nomenclature system that gives each type of organism a genus and species name. At the present time, the taxonomic hierarchy of the classification system includes eight ranks from general to specific: domain, kingdom, phylum, class, order, family, genus, and species. A taxon (plural: taxa) is a group of organisms that are classified as a unit. This can be specific or general. For example, all humans form a taxon at the species level and all primates form a taxon at the order level. Species and orders are both examples of taxonomic ranks, which are relative levels of grouping organisms in a taxonomic hierarchy [90].

The NCBI Taxonomy database was developed to include a curated classification and nomenclature for all of the organisms in the public sequence databases of GenBank, EMBL, and DDBJ [91]. In the NCBI Taxonomy database, the taxa are arranged in a hierarchy from kingdom to subspecies. A given taxon usually includes several taxa of lower ranks. The GenBank formatted records of all nucleotide and protein sequences are provided with organism name and taxonomic classification in the SOURCE field. A taxon ID is also in the FEATURE section of the GenBank record as shown in Figure 3.154.

The formal names used in taxonomy are based on rules determined by four codes of nomenclature: (1) the International Code of Nomenclature of Prokaryotes (ICNP), (2) the International Code of Nomenclature for

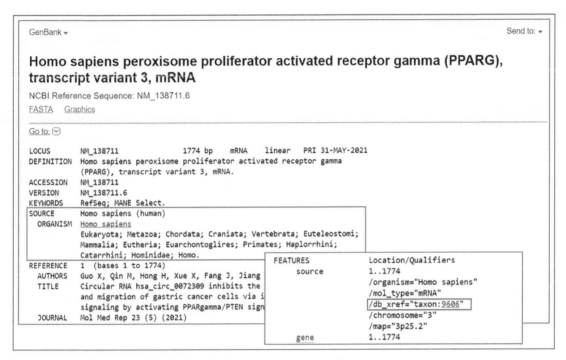

FIGURE 3.154   GenBank record showing taxonomic classification and taxon ID.

TABLE 3.41   NCBI Taxonomy Indexed Fields

Long Field Name	Short Field Name	Long Field Name	Short Field Name
All Fields	ALL	Organism	ORGN
Ancestor	ANCS	Protein Accession	PRAC
Domain Name	DOM	Properties	PROP
Filter	FILT	Protein UID	PUID
Gene Description	GDSC	Title	TITL
Gene Name	GENE	UniGene ID	UGID
Gene ID	GNID	UID	UID
Nucleotide Accession	NCAC	Text Word	WORD
Nucleotide UID	NUID		

algae, fungi, and plants (ICNafp), (3) the International Code of Zoological Nomenclature (ICZN), and (4) the International Code of Virus Classification and Nomenclature (ICVCN). Each entry in any one of the INSDC databases (GenBank, EMBL, and DDBJ) maps onto an entry in the NCBI Taxonomy database at the level of species or below. An NCBI Taxonomy entry is called TaxNode, which has a public unique taxonomy identifier (TaxId). The TaxId is shared by all names for a specific TaxNode. A TaxId has either formal or informal primary name that is used on the NCBI records (e.g. *Homo sapiens* NCBI:txid9606).

The NCBI Taxonomy database can be accessed by using the NCBI Taxonomy Browser, which is available at www.ncbi.nlm.nih.gov/Taxonomy/Browser/wwwtax.cgi or from the NCBI Entrez interface at www.ncbi.nlm.nih.gov/taxonomy/. The database can be searched using a formal or informal name, or indexed fields. A search query can be constructed following the Entrez search conventions. Advanced query can be built using indexed fields shown in Table 3.41 or with the help of the Advanced Search Builder.

Assume that we wish to search for the Taxonomy entries for *Plasmodium falciparum UGT5.1*, which is unicellular and the deadliest parasite that causes malaria in humans. The simplest way to search the Entrez Taxonomy database is to use a formal or scientific name of the species. For example, to find the Taxonomy records of this parasite, you can use the following search term:

"Plasmodium falciparum UGT5.1 "[ORGN]

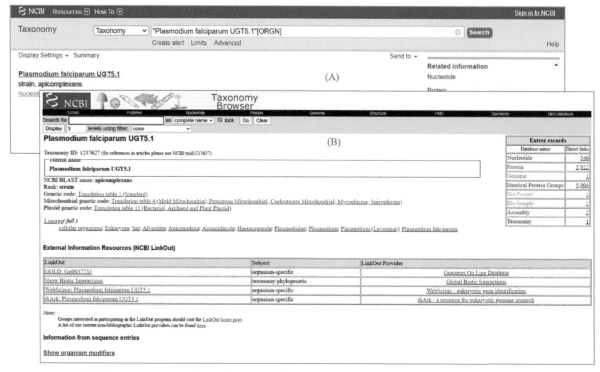

FIGURE 3.155   NCBI taxonomy search results page and taxonomy browser.

This search query will display only one Taxonomy record as shown in Figure 3.155 (A). The item summary on the Taxonomy search results page displays the scientific name, the level of the taxonomy classification, and links to the GenBank Nucleotide and Protein database if that taxonomy entry has links to these two databases.

Click on the name of the species to be forwarded to that species record page on the Taxonomy Browser as shown in Figure 3.155 (B). The Taxonomy record page contains the following section:

- *Description.* This section includes the taxonomic species information including taxonomy ID, current name, genetic codes for the nuclear and mitochondrial genes, and lineage that describes the taxonomic hierarchy of the species.
- *External Information Resources (NCBI LinkOut).* This is a table that contains the external links (LinkOuts) related to the current Taxonomy record, the subjects, and the LinkOut provides.
- *Show organism modifiers.* This section lists the strains and links to NCBI databases such as BioProject, BioSample, Nucleotide, Protein, etc. if available.
- *Entrez records.* This is a table on the top right of the Taxonomy records page. It contains the list of Entrez database names and number of direct links (number of records) related to the current Taxonomy records. *Plasmodium falciparum UGT5.1* as a taxon has 546 Nucleotide sequences, 5922 Protein sequences, a single reference genome, 5904 IPG groups, a single BioProject, a single BioSample, two genome assemblies, and a single Taxonomy record

NCBI LITERATURE DATABASES

Academic research usually begins with the literature review, which provides the foundation of knowledge on the research topic and enables researchers to identify the areas of prior scholarship to avoid duplication and to discover the weakness in the research area. It is crucial to know where the research topic stands, what gaps are there, and what can be done to fill the gaps or to improve the weakness. Such information is obtained only by reviewing the publications in the subject area. Science is a collaborative effort and a product of accumulative academic research and experimentation. Therefore, reporting research findings in manuscripts and reviewing literature are parts of the research itself. Most researchers review the most recent publications in their subject area to avoid doing research that has been done by others and to begin from where other researchers have ended. The NCBI's literature databases are the world's largest repository of medical and scientific abstracts, full-text articles, books, and other reports and documentations. Hence the NCBI's literature databases, including PubMed, PubMed Central (PMC), MeSH, Bookshelf, and other resources, are the right place to begin with for finding biomedical and life science publications.

PubMed

The PubMed database, which was made available by NCBI to the public in 1996, provides access to millions of abstracts and citations of publications collected from numerous biomedical and life science journals. PubMed is not primarily a full-article database but most of the articles in the database have links to the full text of articles made available at the publishers' websites or at the PMC database, which is NCBI's free full-text archive of journal publications. There is no direct submission to the PubMed database, but it is maintained by NCBI from several resources including publications from biomedicine, life sciences, behavioral sciences, chemical sciences, and bioengineering. PubMed also facilitates direct searching across other NCBI literature resources such as MEDLINE, PMC, and Bookshelf. MEDLINE is one of the biggest citations and abstracts provider to PubMed. It is the National Library of Medicine (NLM) bibliographic database that contains millions of indexed citations of journal articles in biomedicine and life sciences. Historically, the NLN founded its first print bibliographic index of medical articles, called Index Medicus, in 1879. In 1963, Index Medicus evolved to a digital version called the Medical Literature Analysis and Retrieval System (MEDLARS) and its content was distributed through computer data tapes. In 1971, MEDLARS evolved to a computerized version called MEDLARS online (MEDLINE), which used the telephone line to provide citations of medical articles published from 1966 and forward to libraries. Since 1997, the content of MEDLINE has been accessed through the Internet via PubMed. One of the greatest features of MEDLINE is that the records are indexed with Medical Subject Headings (MeSH) [92].

NCBI gives a PubMed unique identifier or PMID to the citation that it collects from the different literature resources.

Searching PubMed Database

The PubMed database is searched, as discussed above, by choosing "PubMed" from the database dropdown list, entering search terms, and clicking on the "Search" button. However, the PubMed web page is also available at https://pubmed.ncbi.nlm.nih.gov/. When the searching process starts, PubMed uses a spell-checking feature to suggest alternative correct words and it also uses a fuzzy machine-learning algorithm to find the most relevant records. See above for searching Entrez databases. Table 3.42 lists the PubMed indexed fields that are commonly used in searching for articles.

The searching can be as simple as searching by PMID and free text or can be advanced by using the indexed fields and Boolean operators (AND, OR, and NOT) in uppercase. When a PMID is used, the search is specific, and the record page will open. However, the search will be general when free text is used and more specific when indexed fields are used. When free text is used without quotation marks and without a tagged field, the Automatic Term Mapping (ATM) will be enabled. In PubMed, the ATM is more advanced as it uses three translation tables that index subject words, journal titles, and author names.

Subject Translation Table   The subject translation table is built of the words of subject heading including medical subject headings (MeSH), entry terms (synonyms), article subheadings, supplementary concepts, publication types, and unified medical language system (UMLS), which is a vocabulary system that is comprised of several medical words collected from different disciplines such as the health insurance industry and laboratories.

TABLE 3.42   The Commonly Used PubMed Indexed Fields

Full Field Name	Short Field Name	Description
Affiliation	AFFL	Author affiliation
All Fields	ALL	All field
Author	AUTH	Author of the article
Date – Completion	CDAT	Article completion date
Date – Create	CRDT	The date of record creation
Date – Entrez	EDAT	The date the article made public by Entrez
Electronic Publication Date	EPDT	Date of electronic publication
Author – First	FAUT	First author
Filter	FILT	Filter (e.g. review[FILT]
Investigator – Full	FINV	Investigator full name
Author – Full	FULL	Author full name
Investigator	INVR	Investigator
Journal	JOUR	Journal in which article was published
Language	LANG	Language in which the article was written
Author – Last	LAUT	Author last name
MeSH Terms	MESH	Medical Subject Heading terms
Date – Publication	PDAT	Publication date
Publication Type	PTYP	Publication type (e.g. review[PTYP])
Publisher	PUBN	the publisher
MeSH Subheading	SUBH	Medical Subject Heading Subheading
Title/Abstract	TIAB	Title or Abstract pf the article
Title	TITL	The title of the article
Text Word	WORD	Free text

Journal Translation Table   The journal translation table is built of the full journal titles, MEDLINE title abbreviations, and ISSN numbers of the articles. MEDLINE is the NLM bibliographic database of life sciences and biomedical information for articles from academic journals covering medicine, nursing, pharmacy, dentistry, veterinary medicine, and healthcare.

Author Translation Table   The author translation table is built of author names since 1946. The author names are indexed by last name, space, and initials. PubMed began to index authors' full names in 2002. Therefore, using the last name, space, and initials format in the search will be more comprehensive.

When quotation marks and a tagged field are not used with a search term, PubMed will turn on the ATM feature and will attempt to match that search term against these translation tables in the order: subject table, journal table, and author table. The search for the term will begin first with the subject translation table. If the term is found in this table, then that term will be mapped to the subject table and the search term will be tagged as [MeSH Terms] and the term may be removed from the search queue. If the term does not match any indexed term in the subject table, PubMed will attempt to search for it in the journal table. If the term is found in the journal table, it will be mapped to that table, tagged as [Journal], and then removed from the search queue. Otherwise, PubMed will attempt to search for it in the author translation table. If it is found there, it will be mapped to that table and tagged as [Author]. Otherwise, that term will be searched in all fields and tagged as [All Fields]. PubMed will continue to do the same for each term in the search query until all terms are processed. The results are the intersection of all mapped search terms. However, when you use the ATM feature in PubMed search, you must pay attention that irrelevant tagged field may be added to some search terms, which may add some unwanted records to the results. The mapping created by the ATM process can be checked by viewing the details of the search history as discussed in the introduction.

For example, choose "PubMed" from the database dropdown list, enter "ulcer" into the search box, and click on the "Search" button. Since the term "ulcer" is free text and used without quotation marks and without an indexed field that will turn on the ATM; the results may include thousands of articles. To see how the ATM

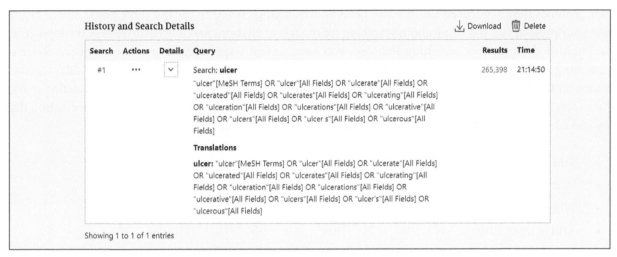

FIGURE 3.156   Search details of a search term.

has processed the search term that you entered, open the Advanced Search Builder by clicking the "Advanced" link below the search bar. In the History and Search Details section, click on the right-facing carat icon (>) for "ulcer" to see the details of the query generated by the ATM (Figure 3.156).

You can notice that the ATM process modified the single search term to the following long query:

"ulcer"[MeSH Terms] OR "ulcer"[All Fields] OR "ulcerate"[All Fields] OR "ulcerated"[All Fields] OR "ulcerates"[All Fields] OR "ulcerating"[All Fields] OR "ulceration"[All Fields] OR "ulcerations"[All Fields] OR "ulcerative"[All Fields] OR "ulcers"[All Fields] OR "ulcer s"[All Fields] OR "ulcerous"[All Fields]

PubMed First searched for "ulcer" in the subject translation table and, because the term was found in the subject table, "ulcer"[MeSH Terms] was added to the query. However, other terms related to "ulcer" were added with [All Fields]. Some of these added terms may be useful and some may be not. When you search PubMed, you need to check the search details to remove any irrelevant terms added to the query. For the above example, you can copy the query and delete the irrelevant search terms leaving only the following:

"ulcer"[MeSH Terms] OR "ulcer"[All Fields] OR "ulcers"[All Fields]

You can copy and paste this on the search box and click on the "Search" button and see how the results will change.

In the above example, "ulcer" is a known subject term so that is why it has been found in the subject translation table and tagged as [MeSH Term]. However, if the term is found in the journal translation table it will be tagged as [journal] and if it is found in the author table it will be tagged as [Author]. You can search PubMed by "biomed res int" and "Ismail HD" without quotation marks and every time check the search details to see how the search terms are tagged.

Understanding how the ATM works will help you to perform efficient searching and obtain more specific and relevant results. If you wish to turn off the ATM, use quotation marks and indexed fields with the search terms.

The following are worked examples for PubMed searching:

Example 1   Assume that you intend to begin a new project about *Salmonella enterica* and that you need to survey some genomic data obtained from *Salmonella enterica* following an outbreak among people and that their genomes were sequenced using whole genome sequencing (WGS) in the last three years. Before beginning your project, you will think about searching for the recent citations and journal articles of the topic from the PubMed database. For searching PubMed, you have several ways to build your search query. Refer to "Searching Entrez Databases" above for building an advanced search query. You also need to consider whether to turn on the ATM by using no quotation marks and tagged fields or to turn it off by using quotation marks and indexed fields. To search for an article for the example topic, there are several pieces of information that you can use to build an efficient search query. Those pieces of information are as follows:

- *Salmonella enterica*
- Human
- Whole-genome sequencing or WGS
- Article since 2010.

An advanced search query can be built from those four pieces of information using indexed fields and Boolean operators as follows:

"Salmonella enterica"[TITLE] AND human[TITLE] AND ("whole-genome sequencing"[TIAB] OR wgs) AND 2010/01/01:2021/04/01[PDAT]

When you search the PubMed database using the above advanced query, you may get the results as shown in Figure 3.157. Only a few records have been found. The reason is that by using the quotation marks and indexed fields, the ATM will be turned off and the search will be restricted to the specified indexed fields rather than all fields or [All Fields]. Using "salmonella enterica"[TITLE] AND human[TITLE], will restrict the searching to these two terms in the article titles only while the search of "whole-genome sequencing" [TIAB] and "wgs" [TIAB] will be in either article titles or abstracts. The entire query instructs the PubMed database to find any article that has both "Salmonella enterica" and "human" in its title and has either "whole-genome sequencing" or "wgs" in its title or abstract, and its publishing date must be between 01/0/2010 and 04/01/2021. If you check the query search details in the history, you will find that the original query does not change. Try to use some of the pieces of information with quotation marks and without indexed fields (e.g., Salmonella enterica AND human AND whole-genome sequencing OR wgs) and check how the query has been modified in the search details.

The layout of PubMed search results looks slightly different from the general Entrez results page discussed above.

Filters The filters on the left side of the page are used to filter the results by Year, Text availability, Article attribute, Article type, and Publication date. Additional filters are also available. However, filtering results by year is provided as a bar graph, which is also a visual representation for the number of records per year. Filtering results by year can be made by clicking on the bar corresponding to the year. The two circles on the graph are used to filter results by a range of years. On the top of the graph there are two icons; the first is used to expand and shrink the graph and the second is used to download the graph data, which is a CSV file consisting of two columns: years and count per year. The MYNCBI FILTERS icon above the filters is the link to the filter manager on MYNCBI, where you can choose up to 15 filters and you can also create a custom filter as discussed in the introduction.

"Save", "Email", and "Send to" Buttons The "Save" button is used to save the results in different formats including summary, PubMed, PMID, Abstract, or CSV. For example, if you wish to save the abstracts of all articles in the results as a text, click on the "Save" button, from the Section dropdown list, select "All results", from the Format dropdown list select "Abstracts", and then click on the "Create file" button. A text file containing the abstracts will be downloaded. The

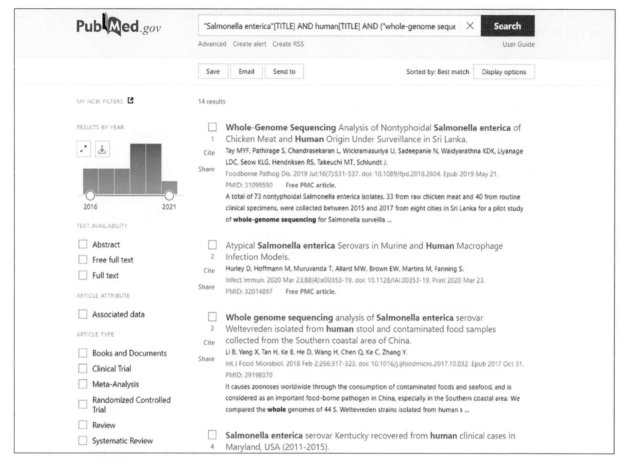

FIGURE 3.157   PubMed results page.

"Email" button is used to send the article summaries or abstracts to an email address. The "Send to" menu allows you to send citations to the clipboard, My Bibliography, Collections, or to a citation manager such as EndNote.

"Display Options" Button   The "Display options" button is used to change the display format, sort by, and the number of records per page.

PubMed can sort the results in different ways including best match sort order, most recent sort order, publication date sort order, first author, and journal. Those sort features are used by PubMed only to organize the search results and not to intervene with the searching process. The best match sort order is the default feature used by PubMed. The best match sort order is an algorithm that tries to match the search terms entered on the search box to the best matches in the list of the search results based on the article title, subject terms, and words in the abstract and then displays them by rank with the most relevant citations appearing at the top. The results show the best matches to the keywords used first on the top with keywords bolded in the titles and abstracts.

"Advanced", "Create Alert", and "Create RSS" Buttons   The "Advanced" button is used to create an advanced search query using the query builder or check the search history as discussed above. The "Create Alert" button is used to create an alert for any update in the search results in the future. Creating an alert requires logging onto MYNCBI account. The alert can be emailed as well. The "Create RSS" button is used to create a link for a web feed to access updates.

Example 2   In this example, you will retrieve PubMed articles by the author's name "Hamid D Ismail", where "Hamid" is the first name, "D" is the middle name initial, and "Ismail" is the last name. The major caveat of searching by an author name is that there may be several authors with the same names. The search by author name can be performed with different author formats as follows:

- If no middle name was provided by the author upon article submission to the journal, the search format can be:

  Last_name+white_space+first_name_initial

  To search for the PubMed articles written by the above author with last name and first name initial, you can use the following search term:

  Ismail H[Author]

  However, the results will not be specific if there are multiple authors with the same last name and first name initial. You may need to check manually on the results for the articles that you are looking for.

- If the middle name was provided by the author, the search term can be as follows:

  last name+white_space+first_initial+middle_initial

  Notice that there is no white space between the first name initial and middle name initial.

  To search for the PubMed articles written by the above author who provided his middle name, you can use the following search term:

  Ismail HD[Author]

  This format is more specific than the first but still irrelevant articles of authors with the same last name and the same first name and middle initials may be found in the results.

- Use the full name as search term. To find the articles of the above author use the following search term:

  Hamid D. Ismail[Author]

  The full name format is the most comprehensive search term for searching by author. However, it is not recommended for old articles since PubMed began to accept the full name of the author in the year 2002. Searching with a full name will miss the articles published prior to 2002.

The search results may include several authors with similar names, but you can check manually the titles and other relevant information such as affiliation to find the articles that you are looking for.

PubMed Record Page

Clicking on the article title on the results page will open the PubMed records page for that article. Abstract is the default display format, and the record page is shown as in Figure 3.158. The following are the descriptions for the record page sections:

(A) The journal name, publication date, pages, and the digital object identifier (doi) of the article. This line may include the type of article at the beginning before ">". The article type usually serves as a label for the article classification.

(B) The title of the article.

(C) The author names. Next to each author name there is a number in superscript referencing the author affiliation in the affiliation list. The author's name is clickable and, when it is clicked, a page of the author's articles on PubMed will open. The author's articles are found with a feature called computed author sort. This feature uses a name disambiguation process to compare citations that have the same author's name, and it also looks at the similarity of co-authors, journal titles, article titles, affiliation, and words from abstract. The articles that are most likely to associate to the author will be displayed at the top of the list and a message saying "Results are displayed in a computed author sort order. Results

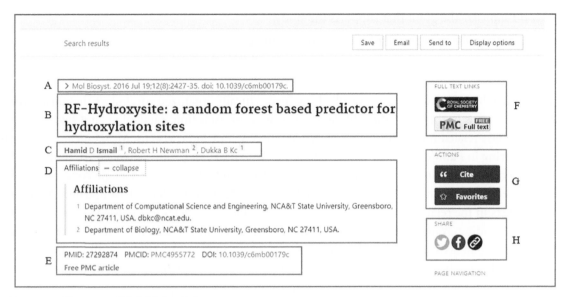

FIGURE 3.158   Top part of PubMed article page.

by year timeline is unavailable" will also be displayed on the top of the PubMed articles to show that the articles are found using a computation process and based on computed author sort.

(D)   Affiliations section displays the affiliations of the author. Click the plus sign "+" to expand the affiliation list. The numbers are referenced by the numbers next the authors.

(E)   This section includes the available unique identifiers and the free full text availability. This article has a unique PubMed identifier (PMID), PMC identifier (PMCID), and a digital object identifier (doi). The free article full text is available at PMC.

(F)   The Full Text Links section shows the links, where the full text is available.

(G)   The actions section includes the "Cite" button and the "Favorites" buttons. The "Cite" button is used to either copy the citation to the clipboard or to download it as a file format that can be opened in citation manager software such as EndNote. The "Favorites" button is used to add the article to the Collections on MYNCBI account.

(H)   Share includes links to share the article on Twitter, Facebook, or to share the article permalink.

In addition to the above section, on the right side of the PubMed record page, there is a navigation page that includes links to the following sections:

(1)   *Abstract.* This is the abstract of the article.

(2)   *Figures.* The figures included on the articles.

(3)   *Similar articles.* This section includes the list and links of PubMed articles like the current article. Usually, they have the same topic.

(4)   *Cited by.* This section includes the list of the PubMed articles that cited this article.

(5)   *References.* Those are the references cited by the article.

(6)   *Publication types.* The publication types that label the current article.

(7)   *MeSH terms.* The list of terms that were indexed as medical subject heading (MeSH).

(8)   *Substances.* The chemical substances that are found in the article.

(9)   *Related information.* Link to the NCBI database.

(10) *Grant support*. The grant that supports the study.

(11) *Link-out to more resources*. Links to external resources.

MeSH

MeSH (Medical Subject Headings) is a controlled and hierarchically organized vocabulary thesaurus produced by NLM for the terms in the biomedical literature. It is used for indexing, cataloging, and searching of biomedical and health-related information such as articles, books, and audio visuals. MeSH includes the subject headings appearing in PubMed, NLM Catalog, and other NLM databases. The controlled vocabulary provides a way to connect the possible variant terms to the preferred term that describes a single concept. The MeSH terms are revised annually and a term may be added as a new MeSH term, deleted, or updated. NLM trained subject specialists in the related fields to be indexers to examine full articles in PubMed and assign the most specific MeSH heading available to describe the topics discussed in the articles. The indexers may assign several headings to an article. When indexing of an article is complete the citation will be indexed for the MEDLINE, which contains bibliographic citations and author abstracts from thousands of medical and life science journals published in the United States and around 70 other countries.

MeSH headings are organized into 16 branches: (1) anatomy, (2) organisms, (3) diseases, (4) chemicals and drugs, (5) analytical, (6) diagnostic and therapeutic techniques and equipment, (7) psychiatry and psychology, (8) phenomena and processes, (9) disciplines, (occupations, anthropology, education, sociology, and social phenomena, (10) technology, industry and agriculture, (11) humanities, (12) information science, (13) named groups, (14) healthcare, (15) publication characteristics, and 16) geographical. The top four branches (anatomy, organism, diseases, and chemicals and drugs are the most commonly used in the search. The MeSH terms are organized into a hierarchical tree, starting from the top level of the tree, with very general terms branching out into more specific terms toward the lower sub-branches.

MeSH terms are classified into four categories:

(1) *Heading*. The heading term represents the general concept.

(2) *Subheading*: Terms, classified as a subheading, that are more specific than the heading.

(3) *Publication types*: Terms, classified as publication type, that describe the type of publications being indexed (review, letter, editorial, etc.) or the type of research described in the article or the source of funding (clinical trials, twin study, etc.).

(4) *Supplementary concept records (SCR)*: Terms, labeled as SCR, that describe substances such as chemicals and drugs.

You have already seen how PubMed uses MeSH terms and how it tags them with [MeSH terms] when the automatic term mapping (ATM) feature is turned on. PubMed begins by searching a term in the MeSH database. If a match is found then that term will be mapped to the MeSH term, which will describe the concept of the term with a preferred term. We will discuss how to use MeSH with PubMed in more details. The term that you use to search PubMed may have synonyms or equivalent terms that describe the concept, and it will be automatically connected to the preferred or official MeSH term. For example, if you search for the word "cancer" without quotation marks in PubMed, the ATM will include "neoplasms[MeSH Terms]". PubMed found the preferred term "neoplasms" and mapped "cancer" to this MeSH term. Very soon, we will understand the automatic explosion feature, which is the inclusion of more specific MeSH terms branching out of the tagged MeSH term.

The MeSH database is searched automatically by PubMed when the ATM feature is turned on. MeSH is also used separately to find MeSH terms – include Headings, Subheadings, Publication Types, and Supplementary concept records – and build a PubMed search strategy. MeSH is available as one of the Entrez databases and available at www.ncbi.nlm.nih.gov/mesh/. Its interface includes the same features available in other Entrez

TABLE 3.43 The Commonly Used MeSH Indexed Fields

Full Field Name	Short Field Name	Description
All Fields	ALL	All fields
See Also	ALSO	See Also section
Filter	FILT	This is used as a filter
MeSH Terms	MESH	The medical Subject heading term
MeSH Unique ID	MHUI	MeSH unique identifier
Scope Note	NOTE	Scope note of term
Registry Number	REG	Registry number
Substance Name	SUBS	The name of the substance
Tree Number	TN	The tree number
Record Type	TYPE	The record type
UID	UID	Unique identifier
Text Word	WORD	Free text

databases and it is also searched using the same methods discussed above. Table 3.43 lists the MeSH indexed fields and their descriptions.

The MeSH database can be searched by a MeSH term such as a MeSH Entry Term, Subheading, Publication Type, or words within a MeSH Scope Note. Terms entered without tagged indexed fields are searched using the ATM feature. For example, choose MeSH from the database dropdown list, enter "breast" into the search box and click on the "Search" button. The MeSH result page will show several items, but "Breast" is the first. When the exact search term is found on the MeSH results page that means the term used is a preferred MeSH term. Otherwise, a preferred synonym will be listed instead. Usually, there may be several items on the MeSH results page but the first is the most relevant term. Click on "Breast" to open the MeSH records page for the term as shown in Figure 3.159. Typical MeSH search results include (1) MeSH term definition, (2) subheadings associated with the term, (3) two checkboxes, (4) Tree Number, MeSH unique ID, and entry terms, which are the term synonyms, and (5) the See Also section, which includes the MeSH tree or trees that show the hierarchy of the preferred MeSH term.

(A) Term definition includes the definition of the term.

(B) The subheadings section includes all subheadings associated with the MeSH preferred term and all these subheadings will be in the scope of search when you use that term tagged as [MeSH Terms] (e.g. breast[MeSH Terms]).

(C) By default, all subheadings will be in the scope of the search. However, if you need to restrict the search to specific topics, select the subheadings you prefer from the list and then select the checkbox "Restricted to MeSH Major Topic". When the checkbox "Do not include MeSH terms found below this term in the MeSH hierarchy" is selected, the search scope does not include the terms below the term in the MeSH tree.

(D) This section includes the tree number or numbers, if there are multiple MeSH trees, MeSH unique ID, and the Entry Terms or the term synonyms. In case of "breast" there is no synonym. When there are synonyms, using any one of them will also be replaced by the preferred MeSH term and tagged as [MeSH Term].

(E) Under "See Also", you will find the MeSH tree of the term. The MeSH tree shows the hierarchy and branching of the term. The tree begins from the category level and branches out into sub-branches. A term may be found in multiple sub-branches. Sometimes, you may find sub-branches emerging from the term. In this case, the terms above the search term are broader in describing the concept (less specific) while the terms below the term are narrower (more specific) in describing the concept. When a search term is tagged as [MeSH Terms] in PubMed, by default all the terms below the search

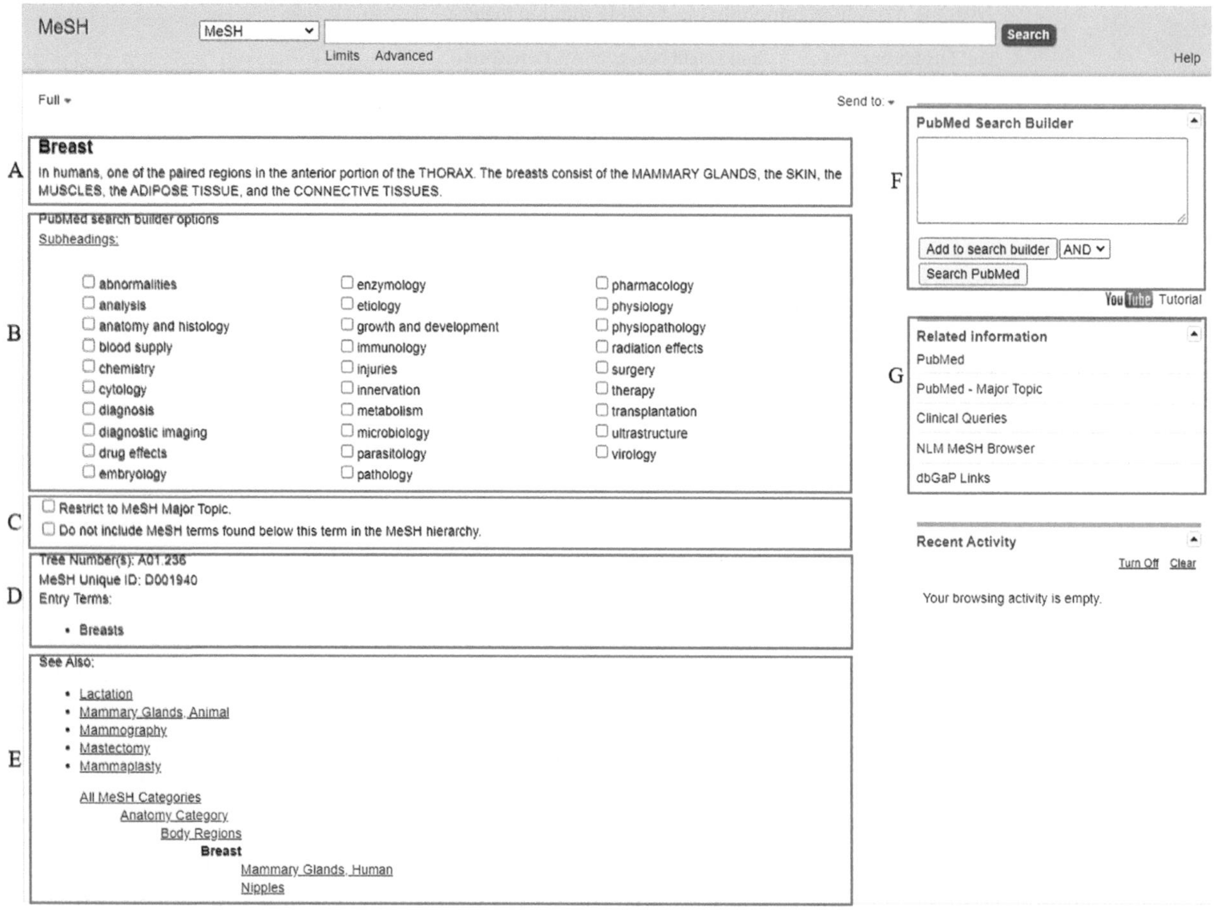

FIGURE 3.159   MeSH term page.

term in the MeSH tree will also be included in the search scope. This feature is known as the automatic explosion. If we need to exclude the terms below the search term from searching, select the "Do not include MeSH terms found below this term in the MeSH hierarchy" checkbox. In the example, from "Breast" branched "Mammary Glands human" and "Nipples" using "Breast[MeSH Term]" for searching, the search scope will explode to include these two branched terms unless the automatic explosion is disabled as described above.

(F)   The PubMed Search Builder on the top right is used to build a simple or advanced PubMed search query to use it to search the PubMed database. Click on the "Add to search builder" button to add the MeSH term ("Breast"[Mesh]) to the Search Builder box. You can enter multiple terms using the dropdown list of Boolean operators. When you have finished adding the terms that you need to use in the PubMed search, click on the "Search PubMed" button to begin the search. The results will be shown in the PubMed Results page.

(G)   The Related Information section indicates that from the MeSH term page, you can use the MeSH term to search PubMed database for MeSH term, MeSH major topic, clinical queries, and to connect to NLM MeSH Browser and dbGaP.

Check the search history and query details on the PubMed Advanced Search Builder. In the details you may find "Breast"[MeSH Terms], which means that searching will automatically explode to include the branched terms, which are more specific. Move back to the MeSH term page, clear the content of the PubMed Search Builder, check the checkbox "Do not include MeSH terms found below this term in the MeSH hierarchy", and click on "Add to search builder" button to add the search term. You will notice that ""Breast"[Mesh:NoExp]" has been added to the query box. Now click on the "Search PubMed" button. You may notice that the number of items in the search results has been greatly reduced because the automatic explosion was turned off and the search excluded all MeSH terms below "Breast" in the MeSH tree.

You may need to be careful when you turn off the automatic explosion because relevant results may be missing.

You may also intend to restrict searching to a specific topic or topics from the subheadings. Move back to the MeSH term page, clear the search query in the query box of the PubMed Search Builder, deselect any checkbox in section C, from the Subheading list select a subheading or subheadings (e.g., Pathology), check the "Restrict to MeSH Major Topic" checkbox, and click the "Add to search builder" button to add the search term to the PubMed query box. You will notice that the search term added is ""Breast/pathology"[Majr]". When you search PubMed with this search term, the searching will be restricted only to the Pathology subject heading.

Generally, to use MeSH terms to conduct PubMed search strategy, you need to do the following:

(1) Identify the MeSH term(s) for your topic, which may be a disease or a disorder (e.g., breast cancer).

(2) Identify any additional aspects of your topic that can narrow the search results. This is done by finding the synonyms of the term (e.g., breast Neoplasm, breast tumor, mammary cancer, human mammary carcinomas, malignant tumor, etc.).

(3) Combine the separate concepts together by using Boolean operators (AND, OR, and NOT). For example, (breast cancer[Mesh Terms] OR breast Neoplasm[Mesh Terms] AND malignant tumor[Mesh Terms]).

(4) Look at the MeSH terms assigned to them and see if there are any additional terms that might improve your search strategy.

PubMed Central

PubMed Central (PMC) is a free resource for full-text articles of biomedical and life sciences journals. The PMC archive was founded as response to the NIH public access policy issued by the US Congress in 2009 and requires that any publications that come out of the research supported by an NIH grant must be made available to the public for free. In keeping with NLM's legislative mandate to collect and preserve biomedical literature, PMC serves as a digital counterpart to NLM's extensive print journal collection. PMC is managed by the NCBI. As of this time, PMC contains 6,760,696 full-text articles published by journals from around the world.

Articles are added to the PMC archive through journal and publisher deposit, author manuscript deposit, and digitization projects. In the journal and publisher program, journals, publishers, scholarly societies, and other content owners have agreement with NLM to deposit articles directly to PMC. Authors of scientific research funded by some institutions must deposit their articles to PMC in compliance with funder policies. NLM also collaborates with some organizations to preserve historical literature through scanning of article content and to be deposited to PMC. Although the articles available on PMC are free, they are protected by US and/or foreign copyright laws.

Article content on PMC is converted into and stored in XML format because this format represents the structure and content of an article in a human and computer-readable form. Copies of PMC articles are maintained in some international archives that share the goals of PMC in foreign countries as part of the PMC International. The PMC articles are very well integrated with other NCBI resources and can be searched from within PubMed. The page of PMC archive can be accessed by choosing PMC from the NCBI database drop-down list from Entrez web page or from www.ncbi.nlm.nih.gov/pmc/.

A journal in PMC may participate at the full participation level, which allows access for the text of all articles of each issue, or at the participation level of "NIH Portfolio", which allows only articles that were funded

TABLE 3.44   The Commonly Used PMC Indexed Fields

Long Field Name	Short Field Name	Long Field Name	Short Field Name
Abstract	ABST	Journal Title	JOUR
Acknowledgements	ACK	MeSH Major Topic	MAJR
Affiliation	AFFL	MeSH Subheadings	SUBH
All Fields	ALL	MeSH Terms	MESH
Author	AUTH	Methods – Key Terms	METH
Article Body – All Words	ARTI	Organism	ORGN
Article Body – Key Terms	KWD	Publication Date	PDAT
DOI	DOI	PubMed ID	PMID
Electronic Publication Date	EPDT	Reference Author	REFA
Filter	FILTER	Title	TITL
Full Author Name	FULL		

by NIH, or selective deposit for publishers who offer a hybrid publishing model of subscription-based journals in which selected articles are published as Open Access. The "Journal List" link under the search bar on the PMC web page displays the list of all journals that deposit all or some of their articles in the PMC archive, in alphabetical order. Research articles that were funded by institutions whose policies require articles to be deposited in PMC are labeled as "author manuscripts" in PMC.

The PMC Journal List includes journal ISSNs, titles, latest and first volume date, holdings, the title of free access after issuing, and participation level. The journal list can be downloaded in CSV (comma-separate value) format, which can be opened in a text editor or Excel spreadsheet. A peer-reviewed final manuscript, accepted publication, is submitted to the PMC with the help of NIH library staff. More information about submitting a transcript to the PMC is available at www.nihlibrary.nih.gov/services/editing.

The PMC archive is searched as PubMed. Entering a search term without quotation marks and tagged field will turn on the ATM. However, the PMC search bar is provided with an autocompletion feature, which can be turned off by clicking on "Turn off" at the button right corner of the dropdown list of the suggested completion items. The most commonly used PMC indexed fields are listed in Table 3.44.

Assume that you intend to find the full-text articles about SARS coronavirus published between 2019 and 2021 and that the study included the whole genome sequencing of the virus. You can use the following query:

SARS coronavirus[TITL] OR SARS-CoV[TITL] AND 2019:2021[PDAT] AND whole-genome sequencing[ABST]

The PMC results page is a typical Entrez results page as discussed previously.

Click on the title of an item to open the PMC article page. The article page includes the full text of the article on the page. Under Formats on the top right, you will find the links to the full text in different formats including PubReader, ePub (beta), PDF, and citation. You may prefer to download the article in PDF file format. The citation is available in different formats. You can copy the citation, or you can download it to an NBIB file that can be opened in citation management software like EndNote.

Other sections of the PMC article page are like PubMed article page and other Entrez record page.

Bookshelf

The NCBI bookshelf or Books started in 1999 with only one book and then grew rapidly to include up to 990,206 titles as of January 2021. It provides a collection of electronic biomedical books and documents in life sciences and healthcare with searchable content. They are integrated with other NCBI databases and can be used to provide reference information for biological data. Books authors holding the copyright can apply for inclusion of their books on the NCBI Bookshelf. However, all parties, which have rights in the book, must agree on the submission. The submission application can be downloaded from the NCBI website, completed,

TABLE 3.45   Bookshelf Indexed Fields

Full Field Name	Short Field Name	Full Field Name	Short Field Name
All Fields	ALL	MeSH Major Topic	MAJR
Attribute	ATTR	MeSH Terms	MESH
Author	AUTH	Publication Year	PDAT
Book Accession ID	BACI	PMID	PMID
Book	BOOK	Protein Name	PN
Corporate Author	CA	Publication Type	PTYP
Chapter Accession ID	CHID	Publisher	PUBN
Concept Phrases	CONP	Release Date	RD
Disease	DN	Rid	RID
Editor	EDIT	RefPMID	RMID
Full Author Name	FA	Resource Type	RT
Full Editor Name	FE	Full Text	STXT
Filter	FILT	MeSH Subheading	SUBH
Grant Number	GRNT	Title	TITL
Gene Name	GS	Type	TYPE
ISBN	ISBN	UID	UID

and emailed to the Bookshelf with copies of the book for review. The link for the complete information for a book submission is available at the Bookshelf website, which can be opened either by choosing Books from the Entrez database dropdown list or by using the direct link www.ncbi.nlm.nih.gov/books/.

The search strategies discussed with PubMed and PMC can also be used with Bookshelf archive. Table 3.45 lists the Bookshelf indexed fields.

REFERENCES

1. Bethesda (MD): National Library of Medicine (US), N.C.f.B.I. *National Center for Biotechnology Information (NCBI)* [cited 2021 4/6/2021]. www.ncbi.nlm.nih.gov/. 1988.
2. Benson, D.A., et al., *GenBank.* Nucleic Acids Res, 2018. **46**(D1): pp. D41–D47.
3. Tatusova, T., et al., *NCBI prokaryotic genome annotation pipeline.* Nucleic Acids Res, 2016. **44**(14): pp. 6614–6624.
4. Murphy, M.B.G., C. Wallin, et al. *Gene Help: Integrated Access to Genes of Genomes in the Reference Sequence Collection* [updated 2021] [cited 2021 5/1/2021]. www.ncbi.nlm.nih.gov/books/NBK3841/. 2006.
5. Anders, S., P.T. Pyl, and W. Huber, *HTSeq—a Python framework to work with high-throughput sequencing data.* Bioinformatics, 2015. **31**(2): pp. 166–9.
6. Sharma, S., et al., *The NCBI BioCollections Database.* Database, 2019.
7. Sharma, S., et al., *The NCBI BioCollections Database.* 2018. Oxford: Database (Oxford).
8. Figueira, R. and F. Lages, *Museum and Herbarium Collections for Biodiversity Research in Angola*, in *Biodiversity of Angola: Science & Conservation: A Modern Synthesis*, B.J. Huntley, et al., Editors. 2019. Cham: Springer International Publishing: pp. 513–542.
9. Martin, N.A., *Voucher specimens: A way to protect the value of your research.* Biology and Fertility of Soils, 1990. **9**(2): pp. 93–94.
10. Labeda, D.P., *Culture Collections: An Essential Resource for Microbiology*, in *Bergey's Manual® of Systematic Bacteriology: Volume One: The Archaea and the Deeply Branching and Phototrophic Bacteria*, D.R. Boone, R.W. Castenholz, and G.M. Garrity, Editors. 2001. New York: Springer New York: pp. 111–113.
11. NCBI Resource Coordinators, *Database resources of the National Center for Biotechnology Information.* Nucleic Acids Res, 2018. **46**(D1): pp. D8–D13.
12. Koonin, E.V., *Orthologs, paralogs, and evolutionary genomics.* Annu Rev Genet, 2005. **39**: pp. 309–338.
13. Klimke, W., et al., *The National Center for Biotechnology Information's Protein Clusters Database.* Nucleic Acids Res, 2009. **37**(Database issue): pp. D216–223.
14. Belouzard, S., et al., *Mechanisms of coronavirus cell entry mediated by the viral spike protein.* Viruses, 2012. **4**(6): pp. 1011–1033.

15. Marchler-Bauer, A., et al., *CDD: conserved domains and protein three-dimensional structure*. Nucleic Acids Res, 2013. **41**(Database issue): pp. D348–352.

16. Corrales, P., A. Vidal-Puig, and G. Medina-Gomez, *PPARs and Metabolic Disorders Associated with Challenged Adipose Tissue Plasticity*. Int J Mol Sci, 2018. **19**(7).

17. Wu, C.H., et al., *The Protein Information Resource*. Nucleic Acids Res, 2003. **31**(1): pp. 345–347.

18. Barker, W.C., F. Pfeiffer, and D.G. George, *Superfamily classification in PIR-International Protein Sequence Database*. Methods Enzymol, 1996. **266**: pp. 59–71.

19. Johnson, L.S., S.R. Eddy, and E. Portugaly, *Hidden Markov model speed heuristic and iterative HMM search procedure*. BMC Bioinformatics, 2010. **11**: p. 431.

20. Punta, M., et al., *The Pfam protein families database*. Nucleic Acids Res, 2012. **40**(Database issue): pp. D290–301.

21. Sigrist, C.J., et al., *PROSITE: a documented database using patterns and profiles as motif descriptors*. Brief Bioinform, 2002. **3**(3): pp. 265–274.

22. Sigrist, C.J., et al., *New and continuing developments at PROSITE*. Nucleic Acids Res, 2013. **41**(Database issue): pp. D344–347.

23. Sigrist, C.J., et al., *ProRule: a new database containing functional and structural information on PROSITE profiles*. Bioinformatics, 2005. **21**(21): pp. 4060–4066.

24. Murzin, A.G., et al., *SCOP: a structural classification of proteins database for the investigation of sequences and structures*. J Mol Biol, 1995. **247**(4): pp. 536–540.

25. Huang, H., et al., *iProClass: an integrated database of protein family, function and structure information*. Nucleic Acids Res, 2003. **31**(1): pp. 390–392.

26. Haft, D.H., et al., *RefSeq: an update on prokaryotic genome annotation and curation*. Nucleic Acids Res, 2018. **46**(D1): pp. D851–D860.

27. Schuster-Böckler, B., J. Schultz, and S. Rahmann, *HMM Logos for visualization of protein families*. BMC Bioinformatics, 2004. **5**(1): p. 7.

28. Li, W., et al., *RefSeq: expanding the Prokaryotic Genome Annotation Pipeline reach with protein family model curation*. Nucleic Acids Res, 2021. **49**(D1): pp. D1020–D1028.

29. Geer, L.Y., et al., *CDART: protein homology by domain architecture*. Genome Res, 2002. **12**(10): pp. 1619–1623.

30. *HomoloGene*, in *Encyclopedia of Genetics, Genomics, Proteomics and Informatics*. 2008. Dordrecht: Springer Netherlands. pp. 899–899.

31. Barrett, T., et al., *BioProject and BioSample databases at NCBI: facilitating capture and organization of metadata*. Nucleic Acids Res, 2012. **40**(Database issue): pp. D57–63.

32. Field, D., et al., *The Genomic Standards Consortium*. PLOS Biology, 2011. **9**(6): pp. e1001088.

33. Field, D., et al., *The minimum information about a genome sequence (MIGS) specification*. Nat Biotechnol, 2008. **26**(5): pp. 541–547.

34. Bowers, R.M., et al., *Minimum information about a single amplified genome (MISAG) and a metagenome-assembled genome (MIMAG) of bacteria and archaea*. Nat Biotechnol, 2017. **35**(8): pp. 725–731.

35. Yilmaz, P., et al., *Minimum information about a marker gene sequence (MIMARKS) and minimum information about any (x) sequence (MIxS) specifications*. Nat Biotechnol, 2011. **29**(5): pp. 415–420.

36. Roux, S., et al., *Minimum Information about an Uncultivated Virus Genome (MIUViG)*. Nature Biotechnology, 2019. **37**(1): pp. 29–37.

37. Sherry, S.T., et al., *dbSNP: the NCBI database of genetic variation*. Nucleic Acids Res, 2001. **29**(1): pp. 308–311.

38. Smigielski, E.M., et al., *dbSNP: a database of single nucleotide polymorphisms*. Nucleic Acids Res, 2000. **28**(1): pp. 352–355.

39. National Center for Biotechnology Information, N.L.o.M. *dbSNP Submission Documentation Overview*. www.ncbi.nlm.nih.gov/snp/docs/submission/. 2017.

40. Kitts, A.P.L., M. Ward, et al., *The Database of Short Genetic Variation (dbSNP)*. 2nd ed. The NCBI Handbook [Internet]. 2013. Bethesda, MD: National Center for Biotechnology Information (US).

41. L. Phan, Y.J.H. Zhang, W. Qiang, E. Shekhtman, D. Shao, D. Revoe, R. Villamarin, E. Ivanchenko, M. Kimura, Z. Y. Wang, L. Hao, N. Sharopova, M. Bihan, A. Sturcke, M. Lee, N. Popova, W. Wu, C. Bastiani, M. Ward, J. B. Holmes, V. Lyoshin, K. Kaur, E. Moyer, M. Feolo, and B. L. Kattman. *ALFA: Allele Frequency Aggregator* [cited 2021 5/14/2021]. www.ncbi.nlm.nih.gov/snp/docs/gsr/alfa/. 2020.

42. Bomba, L., K. Walter, and N. Soranzo, *The impact of rare and low-frequency genetic variants in common disease.* Genome Biology, 2017. **18**(1): p. 77.

43. Fernandez-Moya, A., et al., *Germline Variants in Driver Genes of Breast Cancer and Their Association with Familial and Early-Onset Breast Cancer Risk in a Chilean Population.* Cancers (Basel), 2020. **12**(1).

44. Kap, M., et al., *Histological assessment of PAXgene tissue fixation and stabilization reagents.* PLoS One, 2011. **6**(11): p. e27704.

45. den Dunnen, J.T., et al., *HGVS Recommendations for the Description of Sequence Variants: 2016 Update.* Hum Mutat, 2016. **37**(6): pp. 564–569.

46. Auton, A., et al., *A global reference for human genetic variation.* Nature, 2015. **526**(7571): pp. 68–74.

47. Karczewski, K.J., et al., *The mutational constraint spectrum quantified from variation in 141,456 humans.* Nature, 2020. **581**(7809): pp. 434–443.

48. Karczewski, K.J., et al., *The ExAC browser: displaying reference data information from over 60 000 exomes.* Nucleic Acids Res, 2017. **45**(D1): pp. D840–D845.

49. Taliun, D., et al., *Sequencing of 53,831 diverse genomes from the NHLBI TOPMed Program.* Nature, 2021. **590**(7845): pp. 290–299.

50. Lappalainen, I., et al., *DbVar and DGVa: public archives for genomic structural variation.* Nucleic Acids Res, 2013. **41**(Database issue): pp. D936–941.

51. Kusenda, M. and J. Sebat, *The role of rare structural variants in the genetics of autism spectrum disorders.* Cytogenet Genome Res, 2008. **123**(1–4): pp. 36–43.

52. Landrum, M.J., et al., *ClinVar: improvements to accessing data.* Nucleic Acids Res, 2020. **48**(D1): pp. D835–D844.

53. Brookes, A.J. and P.N. Robinson, *Human genotype–phenotype databases: aims, challenges and opportunities.* Nature Reviews Genetics, 2015. **16**(12): pp. 702–715.

54. Holmes, J.B., et al., *SPDI: data model for variants and applications at NCBI.* Bioinformatics, 2020. **36**(6): pp. 1902–1907.

55. Landrum, M.J., et al., *ClinVar: improving access to variant interpretations and supporting evidence.* Nucleic Acids Res, 2018. **46**(D1): pp. D1062–D1067.

56. Tarca, A.L., R. Romero, and S. Draghici, *Analysis of microarray experiments of gene expression profiling.* Am J Obstet Gynecol, 2006. **195**(2): pp. 373–388.

57. Wong, M.L. and J.F. Medrano, *Real-time PCR for mRNA quantitation.* BioTechniques, 2005. **39**(1): pp. 75–85.

58. Teng, M., et al., *A benchmark for RNA-seq quantification pipelines.* Genome Biology, 2016. **17**(1): p. 74.

59. Edgar, R., M. Domrachev, and A.E. Lash, *Gene Expression Omnibus: NCBI gene expression and hybridization array data repository.* Nucleic Acids Res, 2002. **30**(1): pp. 207–210.

60. Barrett, T., et al., *NCBI GEO: archive for functional genomics data sets—update.* Nucleic Acids Research, 2012. **41**(D1): pp. D991–D995.

61. Reinartz, J., et al., *Massively parallel signature sequencing (MPSS) as a tool for in-depth quantitative gene expression profiling in all organisms.* Briefings in Functional Genomics, 2002. **1**(1): pp. 95–104.

62. Alfred, J., *Golden path to genome.* Nature Reviews Genetics, 2000. **1**(2): p. 87.

63. Simao, F.A., et al., *BUSCO: assessing genome assembly and annotation completeness with single-copy orthologs.* Bioinformatics, 2015. **31**(19): pp. 3210–3212.

64. Consortium, G.R. *GRC and Collaborators.* www.ncbi.nlm.nih.gov/grc/credits/. 2021.

65. *Regular Expressions Quick Start* [cited 2021 5/23/2021]. www.regular-expressions.info/quickstart.html. 2020.

66. Birney, E. and N. Soranzo, *The end of the start for population sequencing.* Nature, 2015. **526**(7571): pp. 52–53.

67. Fairley, S., et al., *The International Genome Sample Resource (IGSR) collection of open human genomic variation resources.* Nucleic Acids Research, 2019. **48**(D1): pp. D941–D947.

68. *Online Mendelian Inheritance in Man, OMIM®* [cited 2021 5/26/2021]. https://omim.org/. 2021.

69. Amberger, J.S., et al., *OMIM.org: Online Mendelian Inheritance in Man (OMIM(R)), an online catalog of human genes and genetic disorders.* Nucleic Acids Res, 2015. **43**(Database issue): pp. D789–798.

70. *Database resources of the National Center for Biotechnology Information.* Nucleic Acids Res, 2013. **41**(Database issue): pp. D8–D20.

71. Larkin, M.A., et al., *Clustal W and Clustal X version 2.0.* Bioinformatics, 2007. **23**(21): pp. 2947–2948.

72. Edgar, R.C., *MUSCLE: multiple sequence alignment with high accuracy and high-throughput.* Nucleic Acids Res, 2004. **32**(5): pp. 1792–1797.

73. Di Tommaso, P., et al., *T-Coffee: a web server for the multiple sequence alignment of protein and RNA sequences using structural information and homology extension.* Nucleic Acids Res, 2011. **39**(Web Server issue): pp. W13–W17.

74. Nelson, David L. and M.M. Cox, *Lehninger principles of biochemistry.* 15th ed. 2008. New York: W.H. Freeman.

75. Tardito, D., et al., *Signaling pathways regulating gene expression, neuroplasticity, and neurotrophic mechanisms in the action of antidepressants: a critical overview.* Pharmacol Rev, 2006. **58**(1): pp. 115–134.

76. Ochsner, S.A., et al., *The Signaling Pathways Project, an integrated 'omics knowledgebase for mammalian cellular signaling pathways.* Scientific Data, 2019. **6**(1): p. 252.

77. Kanehisa, M., et al., *KEGG for linking genomes to life and the environment.* Nucleic Acids Res, 2008. **36**(Database issue): pp. D480–D484.

78. *BioCarta.* Biotech Software & Internet Report, 2001. **2**(3): pp. 117–120.

79. Karp, P.D., et al., *Expansion of the BioCyc collection of pathway/genome databases to 160 genomes.* Nucleic Acids Res, 2005. **33**(19): pp. 6083–6089.

80. Thomas, P.D., et al., *PANTHER: a browsable database of gene products organized by biological function, using curated protein family and subfamily classification.* Nucleic Acids Res, 2003. **31**(1): pp. 334–341.

81. Schaefer, C.F., et al., *PID: the Pathway Interaction Database.* Nucleic Acids Res, 2009. **37**(Database issue): pp. D674–D679.

82. Matthews, L., et al., *Reactome knowledgebase of human biological pathways and processes.* Nucleic Acids Res, 2009. **37**(Database issue): pp. D619–D622.

83. Pico, A.R., et al., *WikiPathways: pathway editing for the people.* PLoS Biol, 2008. **6**(7): p. e184.

84. Gene Ontology Consortium, *The Gene Ontology project in 2008.* Nucleic Acids Res, 2008. **36**(Database issue): pp. D440–D444.

85. Geer, L.Y., et al., *The NCBI BioSystems database.* Nucleic Acids Res, 2010. **38**(Database issue): pp. D492–D496.

86. *NCBI BioSystems Database* [cited 2021 5/29/2021]. www.ncbi.nlm.nih.gov/Structure/biosystems/docs/biosystems_about.html.

87. Tryka, K.A., et al., *NCBI's Database of Genotypes and Phenotypes: dbGaP.* Nucleic Acids Res, 2014. **42**(Database issue): pp. D975–D979.

88. Mailman, M.D., et al., *The NCBI dbGaP database of genotypes and phenotypes.* Nat Genet, 2007. **39**(10): pp. 1181–1186.

89. Sweetlove, L., *Number of species on Earth tagged at 8.7 million.* Nature, 2011.

90. *The Levels of Classification.* 2021.

91. Schoch, C.L., et al., *NCBI Taxonomy: a comprehensive update on curation, resources and tools.* Oxford: Database (Oxford), 2020.

92. NLM. *MEDLINE: Overview* [cited 2021 4/16/2021]. www.nlm.nih.gov/medline/medline_overview.html. 2021.

## CHAPTER 4

NCBI Entrez E-Utilities and Applications

INTRODUCTION

In Chapter 3 we discussed the NCBI Entrez databases along with their Internet interfaces, indexed fields, search results pages, records pages, and uses.

The Entrez common database interface may be sufficient for most users who intend to use the NCBI databases for simple searching, viewing, and data retrieval. However, advanced Entrez databases' users and bioinformatics' programmers may need to use an application programming interface (API) that enables them to search and retrieve data from the Entrez databases. For those users, NCBI developed the Entrez Programming Utilities (E-utilities or E-utils), which is an API that includes a set of rules, protocols, and tools for developing software and applications. The E-utilities allows users to search the NCBI databases through programs with more capability and usability and allows programmers to extend its functionality to retrieve, manipulate, and extract data [1–3]. The purpose of this chapter is to discuss how the E-utilities programs work for those who may wish to use them in their own software, applications, and websites and it also serves as an introduction to the programming packages and bioinformatics tools that implemented these E-utilities such as E-Direct, BioPython, and R Entrez package, which we will discuss in the next chapters.

The E-utilities programs reside on the NCBI server (server-side). Those programs include EInfo, EFetch, ELink, EGQuery, ESearch, ESummary, EPost, ECitMatch, and ESpell. Users communicate with the E-utilities API by sending URL requests using the HTTP protocols (GET or POST). Therefore, using E-utilities or even using a program using those utilities requires an Internet connection. A URL request will include the name of the E-utilities program and the parameters. Each program has its parameters as will be discussed later. The request received by the E-utilities API will be directed to the destination E-utilities program, which will respond to the valid request by sending back an output in Extensible Markup Language (XML) format. Developing software communicating with the E-utilities depends on these two features: sending the URL request and receiving an output in XML format. So, if you are a programmer, you can use any computer programming language to develop an application or a wrapper program using these features.

Before delving into E-utilities, users must know about the NCBI application programming interface key (API key) and NCBI History Server.

NCBI APPLICATION PROGRAMMING INTERFACE KEY

The NCBI application programming interface key, or API key for short, is a unique string that can be generated when you log into your MYNCBI account. It is included in the HTTP requests to identify the user to the NCBI servers. The NCBI have strict policies about the use of E-utilities. It does not allow a user without providing

DOI: 10.1201/9781003226611-4

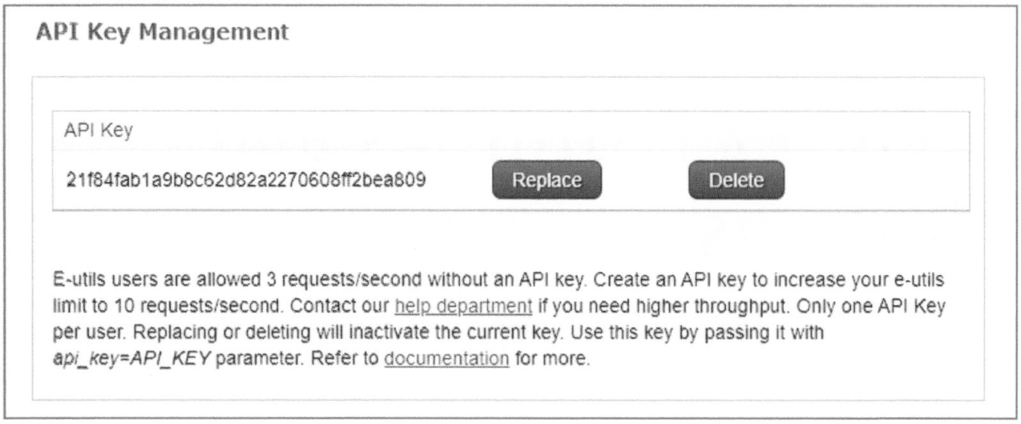

API Key Management

API Key

21f84fab1a9b8c62d82a2270608ff2bea809   [Replace]   [Delete]

E-utils users are allowed 3 requests/second without an API key. Create an API key to increase your e-utils limit to 10 requests/second. Contact our help department if you need higher throughput. Only one API Key per user. Replacing or deleting will inactivate the current key. Use this key by passing it with *api_key=API_KEY* parameter. Refer to documentation for more.

FIGURE 4.1   Generated API key.

an API key to send more than three requests per second or to receive large results when using any E-utilities programs. When you provide an API key with an E-utilities program, you will be allowed to send ten URL requests per second for the activities of that API even if the requests are sent from computers with different IP addresses. Submitting requests more than the allowed number of times in both cases will generate errors. Only a single API key is generated for an account. You can use the NCBI E-utilities as anonymous without providing an API key if your number of requests are limited. However, it is recommended that users provide their emails when they use E-utilities to receive emails that NCBI policies are violated if your request is above the limit. Sometimes, violations may result in blocking the user's IP address from accessing the NCBI services.

To create an API key, you need to create a MyNCBI account or log into your account if you have one. MyNCBI web page is at www.ncbi.nlm.nih.gov/account/. When you log in, click on your username on the top right and then scroll down to the "API Key Management" box and click the "Create an API Key" button to generate the API key as shown in Figure 4.1.

The new API key will be available on your account unless you delete or replace it. You can provide the API key as a parameter to the E-utilities program as you will see. You can save your API key in a text file to come in handy when needed.

NCBI HISTORY SERVER

The NCBI History Server is a dedicated server to store the sets of the unique identifiers (UIDs), of an Entrez database, retrieved due to an URL request. The server stores the UIDS temporarily so that they can be combined or used by a subsequent E-utilities program, or otherwise manipulated as we will see in examples. When UIDs are stored on the History server, the server assigns each set of UIDs an integer label called a query key (query_key) and an encoded server address called a Web environment (WebEnv). Both the query key number and the Web environment string will be displayed in the XML output for the request that retrieved the UIDs. The query key and Web environment string can then be provided as parameters in place of UIDs for ESummary, EFetch, and ELink programs. The History Server helps users who deal with many database records. NCBI limits the maximum number of records that can be displayed at a time. The user can upload all UIDs to the History Server and then access some of them iteratively until all records are accessed.

E-UTILITIES PROGRAMS

There are nine E-Utilities programs that reside on the NCBI server and they can be requested by users by sending URL requests. Table 4.1 contains the E-utilities programs and their descriptions.

To send a request to any of these E-utility programs, the request must be sent through a URL. This URL is https://eutils.ncbi.nlm.nih.gov/entrez/eutils/. The URL request is usually sent through the address bar of an Internet browser but when you are using a computer programming language like C++, Perl, or Python, that

TABLE 4.1   E-Utilities Programs and Their Descriptions

E-Utilities Program	Description
EInfo (einfo.fcgi)	EInfo provides the list of Entrez databases, information of the indexed fields, the last update date of the database, and the links from the database to other Entrez databases.
Gquery (gquery.fcgi)	For a given search query, Gquery responds with the number of records that match the query.
ESearch (esearch.fcgi)	For a given search query, ESearch responds with the list of UIDs that match the query.
ESummary (esummary.fcgi)	ESummary is requested to retrieve the document summaries of a list of UIDs provided as parameters or obtained from the History Server.
EFetch (efetch.fcgi)	EFetch is requested to retrieve the data of a list of UIDs provided as parameters or obtained from the History Server.
EPost (epost.fcgi)	EPost posts a list of UIDs to the History Server and responds with the corresponding query key and Web environment for subsequent use.
ELink (elink.fcgi)	ELink provides a list of UIDs in a database with a list of related IDs in the same database or another Entrez database.
ECitMatch (ecitmatch.fcgi)	ECitMatch searches PubMed for a series of citation strings.
ESpell (Espell.fcgi)	ESpel provides suggestions to a misspell search term.

language will provide a way to use the HTTP protocol to send the URL request without using an Internet browser like Internet Explorer. But both the programmers, who use a programming language to communicate with E-utilities API, and the users, who use E-utilities programs through Internet browsers, must follow the rules to build a URL request. Those rules are as follows:

(1)   Any request should begin with the absolute base E-utilities URL:

https://eutils.ncbi.nlm.nih.gov/entrez/eutils/

(2)   The requested E-utilities program will be entered immediately after the E-utility base URL without any space and the E-utilities program is followed by a question mark "?". Assume that "E-utility" is any program of the E-utilities, the base URL and an E-utilities program is written as follows:

https://eutils.ncbi.nlm.nih.gov/entrez/eutils/E-utility?

(3)   Any of the E-utilities programs has its parameters. The first parameter is added to the above request immediately after the question mark. No whitespace is allowed in the URL request. Assume that "PARAM1" is a parameter of the requested E-utilities program, the first parameter will be added as follows:

https://eutils.ncbi.nlm.nih.gov/entrez/eutils/E-utility?PARAM1

(4)   Some parameters may take values. So, to add a parameter with its value, an equal sign "=" is added after the parameter and then the value is added after the equal sign. No whitespace is allowed. Assume that "PARAM1" parameter has a "VALUE1" value, these will be added as:

https://eutils.ncbi.nlm.nih.gov/entrez/eutils/E-utility?PARAM1=VALUE1

(5)   Multiple parameters can be added to the URL requests. They must be separated by the ampersand sign "&" as follows:

https://eutils.ncbi.nlm.nih.gov/entrez/eutils/E-utility?PARAM1=VALUE1&PARAM2=VALUE2

(6)   A numeric value of parameter is added as a number (e.g., PARAM1=2) but a string value is added as string between quotation marks (e.g., PARAM1="VALUE1").

(7)   No whitespace is allowed at all in the URL request. If the string value has a white space, use the plus sign in the place of the whitespace (e.g., PARAM1= "VALUE+VALUE+VALUE").

(8)   If you need to add the API key discussed above, use the parameter "api_key=" as follows:

https://eutils.ncbi.nlm.nih.gov/entrez/eutils/E-utility?PARAM1=VALUE1&api_key="Your_API_Key"

(9) All E-utilities parameters must be in lower case except one parameter (&WebEnv).

(10) The order of parameters is not important; they can be in any order.

In the following sections, we will discuss the use of each of the E-utilities programs

EInfo

EInfo E-utility (einfo.fcgi) provides information of the Entrez databases and of an individual Entrez database. EInfo has the "db=" parameter whose value is any valid Entrez database, as shown in Table 4.2, and "retmode=", which can take either "XML" (the default) or "json". When EInfo is used without any parameter, it will respond with the list of the Entrez database names. Enter the following URL request onto the address bar of an Internet browser:

https://eutils.ncbi.nlm.nih.gov/entrez/eutils/einfo.fcgi

The EInfo program will respond with the list of the Entrez database names in XML format. Any database name is enclosed between <DbName> and </DbName> as shown in Figure 4.2.

XML format is a simple text-based format for representing structured data. The data are strictly between XML opening and closing tags. An XML document must contain one root element that is the parent of all other elements. In the above output, all database names are between the root elements <eInfoResult> and </eInfoResult>. The XML tags are case sensitive.

Table 4.2 shows the names and descriptions of the Entrez databases. When they are provided to an E-utilities program as a parameter, they must be provided in lowercase as shown in the table.

The EInfo program can also be used to provide information of a specified Entrez database and its indexed fields when it is used with "db=" parameter. For example:

https://eutils.ncbi.nlm.nih.gov/entrez/eutils/einfo.fcgi?db=protein

There are three pieces of information that you can obtain when you use EInfo with the "db=" option, where the value is any valid Entrez database name. These three pieces of information are (1) information of the specified database, (2) information of the indexed fields of the database, and (3) information of other links of the databases related to the specified database.

The XML response of the above EInfo program is the information of the Entrez protein database as shown in Figure 4.3 and described as follows:

(A) This section shows the general information of the Entrez database specified in "db=" parameter of the EInfo program. This information includes the database name, the database name as it appears in the dropdown menu of the Entrez database, description of the database, database build, number of entries

```
<eInfoResult>
    <DbList>
        <DbName>pubmed</DbName>
        <DbName>protein</DbName>
        <DbName>nuccore</DbName>
        . . . . . . . . . . . .
        <DbName>biocollections</DbName>
        <DbName>gtr</DbName>
    </DbList>
</eInfoResult>
```

FIGURE 4.2 XML formatted database name list.

TABLE 4.2 NCBI Entrez Databases

Database	Description
assembly	Assembly database for genomic assemblies (Assembly)
biocollections	Database for historical and museum specimens (BioCollections)
bioproject	Database for biological project (BioProjects)
biosample	Database for samples used in experiments (BioSample)
biosystems	Biological pathways of genes and phenotypes (BioSystems)
books	Books in bioscience that support the databases (Books)
cdd	Conserved Domains Database (CDD) of proteins
clinvar	Aggregates info about genomic variation and its disease (ClinVar)
dbvar	Human genomic structural variation (>50 bp) (dbVar)
gap	Database of genotypes and phenotypes (dbGaP)
gds	GEO DataSets stores curated gene expression data sets
gene	Database for gene information for many species (Gene)
genome	Genomic (sequences, maps, chromosomes, assemblies, and annotations) (Genome)
geoprofiles	Individual gene expression profiles from curated GEO DataSets (GEO Profiles)
gtr	Genetic testing registry database (GTR)
homologene	Putative homology groups from the complete gene sets for some eukaryotes (HomoloGene)
ipg	Identical Protein Groups resource (a single entry for each protein)
medgen	Information related to human medical genetics (MedGen)
mesh	Medical Subject Headings (MeSH)
ncbisearch	Search the NCBI website for content (NCBI Web Site)
nlmcatalog	provides access to NLM bibliographic data (NLM Catalog)
nuccore	Collection of sequences from GenBank, RefSeq, TPA and PDB (Nucleotide)
nucleotide	Collection of sequences from GenBank, RefSeq, TPA and PDB (Nucleotide)
omim	Authoritative database of human genes and genetic phenotypes (OMIM)
pmc	Biomedical and life sciences journal literature (PMC)
popset	collection of related DNA sequences derived from population, phylogenetic, mutation and ecosystem studies (PopSet)
protein	Database for protein sequences (Protein)
proteinclusters	collection of related protein sequences (Archaea, Bacteria, Plants, Fungi, Protozoans, and Viruses) (Protein Clusters)
pubmed	Biomedical and life sciences journal literature (PubMed)
snp	human single nucleotide variations (SNPs and small variation) (SNP)
sparcle	Subfamily Protein Architecture Labeling Engine (Sparcle)
sra	Sequence Read Archive (SRA) for raw sequencing data and alignment information (SRA)
structure	Three-dimensional structures of proteins (Structure)
taxonomy	curated classification and nomenclature for all the organisms in the public sequence databases (Taxonomy)

in the database, and the date of the last update. You can use this section to know how many entries are in the database and when the database was updated.

(B) This section shows only one indexed field. However, the other indexed fields are listed in the same pattern. The information in the field section includes field short name, field full name, field description, the number of the field indexed terms; other elements set the rules about the field.

(C) This section includes the information of the link to another database. It shows the information of only one link, but the information of the other links follows the same pattern.

The output format of the EInfo can be changed to JSON by using the "retmode=json" parameter.

In conclusion, you can also run an EIfno request to provide you with the list of database names and information of any Entrez database as shown above.

Gquery

Gquery (gquery.fcgi) is used to send a URL request to find the number of entries in all entrez databases. Using the Gquery command is like choosing "All Databases" from the database dropdown menu and entering a

```
<eInfoResult>
    <DbInfo>
          <DbName>protein</DbName>
          <MenuName>Protein</MenuName>
          <Description>Protein sequence record</Description>
   (A)    <DbBuild>Build210603-0611m.1</DbBuild>
          <Count>944803861</Count>
          <LastUpdate>2021/06/04 23:26</LastUpdate>
        <FieldList>
            <Field>
                <Name>ALL</Name>
                <FullName>All Fields</FullName>
                <Description>All terms from all searchable fields</Description>
                <TermCount>4979119536</TermCount>
   (B)      <IsDate>N</IsDate>
                <IsNumerical>N</IsNumerical>
                <SingleToken>N</SingleToken>
                <Hierarchy>N</Hierarchy>
                <IsHidden>N</IsHidden>
            </Field>
            <Field>
                . . . . . . . . . . .
            </Field>
            . . . . . . . . . . .
        </FieldList>
        <LinkList>
            <Link>
                <Name>nuccore_protein_wp</Name>
                <Menu>Links to autonomous proteins</Menu>
   (C)        <Description>Autonomous protein records</Description>
                <DbTo>nuccore</DbTo>
            </Link>
            <Link>
                . . . . . . . . .
            </Link>
        </LinkList>
    </DbInfo>
</eInfoResult>
```

FIGURE 4.3   XML formatted output of EInfo.

search term into the search box and clicking the "Search" button. The Gquery program has the "term=" parameter that serves like the Entrez search box on the Entrez web page and the "tretmode=" parameter that determines the display of the content. The "term=" parameter accepts any search term that complies with Entrez search query conventions as discussed in Chapter 3. You are allowed to use free text, indexed fields, and Boolean operators (AND, OR, and NOT) to construct a search query but you have to abide by the E-utilities rules mentioned above; no whitespace is allowed in between the query terms, but they can be replaced by plus sign "+". After sending a valid Gquery request with a valid search query, the global results will be displayed on the web browser by default unless the "retmode=xml" parameter is used. If this parameter is added to the request, the results will be displayed in XML format.

Assume that you wish to find the number of records, in all Entrez databases, that mentioned genomics studies in lung cancer in the human. If you were using the Entrez search box, you would enter the following search query:

"lung cancer"[TITL] AND human[ORGN]

However, the Gquery request with that search query will written as follows:

https://eutils.ncbi.nlm.nih.gov/gquery?term="lung+cancer"[TITL]+AND+human[ORGN]

The results include the name of the database, the number of entries in the database, and description of the database. So, the Gquery program is useful for obtaining the entry counts in all Entrez databases that match a specified search term or a search query.

Instead of displaying the output on a formatted web page, we can use "retmode=xml" parameter to display the output in XML format as follows.

https://eutils.ncbi.nlm.nih.gov/gquery?term="lung+cancer"[TITL]+AND+human [ORGN]&retmode=xml

ESearch

ESearch (esearch.fcgi) is used to search any of the valid Entrez databases that are shown in Table 4.2. The Esearch parameters include "db=", "term=", "retstart=", "retmax=", "usehistory=", "WebEnv=", "query_key=", "rettype=", "retmode=", "field=", "idtype=", "datetype=", "reldate=", "mindate=", and "maxdate=". All those parameters are optional except "db=" and "term=". ESearch requires a target database to be specified in the "db=" parameter and a search query to be provided to the "term=" parameter. The building of a search query follows the Entrez search query rules; and you can use any of the indexed fields, discussed in Chapter 3, of the target database. Always remember that you can use the EInfo E-utilities program to list the valid Entrez database names and the indexed fields of any database. The search query also follows the E-utilities rules that no whitespace is allowed.

The "db=" parameter is used by adding a valid database name after the equal sign (e.g., db=protein). The "term=" parameter is like that of Gquery (e.g. term=human[ORGN]+AND+" lung+cancer"[TITL]). Notice that whitespaces are replaced with plus signs "+".

Whenever you use the "term=" parameter with ESearch and other E-utilities programs that have this parameter, the rules of search queries you learned in Chapter 3 for any of the Entrez databases are also applied. Therefore, revisit Chapter 3 to follow the same search examples with ESearch. Try the following ESearch examples:

(1) Search the Entrez Nucleotide database for the human BRCA1 gene records:

https://eutils.ncbi.nlm.nih.gov/entrez/eutils/esearch.fcgi?db=nucleotide&term=brca1[gene]+AND+human[orgn]

This will return hundreds of UIDs of the redundant BRCA1 nucleotide records.

(2) Search the Entrez Nucleotide database for the RefSeq BRCA1 gene record:

https://eutils.ncbi.nlm.nih.gov/entrez/eutils/esearch.fcgi?db=nucleotide&term=brca1[gene]+AND+human[orgn]+ AND+ refseqgene[Filt]

This will return a single reference BRCA1 gene UID, since there is only one reference gene of an organism.

(3) Search the Entrez Nucleotide for the RefSeq BRCA1 transcripts records:

https://eutils.ncbi.nlm.nih.gov/entrez/eutils/esearch.fcgi?db=nucleotide&term=brca1[gene]+AND+human [orgn]+AND+refseq[Filt]+AND+biomol_ mrna[Properties]

This will return five UIDs of reference BRCA1 transcripts, since BRCA1 gene has five transcript variants.

(4) Search the Entrez Protein database for BRCA1 protein records:

https://eutils.ncbi.nlm.nih.gov/entrez/eutils/esearch.fcgi?db=protein&term=brca1[gene]+AND+human[orgn]

This search request will return hundreds of UIDs of redundant BRCA1 protein records.

(5) Search the Entrez Protein database for RefSeq BRCA1 protein records:

https://eutils.ncbi.nlm.nih.gov/entrez/eutils/esearch.fcgi?db=protein&term=brca1[gene]+AND+human[orgn]+AND+refseq[Filt]

This search request will return five UIDs for RefSeq BRCA1 protein records. Since there are five RefSeq BRCA1 transcript variants there are also five BRCA1 protein isoforms.

(6) Search PubMed for review articles about lung cancer in the human and have available PMC full-text:

https://eutils.ncbi.nlm.nih.gov/entrez/eutils/esearch.fcgi?db=pubmed&term="lung+cancer"[titl]+ AND+human[titl]+AND+review[PTYP]+AND+"pubmed+pmc"[Filter])

This will return the PMIDs of review articles about lung cancer and have free full text available at the PMC database.

(7) Search for COVID-19 (SARS-CoV-2) complete genome assemblies without any anomalies and with annotations.

https://eutils.ncbi.nlm.nih.gov/entrez/eutils/esearch.fcgi?db=assembly&term="sars-cov-2"[orgn]+ AND+(latest[filt]+AND+"complete+genome"[filt]+AND+all[filter]+NOT+anomalous[filt]+ AND+"has+annotation"[prop])

This will return the UIDs of the SARS-CoV-2 complete genome assemblies that have annotations and have no anomalies.

(8) Search for *Salmonella enterica* projects (BioProjects) that sequenced the whole genome of the bacteria and the data for which is available on the Entrez SRA database.

https://eutils.ncbi.nlm.nih.gov/entrez/eutils/esearch.fcgi?db=bioproject&term="salmonella+ enterica"[orgn]+AND+("genome+sequencing"[filt]+AND+"bioproject+sra"[filt])

This will return the UIDs of all Entrez BioProjects that sequence the whole genome of *Salmonella enterica* and for which the data are archived on the SRA database.

(9) Search datasets for phylogenetic studies in coronaviruses on the Entrez PopSet database:

https://eutils.ncbi.nlm.nih.gov/entrez/eutils/esearch.fcgi?db=popset&term="severe+ acute+respiratory+syndrome-related+ coronavirus"[orgn]+AND+"phylogenetic+ study"[prop]

This will return the UIDs of the PopSet series records of phylogenetic studies in coronaviruses.

(10) Search for the ClinVar records associated with sickle cell disease in the human.

https://eutils.ncbi.nlm.nih.gov/entrez/ eutils/esearch.fcgi?db=clinvar&term= "sickle+cell"[dis]

The above are a few examples of searching with ESearch, which is another way for searching the Entrez databases using search queries. However, the results are in XML format and the output of ESearch is a list of unique identifiers (UIDs) of the records matching the search query on the target database. This seems strange for the first time as no other information other than the UIDs will be displayed. You may remember that when you used the Entrez web interface, the results were displayed in summary format. Remember that the sole job of the ESearch E-utilities program is to respond with UIDs of the records that match your search query. Displaying summaries and detailed information of the returned records are the jobs of other E-utilities programs.

Figure 4.4 shows the XML output of ESearch for searching the ClinVar database. Generally, the ESearch XML output is as illustrated in Figure 4.4:

(A) This section shows the number (count) of records matching the search query on the database, the maximum number of UIDs that can be displayed (RetMax), and the index of the first UID that the count will start from (RetStart). Later, you will know that you can set both "retmax=" and "retstart=" parameters.

(B) The UIDs are listed between <IdList> and </IdList> and each UID is between <Id> and </Id>. In this example, the number of records found by the search is three and the number of the UIDs listed is three. However, this will not be the case all the time. The number of records found may be larger than the number specified between <RetMax> and </RetMax>. In such case, the maximum number of UIDs listed will be equal to the number specified by "<RetMax>" while the unlisted UIDs will disappear. For example, if your search results are 100 records and the "retmax=" parameter is set to 20

```
<eSearchResult>
    ┌<Count>3</Count>
    │<RetMax>3</RetMax>
(A)─┤<RetStart>0</RetStart>
    │<IdList>
    └      <Id>446736</Id>
(B)─┤      <Id>15333</Id>
    │      <Id>15292</Id>
    └</IdList>
    <TranslationSet/>
    <TranslationStack>
        ┌<TermSet>
        │    <Term>"sickle cell"[dis]</Term>
(C)─────┤    <Field>dis</Field>
        │    <Count>3</Count>
        │    <Explode>N</Explode>
        └</TermSet>
        <OP>GROUP</OP>
    </TranslationStack>
 (D)<QueryTranslation>"sickle cell"[dis]</QueryTranslation>
</eSearchResult>
```

FIGURE 4.4   XML output of ESearch.

(i.e., <RetMax>20</RetMax>), only the UIDs of the first 20 records will be displayed on the ESearch output and the other 80 records will be ignored.

(C)   The term set section will detail the searching steps; each time it lists a search term and the number of records matching that term. In this example, we have only one term but if there are multiple terms, they will be listed along with the number of records matching that term. The final number of records returned will be the intersection of all search terms.

(D)   This will include the original search query.

Figure 4.4 shows the typical XML structure of the output of ESearch E-utilities program.

In the above ESearch examples, we used only the mandatory parameters with ESearch ("db=" and "term="). The following are additional ESearch parameters:

The "retmax=" parameter determines the maximum number of UIDs to be displayed on the output. The default is "retmax=20". The maximum number that can be set to this parameter is 100000 (i.e., retmax=100000). If the number of the records found is more than specified by the retmax parameter, only the first UIDs will be displayed, while the others will be ignored.

In the following example, we will use ESearch to find the identical protein groups on the Entrez Identical Protein Groups database (IPG):

https://eutils.ncbi.nlm.nih.gov/entrez/eutils/esearch.fcgi?db=ipg&term="nuclear+receptor"[TITL]& retmax=50

The number of IPG records found by the above request is 45,832, but because we set the "retmax=" parameter to 50, only 50 UIDs will be displayed on the output while the remaining UIDs will be ignored.

The "retstart=" parameter is the index of the first UID to be displayed in the output and the count of the UIDs starts from that index. The default is "retstart=0", which means that the display of the UIDs starts from the first record found by the search. This parameter is useful when the number of records found by ESearch is very large and you intend to retrieve all numbers in batches as demonstrated in the following examples:

https://eutils.ncbi.nlm.nih.gov/entrez/eutils/esearch.fcgi?db=ipg&term="nuclear+receptor"[TITL]& retmax=10000& retstart=0 *https*://eutils.ncbi.nlm.nih.gov/entrez/eutils/esearch.fcgi?db=ipg&term="nuclear+receptor"[TITL]& retmax=1000& retstart=9999

https://eutils.ncbi.nlm.nih.gov/entrez/eutils/esearch.fcgi?db=ipg&term="nuclear+receptor"[TITL]& retmax=1000& retstart=19999

https://eutils.ncbi.nlm.nih.gov/entrez/eutils/esearch.fcgi?db=ipg&term="nuclear+receptor"[TITL]& retmax=1000& retstart=29999

https://eutils.ncbi.nlm.nih.gov/entrez/eutils/esearch.fcgi?db=ipg&term="nuclear+receptor"[TITL]& retmax=1000& retstart=39999

https://eutils.ncbi.nlm.nih.gov/entrez/eutils/esearch.fcgi?db=ipg&term="nuclear+receptor"[TITL]& retmax= 1000&retstart=49999

Notice that the "retstart=" parameter is incremented in each ESearch request to retrieve all UIDs of the records found by the search query.

The "usehistory=" parameter is either "usehistory='y'" for yes or "usehistory='n'" for no. The default setting is "usehistory='n'". When "usehistory='y'", the UIDs of the records returned by ESearch will be posted to the NCBI History Server and they will be available for the use by a subsequent E-utilities program. When "usehistory='y'", other elements will be added to the ESearch output.

https://eutils.ncbi.nlm.nih.gov/entrez/eutils/esearch.fcgi?db=ipg&term="nuclear+receptor"[TITL]& retmax= 3&usehistory="y"

Because "usehistory=y", the query key (QueryKey) and WebEnv string will be added to the output (as shown in Figure 4.5), so you can provide them to another E-utilities program (ESearch, EFetch, ESummary, or ELink) for extra processing such as viewing the summary, the complete records, or part of records as we will see.

The "WebEnv=" parameter is the parameter that accepts the Web Environment (WebEnv) string generated by a previously executed E-utilities program with "usehistory='y'". This parameter works together with the "query_keys=" parameter.

```
<eSearchResult>
    <Count>45832</Count>
    <RetMax>3</RetMax>
    <RetStart>0</RetStart>
    <QueryKey>1</QueryKey>
    <WebEnv>MCID_60bee6183722520f7c1c8c59</WebEnv>
    <IdList>
        <Id>62067034</Id>
        <Id>33635914</Id>
        <Id>34434862</Id>
    </IdList>
    <TranslationSet/>
    <TranslationStack>
        <TermSet>
            <Term>"nuclear receptor"[TITL]</Term>
            <Field>TITL</Field>
            <Count>45832</Count>
            <Explode>N</Explode>
        </TermSet>
        <OP>GROUP</OP>
    </TranslationStack>
    <QueryTranslation>"nuclear receptor"[TITL]</QueryTranslation>
</eSearchResult>
```

FIGURE 4.5   XML output of ESearch showing Query Key and WebEnv string.

The "query_key=" parameter accepts an integer returned by a previously executed E-utility program with "usehistory='y'". The WebEnv=" and "query_key" work together. They are used with ESearch to find the intersection of the set of the UIDs, on the History Server, specified by query_key and WebEnv returned in a previous operation and the set of UIDs returned by the search query on the current ESearch operation. This will be better explained with a worked example.

https://eutils.ncbi.nlm.nih.gov/entrez/eutils/esearch.fcgi?db=ipg&term="nuclear+receptor"[titl]&retmax=3&usehistory="y"

https://eutils.ncbi.nlm.nih.gov/entrez/eutils/esearch.fcgi?db=ipg&term=human[orgn]&query_key=1&WebEnv=MCID_60bf5fe9f80a1252067df53e& retmax=3

Notice that the WebEnv changes every time you run the same ESearch request. As shown in Figure 4.6 (A), the first ESearch, which used the "term=nuclear+receptor[titl]" search term, returned 45,832 records and posted their UIDs to the History Server since the "usehistory='y'" parameter was used.

The second ESearch request found 178,6569 records (Figure 4.6 (B)) for the "term=human[orgn]" search term but it intersected that with the results of the first ESearch by using the QueryKey and WebEnv string. The final number of records returned by the second ESearch after the intersection was only 343 as shown in Figure 4.6 (B).

The "rettype=" parameter determines the retrieval type for the output. The default setting for this parameter is "rettype=uilist", which displays the unique identifier list (UIDs). This parameter can be set as "rettype=count" to display the number of records returned by the search query only; the list of UIDs will not be displayed on the output. Try the following search request:

```
<eSearchResult>                              (A)
    <Count>45832</Count>
    <RetMax>3</RetMax>
    <RetStart>0</RetStart>
    <QueryKey>1</QueryKey>
    <WebEnv>MCID 60bf5fe9f80a1252067df53e</WebEnv>
    <IdList>      <eSearchResult>
        <Id>.         <Count>346</Count>              (B)
    </IdList>         <RetMax>3</RetMax>
    <Translatio       <RetStart>0</RetStart>
    <Translatio       <IdList>
        <TermS            <Id>. . . </Id>
            <T        </IdList>
            <F        <TranslationSet>
            <C            <Translation>
            <E                <From>human[orgn]</From>
        </Term                <To>"Homo sapiens"[Organism]</To>
        <OP>GR            </Translation>
    </Translati       </TranslationSet>
    <QueryTrans       <TranslationStack>
</eSearchResult           <OP>GROUP</OP>
                          <TermSet>
                              <Term>"Homo sapiens"[Organism]</Term>
                              <Field>Organism</Field>
                              <Count>1786569</Count>
                              <Explode>Y</Explode>
                          </TermSet>
                          <OP>AND</OP>
                          </TranslationStack>
                          <QueryTranslation>(#1) AND "Homo sapiens"[Organism]</QueryTranslation>
                      </eSearchResult>
```

FIGURE 4.6 XML output of ESearch showing intersection between two queries.

https://eutils.ncbi.nlm.nih.gov/entrez/eutils/esearch.fcgi?db=nucleotide&term="breast+cancer" [titl]+AND+human[orgn]&retmax=5&rettype=count

The "retmode=" parameter determines the retrieval mode of the data, and it can be set either to "xml" or "json". The default retrieval mode is "retmode=xml". This is why the output in the previous example was displayed in XML format. However, you can change the display to the JSON format by using "retmode=json".

The "sort" parameter is used to sort the UIDs in the ESearch output.

The "field=" parameter is used to limit the search to a specific indexed field instead of searching on all fields. This is like using an indexed field in the search query. For example, "field=organism" is the same as using "[organism].

https://eutils.ncbi.nlm.nih.gov/entrez/eutils/esearch.fcgi?db=nucleotide&term="breast+cancer" &field=title&retmax=5

The "idtype=" parameter specifies the type of the identifier to be returned. The possible values are either 'gi' for GenBank identifier or 'acc' for accession number.

https://eutils.ncbi.nlm.nih.gov/entrez/eutils/esearch.fcgi?db=nucleotide&term="breast+cancer"& field=title&retmax=5&idtype=acc

The "datetype=" parameter specifies which date field of the indexed date fields to use to limit the search results (e.g., datetype=pdat). This parameter is used with "mindate=" and "maxdate=" parameters.

The "mindate=" and "maxdate=" parameters specify the date range used to limit the search results by the date specified by the "datetype=".

https://eutils.ncbi.nlm.nih.gov/entrez/eutils/esearch.fcgi?db=nucleotide&term="breast+cancer"& field=title&retmax=5&datetype=pdat&mindate=2015/12/31&maxdate=2020/9/27

The "reldate=" can be set to an integer n so the search will return the items that have a date specified by "datetype" parameter and within the last n days of the specified date.

EPost

The ESearch responds by returning the UIDs of the records matching the search query and it can also post the UIDs to the History Server if "usehistory=" parameter is set to "y". You may already have run out of patience waiting to learn how to view records rather than displaying the UIDs or sending them to the History Server. That will be revealed in the next section. In this section we assume that you have a list of UIDs of Entrez database records and you intend to upload them to the NCBI History Server. The EPost (epost.fcgi) is used for that; it posts a list of UIDs to the History Server so that list can be used by other E-utilities programs. EPost's parameters include "db=", "id=", "query_key=", and "WebEnv=". The most important parameters are "db=" and "id=". The "db=" parameter species the Entrez database to which the UIDs that you intend to upload belong. This target database can be any valid Entrez database name as shown in Table 4.2. The "db=" parameter specifies the UIDs that you intend to upload to the NCBI History Server. This parameter accepts a single UID or a comma-delimited list of UIDs without whitespaces in between. There is no way to provide the UIDs to EPost from a text file. You may ask why NCBI did not provide that feature, especially when you have a list of many UIDs and typing them on the web browser address bar is not practical. Remember that E-utilities programs are APIs developed to allow programmers to build wrapper programs around them or to integrate them in web-based applications so the Entrez database will be accessible through interfaces developed by programmers. Therefore, NCBI left that feature to the programmers when they use E-utilities in their software.

```
<ePostResult>
    <QueryKey>1</QueryKey>
    <WebEnv>MCID_60bffc26393b203a2d296258</WebEnv>
</ePostResult>
```

FIGURE 4.7   EPost output.

You may be not a programmer, but knowing this will help you understand the three programs that implement the E-utilities and will be discussed in next chapters.

Assume that you have the following Nucleotide UIDs, and you wish to upload them to the NCBI History Server so other E-utilities programs can use them.

1483432502, 1483432501, 1483432500, 148343 2499, 1483432498, 1483432497, 1483432496, 148343 2495,1483432494, 1483432493

When you provide this list to the "id=" parameter make sure that there is no whitespace inbetween.

https://eutils.ncbi.nlm.nih.gov/entrez/eutils/epost.fcgi?db=nucleotide&id=1483432502,1483432501,1483432500, 1483432499,1483432498,1483432497,1483432496,1483432495,1483432494,1483432493

The output of EPost is shown in Figure 4.7. The output contains the query key (QueryKey) and the Web Environment string (WebEnv) that serve as an address mapped to the posted lists of UIDs on the History Server. In the coming examples, you will learn how to use these two elements in more advanced operations.

ESummary

ESearch responds with a list of UIDs in XML format by default and it can also post the complete lists of the UIDs of the records matching the search query to the History Server. The ESummary (esummary.fcgi) provides summary information of the records specified by the "id=" parameter and those records from a target database specified by the "db=" parameter. The UIDs can either be provided directly to the "id=" parameter or imported to the ESummary from the History Server using the query key and Web Environment string generated by a previous E-utilities command like ESearch or EPost. When the UIDs are imported from the History Server, ESummary must use the "query_key=" and "WebEnv=" parameters and the "id=" will not be used. In other words, ESummary either uses the "id=" parameter or "query_key=" and "WebEnv=" parameters.

If you are familiar with HTML and HTTP protocol, you will notice that those E-utilities URL requests are sent using the HTTP GET method. The maximum number of UIDs that can be sent in the ESummary request using the "id=" parameter is 200. To retrieve the summaries of more than 200 UIDs, you most post those UIDs to the History Server first by using EPost, which uses the HTTP POST method. Most times you may use ESearch with "usehistory='y'" to post the UIDs to the History Server.

ESummary has other parameters including "retstart=", "retmax=", and "retmode=", which are used the same way as discussed above.

Now we will try worked examples for using UIDs directly and importing UIDs from the History Server.

Assume that you have UIDs of two Entrez Nucleotide records (60391443 and 798959876) and you wish to retrieve the document summaries of these two records. You can use the following ESummary request:

https://eutils.ncbi.nlm.nih.gov/entrez/eutils/esummary.fcgi?db=nucleotide&id=60391443,798959876

Figure 4.8 shows the document summaries (DocSum) of the Nucleotide records with the above two UIDs.

The summary provided by ESummary is called DocSum, which is in XML format as shown in Figure 4.8. The root XML elements for each record are <DocSum> and </DocSum>. The summary of a record starts with the record UID (<Id> </Id>). The other elements of the summary are contained in <Item> XML tags, each with "Name=" and "type=" XML attributes.

```
▼<eSummaryResult>
  ▼<DocSum>
    <Id>60391443</Id>
    <Item Name="Caption" Type="String">AB032710</Item>
    <Item Name="Title" Type="String">Homo sapiens BRAP1 gene for breast cancer associated protein BRAP1, complete cds</Item>
    <Item Name="Extra" Type="String">gi|60391443|dbj|AB032710.2|[60391443]</Item>
    <Item Name="Gi" Type="Integer">60391443</Item>
    <Item Name="CreateDate" Type="String">1999/12/07</Item>
    <Item Name="UpdateDate" Type="String">2004/10/19</Item>
    <Item Name="Flags" Type="Integer">0</Item>
    <Item Name="TaxId" Type="Integer">9606</Item>
    <Item Name="Length" Type="Integer">10837</Item>
    <Item Name="Status" Type="String">live</Item>
    <Item Name="ReplacedBy" Type="String"/>
   ▼<Item Name="Comment" Type="String">
      <![CDATA[ ]]>
    </Item>
    <Item Name="AccessionVersion" Type="String">AB032710.2</Item>
  </DocSum>
  ▼<DocSum>
    <Id>798959876</Id>
    <Item Name="Caption" Type="String">NR_131222</Item>
    <Item Name="Title" Type="String">Homo sapiens breast cancer anti-estrogen resistance 4 (BCAR4), transcript variant 5, long non-coding RNA</Item>
    <Item Name="Extra" Type="String">gi|798959876|ref|NR_131222.1|[798959876]</Item>
    <Item Name="Gi" Type="Integer">798959876</Item>
    <Item Name="CreateDate" Type="String">2015/04/01</Item>
    <Item Name="UpdateDate" Type="String">2021/04/26</Item>
    <Item Name="Flags" Type="Integer">512</Item>
    <Item Name="TaxId" Type="Integer">9606</Item>
    <Item Name="Length" Type="Integer">728</Item>
    <Item Name="Status" Type="String">live</Item>
    <Item Name="ReplacedBy" Type="String"/>
   ▼<Item Name="Comment" Type="String">
      <![CDATA[ ]]>
    </Item>
    <Item Name="AccessionVersion" Type="String">NR_131222.1</Item>
  </DocSum>
</eSummaryResult>
```

FIGURE 4.8   Document summaries for two nucleotide records.

The ESummary provides only the document summary that includes the pieces of information shown in the figure.

In a new example, instead of providing UIDs using the "id=" parameter, this time you will use ESearch to find the RefSeq BRCA1 protein records and to post their UIDs to the History Server, and then you use ESummary to retrieve the document summaries of the records:

> https://eutils.ncbi.nlm.nih.gov/entrez/eutils/esearch.fcgi?db=protein&term=brca1[gene]+AND+human[orgn]+ AND+refseq[Filt]&usehistory="y"

The output of the above ESearch request in Figure 4.9 shows the query key and Web Environment string. You can use these in the subsequent ESummary request. Pay attention to that every time you run the above request the Web Environment String will change.

> https://eutils.ncbi.nlm.nih.gov/entrez/eutils/esummary.fcgi?db=protein&query_key=1&WebEnv= MCID_60c02d5bd5f198028d3a6681&retmax=5

This will display the document summaries of the five RefSeq BRCA1 proteins.

EFetch

ESummary retrieves only the document summary or DocSum of a record. However, you may need to retrieve all the record or a section of it. EFetch (efetch.fcgi) provides you with all those features as it can be used to retrieve information of records of an Entrez database. Like ESummary, the target database is specified by "db=" parameter and the record UIDs can either be provided explicitly in the "id=" parameter or implicitly by using the "query_key=" and "WebEnv=" parameters. However, EFetch has more parameters that provide more options as we will see. Other EFetch parameters include "retstart=", "retmode=", "rettype=", "retmax=",

```
▼<eSearchResult>
    <Count>5</Count>
    <RetMax>5</RetMax>
    <RetStart>0</RetStart>
    <QueryKey>1</QueryKey>
    <WebEnv>MCID_60c02d5bd5f198028d3a6681</WebEnv>
  ▼<IdList>
      <Id>237681123</Id>
      <Id>237681121</Id>
      <Id>237681119</Id>
      <Id>6552299</Id>
      <Id>237681125</Id>
    </IdList>
  ▼<TranslationSet>
```

FIGURE 4.9   ESearch output showing QueryKey and WebEnv.

TABLE 4.3   Retrieval Modes (Retmode) of Some Databases

"db="	"retmode="
All database	Xml
Gene	xml, text, asn.1
Homologene	xml, text, asn.1
Mesh	xml, text
Protein	xml, text, asn.1
Nuccore/nucleotide	xml, text, asn.1
Nucest	xml, text, asn.1
Nucgss	xml, text, asn.1
Pmc	xml, text
Pubmed	xml, text, asn.1
Sequences	xml, text
Snp	xml, text, asn.1
Sra	Xml

"strand=", "seq_start=", "seq_stop=", and "complexity=". The first three parameters have already been discussed, except that "retmode=" and "retype=" have more options when they are used with EFetch.

Before digging deeper into EFetch uses, let us see how EFetch can either use the "id=" parameter or "query_key=" and "WebEnv=" parameters but it cannot use both in the same request.

Assume that you wish to retrieve the Entrez Protein record with the "6552299" UID using EFetch. You can use the following request:

https://eutils.ncbi.nlm.nih.gov/entrez/eutils/efetch.fcgi?db=protein&id=6552299

The file of the protein record will be downloaded to your local drive. The file is in asn.1 file format, which is the default format but later we will show you how to change the retrieval mode to other formats using "retmode=".

The output of EFetch is variable depending on the Entrez database since each type of database record has certain content structure that differs from the others.

Instead of providing UIDs in "id=" parameter, you can import the UIDs from the History Server using "query_key=" and "WebEnv=". Refer to the ESummary above; the same applies for EFetch.

You can control the display format of the records you retrieve with EFetch by using the "retmode=" parameter. Table 4.3 shows the retrieval modes for some databases [2]. Notice that the records of all databases can be displayed as XML and using "retmode=text" may display the UID of the records.

https://eutils.ncbi.nlm.nih.gov/entrez/eutils/efetch.fcgi?db=homologene&id=5276&retmode=xml

TABLE 4.4   The Retrieval Type (Rettype) of Some Entrez Databases

"db="	"rettype="
All database	docsum, uilist
Gene	gene_table, docsum, uilist
Homologene	fasta, homologene, alignmentscores, docsum, uilist
Mesh	full, docsum, uilist
Protein	acc, fasta, seqid, ft
Nuccore/Nucleotide	acc, fasta, seqid, gb, ft, fasta_cds_na, fasta_cds_aa
Nucest	Est, docsum, uilist
Nucgss	gss, docsum, uilist
Pmc	medline, docsum, uilist
Pubmed	medline, uilist, abstract
Sequences	fasta, seqid, docsum, uilist
Snp	flt, fasta, rsr, chr, docsum, uilist

You may wish to retrieve a certain type of data from the database records. For example, you may need to retrieve only record sequences in FASTA format from database such as Entrez Nucleotide or Protein, or you may need to retrieve the abstracts of some PubMed articles. To achieve that you can use the "rettype=" parameter, which controls the retrieval type. The options for this parameter are variable depending on the database type. Table 4.4 shows the retrieval types "rettype" for some databases [2].

Notice that all databases have the docsum (document summary) and uilist (list of UIDs) retrieval types. The docsum is similar to the ESummary output. The following EFetch request will retrieve the docsum of two Nucleotide records (60391443 and 798959876):

https://eutils.ncbi.nlm.nih.gov/entrez/eutils/efetch.fcgi?db=nucleotide&id=60391443,798959876&rettype=docsum

You can also retrieve the FASTA sequence of the records of the sequence databases such as the Nucleotide, Protein, and HomoloGene databases.

The following EFetch request will retrieve the FASTA sequences of the above two Nucleotide records. The sequences may be downloaded as a file:

https://eutils.ncbi.nlm.nih.gov/entrez/eutils/efetch.fcgi?db=nucleotide&id=60391443, 798959876&rettype=fasta

You can use EFetch to retrieve the nucleotide coding sequencing of a Nucleotide record in FASTA format by using "rettype=fasta_cds_na". Assume that you wish to download the FASTA file for the nucleotide coding sequence of the BRCA1 transcript variant1 (GI=1732746264). You can use the following:

https://eutils.ncbi.nlm.nih.gov/entrez/eutils/efetch.fcgi?db=nucleotide&id=1732746264&rettype=fasta_cds_na

Instead of the nucleotide coding sequence of a Nucleotide record, you can also retrieve the amino acid translation of the coding sequence in FASTA format by using "rettype=fasta_cds_aa":

https://eutils.ncbi.nlm.nih.gov/entrez/eutils/efetch.fcgi?db=nucleotide&id=1732746264&rettype=fasta_cds_aa

You can also use EFetch to retrieve or download only the feature table of a Nucleotide record:

https://eutils.ncbi.nlm.nih.gov/entrez/eutils/efetch.fcgi?db=nucleotide&id=1732746264&rettype=ft

For both the records of the PubMed and PMC databases, you can use EFetch to retrieve the abstracts or MEDLINE format of the articles. Assume that you wish to retrieve the abstracts of the PubMed articles 27292874 and 27066500. You can use the following EFetch request to retrieve the abstracts of these two articles in XML format:

https://eutils.ncbi.nlm.nih.gov/entrez/eutils/efetch.fcgi?db=pubmed&id=27292874,27066500&rettype=abstract

You have noticed that "rettype=" parameter can control the output of EFetch E-utilities program and that the retrieval types vary with the database. Refer to Table 4.4 to find the right retrieval type option for each database.

The "retmax=" parameter determines the maximum number of records to be retrieved by EFetch and the use of the "restart=" parameter has already been discussed above.

The "strand=" parameter can be used if the database record is a DNA sequence such as Nucleotide. This parameter specifies which DNA strand to retrieve. The "strand=1" setting is for the plus DNA strand and "strand=2" is for the complementary or minus strand.

The "seq_start" and "seq_stop" parameters are used with sequence records such as that of Nucleotide and Protein databases. They are used to specify a range of the sequence to retrieve. Those two parameters are especially useful if you wish to retrieve a gene sequence from a chromosome; users usually do this if they need to design PCR primers, to identify gene structure, to use the sequence to find similar sequence, etc. Assume that you need to retrieve the complete genomic sequence of the human BRCA1 gene. You can search the Entrez Gene database to find the coordinates of the sequence of this gene. After you check the BRCA1 gene record on the Gene database you will find that it is between 43044295 and 43125364 in the reference sequence of chromosome 17 (NC_000017.11). You can use this information to download the complete sequence of the human BRCA1 gene in FASTA format as follows:

https://eutils.ncbi.nlm.nih.gov/entrez/eutils/efetch.fcgi?db=nucleotide&id=NC_000017.11&rettype=fasta&seq_start=43044295&seq_stop=43125364

ELink

The database records are integrated, and the related records are linked across the Entrez databases. In Chapter 3, when we discussed the Entrez search results web pages and record pages, we pointed out the Related Information that includes the links to the related records from other Entrez databases and external resources (LinkOuts). ELink (elink.fcgi) is the E-utilities API program that can be used to find those related records from the same database, a different database, and the LinkOuts. When it is requested, it responds with the list of UIDs. The parameters of ELink include "dbfrom=", "db=", "id=", "query_key=", "WebEnv=", "cmd=", "retmode=", "idtype=", "linkname=", "term=", "holding=", "datetype=", "reldate=", "mindate=" and "maxdate=".

ELink requires three elements provided by three parameters: (1) the UIDs ("id=") of the records, to which you wish to find the related information (related Entrez database records), (2) the database ("dbfrom=") that contains the input UIDs, and (3) the target database ("db="), from which you need to find the related records.

```
<eLinkResult>
    <LinkSet>
        <DbFrom>gene</DbFrom> (A)
       ┌<IdList>
   (B)─┤        <Id>672</Id>
       └</IdList>
       ┌<LinkSetDb>
       │    <DbTo>protein</DbTo>  (D)
       │    <LinkName>gene_protein</LinkName> (E)
       │    ┌<Link>
       │    │        <Id>2043420544</Id>
   (C)─┤(F)─┤</Link>
       │    │<Link>
       │    │        ...
       │    └</Link>
       │        ...
       └</LinkSetDb>
       ┌<LinkSetDb>
       │    <DbTo>protein</DbTo>  (D)
       │    <LinkName>gene_protein_refseq</LinkName>(E)
       │    ┌<Link>
       │    │        <Id>237681125</Id>
   (C)─┤(F)─┤</Link>
       │    │<Link>
       │    │        ...
       │    └</Link>
       │        ...
       └</LinkSetDb>
    </LinkSet>
</eLinkResult>
```

FIGURE 4.10   ELink output.

For example, the BRCA1 gene ID is 672. If we need to find the protein records linked to the BRCA1 gene, then we need to provide ELink with "id=672", "dbfrom=gene", and "db=protein" as follows:

   https://eutils.ncbi.nlm.nih.gov/entrez/eutils/elink.fcgi?id=672&dbfrom=gene&db=protein

ELink responds with a list of UIDs of the records linked from the target database (specified by "db=") to the UIDs on hand (specified by "id=") contained on the database (specified by "dbfrom=").

The components of the XML output of the ELink are illustrated in Figure 4.10 and described as follows:

(A) This element shows the database that contains the UIDs on hand and is specified by the "dbfrom=" parameter.

(B) This includes the list of UIDs to which you wish to find the related records from a target database. In this example, you used a single UID (672 for the human BRCA1 gene).

(C) This section includes three pieces of information: (D) the target database that you have provided to ELink in the "db=" parameter, (E) link name, and (F) the UID list of the protein records linked to the BRCA1 gene. The link name is introduced to categorize the linked records and to help users to use it as a filter to restrict the output to certain kinds of linked records. Each Entrez database has its own link names as we will discuss below. The Protein database has two link names: gene_protein (gene to protein) and gene_protein_refseq (gene to reference sequence protein). Under each of these two link names there is a UID list of the records linked to the BRCA1 gene. The results of the above ELink request include many UIDs. Later, you can use the "linkname=" parameter to filter the results.

In the previous example, we provided ELink with both a UID using the "id=" parameter and the database containing that UID by using the "dbfrom=" parameter. This time, instead of providing the UIDs and

```
▼<eSearchResult>
   <Count>5</Count>
   <RetMax>5</RetMax>
   <RetStart>0</RetStart>
   <QueryKey>1</QueryKey>
   <WebEnv>MCID_60c179be08140d65b757a954</WebEnv>
 ▼<IdList>
      <Id>1732746264</Id>
      <Id>1677529721</Id>
      <Id>1677501432</Id>
      <Id>1677500831</Id>
      <Id>237681122</Id>
   </IdList>
 ▶<TranslationSet>
   ...
   </TranslationSet>
 ▶<TranslationStack>
   ...
   </TranslationStack>
   <QueryTranslation>brca1[gene] AND "Homo sapiens"[Organism] AND refseq[Filt] AND
   biomol_mrna[Properties]</QueryTranslation>
</eSearchResult>
```

FIGURE 4.11 ESearch output.

the database containing the UIDs they will be imported, from the History Server from a previous E-utilities program operation, by using the "query_key=" and "WebEnv=" parameters. In this example, first, you will use ESearch to find the refseq BRCA1 transcripts and to post their UIDs to the History Server ("usehistory='y'") and then you will use ELink to find the UID of the gene record linked to the refseq BRCA1 transcripts by importing their UIDs from the History Server using the query key ("query_key=") and Web Environment string ("WebEnv=") as follows:

https://eutils.ncbi.nlm.nih.gov/entrez/eutils/esearch.fcgi?db=nucleotide&term=brca1[gene]+ AND+human[orgn]+AND+refseq[Filt]+AND+biomol_mrna[Properties]&usehistory=y

After running the above request (Figure 4.11), you can use ELink with the "query_key=" and "WebEnv=" parameters as follows:

https://eutils.ncbi.nlm.nih.gov/entrez/eutils/elink.fcgi?query_key=1&WebEnv=MCID_60c179be 08140d65b757a954&db=gene

This ELink request responds with a single UID (672), which is the only gene linked to the refseq BRCA1 transcripts.

Notice that you do not need to use "id=" and "dbfrom=" parameters when you use a query key and a Web Environment string as the UIDs and the database containing the UIDs will be imported from the History Server. Also, remember that the Web Environment string will change every time you run the ESearch request.

The "cmd=" parameter is called the ELink command mode. It is used to specify a function to be performed by ELink. The default output of ELink is the list of UIDs in the database specified by the "db=" parameter and linked to the input UIDs in the database specified by the "dbfrom=" parameter. That ELink output is because the "cmd=neighbor" setting is the default. The following ELink request will return UIDs:

https://eutils.ncbi.nlm.nih.gov/entrez/eutils/elink.fcgi?id=672&dbfrom=gene&db=protein

```
▼<eLinkResult>
  ▼<LinkSet>
     <DbFrom>pubmed</DbFrom>
    ▼<IdList>
        <Id>27292874</Id>
     </IdList>
    ▼<LinkSetDb>
        <DbTo>pubmed</DbTo>
        <LinkName>pubmed_pubmed</LinkName>
       ▼<Link>
          <Id>25534958</Id>
          <Score>29667028</Score>
        </Link>
       ▼<Link>
          <Id>26957000</Id>
          <Score>28157148</Score>
        </Link>
```

FIGURE 4.12   ELink neighbor_score command mode.

TABLE 4.5   The Elink Command Mode (cmd=) Functions

Cmd Value	Output Returned by ELink
neighbor	UIDs linked to the specified input UIDs
neighbor_score	UIDs and scores within the same database
neighbor_history	UIDs will be posted to Entrez History server and query_key and WebEnv for the neighbor set will be displayed.
acheck	Links available for a set of UIDs
ncheck	checks existence of links within the same database for a set of UIDs.
lcheck	checks the existence of external links for a set of UIDs
llinks	lists the URLs and attributes for external links for each UID.
llinkslib	lists the URLs and attributes for external links and libraries for each UID.
prlinks	lists the primary external links for each UID.

This ELink is the same as:

> https://eutils.ncbi.nlm.nih.gov/entrez/eutils/elink.fcgi?id=672&dbfrom=gene&db=protein&cmd= neighbor

However, this default ELink command mode can be changed by setting the "cmd=" parameter to any of the options shown in Table 4.5. Some option may not work with some databases.

The "cmd=neighbor_score" setting instructs ELink to return the UIDs with the same database as the input UIDs along with computed similarity scores. This mode is used for the PubMed database to find similar articles within PubMed with their similarity scores as shown in Figure 4.12 for the following ELink request:

> https://eutils.ncbi.nlm.nih.gov/entrez/eutils/elink.fcgi?id=27292874&dbfrom=pubmed&cmd= neighbor_score

When you use "cmd=neighbor_score" there is no need to provide the "db=" parameter.

The "cmd=neighbor_history" setting will instruct ELink to post the UIDs to the NCBI History Server and to return a query key for each UIDs list of a link name and a WebEnv string for all sets.

> https://eutils.ncbi.nlm.nih.gov/entrez/eutils/elink.fcgi?id=27292874&dbfrom=pubmed&cmd= neighbor_history

The output of the above ELink request includes several link names. Each link name has a query key for the set of UIDs of that link name. To use the UIDs of a certain link name in a subsequent E-utilities program, you can use the query key of that link name and the WebEnv string with the "query_key=" and "WebEnv=" parameters of the E-utilities program.

The "cmd=acheck" setting instructs ELink to list all the links available for a set of UIDs. For example, the following ELink request will list all possible links (link names) from the human BRCA1 gene (ID=672) to Protein.

> https://eutils.ncbi.nlm.nih.gov/entrez/eutils/elink.fcgi?id=672&dbfrom=gene&db=protein&
> cmd=acheck

The "cmd=ncheck" setting instructs ELink to check for the existence of links within the same database for a set of UIDs. There is no need to provide the "db=" parameter. The following ELink request checks whether or not the PubMed article (PMID=27292874) has links in the PubMed database.

> https://eutils.ncbi.nlm.nih.gov/entrez/eutils/elink.fcgi?id=27292874&dbfrom=pubmed&cmd=ncheck

The output will indicate that there are links (<Id HasNeighbor="Y">27292874</Id>).

The "cmd=lcheck" setting will instruct ELink to check for the existence of external links (LinkOut) for a set of UIDs. The following ELink request checks whether the PPAR-gamma (id= 1823752945) has any external link or LinkOut.

> https://eutils.ncbi.nlm.nih.gov/entrez/eutils/elink.fcgi?id=1823752945&dbfrom=protein&cmd=
> lcheck

This output of the above request includes "<Id HasLinkOut="N">1823752945</Id>", which indicates that there is no LinkOut for that protein record.

The "cmd=llinks" setting will instruct ELink to list the URLs and attributes for the external link providers not including libraries. If there is no LinkOut, the output will show the message "No LinkOut links available for UID". The following request will list the URLs and attributes for the external providers (no libraries) for the PubMed article with "27292874" PMID. The attributes for the PubMed article may include online full text, publisher of information in URL, subscription/membership/fee, etc.

> https://eutils.ncbi.nlm.nih.gov/entrez/eutils/elink.fcgi?id=27292874&dbfrom=pubmed&cmd=
> llinks

The "cmd=llinkslib" setting will instruct the ELink to list the URLs and attributes of the external link providers including libraries. The following request lists the URLs and attributes of all external link providers.

> https://eutils.ncbi.nlm.nih.gov/entrez/eutils/elink.fcgi?id=27292874&dbfrom=pubmed&cmd=
> llinkslib

The "cmd=prlinks" setting will instruct ELink to list the primary external link provider for each input UID or to link to the external link provider's website for a single UID if "retmode=ref" setting is used with ELink. The following ELink request lists the website of the primary external link provider.

> https://eutils.ncbi.nlm.nih.gov/entrez/eutils/elink.fcgi?id=27292874&dbfrom=pubmed&cmd=prlinks

However, you can display the article link on the provider's website if you add the "retmode=ref" to the above request as follows:

> https://eutils.ncbi.nlm.nih.gov/entrez/eutils/elink.fcgi?id=27292874&dbfrom=pubmed&cmd=prlinks&retmode=ref

This request will direct you to the article on the provider's website.

The "retmode=" parameter can accept both the "xml" and "json" option to change the retrieval mode of ELink accordingly.

Adding the "idtype=" parameter will determine the type of UID to return. This parameter works for sequence databases such as Nucleotide, Protein, and PopSet, etc. The "idtype=acc" will let ELink return accession numbers.

The "term=" parameter is used to provide the search query. We have already discussed this parameter above. When it is used with ELink to limit the set of linked UIDs returned, the "dbfrom=" and "db=" parameters must set to the same database. The following request will find all related article for the PMID article with PMID=27292874.

> https://eutils.ncbi.nlm.nih.gov/entrez/eutils/elink.fcgi?id=27292874&dbfrom=pubmed&db=pubmed

After adding the "term=" parameter, only the PMIDs of review articles related to that PubMed article will be returned.

> https://eutils.ncbi.nlm.nih.gov/entrez/eutils/elink.fcgi?id=27292874&dbfrom=pubmed&db=pubmed&term=review

The "datetype=" parameter is used to determine the indexed date used to limit the returned UIDs (e.g., datetype=pdat). Any indexed date field for the database is valid.

The "mindate=" and "maxdate=" are used to restrict the linked UIDs to a specific range of dates as discussed above.

The "reldate=" parameter, which accepts an integer, limits the UIDs returned by ELink to be within the range of the number of days specified by the parameter from the date specified by the "datetype=" parameter.

The "holding=" parameter works only when the "cmd=" parameter is set to either "llinks" or "llinkslib" as it allows the provider specified by "holding=" only to be returned. The value must be an abbreviation of the LinkOut provider's name.

Finally, we will discuss the "linkname=" parameter. We have already shown the link name in Figure 4.10 and said that link names are part of the ELink output structure as the returned UIDs are categorized into link names. Links of records of a database to another fall under several link names depending on the databases. Those link names serve as filters that can be used to limit the returned UIDs to a certain link name. You can display the possible link names by viewing the output of the ELink. For example, assume that you wish to know the link name that will categorize the linked UIDs from a record of Protein to Nucleotide.

> https://eutils.ncbi.nlm.nih.gov/entrez/eutils/elink.fcgi?id=ALQ33725.1&dbfrom=protein&db=nucleotide

Figure 4.13 shows the link names of a protein record that categorize the returned Nucleotide UIDs. The link names for this ELink request are "protein_nuccore" and "protein_nuccore_mrna" as indicated in Figure 4.13.

```
▼<eLinkResult>
  ▼<LinkSet>
      <DbFrom>protein</DbFrom>
    ▼<IdList>
        <Id>957950005</Id>
      </IdList>
    ▼<LinkSetDb>
        <DbTo>nuccore</DbTo>
        <LinkName>protein_nuccore</LinkName>
      ▼<Link>
          <Id>957950004</Id>
        </Link>
      </LinkSetDb>
    ▼<LinkSetDb>
        <DbTo>nuccore</DbTo>
        <LinkName>protein_nuccore_mrna</LinkName>
      ▼<Link>
          <Id>957950004</Id>
        </Link>
      </LinkSetDb>
    </LinkSet>
  </eLinkResult>
```

FIGURE 4.13   The link name of protein-nucleotide for a protein record.

There are different link names for each database-database or (dbfrom-db). You can either display those link names using the above method, or you may find the complete list of the link names for any two databases at www.ncbi.nlm.nih.gov/entrez/query/static/entrezlinks.html.

The "linkname=" parameter can be used to limit the UIDs to a specific link name. To clarify this, let us revisit the first ELink example that has the output shown in Figure 4.10.

https://eutils.ncbi.nlm.nih.gov/entrez/eutils/elink.fcgi?id=672&dbfrom=gene&db=protein

This ELink example returns several protein UIDs linked to the BRCA1 gene (id=672). Those returned UIDs are categorized into two link names: gene_protein (this list includes numerous redundant non-reference protein records) and gene_protein_refseq (includes a few non-redundant refseq proteins). Assume that you need to limit the ELink output to only the set of UIDs in gene_protein_refseq; then you can use the "linkname=" parameter with ELink as follows:

https://eutils.ncbi.nlm.nih.gov/entrez/eutils/elink.fcgi?id=672&dbfrom=gene&db=protein&linkname=gene_protein_refseq

After running the above ELink request, you will notice that the output includes only five refseq BRCA1 protein isoforms.

ESpell

The ESpell (espell.fcgi) E-utilities program acts as a spell checker for the search terms that the user wishes to use for searching the Entrez database. ESPell checks the term and if it finds that there may be a possible mistake it will provide correction suggestions. ESpell has two parameters: "db=" and "term=". The use of those terms was discussed in previous E-utilities programs. Try the following example to see how ESpell suggests a correction for the term "brest cancar".

https://eutils.ncbi.nlm.nih.gov/entrez/eutils/espell.fcgi?db=pubmed&term=brest+cancar

```
Mol Biosyst|2016|12|2427|Hamid D Ismail|doi: 10.1039/c6mb00179c|27292874
IEEE/ACM Trans Comput Biol Bioinform|2018|15|1844|Hamid D Ismail|doi:10.1109/TCBB.2017.2773063|29990125
Biomed Res Int|2016|2016|3281590|Hamid D Ismail|doi:10.1155/2016/3281590|27066500
BMC Bioinformatics|2017|18|577|Hamid D Ismail|doi:10.1186/s12859-017-1972-6|29297322
```

FIGURE 4.14   ECitMatch output.

ECitMatch

ECitMatch (ecitmatch.fcgi) is specific for the PubMed database. It retrieves PubMed identifiers (PMIDs) for the citations specified by "bdata=" parameter. This E-utilities program is used to find the PMIDs of known citations. The parameters of ECitMatch include "db=", "rettype=", and "bdata=".

The "db=pubmed" is the only parameter setting for ECitMatch.

The "rettype=" parameter is for retrieval type (e.g., rettype=xml).

The "bdata=" parameter specifies the citation string, which must be in the following format:

journal_title|year|volume|first_page|author_name|your_key|

Multiple citation strings are allowed by separating the strings with a carriage return character (%0D). The "your_key" value is provided by the user. A space must be replaced by a plus sign "+" and that citation strings should end with a final vertical bar "|". The following URL request will find the PMIDs of four citations given the citation strings (Figure 4.14).

https://eutils.ncbi.nlm.nih.gov/entrez/eutils/ecitmatch.cgi?db=pubmed&retmode=xml&bdata=
Mol+Biosyst|2016|12|2427|Hamid+D+Ismail|doi:+10.1039/c6mb00179c%0DIEEE/ACM+Trans+
Comput+Biol+Bioinform|2018|15|1844|Hamid+D+Ismail|doi:10.1109/TCBB.2017.2773063%0DBiomed+
Res+Int|2016|2016|3281590|Hamid+D+Ismail|doi:10.1155/2016/3281590%0DBMC+Bioinformatics
|2017|18|577|Hamid+D+Ismail|doi:10.1186/s12859-017-1972-6

The ECitMatch output shows the PMIDs of the four citation strings: 27292874, 29990125, 27066500, and 29297322.

REFERENCES

1. NCBI Resource Coordinators, *Database resources of the National Center for Biotechnology Information.* Nucleic Acids Res, 2018. **46**(D1): p. D8–D13.

2. Sayers, E., *A General Introduction to the E-utilities.* Entrez Programming Utilities Help [cited 2021 6/6/2021]. www.ncbi.nlm.nih.gov/books/NBK25497/. 2010.

3. Sayers, E., *The E-utilities In-Depth: Parameters, Syntax and More.* Entrez Programming Utilities Help 2009 5/15/ 2021 [cited 2021 6/25/2021]. https://www.ncbi.nlm.nih.gov/books/NBK25499/.

## CHAPTER 5

The Entrez Direct

INTRODUCTION

In Chapter 4, we discussed the NCBI Entrez Programming Utilities, or E-utils, that enable software developers to build their bioinformatics tools on the top of those E-utilities programs [1, 2]. Several programs have been developed using the E-utils API to communicate with the Entrez databases. The use of the E-utilities programs as you experienced in the previous chapter is primitive as the requests are built as a URL and sent via the HTTP protocol and the response is obtained mainly as XML output. These two features allow users to access the Entrez programs from a programming environment. The NCBI introduced Entrez Direct (EDirect) [3] as Linux-based command-line programs for advanced Entrez database users. EDirect allows user to search the Entrez databases and to retrieve data more easily. The Linux environment also adds to the EDirect functionality as users can integrate bash Linux shell commands and scripting with the EDirect functions to perform complex operations that cannot be accomplished with the E-utilities programs only.

In the following sections, you will be shown how to install EDirect on Linux, Mac OS, and Windows. Then the use of each EDirect function will be discussed. At the end of the chapter, you will be shown how to use Linux shell commands and bash scripting language to extend the use of EDirect functions.

EDIRECT INSTALLATION

EDirect works only on a Linux environment. But it can also work on other platforms such as MacOS that uses a Linux shell and Windows after installing the Linux environment provided by Cygwin. The EDirect programs are available for downloading from the NCBI's FTP server at https://ftp.ncbi.nih.gov/entrez/entrezdirect/. The EDirect requires Perl scripting language to be installed. However, the Mac Terminal and many Linux distributions come with Perl pre-installed.

Installing EDirect on Linux and MacOS

The vast majority of Mac OS will be using the bash Linux shell by default. If the bash shell is not the current one you can set it to bash shell easily by changing the preferences inside the Mac. You will follow the same steps to install EDirect on both Linux and Mac OS.

To install EDirect on Linux and MacOS, you can either follow the instructions available at www.ncbi.nlm.nih.gov/books/NBK179288/ or simply install it using the following commands if you have Linux "sudo" privilege:

```
$ sudo apt-get update -y
$ sudo apt-get install -y ncbi-entrez-direct
```

The first command will update the package and the second one will install EDirect on Linux and a Linux-like system and configure it so it will be ready for use.

DOI: 10.1201/9781003226611-5

Installing EDirect on Windows 10

To install EDirect on Windows, you need to install Cygwin first. Cygwin is the software that provides a Linux environment emulator on Windows. After installing Cygwin, you need to install the Perl package on the Linux environment. In the following steps you will learn how to install Cygwin on Windows 10 and then how to install and configure EDirect on the Cygwin Linux environment:

- Open the Cygwin home page, which is available at www.cygwin.com/.
- On the Cygwin, you may need to scroll down to "Installing Cygwin", as shown in Figure 5.1, and click on the "setup-x86_64.exe" link to begin downloading the Cygwin program file. The file may be downloaded in the Download folder on your Windows system.
- Once the file has been downloaded on your local drive, double click on it. The Cygwin Setup dialog box will pop up asking you to choose a download source. Choose "Install from Internet" as this option will install the software directly from its server without downloading it to the local drive. Click on the "Next" button and the Cygwin installer will begin installing the software on your computer.
- The Cygwin Setup dialog box will prompt you to choose the installation folder (root directory). You can browse to the folder where you want to install Cygwin or accept the suggested folder name. It is recommended to choose the "All Users" option so users with other accounts on the computer can use Cygwin as well. Click on the "Next" button.
- The Cygwin Setup dialog box will ask you to choose the Internet connection type. Use the direct connection and click on the "Next" button.
- The next Cygwin Setup dialog box will ask you to choose a site or mirror, from which you wish to download the Cygwin software and packages. Choose a site and click on the "Next" button.

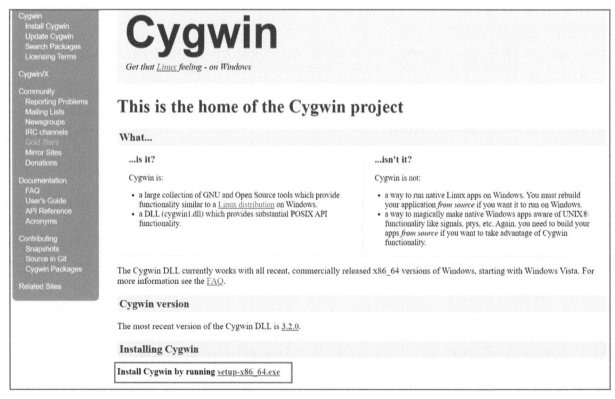

FIGURE 5.1   Cygwin page.

- The Cygwin Setup will prompt to select the package that you need to install on the Cygwin. You need to install the Perl and gzip packages. You can use the search box to search for these two packages and select them by checking their check boxes and then click on the "Next" button.

- The setup dialog box will ask you to review and confirm change. Click on the "Next" button to continue.

- The setup progress box will display the progress of the installation, which may take some time depending on your internet connection.

- Once the installation has been completed successfully you will be asked if you need the Cygwin icons to be added to the Windows Desktop and Start Menu. You can check both and click on the "Finish" button.

Once you have installed the Cygwin, you will have full functional Linux environment emulator. Open the Terminal by double-clicking on the Cygwin icon on the Windows Desktop. A dark Linux-like Terminal, as shown in Figure 5.2, will open with a command line prompt "$", where you type and enter the commands.

If you have reached this stage successfully, then you are ready to install EDirect software on your Windows system.

To download the Entrez EDirect, open www.ncbi.nlm.nih.gov/books/NBK179288/ and copy the bash script from there or just copy the following script and paste it on the Cygwin terminal (The script may change).

```
cd ~
  /bin/bash
  perl -MNet::FTP -e \
    '$ftp = new Net::FTP("ftp.ncbi.nlm.nih.gov" , Passive => 1);
    $ftp->login; $ftp->binary;
    $ftp->get("/entrez/entrezdirect/edirect.tar.gz");'
  gunzip -c edirect.tar.gz | tar xf -
  rm edirect.tar.gz
  builtin exit
  export PATH=${PATH}:$HOME/edirect >& /dev/null || setenv PATH
"${PATH}: $HOME/edirect"
  ./edirect/setup.sh
```

The script will be executed, and the execution may stop on the last script line ./edirect/setup.sh. Press the "Enter" key to finish the installation. The finishing may take some time. When installation has been completed, the terminal will display a message saying "Entrez Direct has been successfully downloaded and installed" as shown in Figure 5.3.

After installing EDirect on Cygwin, you may need to add EDirect to the path before you use it. First, you may need to know where the EDirect has been installed by using the "which" Linux command with one of the EDirect programs as follows:

$ which esearch

FIGURE 5.2   Cygwin terminal.

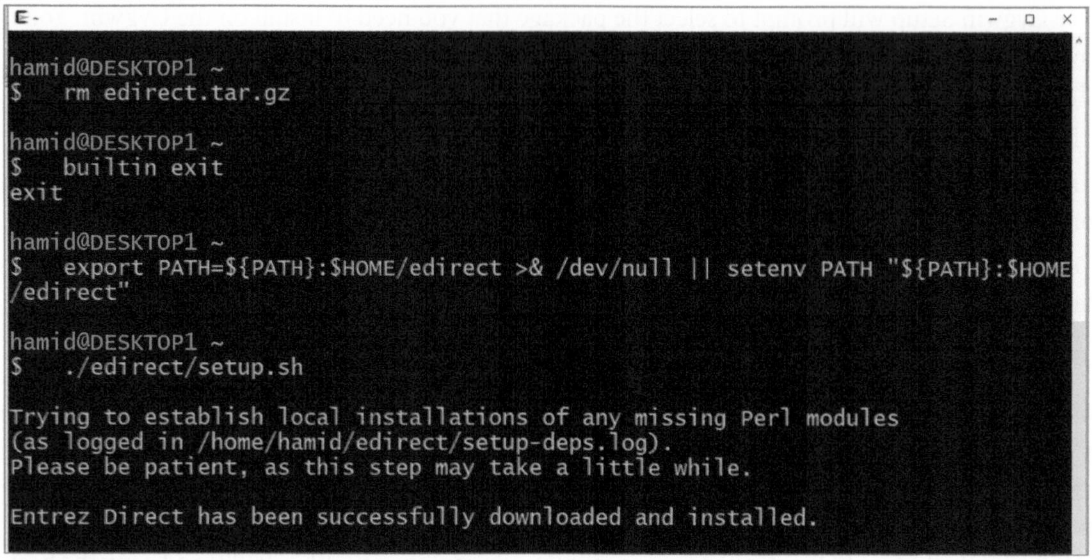

FIGURE 5.3   Cygwin terminal showing EDirect has been installed.

FIGURE 5.4   Using "which" Linux command to find EDirect path.

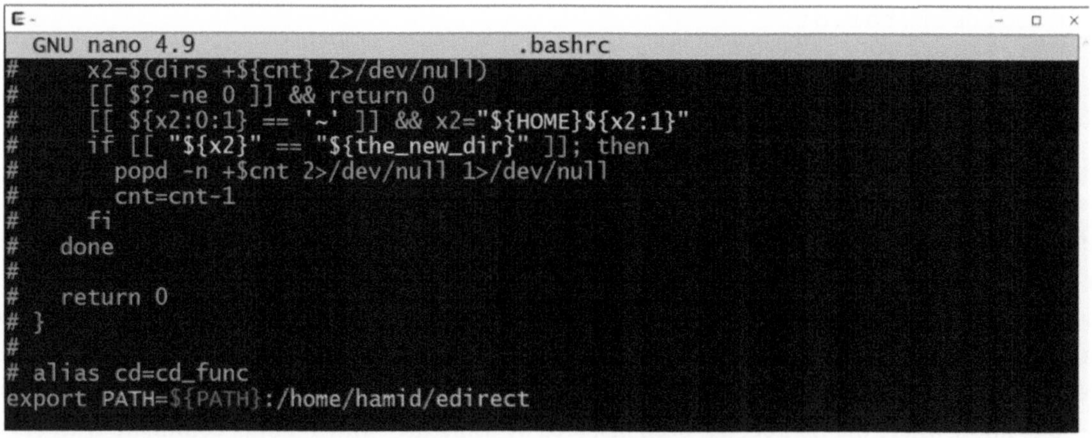

FIGURE 5.5   Adding EDirect path to ".bashrc" file.

From Figure 5.4, the EDirect has been installed on "/home/hamid/edirect". The second step, you need to add this path to the hidden ".bashrc" file in the default working directory when we open the terminal. You can use any text editor such as nano or vim text editor to open the ".bashrc" file.

$ nano .bashrc

At the end of ".bashrc" file add the following line as shown in Figure 5.5:

export PATH=${PATH}:/home/hamid/edirect

FIGURE 5.6   Checking the EDirect version.

TABLE 5.1   EDirect Executable Programs

Edirect Function	E-Utilities Program
einfo	EInfo (einfo.fcgi)
Esearch	ESearch(esearch.fcgi)
Elink	ELink (elink.fcgi)
Efetch	EFetch (efetch.fcgi) and ESummary (esummary.fcgi)
Epost	EPost (epost.fcgi)
Efilter	Filters results returned by a previous query
Nquire	Sends a URL request to the Entrez server
Xtract	Extracts data from XML output

Then save the file and exit.

Now you can run the following command that checks the EDirect version but it also tells you if EDirect is on the path and ready to use.

    $ esearch -version

Figure 5.6 shows that the current EDirect version is 13.9. The EDirect has been installed and configured successfully and is ready to use.

USING EDIRECT

The EDirect programs are nothing other than Perl-based wrapper functions around the E-utilities programs and availing of the Linux bash shell to extend the functionality and usability of the E-utilities programs discussed in Chapter 4. We may refer to EDirect programs as functions, commands, or executables as well.

EDirect has eight command line executables as shown in Table 5.1. Five of them are direct wrapper functions around the Entrez E-utilities programs. EFilter is developed to serve as a filter to limit the results returned by one of EDirect commands. NQuire can be used to send a URL request like the ones we discussed in the previous chapter. XTract extracts data from the XML formatted output returned by EFetch. Table 5.1 contains the EDirect functions and the corresponding E-utilities program.

An EDirect function is executed by entering it on the prompt of the command line on Terminal on both Linux and MacOS and Cygwin Terminal on Windows. Remember that each E-utilities program has parameters as discussed in Chapter 4. Since most of EDirect programs are wrappers for E-utilities API, almost the same parameters of the E-utilities programs will be provided to the EDirect functions as well. However, those parameters are called arguments when they are used with EDirect

For those, who did not use the MS-DOS or Linux shell commands, the command line is a user interface where the user can enter a command at a command prompt. A command is a compiled executable file that contains valid instructions to the computer, and it is executed when the user presses the "Enter" key. Most commands have arguments that pass some information to the command so the command can convey the instruction correctly to the computer. This is the case with EDirect functions as they are commands or executables and each one of them has arguments to pass the parameters required by the E-utilities programs that were discussed in Chapter 4.

The general syntax of an EDirect command is as follows:

$ function -argumen1 value1 [-agument2 value2] […]

The dollar sign '$' is only to differentiate the command line from other text line and it should not be included when you enter the command onto the command-line prompt of a Linux or Cygwin Terminal, "function" is any EDirect function, "-argument1", "argument2", etc., are any arguments (those are like parameters in E-utilities), and "value1", value2, etc. are the values of the argument (those are parameter options).

The following are some differences between the use of EDirect functions and E-utilities programs:

- The EDirect functions are executed on a command line of Linux or a Linux-like Terminal while the E-utilities programs are sent as URL request through a web browser. There must be an Internet connection in both cases.

- The command line of an EDirect function is built as shown by the above syntax. There must be a whitespace between the function, and the argument must be preceded by a dash "-", and there is no whitespace between the dash and the argument. There must be a whitespace between the argument and its value and that value can be numeric or string. When the value is a string, it must be between quotation marks. On the other hand, in case of E-utilities programs that we discussed in Chapter 4, there are very strict rules about writing the E-utilities URL request and whitespace. Refer to Chapter 4 for E-utilities rules.

- EDirect exploits Linux piping. A pipe is a form of redirection or transfer of standard output to some other destination. It is used in Linux and other Unix-like operating systems to send the output of one command to another command for further processing. This Linux piping extends the usability of E-utilities as you can combine multiple EDirect function in one line using fewer arguments. Piping is achieved by using the pipe character '|' to transfer an output of an EDirect function to another. The general form of piping is as follows:

$ function1 –argumen1 value1 | function2 –argumen2 value2

In the above piping form, the output of function1 will be transferred to function2 provided that the output of function1 is a valid input for function2.

- The command line that includes multiple functions combined by a pipe may become long. For readability the functions can be written in multiple lines by using the backslash '\' immediately before pressing the "Enter" key for a new line as follows.

$ function1 –argumen1 value1 | \
  function2 –argumen1 value1 | \
  function3 –argumen1 value1

Soon you will notice that the Linux pipe '|' and '\' will be used to build multi-step, multi-line request that makes retrieving information from an Entrez database more efficient than using E-utilities programs only.

Since EDirect functions operate on a Linux environment, Linux Bash scripting language can be used to extend the usability and functionality of E-utilities programs to beyond what E-utilities programs alone can do.

In Chapter 4, we explained how to generate an NCBI API key and why it is important to provide it to NCBI so as to identify you. For EDirect, you provide your API key to the Linux environment by running the "export" Linux command as follows.

$ export NCBI_API_KEY='your_key'

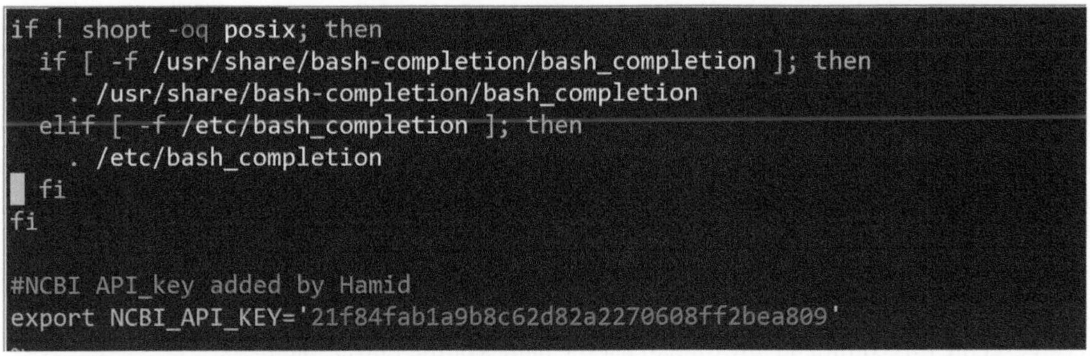

```
if ! shopt -oq posix; then
  if [ -f /usr/share/bash-completion/bash_completion ]; then
    . /usr/share/bash-completion/bash_completion
  elif [ -f /etc/bash_completion ]; then
    . /etc/bash_completion
  fi
fi

#NCBI API_key added by Hamid
export NCBI_API_KEY='21f84fab1a9b8c62d82a2270608ff2bea809'
```

FIGURE 5.7   Defining the NCBI API_key in ".bashrc" file.

Replace your_key' with your NCBI API_key as described in Chapter 4. However, when you define the API key as you did above you will need to run that command every time you open the terminal. To avoid this you can add the above command to the '.bashrc' file, which is a hidden bash script file run by the computer whenever you open the Linux Terminal. To add the API key to the ".bashrc", first you need to change to the home directory, if you are not currently in the home directory, by running the following command.

   $ cd $HOME

Then use a text editor such as nano or vim to open the ".bashrc" file as follows:

   $ nano .bashrc

To the end of the file, add the above "export" command with your NCBI API_key as shown in Figure 5.7, save the file and exit.

We may need to restart the terminal or force Linux to reload the ".bashrc" file by running:

   $ source .bashrc

The above are the key points about using EDirect and what makes its use different from that of the URL-based E-utilities programs. Since we have already discussed E-utilities program in Chapter 4, the use of EDirect functions will be very familiar. However, they provide flexibility and easiness in use and the extra mile in data retrieval and data extraction from the Entrez databases.

In the following sections we will discuss the use of each of the EDirect functions and we will provide worked examples. To use EDirect, you need to open the Terminal if you are using Linux or MacOS, or open the Cygwin Terminal if you are using Windows. The EDirect function is entered onto the Terminal command line and executed by pressing the "Enter" key.

EInfo

EInfo is a wrapper for the "einfo.fcgi" E-utility. It is used (1) to list the names of Entrez databases, (2) to display summary information of a specific database, (3) to list the names and descriptions of the indexed fields of a specific Entrez database, and (4) to list the link names of the database. The following is the general syntax of the EInfo function and its arguments.

```
$ einfo [-help] [-db name] [-dbs] [-fields] [-links]
```

Whenever you need to know about EInfo arguments, use the "-help" argument as follows:

$ einfo -help

Listing the Names of Entrez Databases The "-dbs" argument is used with EInfo to display the list of available Entrez databases. This argument does not need any value.

$ einfo -dbs

You can execute this command any time to list the names of the Entrez database.

Displaying Summary Information of an Entrez Database Using the "-db name" argument, "name" can be replaced with any valid Entrez database (e.g., -db protein). If it is used alone with the EInfo function, the output will be like that of the EInfo E-utilities program as shown in Figure 4.3.

$ einfo -db protein

The output is an XML format that includes the number of records on the specified database, the last update of the database, and then the list of the fields, number of indexed terms for each field, and links (see Figure 4.3).

Listing the Indexed Fields of an Entrez Database The "-fields" argument has no options, and it is used together with the "-db" argument to instruct EInfo to list the names and descriptions of the indexed fields of the specified database. The following EInfo will list the names and descriptions of the indexed fields of the Protein database.

$ einfo -db protein -fields

You can run this command to list the names of the indexed fields of any Entrez database.

Listing the Link Names of an Entrez Database The "-links" argument is used together with "-db" to list the link names of an Entrez database. The following command lists the link names of the Protein database.

$ einfo -db protein -links

The link names are used to filter the records UIDs returned by ELink. You can refer to Chapter 4 to learn more about the link names.

ESearch

The ESearch function is a wrapper for "esearch.fcgi" E-utilities program. It is used to search an Entrez database provided as a value for the "-db name" argument using a search query provided as value for the "-query str" argument. The ESearch responds by returning UIDs for the records matching the search query. The general syntax for ESearch is as follows:

```
$ esearch  [-help] -db name -query str [-sort field]
            [-datetype field] [-min date date] [-maxdate date]
            [-field field] [-pairs field] [-label name]
```

The arguments between square brackets are optional. Only "-db name" and "-query" are mandatory and they must be provided.

You can use the "-help" argument whenever you need to display the description of these options.

$ esearch -help

Providing Target Database   ESearch always requires a target database specified by the "-db name" argument, where "name" can be replaced by any valid Entrez database name (e.g., -db protein). For the valid database name, run the "einfo -dbs" command as shown above.

Providing a Search Query   ESearch requires a search query to be specified in "-query str", where "str" stands for a string. The query string is an Entrez search query that can be built from a single term or multiple terms combined with Boolean operators (AND, OR, and NOT). A term can be free text or text with a tagged indexed field. You can list the indexed fields of any database by using "einfo -db name -fields". The search query is built exactly as we discussed in Chapter 3. Assume that you wish to search the PubMed database for articles on human lung cancer. You can enter the following ESearch command on the Terminal command line:

$ esearch -db pubmed -query "lung cancer [TITL] AND human[ORGN]"

The output of the above ESearch command is as shown in Figure 5.8. The ESearch output is in XML format, and it contains only a Web Environment string (WebEnv), query key (QueryKey), the total number (Count) of records matching the search query, and the number of steps (Step). You can notice that although 85,824 records have been found, no list of UIDs is displayed. ESeaech posts the list of UIDs of the records matching the search query to the NCBI History Server and returns the WebEnv and QueryKey to be used by a subsequent EDirect command. Soon we see some examples using ESearch results. But first let us discuss the other arguments.

Sorting the Results   The "-sort field" argument is used to sort ESearch results by a specified field. For example, "-sort pdat" will sort the results by the publishing date.

$ esearch -db pubmed -query "lung cancer [TITL] AND human[ORGN]" -sort pdat

The returned results will be sorted by the publishing date and posted to the History Server.

Limiting Results by Dates   The "-datetype field" argument is used to specify an indexed date field to be used by "-mindate date" and "-maxdate date" arguments. The indexed date field for any database will be in the list of the indexed fields that can be displayed by running "einfo -db name -fields" such as the publishing date (pdat). The "-mindate date" and "-maxdate date" arguments are used to limit the ESearch results to a specific range of dates determined by the "-datetype field" argument. For example, the following ESearch command will return

```
hamid@DESKTOP1 ~
$ esearch -db pubmed -query "lung cancer[TITL] AND human[ORGN]"
<ENTREZ_DIRECT>
  <Db>pubmed</Db>
  <WebEnv>MCID_60c3ed96d7a7a705c46b6bb4</WebEnv>
  <QueryKey>1</QueryKey>
  <Count>85824</Count>
  <Step>1</Step>
</ENTREZ_DIRECT>
```

FIGURE 5.8   ESearch output.

the PubMed articles on human lung cancer, and they were published between 2015 and 2020 and sorted by publishing date:

$ esearch -db pubmed -query "lung cancer [TITL] AND human[ORGN]" -datetype pdat -mindate 01/01/2015 -maxdate 12/31/2020 -sort pdat

The above search can also be written as follows:

$ esearch -db pubmed -query "lung cancer[TITL] AND human[ORGN] AND 01/01/2015:12/31/2020[PDAT]" -sort pdat

Limit Searching to a Field   The "-field field" is used to limit the search to a specific indexed field rather than all fields. You can use this argument when no tagged indexed field is used in the query search. The "field" is any valid indexed field for the target database. Assume that you wish to find the BRCA1 records in GenBank. You can use the following ESearch command.

$ esearch -db nucleotide -query "brca1" -field gene

The above ESearch command is the same as:

$ esearch -db nucleotide -query "brca1 [GENE]"

You may find using the search query that we discussed in Chapter 3 convenient to combine different terms. But, EDirect has its way to do the same, as you will see soon.

Labeling Query Steps   The "-label name" argument is used to label a query search. This is useful when multiple search steps are involved, as we will see in coming examples. To show how a label is added to a query step in ESearch output, we can use the ESearch example whose output is shown in Figure 5.8.

$ esearch -db pubmed -query "lung cancer[TITL] AND human[ORGN]" -label lung_cancer

The output is shown in Figure 5.9. Notice that a label has been added to step 1.

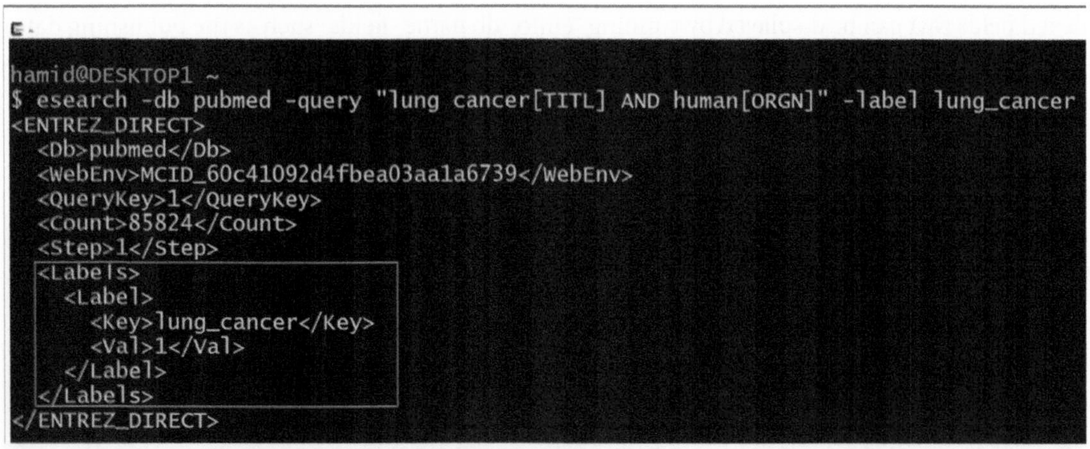

```
E.

hamid@DESKTOP1 ~
$ esearch -db pubmed -query "lung cancer[TITL] AND human[ORGN]" -label lung_cancer
<ENTREZ_DIRECT>
  <Db>pubmed</Db>
  <WebEnv>MCID_60c41092d4fbea03aa1a6739</WebEnv>
  <QueryKey>1</QueryKey>
  <Count>85824</Count>
  <Step>1</Step>
  <Labels>
    <Label>
      <Key>lung_cancer</Key>
      <Val>1</Val>
    </Label>
  </Labels>
</ENTREZ_DIRECT>
```

FIGURE 5.9   ESearch output Showing a step label.

FIGURE 5.10   The output of four ESearch commands.

Uploading the results to the History Server and returning an output with a Web Environment string and query key can be used to combine multiple ESearch queries. Two or more search queries with multiple ESearch commands can be combined by using the query keys and Boolean operators (AND, OR, and NOT). Assume that we have multiple ESearch queries. Consider the following four different ESearch commands:

$ esearch -db nucleotide -query "brca1" -field gene

$ esearch -db nucleotide -query "human" -field organism

$ esearch -db nucleotide -query "refseq" -field filter

$ esearch -db nucleotide -query "biomol_genomic" -field property

The outputs of the above ESearch commands are shown in Figure 5.10. Notice that each ESearch query returned a total number (count) of matching records. Assume that you need to combine these four ESearch command to find only the refseq human BRCA1 transcript variants (no non-reference sequence and no genomic BRCA1 DNA). You can combine those commands by using the Linux pipe character "|", query keys, and Boolean operators as follows (Figure 5.11):

$ esearch -db nucleotide -query "brca1" -field gene | \
    esearch -db nucleotide -query "human" -field organism | \
    esearch -db nucleotide -query "refseq" -field filter | \
    esearch -db nucleotide -query "biomol_genomic" -field property | \
    esearch -query "(#1) AND (#2) AND (#3) NOT (#4)"

```
E
hamid@DESKTOP1 ~
$ esearch -db nucleotide -query "brca1" -field gene | \
>     esearch -db nucleotide -query "human" -field organism | \
>     esearch -db nucleotide -query "refseq" -field filter | \
>     esearch -db nucleotide -query "biomol_genomic" -field property | \
>     esearch -query "(#1) AND (#2) AND (#3) NOT (#4)"

<ENTREZ_DIRECT>
  <Db>nucleotide</Db>
  <WebEnv>MCID_60c422c19e805c0b221429fc</WebEnv>
  <QueryKey>5</QueryKey>
  <Count>8</Count>
  <Step>5</Step>
</ENTREZ_DIRECT>
```

FIGURE 5.11   ESearch output.

In the above, the first three commands are combined with the "AND" Boolean operator, then the genomic DNA in the fourth command is excluded with the "NOT" operator.

The above is the EDirect way to create an advanced search query. The above results can also be obtained by using the Entrez query style as follows:

$ esearch -db nucleotide -query "brca1[GENE] AND human[ORGN] AND refseq[FILT] NOT biomol_genomic[PROP]"

Instead of combining multiple Esearch command using the query keys, you can use the labels, which make tracking easier in a complex search.

$ esearch -db nucleotide -query "brca1" -field gene -label gn | \

esearch -db nucleotide -query "human" -field organism -label orgn | \

esearch -db nucleotide -query "refseq" -field filter -label ref | \

esearch -db nucleotide -query "biomol_genomic" -field property -label dna| \

esearch -query "(#gn) AND (#orgn) AND (#ref) NOT (#dna)"

As a reminder, ESearch posts the UIDs of the records matching the query to the History Server and returns the WebEnv, query key, and the number of records found. EDirect functions like EFetch and ELink can use the UIDs stored on the History Server as we will discuss next.

EFetch

EFetch is the wrapper function for both "efetch.fcgi" and "esummary.fcgi" E-utilities programs. It is used to retrieve records, specified by their UIDs, from an Entrez database specified by the "-db name" argument. The following is the syntax of the EFetch function and its arguments

```
$efetch  [-help] [-format fmt] [-mode mode] [-db name] [-id ID]
         [-seq_start N] [-seq_stop N] [-strand N] [-chr_start N]
         [-chr_stop N] [-complexity N] [-extend N] [-extrafeat N]
```

Use the "-help" argument to obtain the full list of the arguments and their descriptions.

$ efetch -help

Providing a Target Database   Efetch requires a target database that contains the records UIDs. The database is provided to EFetch in the "-db name" argument, where "name" is any valid Entrez database name. You can list the Entrez database names by running "einfo -dbs".

Providing the Record UIDs   EFetch requires a single UID or a list of UIDs to retrieve their records. The UIDs are provided either directly by (1) using "-id" argument or (2) by transferring them with piping from a previous EDirect command.

Using "-id" Argument   You can pass a single UID or a list of UIDs to EFetch command through the "-id ID" argument. For example, to retrieve the Nucleotide record of the human PPAR alpha gene transcript whose UID (GI) is 1677538777, you can use the following EFetch command:

    $ efetch -db nucleotide -id 1677538777

The above EFetch command retrieves the complete record of the human PPARA gene transcript in JSON format, which is the default retrieval mode "-mode json" for the Nucleotide database. You can retrieve multiple records by providing a comma separated list of UIDs without whitespace as follows:

    $ efetch -db nucleotide -id 1677538777,283132453

Transferring UIDs by Piping   An EDirect function like ESearch posts the UIDs of the records matching the query search to the History Server and returns a WebEnv string and a query key to be used by a subsequent EDirect function. The WebEnv string and query key can be transferred to EFetch by piping. The following command line first uses ESearch to find the human refseq BRCA1 gene transcripts and then transfers the ESearch output by piping to EFetch, which retrieves the records found by ESearch.

    $ esearch -db nucleotide -query "brca1[GENE] AND refseq[FILT] AND biomol_rna[PROP] AND human[ORGN]" | efetch

Retrieval Modes   The above outputs of EFetch were displayed in JSON format. The default retrieval mode varies with the database. The retrieval mode of EFetch can be specified by using the "-mode mode" argument. This argument corresponds to the "retmode=" parameter of EFetch E-utilities program discussed in Chapter 4. The records of all databases can be retrieved in json. The possible retrieval modes for some Entrez databases are shown in Table 5.2. For example, to retrieve a nucleotide record in XML format, you can use the following:

    $ efetch -db nucleotide -id 1677538777 -mode xml

Retrieval Formats   Instead of retrieving the entire database record, you may need to retrieve a specific portion of the record or to retrieve the record in a specific format. You can use the "-format format" argument for that purpose. This argument corresponds to the "rettype=" parameter of EFetch E-utilities program discussed in Chapter 4. Since the records of each Entrez database may have different structure, formats may vary by the database as well as shown in Table 5.2.

Sequence databases such as Nucleotide and Protein may have a similar format. For example, assume that you need to retrieve the FASTA sequence of the human PPAR-alpha transcript. You can use the following EFetch command:

    $ efetch -db nucleotide -id 1677538777 -format fasta

TABLE 5.2   EFetch Formats and Modes for Some Entrez Databases

"-db name"	"-mode mode"	"-format format"
All	Json	docsum, full, uid, url, xml
Gene	asn.1, xml	gene_table, tabular
Homologene	asn.1, xml	alignmentscores, fasta, homologene
Mesh	Xml	Full
Pmc	Xml	medline, native
Pubmed	asn.1, xml	abstract, medline, native
Sequence	Xml	acc, est, fasta, fasta_cds_aa, fasta_cds_na, ft, gb, gpc, gss, ipg
Snp	asn.1, xml	chr, docset. Fasta, flt, rsr, native, ssexemplar
Sra	Xml	native, runinfo
Structure	Xml	mmdb, native
Taxonomy	Xml	Native

You can retrieve the FASTA sequence of multiple Nucleotide records. For example, the following command retrieves the FASTA sequences of six refseq BRCA1 gene transcripts:

```
$ esearch -db nucleotide -query "brca1[GENE] AND refseq[FILT] AND biomol_rna[PROP] AND human[ORGN" | efetch -format fasta
```

If you need to retrieve a Nucleotide or Protein record in GenBank format (gb), use "-format gb" as follows:

```
$ efetch -db nucleotide -id 1677538777 -format gb
```

You may also need to retrieve the FASTA sequence of the coding region of a Nucleotide record by using "-format fasta_cds_na"

```
$ efetch -db nucleotide -id 1677538777 -format fasta_cds_na
```

Similarly, you may need to retrieve the FASTA sequence of the translated protein of a Nucleotide record.

```
$ efetch -db nucleotide -id 1677538777 -format fasta_cds_aa
```

Since you are using a Linux environment, you can redirect (save) the standard output (stdout) of any command to a text file by using the ">" symbol or append the output of a command to the end of an existing file by using ">>".

Assume that we wish to find the PubMed articles on the COVID-19 vaccine and then write the abstracts to a text file named "covid19.txt".

```
$ esearch -db pubmed -query "covid-19[TITL] AND vaccine[TITLE]" | efetch -format abstract > covid19.txt
```

You can open the file using any text editor such as vim or nano text editor.

EFech can also retrieve the document summary (docsum) of records by using "-format docsum". However, the structure of this docsum XML format is different from the docsum of Esummary of the E-utilities discussed in Chapter 4. More information is included in EFetch docsum and you will use this format frequently to extract data using Xtract.

Retrieving a Sequence Range   The "-seq_start N1" and "-seq_stop N2" arguments correspond to "seq_start=" and "seq_stop" of the EFetch utilities program in Chapter 4. These two arguments are used with sequence databases such as the Nucleotide and Protein database. They are used to specify a range of sequence to retrieve. Assume that you wish to retrieve the complete sequence of the human BRCA1 gene. First, you need to determine the gene coordinates from the Entrez Gene database. You can either use the Entrez Gene web page or you can find the coordinates using the following command:

$ esearch -db gene -query "brca1[gene] AND human[ORGN]" | efetch | grep Annotation

The output of the above command will be as follows:

Annotation: Chromosome 17 NC_000017.11 (43044295..43125364, complement)

The complete sequence of the human BRCA1 gene is between 43044295 and 43125364 in the reference sequence of chromosome 17 (NC_000017.11). You can use this information to retrieve the complete sequence of the human BRCA1 gene in FASTA format and write the sequence to a file "brca1_gene1.fasta" as follows:

$ efetch -db nucleotide -id NC_000017.11 -seq_start 43044295 -seq_stop 4312536 -format fasta > brca1_gene1.fasta

EFetch can uses "-chr_start N1" and "-chr_stop N2" arguments to specify the sequence range from 0-based coordinates in the gene docsum GenomicInfoType object. We will revisit these two arguments when we discuss the Xtract function. The following example retrieves the FASTA sequence of the human BRCA1 gene using 0-based coordinates.

$ efetch -db nucleotide -id NC_000017.11 -chr_start 43044295 -chr_stop 4312536 -format fasta > brca1_gene2.fasta

Determining DNA Strand   You may need to specify a DNA strand to retrieve the plus DNA strand (5` → 3`) or its complementary strand. The "-strand N" argument is used to determine which strand to use. The "-strand 1" setting is for the plus DNA strand and "-strand 2" is for the minus DNA strand.

ELink

The ELink function is the wrapper for the "elink.fcgi" E-utilities program. For a specific database record, ELink finds the UIDs of the related records from the same database or from one of the other Entrez databases. It requires three mandatory elements: (1) the UIDs of the records to which you need to find the linked records, (2) the database containing these UIDs, and (3) a target database in which you need to find the linked records. The following is the ELink syntax and some arguments.

```
elink  [-help] [-related] [-target dbname] [-name name]
       [-db name] [-id ID(s)] [-cmd command] [-mode ref]
       [-holding provider] [-batch] [-label name]
```

Providing the Record UIDs   The UIDs of the records, to which you need to find the linked records, can be provided either directly by using the "-id" argument or by transferring them with piping from a previous EDirect command.

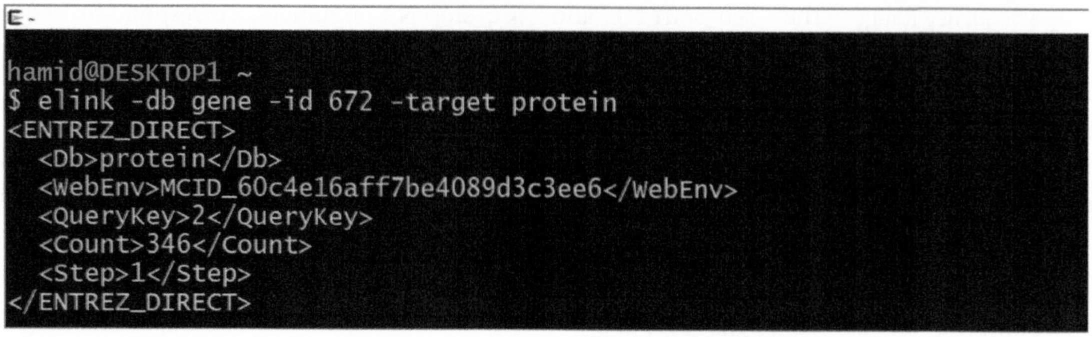

```
E -
hamid@DESKTOP1 ~
$ elink -db gene -id 672 -target protein
<ENTREZ_DIRECT>
  <Db>protein</Db>
  <WebEnv>MCID_60c4e16aff7be4089d3c3ee6</WebEnv>
  <QueryKey>2</QueryKey>
  <Count>346</Count>
  <Step>1</Step>
</ENTREZ_DIRECT>
```

FIGURE 5.12   ELink output.

Providing the Database Containing the UIDs   ELink requires the database that contains the UIDs. The "-db name" argument is used to provide this database. This argument corresponds to the "dbfrom=" parameter of the ELink E-utilities program.

Providing a Target Database   ELink requires a target database, in which it searches for the records related to the records of the specified UIDs. The "-target name" argument is used to provide the target database. It can be any valid Entrez database name.

For example, to find the protein records linked to the human BRCA1 gene, you can use the following ELink command:

$ elink -db gene -id 672 -target protein

Figure 5.12 shows the output of the ELink function that posts the results to the History Server and returns a WebEnv string, a query key, the number of UIDs returned, and the number of steps. The results can be used by a subsequent EDirect function like EFetch.

Instead of providing the "-db" and "-id" parameters, you can use Linux piping to transfer the UIDs returned by a previous EDirect function such as ESearch. The above ELink results can be achieved by the following ESearch and ELink command line:

$ esearch -db gene -query "BRCA1[GENE] AND human[ORGN]" | elink -target protein

You can use EFetch to retrieve the records, sequences, UIDs, feature tables, etc. as mentioned above. The following are some examples for retrieving data from the above protein records linked to the human BRCA1 gene:

(1)   Retrieving the UIDs of linked protein records and writing them to a file:

   $ esearch -db gene -query "BRCA1[GENE] AND human[ORGN]" | elink -target protein | efetch -format uid > linked_prot_uid.txt

(2)   Retrieving the FASTA sequences of the linked protein records and writing them to a file:

   $ esearch -db gene -query "BRCA1[GENE] AND human[ORGN]" | elink -target protein | efetch -format fasta > linked_prot_seqs.fasta

(3)   Retrieving the GenBank records of the linked protein and writing them to a file:

   $ esearch -db gene -query "BRCA1[GENE] AND human[ORGN]" | elink -target protein | efetch -format gb > linked_prot_gb.gb

```
gene_pmc_nucleotide      Full text in PMC (nucleotide)
gene_probe        Probe Links
gene_protein      Protein Links
gene_proteinclusters      Protein Cluster Links
gene_protein_refseq       RefSeq Protein Links
gene_protfam      Protein Family Models
gene_pubmed       PubMed Links
gene_pubmed_citedinomim PubMed (OMIM) Links
gene_pubmed_pmc_nucleotide      PubMed (nucleotide/PMC)
```

FIGURE 5.13   Partial list of the link names of gene database.

```
E -
hamid@DESKTOP1 ~
$ esearch -db gene -query "BRCA1[GENE] AND human[ORGN]" | elink -target protein -name gene_protein_refseq
<ENTREZ_DIRECT>
  <Db>protein</Db>
  <WebEnv>MCID_60c4fa77d40d8c1a24509728</WebEnv>
  <QueryKey>3</QueryKey>
  <Count>5</Count>
  <Step>2</Step>
</ENTREZ_DIRECT>
```

FIGURE 5.14   ELink output.

Filtering Linked Records by Link Names   The results found by ELink are categorized by the link names as discussed in Chapter 4. You can also list the link names of an Entrez database by running "einfo -db name -links". For example, you can run the following to list the link names of the Gene database and save them into a text file:

$ einfo -db gene -links > geneLinks.txt

This will save the possible link names of a gene record to the "genLinks.txt" file, which can be displayed in a text editor as shown in Figure 5.13. Then you can find the right link name and use it with the ELink function to filter a specific type of linked record.

Notice that Figure 5.12 shows that there are 346 protein records linked to the human BRCA1 gene. You can use the "-name name" parameter to filter the linked records to a specific category. For example, to filter the refseq protein records linked to the human BRCA1 gene, you can use "-name gene_protein_refseq" as follows:

$ esearch -db gene -query "BRCA1[GENE] AND human[ORGN]" | elink -target protein -name gene_protein_refseq

Figure 5.14 shows that there are only five refseq protein records linked to the human BRCA1 gene. You can save the FASTA sequences of these proteins in a file as follows:

$ esearch -db gene -query "BRCA1[GENE] AND human[ORGN]" | elink -target protein -name gene_protein_refseq | efetch -format fasta > brca1_prots.fasta

Finding Neighboring Records   The neighbors of a database record are the linked records from the same database. This is usually used with PubMed to find similar articles. The "-related" argument is used to instruct ELink to find the neighbors. You do not need to specify a target database. For example, to find the similar PubMed articles for the article with PMID: 27292874, you can use the following ELink command.

$ elink -db pubmed -id 27292874 -related | efetch -format abstract > hydroxy_rel.txt

The abstracts of the articles similar to PubMed article 27292874 will be saved to a text file.

ELink Command Mode   An ELink command mode instructs ELink to perform a specific function as discussed in Chapter 4. The "-cmd command" argument is used to specify a command mode. The possible options include neighbor, neighbor_score, neighbor_history, acheck, ncheck, lcheck, llinks, llinkslib, and prlinks. These command modes and their descriptions are listed in Table 4.5 in Chapter 4. The following ELink command will provide the list of similar PubMed articles and neighbor scores.

    $ elink -db pubmed -id 27292874 -related -cmd neighbor_score

Finding Article Citations   The "-cited" argument can be used with ELink to find the UID list of the articles that cited a specified article. For example, the following ELink will return the UIDs of the articles that cited the PubMed article with UID 27292874.

    $ elink -db pubmed -id 27292874 -cited | efetch -format uid

EFilter

The EFilter function is used to filter the results posted to the History Server. The filter is enforced by using a number of filter arguments and the results are posted to the History Server to be used by a subsequent EDirect function. The following is the EFilter syntax and some of its arguments.

```
efilter  [-help] [-query str] [-sort field] [-days N]
         [-datetype field] [-mindate date] [-maxdate date]
         [-field field] [-pairs field] [-spell] [-pub type]
         [-feature type] [-location type] [-molecule type]
         [-organism type] [-source type] [-status alive]
         [-type type] [-label name]
```

Query String   The query string is the same as the one discussed above with ESearch. The query is built by following the Entrez conventions that we discussed in Chapter 3. It is provided to EFilter by using the "-query string" argument. Assume that you began your search by using ESearch to find the Nucleotide records of the BRCA1 gene as follows:

    $ esearch -db nucleotide -query "BRCA1 [GENE]"

As of this date, this ESearch command resulted in 6,974 nucleotide records.

   You can use EFilter function to obtain more specific results. Assume that you wish to limit the above ESearch results to the human BRCA1 records only, so you can use the following EFilter:

    $ esearch -db nucleotide -query "BRCA1 [GENE]" | efilter -query "human[ORGN]"

The results after enforcing that filter became 644 Nucleotide records as of this date. You may also think to limit the results to the mRNA nucleotide only so you can add another term to the above filter query:

    $ esearch -db nucleotide -query "BRCA1 [GENE]" | efilter -query "human[ORGN] AND biomol_
    mrna[PROP]"

There are 74 mRNA nucleotide sequences for the human BRCA1. You can keep adding more terms to the query until you reach the results that you are looking for. For example, assume that you want to limit the above results to the RefSeqs only:

$ esearch -db nucleotide -query "BRCA1 [GENE]" | efilter -query "human[ORGN] AND biomol_mrna[PROP] AND refseq [FILT]"

The results now are only five refseq human BRCA1 mRNA records. You may think to print their UIDs, to save their FASTA sequences, or to save their FASTA translated protein sequences as follows respectively:

$ esearch -db nucleotide -query "BRCA1 [GENE]" | efilter -query "human[ORGN] AND biomol_mrna[PROP] AND refseq [FILT]" | efetch -format uid

$ esearch -db nucleotide -query "BRCA1 [GENE]" | efilter -query "human[ORGN] AND biomol_mrna[PROP] AND refseq [FILT]" | efetch -format fasta > brca1_ref_mRNA.fasta

$ esearch -db nucleotide -query "BRCA1 [GENE]" | efilter -query "human[ORGN] AND biomol_mrna[PROP] AND refseq [FILT]" | efetch -format fasta_cds_aa > brca1_prot.fasta

Limiting the Search Query to a Field   In the above examples, you followed the Entrez rules to build a search query. However, EDirect has its own way as well. EFilter function can use "-field field" to limit the search to a specific indexed field. The above human refseq BRCA1 mRNA records can be found using the following EDirect ESearch and EFilter commands:

$ esearch -db nucleotide -query "BRCA1 [GENE]" \
   | efilter -query "human" -field organism \
   | efilter -query "biomol_mrna" \
   | efilter -query "refseq" -field filter

Filtering by Date   You have already learnt how to filter the ESearch results with date. Using EFilter to filter the results by date is exactly the same. If you need to specify a specific date type you can use "-datetype field" argument (e.g. -datetype pdat). You can also use "-mindate date" and "-maxdate date" to specify a date range. The "-sort field" argument can be used to sort the results by an indexed field such as the publishing date (e.g., -sort pdat). The following commands find the PubMed articles on lung cancer published between 2015 and 2020. The results show that there are 40,099 articles.

$ esearch -db pubmed -query "lung cancer[TITL]" | efilter -datetype pdat -mindate 2015 -maxdate 2020 -sort pdat

Filtering by Publication Type for PubMed Results   The "-pub type" argument is a specific filter for the literature databases (PubMed). You can filter PubMed articles by publication types including abstract, clinical, English, free, historical, journal, last_week, last_month, last_year, preprint, review, and structured. In the previous example, the results were 40,099 articles on lung cancer. Assume that you need to limit the results to clinical articles only. You can add the "-pub type" filter to the above command line as follows:

$ esearch -db pubmed -query "lung cancer[TITL]" | efilter -datetype pdat -mindate 2015 -maxdate 2020 -pub clinical

PubMed clinical articles, which were published between 2015 and 2020 on lung cancer, are 4,387 as of this date.

Other Filters   EFilter has other arguments that can be used to enforce filters on the results of a previous EDirect function. Although these filters can be enforced using the conventional Entrez query, those argument can help to create a complex search query and refined results.

The "-feature type" argument is used to filter the results of sequence databases such as the Nucleotide and Protein databases. The possible features include gene, mrna, cds, and mat_peptide.

In the following example, you will search for the EGFR gene that encodes the epidermal growth factor receptor. This gene is one of the lung cancer driver genes. In the following, ESearch will search for EGFR records on the Nucleotide database and the EFilter limits the results to EGFR coding sequences only:

```
$ esearch -db nucleotide -query "EGFR[GENE]" | efilter -feature cds
```

The "-molecule type" argument is used to specify the molecule type. The possible values are: genomic, mrna, trna, rrna, and ncrna. This argument is used for limiting the results to a specific molecule type. In the following example, EFilter limits the ESearch results to EGFR mRNA records only.

```
$ esearch -db nucleotide -query "EGFR[GENE]" | efilter -molecule mrna
```

The "-source type" argument is used to filter the results by the source of the sequence records. The possible values are: genbank, insd, pdb, pir, refseq, swissprot, and tpa. Assume that you wish to limit the search results to the reference EGFR nucleotide records only; you can use the following:

```
$ esearch -db nucleotide -query "EGFR[GENE]" | efilter -source refseq
```

You may also wish to find the protein records that were collected from the Protein Data Bank Database (PDB) to make sure that they have 3D structure. In the following, ESearch searches for human protein records whose titles include "nuclear receptor" and then EFilter limits the results to those that were collected on the Entrez Protein database from the Protein Data Bank.

```
$ esearch -db protein -query "nuclear receptor[TITL] AND human[ORGN]" | efilter -source pdb
```

The "-organism type" argument is used to limit the results by an organism type. The possible organism types are animals, archaea, bacteria, eukaryotes, fungi, human, insects, mammals, plants, prokaryotes, protists, rodents, and viruses. For example, the results of the above search include the refseq EGFR nucleotide records of various organisms. You can limit the results to the records of humans only as follows:

```
$ esearch -db nucleotide -query "EGFR[GENE]" | efilter -source refseq -organism human
```

The "-type type" argument limits the results by the type of a gene whether it is a coding gene or a pseudogene. There are two possible types: coding or pseudo. In the following example, you will search for BRAF, which is the gene that encodes the B-Raf protein. Some mutations in this gene are associated with cancer. In the following, ESearch will search for human BRAF gene records and then EFilter limits the results to BRAF human pseudogene only.

```
$ esearch -db gene -query "BRAF*[GENE] AND human[ORGN]" | efilter -type pseudo | efetch -format uid
```

The "-status alive" argument is used to limit the results to current records only. The results of the previous example include some obsolete records. In the following example, EFilter limits the results to the current records only.

$ esearch -db gene -query "BRAF AND human[ORGN]" | efilter -type pseudo -status alive| efetch -format uid

The "-location type" argument is used to limit the results by the location of the DNA. The type is an organelle name such as mitochondrion, chloroplast, plasmid, and plastid, etc. In the following example, ESearch searches for *Escherichia coli* protein records, whose titles include "streptomycin resistance" and then EFilter limits the results to only proteins localized in the plasmid. The results then were written to a file.

$ esearch -db protein -query "streptomycin resistance[TITL] AND Escherichia coli[ORGN]"| efilter -location plasmid |efetch -format uid > strep_coli_plasmid.txt

Labeling EFilter Steps   The "-label label" argument can be used to add a label to each EFilter step. The step labels can be used to combine the filters using Boolean operators (AND, OR, and NOT) as explained above.

$ esearch -db nucleotide -query "BRCA1[GENE]" \
   | efilter -query "human" -field organism -label org\
   | efilter -query "biomol_mrna" -label biomol \
   | efilter -query "refseq" -field filter -label ref

Epost

Epost is a wrapper function for the epost.fcgi E-utilities program. It is used to upload a batch of UIDs of an Entrez database to the History Server and returns a query key and a Web Environment string to be used by a subsequent EDirect function. EPost syntax and arguments are as follows:

```
$ epost [-help] [-db name] [-id ID(s)] [-format fmt]
        [-input filename] [-label name]
```

The "-db name" argument provides the database that contains the batch of the UIDs. It can be any valid Entrez database. Use "einfo -dbs" to list the valid database names.

The "-id IDs" argument is used to pass the list of UIDs to EPost to upload them to the History Server. The list is comma separated without a whitespace. Consider the following example, which posts a number of PubMed UIDs (PMIDs) to the History Server.

$ epost -db pubmed -id 29990125,27292874,27066500,29297322

EDirect provides the "-input filename" argument to import the UID list from a text file instead of using the "-id IDs" argument. This argument adds a new feature to the E-utilities EPost. The text file that contains the UID list can be created with any text editor such as vim and nano text editor.

The UIDs are entered in a single column; each UID in a new line as follows:

29990125
27292874
27066500
29297322

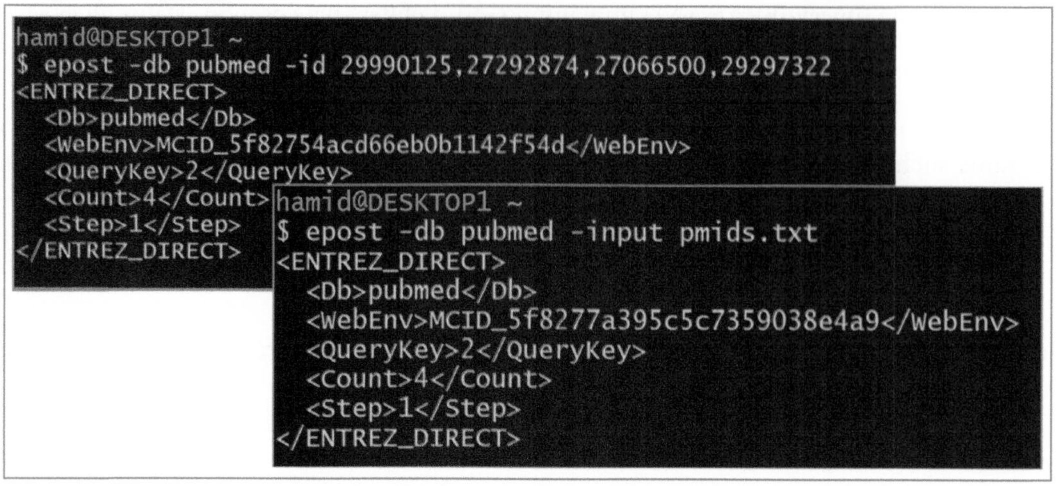

```
hamid@DESKTOP1 ~
$ epost -db pubmed -id 29990125,27292874,27066500,29297322
<ENTREZ_DIRECT>
  <Db>pubmed</Db>
  <WebEnv>MCID_5f82754acd66eb0b1142f54d</WebEnv>
  <QueryKey>2</QueryKey>
  <Count>4</Count>  hamid@DESKTOP1 ~
  <Step>1</Step>   $ epost -db pubmed -input pmids.txt
</ENTREZ_DIRECT>    <ENTREZ_DIRECT>
                      <Db>pubmed</Db>
                      <WebEnv>MCID_5f8277a395c5c7359038e4a9</WebEnv>
                      <QueryKey>2</QueryKey>
                      <Count>4</Count>
                      <Step>1</Step>
                    </ENTREZ_DIRECT>
```

FIGURE 5.15   EPost output.

Enter the above PubMed UIDs in a text file, save it as "pmids.txt", and then you can use the following EPost command to post those UIDs to the History Server.

$ epost -db pubmed -input pmids.txt

Figure 5.15 shows the outputs of the above two examples. After posting the UIDs to the History Server, EPost returns a WebEnv string, a query key, the number of records posted, and the step number.

You can add a label to the EPost step with the "-label name" argument as discussed above.

$ epost -db pubmed -input pmids.txt -label step1

The "-format format" argument specifies the input UID format. The possible values are "uid"' and "acc" when applicable.

Remember that the UIDs are posted to the History Server to be used by other subsequent EDirect functions. In real life and if you work in a project that requires literature review or dealing with searching in massive data, you may save a large number of UIDs in a text file and then you will need to upload those UIDs to the History Server to retrieve data from them.

$ epost -db pubmed -input pmids.txt | efetch -format abstract

Nquire

The Nquire function creates a URL to query a web server based on your specified request. This function can provide extensibility to EDirect as it can be used to bypass the EDirect commands and to create an E-utilities API URL manually. Nquire also allows users to incorporate non-E-utilities API calls onto your EDirect scripts to obtain data from other parameter-based or common gate interface (CGI) services. The NQuire syntax and argument are as follows:

```
nquire [-help] [-get] [-url URL] [-eutils] [component ...] [-tag value ...]
```

Using NQuire to Bypass EDirect   You can use NQuire to bypass EDirect and use the E-utilities program directly. You can use the "-url URL" argument to specify the E-utilities URL address. For example, assume that you wish to search the PubMed database for articles on lung cancer. You can use the following NQuire command:

$ nquire -url "https://eutils.ncbi.nlm.nih.gov/entrez/eutils" esearch.fcgi -db pubmed -term "lung cancer[TITL]"

By bypassing EDirect, you can use the same E-utilities program parameters but with EDirect rules. As you see the whitespace is allowed. The following example is to fetch a nucleotide record.

$ nquire -url "https://eutils.ncbi.nlm.nih.gov/entrez/eutils" efetch.fcgi -db nucleotide -id 1677538777

Instead of providing the E-utilities URL, you can use "-utils" arguments as a shorthand for "-url https://eutils.ncbi.nlm.nih.gov/entrez/eutils". The above examples can be rewritten as follows:

$ nquire -eutils esearch.fcgi -db pubmed -term "lung cancer[TITL]"
$ nquire -eutils esearch.fcgi -db pubmed -term "lung cancer[TITL]"

Using NQuire to Retrieve Data from an External Server   The "-get" argument is used to send a request for retrieving data from a specified web resource. This parameter can be used to send a SPARQL query to request specific information. SPARQL is a query language that retrieves and manipulates data stored in Resource Description Framework (RDF) format. In the following example, Nquire sends a request to https://query.wikidata.org/ to request the number of humans in Wikidata.

$ nquire -get "https://query.wikidata.org/sparql" -query "SELECT (COUNT(?item) AS?count) WHERE {?item wdt:P31/wdt:P279* wd:Q5 .}"

In the following example, you will use NQuire to retrieve information of a breast cancer pathway with a "WP4262" Wikipathways id.

$ nquire -get -j2x -url "https://mygene. info/v3" query -q "pathway.wikipathways.id: WP4262" -fetch_ all true

Xtract

The Xtract function is not one of the E-utilities programs, but was added by EDirect to extract data from the XML formatted output generated by EFetch function. The following is the Xtraxt syntax and some of its arguments:

```
xtract [-input filename] [-pattern expr] [-group expr]
       [-block expr] [-subset expr] [-ret str] [-tab str]
       [-sep str] [-pfx str] [-sfx str] [-clr] [-lbl str]
       [-element element] [-first element] [-last element]
       [-NAME] [-title element] [-terms element] [-format fmt]
```

Xtract has numerous arguments. Instead of listing and describing all arguments we will focus only on the most commonly used. However, if you need to learn about the other arguments and their use, you can simply run the following command:

$ xtract -help

The Xtract arguments are divided into functional categories, including: processing flags, exploration argument hierarchy, conditional execution, string constraints, numeric constraints, format customization, element selection, numeric processing, string processing, phrase processing, phrase filtering, sequence coordinates, command generator, and miscellaneous parameters. Understanding the use of these arguments will help users to create efficient tabular reports from data fetched by EFetch from Entrez databases. However, the most commonly used arguments for tabular report are "-pattern" argument, which creates rows, and "-element" argument, which controls the placement of data into columns. We will discuss some of the Xtract arguments in worked examples.

XML Structure of Entrez Database Records and Data Types

From now on and until the end of this chapter we will focus on extracting data from EFetch output. The EDirect functions including ESearch, Elink, and Epost upload their results to the History Server. EFetch can retrieve data from the records returned by those three EDirect functions in several formats depending on the database of records. EFetch can retrieve records from all Entrez databases in Extensible Markup Language (XML) format, which is a markup format created by the World Wide Web Consortium (W3C) to define a syntax for encoding documents that both humans and machines could read. The structure of document is defined by the XML tags that are organized in hierarchical structure. Data can be extracted easily from an XML formatted text. Xtract is a Perl script and command-line program developed by NCBI to extract data from any XML document. The XML data can either transferred to Xtract function by piping "|" from the EFetch function (e.g., efetch … | extract …) or can be provided as a file to Xtract using the "-input filename" argument (e.g., xtract -input test.xml …). For example, the following retrieves a PubMed article from PubMed data as XML and writes to an XML file named "pub_29990125.xml".

```
$ efetch -db pubmed -id 29990125 -format xml > pub_29990125.xml
```

You can open the file and study its content and structure carefully. Any database has its XML elements defined by tags but the XML elements are self-defined and organized in similar structures as shown in Figure 5.16, which includes the general XML structure of PubMed, Gene, and GenBank records. An XML document has root opening and closing elements as indicated by (A) that may contain multiple database records. Each database record is also contained between opening and closing elements as indicated by (B). There may be multiple nested elements to include multiple types of data.

The data of a database record are organized in XML elements. The element names describe the content of the element, and the structure describes the relationship between the elements. There are two kinds of data in an XML document:

(1) The data that is between the opening and closing element such as the "Journal Article" shown below:

<PublicationType>**Journal Article**</PublicationType>

(2) The attribute data that is found within the opening element tag. Such data will be in the form of "attribute=value" such as shown below. The attribute is "UI" and the attribute value is "D016428":

<PublicationType **UI="D016428"**>Journal Article</PublicationType>

The extraction of data from a database record depends on the structure of that record. Therefore, before extracting data you need to display and study the structure of the XML document and the elements that store the data you need to extract. Soon you will learn how to extract these two types of data using Xtract.

Identifying Patterns and Elements in an XML Document

For very basic extraction of data from an XML document using the Xtract function, you need to provide two things: a pattern that serves as a container for each record in the document and an element that stores the data.

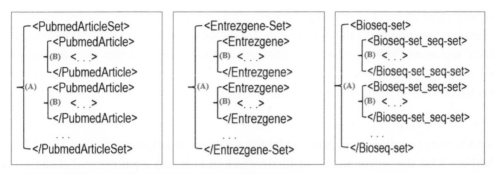

FIGURE 5.16   XML root element of PubMed, Gene, and GenBank records.

```
<PubmedArticleSet>
<PubmedArticle>
    <MedlineCitation Status="MEDLINE" Owner="NLM">
        <PMID Version="1">29990125</PMID>
        <Article PubModel="Print-Electronic">
            <Journal>
                <ISSN IssnType="Electronic">1557-9964</ISSN>
                <JournalIssue CitedMedium="Internet">
                    <Volume>15</Volume>
                    <Issue>6</Issue>
                    <PubDate>
                        <MedlineDate>2018 Nov-Dec</MedlineDate>
                    </PubDate>
                </JournalIssue>
                <Title>Journal title</Title>
                <ISOAbbreviation>Journal abbreviation</ISOAbbreviation>
            </Journal>
            <ArticleTitle>The article title is here</ArticleTitle>
            <Pagination>
                <MedlinePgn>1844-1852</MedlinePgn>
            </Pagination>
            <ELocationID EIdType="doi" ValidYN="Y">Number is here</ELocationID>
            <Abstract>
                <AbstractText>The abstract is here</AbstractText>
            </Abstract>
```

FIGURE 5.17   Partial XML document of PubMed database.

When an XML document of a database contains multiple records, XML elements with the same names (parent and child elements) will be repeated for each record. For example, for the PubMed database, "PubmedArticle" element (Figure 5.16) is a parent element that contains multiple nested elements that store data. The article data are contained in multiple child elements. This parent element ("PubmedArticle") is repeated for each PubMed article therefore, it creates a pattern that can be provided to the Xtract function in the "-pattern pattern" argument. Figure 5.17 shows a partial XML document of the PubMed database. Notice that <PubmedArticleSet> is the root element for the entire XML document. Therefore, it does not create a pattern. But <PubmedArticle> is the parent element for each article in the XML document. Therefore, it creates a pattern. In Figure 5.17, you can also notice that <MedlineCitation> is a child element for <PubmedArticle> but a parent element of <PMID>. You can also notice that <PMID> contains data "<PMID Version="1">29990125</PMID>. So, <PMID> is a pure child element that contains data and it is not a parent for any element. The data contained between the opening and closing tags of a pure element can be extracted using the Xtract function by providing the name of these elements to the "-element element" argument.

You can also notice that <Article> is a child of <MedlineCitation>, and that <Journal>, <ArticleTitle>, <Pigination>, <ElocationID, and <Abstract> are children of <Article>. However, <Journal> is a parent for multiple pure child elements that contain data.

Generally, any child element containing data can be provided to the Xtract function in the "-element element" argument. Now you know that for the PubMed database, you can provide <PubmedArticle> to the "-pattern pattern" argument since it contains an entire article and the element that contains data such as PMID, Title, ISOAbbreviation, ArticleTitle, ELocationID, AbstractText, etc. as an element since they contain data. You can open the XML document of any database and identify patterns and elements that store data.

Extracting XML Child Elements

In the previous section you discovered how to identify a pattern and elements for the Xtract function. Try to open any PubMed XML document and study its structure and identify a pattern and elements. For example, you can run the following:

```
$ efetch -db pubmed -id 29990125 -format xml > pub_29990125.xml
$ vim pub_29990125.xml
```

Xtract extracts data from XML document retrieved by EFetch by providing a pattern in the "-pattern" argument and the element, from which you wish to extract data, in the "element" argument. Assume that after studying the above PubMed structure you decided to search for PubMed review articles on the COVID-19 vaccine and to create a tabular report including the PMID and the article title. You can use the following EDirect commands:

```
$ esearch -db pubmed -query "COVID-19 vaccine[TITL] and review[FILT]" \
  | efetch -format xml \
  | xtract -pattern PubmedArticle -element PMID ArticleTitle > covid19.txt
```

This will extract PMIDs and the article titles as shown in Figure 5.18.

Sometimes, there are multiple elements with the same name but they have different parents. For example, in PubMed records, there are multiple elements with the names: Year, Month, Day as shown in Figure 5.19.

```
34064726    Targeting COVID-19 Vaccine Hesitancy in Minority Populations in the US: Implications for Herd Immunit
34019911    Covid-19 vaccine- induced thrombosis and thrombocytopenia-a commentary on an important and practicala.
34019801    Ongoing and future COVID-19 vaccine clinical trials: challenges and opportunities.
34015363    The COVID-19 vaccine development: A pandemic paradigm.
33987882    COVID-19 vaccine-associated immune thrombosis and thrombocytopenia (VITT): Diagnostic and therapeu
33973199    The COVID-19 Vaccine Landscape.
33945504    Is complement the culprit behind COVID-19 vaccine-related adverse reactions?
33936564    An overview of current COVID-19 vaccine platforms.
33913206    Potential 3-chymotrypsin-like cysteine protease cleavage sites in the coronavirus polyproteins pp1a
33907509    Review of Covid-19 vaccine clinical trials - A puzzle with missing pieces.
33877041    COVID-19 Vaccine Concerns: Fact or Fiction?
33820678    COVID-19 vaccine challenges: What have we learned so far and what remains to be done?
33814753    Adverse Events Reported From COVID-19 Vaccine Trials: A Systematic Review.
33801651    A Rapid Review of COVID-19 Vaccine Prioritization in the U.S.: Alignment between Federal Guidance ice.
33746182    COVID-19 vaccine research focusses on safety, efficacy, immunoinformatics, and vaccine production wer.
33728097    Current Status of COVID-19 Vaccine Development: Focusing on Antigen Design and Clinical Trials on ges.
```

FIGURE 5.18 Partial output of PubMed extracted data.

```
<DateCompleted>
    <Year>2019</Year>
    <Month>07</Month>
    <Day>01</Day>
</DateCompleted>
<DateRevised>
    <Year>2019</Year>
    <Month>07</Month>
    <Day>01</Day>
</DateRevised>
```

FIGURE 5.19 Partial PubMed XML document.

```
34064726    2021  2021  2021  2021  2021  2021  2021  2021
34019911    2021  2021  2021  2021  2021  2021
34019801    2021  2021  2021  2021  2021  2021  2021  2021
34015363    2021  2021  2021  2021  2021  2021  2021  2021
33987882    2021  2021  2021  2021  2021  2021  2021  2021
33973199    2021  2021  2021  2021  2021  2021
33945504    2021  2021  2021  2022  2021  2021  2021
33936564    2021  2021  2021  2021  2021  2021  2021  2021
33913206    2021  2021  2021  2021  2021  2021  2021  2021
33907509    2021  2021  2021  2021  2021  2021  2021  2021
33877041    2021  2021  2021  2021  2021  2021
33820678    2021  2021  2021  2020  2021  2021  2021  2021
33814753    2021  2021  2021  2021  2021  2021  2021  2021
33801651    2021  2021  2021  2021  2021  2021  2021  2021
33746182    2021  2021  2021  2021  2021  2021  2021
33728097    2021  2021  2021  2021  2021  2021  2021  2021
```

FIGURE 5.20 Partial Xtract output from PMID and year.

```
33034449    2020
33012020    2021
32978861    2020
32893468    2021
32887954    2020
```

FIGURE 5.21 Extracting elements.

If you use Year, Month, or Day as the element in the "-element" argument you may get multiple values for a single record. Try to extract PMID and Year as follows:

```
$ esearch -db pubmed -query "COVID-19 vaccine[TITL] and review[FILT]" \
  | efetch -format xml \
  | xtract -pattern PubmedArticle -element PMID Year
```

Figure 5.20 shows each row has a single PMID but has multiple columns of year. The reason is that the document contains several elements with the name "Year" as shown in Figure 5.20.

However, you may need a specific date type instead of all dates in the document. For example, assume that you need only the <DateCompleted>. To show only <Year> whose parent is <DateCompleted> you need to provide the full path to the "-element" argument as "-element parent/child" as follows:

```
$ esearch -db pubmed -query "COVID-19 vaccine[TITL] and review[FILT]" \
  | efetch -format xml \
  | xtract -pattern PubmedArticle -element PMID DateCompleted/Year
```

This will provide a single column for Year as shown in Figure 5.21.

Another example, you can open any Taxonomy XML document and study its structure. Assume that you wish to create a tabular report for all *Salmonella* showing the TaxID and the scientific name. You can use the following to display the TaxID and the names of all *Salmonella* species and subspecies:

```
$ esearch -db taxonomy -query "salmonella *" \
  |efetch -format xml \
  |xtract -pattern Taxon -element TaxId ScientificName
```

You can use Xtract function to extract data from any Entrez database record. However, you need to study the structure of the XML document first to identify a pattern and elements.

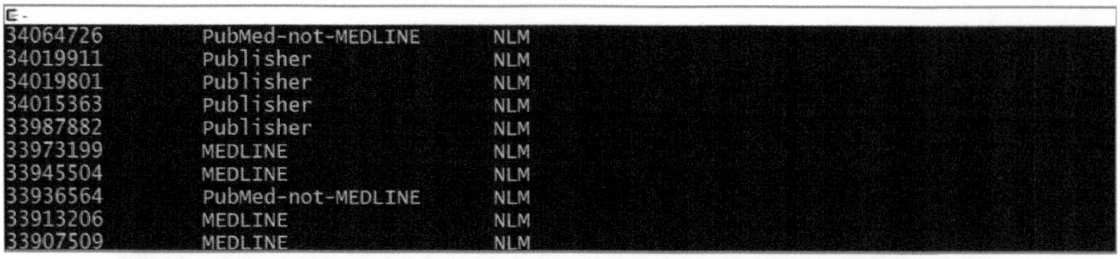

FIGURE 5.22   Extracting attributes.

Extracting XML Attribute

You may need to extract attribute data from the XML document of an Entrez database. Above, we described the attribute data as the data contained within an opening element tag and it is in the "attribute=value" form as follows.

<PubmedArticle>

<MedlineCitation Status="MEDLINE" Owner="NLM">

…………….. ..

</PubmedArticle>

The attribute data are extracted by using "xtract -element element@attribute" form, where the "element" is the element that contains the attribute and the "attribute" in the attribute name. For example, to extract the PMID, "Status" attribute and "Owner" attribute you can use the following (Figure 5.22):

$ esearch -db pubmed -query "COVID-19 vaccine[TITL] and review[FILT]" \

| efetch -format xml \

| xtract -pattern PubmedArticle -element PMID MedlineCitation@Status MedlineCitation@Owner

Formatting Columns

The Xtract function also has format customization arguments such as "-tab" and "-sep", which are used to format the spaces between columns. We will continue with the PubMed database as an example; but, you can apply this to any Entrez database XML document.

An article may have multiple authors, which are organized in the PubMed XML document as shown in Figure 5.23. Each author's last name, forename, and initial is under <Author> as a parent element.

Assume that you need to extract the PMID, completion year, and authors of some PubMed articles returned by ESearch. You can run the following command line (Figure 5.24):

$ esearch -db pubmed -query "Hamid D. Ismail[AUTH]" \

|efetch -format xml \

|xtract -pattern PubmedArticle -element PMID DateCompleted/Year LastName

Notice that PMID and Year have a single column each but LastName has several multiple columns, although only one LastName has been defined in the "-element" argument. Of course, the reason is there are multiple LastName data elemets. Xtract has arguments for formatting the space between columns of different elements such as PMID and Year and also for the spaces between the columns of a single element such as LastName.

For formatting the space between columns of different elements you can use the "-tab" argument, which is used to create a separator between columns (PMID, Year, and LastName (as all) but not between the columns of LastName. In the following example, you will place "**" between the major columns (Figure 5.25).

```
            <AuthorList CompleteYN="Y">
                <Author ValidYN="Y">
                    <LastName>Ismail</LastName>
                    <ForeName>Hamid D</ForeName>
                    <Initials>HD</Initials>
                </Author>
                <Author ValidYN="Y">
                    <LastName>Saigo</LastName>
                    <ForeName>Hiroto</ForeName>
                    <Initials>H</Initials>
                </Author>
                <Author ValidYN="Y">
                    <LastName>Kc</LastName>
                    <ForeName>Dukka B</ForeName>
                    <Initials>DB</Initials>
                </Author>
            </AuthorList>
```

FIGURE 5.23   Partial PubMed record in XML format.

```
29990125      2019     Ismail  Saigo  Kc
29297322      2018     White   Ismail Saigo   Kc
27292874      2017     Ismail  Newman Kc
27066500      2016     Ismail  Jones  Kim     Newman  Kc
```

FIGURE 5.24   Xtract tabular report.

```
29990125**2019**Ismail  Saigo   Kc
29297322**2018**White   Ismail  Saigo   Kc
27292874**2017**Ismail  Newman  Kc
27066500**2016**Ismail  Jones   Kim     Newman  Kc
```

FIGURE 5.25   Xtract formatted report (placing a separator between major columns).

```
29990125**2019**Ismail|Saigo|Kc
29297322**2018**White|Ismail|Saigo|Kc
27292874**2017**Ismail|Newman|Kc
27066500**2016**Ismail|Jones|Kim|Newman|Kc
```

FIGURE 5.26   Xtract formatted report (placing a separator between elements of a single column).

```
$ esearch -db pubmed -query "Hamid D. Ismail[AUTH]" \
|efetch -format xml \
|xtract -pattern PubmedArticle -tab '**' -element PMID DateCompleted/Year LastName
```

For formatting the space between the columns of a single element like LastName, you can use "-sep" argument. Assume that you need to add "|" as a separator between the LastName columns. You can use the following (Figure 5.26):

```
$ esearch -db pubmed -query "Hamid D. Ismail[AUTH]" \
|efetch -format xml \
|xtract -pattern PubmedArticle -tab '**' -sep '|' -element PMID DateCompleted/Year LastName
```

Both "-tab" and "-sep" help in formatting the report for better readability. In the following example, the tabular report is formatted by adding three whitespaces between major columns and "/" between the last names (Figure 5.27).

FIGURE 5.27   Xtract formatted report (placing a separator between major columns and elements of a single column).

FIGURE 5.28   Xtract report (messy report).

FIGURE 5.29   Xtract report (organized report).

$ esearch -db pubmed -query "Hamid D. Ismail[AUTH]" \

|efetch -format xml \

|xtract -pattern PubmedArticle -tab ' ' -sep '/' -element PMID DateCompleted/Year LastName

Grouping of Child Elements by Parents

Referring to the author elements in Figure 5.23, assume that you wish to create a report including the PMID, last name, forename, and initials of all authors on the four PubMed articles. You may run the following (Figure 5.28):

$ esearch -db pubmed -query "Hamid D. Ismail" \

|efetch -format xml \

|xtract -pattern PubmedArticle -element PMID LastName Forename Initials

However, the report is not as it is intended to be, as the last name, first name, and initial of each author are not grouped together. For example, the first row should be like this: Ismail HD, Saigo H, and KC DB. This can be fixed by grouping the information of the same author together with the '-block' argument, which groups the elements by their parent element. The last name, first name, and initial for each author together can be grouped by "Author" using "-block Author" with the Xtract function. The "-block" argument works the same way as "-pattern"; the only difference is that "-block" groups columns inside "-pattern" (Figure 5.29).

$ esearch -db pubmed -query "Hamid D. Ismail" | efetch -format xml | xtract -pattern PubmedArticle -element PMID -block Author -element LastName Initials

You can notice that the last name, forename, and initials have been grouped by "Author". You can format the above results by using the "-tab" and "-sep" arguments, which come before the "-element" argument. When you use "-tab" and "-sep" before "-element" of "-block", the grouped elements must be separated by a comma and no space as follows (Figure 5.30):

```
29990125    Ismail,HD    Saigo,H    Kc,DB
29297322    White,C    Ismail,HD    Saigo,H    Kc,DB
27292874    Ismail,HD    Newman,RH    Kc,DB
27066500    Ismail,HD    Jones,A    Kim,JH    Newman,RH    Kc,DB
```

FIGURE 5.30   Xtract report (formatted report).

```
Christensen,BC
Mouliere,F          0000-0001-7043-0514
Chandrananda,D      0000-0002-8834-9500
Piskorz,AM          0000-0002-7171-1120
Moore,EK            0000-0002-2728-3202
Morris,J
Ahlborn,LB
Mair,R
Goranova,T          0000-0003-3848-2968
Marass,F            0000-0002-8993-7320
Heider,K            0000-0003-4035-1668
Wan,JCM             0000-0003-0001-1802
Supernat,A
Hudecova,I          0000-0003-3823-9896
Gounaris,I
```

FIGURE 5.31   Xtract report (without "-if").

$ esearch -db pubmed -query "Hamid D. Ismail" \

|efetch -format xml \

|xtract -pattern PubmedArticle -tab ' ' -element PMID -block Author -tab ' ' -sep ',' -element LastName, Initials

Using Xtract Conditional Arguments with Elements

The conditional expressions are the features of the programming languages. With EDirect Xtract, conditional arguments (-if, -unless, -and, -or, -else, and -position) can be used to limit the output to only data that match the condition specified by the conditional argument. The following example shows the use of the "-if" argument. Assume that you wish to search for PubMed articles on breast cancer, but you need to create a report that lists only the authors who have identifiers. The following ESearch command returns all UIDs records that satisfy the search query. Some authors may not have identifiers, which are unique numbers assigned to an author (e.g., ORCID). Before using the "-if" argument with Xtract, you run the following command line to see the output before implementing that conditional argument (Figure 5.31):

$ esearch -db pubmed -query "breast cancer AND mutations AND machine learning" \

|efetch -format xml \

|xtract -pattern Author -sep "," -element LastName, Initials Identifier

You can notice that there are some authors who do not have identifiers. To limit the list of the authors to only those who have identifiers you can use "-if" conditional argument with Xtract. The "-if" should be before the "-element" argument as follows (Figure 5.32):

$ esearch -db pubmed -query "breast cancer AND mutations AND machine learning" \

|efetch -format xml \

|xtract -pattern Author -if Identifier -sep "," -element LastName, Initials Identifier

```
Funnell,T          0000-0003-1612-5644
Zhang,AW           0000-0002-7606-089X
Mouliere,F         0000-0001-7043-0514
Chandrananda,D     0000-0002-8834-9500
Piskorz,AM         0000-0002-7171-1120
Moore,EK           0000-0002-2728-3202
```

FIGURE 5.32   Xtract report (with "-if").

```
33311458   MEDLINE   Deep learning-based cross-classifications reveal conserved spatial be
33307492   MEDLINE   Understanding the organ tropism of metastatic breast cancer through t
33203356   MEDLINE   The MOBSTER R package for tumour subclonal deconvolution from bulk DNA
33121438   MEDLINE   Feature selection algorithm based on dual correlation filters for can
32967061   MEDLINE   A lncRNA prognostic signature associated with immune infiltration and
32723974   MEDLINE   Identifying CpG methylation signature as a promising biomarker for re
32604779   MEDLINE   Concise Polygenic Models for Cancer-Specific Identification of Drug-S
32594207   MEDLINE   Improved characterization of sub-centimeter enhancing breast masses o
32429832   MEDLINE   Direct comparison shows that mRNA-based diagnostics incorporate infor
32366478   MEDLINE   A Premalignant Cell-Based Model for Functionalization and Classificat
32245405   MEDLINE   pyCancerSig: subclassifying human cancer with comprehensive single nu
```

FIGURE 5.33   Using string constraints.

Figure 5.32 shows only the authors that have ORCID number. Xtract conditional arguments are very useful in creating advanced reports from Entrez database records.

Using Xtract Conditional Arguments with String Constraints

The string constraint arguments of the Xtract function can be used with the conditional arguments to limit the results to those that meet a specified condition. The string constraint arguments of Xtract include "-equals", "-contains", "-starts-with", "-ends-with", and "-is-not".

In the following example, the "Status" attribute in the PubMed MedlineCitation element is used to restrict the results. There are different MedlineCitation statuses, which include In-Data-Review, In-Process, MEDLINE, OLDMEDLINE, PubMed-not-MEDLINE, Publisher, and Completed (see Figure 5.17).

Assume that you wish to extract the PMIDs Status, and the article title of the PubMed records but you need to limit the results to those with MEDLINE status (i.e., <MedlineCitation Status= "MEDLINE">). Since PMID is a child element for MedlineCitation it can be extracted by "MedlineCitation/PMID" and Status is an attribute in MedlineCitation tag so it can be extracted by MedlineCitation@Status. To limits the PubMed records to only those with MEDLINE status, you can use "-if" and "-equals" arguments as "-if MedlineCitation@Status -equals MEDLINE" before "-element" argument as follows (Figure 5.33).

```
$ esearch -db pubmed -query "breast cancer AND mutations AND machine learning" \
    |efetch -format xml \
    |xtract -pattern PubmedArticle -if MedlineCitation@Status -equals MEDLINE \
        -element MedlineCitation/PMID title MedlineCitation@Status ArticleTitle
```

Figure 5.33 shows that only the PMIDs and titles of the articles with MEDLINE status were printed.

The "-equals" in the above example can be replaced by any of the other string constraint arguments. The following extracts data from PubMed records, in which the author affiliation is in the United States.

```
$ esearch -db pubmed -query "breast cancer AND mutations AND machine learning" \
    |efetch -format xml \
    |xtract -pattern PubmedArticle -if Affiliation -contains USA \
```

```
<ArticleIdList>
    <ArticleId IdType="pubmed">32604779</ArticleId>
    <ArticleId IdType="pii">biom10060963</ArticleId>
    <ArticleId IdType="doi">10.3390/biom10060963</ArticleId>
    <ArticleId IdType="pmc">PMC7356608</ArticleId>
```

FIGURE 5.34 ArticleIdList nested elements.

```
30761181        Frontiers in genetics
30704458        BMC medical genomics
30683142        Breast cancer research : BCR
30404863        Science translational medicine
30230586        Journal of cellular biochemistry
30071039        PloS one
29949979        Bioinformatics (Oxford, England)
29616660        Physics in medicine and biology
29322935        BMC medical genomics
29277326        Biochimica et biophysica acta. Molecular basis of disease
29215763        Cancer science
29168353        Cancer medicine
29162841        Scientific reports
28389083        Computational biology and chemistry
27912731        BMC bioinformatics
27902695        PLoS computational biology
27587275        BMC systems biology
27197545        Briefings in bioinformatics
27121612        Journal of the American Medical Informatics Association : JAMIA
```

FIGURE 5.35 Partial output (using "-if -X -or").

-element MedlineCitation/PMID Medline Citation@Status ArticleTitle

The conditional and constrain arguments can be combined. To show this, study the article list (ArticleIdList) in the PubMed XML document in Figure 5.34. This section of a PubMed article XML document includes the unique identifier of the articles for different literature resources (PubMed, PII, DOI, PMC).

Assume that you wish to extract the PMIDs and journal titles of the PubMed articles that are either "pmc" or "doi". When you need the results that match either one of two conditions, you can use the "-if -X -or" argument, where "-X" represents any string constrain argument (Figure 5.35).

```
$ esearch -db pubmed -query "breast cancer AND mutations AND machine learning" \
  |efetch -format xml \
  |xtract -pattern PubmedArticle -if ArticleId@IdType -equals pmc -or ArticleId@IdType \
        -equals doi -element MedlineCitation/PMID Title
```

You will use "-and" argument if you wish to extract the results that match both conditions. The following script will extract the PMIDs and journal title of PubMed articles that are both "pmc" and "doi".

```
$ esearch -db pubmed -query "breast cancer AND mutations AND machine learning" \
  |efetch -format xml \
  |xtract -pattern PubmedArticle -if ArticleId@IdType -equals pmc -and ArticleId@IdType \
        -equals doi -element MedlineCitation/PMID Title
```

The "-position first/last/any integer" conditional arguments can be used with the "-block" argument to limit the extraction to only the first (-position first) or last (-position last) value in a block of values or you

```
31077166	Cheloshkina	Poptsova
31056464	Gautam	Jaiswal	Aittokallio	Al-Ali	Wennerberg
31014259	Ruffalo	Bar-Joseph
30988514	Gulhan	Lee	Melloni	Cortés-Ciriano	Park
30982079	Jordan	Patil	Suresh	Park	Mosse	Lemmon	Radhakrishnan
30794536	Funnell	Zhang	Grewal	McKinney	Bashashati	Wang	Shah
30761181	Luo	Ding	Lei	Wu
30704458	Chiu	Chen	Zhang	Zhang	Gorthi	Wang	Huang	Chen
30683142	Chen	Wang	Salas	Miller	Mark	Marotti	Kettenbach	Cheng	Chris
30404863	Mouliere	Chandrananda	Piskorz	Moore	Morris	Ahlborn	Mair	Gorar
```

FIGURE 5.36 Extracting PubMed authors without "-position first".

```
31077166	Cheloshkina
31056464	Gautam
31014259	Ruffalo
30988514	Gulhan
30982079	Jordan
30794536	Funnell
30761181	Luo
30704458	Chiu
30683142	Chen
30404863	Mouliere
```

FIGURE 5.37 Extracting the last name of PubMed article first author using "-position first".

can use an integer for position. This argument is especially useful when you have multiple values for an element and you need only the first or last value. For example, in a PubMed record there may be multiple authors but you may need to extract only the first author or last author (the corresponding author). The following two scripts extract the PMID and first author's last name. The first script does not use any constraint (Figure 5.36), while the second uses the "-position first" argument to limit the last name to the first author only (Figure 5.37).

```
$ esearch -db pubmed -query "breast cancer AND mutations AND machine learning" \
  |efetch -format xml \
  |xtract -pattern PubmedArticle -element MedlineCitation/PMID -block Author -element LastName
```

```
$ esearch -db pubmed -query "breast cancer AND mutations AND machine learning" \
  |efetch -format xml \
  |xtract -pattern PubmedArticle -element MedlineCitation/PMID -block Author \
        -position first -element LastName
```

Extracting Data from Docsum Format

The EFetch function can also fetch records of all Entrez databases in docsum format, which is a document summary in an XML format. In the docsum format, DocumentSummary is the parent element of all elements of a single record for all Entrez databases.

Studying the structure of the docsum format of a database record will help you to design the right Xtract command for data extraction. You can either view the docsum retrieved by EFetch or you can use the "-outline" Xtract argument to view the outlines of the docsum structure as follows (Figure 5.38).

```
$ efetch -db pubmed -id 27292874 -format docsum > docsum.xml
$ efetch -db pubmed -id 27292874 -format docsum | xtract -outline > outlines.txt
```

```
DocumentSummary
  Id
  PubDate
  EPubDate
  Source
  Authors
    Author
      Name
      AuthType
      ClusterID
    Author
      Name
      AuthType
      ClusterID
    Author
      Name
      AuthType
      ClusterID
  LastAuthor
  Title
  SortTitle
  Volume
```

FIGURE 5.38 The outline of XML PubMed docsum using "xtract -outline".

```
29996917    2018 Jul 11    Hum Genomics
29891518    2018 Jun       J Natl Compr Canc Netw
29802286    2018 May 25    Sci Rep
29797126    2018 May       Bull Exp Biol Med
29486751    2018 Feb 27    BMC Cancer
29346284    2018 Jan 18    Int J Mol Sci
29292184    2018 Aug       Clin Breast Cancer
28796549    2017 Oct       AJR Am J Roentgenol
28766224    2017 Oct       Ann Surg Oncol
28471621    2016 Oct       Isr Med Assoc J
28439188    2017 Spring    Ethn Dis
28438622    2017 Oct       Hum Pathol
29938981    2016 Dec       Invest Clin
27623252    2016 Nov       Gynecol Oncol
27364506    2016 Oct       Ann Surg Oncol
27363726    2016 Jul 1     BMC Genet
27153395    2016 May 5     Am J Hum Genet
26888582    2016 Jul 1     J Vet Med Sci
26774741    2016 Mar       Acad Radiol
26700035    2017 Aug       Breast Cancer Res Treat
26679809    2015 Dec       Res Vet Sci
```

FIGURE 5.39 Tabular report from PubMed docsum format.

The "-outline" argument displays the outline of the docsum document and enables you to design the xtract command. Since docsum is an XML format, you can use the same methods used above to extract data elements from a docsum of an Entrez database. You can provide "DocumentSummary" as a pattern in the "-pattern" Xtract argument and then use any of the child elements as an element in the "-element" arguments. For example, let us pick the child elements: Id, PubDate, and Source from Figure 5.38. Pay attention to that the docsum elements are case sensitive. The following example shows how to extract data contained in these child elements of the PubMed docsum format. In the following example, ESearch is used to search for articles on human breast cancer and the articles were published between 2015 and 2020. The EFilter is used to filter the ESearch results to only articles that mentioned "BRCA1 mutations". Then, EFetch is used to retrieve the records, which are filtered by EFilter, in docsum. Finally, Xtract is used to extract the article ID, publication date, and source. A partial output is shown in Figure 5.39.

```
$ esearch -db pubmed -query "breast cancer AND benign AND human[ORGN] AND 2015:
2020[PDAT]" \
    |efilter -query "BRCA1 mutations" \
    |efetch -format docsum \
    |xtract -pattern DocumentSummary -element Id PubDate Source
```

Above, you used PubMed only as an example, but that is applicable for any Entrez database docsum format. First, you need to study the structure outlines of the database records and then you can design a report that answers your needs.

Extracting Data from INSDSeq Format

INSDSeq is the official supported XML format of the International Nucleotide Sequence Database Collaboration (INSDC). The INSDSeq format provides the elements of a sequence as presented in the GenBank/EMBL/DDBJ-style flat file formats with some additional elements. You have already learnt that EFetch can retrieve data from Entrez sequence databases (Nucleotide and Protein) in an XML or GenPept flat file. All records of sequence databases can also be retrieved by EFetch in INSDSeq format using "efetch -format gpc". The INSDSeq is a useful format for extracting sequence information from the records of sequence databases.

Since INSDSeq is an XML format, all methods discussed above about extracting data from the XML document are also applicable for INSDSeq. However, there is an extra method for extracting data from features of GenBank records which will be discussed later. First, you need to study the structure of the INSDSeq format of a GenBank record. Consider the following commands, which search for the protein records in the Protein database that are associated with human benign breast cancer and those protein records were submitted in the period between 1/1/2015 and 06/30/2021. The found records then are retrieved by EFetch in the INSDSeq format (gpc) and saved in an XML file.

```
$ esearch -db protein -query "benign breast cancer AND Homo sapiens [ORGN]"\
            -datetype pdat -mindate 2015/1/1 -maxdate 2020/06/30 \
    |efetch -format gpc > gpc.xml
```

A partial protein record in INSDSeq format is shown in Figure 5.40. The structure of the INSDSeq format makes extraction of data from sequence databases very easy. Data from this format can be extracted with the same methods used with regular XML. For example, in the following command line, ESearch searches for protein records associated with human benign breast cancer, EFetch retrieves the returned records in INSDSeq format and, finally, Xtract creates a tabular report including the locus (INSDSeq_locus), sequence length (INSDSeq_length), GenBank division (INSDSeq_division), and submission date (INSDSeq_create-date) (Figure 3.41).

```
$ esearch -db protein -query "benign breast cancer AND Homo sapiens[ORGN]" \
            -datetype pdat -mindate 2015/1/1 -maxdate 2020/06/30 \
    | efetch -format gpc \
    | xtract -pattern INSDSeq \
            -element INSDSeq_locus INSDSeq_length INSDSeq_division INSDSeq_create-date
```

```
<INSDSet>
 <INSDSeq>
   <INSDSeq_locus>NP_001357055</INSDSeq_locus>
   <INSDSeq_length>144</INSDSeq_length>
   <INSDSeq_moltype>AA</INSDSeq_moltype>
   <INSDSeq_topology>linear</INSDSeq_topology>
   <INSDSeq_division>PRI</INSDSeq_division>
   <INSDSeq_update-date>02-AUG-2020</INSDSeq_update-date>
   <INSDSeq_create-date>26-APR-2019</INSDSeq_create-date>
   <INSDSeq_definition>kallikrein-12 isoform 4 [Homo sapiens]</INSDSeq_definition>
   <INSDSeq_primary-accession>NP_001357055</INSDSeq_primary-accession>
   <INSDSeq_accession-version>NP_001357055.1</INSDSeq_accession-version>
   <INSDSeq_other-seqids>
     <INSDSeqid>ref|NP_001357055.1|</INSDSeqid>
     <INSDSeqid>gi|1625649079</INSDSeqid>
   </INSDSeq_other-seqids>
   <INSDSeq_secondary-accessions>
     <INSDSecondary-accn>XP_005259007</INSDSecondary-accn>
   </INSDSeq_secondary-accessions>
   <INSDSeq_keywords>
     <INSDKeyword>RefSeq</INSDKeyword>
   </INSDSeq_keywords>
```

FIGURE 5.40   INSDSeq format.

```
NP_001366598    690    PRI    10-APR-2020
NP_001366597    690    PRI    10-APR-2020
NP_001366605    521    PRI    10-APR-2020
NP_001366599    690    PRI    10-APR-2020
NP_001366602    690    PRI    10-APR-2020
NP_001366596    690    PRI    10-APR-2020
NP_001366603    690    PRI    10-APR-2020
NP_001366604    595    PRI    10-APR-2020
```

FIGURE 5.41   Tabular report from INSDSeq document.

```
NP_001308008.1    NP_001308008    753     PRI    18-MAR-2016
NP_001308011.1    NP_001308011    707     PRI    18-MAR-2016
NP_001308010.1    NP_001308010    738     PRI    18-MAR-2016
NP_001351227.1    NP_001351227    1086    PRI    27-AUG-2018
NP_001351226.1    NP_001351226    1097    PRI    13-JUN-2018
NP_001371061.1    NP_001371061    207     PRI    01-JUN-2020
NP_001371056.1    NP_001371056    750     PRI    01-JUN-2020
NP_001371059.1    NP_001371059    673     PRI    01-JUN-2020
NP_001371055.1    NP_001371055    887     PRI    01-JUN-2020
NP_001371060.1    NP_001371060    207     PRI    01-JUN-2020
NP_001371057.1    NP_001371057    750     PRI    01-JUN-2020
```

FIGURE 5.42   Partial tabular report from INSDSeq document using "-insd" argument.

When extracting data from INSDSeq format, you can use the "-insd" argument instead of "-pattern" and "-element" to extract any descriptor. The following command line extracts the same data above but using the "insd" argument (Figure 5.42).

$ esearch -db protein -query "benign breast cancer AND Homo sapiens [ORGN]" \
        -datetype pdat -mindate 2015/1/1 -maxdate 2020/06/30 \
|efetch -format gpc \
|xtract -insd INSDSeq_locus INSDSeq_length INSDSeq_division INSDSeq_create-date

You may wish to extract certain data from the feature tables of GenBank records. As usual, you need to study the structure for designing your report. The following is the structure of the parent and child elements of the feature table of a GenBank record in INSDSeq format:

```
<INSDSeq_feature-table>
    <INSDFeature>
            .................
    </INSDFeature>
    <INSDFeature>
            .................
    </INSDFeature>
    <INSDFeature>
            .................
    </INSDFeature>
            ....................
</INSDSeq_feature-table>
```

The feature elements are enclosed between <INSDFeature> and </INSDFeature>. As shown in Figure 5.43, there may be multiple features in a single GenBank sequence record. A feature has (1) a feature key enclosed between <INSDFeature_key> and </INSDFeature_key>, (2) a feature location enclosed between INSDFeature_location> and </INSDFeature_location>, (3) feature intervals enclosed between INSDFeature_intervals> and </INSDFeature_intervals>, and (4) feature qualifiers enclosed between INSDFeature_quals> and </INSDFeature_quals>. A feature qualifier has both a name and value (name/value pair).

Data from GenBank record features can be extracted with the Xtract function and "-insd" argument. The qualifiers are in name/value pair. The qualifier names are used to retrieve the qualifier values. For example, for the CDS (coding sequence) feature shown in Figure 5.43, you can extract gene (gene symbol), gene_synonym (gene aliases), and coded_by (RefSeq mRNA that encodes the CDS and the CDS interval) as follows (Figure 5.44):

```
<INSDFeature>
  <INSDFeature_key>CDS</INSDFeature_key>
  <INSDFeature_location>1..144</INSDFeature_location>
  <INSDFeature_intervals>
    <INSDInterval>
      <INSDInterval_from>1</INSDInterval_from>
      <INSDInterval_to>144</INSDInterval_to>
      <INSDInterval_accession>NP_001357055.1</INSDInterval_accession>
    </INSDInterval>
  </INSDFeature_intervals>
  <INSDFeature_quals>
    <INSDQualifier>
      <INSDQualifier_name>gene</INSDQualifier_name>
      <INSDQualifier_value>KLK12</INSDQualifier_value>
    </INSDQualifier>
    <INSDQualifier>
      <INSDQualifier_name>gene_synonym</INSDQualifier_name>
      <INSDQualifier_value>KLK-L5; KLKL5</INSDQualifier_value>
    </INSDQualifier>
    <INSDQualifier>
      <INSDQualifier_name>coded_by</INSDQualifier_name>
      <INSDQualifier_value>NM_001370126.1:447..881</INSDQualifier_value>
    </INSDQualifier>
    <INSDQualifier>
```

FIGURE 5.43 GenBank features in INSDSeq XML format.

```
NP_001294881.1  HAPLN3   EXLD1; HsT19883 NM_001307952.2:87..1355
NP_001291410.1  FGD4     CMT4H; FRABP; ZFYVE6     NM_001304481.1:163..2718
NP_001317303.1  FGD4     CMT4H; FRABP; ZFYVE6     NM_001330374.1:513..2534
NP_001317302.1  FGD4     CMT4H; FRABP; ZFYVE6     NM_001330373.1:637..2658
NP_001308008.1  EZH1     KMT6B                    NM_001321079.2:24..2285
NP_001308011.1  EZH1     KMT6B                    NM_001321082.2:133..2256
NP_001291413.1  FGD4     CMT4H; FRABP; ZFYVE6     NM_001304484.1:1693..2961
NP_001291412.1  FGD4     CMT4H; FRABP; ZFYVE6     NM_001304483.1:1386..2801
NP_001308010.1  EZH1     KMT6B                    NM_001321081.2:133..2349
NP_001353633.1  MAS1     MAS; MGRA                NM_001366704.1:233..1210
NP_001302462.1  PDE9A    HSPDE9A2                 NM_001315533.1:284..1741
NP_001371061.1  FGD4     CMT4H; FRABP; ZFYVE6     NM_001384132.1:423..1046
```

FIGURE 5.44   Extracting data from feature tables of GenBank records.

$ esearch -db protein -query "benign breast cancer AND Homo sapiens [ORGN]" \
        -datetype pdat -mindate 2015/1/1 -maxdate 2020/06/30 \
    |efetch -format gpc \
    |xtract -insd complete CDS gene gene_synonym coded_by

The "complete" keyword is used for the complete feature. The "partial" keyword is used for a partial feature.

Extending EDirect with Bash Shell Script

EDirect uses the Linux environment to take advantage of the great features that the Linux environment introduces. One of these features is the bash scripting language, which can be used to extend the ability of EDirect in retrieving and manipulating the data stored on the Entrez databases. Several Linux shell commands can be used with EDirect functions to build complex, multi-step data retrieval and extraction scripts. This section does not aim to teach bash scripting language but to provide readers with some bash commands and scripts that can help in Entrez data retrieval and manipulation. Bash scripting can extend EDirect usability and functionality because users can use the bash programming features such as shell commands, loops, and conditional statements. In the following we will discuss some of these bash commands and programming features.

Use of Bash Commands   A shell is a program that provides an interface to the user to use operating system services. Shell commands are human-readable commands that can be run from the command-line prompt to instruct the computer to perform a specific task. The Linux system has several shell programs but bash is the default shell on a computer with a Linux system or Linux environment. Bash stands for Borne Again Shell. The shell gets started when the user starts the terminal.

In the following sections you will learn how to use "cat", "sort", "nl", "grep", "uniq", "sed", "cut", and "awk" shell commands with EDirect functions.

Use of "cat" Linux Command   The "cat" Linux command is used to concatenate files and to print on the standard output (screen). Its syntax is as follows:

```
cat [OPTION] [FILE1] [FILE2] …
```

For example, the following are four command lines. In the following, you will use EFetch to retrieve the FASTA sequences of three PPARG protein isoforms. Each sequence will be saved in a separate file. Then, you will use the "cat" command to concatenate the three FASTA sequence files into a single one.

$ efetch -db protein -id NP_001341595.2 -format fasta > pparg1.fasta
$ efetch -db protein -id NP_056953.2 -format fasta > pparg2.fasta

$ efetch -db protein -id NP_001361191.2 -format fasta > pparg3.fasta

$ cat pparg1.fasta pparg2.fasta pparg3.fasta > ppargs.fasta

If the above "cat" command line is used without "> ppargs.fasta", the content will be displayed on the screen.

The "cat" command can be used to extend the usability of ESearch, EFilter which have "-query" argument. With the "cat" command, you can read the query from a text file instead of providing it in line. The following syntax shows you how to import a query from a text file into an ESearch "-query" argument.

$ esearch -db pubmed -query "$(cat query.txt)"

The "query.txt" can be any plain text file containing a valid search query. The "cat" command will read the content of the text file and will pass it to the "-query" argument.

For example, open a text editor such as vim or nano and enter and save the following search query in a text file (e.g., query.txt):

((breast cancer) OR ('benign breast cancer) AND (human OR Homo sapiens OR women OR woman) AND (mutation OR mutations)) AND ((whole genome sequencing) OR WGS OR wgs) AND 2018:2020[PDAT]

The following ESearch command uses the "cat" command to import the search query from a text file. The results of the search are retrieved and saved in a text file (abstracts.txt).

$ esearch -db pubmed -query "$(cat query.txt)" | efetch -format medline > abstracts.txt

Use of "sort" Linux Command   The 'sort' Linux command is used to sort the tabular results and also to remove duplicate lines. In the following example, the "sort" Linux command is used to sort the results by the third column (-k 3) and to remove any duplicate article (-u). The results will be saved in a text file

```
$ esearch -db pubmed -query "$(cat query.txt)" \
  | efetch -format xml \
  | xtract -pattern PubmedArticle -tab " " -element MedlineCitation/PMID PubDate/Year \
                                    -block Author -position first -element LastName \
  | sort -k 3 -u > pubs.txt
```

Use of "nl" Linux Command   The 'nl' Linux command adds serial numbers to the rows of the output. In the following example (Figure 5.45), the "nl" command is used to number the rows of the output of the previous example.

```
 1  31697689 2019 Abécassis
 2  30925164 2019 Adamovich
 3  31448780 2019 Adams-Reyes
 4  31570896 2019 Angus
 5  28892047 2018 Anjanappa
 6  30415991 2019 Ashley
 7  29996881 2018 Barrett
 8  31361912 2019 Beca
 9  30755730 2019 Block
10  30610487 2019 Bowden
```

FIGURE 5.45   Numbering rows with "nl" command.

```
$ esearch -db pubmed -query "$(cat query.txt)" \
  |efetch -format xml \
  |xtract -pattern PubmedArticle \
        -tab " " -element MedlineCitation/PMID PubDate/Year \
        -block Author -position first -element LastName \
  |sort -k 3 -u \
  |nl > pubs.txt
```

Use of "grep" Linux Command The "grep" command is a command-line program for searching plain-text datasets for lines that match a regular expression. It is available for all Unix-like systems and systems with a Linux environment. By default, "grep" will search for the exact specified pattern within the input file and returns the lines containing the pattern. You can also use optional flags to change its behavior. The following are the general syntaxes of "grep" command.

```
grep [OPTIONS] PATTERN [FILE...]
grep [OPTIONS] -e PATTERN ... [FILE...]
grep [OPTIONS] -f FILE ... [FILE...]
... | grep [OPTIONS] ...
```

Any one of the above three syntaxes can be used. If you use the syntax with '-e PATTERN', you can provide an inline pattern, but if you use the syntax with '-f FILE' you must provide a file containing the pattern. The most commonly used options include '-i' to ignore case, '-c' to perform counting, '-A X' to print X lines of trailing context after matching lines (e.g., grep -A 3), which means to print three lines, and '-B X' to print X lines before context.

The "grep" command can be used in several ways with EDirect. One of the "grep" uses is to search a pattern in the Xtract's tabular report. The Xtract output can be used as input for the "grep" command to limit the output to selected rows. For example, the Xtract output in Figure 5.45 contains different years in the Year column. You can use "grep" to limit the report to the year 2019 only as follows (Figure 5.46):

```
$ esearch -db pubmed -query "$(cat query.txt)" \
  |efetch -format xml \
```

```
31419696 2019 Ferreira
31019444 2019 Fremd
30988514 2019 Gulhan
30843125 2019 Hayashi
31221724 2019 Jager
31464824 2019 Johansson
31422574 2019 Kraemer
31181796 2019 Kwon
30417574 2019 Kyrochristos
31174159 2019 Masoodi
31570656 2019 Megquier
30789657 2019 Nguyen
31090900 2019 Nones
30704472 2019 Nono
```

FIGURE 5.46 Using "grep" command for row selection.

|xtract -pattern PubmedArticle -tab " " -element MedlineCitation/PMID PubDate/Year -block Author \

        -position first -element LastName \

|sort -k 3 -u \

|grep 2019 > pubs_2019.txt

The output will be saved in "pubs_2019.txt" file, which you can open using any text editor.

The "grep" command can also be used to count a specific keywork. The following command counts the number of exon features in a GenBank record.

$ efetch -db nuccore -id 262359905 -format gpc | grep exon -c

The output will be the number of exons in the GenBank sequence.

You can also use "grep" to display the exon locations, which is the second line after the "exon" keyword as follows (Figure 5.47):

$ efetch -db nuccore -id 262359905 -format gpc | grep exon -A 1

The "grep" command can also be used with the regular expression and that pattern can be read from an input file. Table 5.3 includes some special characters that can be used in the "grep" pattern:

```
hamiddafa@dax:~$ efetch -db nuccore -id 262359905 -format gpc | grep -e '>exon<' -A 1
        <INSDFeature_key>exon</INSDFeature_key>
        <INSDFeature_location>92501..92713</INSDFeature_location>

        <INSDFeature_key>exon</INSDFeature_key>
        <INSDFeature_location>93869..93967</INSDFeature_location>

        <INSDFeature_key>exon</INSDFeature_key>
        <INSDFeature_location>102205..102258</INSDFeature_location>

        <INSDFeature_key>exon</INSDFeature_key>
        <INSDFeature_location>111451..111528</INSDFeature_location>
```

FIGURE 5.47   Displaying exon locations in a GenBank record using "grep".

TABLE 5.3   Special Characters Used for Regular Expression with "grep" Command

Pattern	Description
"^WORD"	To find the pattern that begins with WORD, WORD is any word
"WORD$"	to find the pattern that ends with WORD
"..WORD"	The period character "." is a wild card that is used to represent any single character at the location
"W[OR]D"	Any one of the characters within the brackets. For example, grep "wom[ae]n", will search for both "woman" or "women"
"^[A-Z]"	the pattern begins with any capital letter from A to Z
"^[A-Za-z]"	the pattern begins with any capital or small letter from A to Z
"*"	This repeats the previous character or expression zero or more times
.|*?+(){}[]^$\	Those characters have special meaning in regular expression and they will match themselves when preceded by a \
"{n}"	This specifies the number of times that a match is repeated
"?"	To match a character zero or one time
"+"	Matches an expression one or more times

In the following the "grep" command uses EFetch output to print the sequence of a GenBank nucleotide record. The sequence in INSDSeq format begins with whitespace and "<INSDSeq_sequence>"

$ efetch -db nuccore -id 262359905 -format gpc | grep "^ *<INSDSeq_sequence>"

Use of "uniq" Linux Command   The "uniq" Linux command reports or omits repeated lines. Its syntax is as follows:

uniq [OPTION]… [INPUT [OUTPUT]]

The most commonly used options include "-c", which counts the lines of occurrence, "-f N", which skips field N, and "-u", which prints unique lines only.

The following command line searches the protein database for records associated with sickle cell disease and then it searches PubMed articles linked to the proteins records and prints the PMIDs and names of the first authors, counts the occurrence of authors, and removes any line with a duplicate author name.

```
$ esearch -db protein -query "sickle cell disease AND human[ORGN] AND refseq[FILTER]" \
    |elink -target pubmed \
    |efetch -format docsum \
    |xtract -pattern DocumentSummary -element Id SortFirstAuthor \
    |sort -k 2 \
    |uniq -c -f 1
```

Use of "sed" Linux Command   The "sed" Linux command, which stands for Stream EDitor, is mainly used for the text substitution and text finding and replacing, in addition to others uses such as text manipulations like insertion, deletion, search etc. With the "sed" command, you can edit a complete file without opening it. It also supports the use of regular expressions. Its syntax is as follows:

```
sed [OPTION]…[input-file].. or …| sed [OPTION]
```

The "sed" command can be used with "-e SCRIPT" option to add a script to the command and "-n" to suppress printing of all lines. The following are some examples of the uses of the "sed" command:

- Printing lines 10 to 20 from a text in a file

$ sed -n 10,20p file.txt

- Displaying all lines in a text file except lines 10 and 20:

$ sed 10,20d file.txt

- Deleting line 20 in a text file:

$ sed 20d file.txt

- Deleting all lines in a text file except 25–30:

$ sed '25,30!d' testfile.txt

- Starting from line 5 and printing any 4th line:

$ sed -n '5~4p' file.txt

- Adding a blank line after every line printed:

$ sed G file.txt

- Finding "keyword1" and replacing it with "keyword2" on every line for the first occurrence only:

$ sed 's/keyword1/keyword2/' file.txt

- Finding "keyword1" and replacing it with "keyword2" on every line for all occurrence:

$ sed 's/keyword1/keyword2/g' file.txt

- Finding "keyword1" and replacing it with "keyword2" on the second occurrence only:

$ sed 's/ keyword1/keyword2/2' file.txt

- Finding "keyword1" and replacing it with 'keyword2' on the second occurrence for all lines in the text file:

$ sed 's/keyword1/keyword2/2g' file.txt

- Replacing "keyword1" with "keyword2" in the 4th line:

$ sed '4 s/keyword1/keyword2/' file.txt

- Adding a new line with some content after every pattern match:

$ sed '/keyword/a "text here"' file.txt

- Adding a new line with some content before every pattern match:

$ sed '/keyword/i "text here"' file.txt

- Changing the line content with a new content when a keyword is found:

$ sed '/keyword/c "new line content" ' file.txt

- Deleting a line starting with a particular string and ending with another string:

$ sed -e 's/^keyword1.*keyword2$//g' file.txt

- Adding some content before every line:

$ sed -e 's/.*/this test &/' file.txt

- Using "-e" for multiple sed commands:

$ sed -e 's/keyword1/ keyword2/g' -e 's/ keyword3/ keyword4/' file.txt

In the following example, EFetch retrieves a Nucleotide record and then Linux commands are used to extract the FASTA sequence and save it in a text file.

```
$ efetch -db nuccore -id 262359905 -format gpc \
  |grep "^ *<INSDSeq_sequence>" \
  |sed -e "/<INSDSeq_sequence>/i >gene_sequence" \
    -e "s/^ *<INSDSeq_sequence>//g" -e "s/<\/INSDSeq_sequence>//g" > myseq1.fasta
```

Use of "cut" Linux Command The "cut" Linux command removes sections from each line of a file and can be used to extract fields. Its syntax is as follows:

```
$ cut [OPTION]… [FILE]… or …| cut [OPTION]
```

The most commonly used options include "-f N" to select the field N and "-d" to use a delimiter instead of TAB. The following are some examples

- Displaying the first field in the file:

$ cut -f1 file.txt

- Displaying the 2nd field of each line, using colon as the field separator:

$ cut -d: -f2 file.txt

- Displaying the third field and other fields after:

$ cut -d" " -f3- file.txt

In the following example, EFetch retrieves a gene table of a gene record and displays only the "Gene Interval Exon" of the BRCA1 gene.

$ efetch -db gene -id 672 -format gene_table | sed -n 11,33p | cut -f 3

Use of "awk" Command AWK is a general-purpose program in UNIX/Linux. It is designed to create filters, transform data, and send data to a standard output. Therefore, it is used for developing report generators, and tools used to reformat data. Its syntax is as follows:

```
$ awk [-F value] [-f program-file] [--] [file …]
```

The "-F" option is used as an input field separator and "-f" option is used for the awk script file if you have the awk script in a file.

The "awk" command has rules consisting of (1) patterns and (2) actions. The action is executed on the text that matches the pattern. Actions and patterns are enclosed in curly braces ({}). Together, a pattern and an action form a rule. The entire "awk" program is enclosed in single quotes ('). By default, "awk" considers a field to be a string of characters surrounded by whitespace, the start of a line, or the end of a line. Fields are identified by a dollar sign ($) and a number. So, $1 represents the first field, $0 represents all lines of text, and $NF, which stands for "number of fields", represents the last field. The following are some examples of AWK uses.

(1) *Printing columns/fields*

- Printing the 3rd field/column

$ awk '{print $3}' file.txt

- Printing the 2nd and 7th fields

$ awk '{print $2,$7}' file.txt

(2) *Adding custom separator*

The default output separator is a whitespace, which can be replaced by 'OFS="SEP"'. The following will replace the whitespace with '|')

$ awk 'OFS="|"{print $4, $2}' file.txt.

(3) *Adding text to the beginning and end*

You can add a text to the beginning and end of awk action by using "BEGIN" and "END".

$ awk 'BEGIN {print "Gene list\n------------"} {print $3,$4}' file.txt

(4) *Adding a condition to filter rows*

$ Awk '$2>500 {print $0}' file.txt

(5) *Using a regular expression to find a specific pattern*

$ awk '/KLK12/{print $0}' file.txt

The "awk" script can also be saved in a file and run using "-f" option.

The following script searches the Protein database for protein records associated with human benign breast cancer and then extracts the "coded_by" field, and separates and prints the refseq mRNA accession (Figure 5.48).

$ esearch -db protein -query "benign breast cancer AND Homo sapiens [ORGN]"\

-datetype pdat -mindate 2015/1/1 -maxdate 2020/06/30 \

```
NM_001370126.1
NM_001370128.1
NM_001370127.1
NM_001370125.1
NM_001375890.1
NM_001375889.1
NM_001375888.1
NM_001364298.2
NM_001364297.2
NM_001370298.3
NM_001379671.1
NM_001379669.1
```

FIGURE 5.48   mRNA accession list.

```
|efetch -format gpc \
|xtract -insd complete CDS coded_by \
|awk '{print $NF}' \
|awk -F: '{print $1}'
```

Bash Shell Program   The bash program or bash script is a sequence of valid shell commands saved in a plain text file and executed by entering the name of the script file on the command-line prompt. To create a bash shell program, open a new empty file in a plain text editor such as vim, emacs, nano, etc., and type valid shell commands, save the file, and exit. The shell script file then can be run from the Linux terminal command prompt as follows:

```
$ sh shellFile
```

There are no data types in Bash scripting language in contrast to many computer programming languages. A variable can contain a number, a character, or a string of characters without declaration. In the following script a protein accession number is assigned to a variable named "id" (no whitespace is allowed) and then the EFetch function is used with "-id $id" instead of providing the accession number. Save the following script in a plain text file with the "test.sh" name.

```
id=NP_001013434.1
efetch -db protein \
        -id $id \
        -format gpc
```

You can run the bash script program as

```
$ sh test.sh
```

The above bash program will retrieve the record with 'NP_001013434.1' accession in INSDSeq format.

All these Linux commands can be used with EDirect functions to create a bash program for retrieving data from the Entrez databases. The following are some examples of the uses of bash scripting language to retrieve data from Entrez database.

Retrieving Gene List and Transcript Sequences The following bash script uses 'sort', 'cut', 'nl', 'xargs', and 'sed' along with EDirect commands to retrieve the RefSeq transcript sequences associated with the sickle cell disease in humans. The script can be saved in a file named "sickle.sh".

```bash
#!/bin/bash
#file:sickle.sh
fileName="list_sickle_genes.txt"
myQuery="sickle cell disease AND human[ORGN] AND refseq[FILT]"
#Create file containing protein IDs, gene names, gene acc, cds position
esearch -db protein -query "$myQuery" |\
    efetch -format gpc | \
    xtract -insd complete CDS gene coded_by | \
    sort -k 2 -u | nl | sed 's/:/\t/g' > $fileName;
#Extract the gene uids and store them in a variable
ids=$(cut -f4-4 $fileName | xargs | sed -e 's/ /,/g');
#upload the gene uids to the History server and retrieve sequences
epost -db nucleotide -id=$ids -label post1 | \
    efetch -format fasta > seq_sickle_gene1.fasta;
```

The bash script file can be run on Linux terminal as

```
$ sh sickle.sh
```

The first line in the script file "#!/bin/bash" indicates that this file should always be run with bash rather than another Linux shell. The hash sign "#" indicates the line is a comment and will be ignored and not interpreted by the computer. So the "#file:sickle.sh" line is just a comment and will not be interpreted. The "fileName="list_sickle_genes.txt"" is a variable named "filename" and then it was assigned to "list_sickle_genes.txt" file name. In the same way, the "myQuery" variable was created for the search query. The ESearch function became short because the "-query" argument has the string variable "$myQuery" ('-query "$myQuery"' is the same as "-query sickle cell disease AND human [ORGN] AND refseq [FILT]"). The results returned by Esearch were transferred by piping to EFetch, which retrieved the protein records in INSDSeq format. The INSDSeq formatted results were then transferred by piping to the Xtract function, which extracted the gene name (gene) and gene accession number (coded_by). The results were then transferred by piping to the Linux "sort" command, which sorted the results by gene name in the second columns (sort –k 2) and removed any line with a duplicate gene name (-u). The sorted and refined results were then transferred by piping to the Linux command "nl" to number the lines. Each line in the results, so far, looks like the following:

```
1 NP_001305150.1 AHSP NM_001318221.2:64..372
```

Notice that the mRNA accession number and the interval are separated by the colon sign ":". This output was transferred to the Linux stream editor command 'sed "s/:/\t/g"', which searched all the results for ':' and replaced it with a tab "\t". The output is then saved in a text file using "> $fileName"; this phrase is translated before interpretation to "> list_sickle_genes.txt". A text file with that name was saved in the current directory.

The comment line after saving the tabular report file is a comment about the next step, which extracts the accession column or column 4 "cut -f4-4 $fileName" of the saved file. The results were then transferred by piping to "xargs | sed -e 's/ /,/g')" to convert the entire accession column to a single comma-delimited line, which was assigned to the variable "ids". The "ids" variable was used to provide UIDs to the EFetch function. In the final step, a FASTA file (seq_sickle_gene1.fasta) containing the sequences of gene reference transcripts (mRNA) was saved in the current directory.

Retrieving CDD Information   In the following example, you will learn how to use the Xtract function and "grep" command to extract the conserved domain data from a protein feature table. The data of the conserved domains of a protein record is found in the Conserved Domain Database (CDD), which is a protein annotation resource that consists of a collection of well-annotated multiple sequence alignment models for ancient domains and full-length proteins. The following bash program will print the Entrez Protein accession, start and end position of the conserved domain in a protein sequence, name of the domain, and CDD UID. As usual, you need to study the structure of the database record to better design the extraction report. Since you will extract the data from a protein record, you need to study the structure of the Entrez Protein INSDSeq format. Fetching a sequence record in gpc format will allow you to retrieve GenBank features as discussed earlier. See above for the INSDSeq structure and the element of the gene table in a GenBank record. The following are the INSDSeq elements from which we need to extract data.

```
<INSDInterval_from>448</INSDInterval_from>
<INSDInterval_to>540</INSDInterval_to>
<INSDInterval_accession>XP_024832014.1</INSDInterval_accession>
…
<INSDQualifier_name>region_name</INSDQualifier_name>
<INSDQualifier_value>Evr1_Alr</INSDQualifier_value>
…
<INSDQualifier_name>db_xref</INSDQualifier_name>
<INSDQualifier_value>CDD:309769</INSDQualifier_value>
```

Use the text editor of your choice and save the following bash script in a plain text file (cdd.sh).

```
#!/bin/bash
#file: cdd.sh
myquery="$1*[GENE]
        AND   $2[ORGN]
        AND alive[PROP]"
esearch -db gene -query "$myquery" \
| elink -db gene \
        -target protein \
        -name gene_protein_refseq \
| efetch -db protein \
        -format gpc \
| xtract -insd Region \
        INSDInterval_from \
        INSDInterval_to \
```

```
        region_name \
        db_xref \
  | grep 'CDD:'
```

Running the above bash program requires two command-line arguments: (1) a valid gene symbol and (2) a name of an organism. The name can be a common or scientific name between quotation marks. The command-line arguments make the program reusable without changing the script. For example, to run the Bash program for the bovine COX1 gene, you can use any of the following command lines.

```
$ sh cdd.sh COX1 cow
$ sh cdd.sh COX1 "Bos taurus"
```

You can also run the same program for the human BRCA1 using any of the following command lines:

```
$ sh cdd.sh BRCA1 human
$ sh cdd.sh BRCA1 "Homo sapiens"
```

The script starts with myquery ="$1*[GENE] AND $2[ORGN] AND alive [PROP]", which is the query string. The "$1" and "$2" will be substituted with the first and second command-line arguments, respectively upon the execution of the script. The first argument must be a gene symbol and the second argument must be an organism name. For example, when we run "sh cdd.sh BRCA1 human", the "$1" will be replaced with "BRCA1" and "$2" will be replaced with "human". The asterisk "*" is a wild card. The ESearch function searches the Gene database for the query terms and returns the UIDs. The ESearch results are transferred by piping to the ELink function to find the Protein records linked to the Gene UIDs. The Protein UIDs returned by ELink are then transferred to the EFetch function to retrieve the Protein records in INSDSeq XML format (gpc). The results then are transferred to the Xtract function, which extracts the accession number, start and end position of feature regions, name of the region. Finally, the extracted results are transferred to the 'grep' command to filter the regions with "CDD:" as shown in Figure 5.49.

Extracting the FTP of the Latest Assembly   Sometimes, you may need to know the FTP address of the latest Genome Assembly database to download a reference genome. The following example shows you how to use the bash program to extract the ftp address of the latest genome assembly on the Assembly database. First, you need to study the structure of any Assembly record to determine the locations of the data we need. Use EFetch to retrieve any record in docsum, save it in a text file, and then open the file to study the file content and structure as follows.

```
$ efetch -db assembly -id 7292811 -format docsum > test.xml
```

Figure 5.50 shows that the ftp address of the reference assembly is in between <FtpPath_RefSeq> and </FtpPath_RefSeq> and the ftp address of the GenBank assembly is in between <FtpPath_GenBank> and </FtpPath_GenBank>. Then, you can use the following script to display the ftp address of the reference

```
NP_009231.2    1671    1745    BRCT    CDD:237994
NP_009231.2    1779    1863    BRCT    CDD:214602
NP_009229.2    23      68      RING    CDD:238093
NP_009229.2    546     620     BRCT    CDD:237994
NP_009229.2    654     738     BRCT    CDD:214602
```

FIGURE 5.49   Retrieving CDD information from GenBank records.

```
<DocumentSummary>
<Id>7292811</Id>
    <RsUid></RsUid>
    <GbUid>20129198</GbUid>
    <AssemblyAccession>GCA_013364835.1</AssemblyAccession>
    <LastMajorReleaseAccession>GCA_013364835.1</LastMajorReleaseAccession>
    <Primary>20129158</Primary>
    <FtpPath_GenBank>ftp://ftp.ncbi.nlm.nih.gov/genomes/all/...</FtpPath_GenBank>
    <FtpPath_RefSeq></FtpPath_RefSeq>
    <FtpPath_Assembly_rpt>ftp://ftp.ncbi.nlm.nih.gov/genomes/all/...</FtpPath_Assembly_rpt>
    <FtpPath_Stats_rpt>ftp://ftp.ncbi.nlm.nih.gov/genomes/all/...</FtpPath_Stats_rpt>
    <FtpPath_Regions_rpt></FtpPath_Regions_rpt>
    <SortOrder>5C5X974497055013364835900</SortOrder>
```

FIGURE 5.50   Assembly record docsum format.

assembly of an organism. When you run the script, you should provide a scientific or common name or an organism as a command-line argument. You can save the following script in a text file named "assembly.sh".

```
#!/bin/bash
#file:download.sh
#the latest assembly download ftps
myQuery="[ORGN] AND latest[FILT]"
esearch -db assembly -query "$1$myQuery" \
    | efetch -format docsum \
    | xtract -pattern DocumentSummary \
            -element AssemblyAccession,FtpPath_RefSeq
```

For example, the following will display the ftp address of the latest cat (Felis catus) assembly.

```
$ sh assembly.sh "Felis catus"
```

Using Bash Loop   Almost all programming languages provide a loop concept that helps in executing one or more statements up to a desired number of times. The following are some loop statements used by bash.

For Loop   The "for loop" iterates over a list of items and performs the given set of commands. The form of the "for loop" in bash is as follows:

```
for item in [LIST]
do
    [COMMANDS]
done
```

The list [LIST] can be a series of words separated by whitespaces, a range of numbers, an output of a command, or an array. The bash commands between "do" and "done" are repeated according to the number of list items.

For example, assume that you have three Protein UIDs: NP_001013434.1, NP_036646.1, and NP_848668.1 and you wish to retrieve the FASTA sequence and to remove the description information from the FASTA sequence but you want to keep only the accession number in the definition line (defline). You can save the following bash script in a text file and run it using "sh" command.

```
ids="NP_001013434.1 NP_036646.1 NP_848668.1"
for id in $ids;
    do
        efetch -db protein \
            -id $id \
            -format fasta \
        | perl -p -i -e 's/>(.+?) .+/>$1/g'
    done
```

The "for loop" runs the commands between "do" and "done" for each accession number in the "ids" list. Each time the FASTA sequence is fetched by the EFetch function and the "perl" command removes the description in FASTA sequence and replaces it with the accession number.

While Loop   The "while loop" does the same as "for loop" but it requires a condition. The commands between "do" and "done" will be executed repeatedly until the condition is fulfilled.

Assume that you have the above accession numbers in a plain text file "acc.txt"; each accession number in a separate line as follows:

```
NP_001013434.1
NP_036646.1
NP_848668.1
```

The following bash script will take a file name as a command-line argument "FILE=$1". The lines 'exec 3<&0' and 'exec 0<$FILE' direct the standard input (stdin) to the file so the file given as an argument will be opened and the accessions in the file will be read sequentially. The "while loop" assigns a single accession number to "id" each time and passes it to the EFetch function to retrieve the FASTA sequence. The FASTA sequence is then passed to "perl" to replace the FASTA definition line with the accession number. The "while loop" will repeat this process until the end of file (EOF) is reached.

Save the following script in a plain text file (e.g., myscript.sh).

```
FILE=$1
exec 3<&0
exec 0<$FILE
while read id
    do
        efetch -db protein \
            -id $id \
            -format fasta \
        | perl -p -i -e 's/>(.+?) .+/>$1/g'
    done
```

Then you can run the bash program with "acc.txt" file as an argument as follows.

    $ sh myscript.sh acc.txt

The "while loop" is useful and can be used with the Xtract function to perform complex tasks using conditional execution arguments (-if, -unless, -else, etc.).

In the following example, you will learn the use of Xtract conditional execution arguments with "while loop". Instead of an external data file, you will use pipe "|" to pass the results of a previous command. The script will retrieve gene sequences from chromosomes. The information of gene records in NCBI database are stored on the Entrez Gene database. The document summary (docsum format) of a gene record contains the elements of genomic information enclosed between "<GenomicInfo>" and "</ GenomicInfo>" XML tags. The genomic information elements include the chromosome (ChrLoc), chromosome accession (ChrAccVer), starting position of the gene sequence (ChrStart), the end position of the gene sequence (ChrStop), and the number of exons. The location of the genes marks that gene locus in the specified chromosome. We can use the above information to retrieve the genomic nucleotide sequence of the gene from the chromosome.

As usual, first you will need to study the structure of the docsum format of the gene record. The following EFetch command retrieves the gene tumor protein 53 gene (TP53) record in docsum format, and a partial output is shown in Figure 5.51.

    $ efetch -db gene -id 7157 -format docsum

Figure 5.51 displays the structure of the genomic data elements of a gene record. You can then create a bash program on a file to retrieve the genomic gene sequence from the chromosome. For re-usability you can create

```
<DocumentSummary>
<Id>7157</Id>
        <Name>TP53</Name>
        <Description>tumor protein p53</Description>
        <Status>0</Status>
        <CurrentID>0</CurrentID>
        <Chromosome>17</Chromosome>
        <GeneticSource>genomic</GeneticSource>
        <MapLocation>17p13.1</MapLocation>
        <OtherAliases>BCC7, BMFS5, LFS1, P53, TRP53</OtherAliases>
        <OtherDesignations>cellular tumor antigen p53|antigen NY-CO-13</OtherDesignations>
        <NomenclatureSymbol>TP53</NomenclatureSymbol>
        <NomenclatureName>tumor protein p53</NomenclatureName>
        <NomenclatureStatus>Official</NomenclatureStatus>
        <Mim>
                <int>191170</int>
        </Mim>
        <GenomicInfo>
                <GenomicInfoType>
                        <ChrLoc>17</ChrLoc>
                        <ChrAccVer>NC_000017.11</ChrAccVer>
                        <ChrStart>7687549</ChrStart>
                        <ChrStop>7668401</ChrStop>
                        <ExonCount>12</ExonCount>
                </GenomicInfoType>
        </GenomicInfo>
```

FIGURE 5.51   Docsum structure of the BRCA1 gene record.

a bash program that can be used with a command-line argument to pass the gene symbol. You have to bear in mind that a pseudogene will have a similar symbol as the functional gene. According to HGNC (HUGO Gene Nomenclature Committee) guidelines a pseudogene is defined as the sequence that is incapable of producing a functional protein product but has a high level of homology to a functional gene. Only the pseudogenes that retain homology to a significant proportion of the functional ancestral gene are given names based on the specific parent gene, with a "P" and number appended to the parent gene symbol (e.g., NACAP10, "NACA pseudogene 10"). The numbering is usually species-specific.

The following bash script retrieves any gene sequence, given a gene symbol and organism name as arguments. You can save the following script in a text file (e.g., gene_seq.sh).

```
#!/bin/bash
#file name: gene_seq.sh
esearch -db gene -query "$1[Gene Symbol] AND $2[ORGN] AND alive[PROP]" | esummary \
    | xtract -pattern DocumentSummary \
        -if GenomicInfoType -element Id \
        -block GenomicInfoType \
        -element ChrAccVer ChrStart ChrStop \
        | while read -r gene_id chr_acc chr_start chr_stop ;
            do
                efetch -db nuccore \
                -id $chr_acc \
                -chr_start $chr_start \
                -chr_stop $chr_stop \
                -format fasta ;
            done
```

When you run the Bash script, you must provide two arguments: a valid gene symbol and organism name. The organism's name is either a common or scientific name. When you use a scientific name, it must be between two quotation marks. Any one of the following commands can retrieve the genomic sequence of the human breast cancer gene (BRCA1).

```
$ sh gene_seq.sh BRCA1 human > brca1_gene1.fasta
$ sh gene_seq.sh BRCA1 "Homo sapiens"> brca1_gene1.fasta
```

The genomic sequence of the mouse Peroxisome Proliferator Activated Receptor Gamma (PPARG) gene can be retrieved by using any of the following commands:

```
$ sh gene_seq.sh PPARG mouse > pparg_gene1.fasta
$ sh gene_seq.sh BRCA1 "Mus musculus"> pparg_gene1.fasta
```

The sequence extracted using the location information obtained from the record of the Gene database is the complete genomic sequence that includes all parts of the gene.

REFERENCES

1. Sayers, E., *A General Introduction to the E-utilities*. Entrez Programming Utilities Help [cited 6/6/2021]. www.ncbi.nlm.nih.gov/books/NBK25497/. 2010.

2. Sayers, E., *The E-utilities In-Depth: Parameters, Syntax and More*. Entrez Programming Utilities Help [cited 6/25/2021]. www.ncbi.nlm.nih.gov/books/NBK25499/. 2009.

3. Kans, J., *Entrez Direct: E-utilities on the Unix Command Line*. In: Entrez Programming Utilities Help [Internet] [cited 6/25/2021]. www.ncbi. nlm.nih.gov/books/NBK179288/. 2013 updated 2021.

## CHAPTER 6

R and Python Packages for the NCBI E-Utilities

INTRODUCTION

The E-utilities APIs [1], which were discussed in Chapter 4, allow programmers to use the programming languages of their choice to develop stand-alone applications, web-based applications, or modules that serve as interfaces for searching and retrieving data from Entrez databases. In this chapter we will discuss both the R Entrez package and BioPython, which use E-utilities APIs and make accessing the Entrez databases possible to users and programmers who use their programming environment. Both R and Python are widely used by students and researchers from diverse disciplines because they are open-source, easy to use, powerful, and available for Linux, MacOS and Windows. Therefore, learning both R and Python or at least one of them has become one of the basics in bioinformatics because they pervade all aspects of bioscience from sequence-based bioinformatics and molecular evolution to phylogenomics, systems biology, structural biology, and beyond.

Since you have reached this point, you are already familiar with the E-utilities programs, their parameters, and their uses. Therefore, this chapter will focus only on how to use the R Entrez functions and BioPython to perform the same operations that were discussed in the last three chapters. As a prerequisite, you may need to know how to use R and Python on the computer platform that you are using.

R ENTREZ PACKAGE

R is a free software program for statistical computing and graphics and open-source language and computing environment for Windows, Macintosh, UNIX, and Linux platforms. R performs a wide variety of basic to advanced statistical and graphical techniques and has become one of the most commonly used programming environments for bioinformatics. Several R packages integrate the NCBI's E-utilities API to allow R users to search Entrez databases and to retrieve database data onto the R sessions for further processing using R programming capability. R can be downloaded for all computer platforms, including Linux, MacOS, and Windows, from the CRAN-R-project website at https://cran.r-project.org/ and can then be installed following the instructions. There is an easier way to install R in Linux and Linux-like platforms by using "sudo apt-get install r-base" and then you can run R by entering R on the command-line prompt of the Linux terminal. The R installation in Windows is achieved by downloading and running the R installer, which installs the R-base and creates an R shortcut icon on the desktop. Once R has been installed, you can install any stable R packages by entering "install.packages(package_name)" on the R command-line prompt.

In R, there are many packages for searching and retrieving data from Entrez databases but R Entrez (rentrez) [2, 3] is the most popular and stable. The rentrez package provides functions that serve as interface for the NCBI E-utilities to search and retrieve data from the Entrez databases onto an R environment.

DOI: 10.1201/9781003226611-6

TABLE 6.1   R Entrez Functions

Rentrez Function	E-utility Program	Description
entrez_dbs()	Einfo.fcgi	Lists the Entrez databases
entrez_db_summary()	Einfo.fcgi	Prints the summary of an Entrez database
entrez_db_searchable()	Einfo.fcgi	Lists the indexed fields and descriptions of a database
entrez_search()	esearch.fcgi	Searches Entrez database
entrez_summary()	esummary.fcgi	Retreives summary data from database records
entrez_db_links()	Elinkfcgi	Finds links to Entrez database records
entrez_fetch()	efetch.fcgi	Retrieves data from Entrez database records
extract_from_esummary()		Extracts a record summary

The "rentrez" is on the CRAN packages and you can install the latest stable release for Windows with install. packages("rentrez") as follows:

> install.packages("rentrez")

However, for Linux and a Linux environment, you need to run the following commands on the Linux terminal command-line prompt:

$ sudo apt-get update -y
$ sudo apt-get install -y r-cran-rentrez

After the installation of the rentrez package you will be able to search and retrieve data from the Entrez databases.

The rentrez package includes eight functions. Table 6.1 lists these functions and their corresponding E-utilities programs.

You are already familiar with the uses of these functions and their parameters, which were discussed in detail in both Chapters 4 and 5. We will not spend time in repeating the discussion on what these functions do, nor on explaining their parameters. The focus will be on how to use these functions.

In any new R session, you will need to load the "rentrez" package to be able to use its functions. You can load the "rentrez" package by running the following function:

> library(rentrez)

Before using any rentrez function you may need to list that function's arguments. You can list the argument of any function in R by using the "args()" function. For example, to list the arguments of "entrez_search()" function you can run the following:

> args(entrez_search)

Always use this function to see the arguments of any one of the entrez functions.

You may also need to use your NCBI API key, which has been discussed in Chapters 4 and 5. Use the "api_key=" argument of a rentrez function to provide your key. For example, to pass your API key to the "entrez_search()" function, you can provide it as follows:

> entrez_search(……, api_key ='Your_key')

In the following section, we will discuss the use of each of the rentrez functions.

```
> library(rentrez)
> entrez_dbs()
 [1] "pubmed"          "protein"          "nuccore"          "ipg"
 [5] "nucleotide"      "structure"        "genome"           "annotinfo"
 [9] "assembly"        "bioproject"       "biosample"        "blastdbinfo"
[13] "books"           "cdd"              "clinvar"          "gap"
[17] "gapplus"         "grasp"            "dbvar"            "gene"
[21] "gds"             "geoprofiles"      "homologene"       "medgen"
[25] "mesh"            "ncbisearch"       "nlmcatalog"       "omim"
[29] "orgtrack"        "pmc"              "popset"           "proteinclusters"
[33] "pcassay"         "protfam"          "biosystems"       "pccompound"
[37] "pcsubstance"     "seqannot"         "snp"              "sra"
[41] "taxonomy"        "biocollections"   "gtr"
>
```

FIGURE 6.1   The list of Entrez database names.

```
> library(rentrez)
> entrez_db_summary(db="protein")
 DbName: protein
 MenuName: Protein
 Description: Protein sequence record
 DbBuild: Build210613-0506m.1
 Count: 948613763
 LastUpdate: 2021/06/14 18:36
>
```

FIGURE 6.2   Protein database summary.

List the NCB Databases

For the listing of the Entrez databases it is important to know the valid database names, which will be provided in the "db=" argument of some rentrez functions. The valid entrez database names are listed by using "entrez_dbs()" as follows.

> library(rentrez)
> entrez_dbs()

Whenever you need to know the valid name of a database to use with a rentrez function you use "entrez_dbs()", which will display the database names as shown in Figure 6.1.

Displaying a Database Summary

The rentrez package provides the "entrez_db_summary()" function to display the summary of an Entrez database specified in the "db=" argument. The summary, as shown in Figure 6.2, includes the database name, the database menu name as chosen from the Entrez dropdown menu on the Entrez web interface, the description of the database, the database build, the number of entries on the database, and the date of last update. The syntax of using this is as follows:

> entrez_db_summary(db= "database_name")

For example, the following R script displays the summary information of the Protein database.

> entrez_db_summary(db="protein")

As of the date of running the above command, the Entrez Protein database has 948,613,763 protein records. The database was last updated on June 14, 2021. The number of records in a database may change with time since new records will be added to the database.

```
> entrez_db_searchable(db="taxonomy")
Searchable fields for database 'taxonomy'
  ALL    All terms from all searchable fields
  UID    Unique number assigned to publication
  FILT   Limits the records
  SCIN   Scientific name of organism
  COMN   Common name of organism
  TXSY   Synonym of organism name
  ALLN   All aliases for organism
  NXLV   Immediate parent in taxonomic hierarchy
  SBTR   Any parent node in taxonomic hierarchy
  LNGE   Lineage in taxonomic hierarchy
  GC     Nuclear genetic code
  MGC    Mitochondrial genetic code
  PGC    Plastid genetic code
  TXDV   GenBank division
  RANK   Hierarchical position (e.g., order, genus)
  EDAT   Date record first accessible through Entrez
  MDAT   Date of last update
  PROP   Property defined on particular node (e.g., terminal node)
  WORD   Free text associated with record
  NTOK   Name tokens associated with organism names
  HGC    Hydrogenosome genetic code
>
```

FIGURE 6.3   Indexed fields and descriptions of taxonomy database.

Displaying the Field List of a Database

Another important thing you may need to know before building a search query is the list of the indexed fields of an Entrez database. You can use the "entrez_db_searchable()" function to list the indexed fields and their description for a database, the name of which you can specify in the "db=" argument. The following is the list of the indexed fields for the Protein database.

> library(rentrez)

> entrez_db_searchable(db="protein")

Any time you need to list the indexed fields of an Entrez database, you can run the above function, which displays the indexed fields as shown in Figure 6.3.

Searching Entrez Databases

Searching the Entrez databases is the main purpose of any program serving as an interface for the E-utilities. Rentrez package introduces "entrez_search()" as an interface for sending a search query to a specific database and then returning the request response, which is the list of the UIDs of the records matching the search query. Whenever you need the argument list of a function you can always run the "args()" function. The following is the general syntax of entrez_search():

entrez_search(db, term, config = NULL, retmode = "xml", retmax=20, use_history = FALSE, …)

The "entrez_search()" function always requires a target database "db=" to search and a search query "term=" that set the criteria for database records that you are looking for. The target database is any valid Entrez database name and the search query follows the Entrez conventions we discussed in Chapter 3. By default, the "retmode=" is set to "xml" and "retmax=" is set to 20, and "use_history=" is set to FALSE. The "retmode=" argument determines the retrieval mode as either "xml" or "json". The "retmax=" argument determines the maximum number of UIDs that can be returned by the function. The "use_history=" is a Boolean argument that takes either FALSE or TRUE. If it is set to TRUE, the function will upload the UIDs of the records matching the search query to the NCBI History Server. If "use_history=" is set to FALSE, only the number of

FIGURE 6.4   The data items returned by entrez_search() function.

UIDs specified by "retmax", if it is less than the number allowed by NCBI, will be returned. If the number of records returned by the function is more than that specified by "retmax=", the remaining UIDs will be ignored. To learn more about these arguments, you can refer to both Chapters 4 and 5.

In the following example, you will search the Nucleotide database for nucleotide records for the human breast cancer gene (BRCA1).

> library(rentrez)

> s_results <- entrez_search(db="nucleotide", term="BRCA1[GENE] AND human [ORGN]", retmax=20)

The results will be directed to the "s_results" variable, which is a way of storing data in the programming environment for further processing. You can use the "summary()" function to display the types of data stored in that variable.

> summary(s_results)

As shown in the summary of the "s_results" variable (Figure 6.4) that "s_results" is a containter for five items – "id", "count", "retmax", "QueryTranslation", and "file". Each of these items has a length, class, and mode. The "ids" item has a character data type and it stores the UIDs. The "count" item stores a single numeric value, which is the number of UIDs matching the search query. The "retmax" item stores a numeric value provided by the user in "retmax=" argument. The "QueryTranslation" item stores the string search query provided by the user in "term=" argument. The "file" element stores the XML output generated by the original E-utilities ESearch program. The "s_results" is just a container that holds those mentioned items and each of these items holds certain data.

In the following, we will run the same above search but this time with "use_history=TRUE".

> query <- "BRCA1[GENE] AND human[ORGN]"

> s_results <- entrez_search(db="nucleotide", term=query, retmax=20, use_history=TRUE)

> summary(s_results)

In the above script, instead of providing the query directly to the "term=" argument, we created a string variable "query" that holds the search query and then we provided that variable to the "term=" argument. This will make the script more readable. You can also notice that because "use_history=TRUE" was added to the entrez_search() function, the "web_history" item, which is a list of two items, was added to the results as shown in Figure 6.5.

So far, the search results are stored in the "s_results" variable, which contains six data items. You can display the content of any of these items by entering "s_results$item_name", where "item_name" is any one of the items listed above by the variable summary.

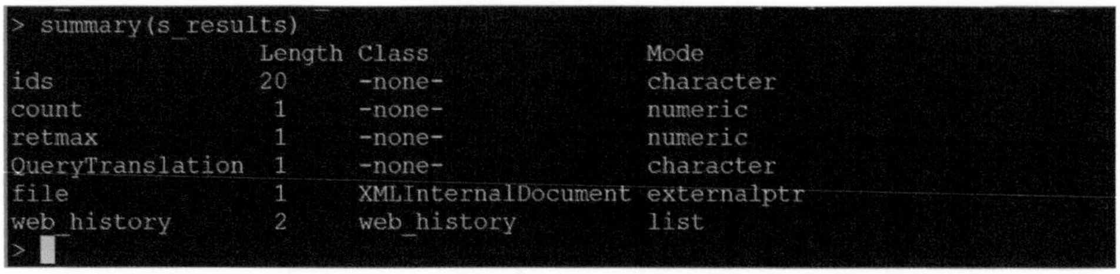

```
> summary(s_results)
          Length Class             Mode
ids           20  -none-           character
count          1  -none-           numeric
retmax         1  -none-           numeric
QueryTranslation 1  -none-         character
file           1  XMLInternalDocument externalptr
web_history    2  web_history      list
>
```

FIGURE 6.5   The data items returned by entrez_search() function with "use_ history=TRUE".

To list the 20 UIDs in the search results, enter:

> s_results$ids

To see the total number of records matching the search query, enter:

> s_results$count

To display the original XML file returned by E-utilities ESearch, enter:

> s_results$file

To display both QueryKey and WebEnv string, enter:

> s_results$web_history

Refer to Chapters 4 and 5, where we discussed in detail the ESearch function and its arguments and XML output. The search query follows the Entrez rules so you can create an advanced search query using the indexed fields of the target database. Since R session is a programming environment, you can save the search query in an external file and then upload it. This is useful when the search query is long. For example, you can save "BRCA1[GENE] AND human[ORGN]" in a text file (e.g. query.txt) in your working directory and then you can use the search query in that text file as follows:

```
> query <- readLines("query.txt")
> s_results <- entrez_search(db="nucleotide", term=query, retmax=20, use_history =TRUE)
> summary(s_results)
```

As an R programmer, you can use the results of the entrez_search() function in various ways since the results include the UID list, the total number of records matching the search query, the XML file, and the query key and WebEnv string. NCBI restricts the number of records per request. However, you can use your API key as explained above and also you can use "use_history=TRUE" setting to upload all the UIDs of the records matching the search query to the History Server and then you can retrieve them from there. We will cover that soon.

Getting Summary Data from Records

The "entrez_summary()" function retrieves the summary of an Entrez database record. It requires a target database and UIDs. Its syntax is as follows:

```
entrez_summary(db=, id = NULL, web_history = NULL, version = c("2.0", "1.0"), always_return_list
= FALSE, retmode = NULL, config = NULL, …)
```

```
> summary(brca1_summary)
                    Length Class      Mode
uid                 1      -none-     character
name                1      -none-     character
description         1      -none-     character
status              1      -none-     character
currentid           1      -none-     character
chromosome          1      -none-     character
geneticsource       1      -none-     character
maplocation         1      -none-     character
otheraliases        1      -none-     character
otherdesignations   1      -none-     character
nomenclaturesymbol  1      -none-     character
nomenclaturename    1      -none-     character
nomenclaturestatus  1      -none-     character
mim                 1      -none-     character
genomicinfo         5      data.frame list
geneweight          1      -none-     numeric
summary             1      -none-     character
```

FIGURE 6.6 Partial summary information of a gene record.

```
> brca1_summary$genomicinfo
  chrloc    chraccver chrstart  chrstop exoncount
1     17 NC_000017.11 43125363 43044294        24
>
```

FIGURE 6.7 Genomic information of BRCA1 gene.

The target database can be provided to the "db=" argument and the UIDs are provided to the "id=" argument. However, the UIDs can also be imported from the History Server using the "web_history=" argument.

The following script retrieves the summary information of the human BRCA1 gene (id=672).

```
> brca1_summary <- entrez_summary (db="gene", id="672")
> summary(brca1_summary)
```

In the first line, the results of the entrez_summary() function were stored in the "brca1_summary" variable. In the second line the summary() function will print the list of the items stored in that variable, their length, class, and mode (data type) as shown in Figure 6.6. However, this time, the items store summary information of the database records and the items vary by the database type. The summary information stored in any item can be displayed by running "brca1_summary$item_name", where "item_name" is any one of the items listed in the summary above. For example, to display the genomic information of the gene, you can run the following:

```
> brca1_summary$genomicinfo
```

As shown in Figure 6.7, the human BRCA1 gene is found in chromosome 17, its location is between 43125363 and 43044294 on the chromosome reference sequence (NC_000017.11), and it has 24 exons.

You can use the above format to retrieve the summary information you need. The above is just an example; you can obtain the summary information of any database record using this method.

In the above example, you provided the UID in the "id=" argument of the function. You can import the UID from the History Server as well. In the following example, you will use entrez_search() function, which searches for the BRCA1 gene in the Gene database and then posts the UID to the History Server. The "webenv" variable stores the query key and WebEn string, which are generated by the entrez_search() function. Then that variable is provided to the entrez_summary() function in the "web_history=" argument.

```
> query <- "BRCA1[GENE] AND human[ORGN]"
> s_results <- entrez_search(db="gene", term=query, retmax=20, use_history=TRUE)
```

```
> webenv <- s_results$web_history
> brca1_summary <- entrez_summary (db="gene", web_history= webenv)
> brca1_summary$genomicinfo
```

In the above, you retrieved the summary of only one record. You can retrieve the summaries of multiple records by providing their UIDs. You can either provide the UIDs as a list to the "id=" argument or you can import them from the History Server. In the following scripts, you will store the RefSeq BRCA1 transcripts 1, 2, 3, and 4 (with ids, 732746264, 1677529721, 1677500831, and 237681122, respectively) as a vector assigned to "ids" variable and then you provide that variable to the entrez_summary () as follows:

```
> ids <- c("732746264", "1677529721", "1677500831", "237681122")
> brca1_summary <- entrez_summary (db="nucleotide", id=ids)
> summary(brca1_summary)
```

Because the "brca1_summary" variable stores summary information of multiple records, the summary() function displays the UID list and each UID with length (33), class (esummary), and mode (list) as shown in Figure 6.8.

You can list the summary items of each UID by using "brca1_summary$"UID". For example, to list the summary items of 732746264, you can use:

```
> brca1_summary$"732746264"
```

The summary items of the BRCA1 transcript 1 are 32 as shown in in Figure 6.9.

To print the content of a summary item of a record, you can use the form "brca1_summary$"UID"$item_name". For example, for the sequence length of each of the four human BRCA1 variants, you can run the following:

```
> brca1_summary$"732746264"$slen
> brca1_summary$"1677529721"$slen
> brca1_summary$"1677500831"$slen
> brca1_summary$"237681122"$slen
```

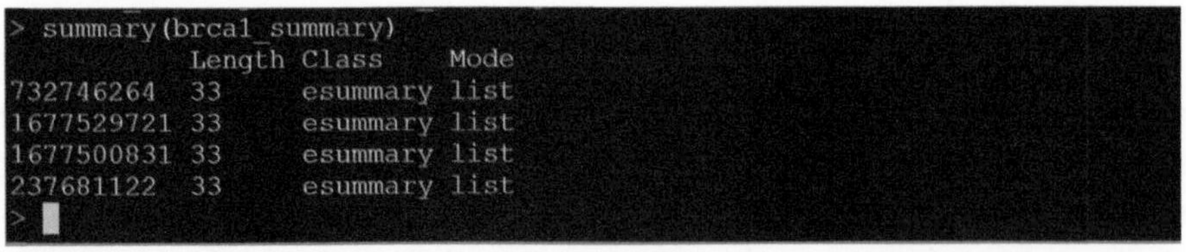

FIGURE 6.8   Summary of multiple records.

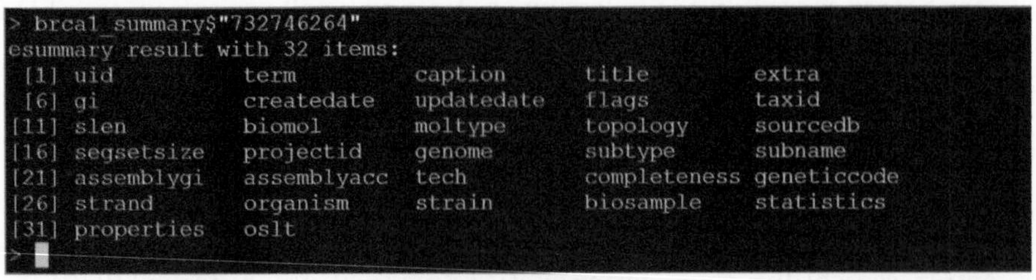

FIGURE 6.9   Summary items of a single record.

FIGURE 6.10   Sequence lengths of four BRCA1 transcript variants.

FIGURE 6.11   Using extract_from_summary() to print multiple summary items.

Extracting Summary Data from Records

In the previous section, you used the "variablName$Item_name" format to display the content of a summary item. However, the "extract_from_esummary()" function will allow you to extract summary information from multiple summary items and to create a tabular report. It has the following syntax:

> extract_from_esummary(esummaries, elements, simplify = TRUE)

The "esummaries" is any Esummary variable storing the summary of a single records or multiple records. For example, to extract the sequence length of the four BRCA1 transcripts you can run the following R script whose output is shown in Figure 6.10:

> extract_from_esummary(brca1_summary, c("slen"))

You can extract multiple summary items as follows:

> extract_from_esummary(brca1_summary, c("uid", "slen", "moltype", "biomol", "taxid"))

The above R script displays multiple summary items as shown in Figure 6.11.

There are several R packages that can be installed and used to create more organized tabular reports from the output of extract_from_essummary() function. One of these packages is "knitr" which has the "kable()" function that can be used to organize the above output into a more organized table.

Install the "knitr" R package by running the following:

> install.packages("knitr")

Once it has been installed, you need to load the packages to use the "kable" function:

> library(knitr)

Using the following script you will organize the above in a table using "kabke()" as follows and the output is shown in Figure 6.12:

> Brca1_summs <- extract_from_esummary (brca1_summary, c("uid", "slen", "moltype", "biomol", "taxid"))
> kable(head(t(Brca1_summs)), row.names= FALSE)

```
|uid        |slen |moltype |biomol   |taxid |
|:----------|:----|:-------|:--------|:-----|
|732746264  |1163 |dna     |genomic  |61180 |
|1677529721 |7151 |rna     |mRNA     |9606  |
|1677500831 |7028 |rna     |mRNA     |9606  |
|237681122  |3699 |rna     |mRNA     |9606  |
>
```

FIGURE 6.12   Organizing extracted record summary in a tabular report.

```
>NP_009230.2 breast cancer type 1 susceptibility protein isoform 5
[Homo sapiens]
MDLSALRVEEVQNVINAMQKILECPICLELIKEPVSTKCDHIFCKFCMLKLLNQKKGPSQCPLCKNDITK
RSLQESTRFSQLVEELLKIICAFQLDTGLEYANSYNFAKKENNSPEHLKDEVSIIQSMGYRNRAKRLLQS
EPENPSLQETSLSVQLSNLGTVRTLRTKQRIQPQKTSVYIELGSDSSEDTVNKATYCSVGDQELLQITPQ
GTRDEISLDSAKKAACEFSETDVTNTEHHQPSNNDLNTTEKRAAERHPEKYQGEAASGCESETSVSEDCS
GLSSQSDILTTQQRDTMQHNLIKLQQEMAELEAVLEQHGSQPSNSYPSIISDSSALEDLRNPEQSTSEKV
LTSQKSSEYPISQNPEGLSADKFEVSADSSTSKNKEPGVERSSPSKCPSLDDRWYMHSCSGSLQNRNYPS
QEELIKVVDVEEQQLEESGPHDLTETSYLPRQDLEGTPYLESGISLFSDDPESDPSEDRAPESARVGNIP
SSTSALKVPQLKVAESAQSPAAAHTTDTAGYNAMEESVSREKPELTASTERVNKRMSMVVSGLTPEEFML
VYKFARKHHITLTNLITEETTHVVMKTDAEFVCERTLKYFLGIAGGKWVVSYFWVTQSIKERKMLNEHDF
EVRGDVVNGRNHQGPKRARESQDRKIFRGLEICCYGPFTNMPTGCPPNCGCAARCLDRGQWLPCNWADV
>
```

FIGURE 6.13   The FASTA sequence of BRCA1 protein isoform 5.

Fetching Database Records

The "entrez_fetch()" function retrieves data from Entrez database records. It behaves similarly to EFetch, as described in Chapters 4 and 5. It requires a target Entrez database and a UID or a list of UIDs. The database is provided to the "db=" argument and the UIDs are either provided to the "id=" argument or imported from the History Server by providing the query key and WebEnv string as a list to the "web_history" argument. The following is the syntax of the function:

> entrez_fetch(db, id=NULL, web_history=NULL, rettype, retmode ="", parsed = FALSE, config = NULL, …)

Refer to Chapter 5 for the use of EFetch and to Table 5.2 to review the valid options of the retrieval type (rettype) and retrieval mode (retmode). The "rettype" is used to retrieve data from database records. For example, for sequence databases such as Nucleotide and Protein you can use the "rettype=fasta" setting to retrieve only the sequences in FASTA format. The following script retrieves the FASTA sequence of the BRCA1 protein isoform 5 whose id is 237681125.

> entrez_fetch(db="protein", id=237681125, rettype="fasta")

The sequence will contain "\n" which is the escape sequence for a new line feed. You can get rid of the new line escape sequence either by saving the sequence to a text file using "write()" function or by using "cat(strwrap(substr()), sep="\n")" as follows and the output is shown in Figure 6.13:

> seq <- entrez_fetch(db="protein", id=237681125, rettype="fasta")
> cat(strwrap(substr(seq, 1, 1000)), sep="\n")

You can also retrieve sequences from multiple records. In the following example, you will fetch the FASTA sequences of the five RefSeq BRCA1 protein isoforms. After fetching the sequences, you can display them on screen and also save them in a file in your working directory.

> query <- "BRCA1[GENE] AND human[ORGN] AND refseq[FILT]"
> search_res <- entrez_search(db="protein", term=query, retmax=20)

```
> brca1_isoforms <- entrez_fetch(db= "protein", id=search_res$ids, rettype="fasta")
> cat(strwrap(substr(brca1_isoforms, 1, 10000)), sep="\n")
> write(brca1_isoforms,file="brca1_isofor ms.fasta")
```

In the above "entrez_fetch", you provided the UIDs as "id=search_res$ids". Instead of that you can import the UIDs from the History Server by setting "use_history=TRUE" in "entrez_search" and "web_history=TRUE" in "entrez_fetch" as follows:

```
> query <- "BRCA1[GENE] AND human[ORGN] AND refseq[FILT]"
> search_res <- entrez_search(db= "protein", term=query, use_history=TRUE, retmax=20)
> brca1_isoforms <- entrez_fetch(db="protein", web_history=search_res$web_history, rettype="fasta")
> write(brca1_isoforms,file="brca1_isofor ms2.fasta")
```

In another example, we can fetch the abstracts from PubMed articles returned by "entrez_search" and store them in a file.

```
> query <- "(breast cancer[MeSH]) AND (BRCA1 mutation[MeSH]) AND 2010:2015[PDAT]"
> bcancer_search <- entrez_search(db = "pubmed", term =query, retmax=20, use_history=TRUE)
> absts <- entrez_fetch(db="pubmed", web_history=bcancer_search$web_history, rettype="abstract")
> write(absts, file="absts.txt")
```

NCBI restricts the number of records to retrieve per time. However, the UIDs can be uploaded to the History Server and then their records can be retrieved iteratively by setting the value of the "retstart=" argument to a new start index until all records are retrieved. We have already discussed this in Chapters 4 and 5. This time, you can use programming feature like "for-loop". In the following example, the entrez_search() function will find a large number of matching protein records to the refseq PPARG proteins. The query does not specify any organism; therefore, the refseq PPARG protein records of various organisms will be included in the search results. The UIDs will be uploaded to the History Server. Then the entrez_fetch() function will import the UIDs from the History Server repeatedly using the "for-loop", but every time the start is incremented by 499 and the number of retrieved records is 500. The entrez_fetch() function retrieves the FASTA protein sequences, which will be appended to a file. The process is repeated until all records are retrieved. The following R codes are written as a script, which can be typed on the script editor or a text editor. Then it can be either run as a script in R or can be copied and pasted on the R command-line prompt.

```
library(rentrez)
query <- "PPARG[GENE] AND refseq[FILT]"
pparg <- entrez_search(db="protein", term=query, use_history=TRUE)
webenv <- pparg$web_history
for(start in seq(1,1500,500))
{recs <- entrez_fetch(db="protein",
    web_history=webenv,
    rettype="fasta",
    retmax=500,
    retstart=start)
```

```
# create a new file if this is the first sequence
if(start==1){
    cat(recs, file="pparg.fasta")
}else{
    cat(recs, file="pparg.fasta", append=TRUE)
}
# print status to console
cat(start+499, "sequences have been downloaded\n")
}
```

The FASTA file "pparg.fasta" containing the sequences of the refseq PPARG protein will be saved in the working directory.

Listing Linked Databases and Records

The "entrez_db_links()" function lists the Entrez database that are linked to the target database specified in the "db=" argument. To find the list of databases linked to the Entrez protein database, enter the following:

```
> entrez_db_links(db="protein")
```

The linked database records to a specific database record are found by the "entrez_link()" function, which interacts with the "elink.fcgi" E-utilities API. Its syntax is as follows:

```
entrez_link(dbfrom, web_history = NULL, id = NULL, db = NULL, cmd = "neighbor", by_id = FALSE)
```

Refer to Chapters 4 and 5, where this function was discussed in detail. It requires the UIDs that you need to find the linked records, the database that contains the UIDs (dbfrom=), and the target database (db=) on which you wish to search for the linked records. The UIDs can either be provided in the "db=" argument or can be imported from the Server History using the "web_history=".

The following script will find the protein records linked to the human BRCA1 gene (id=672).

```
> gene_links <- entrez_link(dbfrom="gene", id="672", db="protein")
```

The protein records found by this script is stored in the "gene_links" variable. From the previous chapter, remember that any "dbfrom-db" linked records has link names that can be used to filter the linked records. To display the link names for "gene-protein", enter the following:

```
> gene_links$links
```

Figure 6.14 shows that there are two link names: (1) gene_protein, which includes non-refseq protein records, and (2) gene_protein_refseq, which includes the refseq protein records.

To list the record UIDs in any of these two link names, enter the following:

```
> gene_links$links$gene_protein
> gene_links$links$gene_protein_refseq
```

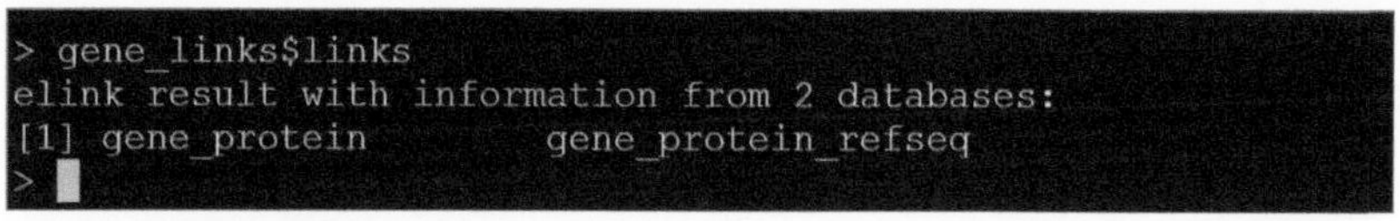

```
> gene_links$links
elink result with information from 2 databases:
[1] gene_protein          gene_protein_refseq
>
```

FIGURE 6.14   Gene-protein link names.

In the following script, "entrez_link" finds the protein linked to the human BRCA1 gene. The second line filters only the refseq BRCA1 protein records. Then, the ids of that record are provided to "entrez_fetch" to retrieve their FASTA sequences. Finally, the FASTA sequences are saved in a text file.

gene_links <- entrez_link(dbfrom="gene", id="672", db="protein")

brca1_refP <- gene_links$links$gene_protein_refseq

ids <- paste0(brca1_refP, collapse=",")

seq <- entrez_fetch(db="protein", id= ids, rettype="fasta")

write(seq,file="brca1_isoforms.fasta")

The "entrez_link" can also be used to list all the link names of an Entrez database record. The following script will print all the possible link names of the BRCA1 gene.

> gene_links <- entrez_link(dbfrom="gene", id=672, db="all")

> gene_links$links

USING BIOPYTHON FOR ENTREZ DATABASES

In the previous section, we discussed the use of the R Entrez (rentrez) package for Entrez databases. In this section, we will discuss the modules used by BioPython to search the Entrez databases and to retrieve data from their records. Python has emerged as the most commonly used scripting language in bioinformatics, taking the lead from Perl, which has been used for a long time. Many people think that Python over-performs R because it is a scripting language with a full programming capability that can be used to develop desktop and web-based applications and to create a graphical user interface (GUI). Since Python, as a whole, is a general-purpose programming language, it is very fluent for developing bioinformatics tools – regardless of BioPython, which is the topic of this section. Learning Python is a great asset for those who wish to excel in bioinformatics. Learning Python is beyond the scope of this book. This section is for those who use Python and wish to use BioPython to retrieve Entrez databases.

Most bioinformatics in Python can be done through the BioPython package, which is a set of freely available tools for biological computation written in Python by an international team of developers [4]. BioPython avails of the two features the NCBI E-utilities API introduces – URL-based requests and XML responses to the requests – which are the features that any programming language can use to interact with the E-utilities programs for database searching and data retrieval. Python also has several XML parsers as standard libraries that can be used to parse the output for data manipulation.

Since BioPython has a large scope in bioinformatics, our focus in this book will be on using "Bio.Entrez", which provides several functions that interact with the E-utilities APIs and returns data as a handle object.

Python can either be used in either interactive or script mode. In interactive mode, Python statements are run on the Python command line and feedback is given immediately for each statement. In script mode, Python statements are saved in a script file with the ".py" name extension and the script file then can be run from a command prompt of a Linux terminal or Windows Command Prompt window using the "python script.py" form, where "script.py" can be any valid file name with the ".py" extension. Python must be installed on the computer and it is on the path for the Python script file to be run. In this section, you will use script mode most of the time because it allows you to focus more on the script writing. But you may also use the interactive mode to test the Python statement.

Installing Python

Python may be already installed by default on Linux and Linux-like platforms. Python comes in two types of releases: Python 2 and Python 3. You will use Python 3 release (the latest stable version as of the time of writing this book is Python 3.8.0) since Python 3 is strongly recommended for any new development. Python 2 is in the process of retiring and there will be no ongoing support for it from the community. Python installation has never been easier. Its installation is straightforward and fast.

Installing Python and BioPython on Linux

Python is installed by default on a computer with Linux or a Linux environment such as MacOS. You can check whether Python 3 is installed or not by opening the Linux terminal and run the Python command as follows:

$ python3

If Python 3 is installed on the Linux of your machine, you will see the Python shell screen as shown in Figure 6.15.

Pay attention to the Python version when you run the python command. You may have different python versions installed on your computer. You can exit from the Python shell by pressing "Ctrl+z".

Some Linux machines may have only Python 2 installed or may have an old version of Python 3. You can install or upgrade Python 3 as follows:

$ sudo apt-get update

$ sudo apt-get install python3.8

If Python3 is installed on your machine, then you can install the BioPython package. Since you may have different Python releases or versions on your computer, it is better always to specify the release and version of Python you use in any package installation. For BioPython you will use "pip", which is a standard package-management system used to install and manage software packages written in Python. You can install the BioPython package in Python3.8 as follows:

$ python3.8 -m pip install biopython

After the successful installation you can check if BioPython works properly by opening the Python shell using the following command.

$ python3.8

On the Python shell run "import Bio" and then "print(Bio.__version__)", which will display the BioPython version as shown in Figure 6.16 if BioPython is installed.

You may use the interactive mode as the above occasionally but you will use the script mode because it provides more flexibility and reusability. If you wish to use the script mode for the above, first you will exit the

```
hamiddafa@dax:~$ python3.8
Python 3.8.0 (default, Oct 28 2019, 16:14:01)
[GCC 8.3.0] on linux
Type "help", "copyright", "credits" or "license" for more information.
>>>
```

FIGURE 6.15 **Python 3 shell.**

FIGURE 6.16   BioPython version in Python interactive mode.

FIGURE 6.17   BioPython version in Python script mode.

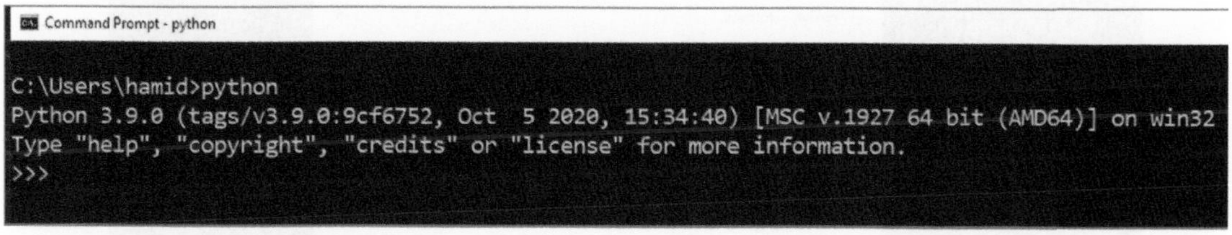

FIGURE 6.18   Python's shell on Windows 10.

Python shell by pressing "Ctrl+z" and on the command line of the Linux terminal, create a file (e.g., version.py) using the vim or nano text editor. Then type the following on the file, save it, and exit.

```
#file: version.py
import Bio
ver = Bio.__version__
print(ver)
```

After saving the above in a text file with "version.py" name, you can run the python script file on the command line as follows and the output is shown in Figure 6.17:

```
$ python3.8 version.py
```

Installing Python and BioPython on Windows

Installing Python on a Windows machine has also never been easier. Visit the Python website www.python.org/downloads/, download the latest Python 3 version to your Windows local drive and double-click on the installer. The installer will start to install Python on your computer. The installer may ask you for permission to make some change to set Python on the path. Follow the instructions until the installation is completed. Although there are several Python IDEs (integrated development environments) for Windows, you will use the Windows Command Prompt (CMT) for the script mode. After installing Python 3, open the Windows Command Prompt and type "python" on the command line and press the "Enter" key. If Python has been installed successfully, the Python shell will open as shown in Figure 6.18.

```
> python
```

You can press "Ctrl+z" to exit the Python shell to the command prompt. Now you can install the BioPython package on the Python by running the following command on the Window command line.

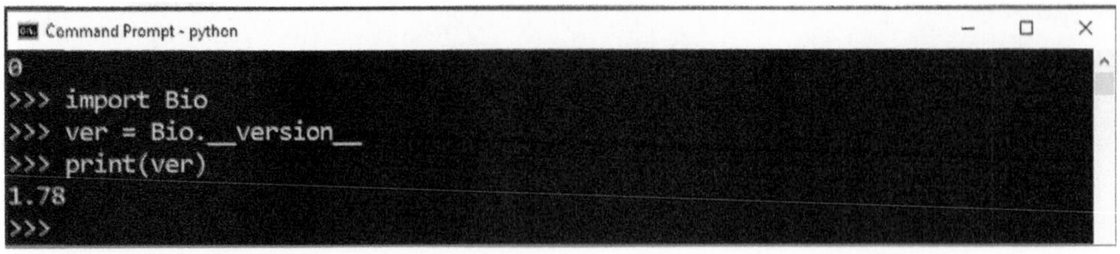

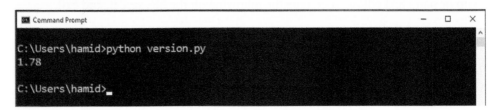

FIGURE 6.19   BioPython version in Python interactive mode.

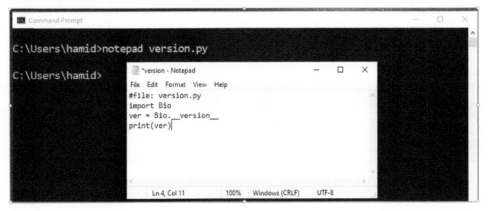

FIGURE 6.20   Python script in a file opened on notepad on Windows.

```
Command Prompt                                      —  □  ×

C:\Users\hamid>python version.py
1.78

C:\Users\hamid>
```

FIGURE 6.21   BioPython version in Python script mode.

> pip install biopython

If you get an error, you may need to download and install Microsoft Build Tools for Visual Studio from the Visual Studio website at https://visualstudio.microsoft.com/downloads/. You may need to restart your computer after installing Microsoft Build Tools. Once your computer has been restarted, open the Command Prompt window and then try to install BioPython again as above.

When BioPython has been installed successfully without any error, run python on the command line on the interactive mode using "> python" and on the Python shell run "import Bio" and then "print(Bio.__version__)" to display the BioPython version, as shown in Figure 6.19, if BioPython is installed.

You can also check the BioPython version by using Python script mode as you did above on the Linux system. On the command line, open the Windows text editor "Notepad" as follows:

> notepad version.py

Type the same above script in the text file as shown in Figure 6.20, save the file, and exit.

After typing or copying the above in the text file, save the file in the current directory and exit. You can run Python script as follows and the output will be as shown in Figure 6.21:

> python version.py

Whether you are using a Linux terminal or Windows Command Prompt, the use of Python and BioPython will be almost the same, except for some rules based on the operating system, such as shell commands and file path.

Using BioPython Entrez Package

If you did not skip the previous chapters, you would have a clear picture about what BioPython Entrez functions do. The BioPython Entrez functions are the ones that interact with the NCBI's E-utilities APIs. They allow Python programmers to develop programs that can be used for searching the Entrez databases and to retrieve data for further processing and manipulation. The BioPython functions are included in "Bio.Entrez" Python module and shown in Table 6.2.

In the following we will discuss each of the above functions. Sometimes, you may use the Python interactive mode but you will use the script mode most of the time. For the examples in this chapter, when the interactive mode is used, the Python statements will be written after the Python shell prompt ">>>" as an indication for the interactive model. Writing Python script statements without ">>>" will indicate that the script must be typed in a text file with ".py" extension and the script file will be run on the command line using "python script.py".

Before you start running any BioPython Entrez function, it is important to let NCBI know your email. You can also provide your NCBI API key, which will help you to make ten queries per second instead of only three. If you are using interactive mode, you may need to tell NCBI about your email and API key just once at the beginning of the interactive session, which starts when you open Python shell. If you are using the script mode you can define both email and API key once at the beginning of the script. Both "email" and "api_key" are attributes in "Bio.Entrez" module. Notice that we used parameters with E-utilities, argument with the EDirect and R Entrez package, and with Python we will use attributes as each program has its different jargon for the same thing. The definition of an attribute in a Python module is a variable that can be either set to a value or get a value from or both. Interactively, you can define both email and API key as follows:

```
>>> from Bio import Entrez
>>> Entrez.email = "yourEmail@example.com"
>>> Entrez.api_key = "yourApiKey"
```

You will need to provide your real email and API key. If you do not have an API key, you can obtain one from the MyNCBI website as discussed in Chapter 4.

In the script mode, you can type the above statements without ">>>" at the beginning of the script text file as you will see in coming examples.

TABLE 6.2 BioPython Entrez Functions

Entrez Function	Description
Bio.Entrez.einfo()	provides indexed field names of a database and other information
Bio.Entrez.epost()	posts UIDs to the History Server
Bio.Entrez.esearch()	searches databases and returns UIDs of the matching records
Bio.Entrez.esummary()	retrieves document summaries of database records
Bio.Entrez.efetch()	retrieves data from database records
Bio.Entrez.elink()	finds the records linked to database records
Bio.Entrez.egquery()	provides records counts on all databases for a specific search term
Bio.Entrez.espell()	provides correction suggestions for mistakenly written search terms
Bio.Entrez.ecitmatch()	retrieves PubMed PMIDs that correspond to a set of input citation strings
Bio.Entrez.read(handle)	parses an XML file from the NCBI Entrez Utilities into python objects
Bio.Entrez.parse(handle)	parses an XML file from the NCBI Entrez Utilities into python objects

In the above statements, first you imported the "Entrez", which is a sub-module in the "Bio" module. Secondly, you set the "email" and "api_key", which are attributes of the "Entrez" sub-module. Python 3 is an object-oriented programming (OOP), therefore, functions and attributes within a module can be accessed using the period "." between the module and an attribute and function name.

All Entrez functions are included in the "Bio.Entrez" module. Therefore, you need to import the "Entrez" module as follows:

>>> from Bio import Entrez

In script mode, this statement must be at the beginning of the script file before using any Entrez function. Once you run the above statement in Python interactive mode, you can then use the Entrez functions as long as you are using the session.

The Entrez functions in BioPython work through handles, which are created by calling the Entrez functions. Handles are pointers to Python object types. A BioPython Entrez handle is created using the following general form:

>>> handle = Entrez.FunctionName()

In the above statement, "handle" is a variable name and can be any other valid name of your choice. "FunctionName()" is any "Bio.Entrez" function. The handle points to the results of the Entrez function. Once a handle has been created, it can be read using any one of the following two forms:

>>> output = handle.read()
>>> output = Entrez.read(handle)

In the coming examples, you will come across each form and you will notice the difference.

The above statements will read the returned results in the "output" variable. When you read the handle, do not forget to close it to free the memory holding the handle as follows:

>>> handle.close()

In the following, you will use the above basic statement forms to use each of the BioPython Entrez functions. From now on, you have to pay attention to that any python script must be saved in a text file using a plain text editor of your choice. On Linux you can use vim or nano text editor on the Linux terminal (e.g., $ vim myfile. py). On Windows, you can use Notepad on the command prompt (e.g., > notepad myfile.py). After saving the python script file, it can be executed using "$ python myfile". Also notice that we use ">", "$", and ">>>" just to show you that we run the statement from Windows command prompt, Linux terminal, or Python shell, respectively. Those symbols are not part of the statement and you should not type them when you run the statements. Sometimes there may be multiple python releases or versions on your computer. Always use the python version in which you installed BioPython (e.g., python3 myfile.py). If you do not have multiple python releases on your computer you may execute your python file using "python myfile.py". If you get an error when you execute the python script file then you might have used a wrong release. Also, you need to pay attention that the python statements are the same for all computer platforms (Linux, Mac, and Windows). However, there are some operating system rules you need to follow such as file path on Linux ("/" is used) and Windows ("\" is used).

Getting Information of Entrez Databases

The "Bio.Entrez.Einfo()" function is used to obtain the list of the Entrez databases or the list of indexed fields of a specified database and their descriptions.

In the following script, "Entrez" is imported from the "Bio" module. The "Entrez" sub module has "email=" and "api_key=" attributes, where you can provide your email and your API key if you have one. The line of the API key is commented to be ignored by the interpreter. Remove the comment symbol "#" and type your valid API key if you have one. Otherwise leave the line commented. In the fifth line, a handle is created by "Entrez.einfo()", which will send a request to the NCBI database via the E-utilities API and will receive the XML response, which is stored on a handle "handle". The handle then will be read onto the "output" variable using the "Entrez.read()" function. The "Entrez.read()" reads the XML response and reformats it into a Python dictionary containing the Entrez databases. Once the handle is read, you can close it to free the memory.

Open a text editor, enter the following script, and save the file with a "dbinfo1.py" file name.

```
#File: dbeinfo1.py
from Bio import Entrez
Entrez.email = "myemail@example.com"
#Entrez.api_key = "yourApiKey"   #enter a valid API key and remove "#"
handle = Entrez.einfo()
output = Entrez.read(handle)
handle.close()
print(output)
```

Save the script file and exit. The "dbeinfo1.py" python file then can be executed from either Windows command-line prompt or Linux terminal command line as follows:

```
$ python3 dbeinfo1.py
```

After running "dbeinfo1.py", the Entrez databases will be displayed in a Python dictionary as shown in Figure 6.22. A python dictionary is formed of key-value pairs contained within curly braces "{"key1": value1, "key2": value2, …}, keys are the names and values are the values of the keys. A value of a dictionary can be simple data type like a number or a string or can be a complex data structure like a list, a tuple, or a nested dictionary. The output read from "Entrez.einfo()" handle is a dictionary of a single key "DbList" whose value is the list of the Entrez databases.

The database list contained in the "DbList" key can be obtained with "output["DbList"]" and the results will be a Python string list. You can add statements to the above script to obtain the database list and then use "for-loop" to print the database names as follows:

```
#File: dbeinfo2.py
#the program will list the Entrez databases
```

```
{'DbList': ['pubmed', 'protein', 'nuccore', 'ipg', 'nucleotide', 'structure', 'genome',
 'annotinfo', 'assembly', 'bioproject', 'biosample', 'blastdbinfo', 'books', 'cdd', 'cl
invar', 'gap', 'gapplus', 'grasp', 'dbvar', 'gene', 'gds', 'geoprofiles', 'homologene',
 'medgen', 'mesh', 'ncbisearch', 'nlmcatalog', 'omim', 'orgtrack', 'pmc', 'popset', 'pr
oteinclusters', 'pcassay', 'protfam', 'biosystems', 'pccompound', 'pcsubstance', 'seqan
not', 'snp', 'sra', 'taxonomy', 'biocollections', 'gtr']}

C:\Users\hamid\py>
```

FIGURE 6.22   **BioPython version in Python script mode.**

```
from Bio import Entrez
Entrez.email = "myemail@example.com"

handle = Entrez.einfo()
output = Entrez.read(handle)
handle.close()
for db in output["DbList"]:
    print(db)
```

You may need to pay attention to that python is very strict in the statement indentation. Also notice that the lines that begin with "#" will be considered as comments and will be ignored by the interpreter. When you execute the "dbeinfo2.py", the database names containing in "DbList" will be printed.

The word argument is used in python if you pass a value to a python function. When the "db=" argument is used with "Bio.Entrez.einfo()", the response will be the information about the database specified in that argument. The database name can be any valid database name as listed above. The following script creates a handle that points to the information of the Protein database, reads the handle, and prints the output. Enter the script in a text file (e.g., dbeinfo3.py) and execute it on the command-line prompt as above.

```
#File: dbeinfo3.py
from Bio import Entrez
Entrez.email = "myemail@example.com"
handle = Entrez.einfo(db="protein")
output = Entrez.read(handle)
print(output)
```

The output is a python dictionary with a single key "DbInfo" that contains nested dictionaries as a value. The following script will list the dictionary keys nested in "DbInfo". Save the script in a file "dbeinfo4.py" and execute it.

```
#File: dbeinfo4.py
#list the key inside "DbInfo"
from Bio import Entrez
Entrez.email = "myemail@example.com"
handle = Entrez.einfo(db="protein")
output = Entrez.read(handle)
for key in output["DbInfo"]:
    print(key)
```

The list of the dictionary keys in "DbInfo" are shown in Figure 6.23. The names of the keys are self-explanatory; however, the keys that store important information that we may need to know is "Count", which stores the total number of entries on the database, "FieldList", which stores the indexed fields of the database, and "LinkList", which stores the link names of the database. Figure 6.23 shows the general keys of the "DbInfo". Therefore, you can use Python programming capability to print a report displaying the name and the number of entries for each Entrez database by using the following script.

```
C:\Users\hamid\py>python dbinfo4.py
DbName
MenuName
Description
DbBuild
Count
LastUpdate
FieldList
LinkList

C:\Users\hamid\py>
```

FIGURE 6.23 Dictionary keys in "DbInfo".

No.	Database	Count
1	pubmed	32683616
2	protein	948830666
3	nuccore	468285993
4	ipg	427644177
5	nucleotide	468285993
6	structure	178982
7	genome	77638
8	annotinfo	1306
9	assembly	1067247
10	bioproject	520257
11	biosample	18107706
12	blastdbinfo	11480379
13	books	1026525
14	cdd	62852
15	clinvar	1033703
16	gap	363665
17	gapplus	136796
18	grasp	7862970
19	dbvar	6855127
20	gene	52095440
21	gds	4664115
22	geoprofiles	12841405
23	homologene	141268
24	medgen	203655
25	mesh	348681
26	ncbisearch	3941
27	nlmcatalog	1627233
28	omim	27240
29	orgtrack	7382
30	pmc	7194960
31	popset	363342
32	proteinclusters	1137329
33	pcassay	1366335
34	protfam	179613
35	biosystems	983968
36	pccompound	109923443
37	pcsubstance	282878078
38	seqannot	305152
39	snp	1076992604
40	sra	14855804
41	taxonomy	2470058
42	biocollections	8458
43	gtr	77398

FIGURE 6.24 The NCBI Entrez database names and the number of records on each database.

```
#File: dbeinfo5.py
from Bio import Entrez
Entrez.email = "myemail@example.com"
handle = Entrez.einfo()
output = Entrez.read(handle)
handle.close()
print(f'{"Database":20} {"Count":15}')
for db in output["DbList"]:
    handle = Entrez.einfo(db=db)
    dbinfo = Entrez.read(handle)
    dbCount = dbinfo["DbInfo"]["Count"]
    #print(db + "\t\t\t" + dbCount)
    print(f'{db:20} {dbCount:15}')
```

The output of the above script is shown in Figure 6.24. The output shows the name and number of entries of each Entrez database as of June 2021.

Since the database indexed fields are stored in "FieldList", you can unpack this nested dictionary into "Name" (for field short name), "FullName" (for field full name), "Description" for the indexed field description. The following script prints the indexed list of the Protein database.

```
#File: dbeinfo6.py
#displays the short field name, full field name
#and description.
from Bio import Entrez
Entrez.email = "myemail@example.com"
handle = Entrez.einfo(db="protein")
output = Entrez.read(handle)
for field in output["DbInfo"]["FieldList"]:
    #print("%(Name)s\t %(FullName)s\t %(Description)s" % field)
    print("%(Name)s\t %(FullName)s" % field)
```

You can also unpack "LinkList" into "Name" (for link name) and "DbTo" (for target database). The following script prints the link names of the Protein database and the target database for each link name.

```
#File: dbeinfo7.py
#displays the link list.
from Bio import Entrez
Entrez.email = "myemail@example.com"
handle = Entrez.einfo(db="protein")
output = Entrez.read(handle)
for link in output["DbInfo"]["LinkList"]:
    print("%(Name)s\t\t\t %(DbTo)s" % link)
```

Searching Entrez Databases

In Chapters 4 and 5, we discussed how ESearch is the function that searches a specified Entrez database for records that match a search query. The "Bio.Entrez.esearch()" BioPython function does exactly the same and it uses "db=", "term=", "retmax=", "retstart=", "usehistory=", and "idtype=" arguments. Refer to Chapters 4 and 5 to learn more about the ESearch arguments. The "db=" argument specifies the target database name. The "term=" argument specifies the search query that follows the Entrez search query rules discussed in Chapter 3. The "retmax=" argument determines the maximum number of UIDs that can be returned by the ESearch function. If the number of records found is more than the maximum number specified by "retmax", only that maximum number of UIDs is returned while the remaining UIDs will be discarded. The "retmax" can be set to a maximum of 100,000 records (i.e., retmax=100000). Retrieving more than 100,000 UIDs requires submitting multiple Esearch requests while incrementing the value of "retstart" as discussed in the previous chapters. The "retstart" argument specifies the index to begin with for retrieving. By default, it is set to zero (i.e., retmax=0). When you set "usehistory" to "y" (i.e., usehistory='y'), the UIDs of the records matching the search query will be stored on the NCBI History Server for the subsequent Entrez function, as we discussed several times in the previous chapters. Finally, the "idtype" argument determines the type of Entrez database UIDs to return (e.g., idtype= "acc" for accession number).

Assume that you are planning for a phylogenetic study on the *Salmonella* species using the 16S ribosomal RNA gene and you need to search on the PopSet database for the available datasets to choose from.

```
#file: dbesearch1.py
from Bio import Entrez
```

```
{'Count': '58', 'RetMax': '50', 'RetStart': '0', 'IdList': ['765560594', '1585575433', '1235120617',
'1044641707', '1031917784', '1159332245', '1093398011', '1073858403', '1049566390', '1040467831', '44
3254246', '971493641', '953268018', '952978868', '950648394', '943876035', '942473043', '848793474',
'669636587', '693302880', '673457816', '673457681', '660450718', '645904436', '374082035', '6478165',
 '385045149', '523540033', '448280734', '302749208', '541990212', '522211744', '514251538', '37876139
9', '501415168', '475678493', '443907010', '440658023', '436432108', '407908785', '407378610', '38409
5086', '382947369', '365268939', '313585768', '299802540', '340366068', '197321162', '110704218', '30
2026073'], 'TranslationSet': [{'From': 'salmonella[ORGN]', 'To': '"Salmonella"[Organism]'}], 'Transla
tionStack': [{'Term': '"Salmonella"[Organism]', 'Field': 'Organism', 'Count': '525', 'Explode': 'Y'},
 {'Term': '16S ribosomal RNA[TITL]', 'Field': 'TITL', 'Count': '45004', 'Explode': 'N'}, 'AND', {'Ter
m': 'phylogenetic study[FILT]', 'Field': 'FILT', 'Count': '225178', 'Explode': 'N'}, 'AND'], 'QueryTr
anslation': '"Salmonella"[Organism] AND 16S ribosomal RNA[TITL] AND phylogenetic study[FILT]'}
```


FIGURE 6.25 ESearch results.

```
Entrez.email = "youremail@example.com"
#Entrez.api_key = "yourApiKey"
query = "salmonella[ORGN] AND 16S ribosomal RNA[TITL] AND phylogenetic study[FILT]"
handle = Entrez.esearch(db="popset", term=query, retmax="50")
#output = handle.read()
output = Entrez.read(handle)
handle.close()
print(output)
```

The above script used the "esearch()" function to search the PopSet database for the records matching the specified query. The output is shown in Figure 6.25, which is a Python dictionary. Whenever the output is a dictionary, you can list the dictionary keys first to help you plan for extracting data from the dictionary.

Use the following script to list the dictionary keys:

```
#file: dbesearch2.py
from Bio import Entrez
Entrez.email = "youremail@example.com"
#Entrez.api_key = "yourApiKey"
query = "salmonella[ORGN] AND 16S ribosomal RNA[TITL] AND phylogenetic study[FILT]"
handle = Entrez.esearch(db="popset", term=query, retmax="50")
#output = handle.read()
output = Entrez.read(handle)
handle.close()
for key in output:
    print(key)
```

After running the above script, you will find that the keys of the dictionary resulted by ESearch include "Count", "RetMax", "RetStart", "IdList", "TranslationSet", "TranslationStack", and "QueryTranslation". This is applicable for all databases.

The "Count" key stores the number of records matching the search query and the "IdList" key stores the list of the UIDs. Since the "retmax=" is set to 50, only 50 UIDs will be returned if the total number of UIDs matching the search query is more than 50. The following script will show the number of records matching the search query and the list of the UIDs.

```
Number of records:58
765560594
1585575433
1235120617
1044641707
1031917784
1159332245
1093398011
```

FIGURE 6.26 PopSet UIDs.

```
#file: dbesearch3.py
from Bio import Entrez
Entrez.email = "youremail@example.com"
#Entrez.api_key = "yourApiKey"
query = "salmonella[ORGN] AND 16S ribosomal RNA[TITL] AND phylogenetic study[FILT]"
handle = Entrez.esearch(db="popset", term=query, retmax="50")
#output = handle.read()
output = Entrez.read(handle)
handle.close()
print("Number of records:" + output ["Count"])
for id in output["IdList"]:
   print(id)
```

The search results show that 58 PopSet datasets were found to match the search query. A partial list of UIDs is shown in Figure 6.26. The returned UIDs are for the datasets of phylogenetic studies. Each dataset will include several sequences.

You can instruct the ESearch in the above example to upload the UIDs to the History Server by adding "usehistory="y"" to ESearch as in the following script, which also prints the keys of the dictionary read from the handle.

```
#file: dbesearch4.py
from Bio import Entrez
Entrez.email = "youremail@example.com"
#Entrez.api_key = "yourApiKey"
query = "salmonella[ORGN] AND 16S ribosomal RNA[TITL] AND phylogenetic study[FILT]"
handle = Entrez.esearch(db="popset", term=query, retmax="50", usehistory="y")
#output = handle.read()
output = Entrez.read(handle)
handle.close()
for key in output:
   print(key)
```

The dictionary keys this time include two additional keys: "QueryKey" and "WebEnv" for query key and Web Environment string, respectively. The values stored in these two keys (output["QueryKey"] and output["WebEnv"] can be used by a subsequent Entrez function.

Uploading UIDs to the History Server
The "Entrez.epost()" function uploads a list of Entrez database UIDs to the NCBI History Server to be used by a subsequent Entrez function as discussed before. The arguments include "db", which specifies the target database and "id", which specifies the list of unique identifiers. The UID list is comma delimited and without whitespace in between. The UID list is usually a long list but, for example, assume that you wish to upload the "29990125, 27292874, 27066500, 29297322" PubMed UIDs (PMIDs) to the History Server. You can use the following script to upload the PMIDs and to print the output, which a Python dictionary whose keys are the query key and Web Environment string.

```
#File: dbepost1.py
from Bio import Entrez
Entrez.email = "myemail@example.com"
uidList = ["29990125", "27292874", "27066500", "29297322"]
handle = Entrez.epost(db="pubmed", id=",".join(uidList))
output = Entrez.read(handle)
print(output)
```

The output is as follows:

```
{'QueryKey': '1', 'WebEnv': 'MCID_5f9f5ef033a8c76cb063a92f'}
```

Instead of providing the UIDs as a list, you can import them from a text file. Type the UIDs in a text file each in a separate line and save the file as "ids.txt" in the working directory and use the following script.

```
#File: dbepost2.py
from Bio import Entrez
Entrez.email = "myemail@example.com"
infile = open("ids.txt", "r")
uidList = infile.read().split()
handle = Entrez.epost(db="pubmed", id=",".join(uidList))
output = Entrez.read(handle)
print("Query key: " + output["QueryKey"])
print("WebEnv: " + output["WebEnv"])
```

Retrieving Records' Summaries
The "Entrez.esummary()" function retrieves summaries of records for specified UIDs of a database. The list of UIDs is provided to the function either as a list to the "id" argument or from the History Server using the query key (QueryKey) and web environment string (WebEnv) generated by ESearch or EPost as shown above. The arguments of "Entrez.esummary()" include "db" for the target database, "id" for the list of identifiers, "webenv" for web environment string, and "query_key" for query key. The structure of the output of Esummary may be different from one database to another. So, you may need to view the output to study the structure and then you will know how to retrieve the summary data. The following are some examples:

Retrieving Summary Data from PubMed   The following script will retrieve the summary of a single PubMed article (PMID=29990125) to view the structure of the output.

```
#File: dbesummary1.py
from Bio import Entrez
Entrez.email = "youremail@example.com"
handle = Entrez.esummary(db="pubmed", id="29990125")
output = Entrez.read(handle)
handle.close()
print(output)
```

When you execute the above script file, the output is a list data structure including a Python dictionary that includes the summary data as values of the dictionary keys. Since there is a single article, the dictionary that includes the summary keys for this article will be obtained as "output[0]" in the following script "dbesummary2.py", which prints the keys of the dictionary.

```
#File: dbesummary2.py
from Bio import Entrez
Entrez.email = "youremail@example.com"
handle = Entrez.esummary(db="pubmed", id="29990125")
output = Entrez.read(handle)
keys=""
for key in output[0]:
    keys = keys + key + ", "
print(keys)
```

The following are the dictionary keys that store the summary data of the PubMed article:

Item, Id, PubDate, EPubDate, Source, AuthorList, LastAuthor, Title, Volume, Issue, Pages, LangList, NlmUniqueID, ISSN, ESSN, PubTypeList, RecordStatus, PubStatus, ArticleIds, DOI, History, References, HasAbstract, PmcRefCount, FullJournalName, ELocationID, SO

You can retrieve the value of any of the above dictionary keys by using "output[0]["key"]", where "key" is any one in the above list. Also, notice that a key value may be a list such as "AuthorList" whose value is a list of authors. The following script will print the PMID, title, first author, journal name, and publication date of the PubMed article as shown in Figure 6.27.

```
#File: dbesummary3.py
from Bio import Entrez
Entrez.email = "youremail@example.com"
handle = Entrez.esummary(db="pubmed", id="29990125")
output = Entrez.read(handle)
uid = output[0]["Id"]
title = output[0]["Title"]
author = output[0]["AuthorList"][0]
journal = output[0]["FullJournalName"]
```

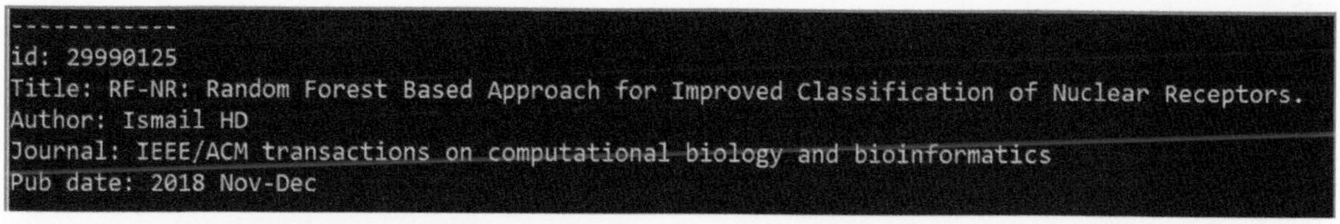

FIGURE 6.27   PubMed article summary data.

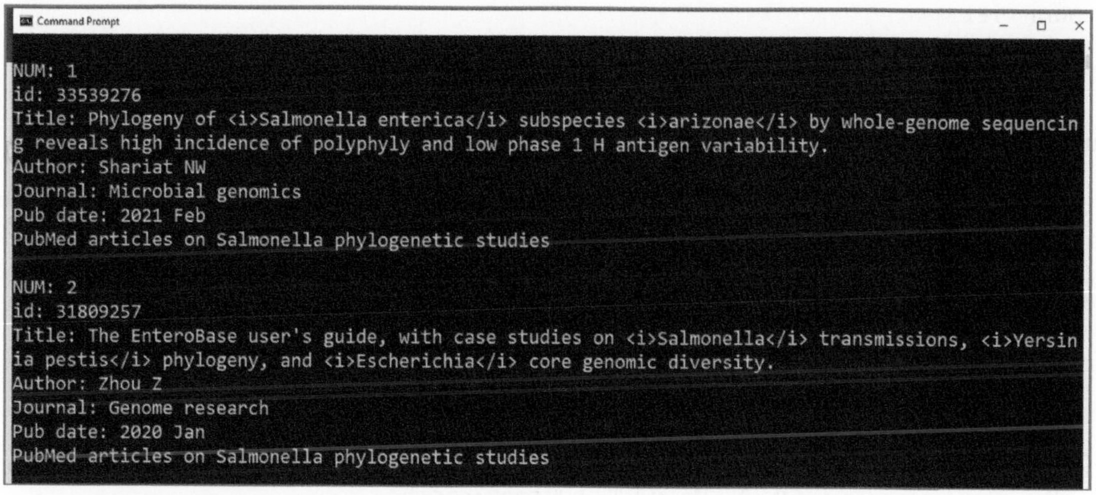

FIGURE 6.28   Partial summary data from multiple articles.

```
pdate = output[0]["PubDate"]
print("------------\nid: {}\nTitle: {}\nAuthor: {}\nJournal: {}\nPub date: {}".format(uid, title, author, journal, pdate))
```

The output is as shown in Figure 6.27.

You can also print summary data for a list of PubMed articles. In this case, you can either provide the list of UIDs to "id=" argument as shown in above examples (as a list or from a file) or can be imported from the History Server using "query_key=" and "webenv=" arguments. In case of multiple articles, the dictionaries of the articles must be accessed by using "for loop" (Figure 6.28).

```
#File: dbesummary4.py
from Bio import Entrez
Entrez.email = "youremail@example.com"
query = "salmonella[TITL] AND phylogeny[TITL]"
handle = Entrez.esearch(db="pubmed", term=query, retmax="20", usehistory="y")
searh_results = Entrez.read(handle)
handle.close()
recCount = int(searh_results["Count"]) #number of records
query_key = searh_results["QueryKey"]
webenv = searh_results["WebEnv"]
handle = Entrez.esummary(db="pubmed", query_key=query_key, webenv=webenv)
output = Entrez.read(handle)
```

```
for i in range(recCount):
    uid = output[i]["Id"]
    title = output[i]["Title"]
    author = output[i]["AuthorList"][0]
    journal = output[i]["FullJournalName"]
    pdate = output[i]["PubDate"]
    num = i+1
    print("PubMed articles on Salmonella phylogenetic studies\n")
    print("NUM: {}\nid: {}\nTitle: {}\nAuthor: {}\nJournal: {}\nPub date: {}".format(num, uid, title,
author, journal, pdate))
```

Retrieving Summary Data from Nucleotide Database   You can follow the same steps you did for PubMed to retrieve summary data from other Entrez databases.

The following script displays the keys of the dictionary that stores nucleotide records.

```
#File: dbsummary5.py
from Bio import Entrez
Entrez.email = "youremail@example.com"
handle = Entrez.esummary(db="nucleotide", id="1732746264")
output = Entrez.read(handle)
keys=""
for key in output[0]:
    keys = keys + key + ", "
print(keys)
```

The following are the keys that store the summary data for the nucleotide records:

Item, Id, Caption, Title, Extra, Gi, CreateDate, UpdateDate, Flags, TaxId, Length, Status, ReplacedBy, Comment, AccessionVersion.

You can retrieve summary data from a single nucleotide record or multiple records from these dictionary keys by following the steps in "dbesummary3.py" and "dbesummary4.py".

Retrieving Summary Data from the Gene Database The structure of the summary of the gene record is different. You can use the following script to view the dictionary keys where the data are stored.

```
#File: dbesummary6.py
from Bio import Entrez
Entrez.email = "youremail@example.com"
handle = Entrez.esummary(db="gene", id="672")
output = Entrez.read(handle)
keys=""
for key in output["DocumentSummarySet"]["DocumentSummary"][0]:
    keys = keys + key + ", "
print(keys)
```

The keys of the dictionary that store the gene record summary are:

Name, Description, Status, CurrentID, Chromosome, GeneticSource, MapLocation, OtherAliases, OtherDesignations, NomenclatureSymbol, NomenclatureName, NomenclatureStatus, Mim, GenomicInfo, GeneWeight, Summary, ChrSort, ChrStart, Organism, LocationHist

The data stored in any one of these keys can be obtained by:

output["DocumentSummarySet"]["DocumentSummary"][0]["key"]

The "key" is any key as listed above. For example, to get the data on "GenomicInfo", you can use:

output["DocumentSummarySet"]["DocumentSummary"][0]["GenomicInfo"]

The following script views and prints the genomic information of the human BRCA1 gene:

```
#File: dbesummary7.py
from Bio import Entrez
Entrez.email = "youremail@example.com"
handle = Entrez.esummary(db="gene", id="672")
output = Entrez.read(handle)
genomicinfo = output["DocumentSummarySet"]["DocumentSummary"][0]["GenomicInfo"]
print(genomicinfo)
```

The output is as follows:

[{'ChrLoc': '17', 'ChrAccVer': 'NC_000017.11', 'ChrStart': '43125363', 'ChrStop': '43044294', 'ExonCount': '24'}]

Notice that the genomic information of a gene record is stored in a dictionary inside a list. You may need the genomic information of a gene to retrieve its complete sequence from the Nucleotide database. The following script prints the chromosome accession and the starting and ending coordinates of the human BRCA1 gene.

```
#File: dbesummary8.py
from Bio import Entrez
Entrez.email = "youremail@example.com"
handle = Entrez.esummary(db="gene", id="672")
output = Entrez.read(handle)
genomicinfo = output["Document SummarySet"]["DocumentSummary"][0]["GenomicInfo"][0]
chrAcc = genomicinfo["ChrAccVer"]
chrStart = genomicinfo["ChrStart"]
chrStop = genomicinfo["ChrStop"]
print("Accession: " + chrAcc)
print("Start: " + chrStart)
print("Stop: " + chrStop)
```

The following script prints the gene name, organism, chromosome accession and the starting and ending coordinates of the gene records matching a search query.

```
#File: dbesummary9.py
from Bio import Entrez
Entrez.email = "youremail@example.com"
query = "16S ribosomal rna[TITL] AND Salmonella enterica subsp. enterica[ORGN]"
handle = Entrez.esearch(db="gene", term=query, usehistory="y")
searh_results = Entrez.read(handle)
handle.close()
#recCount = int(searh_results["Count"]) #number of records
recCount = 20
query_key = searh_results["QueryKey"]
webenv = searh_results["WebEnv"]
handle = Entrez.esummary(db="gene", query_key=query_key, webenv=webenv)
output = Entrez.read(handle)
handle.close()
for i in range(recCount):
    genomicinfo = output["Document SummarySet"]["DocumentSummary"][i]["GenomicInfo"][0]
    name = output["DocumentSummarySet"]["DocumentSummary"][i]["Name"]
    organism = output["Document SummarySet"]["DocumentSummary"][i]["Organism"]["Scientific
Name"]
    chrAcc = genomicinfo["ChrAccVer"]
    chrStart = genomicinfo["ChrStart"]
    chrStop = genomicinfo["ChrStop"]
    print("[" + str(i+1) + "]")
    print("Name: " + name)
    print("Organism: " + organism)
    print("Accession: " + chrAcc)
    print("Start: " + chrStart)
    print("Stop: " + chrStop)
```

We will revisit these examples to retrieve the FASTA genomic sequences of the genes returned by ESearch.

Fetching Data from Entrez Database Records

Sometimes, you may need to retrieve the entire records or certain parts of the records such as sequences. The "Entrez.efetch()" function retrieves database records in different format depending on the database. It uses almost the same arguments that were discussed with EFetch in Chapter 5. The arguments include "db=" for the target database, "id=" for the list of identifiers, "webenv=" for web environment string, "query_key=" for query key, "rettype" for retrieval type, and "retmode" for retrieval mode. To learn about these arguments, you can refer to E-utilities and EDirect in Chapters 4 and 5. The following are some examples for using EFetch.

Fetching a Complete GenBank Record   The following script will retrieve the complete GenBank record of human breast cancer type 1 susceptibility protein isoform 1 (BRCA1 isoform 1).

```
#File: dbefetch1.py
from Bio import Entrez
from Bio import SeqIO
Entrez.email = "myemail@example.com"
handle = Entrez.efetch(db="protein",
                id="NP_009225.1",
                rettype="gb",
                retmode="text")
record = handle.read()
print(record)
```

Fetching FASTA Sequences of GenBank Records   The "Entrez.efetch()" can be used to retrieve a FASTA-formatted sequence of records from the Protein and Nucleotide databases by using "rettype='fasta'". Assume that you wish to download the FASTA sequences of the proteins encoded by the human BRCA1 gene (BRCA1 gene encodes multiple isoforms). You can use "Entrez.esearch()" to search for those protein isoforms and then retrieve their FASTA sequences using "Entrez.efetch()" and save the sequences in a file.

```
#File: dbefetch2.py
#fetching refeseq human BRCA1 proteins fasta sequences
from Bio import Entrez
Entrez.email = "myemail@example.com"
handle = Entrez.esearch(db="protein",
                term="(BRCA1[GENE] AND refseq[FILT]) AND human[ORGN]",
                usehistory="y")
output = Entrez.read(handle)
handle.close()
query_key = output["QueryKey"]
webenv  = output["WebEnv"]
handle = Entrez.efetch(db="protein",
                webenv = webenv,
                query_key = query_key,
                rettype="fasta",
                retmode="text")
brca1_prots = handle.read()
handle.close()
f = open("brca_proy.fasta", "w")
f.write(brca1_prots)
f.close()
print(brca1_prots)
```

The GenBank databases (the Nucleotide and Protein databases) have several retrieval types (rettype). Refer to Table 5.2 for the different options.

Fetching Abstracts from PubMed Articles   The following is an example for retrieving article abstracts from the PubMed database. First, the script searches the PubMed database for articles that have title including colorectal cancer using "Entrez.esearch()". Then "Entrez.efetch()" is used to retrieve the abstracts of those articles.

```
#File: myefetch3.py
#fetching PubMed article abstracts
from Bio import Entrez
Entrez.email = "myemail@example.com"
retmax = 50
handle = Entrez.esearch(db="pubmed",
                term="colorectal cancer[title] AND human[ORGN]",
                retmax=retmax,
                usehistory="y")
output = Entrez.read(handle)
handle.close()
query_key = output["QueryKey"]
webenv  = output["WebEnv"]
handle = Entrez.efetch(db="pubmed",
                webenv = webenv,
                query_key = query_key,
                rettype="abstract",
                retmode="text")
pubs = handle.read().encode('utf-8').decode('latin-1')
handle.close()
print(pubs)
```

If you are using a Linux environment you can redirect the output to a file (e.g. pubs.txt) as follows:

```
$ python3 myefetch3.py > pubs.txt
```

Fetching Genomic Gene Sequences   The following example shows you how you can use BioPython Entrez to retrieve a complete genomic gene sequence from a genome assembly using the genomic information of a gene that we discussed in an above example (dbsummary8.py). You may need to retrieve an entire genomic gene sequence to use it with Primer-BLAST to obtain primers for polymerase chain reaction (PCR) or for other purposes. The following script includes a function, "getGenSequence(GeneSym, organ)", which requires a gene symbol and organism's name as arguments. The gene symbol must be a valid gene symbol and the organism's name must be a common name or a scientific name. The function begins with an "Entrez. esearch()" statement, which searches the Gene database for the gene of the organism. If the gene symbol and organism name are provided correctly, it is expected that the search will return a single or multiple genes. The UIDs of the returned gene will be stored on the History Server. The "Entrez.esummary()" function imports the UIDs from the History Server to retrieve the genomic information of the gene (chromosome accession and coordinates). The "Entrez.efetch()" then uses the genomic information to fetch the gene sequence. The

FASTA sequences will be saved in a file (Gene_seq.fasta) and displayed on the screen. The function is run as "getGenSequence(GeneSym, organ)". For example, to retrieve the human BRCA1 gene sequence we can run "getGenSequence("BRCA1", "human")". Save the script in a file with the name "dbefetch4.py" and run it from the command-line prompt as "$ python dbefetch4.py".

```python
#File: dbefetch4.py
from Bio import Entrez, SeqIO
import os
def getGenSequence(GeneSym, organ):
    Entrez.email = "youremail@example.com"
    #query = "16S ribosomal rna[GENE] AND Salmonella enterica subsp. enterica [ORGN]"
    query = GeneSym + "[GENE] AND " + organ +"[ORGN]"
    handle = Entrez.esearch(db="gene", term=query, usehistory="y")
    searh_results = Entrez.read(handle)
    handle.close()
    recCount = int(searh_results["Count"]) #number of records [edit this]
    #recCount = 20
    query_key = searh_results["QueryKey"]
    webenv = searh_results["WebEnv"]
    handle = Entrez.esummary(db="gene", query_key=query_key, webenv=webenv)
    output = Entrez.read(handle)
    handle.close()
    FileName = "Gene_seq.fasta"
    if os.path.isfile(FileName ):
        os.remove(FileName)
        outFile = open(FileName ,"a")
    else:
        outFile = open(FileName ,"a")
    if recCount <= 0:
        print("No gene is found")
        print(quit)
        quit()
    elif recCount == 1:
        i=0
        genomicinfo = output["DocumentSummarySet"]["DocumentSummary"][i]["GenomicInfo"][0]
        name = output["Document SummarySet"]["DocumentSummary"][i]["Name"]
        organism = output["DocumentSummarySet"]["DocumentSummary"][i]["Organism"]["ScientificName"]
        chrAcc = genomicinfo["ChrAccVer"]
        chrStart = genomicinfo["ChrStart"]
        chrStop = genomicinfo["ChrStop"]
        handle = Entrez.efetch(db="nucleotide",
```

```
                    id=chrAcc,
                    rettype="fasta",
                    strand=1,
                    seq_start=chrStart,
                    seq_stop=chrStop)
        geneSeq = SeqIO.read(handle, "fasta")
        print(">" + name + "-" + organism)
        print(geneSeq.seq)
        handle.close()
        outFile.write(">" + name + "-" + organism + "\n")
        outFile.write(str(geneSeq.seq) + "\n")
        #outFile.close()
    else:
      for i in range(0, recCount-2, 1):
        genomicinfo = output["Document SummarySet"]["DocumentSummary"][i]["GenomicInfo"][0]
        name = output["Document SummarySet"]["DocumentSummary"][i]["Name"]
        organism   =   output["Document   SummarySet"]["DocumentSummary"][i]["Organism"]
        ["ScientificName"]
        chrAcc = genomicinfo["ChrAccVer"]
        chrStart = genomicinfo["ChrStart"]
        chrStop = genomicinfo["ChrStop"]
        handle = Entrez.efetch(db="nucleotide",
                    id=chrAcc,
                    rettype="fasta",
                    strand=1,
                    seq_start=chrStart,
                    seq_stop=chrStop)
        geneSeq = SeqIO.read(handle, "fasta")
        print(">" + name + "-" + organism + " " + str(i+1) + " \ " + str(recCount-2))
        print(geneSeq.seq)
        handle.close()
        outFile.write(">" + name + "-" + organism + "\n")
        outFile.write(str(geneSeq.seq) + "\n")
      outFile.close()

getGenSequence("ppar*", "human")
#getGenSequence("brca1", "human")
```

Fetching Features from a GenBank Record   The following script will retrieve features from a GenBank record. Features extracted from reference sequences are usually meaningful and you may need to use their information for other purposes. The "myefetch5.py" script includes a function "get_features(uid, featType)" that has two arguments: a GenBank accession and feature type (e.g. exon, CDS, etc.). The function fetches the complete GenBank record. The handle of GenBank records will be read as a BioPython SeqIO object (SeqIO. read(handle, "gb")) to retrieve the record features. The features will be limited to the feature type specified by the argument (featType).

```
#File: dbefetch5.py
#Extract feature from a genbank record
#Function arguments:
#   uid: a valid GenBank id as a string
#   featType : a valid feature type as a string (e.g. "exon", "CDS")
from Bio import Entrez
from Bio import SeqIO
Entrez.email = "youremail@example.com"
def get_features(uid, featType):
    handle = Entrez.efetch(db="nuccore",
                    rettype="gb",
                    retmode="full",
                    id=uid)
    seq_record = SeqIO.read(handle, "gb")
    features = seq_record.features
    #uncomments the following two lines to print the possible attributes
    #attributes = [attr for attr in dir(features[0]) if not attr.startswith("_")]
    #print(attributes)
    i = 0
    for feature in features:
        if feature.type == featType:
            i = i + 1
            print("Feature: " + str(i))
            print(feature)
#running the function
#example features - uncomment a line to see its results
get_features("NM_007294.4","CDS")
get_features("NM_007294.4","exon")
```

When executing the script, you can direct the output to a file if you are using Linux.

```
$ python3 myefetch5.py > features.txt
```

Notice that "get_features("NM_007294.4","exon")" will extract exons in the "NM_007294.4" GenBank record. You can extract any valid features from a GenBank record by specifying a GenBank accession and a feature type as arguments. Pay attention to that the arguments are string and must be enclosed between quotation marks.

Finding Related Records in NCBI Databases

In the previous chapters, we discussed that a database record may be linked to records from the same database (neighbors) or other Entrez databases. In BioPython, you can use "Entrez.elink()" function to find the related records. The function arguments include "dbfrom=", "id=", and "db=". The "dbfrom" argument specifies the database that contains the UIDs specified by "id=" argument. The UIDs specified by "id" is of the record for which you wish to find records that are linked to the item from the same or another database specified by the "db=" argument. Refer to Chapters 4 and 5 for more details about "elink" arguments and link names. When "db=" is not used, the "Entrez.elink()" function will search on PubMed. The following script includes a function "Count_links(dbfrom, uid, dbto)" that has "dbto", "uid", and "db" arguments. The function counts the link names and the number of links that belong to each link name. As an example, you can find the number of link names and counts for each link name for the BRCA1 gene (Acc=672) from the protein database.

```python
#File: dbelink1.py
#Link name counts
import os
from Bio import SeqIO
from Bio import Entrez
Entrez.email = "youremail@example.com"
def Count_links(dbfrom, uid, dbto):
    handle = Entrez.elink(dbfrom=dbfrom, id=uid, db=dbto)
    output = Entrez.read(handle)
    handle.close()
    #Number of links
    NumLinks = len(output[0]["LinkSetDb"])
    print("Number of link names: " + str(NumLinks))
    #Link counts
    for linksetdb in output[0]["LinkSetDb"]:
        print(linksetdb["DbTo"],linksetdb["LinkName"], len(linksetdb["Link"]))
#running the function
uid = "672"
dbfrom ="gene"
dbto = "protein"
Count_links(dbfrom, uid, dbto)
```

The output is shown in Figure 6.29.

You can notice that the human BRCA1 gene has two link names from the Protein database: gene_protein (331 links) and gene_protein_refseq (five links). The numbers "331" and "5" for the link names respectively are the number of protein records linked to the human BRCA1 gene from each group. The gene_protein links are the redundant human BRCA1 protein records in the GenBank Protein database while the gene_protein_refseq links are reference protein records (RefSeqs) linked to the human BRCA1 genes. The RefSeq records are non-redundant and curated by the NCBI. Therefore, those five protein records represent the isoforms that are encoded by the same human BRCA1 gene but with different alternative splicing.

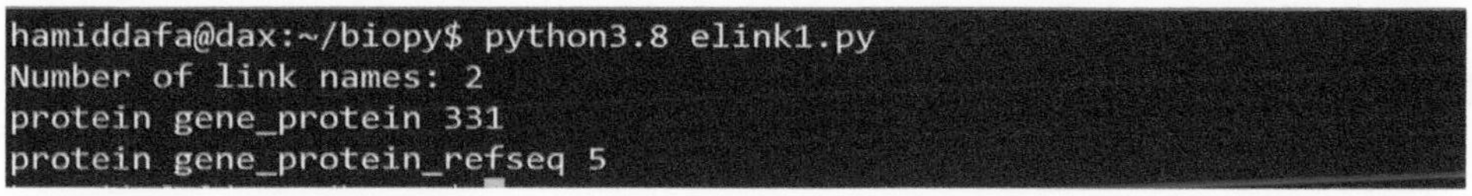

```
hamiddafa@dax:~/biopy$ python3.8 elink1.py
Number of link names: 2
protein gene_protein 331
protein gene_protein_refseq 5
```

FIGURE 6.29   Link names and link counts.

The following script "dbelink2.py" will print the UIDs of the protein records linked to the human BRCA1 gene.

```
#File: dbelink2.py
#Print the UIDs
import os
from Bio import SeqIO
from Bio import Entrez
Entrez.email = "youremail@example.com"
def Count_links(dbfrom, uid, dbto):
    handle = Entrez.elink(dbfrom=dbfrom, id=uid, db=dbto, idtype="acc")
    output = Entrez.read(handle)
    handle.close()
    #Number of links
    #ids of linked from the same db
    for link in output[0]["LinkSetDb"][0]["Link"]:
        print(link["Id"])

#running the function
uid = "672"
dbfrom ="gene"
dbto = "protein"
Count_links(dbfrom, uid, dbto)
```

The above script prints the UIDs of all link names. However, you may need to print the UIDs of a specific link name. The above script can be modified to print the UIDs of a specific link name. The following script "dbelink3.py" added "linkname" as an argument to limit the records to a specific link name. In the example, you will set the link name to "gene_protein_refseq" to print the accession number of the reference proteins (RefSeq) linked to the human BRCA1 gene.

```
#File: dbelink3.py
#Print the UIDs
import os
from Bio import SeqIO
from Bio import Entrez
Entrez.email = "youremail@example.com"
```

```
def Count_links(dbfrom, uid, dbto, linkname):
    handle = Entrez.elink(dbfrom=dbfrom,
                    id=uid, db=dbto,
                    linkname=linkname,
                    idtype="acc")
    output = Entrez.read(handle)
    handle.close()
    #printing the ids
    for link in output[0]["LinkSetDb"][0]["Link"]:
        print(link["Id"])


    #running the function
    uid = "672"
    dbfrom ="gene"
    dbto = "protein"
    linkname = "gene_protein_refseq"
    Count_links(dbfrom, uid, dbto, linkname)
```

The link names of each database were discussed in Chapters 4 and 5, as each database has its link names.

Printing Records Counts of All Entrez Databases

The "Entrez.egquery()" function (also known as the global query function) prints the counts of records of all Entrez database that match a search query specified by the "term=" argument. The following script "dbegquery1. py" includes a function that can be provided with a search query as an argument and it will return the number of records for all databases that have one or more records that match the search query. In the following script, you will use "COVID-19" as a search term. The output of the script is shown in Figure 6.30.

```
#File: dbegquery1.py
#Print global counts for search terms
from Bio import Entrez
```

```
pubmed 144582
pmc 165489
mesh 88
books 2057
omim 2
nuccore 665499
protein 4177189
genome 1
structure 1333
taxonomy 1
dbvar 8298
gene 223
sra 724059
cdd 23
popset 91
gds 3814
pcsubstance 1364
pcassay 29
nlmcatalog 433
gap 5017
bioproject 770
biosample 887892
```

FIGURE 6.30   Entre database record counts for COVID-19 term.

```
Entrez.email = "youemail@example.com"
def GlobalQuery(term):
    handle = Entrez.egquery(term=term)
    output = Entrez.read(handle)
    handle.close()
    for row in output["eGQueryResult"]:
        if row["Count"] != "Error" and  int(row["Count"]) > 0:
            print(row["DbName"], row["Count"])
#Running the function
term = "COVID-19"
GlobalQuery(term)
```

Providing Correction Suggestions

The "Entrez.espell()" function provides a correction suggestion for mistakenly written search terms. The following script prints the correction suggestion for "brest cancar"

```
#File: dbespell1.py
#providing spell suggestions
from Bio import Entrez
Entrez.email = "youremail@example.com"
handle = Entrez.espell(term="brest cancar AND humn")
output = Entrez.read(handle)
output["Query"]
print(output["CorrectedQuery"])
```

The following script shows how to use the "Entrez.espell()" to correct search terms before being used by the "Entrez.esearch()" function, which searches the PubMed database and posts the UIDs of the records that match the search terms to the History Server. The "Entrez.efetch()" fetches the abstracts of the PubMed articles.

```
#File: dbespell2.py
from Bio import Entrez
Entrez.email = "youremail@example.com"
handle = Entrez.espell(term="brest cancar AND humn")
output1 = Entrez.read(handle)
handle.close()
correctedQuery = output1["Corrected Query"]
print(correctedQuery)
handle = Entrez.esearch(db="pubmed",
                term=correctedQuery,
                usehistory="y")
output2 = Entrez.read(handle)
```

```
handle.close()
query_key = output2["QueryKey"]
webenv  = output2["WebEnv"]
handle = Entrez.efetch(db="pubmed",
            webenv = webenv,
            query_key = query_key,
            rettype="abstract",
            retmode="text")
pubs = handle.read().encode("utf-8").decode("latin-1")
handle.close()
print(pubs)
```

If you are using Linux, you can redirect the output to a text file as follows:

```
$ python myespell2.py > abstracts.txt
```

REFERENCES

1. Sayers, E., *The E-utilities In-Depth: Parameters, Syntax and More.* Entrez Programming Utilities Help [cited 6/25/2021]. www.ncbi.nlm.nih.gov/books/NBK25499/. 2009.
2. Winter, D.J., *rentrez: An R package for the NCBI eUtils API.* R Journal, 2017. **9**: pp. 520–526.
3. Winter, D. *Rentrez Tutorial* [cited 2021 6/29/2021]. https://cran.r-project.org/web/packages/rentrez/vignettes/rentrez_tutorial.html. 2020.
4. Cock, P.J., et al., *Biopython: freely available Python tools for computational molecular biology and bioinformatics.* Bioinformatics, 2009. **25**(11): pp. 1422–1423.

## CHAPTER 7

Pairwise Sequence Alignment

INTRODUCTION

Sequence alignment is one of the most important parts of bioinformatics. It is defined as arranging DNA or protein sequences to identify regions of similarity that may be as a result of evolutionary relationships between the sequences. It is widely used in genomic research to predict the function of new genes, the classification of protein into families, inferring evolutionary relationships or phylogeny, sequence annotation, identification of a new sequence, prediction of conserved regions in a protein, to name just a few. The sequence alignment is a major part of bioinformatics that biologists need to know and it also one of the most commonly cited works for its importance to modern research in biology.

The alignment focuses on aligning biological sequences, which are DNA, RNA, or protein sequences. The DNA and RNA sequences are generated from sequencing of DNA or RNA samples. Most protein sequences can be inferred from the translation of RNA sequences. In eukaryotes a single gene may code for several proteins using alternative RNA splicing. However, the mechanism of the alternative splicing is different in prokaryotes because their messenger RNA lacks introns. Proteins are the final products of coding genes and a gene transcript can be inferred from a protein sequence. Whether the biological sequences are of DNA/RNA or protein, similar sequences for a gene or a protein may be found within the species or across species. Genes with similar sequences may code for similar proteins that have a similar structure and perform similar functions. That may lead to an obvious question; is the similarity a consequence of evolution or has it occurred by chance. There is no absolute answer to such a question but science could find ways to answer that question by developing algorithms to find optimal answers and using statistical methods to measure the uncertainty and the level of confidence. Significantly similar sequences may share a common ancestral sequence and such similarity will be a key for inferring several aspects of biological sequences. The technique of arranging sequences for learning sequence similarity is called sequence alignment; it requires the algorithm that best aligns the sequences, the scoring scheme that measures the similarity between the sequences, and the statistical tests that measures the significance of the similarity.

Sequence alignment can be either pairwise sequence alignment or multiple sequence alignment. Pairwise sequence alignment involves only two sequences, where one sequence is aligned to the other. Multiple sequences alignment involves multiple sequences; each sequence is aligned to one another to achieve optimal alignment. Pairwise alignment is the basis of BLAST; therefore, it is implemented in searching sequence databases for finding similar sequences, which are the key elements of many applications in comparative genomics and homology studies. On the other hand, multiple sequence alignment, which is also based on pairwise alignment in its primary steps, is used in several genomic applications including phylogeny, motif discovery, prediction of protein conserved regions, homology modeling for predicting protein structure and function. Since this book focuses on the NCBI databases and sequence alignments, which use mainly the pairwise alignment, the

DOI: 10.1201/9781003226611-7

multiple sequence alignment is beyond the scope of this book; we will use it to build phylogenetic trees, but without delving deep into its theoretical concept.

PAIRWISE SEQUENCE ALIGNMENT

The diversity of sequences of the same gene in the same species and across species is due to mutations, which is an ongoing process but slow in normal conditions. The mutation rate may be faster in some region of the genome than others. The mutation rate in non-protein coding regions is usually faster than the rate in the protein coding region. The regions of DNA or protein sequences, which have very slow mutation rates to preserve their biological functions, are called conserved regions. In eukaryotic genes, which consist of introns and exons, we may find the mutation rate slower in exons. Evolution never stops in living organisms. Mutations may bring new phenotypes, which are either favored by the organism (therefore they remain), or unfavored by the organism (therefore will not survive). The mutation rate may be exceptionally fast in some conditions such as exposure to some chemicals or radiation or in the case of cancer. Slow or fast mutations generate diversity in sequences. Mutations in the evolutionary path have created diverse species. Homology studies seek the relationship between genes that evolved from a common ancestral gene in the same species or across species. The genes that evolved from an ancestral gene in the same species are called paralogs while the genes in different species but evolved from a common ancestral gene during the evolutionary path are called orthologs. A level of similarity may exist between related sequences that allows us to detect the homology. The similarity of sequences does not always mean homology. The homology of two sequences either exists or not (i.e., no level of homology). However, certain level of similarity may suggest homology.

Two DNA or two protein sequences can be compared by aligning the two sequences. In most cases, you will have a single sequence and you wish to find the similar sequences in a bunch of sequences. The process of finding the sequences similar to your sequence starts by aligning your sequence to each sequence in the group. Your sequence in this case is known as query sequence and each sequence in the group is called the subject sequence, and the group of sequences is called the target sequence group (later we will call it a target database).

The pairwise sequence alignment allows you to align the query sequence to each subject sequence in a target group of sequences and to score the level of similarity between the query sequence and any subject sequence. There are two types of pairwise alignments: (1) global sequence alignment; and (2) local sequence alignment. A global alignment is a form of global optimization that forces the alignment to span the entire lengths of the two sequences while local alignments identify only the regions of similarity within long sequences. In the following sections, we will discuss global sequence alignment, local sequence alignment, and BLAST, which is a special version of the local alignment.

Global Sequence Alignment

Global sequence alignment is an attempt to align two sequences and the alignment spans the entire two sequences so that the first sequence is completely aligned to the second. The global alignment is suitable when two sequences have approximately the same length and they are quite similar. It is usually used for comparing evolutionarily related sequences across species. However, in most cases, the two sequences will not have the same length due to insertion and deletion mutation. In global alignment, gaps may be introduced by stretching one of the sequences to maximize the alignment. The alignment also requires scoring measurement to quantify the degree of similarity between the two aligned sequences. For example, consider the following two protein sequences (Seq1 and Seq2):

>Seq1
RETSIEMEESELDAQYLQNTFKVSKRQSFAPFSNPGNAEEECATFSAHSGSLKKQ
>Seq2
RETSIEMEESELDAQYLQNTFKVSKRQSFALFSNPGNPEEECATFSAHCRSLKKQ

The two sequences look closely similar with mismatches in four positions: P-L, A-P, S-C, and G-R. Such difference in closely similar protein sequences is due to base substitutions that changed the coded amino acids. Changes in sequence may also be due to residue deletion or residue insertion, which is difficult to observe when deletion or insertion involves multiple residues. Consider the following two protein sequences:

>Seq3
RETSIEMEESELDAQYLQNTFKVSKRQSFAPFSNPGNAEEECATFSAHSGSLKKQ
>Seq4
RETSIEMEESELQNTFKVSKRQSFALFSNPGNPEEECATFSAHCRSLKKQ

The lengths of the above two sequences are not equal. If we assume that these two sequences are for complete proteins and they originated from a common ancestral sequence, there must be either residue deletion or insertion in the coding sequence of one of them. In this case, to align the two sequences globally, a gap must be introduced in the second so that the two sequences can align properly:

Seq1: RETSIEMEESELDAQYLQNTFKVSKRQSFAPFSNPGNAEEECATFSAHSGSLKKQ

Seq2: RETSIEMEESEL - - Q - - - NTFKVSKRQSFALFSNPGNPEEECATFSAHCRSLKKQ

Aligning two sequences is easy only if the two sequences are short and they are highly similar. Otherwise, aligning two long and distantly related sequences will be complicated and hard to do manually. The complications arise from the fact that there will be many possible alignments when the lengths of the two sequences are not equal. Therefore, a computer and algorithms are required to find all possible alignments and to select the optimal one. We will discuss those algorithms. But we must discuss first the scoring systems used to measure the sequence similarity.

Similarity Scores
The similarity score of two sequences is the number that scores the degree of similarity between two aligned sequences. The similarity of sequences can be measured either by the distance between the two sequences or by using any scoring scheme such as identity or similarity scoring based on substitution matrices.

Levenshtein Distance   Levenshtein distance between two sequences is the minimum number of single-character edits (substitutions, insertions, or deletions) required to change one sequence into the other [1]. For example, the distance between Seq1 and Seq2 above is four; because it takes four substitutions (edits) to transform the first sequence into the second one and vice versa. The distance between Seq3 and Seq4 is nine; it takes four deletion operations and five substitutions to transform the first sequence into the second or it takes four insertions and five substitutions to transform the second sequence into the first.

The Levenshtein distance is the simplest distance metric for scoring the similarity between two sequences.

Percent Identity   The percent identity of two aligned sequences is a measurement metric for scoring the similarity between two sequences. The identity is the extent to which two sequences are invariant and it is defined as the number of the matching residues in the two sequences. The scoring scheme for identity is given a score of one for a matched pair and zero for unmatched pair. The total number of matches is obtained by adding together the alignment scores. The percent identify is defined as the total number of matches divided by the length of the sequence after the alignment.

$$\text{Percent identity} = \frac{\text{Number of matches}}{\text{Length of the shortest sequence}} \times 100 \qquad (7.1)$$

For example, to calculate the identity of Seq1 and Seq2; the number of matched residues is 51 and the length of the sequence is 55 amino acids. So, the percent identity for the pairwise alignment is (51/55) × 100 = 92.72%.

Two sequences are identical if all residues in one sequence are matching to the residues of the sequence of the other. A high percent identity is evidence of a high similarity. However, short sequences may align properly by chance. Therefore, only the percent identity of long sequences is more likely to reflect the relatedness of the two aligned sequences. The sufficiently long sequences with more than 30% identity are likely to have a common ancestral sequence but they diverged upon evolution. In most cases, homologous gene may encode proteins with similar 3D structures. The percent identity of an alignment of two sequences gives an idea to what extent these two sequences are similar. However, similarity of sequences may not be a consequence of evolution all the time. It is possible to find significantly similar sequences without having a common ancestor. Such sequence similarity is due to convergent evolution; the sequences independently evolved and became similar without having a common ancestor [2]. On the other hand, some sequences may have low identity, but they may have a common ancestor. Therefore, to distinguish between homology and convergent evolution, extra information is needed.

Dot-Plot of an Alignment The similarity of two sequences can be viewed graphically by using the dot-plot, on which the residues of one sequence will be presented by the X-axis and the residues of the second sequence will be represented by the Y-axis as shown in Figure 7.1. Each residue of the columns is compared to each residue of the rows. If the residues are identical a dot or one is placed at X-Y point. If the two residues are not identical a blank space or zero is placed. The dot plot of two very closely related sequences will appear as a single line along the diagonal of the plot. When the two sequences are long, the dot-plot may be affected by background noise. However, there are several ways to reduces the noise. Figure 7.1 shows the dot-plot of the two sequences: "RETSIEMEES" and RETSIEMEES".

The dot-plot is also used to detect repetitiveness in a single sequence by plotting the sequence against itself. The regions that share significant similarities will appear as lines off the main diagonal.

Substitution Matrices   The identity describes sequence similarity and relatedness on the basis of the matching and mismatching residues of the sequences. However, sometimes, a mutation in a gene may result in no change in the protein sequence or may result in an amino acid that has similar physicochemical properties. Replacing an amino acid with a similar one is more likely to make no significant change in the property of the protein. Moreover, the sequences diverged from a common ancestral sequence would have already undergone a series of changes including substitution, deletion, and insertion. Identity scoring is not sufficient to capture the information of that changes. Other scoring schemes were proposed to measure sequence similarity by integrating some evolutionary information by using the likelihood that a residue will be substituted by another during the evolutionary path. This scoring system is used mainly for protein sequence alignment because

		\multicolumn{10}{c}{Sequence 1}
		R	E	T	S	I	E	M	E	E	S
	R	*									
	E		*				*		*	*	
	T			*							
Sequence 2	S				*						*
	I					*					
	E		*				*		*	*	
	M							*			
	E		*				*		*	*	
	E		*				*		*	*	
	S				*						*

FIGURE 7.1   Dot-Plot for pairwise sequence alignment.

protein sequences contain more evolutionary information than DNA; the reason is that protein sequences are built up of 20 characters while DNA is built up of only four characters.

The substitution scoring system is based on the probability that an amino acid is substituted by any one of the other amino acids; each amino acid can be replaced by any one of the other 19 amino acids or remain unchanged. Thus, there will be 20 probabilities for each amino acid. These probabilities are better be represented by a 20×20 matrix for amino acids and 4×4 matrix for nucleotides. The value in each matrix cell is the probability that a residue is substituted by another. This matrix is called the probability substitution matrix.

There are several ways to compute the substitution probabilities of amino acids or nucleotides. The most commonly used is the probabilities computed after aligning homologous sequences from numerous species. After computing the substitution probabilities for each residue, the substitution scores are computed as the substitution probabilities divided by the product of the random probabilities. The expected random probability that any amino acid is substituted by another in a protein sequence is 1/20=0.05 and the random probability that any nucleotide in a DNA sequence is substituted by another is 1/4=0.25. The product of the random probabilities of any two residues is the product of their two random probabilities. However, the random probability can be estimated using other ways.

Generally, the substitution scores are based on the nonrandom evolutionary model, which states that sequences are evolutionarily related if there is a high correlation between aligned residues. Thus, the probability of the occurrence of certain residues depends on the residue at the equivalent position in the sequence of the common evolutionary ancestral sequence. In this nonrandom evolutionary model, the probability of aligning a pair of residues i and j is given by $q_{i,j}$, which depends on the evolutionary process. On the other hand, if the mutation is random and not affected by the evolutionary process the probability of aligning a pair of residues i and j will be the product of the probability of i and probability of j or $p_i p_j$ because the two events are independent (probability multiplication rule). Thus, the two pair-aligning probabilities can be computed by dividing the probability due to the evolutionary process by the probability due to the random process, which results in the following odds ratio:

$$\text{Odds ratio} = \frac{q_{i,j}}{p_i p_j} \tag{7.2}$$

If the odds ratio is greater than 1 (i.e., $q_{i,j} > p_i p_j$), then the nonrandom evolutionary model will be more likely to describe the alignment for that pair of residues. The overall score for the alignment of the two sequences is the product of the odds ratios of all aligned pairs in the entire alignment (probability multiplication rule) assuming that the occurrence of each aligned pair is independent from others.

$$\text{Similarity} = \prod_{k}^{L} \left(\frac{q_{i,j}}{p_i p_j} \right)_k \tag{7.3}$$

where L is the number of aligned positions and $k=1,2,\ldots,L$.

To avoid multiplication of odds ratios, we can convert the score of each aligned pair to the logarithm of the odds ratio and then add the scores of the individual pairs to obtain the overall alignment score.

$$S_{i,j} = \log\left[\frac{q_{i,j}}{p_i p_j} \right] \tag{7.4}$$

where $S_{i,j}$ is the substitution score of the residues i and j.

The elements of the substitution matrix are the scores of all possible pairs of residues. A positive score matrix element indicates that $q_{i,j} > p_i p_j$ and vise versa.

The overall alignment score (similarity) is given by

$$\text{Similarity} = \sum_{k}^{L} \log\left(\frac{q_{i,j}}{p_i p_j}\right)_k = \sum_{k}^{L} \left(S_{i,j}\right)_k \tag{7.5}$$

The overall alignment score measures the similarity of the two aligned sequences.

Since the substitution score in the nonrandom mutation model is based on the probability that a residue in a specific position in the sequence is replaced by another, several substitution matrices were developed to score sequence similarity and to explain the sequence homology. Those substitution matrices are grouped into Point Accepted Mutation (PAM) matrices and BLOck Substitution Matrices (BLOSUMs).

PAM Substitution Matrices   Point Accepted Mutation (PAM) matrices are a family of substitution matrices that were first developed by Margaret Dayhoff in 1970s [3]. She constructed a phylogenetic tree from the sequences of closely related proteins from many protein families to infer the common ancestral sequences of the proteins and then she calculated the observed frequencies, with which any amino acid pairs are aligned. The point accepted mutation or PAM is defined as the mutation that has been accepted by natural selection (i.e., the mutation that occurred in a coding region of a gene and adopted by the entire species). The PAM does not include silent mutations, which has no impact on the function of the proteins, and it also does not include mutations of lethal consequences, which are rejected by natural selection.

Based on PAM per sequence length, different PAM substitutions matrices were developed. Each PAM matrix is designed to compare two sequences that are at a specific number of points accepted mutation apart. Consider the following two protein sequences (Seq5 and Seq6), which are at an evolutionary distance of a single point accepted mutation, which means that Seq5 requires one edit operation (substitution) to be transformed into Seq6.

>Seq5

RETSIEMEESELDAQYLQNTFKVSKRQSFAPFSNPGNAEEECATFSAHSGSLKKQ

>Seq6

RETSIEMEESELDAQYLQNTFKVSKRQSFAPFSNPGNPEEECATFSAHSGSLKKQ

Those two sequences will be at evolutionary distance of 1 PAM, if one sequence requires an average of one edit per 100 amino acids. The PAM substitution matrix is 20×20 matrix (as shown in Figure 7.2) filled with substitution scores. An element of this matrix, [Mij], gives the score that the amino acid in column j will be replaced by the amino acid in row i after a given evolutionary interval (e.g., 1 PAM). The PAM substitution matrix for two sequences at an average distance of 1 PAM distance is called PAM1. Thus, we can derive substitution matrices for different evolutionary distance such as an average of 10 PAM per 100 amino acids, 70 PAM per 100 amino acids, or 250 PAM per 100 amino acids. The substitution matrices for those average distances are called PAM10, PAM70, and PAM250 respectively.

Margaret Dayhoff calculated the substitution probabilities for the PAM1 substitution matrix by constructing a phylogenetic tree from closely related protein sequences of an evolutionary distance of 1 PAM and calculated the observed frequency of the substitution of any one of the 20 amino acids.

Dayhoff assumed that the amino acid in column j is substituted by the amino acid in row i with the same frequency that the amino acid in row i is substituted by the amino acid in column j.

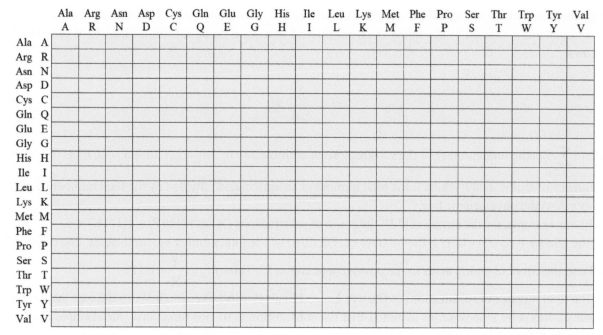

FIGURE 7.2   General format of substitution matrix.

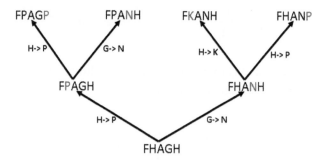

FIGURE 7.3   Phylogenetic tree of closely related sequences.

For explaining how Dayhoff derived PAM1, we will take the following short closely related sequence as examples for sequences of an evolutionary distance of 1 PAM.

FHAGH
FPAGH
FHANH
FPAGP
FPANH
FKANH
FHANP

The first step is to build a simple phylogenetic tree for the protein sequences. The phylogenetic tree (Figure 7.3) is built using the distances between any two sequences as explained in Levenshtein distance above. Then the observed frequency of the substitution of each amino acid for any two aligned sequences is counted. For example, the observed frequency of (H->P) is 3, (H->K) is 1, (G->N) is 2.

Since two sequenced will be aligned, assume that any one of the 20 amino acids in the first sequences is denoted by the column number j=1, 2, 3,…, 20 and any one of the 20 amino acid in the second sequence is denoted by the row number i=1, 2, 3,…, 20, and that the frequency (count) of substituting the amino acid i by any other amino acid in the second sequence in the tree is A_i. Thus, the relative mutability of each one of the 20 amino acids is defined as the ability of an amino acid to mutate (to be substituted), and it is calculated as follows:

$$m_i = \frac{A_i}{\sum A_i} Rf_i \qquad (7.6)$$

where $\sum_i A_i$ is the total number of the substitutions of amino acid i by any other amino acid, Rf_i is the relative frequency of amino acid i, which is the total number of an amino acid i divided by the total number of amino acids across the phylogenetic tree.

In our example, for the amino acid H, the count of substitutions (A_i) is 3 (H→P) + 1(H→K) = 4.

The relative frequency of H is the number of H divided by the total number of amino acids. The count of H is 8 and the count of amino acids in the phylogenetic tree is 35. Thus, $Rf_H = \frac{8}{35} = 0.229$.

The total number of substitutions in the tree $\sum A_{ij} = 12$ substitutions (i.e., 6×2). We multiplied the numbers of substitutions by 2 because we assumed that the substitution is in two directions (for example H→P and P→H). Thus, the relative mutability of H is:

$$m_H = \frac{A_H}{\sum A_{Hj}} Rf_i \times 100 = \frac{4}{12} 0.229 = 0.0763$$

The relative mutability of an amino acid is then used to calculate the substitution probability that the amino acid in row i is substituted by the amino acid in column j.

$$M_{ij} = \frac{m_i A_{ij}}{\sum_i A_{ij}} \left(i \neq j \right) \qquad (7.7)$$

where M_{ij} represents the off-diagonal elements of substitution probability matrix. The diagonal elements of the matrix $(i=j)$, which is the probability that the amino acid is not substituted by another in the phylogenetic tree and it is given as a complementary probability for the relative mutability of that amino acid.

$$M_{ii} = 1 - m_i \qquad (7.8)$$

To calculate the probability that H is replaced by P:

$$m_H = 0.0763$$

A_{HP} (The frequency of (H→P)) = 3.

$\sum_i A_{Hj}$ (The total number of changes involving H) = 4

$$M_{HP} = \frac{m_H A_{HP}}{\sum_i A_{Hj}} \left(H \neq P \right) = \frac{0.0763 \times 3}{4} = 0.057$$

$$M_{HH} = 1 - 0.0763 = 0.924$$

From our above example, the probability that H will be substituted by P is 0.057 and the probability the H remains unchanged is 0.924.

The empty substitution matrix in Figure 7.2, can be filled with the substitution probabilities for all amino acid pairs using Equations 7.7 and 7.8. When the matrix is filled, an element of the matrix will represent the probability that the amino acid in column j is substituted by the amino acid in row i. Sometimes the probability in each cell is multiplied by 10,000.

The probabilities (M_{ij}) in the PAM substitution matrix can also be transformed into a substitution score by dividing them by the relative frequency of the amino acid type j and then taking the logarithm and multiplying it by 10 as follows:

$$R_{ij} = 10 \log \left[\frac{M_{ij}}{Rf_j} \right] \tag{7.9}$$

To calculate the substitution score R_{HP}:
The relative frequency of P: $Rf_P = 5/35 = 0.143$.

$$R_{HP} = 10 \log \left[M_{HP} \times \frac{1}{Rf_P} \right] = 10 \log \left(\frac{0.057}{0.143} \right) = -4$$

$$R_{HH} = 10 \log \left[M_{HH} \times \frac{1}{Rf_H} \right] = 10 \log \left(\frac{0.924}{0.229} \right) = 6$$

Thus, the PAM substitution matrix in Figure 7.2 can also be filled by substitution scores instead of probabilities.

The above demonstration is only meant to show you how to compute PAM1. Since the computation of such substitution matrix is complicated, other PAMs (PAM10, PAM70, PAM250) can be extrapolated from PAM1. Anyway, you may never need to compute PAM or any other substitution matrix, since NCBI computes them, and they are ready to download and use from the NCBI website. The latest PAMs versions are available on the NCBI FTP server at https://ftp.ncbi.nlm.nih.gov/blast/matrices/. Figure 7.4 shows the PAM10 matrix, which can be used to score the pairwise alignment.

As an example, you can align the following two sequences using PAM10 substitution matrix to score the overall alignment.

>Seq7
RETSIEMEESELDAQYLQNTFKVSKRQS
>Seq8
RETSDEMEESELDPQYLQNTFKVSKRSS

Figure 7.5 shows the two aligned sequences and the substitution score for each pair using the PAM10 substitution matrix.

The overall alignment score is obtained by adding up all the individual scores. The overall alignment or similarity score for the alignment is 181. You can convert this similarity score into percent similarity by aligning the first sequence to itself, obtaining the overall score, and then dividing the overall sequence alignment score by the overall score of the aligning of the sequence to itself. In this example, the overall score of aligning the first sequence to itself is 229. Thus, the percent similarly based on PAM10 is 79%.

*	A	R	N	D	C	Q	E	G	H	I	L	K	M	F	P	S	T	W	Y	V	B	Z	X	*
A	7	-10	-7	-6	-10	-7	-5	-4	-11	-8	-9	-10	-8	-12	-4	-3	-3	-20	-11	-5	-6	-6	-6	-23
R	-10	9	-9	-17	-11	-4	-15	-13	-4	-8	-12	-2	-7	-12	-7	-6	-10	-5	-14	-11	-11	-7	-9	-23
N	-7	-9	9	-1	-17	-7	-5	-6	-2	-8	-10	-4	-15	-12	-9	-2	-5	-11	-7	-12	7	-6	-6	-23
D	-6	-17	-1	8	-21	-6	0	-6	-7	-11	-19	-8	-17	-21	-12	-7	-8	-21	-17	-11	7	-1	-9	-23
C	-10	-11	-17	-21	10	-20	-20	-13	-10	-9	-21	-20	-20	-19	-11	-6	-11	-22	-7	-9	-18	-20	-13	-23
Q	-7	-4	-7	-6	-20	9	-1	-10	-2	-11	-8	-6	-7	-19	-6	-8	-9	-19	-18	-10	-6	7	-8	-23
E	-5	-15	-5	0	-20	-1	8	-7	-9	-8	-13	-7	-10	-20	-9	-7	-9	-23	-11	-10	-1	7	-8	-23
G	-4	-13	-6	-6	-13	-10	-7	7	-13	-17	-14	-10	-12	-12	-10	-4	-10	-21	-20	-9	-6	-8	-8	-23
H	-11	-4	-2	-7	-10	-2	-9	-13	10	-13	-9	-10	-17	-9	-7	-9	-11	-10	-6	-9	-4	-4	-8	-23
I	-8	-8	-8	-11	-9	-11	-8	-17	-13	9	-4	-9	-3	-5	-12	-10	-5	-20	-9	-1	-9	-9	-8	-23
L	-9	-12	-10	-19	-21	-8	-13	-14	-9	-4	7	-11	-2	-5	-10	-12	-10	-9	-10	-5	-12	-10	-9	-23
K	-10	-2	-4	-8	-20	-6	-7	-10	-10	-9	-11	7	-4	-20	-10	-7	-6	-18	-12	-13	-5	-6	-8	-23
M	-8	-7	-15	-17	-20	-7	-10	-12	-17	-3	-2	-4	12	-7	-11	-8	-7	-19	-17	-4	-16	-8	-9	-23
F	-12	-12	-12	-21	-19	-19	-20	-12	-9	-5	-5	-20	-7	9	-13	-9	-12	-7	-1	-12	-14	-20	-12	-23
P	-4	-7	-9	-12	-11	-6	-9	-10	-7	-12	-10	-10	-11	-13	8	-4	-7	-20	-20	-9	-10	-7	-8	-23
S	-3	-6	-2	-7	-6	-8	-7	-4	-9	-10	-12	-7	-8	-9	-4	7	-2	-8	-10	-10	-4	-8	-6	-23
T	-3	-10	-5	-8	-11	-9	-9	-10	-11	-5	-10	-6	-7	-12	-7	-2	8	-19	-9	-6	-6	-9	-7	-23
W	-20	-5	-11	-21	-22	-19	-23	-21	-10	-20	-9	-18	-19	-7	-20	-8	-19	13	-8	-22	-13	-21	-16	-23
Y	-11	-14	-7	-17	-7	-18	-11	-20	-6	-9	-10	-12	-17	-1	-20	-10	-9	-8	10	-10	-9	-13	-11	-23
V	-5	-11	-12	-11	-9	-10	-10	-9	-9	-1	-5	-13	-4	-12	-9	-10	-6	-22	-10	8	-11	-10	-8	-23
B	-6	-11	7	7	-18	-6	-1	-6	-4	-9	-12	-5	-16	-14	-10	-4	-6	-13	-9	-11	7	-3	-8	-23
Z	-6	-7	-6	-1	-20	7	7	-8	-4	-9	-10	-6	-8	-20	-7	-8	-9	-21	-13	-10	-3	7	-8	-23
X	-6	-9	-6	-9	-13	-8	-8	-8	-8	-8	-9	-8	-9	-12	-8	-6	-7	-16	-11	-8	-8	-8	-8	-23
*	-23	-23	-23	-23	-23	-23	-23	-23	-23	-23	-23	-23	-23	-23	-23	-23	-23	-23	-23	-23	-23	-23	-23	1

FIGURE 7.4   PAM10 substitution matrix.

#	1	2	3	4	5	6	7	8	9	10	11	12	13	14	15	16	17	18	19	20	21	22	23	24	25	26	27	28
Seq7	R	E	T	S	I	E	M	E	E	S	E	L	D	A	Q	Y	L	Q	N	T	F	K	V	S	K	R	Q	S
					*									*														
Seq8	R	E	T	S	D	E	M	E	E	S	E	L	D	P	Q	Y	L	Q	N	T	F	K	V	S	K	R	S	S
Score	9	8	8	7	-11	8	12	8	8	7	8	7	8	-4	9	10	7	9	9	8	9	7	8	7	7	9	-8	7

FIGURE 7.5   Aligning two sequences using PAM10 substitution matrix.

```
R E T P C E - E D S P S K
N M T S C E K - E S Q S N
D E T P C R M P E S P S L
Q E T R C E - D E S P S I
H E T P C E - - E S P S B
P E T P C E C - E S P S -
S E T P C E P - R S P S Q
G E T P C E - K E S P S A
L E T P C E - - E S P S C
```

FIGURE 7.6   Blocks of nine conserved sequences.

BLOSUM Substitution Matrices   BLOSUM (BLOck Substitution Matrix) is another amino acid substitution matrix, first calculated by Steven Henikoff and Jorja Henikoff (1992) [4]. Only blocks of amino acid sequences with a little difference between them are considered in the calculation of the substitution matrix. The blocks are chosen from the conserved parts of the protein sequences as shown in Figure 7.6.

The first stage of building the BLOSUM matrix is the removal of redundant sequences based on a threshold of percent identity of x% so that sequences of percent identity more than the threshold will be eliminated. Identical sequences are removed to avoid bias of the result in favor of a certain protein. The matrix constructed from blocks with no more the x% of similarity is called BLOSUM-x. For example, the BLOSUM 30 is the amino acid substitution matrix built using sequences with no more than 30% identity. The probability that an amino acid is substituted by another and the alignment score for any aligned pairs of amino acids are computed as shown above for PAM.

	A	R	N	D	C	Q	E	G	H	I	L	K	M	F	P	S	T	W	Y	V	B	Z	X	*
A	4	-1	-2	-2	0	-1	-1	0	-2	-1	-1	-1	-1	-2	-1	1	0	-3	-2	0	-2	-1	0	-4
R	-1	5	0	-2	-3	1	0	-2	0	-3	-2	2	-1	-3	-2	-1	-1	-3	-2	-3	-1	0	-1	-4
N	-2	0	6	1	-3	0	0	0	1	-3	-3	0	-2	-3	-2	1	0	-4	-2	-3	3	0	-1	-4
D	-2	-2	1	6	-3	0	2	-1	-1	-3	-4	-1	-3	-3	-1	0	-1	-4	-3	-3	4	1	-1	-4
C	0	-3	-3	-3	9	-3	-4	-3	-3	-1	-1	-3	-1	-2	-3	-1	-1	-2	-2	-1	-3	-3	-2	-4
Q	-1	1	0	0	-3	5	2	-2	0	-3	-2	1	0	-3	-1	0	-1	-2	-1	-2	0	3	-1	-4
E	-1	0	0	2	-4	2	5	-2	0	-3	-3	1	-2	-3	-1	0	-1	-3	-2	-2	1	4	-1	-4
G	0	-2	0	-1	-3	-2	-2	6	-2	-4	-4	-2	-3	-3	-2	0	-2	-2	-3	-3	-1	-2	-1	-4
H	-2	0	1	-1	-3	0	0	-2	8	-3	-3	-1	-2	-1	-2	-1	-2	-2	2	-3	0	0	-1	-4
I	-1	-3	-3	-3	-1	-3	-3	-4	-3	4	2	-3	1	0	-3	-2	-1	-3	-1	3	-3	-3	-1	-4
L	-1	-2	-3	-4	-1	-2	-3	-4	-3	2	4	-2	2	0	-3	-2	-1	-2	-1	1	-4	-3	-1	-4
K	-1	2	0	-1	-3	1	1	-2	-1	-3	-2	5	-1	-3	-1	0	-1	-3	-2	-2	0	1	-1	-4
M	-1	-1	-2	-3	-1	0	-2	-3	-2	1	2	-1	5	0	-2	-1	-1	-1	-1	1	-3	-1	-1	-4
F	-2	-3	-3	-3	-2	-3	-3	-3	-1	0	0	-3	0	6	-4	-2	-2	1	3	-1	-3	-3	-1	-4
P	-1	-2	-2	-1	-3	-1	-1	-2	-2	-3	-3	-1	-2	-4	7	-1	-1	-4	-3	-2	-2	-1	-2	-4
S	1	-1	1	0	-1	0	0	0	-1	-2	-2	0	-1	-2	-1	4	1	-3	-2	-2	0	0	0	-4
T	0	-1	0	-1	-1	-1	-1	-2	-2	-1	-1	-1	-1	-2	-1	1	5	-2	-2	0	-1	-1	0	-4
W	-3	-3	-4	-4	-2	-2	-3	-2	-2	-3	-2	-3	-1	1	-4	-3	-2	11	2	-3	-4	-3	-2	-4
Y	-2	-2	-2	-3	-2	-1	-2	-3	2	-1	-1	-2	-1	3	-3	-2	-2	2	7	-1	-3	-2	-1	-4
V	0	-3	-3	-3	-1	-2	-2	-3	-3	3	1	-2	1	-1	-2	-2	0	-3	-1	4	-3	-2	-1	-4
B	-2	-1	3	4	-3	0	1	-1	0	-3	-4	0	-3	-3	-2	0	-1	-4	-3	-3	4	1	-1	-4
Z	-1	0	0	1	-3	3	4	-2	0	-3	-3	1	-1	-3	-1	0	-1	-3	-2	-2	1	4	-1	-4
X	0	-1	-1	-1	-2	-1	-1	-1	-1	-1	-1	-1	-1	-1	-2	0	0	-2	-1	-1	-1	-1	-1	-4
*	-4	-4	-4	-4	-4	-4	-4	-4	-4	-4	-4	-4	-4	-4	-4	-4	-4	-4	-4	-4	-4	-4	-4	1

FIGURE 7.7 BLOSUM-62 substitution matrix.

Once again, you may never need to compute any of substitution matrices; BLOSUM matrices of different thresholds are available at https://ftp.ncbi.nlm.nih.gov/blast/matrices/. Figure 7.7 shows BLOSUM-62, which was built of conserved sequence blocks of no more than 62% identity.

Up to this point, we have discussed the most commonly used scoring schemes for pairwise sequence alignments. Identity scoring, which gives 1 for matched pair and 0 for unmatched pair, is used for nucleotide (DNA and RNA) alignments, but it can also be used for protein sequence alignments. The substitution matrices (PAMs and BLOSUMs) are usually used for protein sequence alignments. The question that may arise as to which substitution matrix to use for sequence alignment. For closely related sequences, PAM1, PAM10, PAM30, PAM40 may be good choices since those scoring matrices computed using fewer amino acid substitutions in an average of 100 amino acids. On the other hand, PAM250 is better for distantly related sequences because it is designed for sequences with relatively large number of changes per 100 amino acids. The sequence blocks used to compute BLOSUM matrices are chosen based on percent identity threshold. For closely related sequences it is preferable to use BLOSUM with large threshold such as BLOSUM-100, BLOSUM-80, and BLOSUM-62. For distantly related sequences it is preferable to use BLOSUM-50. Moreover, for alignment of short sequences, you can use matrices that were designed for short evolutionary time scales, such as PAM40 or BLOSUM-80. For long sequences of 100 residues or more you can use matrices designed for longer evolutionary time scales such as PAM250 and BLOSUM-50.

Gaps and Gap Penalty   During the evolution path, in addition to mutation by substitutions, sequences of the same ancestral sequence might mutate by insertions or deletion (InDel), which would result in sequences of variable lengths. When aligning such sequences, gaps must be introduced to substitute insertions and to achieve a correct match. In the sequence alignment, gaps are achieved by pairing up a base of amino acid in one sequence with blank spaces inserted into the other nucleotide or protein sequence to achieve a better match. However, inserting many gaps may produce a wrong alignment with a significant overall alignment score. To avoid such erroneous alignments, a gap penalty is introduced to the scoring scheme so that a penalty is subtracted from the score each time a gap is inserted. Since gap insertions may span to several residues, it was found that it is better to give an initial gap penalty for the new gap and then a smaller penalty for a gap extension called the extension gap penalty. A high gap penalty and high gap extension penalty are usually used for closely related sequences while low penalties are used for distantly related sequences.

Global Alignment Algorithm

So far, we have discussed alignment scoring schemes and gaps. The alignment of sequences may involve long sequences subjected in different kinds of changes including substitution, insertion, or deletion. Therefore, sequence alignments require efficient algorithms for obtaining optimal alignment. In this section, we will discuss pairwise alignment algorithms. The purpose for sequence alignment is either to align an entire sequence to another or to align local parts of a sequence to local parts in another sequence. The latter is usually used for the search of exons, introns, promoter regions in a gene sequence or domains and motifs in protein sequences. More importantly, for any pairwise alignment, especially when insertion and deletion are involved, there may be several alignment possibilities. Therefore, algorithms are required to find the best alignment among these large numbers of alignments. The alignment algorithm used to explore all possible sequence alignments and to find the optimal one is called the dynamic programming algorithm. This algorithm divides the whole alignment into smaller sub-alignments to find the optimum one.

The global alignment for two sequences is achieved by aligning an entire sequence to another so that a residue from one sequence must pair up with a residue from the other. Gaps will be introduced to make the lengths of the two aligned sequences equal. Consider the two sequences: MENSELAQY and MEELDAQY, which can be aligned as follows:

MENSEL-AQY

ME--ELDAQY

Needleman and Wunsch were the first to develop a dynamic programming algorithm for global sequence alignment in the 1970s [5]. The Needleman-Wunsch's algorithm was meant to find the alignment with the highest overall alignment score if similarity is used or with the lowest overall score if evolutionary distance is used. The algorithm begins with forming an alignment scoring matrix with $(m+1)\times(n+1)$ dimension, where m and n are the lengths of the first and second sequence (y and x) respectively. Consider the two sequences are $y=$"MENSELAQY" and $x=$ "MEELDAQY". Any amino acid in y is denoted by y_i, where $i = 1,2,\ldots, m$-1 (so $y_1 = M, y_2 = E, y_3 = N$ and so on). On the other hand, any residue in x is denoted by x_j, where $j=1,2,\ldots, n$-1 (so $x_1 = M, x_2 = E, x_3 = E$ and so on). The goal of the dynamic programming algorithm is to divide the two major sequences y and x into a set of subsequences $y\left[y_1 \ldots y_i\right]$ and $x\left[x_1 \ldots x_j\right]$, to find the scores of the optimal alignments of the subsequences, and to determine the path that maximizes the score and identifies the final alignment.

For the above two sequences, first you need to create an empty matrix of ten rows and nine columns (10×9) and then position the amino acids of the first sequence horizontally as column headers and the amino acids of the second sequence vertically as row headers as shown in Figure 7.8. Notice that each sequence is preceded with a gap.

The second step is to fill the cells of the empty scoring matrix with the alignments (S_{ij}) of the subsequences $y\left[y_1 \ldots y_i\right]$ and $x\left[x_1 \ldots x_j\right]$. You can use any scoring scheme such as identity, PAM, BLOSUM, or distance. But in this example, for simplicity's sake we will use a simple identity scoring scheme as follows:

- Matched pair: +1
- Unmatched pair: -1
- Gap penalty (g): -2

The empty scoring matrix is filled with alignment scores based on the Needleman-Wunsch algorithm for dynamic programming of pairwise sequence alignment. The algorithm has three phases: (1) initialization

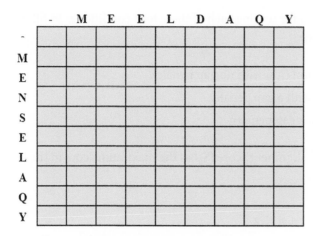

FIGURE 7.8   An empty alignment scoring matrix.

-	-	M	E	E	L	D	A	Q	Y
-	0	-2	-4	-6	-8	-10	-12	-14	-16
M	-2								
E	-4								
N	-6								
S	-8								
E	-10								
L	-12								
A	-14								
Q	-16								
Y	-18								

FIGURE 7.9   An initialized alignment scoring matrix.

of the scoring matrix, (2) filling the matrix cells with alignment scores, and (3) traceback to obtain the final sequence alignment.

Initializing the Scoring Matrix   The empty alignment scoring matrix is initialized by filling the cells of the first row and first column of the matrix beginning from the first cell on the left top corner. This first cell is filled with a zero, which is the score for aligning an initial gap with an initial gap. Then we fill the remaining cells of the first left column and the remaining cells of the first top row with alignment scores. Each amino acid is aligned to a gap; the score of aligning an amino acid to a gap (g) is -2. Based on the algorithm, those cells are filled using the following formulas:
For the cells of the first column:

$$S_{i,1} = S_{i-1,1} + g \qquad (7.10)$$

For the cells of the first row:

$$S_{1,j} = S_{1,j-1} + g \qquad (7.11)$$

For example, for M aligned to a gap in the first column (j=1):

$S_{2,1} = S_{2-1,1} - 2 = S_{1,1} - 2 = -2$, since $S_{1,1} = 0$
$S_{3,1} = S_{3-1,1} - 2 = S_{2,1} - 2 = -4$, since $S_{2,1} = -2$

Other cells of the first column and first row of the matrix are initialized the same. Figure 7.9 shows an initialized alignment scoring matrix.

Filling the Cells of the Scoring Matrix   After initializing the alignment scoring matrix, the next step is to fill the remaining cells of the matrix. We will align an amino acid from y sequence to an amino acid from x sequence as (y_i, x_j). The alignment score for any pair is denoted by $s(y_i, x_j)$ and the scores of the optimal alignments for the subsequences $y[y_1 \ldots y_i]$ and $x[x_1 \ldots x_j]$ are denoted by S_{ij}. When we align any pair of amino acid as (y_i, x_j), there will be four possibilities:

(1) the pair of the amino acids may be matched
(2) the pair of amino acids may be mismatched
(3) a gap may be introduced from the first sequence or
(4) a gap may be introduced from the second sequence.

The dynamic programming algorithm provides a formula for scoring each of these four conditions. To fill the remaining cells there are three paths in the scoring matrix:

(1) A diagonal move from position $(i$-$1, j$-$1)$ to position (i, j) with no gap penalty.

(2) A move from any other position along column j with a gap penalty.

(3) A move from any other position along row i with a gap penalty.

The dynamic programming algorithm finds the optimal alignment score (S_{ij}) as the maximum score in the set $[S_{i-1,j-1} + s(y_i, x_j), S_{i-1,j} + g, S_{i,j-1} + g]$, which is given by:

$$S_{ij} = \text{Max} \begin{cases} S_{i-1,j-1} + s(y_i, x_j) \\ S_{i-1,j} + g \\ S_{i,j-1} + g \end{cases} \tag{7.12}$$

To fill the matrix cell, we will begin with the cell (y_2, x_2), which aligns M from the horizontal sequence with M from the vertical sequence. The pair is matched so the score of the aligned pair is $s(y_2, x_2) = +1$. Thus, to calculate the optimal alignment score for the subsequence up to that cell, we will use Formula (7.12) as follows:

$$S_{2,2} = \text{Max} \begin{cases} 0 + 1 = +1 \\ -2 - 2 = -4 \\ -2 - 2 = -4 \end{cases}$$

Since the diagonal $S_{1,1} + s(y_2, x_2) = +1$ is the maximum among the three scores, the move will be diagonal from (y_1, x_1) to (y_2, x_2) and the score is $S_{2,2} = +1$. The move can be indicated by an arrow as shown in Figure 7.10.

The alignment for (y_3, x_2) is (E, M), which is a mismatch, $s(y_3, x_2) = -1$. Thus:

$$S_{3,2} = \text{Max} \begin{cases} -2 - 1 = -3 \\ +1 - 2 = -1 \\ -4 - 2 = -6 \end{cases}$$

	-	M	E	E	L	D	A	Q	Y
-	0	-2	-4	-6	-8	-10	-12	-14	-16
M	-2	1	-1	-3	-5	-7	-9	-11	-13
E	-4	-1	2	0	-2	-4	-6	-8	-10
N	-6	-3	0	1	-1	-3	-5	-7	-9
S	-8	-5	-2	-1	0	-2	-4	-6	-8
E	-10	-7	-4	-1	-2	-1	-3	-5	-7
L	-12	-9	-6	-3	0	-2	-2	-4	-6
A	-14	-11	-8	-5	-2	-1	-1	-3	-5
Q	-16	-13	-10	-7	-4	-3	-2	0	-2
Y	-18	-15	-12	-9	-6	-5	-4	-2	1

FIGURE 7.10 The filled alignment scoring matrix.

Since the $S_{2,2} + g = -1$ is the maximum, the move will be down from (y_2, x_2) to (y_3, x_2) introducing a gap and $S_{3,2} = -1$.

The alignment for (y_2, x_3) is (M, E), which is a mismatch, $s(y_3, x_2) = -1$. Thus

$$S_{3,2} = \text{Max} \begin{cases} -2 - 1 = -3 \\ -4 - 2 = -6 \\ +1 - 2 = -1 \end{cases}$$

Since $S_{2,2} + g = -1$ is the maximum, the move will be to the right from (y_2, x_2) to (y_2, x_3) introducing a gap and $S_{2,3} = -1$.

The alignment for (y_3, x_3) is (E, E), which is a match, so $s(y_3, x_3) = +1$. Thus

$$S_{3,3} = \text{Max} \begin{cases} +2 + 1 = +2 \\ -1 - 2 = -3 \\ -1 - 2 = -3 \end{cases}$$

So, the move will be diagonal from (y_2, x_2) to (y_3, x_3) and $S_{3,3} = +2$.

We can continue like this until all cells of the scoring matrix are filled with the subsequence optimal alignment scores.

Figure 7.10 shows a filled alignment scoring matrix for the two sequences; the cells of the matrix are filled with the scores of the optimal alignment of the subsequences. The filled matrix also determines the overall optimal alignment score, which is the score in the lowest right corner.

Traceback   Traceback is the process of finding the optimal alignment from the scoring matrix filled by alignment optimal scores using the dynamic programming algorithm. The traceback begins from the lowest right cell (the cell of the overall optimal alignment score) and traces back the optimal alignment by finding the maximum score from the three adjacent cells. Beginning from the lowest right cell of score +1 of (Y, Y), the maximum score of the three adjacent cells is zero of (Q, Q) in the up-diagonal cell. From there (Q, Q) the maximum score is -1 of (A, A) so the move is up diagonal to (A, A). From (A, A), the maxim adjacent score is -1 of (A, D) so the move this time is left horizontal to (A, D). The process of traceback will continue like this until it reaches the cell of the first aligned pair. The complete traceback for the optimal alignment path is shown in Figure 7.11.

The optimal alignment path created by the traceback is used to obtain the optimal sequence alignment for the two sequences as shown in Figure 7.12. You can notice that the dynamic programming algorithm could insert gaps to maximize the alignment.

-	-	M	E	E	L	D	A	Q	Y
-	0	-2	-4	-6	-8	-10	-12	-14	-16
M	-2	1	-1	-3	-5	-7	-9	-11	-13
E	-4	-1	2	0	-2	-4	-6	-8	-10
N	-6	-3	0	1	-1	-3	-5	-7	-9
S	-8	-5	-2	-1	0	-2	-4	-6	-8
E	-10	-7	-4	-1	-2	-1	-3	-5	-7
L	-12	-9	-6	-3	0	-2	-2	-4	-6
A	-14	-11	-8	-5	-2	-1	-1	-3	-5
Q	-16	-13	-10	-7	-4	-3	-2	0	-2
Y	-18	-15	-12	-9	-6	-5	-4	-2	1

FIGURE 7.11   The alignment scoring matrix with traceback for the optimal alignment path.

Sequence x	M	E	N	S	E	L	.	A	Q	Y
	|	|			|	|		|	|	|
Sequence y	M	E	.	.	E	L	D	A	Q	Y
Scores (S)	1	2	1	-1	-1	0	-1	-1	0	1

FIGURE 7.12   Optimal sequence alignment.

After obtaining the optimal sequence alignment, we can use any scoring scheme to give a score to each pair of amino acids and then calculate the overall alignment score by adding up the individual scores as we discussed above.

Significance of a Pairwise Global Alignment   When we align two sequences, there is always a probability that the alignment we obtained might occur by change rather than a consequence of homology. Therefore, there is a need for a metric to measure the uncertainty of the sequence alignment. In other words, we need to know whether an alignment is statistically significant or not. Assume that we wish to align two sequences (Seq1 and Seq2). We can state the hypothesis test as follows:

H_0: the two sequences are not related (Null hypothesis)
H_A: the two sequences are related (Alternative hypothesis)

To test this hypothesis, we need a pool of non-homologous sequences (n subject sequences). The non-homologous sequences can be obtained either from the NCBI sequence database or can be generated randomly using a computer program. The non-homologous subject sequences can be aligned to either the first or second sequence and the *overall alignment score* for each aligned subject sequence is denoted by x_i, where $i=1,2,3,\ldots,n$. From the scores of aligned sequences $[x_1, x_2, x_3, \ldots, x_n]$ we can calculate both the mean ($\bar{x}$) and standard deviation (s) as

$$\bar{x} = \frac{\sum_{i=1}^{n} x_i}{n} \tag{7.13}$$

$$s = \sqrt{\frac{\sum_{i=1}^{n}(x_i - \bar{x})^2}{n-1}} \tag{7.14}$$

From the basic statistics, we know that the central limit theorem states that if we have a population with mean μ and standard deviation σ and we take sufficiently large random samples of size n repeatedly from that population with replacement, then the distribution of the sample means will be approximately normally distributed. Thus, the scores x_i can be standardized as follows:

$$z_i = \frac{x_i - \bar{x}}{s} \tag{7.15}$$

where z_i is the standardized overall score for the alignment i.

To test the above hypothesis about the pairwise alignment of the two sequences (Seq1 and Seq2), we can standardize their overall alignment score using Formula 7.15 and then use the obtained z-score as a test statistic at a significance level of α (usually $\alpha = 0.05$). Using the Standard Normal Table, we can obtain the probability of the z-score (the p-value). A p-value less than α is considered as statistical evidence that the alignment of the two sequences is significant at that significance level.

Local Sequence Alignment and Algorithm

Rather than entire sequences, the local sequence alignment algorithm searches for the local aligned region in the two sequences. This is usually the case when we search sequence databases using BLAST. We can use local alignment to find similar regions or domains in proteins, promoter, exons, or introns in a gene, and also in mapping short sequences generated by the sequences to a reference genome. Local sequence alignment uses the Smith-Waterman algorithm [6], which is a modified version of the global dynamic programming algorithm. In local alignment, the scoring scheme must contain negative scores (e.g., for mismatch or gap) and the scoring matrix is created using the same steps we followed to create the scoring matrix of the global alignment. However, in case of the local alignment scoring matrix, the cells of the first left column and the top row are initialized with zero (instead of a gap penalty). A very important constraint in local alignment is that whenever the score of an optimal subsequence alignment is less than zero it will be rejected and the score is set to zero. Thus, the score of the optimal subsequence alignment is given as the maximum of four possible values as:

$$S_{ij} = Max \begin{cases} S_{i-1.j-1} + s(y_i, x_j) \\ S_{i-1.j} + g \\ S_{i.j-1} + g \\ 0 \end{cases} \qquad (7.16)$$

The score of the random match is required to be negative to ensure that alignments between long unrelated sequences do not have high scores.

In the local alignment, the traceback starts from the highest score wherever it is found and proceeds diagonally up to the left stopping when a cell is reached with a value of zero. The highest score defines the start of an alignment. Multiple alignments may be found.

Let us use the Smith-Waterman algorithm for a local alignment to align these two example protein sequences (x: "AQYLQNTFKV" and y: "NPKLQNTLA"). We can use any alignment scoring scheme (identity, PAM, BLOSUM, etc.) to score the pairwise residue alignment. In this example, we will use the identity scoring scheme of +1 for matched pair, -0.4 for mismatched pair, and -1.4 for a gap. The steps for creating the alignment scoring matrix are: (1) create an empty matrix as described above, (2) fill (initialize) the cells of the first left column and top row with zeros, (3) use Formula 7.16 to fill the other cells of the matrix, and (4) use traceback to identify the local alignments. Figure 7.13 shows the alignment scoring matrix for the two example sequences. Notice that the constraint in the formula sets any scores negative scores to zero and also notice that the traceback begins from the highest score in the matrix and then moves diagonally up and stops at the first zero score.

From the traceback we can identify the aligned local region (LQNT), which represents the optimal alignment of the two sequences (Figure 7.14).

-	-	N	P	K	L	Q	N	T	L	A
-	0	0	0	0	0	0	0	0	0	0
A	0	0	0	0	0	0	0	0	0	1
Q	0	0	0	0	0	1	0	0	0	0
Y	0	0	0	0	0	0	0	0	0	0
L	0	0	0	0	1	0	0	0	0	0
Q	0	0	0	0	0	2	0.6	0	0	0
N	0	0	0	0	0	0.6	3	1.6	0.2	0
T	0	0	0	0	0	0	1.6	4	2.6	1.2
F	0	0	0	0	0	0	0.2	2.6	3.6	2.2
K	0	0	0	1	0	0	0	1.2	2.2	3.2
V	0	0	0	0	0	0	0	0	0.8	1.8

FIGURE 7.13   The alignment scoring matrix with traceback for the optimal local alignment path.

```
Sequence x   A   Q   Y   L   Q   N   T   F   K   V
                         |   |   |   |
Sequence y   N   P   K   L   Q   N   T   L   A   -
```

FIGURE 7.14   The optimal local alignment of the two sequences.

BLAST Algorithm

The Smith-Waterman algorithm always guarantees to find the optimal local alignment of two sequences. However, in a typical use of local alignment we run a query sequence against a large database of target sequences. The time complexity of the Smith-Waterman algorithm is $O(m^2n)$, which makes comparing a sequence to numerous target sequences computationally expensive. The Basic Local Alignment Search Tool or BLAST [7] is an optimized version of the local alignment algorithm that overcomes the downside of time complexity by adopting a heuristic approach to find local alignments in a search against a large number of sequences. Compared to the exhaustive Smith-Waterman method, BLAST may skip some local alignment hits.

The BLAST search is performed with a query sequence, which can be nucleotide or protein sequence in FASTA format. The search will be against a target database, which is formed from concatenated FASTA formatted nucleotide or protein sequences. The NCBI BLAST has several databases to serve different purposes. A user can create a custom database using an NCBI program called "makeblastdb" (older version was "formatdb"), which generates files containing the sequences and indexing information used during the BLAST search.

In this section, we will focus on the BLAST algorithm while the uses of BLAST will be discussed in the next chapter.

We will use a protein sequence as an example to explain the BLAST algorithm. The aim of using BLAST is to align a query sequence to concatenated target sequences to find the regions that align significantly to the query sequence. The BLAST heuristic algorithm has the following steps:

Filtering Low-Complexity Region from Query Sequence   The low-complexity regions of a sequence are the regions that have low compositional complexity or repeated residues, which tend to give a high score that does not reflect the actual sequence similarity. Low-complexity regions and residue repetitiveness can be detected visually using the dot-plot that we have discussed above. Sequence complexity can also be detected by dividing the query sequence into windows (segments) of a length N and computing the compositional complexity in each window using the complexity formula of Wootton and Federhen [8].

$$\text{CWF} = \frac{1}{N}\log_A\left(\frac{N!}{\prod_{i=1}^{A}n_i!}\right) \tag{7.17}$$

where A is the alphabet size (A=4 for DNA and A=20 for proteins) and N is the window size, and n_i is the number of residues in a window, i = 1,…,A.

The complexity can also be detected by using the entropy E of residues [9]:

$$E = \sum_{i=1}^{A}\left(\frac{n_i}{N}\right)\log_A\left(\frac{n_i}{N}\right) \tag{7.18}$$

where N is the window size, n_i is the number of symbols in a window and A is the alphabet size.

The *CWF* and *E* values range between 0 and 1, where 1 is the highest sequence complexity.

The region of low complexity can be marked with an X (for protein sequences) or N (for nucleic acid sequences) and will be ignored by the BLAST program.

Query sequence   N P K L Q N T L A
Query words (W=3) N P K
                            P K L
                               K L Q
                                  L Q N
                                     Q N T
                                        N T L
                                           T L A

FIGURE 7.15   Generation of words (word size =3).

Database sequence	L	N	K	P	E	L	Q	L	N	E	L
Query sequence	-	-	N	P	K	L	Q	N	T	L	A
Alignment score			0	7	1	4	5	-3	0	-3	-1

FIGURE 7.16   Exact match scanning.

Words Generation   Words of a certain length (word size) are formed from the query sequence. Assume that the query protein sequence is "NPKLQNTLA" and the word size that you have chosen is three; the query words will be "NPK", "PKL", "KLQ", LQN", "QNT", "NTL", and "TLA" as shown in Figure 7.15.
When using BLAST, the default word size may be six but can be adjusted by the user.

Neighborhood Words Generation   The words generated in the above step are aligned to the concatenated sequences of the target database to get exact matches. The BLOSUM-62 substitution matrix is used to score the exact match alignments in addition to all possible combinations of the three amino acids in a query word. For each word there are 20×20×20=8000 possible matches. The words are sorted based on their optimal scores from the greatest to the lowest score. Such sorted words are called neighborhood words. A threshold (T) then will be applied to keep only the neighborhood words with optimal score above T while those with lower scores will be discarded. A few words may remain.

Tree Data Structure   The remaining high-scoring query words will be organized into a tree data structure to allow rapid search and comparison of these high-scoring words to the database sequence.

Scanning for Exact Match and Seeding   Each sequence in the database is scanned for an exact match to one of the words. If a match is found, this match is used to seed a possible ungapped alignment between the query and database sequences.

Alignment Extension   The alignment is extended from the matching words in both directions along the sequences forming a long stretch of sequence known as high-scoring segment pair (HSP) with a larger optimal accumulated score as shown in Figure 7.16. Each time the alignment is extended, an alignment score either increases or decreases. The extension stops when the alignment score drops below a predefined threshold S.

The HSP is indicated by the shaded region in Figure 7.16. The optimal accumulated score for HSP is 7+1+4+5=17.

Only HSP with scores above a cut-off will be kept. The cut-off value is usually determined empirically.

Statistical Significance of High-Scoring Segment Pairs   The statistical significance for each HSP will be determined by finding the probability that two random sequences (one with the length of the query sequence and the other with the length of the entire concatenated database sequences), exploiting Gumbel extreme value distribution (EVD), in which the probability of observing a score S equal to or greater than x or $p(S \geq x)$ is given by:

$$p(S \geq x) = 1 - \exp\left(-e^{-\lambda(x-\mu)}\right) \tag{7.19}$$

where $\mu = \dfrac{\log(Km'n')}{\lambda}$, the EVD parameters λ and K depend upon the substitution matrix, gap penalties, and the frequencies of the symbols, m' and n' are the effective lengths of the query sequence and database sequences respectively. Those effective lengths of sequences can be approximated as:

$$m' \approx m - \frac{\ln(Kmn)}{H}, \; n' \approx n - \frac{\ln(Kmn)}{H} \tag{7.20}$$

where H is the average expected score per aligned pair of residues in an alignment of two random sequences.

The EVD parameters (λ and K) and H were estimated as that λ=0.318, K=0.13, and H=0.4 for un-gapped local alignment using BLOSUM62 as a substitution matrix.

The expectation E of observing a score $S \geq x$ in a database of D number of sequences is approximately given by the following Poisson distribution:

$$E \approx 1 - e^{-p(S \geq x)D} \tag{7.21}$$

Furthermore, when $p(S \geq x) < 0.1$, E-value can also be approximated as:

$$p(S \geq x)D \tag{7.22}$$

The E-value, also called the expectation or expect value, is used to assess the significance of the HSP for ungapped local alignment.

Using Smith-Waterman Algorithm for Aligning High-Scoring Segment Pairs   The HSPs with high statistical significance will be aligned to database sequences using the Smith-Waterman algorithm. The old BLAST version (BLAST) produces ungapped alignment for each HSP. The recent BLAST version (BLAST2) produces a single gapped alignment that includes all HSPs.

Reporting the Matched Hits   Every matched hit with E-values less than the specified cut-off E-value will be reported. The BLAST user is allowed to set the cut-off E-value. The default value is 10.

PSI-BLAST

The position-specific-iterated BLAST, or PSI-BLAST [10], is a program that uses BLAST to search for homologous sequences of a query sequence on a target database and then generates a sequence profile, called the position-specific scoring matrix (PSSM), from the multiple sequence alignments of those homologous sequences. The PSSM is then used to generate a sequence used for further searches of the database for new matches that can also be used to form a PSSM for a subsequent iteration. The PSI-BLAST algorithm adjusts the PSSM iteratively using new homologous sequences every time until a certain threshold is reached. The PSSM provides a quantitative description of the degree of sequence conservation at each position and allows the capture of conserved sequence patterns in sequences and distantly related proteins. The PSI-BLAST usually uses protein-protein BLAST (BLASTp) and it is used to search distantly related protein sequences. Evolutionarily related protein sequences may share a limited sequence identity that makes it difficult to detect homology of distantly related sequences using the regular BLAST algorithm.

The following are the general steps undertaken by PSI-BLAST when it is used to search for related sequences of a query sequence on a target sequence database. The PSI-BLAST is usually used for protein search but to better explain those steps and for the sake of simplicity, we will use DNA sequences as example.

Seq1	A	T	G	T	A	T	C
Seq2	C	A	A	G	A	T	G
Seq3	G	G	C	T	A	C	A
Seq4	T	A	A	T	G	T	T
Seq5	C	G	G	A	A	T	G

FIGURE 7.17   Multiple sequence alignment of related sequences.

TABLE 7.1   Positional Relative Frequency and Overall Relative Frequencies

		Positions							**Overall**
		1	**2**	**3**	**4**	**5**	**6**	**7**	
Characters	A	0.2	0.4	0.4	0.2	0.8	–	0.2	0.314
	C	0.4	–	0.2	–	–	0.2	0.2	0.143
	G	0.2	0.4	0.4	0.2	0.2	–	0.4	0.257
	T	0.2	0.2	–	0.6	–	0.8	0.2	0.286

1   The PSI-BLAST uses BLAST to search for related sequences using a query sequence against a target BLAST database. The initial scoring matrix for the alignments of this initial BLAST search can be any substitution matrix. For protein sequences the BLOSUM62 substitution matrix is usually used. This first BLAST search reports the matched sequences detected above a given score threshold.

2   The matched sequences obtained from the initial BLAST search are aligned using multiple sequence alignment. A sequence profile or PSSM is created from the aligned sequences. Again, to keep things simple, we will use DNA to show how a PSSM is created. Assume that we have this set of related DNA sequences: (ATGTATC, CAAGATG, GGCTACA, TAATGTT, CGGAATG). Also assume that those sequences are aligned using one of the multiple sequence alignment algorithms as shown in Figure 7.17. The multiple sequence alignment organizes the residues into columns and each column is a position.

3   We will create a positional relative frequency matrix from the aligned sequences. The matrix will have N number of columns and M number of rows. The columns are numbered from 1 to N; in the example matrix, the column will be indexed from 1 to 7; each number represents a position. The number of rows depends on the number of symbols forming the aligned sequences (4 for DNA and 20 for protein sequences). The rows in the matrix are indexed by the symbols (for DNA: A, C, G, and T; for protein: the 20 amino acid symbols). The elements of the matrix are the relative frequencies of each symbol in each position. The relative frequency of a symbol in a position is calculated as the counts of each symbol in the position (column) divided by the count of all in the position (number of aligned sequences). For example, in position 1 there is 1 A, 2 C, 1 G, and 1 T. Thus, the relative frequencies for these symbols in position1 are 1/5, 2/5, 1/5, and 1/5 for A, C, G, and T respectively since there are 5 sequences. Table 7.1 shows the positional relative frequency matrix for the aligned DNA sequences. The last column of Table 7.1 includes the overall relative frequency for each symbol. The overall relative frequency of a symbol is calculated as the count of the symbol divided by the count of the overall number of symbols in all sequences. In the aligned sequences, there are 11 A, 5 C, 9 G, and 10 T and the total counts of symbols is 35. Thus, the overall relative frequencies of A, C, G, and T are 11/35, 5/35, 9/35 and 10/35 respectively.

4   The next step is to normalize the relative frequencies of the symbols in each position by dividing them by their overall frequencies. For example, each value in the row of A is divided by 0.314. Table 7.2 contains the normalized relative frequencies for the symbols in each position.

5   The next step is to convert the positional normalized relative frequencies into logarithm base of 2 ($\log_2$), forming the PSSM matrix. The PSSM shown in Table 7.3 contains the positional score for each symbol.

TABLE 7.2   Positional-Specific Normalized Relative Frequency

				Positions					
		1	2	3	4	5	6	7	Overall
Characters	A	0.64	1.27	1.27	0.64	2.55	–	0.64	0.314
	C	2.80	–	1.40	–	–	1.40	1.40	0.143
	G	0.78	1.56	1.56	0.78	0.78	–	1.56	0.257
	T	0.70	0.70	–	2.10	–	2.80	0.70	0.286

TABLE 7.3   Positional-Specific Scoring Matrix (PSSM)

				Positions			
		1	2	3	4	5	6	7
Characters	A	−0.651	0.349	0.349	−0.651	1.349	–	−0.651
	C	1.484	–	0.484	–	–	0.484	0.484
	G	−0.362	0.638	0.638	−0.362	−0.362	–	0.638
	T	−0.516	−0.516	–	1.069	–	1.484	−0.516

TABLE 7.4   PSSM with Consensus Sequence

				Positions			
		1	2	3	4	5	6	7
Characters	A	−0.651	0.349	0.349	−0.651	1.349	–	−0.651
	C	1.484	–	0.484	–	–	0.484	0.484
	G	−0.362	0.638	0.638	−0.362	−0.362	–	0.638
	T	−0.516	−0.516	–	1.069	–	1.484	−0.516
Match		C	G	G	T	A	T	G

The alignment of highly conserved positions in the sequences receive high scores and weakly conserved positions receive scores near or below zero.

6   A sequence is created from the highly conserved symbols (symbols of maximum scores). Thus, PSSM captures the conservation pattern in the alignment of related sequences. Table 7.4 shows the maximum log score for the symbol in each position and the sequence formed by the symbols of the maximum scores. The match is CGGTATG and its overall log score is $1.485 + 0.637 + 0.637 + 1.070 + 1.348 + 1.485 + 0.637 = 7.301$, which means that it is $2^{7.301} = 158$ times more likely to be conserved sequence than it is formed by random chance.

7   This consensus sequence (CGGTATG) will serve as a query sequence (instead of the original one) for another round of BLAST searching from Step 1 to search for homologous sequences in the target database. Then the homologous sequences are aligned and a sequence profile or PSSM is created using the same steps until a new sequence match is generated. Those steps can be repeated several times iteratively until the desired results or a convergence is achieved. Convergence is reached when no new related sequences are detected above the defined threshold. Figure 7.18 shows the flow of the PSI-BLAST search.

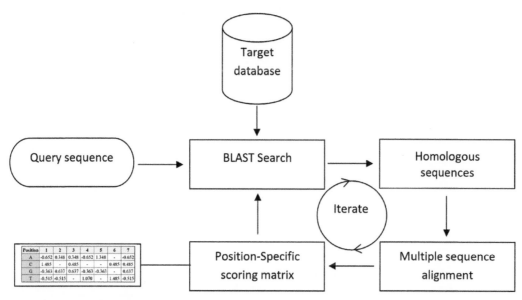

FIGURE 7.18   PSI-BLAST flow chart.

REFERENCES

1. Levenshtein, V., *Binary codes capable of correcting deletions, insertions, and reversals.* Soviet Physics. Doklady, 1965. **10**: pp. 707–710.

2. Sackton, T.B. and N. Clark, *Convergent evolution in the genomics era: new insights and directions.* Philos Trans R Soc Lond B Biol Sci, 2019. **374**(1777): p. 20190102.

3. Dayhoff, M.O., R.M. Schwartz, and B.C. Orcutt, A Model of Evolutionary Change in Proteins, in *Atlas of Protein Sequence and Structure*, M.O. Dayhoff, Editor. 1978. Washington, DC: National Biomedical Research Foundation.

4. Henikoff, S. and J.G. Henikoff, *Amino acid substitution matrices from protein blocks.* Proc Natl Acad Sci USA, 1992. **89**(22): pp. 10915–10919.

5. Needleman, S.B. and C.D. Wunsch, *A general method applicable to the search for similarities in the amino acid sequence of two proteins.* J Mol Biol, 1970. **48**(3): pp. 443–453.

6. Smith, T.F. and M.S. Waterman, *Identification of common molecular subsequences.* J Mol Biol, 1981. **147**(1): pp. 195–197.

7. Altschul, S.F., et al., *Basic local alignment search tool.* J Mol Biol, 1990. **215**(3): pp. 403–410.

8. Wootton, J.C. and S. Federhen, *Statistics of local complexity in amino acid sequences and sequence databases.* Computers & Chemistry, 1993. **17**(2): pp. 149–163.

9. Schmitt, A.O. and H. Herzel, *Estimating the Entropy of DNA Sequences.* Journal of Theoretical Biology, 1997. **188**(3): pp. 369–377.

10. Altschul, S.F., et al., *Gapped BLAST and PSI-BLAST: a new generation of protein database search programs.* Nucleic Acids Res, 1997. **25**(17): pp. 3389–3402.

## CHAPTER 8

Basic Local Alignment Search Tool

INTRODUCTION

In Chapter 7, we discussed the algorithms of the global alignment, local alignment, and BLAST. By now you know the theoretical aspects of BLAST and it is time to put this knowledge to work. The Basic Local Alignment Search Tool (BLAST) is one of the main tools of the National Center for Biotechnology Information (NCBI) [1]. It is the most popular bioinformatics tool used by researchers. The following are just some examples of its uses:

- *Searching for homologous DNA/RNA or protein sequences.* The evolutionarily related sequences are used by researchers for different purposes including construction of phylogenetic trees, machine learning for classification and identification of proteins, motif finding, protein domain detection, detection of conserved regions of a gene or protein, etc.

- *Identifying species using a DNA sequence.* A sequence of DNA, of unknown species, extracted from a sample and sequenced in the lab can be used as a query sequence in BLAST to identify the unknown species. Such identification is common in microbiology, which uses BLAST for the identification of bacterial species and strains from DNA recovered from a sample.

- *Protein domain identification.* A protein or translated nucleotide sequence can be used as a query sequence to identify the protein domain and to infer the structure and functions of a protein.

- *Mapping a sequence to a reference sequence.* There are several uses for sequence mapping including mapping a sequence to a genome assembly or a chromosome to know the location of a sequence.

- *Constructing a phylogenetic tree or distance tree.* BLAST makes it easy to construct a phylogenetic tree from homologous DNA/RNA or protein sequences. This is usually performed by finding the related sequences for a query sequence. BLAST provides the related sequences as results, from which the user can select the sequences of interest and then can either use the tool provided with BLAST for constructing a phylogenetic tree or to save the sequences in a file to use them with a multiple sequence alignment tool such as ClustalW2, MUSCLE, etc. and a phylogenetic tree construction, or to use the sequences with a more advanced scripting programming language such as Python, Perl, or R.

- *Annotation.* BLAST makes annotation easy. Different species may share some common genes. BLAST can be used to map annotations from an organism to another with unannotated sequences.

- *PCR primer designing.* Biologists use BLAST to design primers for specific genes that are used at biology laboratories in a polymerase chain reaction (PCR) to amplify targeted genes.

The BLAST search begins by entering a query sequence as an input or by a GenBank ID if the query sequence is one of the GenBank (Nucleotide or Protein database) records. The query sequence can be a DNA, RNA, or protein. However, there are several BLAST programs, and the choice of BLAST program depends on the type

DOI: 10.1201/9781003226611-8

TABLE 8.1   The Major BLAST Programs

Program	Query Sequence	Database
BLASTn	Nucleotides	Nucleotides
BLASTp	Protein	Protein
BLASTx	Nucleotide (translation)	Protein
tBLASTn	Protein	Nucleotide (translation)
tBLASTx	Nucleotide (translation)	Nucleotide (translation)

of query sequence. See Table 8.1, which lists the BLAST programs and types of sequence accepted as queries. Understanding the use of BLAST programs will help you to choose the right BLAST program and BLAST database for your query sequence.

Once you have obtained the query sequence and determined the BLAST program to use, you will need also to determine the target database. You can use BLAST either at the NCBI website or on your computer from an installed stand-alone BLAST. The stand-alone BLAST will be discussed later in this chapter. For the use of BLAST from the website, several BLAST databases are provided to serve different searching purposes. Therefore, a user must choose the right target database from a list of databases. Moreover, BLAST allows you to set some options such as word size, E-value, masking region of low complexity and others. We discussed most of those options with the BLAST algorithm in Chapter 7.

BLAST programs perform heuristic rather than exhaustive local alignments. Therefore, it is fast but not exact like the Smith-Waterman algorithm, which is accurate but not practical for searches in a database formed of a massive number of sequences.

Once you have entered the query sequence, selected the right target database, and set the BLAST options and launched the search, BLAST will perform the search for related sequences on the target database using the search query (see Chapter 7 for the BLAST algorithm). The sequences, which match the query sequence and pass the threshold E-value, will be reported.

The NCBI BLAST is a family of programs hosted by NCBI and available at the NCBI website for online use or as stand-alone programs that can be downloaded from the NCBI FTP server and installed on your computer. BLAST is also provided by most cloud providers such as Google Cloud as Docker image and cloud-ready. BLAST in the cloud is useful when you have high volume BLAST searches that you cannot do on the NCBI BLAST website, and you want to avoid setting a stand-alone BLAST because of high computing and storage capacity. NCBI also provides BLAST API that can be used with applications programmed by computer languages such as C++, Python, Perl, R, etc.

Generally, BLAST programs allow users to search a query sequence (nucleotide or peptide) against nucleotide or protein sequence databases. The main BLAST programs that do the searches on all platforms are listed in Table 8.1.

- *BLASTn* is used to search for related sequences using a query DNA/RNA sequence against a target nucleotide (DNA/RNA) database. The RNA sequences are usually cDNA, which is a DNA converted from RNA sequences as we discussed in Chapter 2.

- *BLASTp* is used to search for related sequences using a query protein sequence against a target protein database.

- *BLASTx* is used to search for related sequences using a query DNA/RNA sequence against a target protein database. However, BLASTx translates the query nucleotide sequence into protein before conducting the search. The nucleotide sequence is translated into six potential protein sequences based on the six possible open reading frames (ORFs) (see Chapter 1).

- *tBLASTn* is used to search for related sequences using a query protein sequence against a target nucleotide database. However, each of the nucleotide sequences of the target database is translated into six possible proteins before conducting the search. Therefore, the search is a query protein sequence against translated protein sequences.

- *tBLASTx* is used to search for related sequences using a query DNA/RNA sequence against a target DNA/RNA database. However, both query sequence and target database sequence are translated into protein sequences before conducting the search. Therefore, the search is conducted for translated protein sequences (six sequences) against a translated protein database.

Other BLAST programs that serve certain purpose and have slightly different algorithm are available as well.

In this chapter we will discuss the web-based BLAST and stand-alone BLAST installed on a personal computer.

WEB BLAST

The web-based BLAST search interface is available at https://blast.ncbi.nlm.nih.gov/Blast.cgi. It contains the links to the four basic BLAST programs: Nucleotide BLAST (blastn), protein BLAST (blastp), blastx, and tblastn (Figure 8.1). The BLAST Genomes search box has been recently added to the BLAST website to move directly to an organism's BLAST page.

Clicking on any one of the four anchored diagrams will open the BLAST page of that BLAST program. But if you want to use the BLAST databases of a specific organism, enter the organism's name (common name or scientific name) or its taxonomy ID into the BLAST Genome search box and click on the "Search" button to open the BLAST page of that organism.

BLAST Field Description

While you are on the main BLAST page, clicking on "Nucleotide BLAST" will open the Nucleotide BLAST page (BLASTn). At the top you can notice that there are five tabs (blastn, blastp, blastx, tblastn, and tblastx), each for a BLAST program. You can click on any of those tabs to move from one BLAST program to another. Most fields of those BLAST programs are similar except for a few options in the Program Selection section in blastn and blastp.

In the following section, we will discuss the fields and options available for all major BLAST programs.

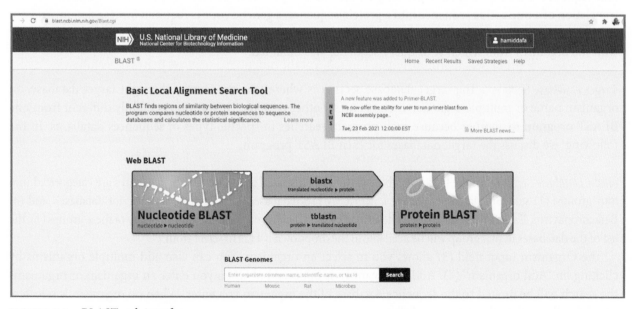

FIGURE 8.1   BLAST web interface.

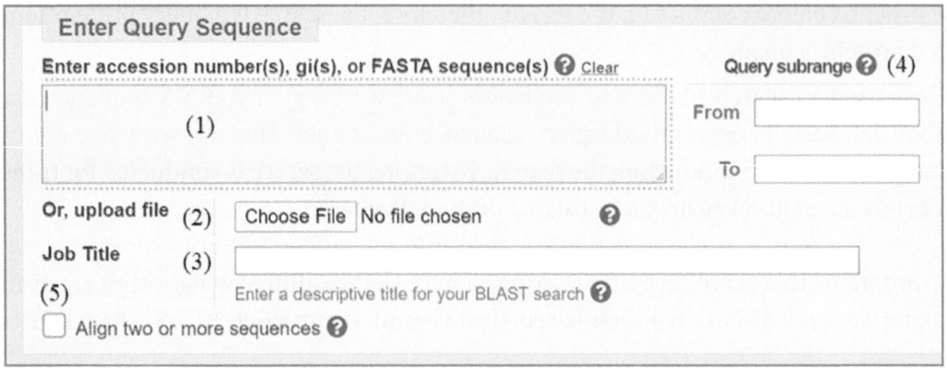

FIGURE 8.2　BLAST query section.

Query Sequence Section　As illustrated in Figure 8.2, the Enter Query Sequence box (1) is used to enter the query sequence, which can be in FASTA format or its GenBank accession number if the query sequence is one of the GenBank records. The query sequence depends on the BLAST program as shown in Table 8.1. For blastn, blastx, and tblastx, the query sequence must be a nucleotide (DNA/RNA) sequence and for blastp and tblastn the query sequence must be a protein sequence. Another option for entering a query sequence is uploading the sequence from a text file. Instead of entering the query sequence into the query box, a plain text file containing a FASTA sequence can be uploaded using the "Choose File" button (2). If a FASTA file with a defline is entered, the definition in the defline will be copied in the Job Title box (3) automatically and it will be used as a title for the search job. The job title can also be edited or entered manually. The query subrange (4) is used to specify a subrange of the entered sequence to be used as a query instead of the whole sequence. This feature is especially useful if your query sequence is a complete gene sequence on a refseq of a chromosome or a feature sequence of a nucleotide record; you need to enter the accession number of the original sequence and then specify the coordinates in the Query subrange. When the check box "Align two or more sequences" (5) is checked, another input box will be opened for entering another sequence called the subject sequence. Select this checkbox only, if you wish to perform a pairwise alignment between the query sequence and a subject sequence.

There is an additional field in blastx and tblastx, the **Genetic code** dropdown list. The purpose of this field is to select the genetic code based on the organism from which the query sequence was obtained. The protein sequence will be translated depending on the selected genetic code (see Chapter 1). Any search requires translation of a nucleotide sequence into a protein sequence, a genetic code is required for translation. You can either leave "Standard (1)", which is the default option, or you can choose the genetic code that works better with the organism from which your query sequence was obtained.

Target Database Section　The target database section is where you can choose the right target database, an organism name or multiple organism names, and set other options. This section is slightly different from one BLAST program to another because each program searches in specific types of sequences databases. In the following, we discuss the target databases for each BLAST program.

blastn Database Section　In the blastn database section as illustrated in Figure 8.3, the databases are categorized into four groups: (1) standard databases (nr etc.), (2) rRNA/ITS databases, (3) Genomic + transcript databases, and (4) Betacoronavirus. Each of these databases is described below. Clicking on the radio button of any of these groups (1), the list of the databases in that group will be available in the dropdown list (2) to select from.

The Organism input field (3) allows you to select an organism. You can also add multiple organisms by clicking on "Add organism" (4). Adding organism is optional but when you enter an organism or organisms the search will be limited to the sequence database of the organism you enter. When no organism is selected, BLAST will search in the database of all organisms.

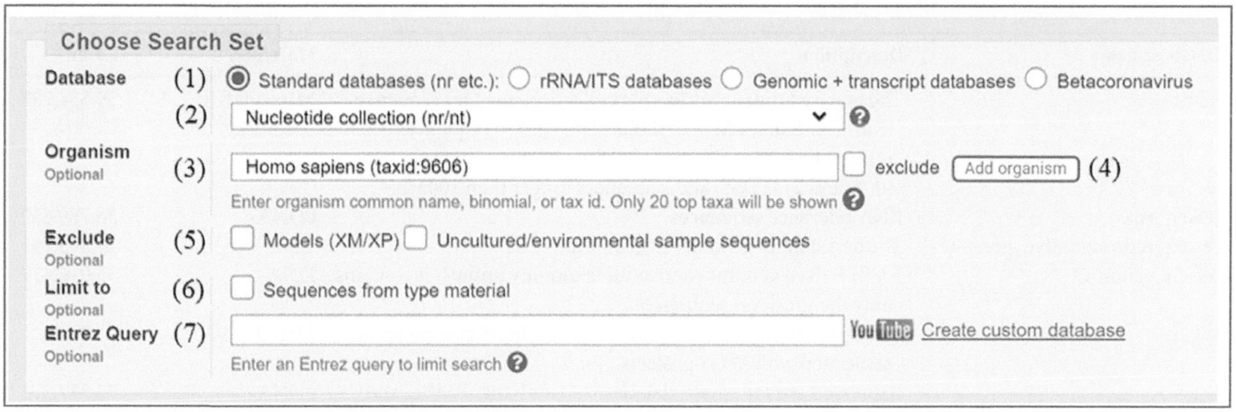

FIGURE 8.3   The blastn target database section.

The Exclude checkboxes (5) can be checked to exclude some sequences from the target database. Selecting the "Models (XM/XP)" checkbox will exclude the model sequences that were generated by computational prediction. Selecting the checkbox "Uncultured/environmental sample sequence" will exclude the microbial sequences obtained from environmental samples rather than cultured isolated bacteria.

Selecting the "Limit to" checkbox (6) will limit the database sequence to a type of material, which is the taxonomic device that ties formal names to the physical specimens that serve as exemplars such as prokaryotic strains submitted to culture collections or eukaryotic specimens submitted to museums or herbaria.

The Entrez Query (7) input box can be used to enter a search query that follows the convention of Entrez search queries, which were discussed in the NCB database chapters. The search query limits the BLAST search to the database sequences that match the search query.

Before we move away from blastn target databases, it is important to understand those four groups of databases: (1) standard databases (nr etc.), (2) rRNA/ITS databases, (3) Genomic + transcript databases, and (4) Betacoronavirus.

Standard Databases (nr etc.)   The standard databases are a collection of non-redundant nucleotide sequence databases. Table 8.2 includes the database names, their descriptions, types of molecules (DNA, cDNA, or mixed), and number of sequences in a database as of the time of writing. You should pay attention to the type of molecules when you choose the database. The eukaryotic genomic DNA sequence may include both introns and exons. The right database choice depends on the purpose of your search. If the query sequence is a genomic DNA and you are looking for similar sequences, a genomic DNA database is the right choice. However, if your intention is to annotate the query sequence with a protein-coding region, the right choice will be a cDNA database. On the other hand, if the query is a cDNA sequence and your goal is to find similar sequences, a cDNA database is the right choice. If your goal is to locate the exons in a reference genome, a genome sequence is the right choice.

You may also need to know the nature of the database. For example, the database HTGS includes sequences produced by high-throughput genomic methods and they have just been submitted to GenBank; therefore, they are in phase 0, 1, or 2 and not stable. If your goal is to find matches that are associated with experimentally determined structures, the PDB database is the right choice.

Ribosomal RNA (rRNA/ITS) Databases   The rRNA/ITS databases are a set of recently added databases for nucleotide reference sequences originated from ribosomal RNA (rRNA) of bacteria, archaea, and fungi. The rRNA genes (the genes that code for rRNA) have well conserved sequences mutated at a very slow rate; therefore, they are used for construction of phylogenetic trees and taxonomic classification [2]. The 16S rRNA gene, which codes for 16S rRNA in prokaryotes, is used for prokaryotic classification and identification and

TABLE 8.2   Standard Nucleotide Databases

Database name	Description	Molecules	Count
nr/nt	The non-redundant nucleotide collection includes sequence from GenBank, EMBL, DDBJ, PDB, RefSeq sequences (except EST, STS, GSS, WGS, TSA), patent sequences, (0, 1, and 2) HTGS, and sequences longer than 100Mb.	Mixed DNA	59,554,787
refseq_rna	RNA reference sequences.	cDNA	36,789,650
refseq_representative_genomes	The best quality genomes available at NCBI.	DNA	13,895,191
refseq_genomes	NCBI Refseq genomes across all taxonomy groups. It contains only the top-level sequences.	DNA	35,016,417
WGS	Whole-Genome-Shotgun contigs but excludes chromosomes associated with WGS projects.	Mixed DNA	N/A
Est	Expressed sequence tags database of GenBank, EMBL, and DDBJ sequences from EST Divisions.	cDNA	77,577,275
SRA	Sequence read archive database.		N/A
TSA	The Transcriptome Shotgun Assembly (TSA) database is an archive of computationally assembled mRNA sequences from primary data such as EST and raw sequence reads.	cDNA	32,318,939
HTGS	Unfinished High Throughput Genomic Sequences (HTGS); Sequences: phases 0,1 and 2	DNA	177,018
PAT	Nucleotide sequences derived from the Patent division of GenBank.	Mixed DNA	37,595,706
PDB	PDB consists of sequences from the Protein Data Bank, which contains information about experimentally determined structures of proteins, nucleic acids, and complex assemblies.	Mixed DNA	28,985
RefSeq_Gene	Human RefSeqGene set.	DNA	6,849
GSS	Genome Survey Sequence (gss) includes single-pass genomic data, exon-trapped sequences, and Alu PCR sequences.	Mixed DNA	40,633,412
Dbsts	Sequence tagged sites (dbsts) includes GenBank, EMBL, and DDBJ sequences from STS Divisions	Mixed DNA	1,304,206

TABLE 8.3   Ribosomal RNA Databases

Database name	Description	Molecules	Count
16S_ribosomal_ RNA	16S ribosomal RNA from bacteria and archaea	Mixed DNA	21632
18S_fungal_sequences	A RefSeq curated dataset for fungal 18S ribosomal RNA sequences (SSU)	rRNA	2478
28S_fungal_sequences	A RefSeq curated dataset for fungal 28S ribosomal RNA sequences (LSU)	rRNA	7243
ITS_RefSeq_Fungi	A RefSeq curated dataset for fungal Internal transcribed spacer region (ITS)	rRNA	11590

for establishing taxonomic relationships between prokaryotic strains with 98.65% similarity as a cutoff [3]. On the other hand, both 18S rRNA and 28S rRNA genes code for 18S rRNA and 28S rRNA in eukaryotes and they are used for fungal identification.

The rRNA/ITS databases, as shown in Table 8.3, are collected from Nucleotide collection (nr/nt) and curated separately to speed up research in prokaryotic and fungal identification and classification.

Genomic + Transcript Databases   The Genomic plus transcript (G+T) databases consist of curated and model RefSeq RNA sequences annotated on the set of genomic RefSeq sequences. Only human and mouse genomic plus transcript databases are currently available as shown in Table 8.4.

Betacoronavirus   Betacoronavirus is a recently added database for coronavirus nucleotide sequences after the outbreak of Covid-19 to provide a backup for researchers to advance research to stop the outbreak of

TABLE 8.4   Genomic + Transcript (G+T) Databases

Database Name	Description	Molecules	Count
human_genome	Human RefSeq RNAs annotated on the set of genomic RefSeqs	cDNA	159998
mouse_genome	Mouse RefSeq RNAs annotated on the set of genomic RefSeqs	cDNA	121318

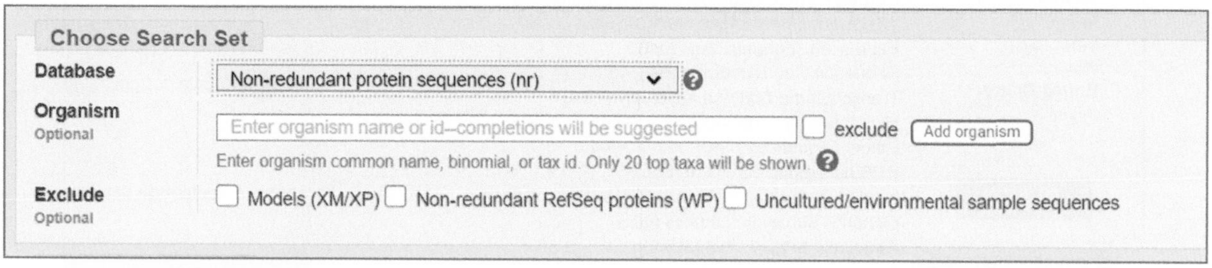

Choose Search Set

Database   Non-redundant protein sequences (nr)   ✔   ❷

Organism   Enter organism name or id—completions will be suggested   ☐ exclude   [Add organism]
Optional
Enter organism common name, binomial, or tax id. Only 20 top taxa will be shown. ❷

Exclude   ☐ Models (XM/XP) ☐ Non-redundant RefSeq proteins (WP) ☐ Uncultured/environmental sample sequences
Optional

FIGURE 8.4   The blastp and blastx target database section.

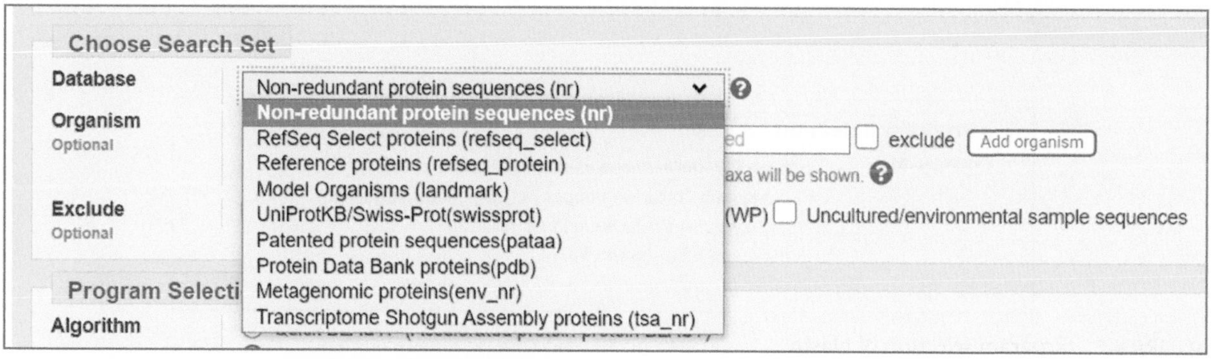

Choose Search Set

Database   Non-redundant protein sequences (nr)   ✔   ❷
            Non-redundant protein sequences (nr)
Organism   RefSeq Select proteins (refseq_select)   ed   ☐ exclude [Add organism]
Optional   Reference proteins (refseq_protein)   axa will be shown. ❷
              Model Organisms (landmark)
              UniProtKB/Swiss-Prot(swissprot)
Exclude   Patented protein sequences(pataa)   (WP) ☐ Uncultured/environmental sample sequences
Optional   Protein Data Bank proteins(pdb)
              Metagenomic proteins(env_nr)

    Program Selecti Transcriptome Shotgun Assembly proteins (tsa_nr)

    Algorithm

FIGURE 8.5   The blastp and blastx target database list.

coronavirus. It consists of GenBank sequences and SRA contigs generated by high-throughput sequencing technologies (current number of sequences is 18,125).

blastp and blastx Database Section   The blastp and blastx database section is simple as it consists of a database dropdown list, organism box, and options to exclude some sequences as explained above (Figure 8.4).

The blastp database list is made up of protein databases that include as shown in Figure 8.5: (1) non-redundant protein sequences (nr), (2) (RefSeq Select proteins (refseq_select), (3) reference proteins (refseq_protein), (4) model organisms (landmark), (5) UniProtKB/Swiss-Prot (swissprot), (6) patented protein sequences (pataa), (7) Protein Data Bank protein (pdb), (8) metagenomic proteins (env_nr), and (9) transcriptome shotgun assembly proteins (tsa_nr).

tblastn and tblastx Database Section   Both tblastn and tblastx use the same target databases. Since the databases of those two BLAST programs are DNA/RNA translated into proteins, they include a collection of non-redundant nucleotides, reference RNA sequences, reference genome sequences, and sequences from other resources as shown in the database dropdown list of tblastn and tblastx in Figure 8.6.

Program Selection   Only blastn and blastp BLAST programs have the Program Selection section. Each of the programs is optimized to serve a specific BLAST purpose. In the blastn program, where the query is a DNA/RNA sequence and the target database is DNA/RNA sequences, for capturing the highly similar nucleotide sequences on a nucleotide database, MegaBlast can be used. For more dissimilar sequences and somewhat similar Discontiguous MegaBlast and blastn are used respectively as shown in Figure 8.7.

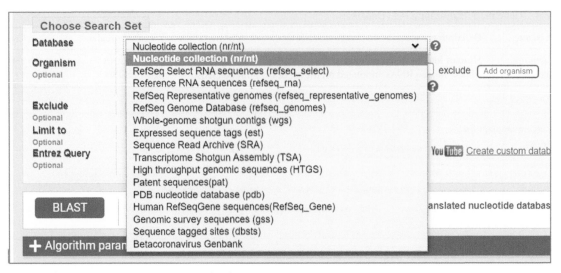

FIGURE 8.6   The Tblastn and Tblastx target database section.

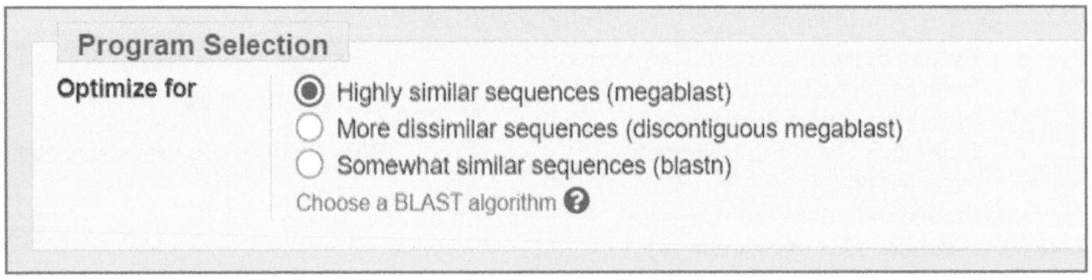

Program Selection
Optimize for   ● Highly similar sequences (megablast)
                  ○ More dissimilar sequences (discontiguous megablast)
                  ○ Somewhat similar sequences (blastn)
                  Choose a BLAST algorithm ❓

FIGURE 8.7   Program selection of blastn.

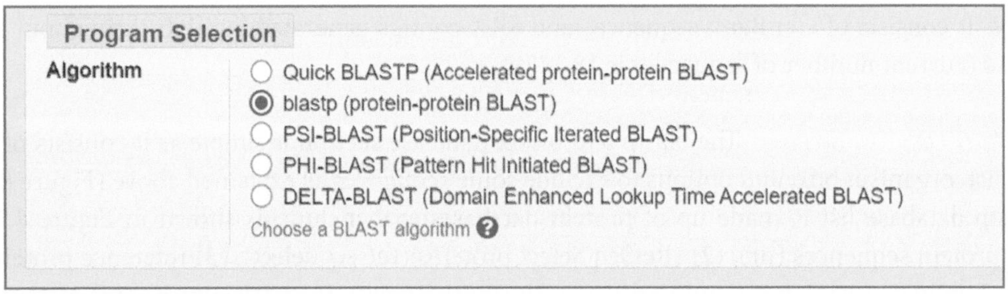

Program Selection
Algorithm   ○ Quick BLASTP (Accelerated protein-protein BLAST)
               ● blastp (protein-protein BLAST)
               ○ PSI-BLAST (Position-Specific Iterated BLAST)
               ○ PHI-BLAST (Pattern Hit Initiated BLAST)
               ○ DELTA-BLAST (Domain Enhanced Lookup Time Accelerated BLAST)
               Choose a BLAST algorithm ❓

FIGURE 8.8   Program selection of blastp.

For blastp, a number of algorithms are available for optimizing the protein-protein search as shown in Figure 8.8. Those algorithms include the blastp (for regular protein search), PSI-BLAST (for distantly related protein), and other optimized variants of those algorithms.

Algorithm Parameters   The algorithm parameters (Figure 8.9) are a number of parameters required by the BLAST algorithm to perform BLAST searching. However, those parameters are set to default values for all BLAST programs, and you can make no change. The algorithm parameters are grouped into General Parameters, Scoring Parameters, and Filter Masking. The following are descriptions of the parameters in each of these three categories:

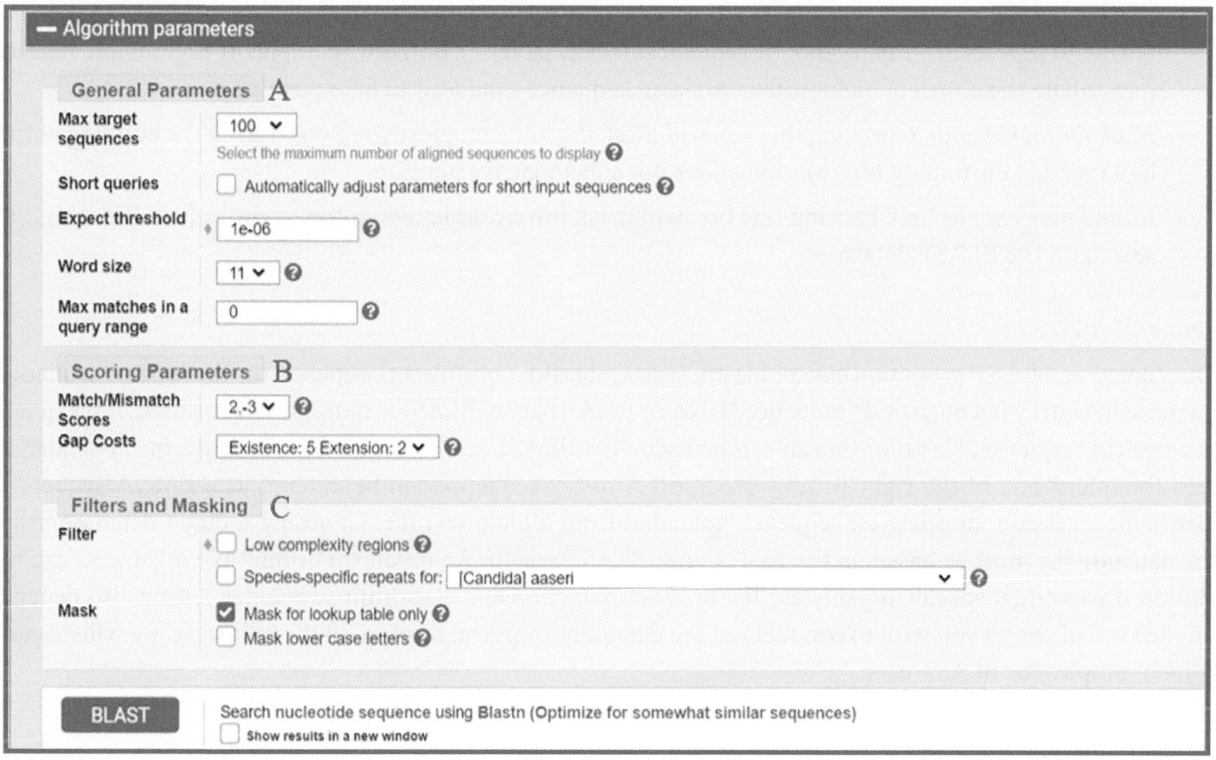

FIGURE 8.9 BLAST algorithm parameters.

General Parameters

- *Max target sequence.* This parameter determines the maximum number of sequences to be displayed in the search results. The dropdown list provides the list of numbers that you can choose from.

- *Short queries.* When the checkbox of this parameter is selected, the BLAST program will automatically adjust the parameters that optimize the search results when the query sequence is short.

- *Expect threshold.* This parameter determines the threshold of E-value, which is the metric for statistical significance of an alignment as explained in Chapter 7. The final BLAST search results will include only the sequences whose E-value is less than the value specified. The default value may be 0.05.

- *Word size.* The word size parameter determines the size of words generated in the BLAST search as illustrated in Chapter 7. The default value may be different from one program to another. MegaBlast has a wide range of values from 16 to 256, Discontiguous MegaBlast has a word size either 11 or 12, and blastn has 7, 11, or 15.

- *Max matches in a query range.* This parameter is used to limit the number of matches to a query range to get rid of the redundant local alignments.

Scoring Parameters

- *Match/mismatch scores:* This parameter determines a reward and penalty for match and mismatch scores.

- *Gap costs:* This parameter determines the existence and extension penalties for the alignment. You can accept the default values.

Filters and Masking

- *Low complexity regions.* Checking the box of this parameter will filter the low-complexity regions (see Chapter 7).

- *Species-specific repeats.* Checking this box will filter the sequence repeats such as LINE's, SINE's, and retroviral repeats in human genomic sequences (see Chapter 1). Both low-complexity regions and repeats may inflate the scores of biologically unrelated sequences and lead to false positive.

- *Mask for lookup only.* Checking this box will mask the low-complexity regions during the building of the lookup table for finding hits. Masking does not affect match extension.

- *Mask lower case letter.* Checking this box will mask lowercase letters in the query sequence during the search on the BLAST databases.

Using BLAST

The choice of BLAST program (blastn, blastp, blastx, tblastn, and tblastx) depends on the type of sequence query. If the query is a nucleotide sequence (DNA or RNA), blastn, BLASTx, or tblastx can be used. If the query is a protein sequence, blastn or tblastn can be used. The BLAST search begins by entering a query sequence into the query box of the right BLAST program. A query sequence can be entered as a FASTA sequence, GenBank accession, or a FASTA sequence uploaded from a plain text file. Choosing a target database from the database list must be based on the goal of your BLAST search. An organism or multiple organisms can be chosen if you target specific organisms. The program selection and algorithm parameter setting also depend on the kind of search you wish to conduct but the default settings can be used. In the following, we will discuss some examples for BLAST uses.

Aligning Two Sequences

BLAST can be used to compare two sequences to assess their similarity as we did in the global sequence alignment. You must enter two sequences of the same types: a query sequence and subject sequence. The subject sequences can be multiple FASTA sequences uploaded from a file.

In the following example as shown in Figure 8.10, you will compare the human PPARG isoform-5 protein (NP_001341598.1) and that of chimpanzee (XP_024211105.1). Since these two sequences are proteins, you

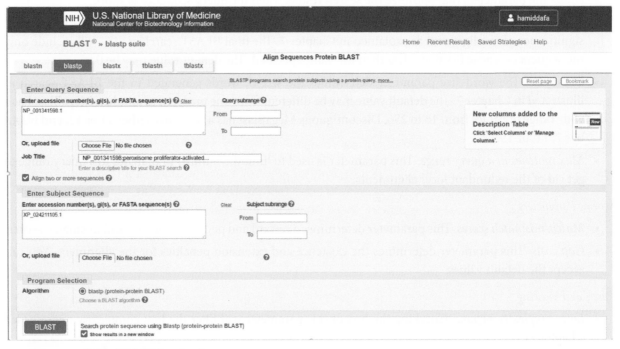

FIGURE 8.10   Using BLAST for aligning two sequences.

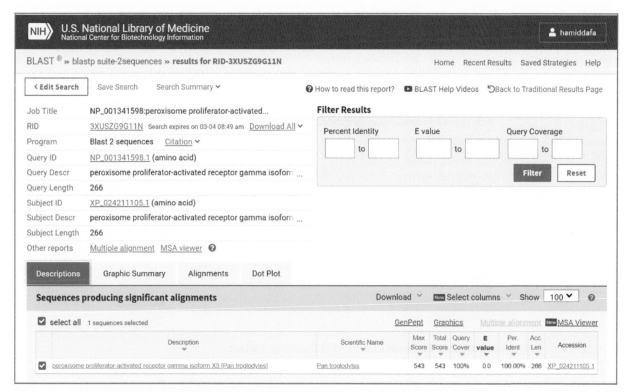

FIGURE 8.11   BLAST results for aligning two protein sequences.

can use blastp. Enter the human PPARG isoform-5 accession number in the Query Sequence box. To enter the subject sequence, check the "Align two or more sequences" checkbox, and then enter the accession of the chimpanzee PPARG isoform-5 into the Subject sequence box and click the "BLAST" button to launch the search.

Figure 8.11 shows the output of the BLAST results for protein pairwise alignment. The first part is a description of the sequences used for the alignment. The report of the alignment is displayed in four tabs: description, graphic summary, alignment, and dot-plot. Click on each of these tabs to study the content. We will discuss these contents in more detail, but the dot-plot (see Chapter 7) is available only when aligning two sequences.

Aligning Multiple Sequences

BLAST can be used to align a query sequence to multiple subject sequences. This is useful if you wish to study how some related sequences are different from a specific sequence. In this example, you will use the *Homo sapiens* peroxisome proliferator activated receptor gamma (PPARG) transcript as an example. The PPARG is a single gene, but it produces several RNA transcript variants by alternative splicing giving rise to several PPARG protein isoforms that vary in structures and functions. Assume that your goal is to align PPARG transcript 1 to the other PPARG transcript variants. First, you need to retrieve either the sequences or the UIDs of the refseq PPARG transcript variants from the NCBI Nucleotide page. Open the Entrez Nucleotide page and enter the following query terms into the search box.

"Homo sapiens"[ORGN] AND pparg[GENE] AND biomol_mrna[PROP] AND refseq [FILT]

The Entrez Nucleotide results will be the human PPARG transcript (mRNA) variants. There are 16 PPARG transcript variants that code for 16 PPARG protein isoforms in human. Those variants may not be sorted by name (Figure 8.12).

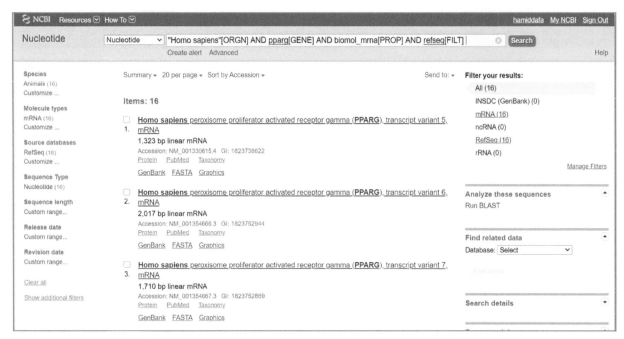

FIGURE 8.12   Entrez nucleotide search results for PPARG transcript variants.

FIGURE 8.13   Changing display format into accession list on nucleotide results page.

Open a new browser window and then open the BLAST Nucleotide page and enter the accession of the PPAR transcript variant1 (NM_138712.5) into the Query sequence box. Check the checkbox "Align two or more sequences" to open the Subject sequence box. Now go back to the Nucleotide results page and select the checkbox of all PPARG variants except variant1 and change the display format on the top left of the page from Summary to Accession List (Figure 8.13).

This will display the accession list of the selected PPARG transcript variants. Copy the accession list and paste it into the Subject Sequence box of the BLAST Nucleotide as in Figure 8.14 and click the "BLAST" button.

The BLAST results page will show the alignment reports in different formats including Graphic summary, Descriptions, and Alignments. Try to study the content of each report in light of what you learnt in Chapter 7.

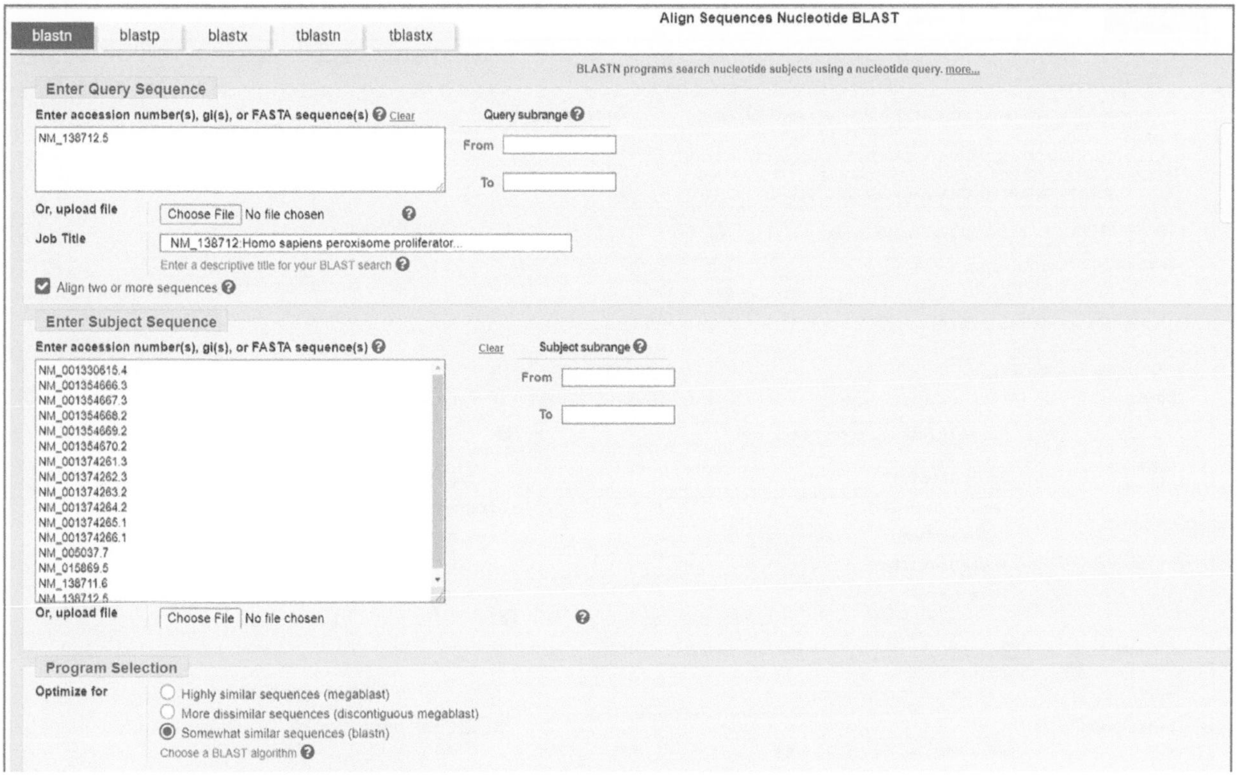

FIGURE 8.14   BLAST nucleotide for aligning a query sequence to multiple sequences.

Identifying a Nucleotide Sequence

Sometimes at the lab, you may have a sequenced PCR product that you may wish to identify or to confirm its identity by using BLAST. Assume that the following mRNA sequence was sequenced using the Sanger sequencing method (Chapter 2). Open the BLAST Nucleotide (blastn) website and enter the content into the Query sequence box as shown in Figure 8.15. For your convience, you can select any mRNA sequence from the Nucleotide database if you are not able to copy this sequence.

>mRNA

ACCCCTCGCCGCACCACACACAGCGCGGGCTTCTAGCGCTCGGCACCGGCGGGCCAGG
CGCGTCCTGCCTTCATTTATCCAGCAGCTTTTCGGAAAATGCATTTGCTGTTCGGAGTTT
AATCAGAAGAGGATTCCTGCCTCCGTCCCCGGCTCCTTCATCGTCCCCTCTCCCCTGTCT
CTCTCCTGGGGAGGCGTGAAGCGGTCCCGTGGATAGAGATTCATGCCTGTGCCCGCGCG
TGTGTGCGCGCGTGTAAATTGCCGAGAAGGGGAAAACATCACAGGACTTCTGCGAATAC
CGGACTGAAAATTGTAATTCATCTGCCGCCGCCGCTGCCTTTTTTTTTTCTCGAGCTCTT
GAGATCTCCGGTTGGGATTCCTGCGGATTGACATTTCTGTGAAGCAGAAGTCTGGGAATC
GATCTGGAAATCCTCCTAATTTTTACTCCCTCTCCCCGCGACTCCTGATTCATTGGGAAG
TTTCAAATCAGCTATAACTGGAGAGTGCTGAAGATTGATGGGATCGTTGCCTTATGCATT
TGTTTTGGTTTTACAAAAAGGAAACTTGACAGAGGATCATGCTGTACTTAAAAAATACAA
CATCACAGAGGAAGTAGACTGATATTAACAATACTTACTAATAATAACGTGCCTCATGAAA
TAAAGATCCGAAAGGAATTGGAATAAAAATTTCCTGCATCTCATGCCAAGGGGGAAACAC
CAGAATCAAGTGTTCCGCGTGATTGAAGACACCCCCTCGTCCAAGAATGCAAAGCACATC
CAATAAAATAGCTGGATTATAACTCCTCTTCTTTCTCTGGGGGCCGTGGGGTGGGAGCTG
GGGCGAGAGGTGCCGTTGGCCCCCGTTGCTTTTCCTCTGGGAAGGATGGCGCACGCTGG
GAGAACAGGGTACGATAACCGGGAGATAGTGATGAAGTACATCCATTATAAGCTGTCGCA

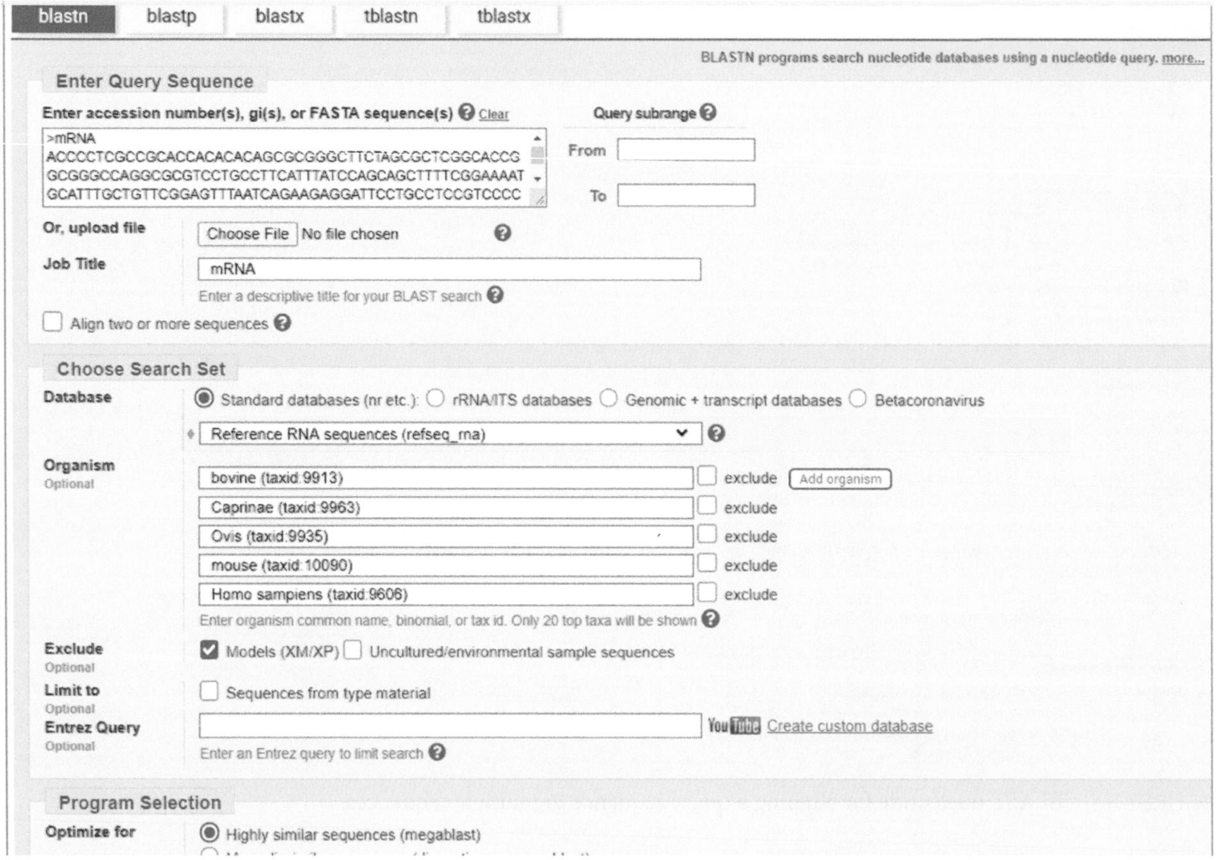

FIGURE 8.15   BLAST nucleotide.

GAGGGGCTACGAGTGGGATGCGGGAGATGTGGGCGCCGCGCCCCCGGGGGCCGCCCCC
GCACCGGGCATCTTCTCCTCCCAGCCCGGGCACACGCCCCATCCAGCCGCATCCCGGGA
CCCGGTCGCCAGGACCTCGCCGCTGCAGACCCCGGCTGCCCCCGGCGCCGCCGCGGGG
CCTGCGCTCAGCCCGGTGCCACCTGTGGTCCACCTGACCCTCCGCCAGGCCGGCGACGA
CTTCTCCCGCCGCTACCGCCGCGACTTCGCCGAGATGTCCAGCCAGCTGCACCTGACGC
CCTTCACCGCGCGGGGACGCTTTGCCACGGTGGTGGAGGAGCTCTTCAGGGACGGGGTG
AACTGGGGGAGGATTGTGGCCTTCTTTGAGTTCGGTGGGGTCATGTGTGTGGAGAGCGT
CAACCGGGAGATGTCGCCCCTGGTGGACAACATCGCCCTGTGGATGACTGAGTACCTGA
ACCGGCACCTGCACACCTGGATCCAGGATAACGGAGGCTGGGTAGGTGCACTTGGTGAT
GTGAGTCTGGGCTGAGGCCACAGGTCCGAGATGCGGGGGGTTGGAGTGCGGGTGGGCTC
CTGGGGCAATGGGAGGCTGTGGAGCCGGCGAAATAAAATCAGAGTTGTTGCT

Since the sequence is mRNA (transcript), you can choose a target mRNA database. There are several databases that you can choose from but always base your choice on the target database that is suitable for your search goal. For this example, you can choose "Reference RNA sequences (refseq_rna)", which are non-redundant and curated sequences. If no organism is chosen, the search will include all organisms. However, in most cases, you may have an organism or organisms in your search plan. The example sequence was obtained from a human sample; therefore, you can choose human "Homo sapiens" as the organism. But you can also add more organisms of interest (if needed) for comparisons. Add bovine (taxid:9913), Ovis (taxid:9935), mouse (taxid:10090), and Homo sapiens (taxid:9606). You may also need to exclude the model sequences; therefore, check the checkbox "Models (XM/XP)". Leave other parameters unchanged and click the "BLAST" button. The results are shown in Figure 8.16.

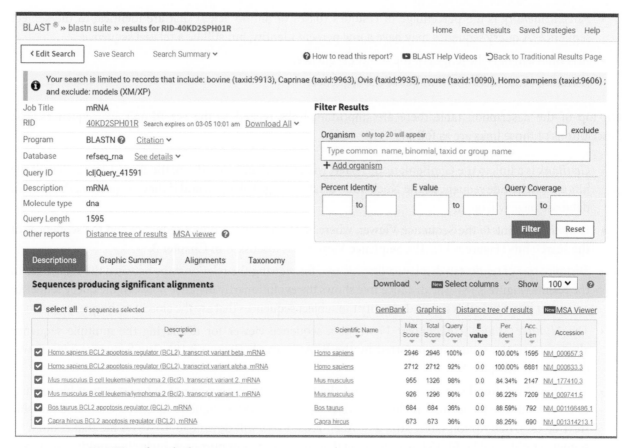

FIGURE 8.16 **BLAST nucleotide descriptions.**

The results page shows summary information about the query sequence, Filter Results box, and the BLAST results. Filter Results is used to filter the BLAST results using organism, percent identity, E-value range, and query coverage range. The BLAST results are in four tabs: Descriptions, Graphic Summary, Alignment, and Taxonomy.

Descriptions Tab   The Descriptions tab has eight default columns: description, scientific name, max score, total score, query coverage, E-value, percent identity, and accession. You can add or remove columns to the table by using the Select columns dropdown menu on the top right of the table. These columns describe the aligned sequences and their significance. The following are descriptions of some of these columns:

- *Description* may include the organism's name and the entity such as gene name, and may include molecule type (genomic DNA, cDNA, mRNA, etc.).
- *Scientific name* is the name of the organism that the subject sequence belongs to.
- *Max score* is the highest alignment score for the query sequence and a sequence extension in the database. The higher the score, the better the alignment.
- *Total score* is the sum of alignment scores calculated over all extensions in the database sequence that match the query sequence. The higher the score, the better the alignment.
- *Query coverage* is the percentage of the query sequence length included in the aligned extensions and calculated over all segments.
- *E-value* indicates the statistical significance of an alignment as it is the number of distinct alignments with a score equivalent to or better than scores that are expected to occur in a database search by chance. The lower the E-value, the more significant the score is.

- *Percent identity* is the percentage of residues (bases or amino acids) that are identical to the subject sequence. A query sequence may have a low percent identity, but still be a related sequence.
- *Accession length* is the length of the subject sequence.
- *Accession* is the accession number of the sequence.

On top of the description table there are important links related to the are BLAST hit sequences. The descriptions of those links are as follows:

- *GenBank* is a link to the GenBank results page, where GenBank records are the BLAST search hits. If the hits are nucleotide sequences, the Nucleotide database page will open and if they are protein, the Protein database page will open.
- *Graphics* is a link to the Sequence Viewer, where you can view the query sequence and the sequences of the search hits (Figure 8.17). The Sequence Viewer was discussed in Chapter 3.
- *Distance tree of results* tab displays a graphic tree for viewing the relationships between the sequences in the results (Figure 8.18). The distance tree shows the evolutionarily distance between the query sequence and other hits. Study this tree and identify the subject sequences that are the closest to the query sequence.
- The *Multiple Sequence Alignment Viewer* is a sequence viewer for displaying the multiple sequence alignment of the sequences reported by the BLAST search (Figure 8.19). The Sequence Viewer was discussed in Chapter 3.
- The *Download* dropdown menu, on the top right, is used to choose one of different output file formats to download. The file formats include: FASTA sequences, FASTA aligned sequences, GenBank, hit table (text or csv), description table, xml, and ASN. Most users will download a FASTA file that contain all sequences obtained by BLAST search to use that file for different purposes, including multiple sequence alignment, phylogenetic tree, conserved sequence detection, etc.

Graphic Summary   The Graphic Summary tab (Figure 8.20) displays the graphic summary reports for the aligned sequences. The query sequence is represented by the top solid dark green bar, and the aligned subject sequences are represented by red solid bars. The alignment bars are color coded by scores. The colored keys are shown on the top with the red color indicating the highest score; black is the lowest. A continuous solid red bar aligned to the query bar is an indication that the entire sequence is aligned to the query sequence (percent identity is 100% and coverage is 100%). The partial red bars that do not cover the query sequence means only the sequence segments represented by that bar are aligned. Remember, BLAST aligns sequences

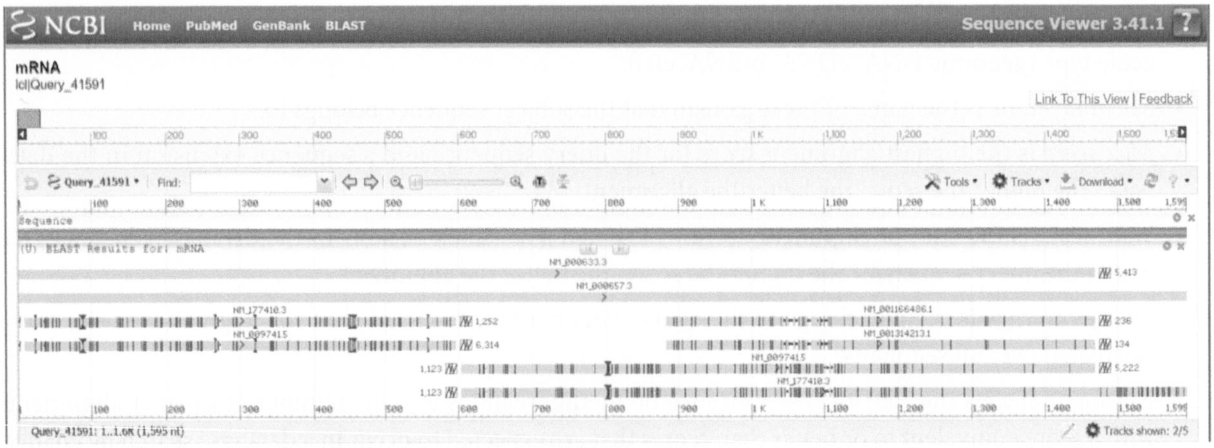

FIGURE 8.17   Sequence viewer showing query sequence and BLAST hits.

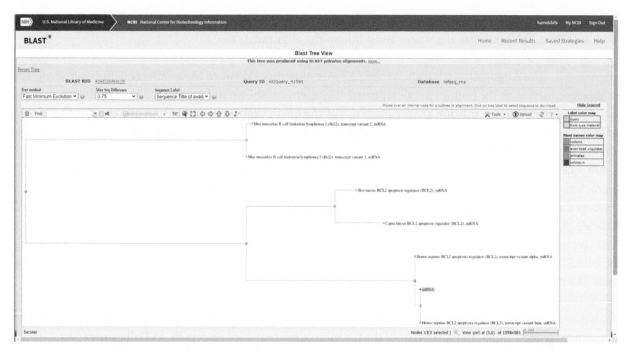

FIGURE 8.18   Distance tree of sequences of the BLAST results.

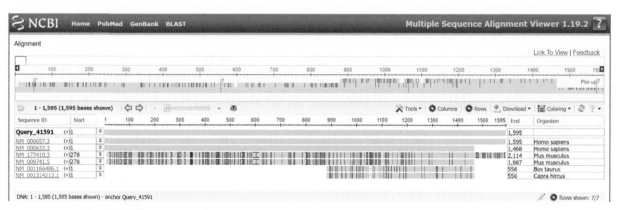

FIGURE 8.19   The multiple sequence alignment viewer.

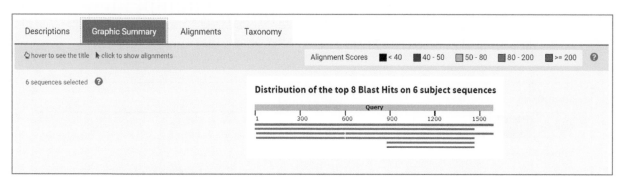

FIGURE 8.20   Graphic summary.

in some regions; therefore, we expect that only some regions of the query sequence may be aligned to a subject sequence. In this case instead of a solid continuous bar, the alignments will be represented by boxes, which may take different color based on their scores and the regions with no significant scores will be represented by a line. In this example, we are dealing with closely related transcript sequences with high identity and coverage; therefore, the alignments are continuous bars.

Pointing the mouse pointer over a bar will display the subject sequence title. Clicking a box will display more information about that alignment and a link to the alignments tab.

Alignments   The Alignments tab displays the pairwise alignment between the query sequence on the top and a subject sequence on the bottom for all reported alignments as shown in Figure 8.21. The numbers on the left and right of each aligned portion are the positions of the query sequence (on the top) and the position on the subject sequence (on the bottom). The alignment metrics including score, E-value, identities, gaps, and strand orientation are on the top of each alignment.

The query-subject pairwise alignment includes a combination of "|" characters and empty spaces. The "|" characters denote the identical matches between the query and the subject residues while an empty space denotes a mismatched residue. If a dash character "-" is found in the query or the subject sequence, it will indicate that a gap was inserted for improving the alignment.

If you have checked the checkboxes for filtering or masking the low-complexity regions before submitting the BLAST search, BLAST would not attempt to match the masked regions to the sequences in the target database. The masked residues may appear as grey lower-case letters or as Xs or Ns.

Taxonomy   The taxonomy reports, as shown in Figure 8.22, consist of Lineage, Organism, and Taxonomy. These three reports provide an overview of the taxonomic relationships among BLAST alignment hits. Lineage

FIGURE 8.21   The pairwise alignments of the BLAST hits.

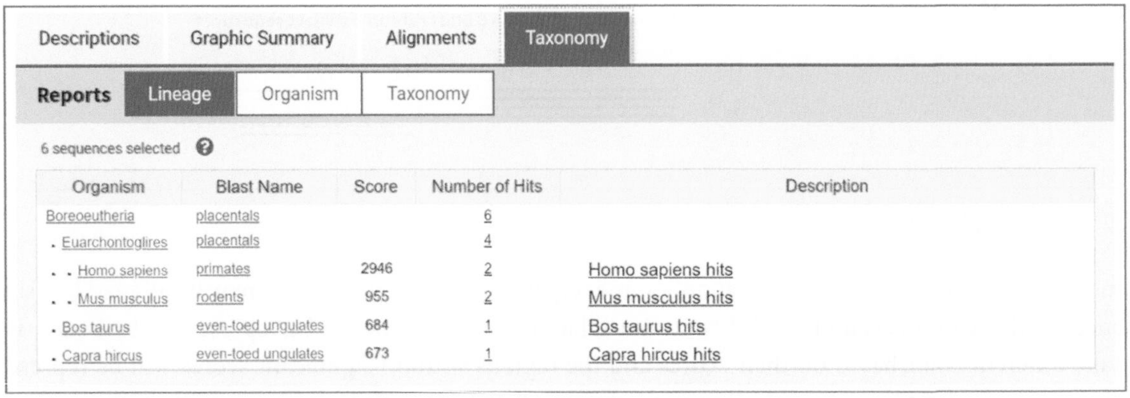

FIGURE 8.22   The BLAST taxonomy reports.

gives an insight about the relationships between the organisms. In the Organism report, the BLAST results are grouped into blocks by species. Within each species block, records are sorted by the BLAST scores. The order of species blocks themselves are based on the BLAST score of the best hit within the block. The Taxonomy report summarizes the relationships among all organisms found in the BLAST results. Using this report, it is easy to see how many records are found within the broad taxonomic groups.

Finding Closely Related Species

The phylogenetic tree is a visual representation that shows the evolutionary relationship across species or across strains of a species. It is used in phylogenetic research, classification, and identification of organisms especially for identification of bacteria and bacterial strains. There are several genes used for the construction of a phylogenetic tree. Those genes have a very slow rate of mutation (very conserved). Therefore, the sequences of such genes vary from one species to another, but they are conserved within the same species because of the slow mutation. Therefore, the sequences of such genes give information about the evolutionary distances between species. Massive studies showed that ribosomal RNA (rRNA) genes have such characteristics and they are used for building phylogenetic trees. The 18S rRNA gene is one of the genes used for studying evolutionary relationship in eukaryotes and also for eukaryotic taxonomy while the 16S rRNA gene is one of the genes used in prokaryotes.

In this example, you will find the species that are closely related to the human. To achieve this goal, you can use the sequence of the human 18S ribosomal RNA (18S rRNA) gene as the query sequence for BLAST to find the closely related sequences from other species.

First, you may need to extract the human 18S ribosomal N1 gene sequence from the latest human reference genome to make sure that the gene sequence is complete, and it includes coding and non-coding regions. The current release of the human reference genome sequence is GRCh38.p13. You need to know the coordinates of the 18S ribosomal N1 gene in this reference genome. You can get the coordinates from the Entrez Gene database using the following query as you learnt in Chapter 3:

RNA18S4[GENE] AND human[ORGN]

The above query will open the record of the 18S ribosomal N1 gene. Find the gene location under the Genomic Context. The location is NC_000021.9 (8436876..8438744), which consists of the chromosome accession number (NC_000021.9) and the gene first base and last base on the reference genome GRCh38.p13 (8436876..8438744).

The next step is to open a new Nucleotide BLAST (blastp) page and enter the chromosome accession number NC_000021.9 into the Query sequence box and under Query subrange enter 8436876 and 8438744 into the fields of "From" and "To" respectively. Change the job title to "Human 18S ribosomal N1 gene". Choose the "Nucleotide collection (nr/nt)" as the target database. Since you are looking for homologous sequences, you do not need to limit search by any organism. You can exclude the model and uncultured/environmental sample sequences because they do not contain information for this search and also to make the search faster. Choose MegaBlast because it is better for closely related sequences and faster. To filter pseudogene and other redundant sequences, enter the following query terms into Entrez Query:

"18S ribosomal"[TITLE] NOT pseudogene [TITLE]

You do not need to adjust the algorithm parameters so leave them unchanged. Finally, click the "BLAST" button to submit the request (Figure 8.23).

On the BLAST results page unselect all and then select only one sequence for each organism (Figure 8.24). You can select up to ten sequences to be viewed easily on the phylogenetic tree.

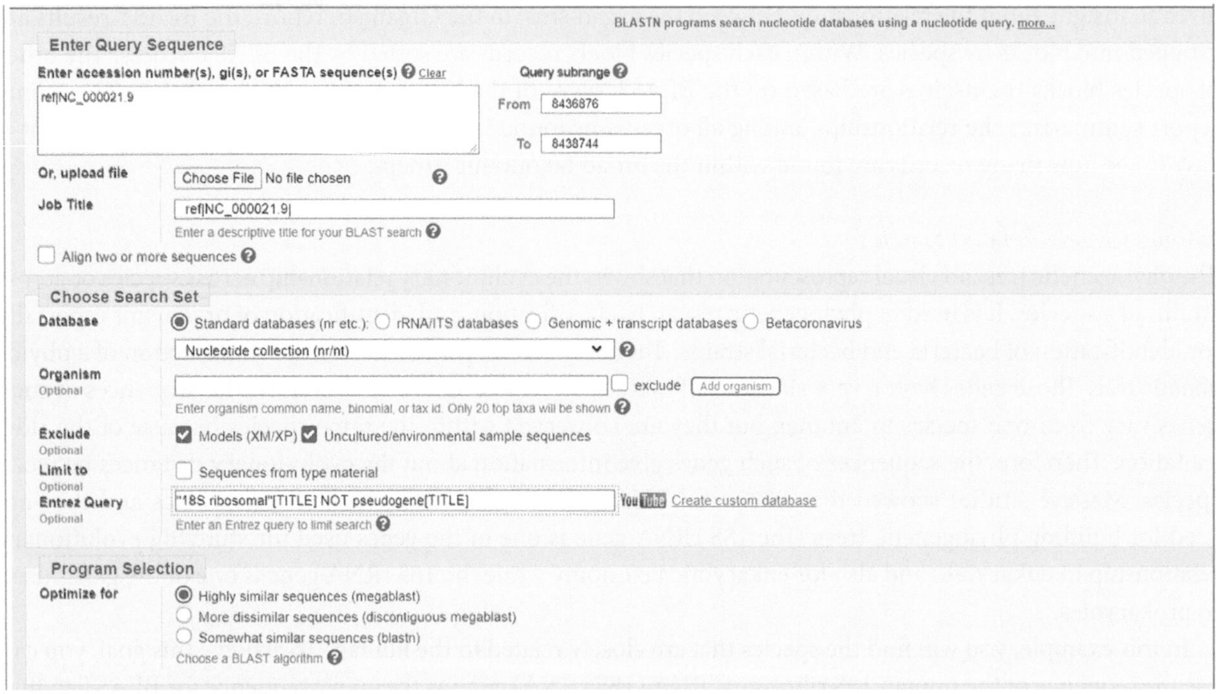

FIGURE 8.23   Nucleotide BLAST search for 18S rRNA related genes.

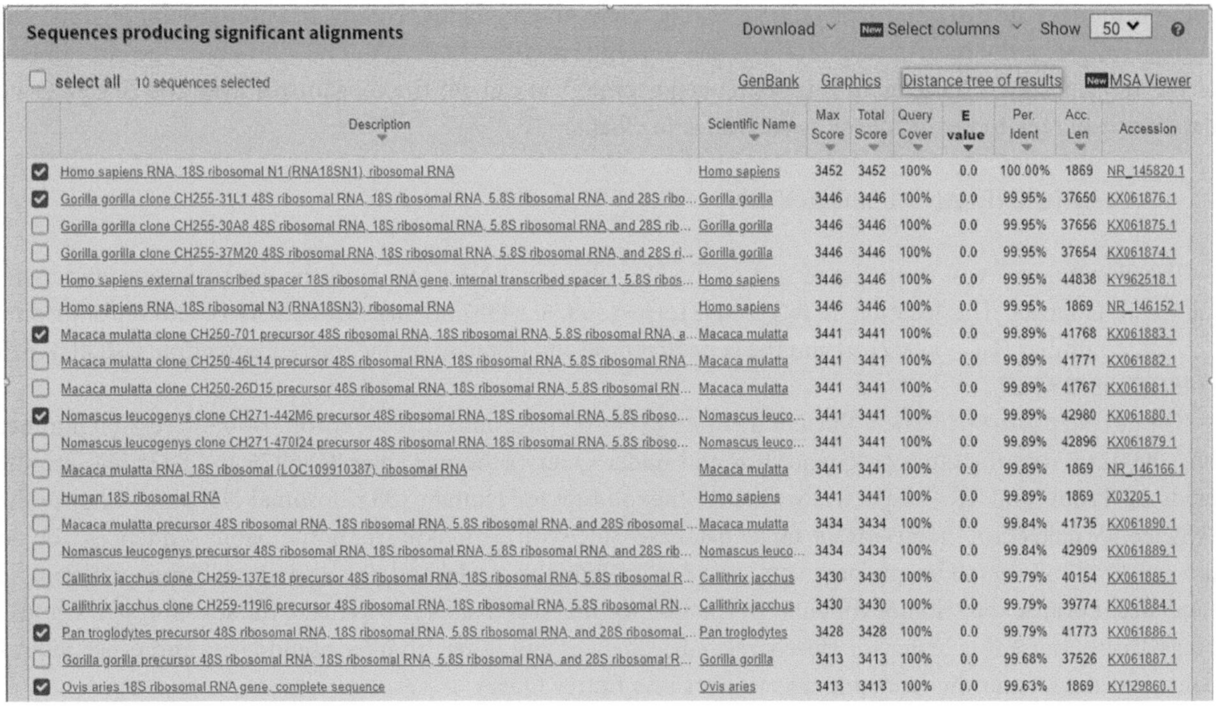

FIGURE 8.24   BLAST search output.

Once you have selected one sequence for each organism, click on "Distance tree of the results". You can save the distance tree into a file (Figure 8.25).

A quick look at the distance tree will give you a clear picture about the evolutionary relationship of the selected species based on 18S rRNA orthologs. You can notice that the house mouse (*Mus musculus*) and the brown mouse (*Rattus norvegicus*) are organized in one group in the tree and they are very closely species.

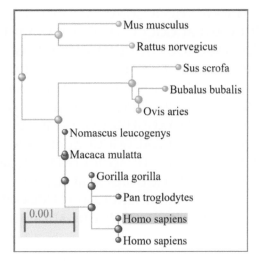

FIGURE 8.25   Distance tree based on 18S rRNA gene orthologs.

The water buffalo (*Bubalus bubalis*) and sheep (*Ovis aries*) are ruminants and they are organized together in a single branch of the tree, but they are also closely related to the wild swine (*Sus scrofa*) and all of them branch out from a single branch. You can also notice that all the primates are grouped together and that *Homo sapiens* (human) and *Pan troglodytes* (chimpanzee) are very closely related. The phylogenetic tree provides a visual description of the evolutionary relationship.

Identifying Unknown Bacteria Using 16S rRNA Sequence

In the modern microbiology lab, bacterial species are identified gnomically by identifying 16S rRNA gene, which is a conserved gene in bacteria and used for bacterial identification. The process begins by extracting DNA from samples and then using the multiplex polymerase chain reaction (PCR) to amplify 16S rRNA sequences. The primers used in the PCR are for multiple 16S rRNA genes of multiple bacteria. The gene product is then sequenced to obtain sequences of the unknown bacteria. Those sequences can be used as query sequences in BLAST against the rRNA database. The BLAST search results will report the matched sequences and their statistical significance. In this example, assume that the following sequence of 16S rRNA gene was obtained from a sequenced PCR product and you wish to identify the unknown bacteria by using BLAST.

>Unknown_bacteria_Seq

AUGUUUGAUCCUGGCUCAGAUUGAACGCUGGCGGCAGGCCUAACACAUGCAAGUCGA
ACGGUAACAGGAAGCAGCUUGCUGCUUCGCUGACGAGUGGCGGACGGGUGAGUAAUG
UCUGGGAAACUGCCUGAUGGAGGGGGAUAACUACUGGAAACGGUAGCUAAUACCGCAU
AACGUCGCAAGACCAAAGAGGGGGACCUUCGGGCCUCUUGCCAUCAGAUGUGCCCAG
AUGGGAUUAGCUAGUAGGUGGGGUAACGGCUCACCUAGGCGACGAUCCCUAGCUGGUC
UGAGAGGAUGACCAGCCACACUGGAACUGAGACACGGUCCAGACUCCUACGGGAGGCA
GCAGUGGGGAAUAUUGCACAAUGGGCGCAAGCCUGAUGCAGCCAUGCCGCGUGUAUG
AAGAAGGCCUUCGGGUUGUAAAGUACUUUCAGCGGGGAGGAAGGCGAUGUGGUUAAU
AACCACGUCGAUUGACGUUACCCGCAGAAGAAGCACCGGCUAACUCCGUGCCAGCAGC
CGCGGUAAUACGGAGGGUGCAAGCGUUAAUCGGAAUUACUGGGCGUAAAGCGCACGCA
GGCGGUCUGUCAAGUCGGAUGUGAAAUCCCCGGGCUCAACCUGGGAACUGCAUCCGA
AACUGGCAGGCUUGAGUCUCGUAGAGGGGGGUAGAAUUCCAGGUGUAGCGGUGAAAU
GCGUAGAGAUCUGGAGGAAUACCGGUGGCGAAGGCGGCCCCCUGGACGAAGACUGAC
GCUCAGGUGCGAAAGCGUGGGGAGCAAACAGGAUUAGAUACCCUGGUAGUCCACGCCG

UAAACGAUGUCGACUUGGAGGUUGUGCCCUUGAGGCGUGGCUUCCGGAGCUAACGCG
UUAAGUCGACCGCCUGGGGGAGUACGGCCGCAAGGUUAAAACUCAAAUGAAUUGACGG
GGGCCCGCACAAGCGGUGGAGCAUGUGGUUUAAUUCGAUGCAACGCGAAGAACCUUA
CCUGGUCUUGACAUCCACAGAACUUUCCAGAGAUGGAUUGGUGCCUUCGGGAACUGU
GAGACAGGUGCUGCAUGGCUGUCGUCAGCUCGUGUUGUGAAAUGUUGGGUUAAGUCC
CGCAACGAGCGCAACCCUUAUCCUUUGUUGCCAGCGGUCCGGCCGGGAACUCAAAGG
AGACUGCCAGUGAUAAACUGGAGGAAGGUGGGGAUGACGUCAAGUCAUCAUGGCCCU
UACGACCAGGGCUACACACGUGCUACAAUGGCGCAUACAAAGAGAAGCAAUCUCGCGA
GAGCUAGCGGACCUCAUAAAGUGCGUCGUAGUCCGGAUUGGAGUCUGCAACUCGACU
CCAUGAAGUCGGAAUCGCUAGUAAUCGUGAAUCAGAAUGUCACGGUGAAUACGUUCC
CGGGCCUUGUACACMCCGCCCGUCACMCCAUGGGAGUGGGUUGCAAAAGAAGUAGGU
AGCUUAACCUUCGGGAGGGCGCUUACCACUUUGUGAUUCAUGACUGGGGUGAAGUCG
UAACAAGGUAACC

Open BLAST Nucleotide and enter or upload the sequence into the Query sequence box. Select the radio button "rRNA/ITS databases" to populate the database dropdown list with the database names of that group. From the database list choose "16S ribosomal; RNA sequences (Bacteria and Archaea)", select both checkboxes "Exclude" to exclude the model sequences and uncultured sample sequences. In program Selection, choose the "Highly similar sequences (megablast)" option. You can also collapse the Algorithm parameters and set the Max target sequence to 10 (Figure 8.26)

Click the "BLAST" button. The ten matched hits will be displayed on the results page as shown in Figure 8.27.

The query sequence matched the 16S rRNA sequences of several bacterial species. However, by identifying the closest to the query sequence, it is possible to establish the most likely identity for the unknown sample. The max score, query coverage, and percent identity are the most important statistics used to make a conclusion about the identity of the unknown bacteria. The unknown sequence is more likely to be 16S rRNA sequence of *Salmonella spp* based on the alignments with maximum metrics.

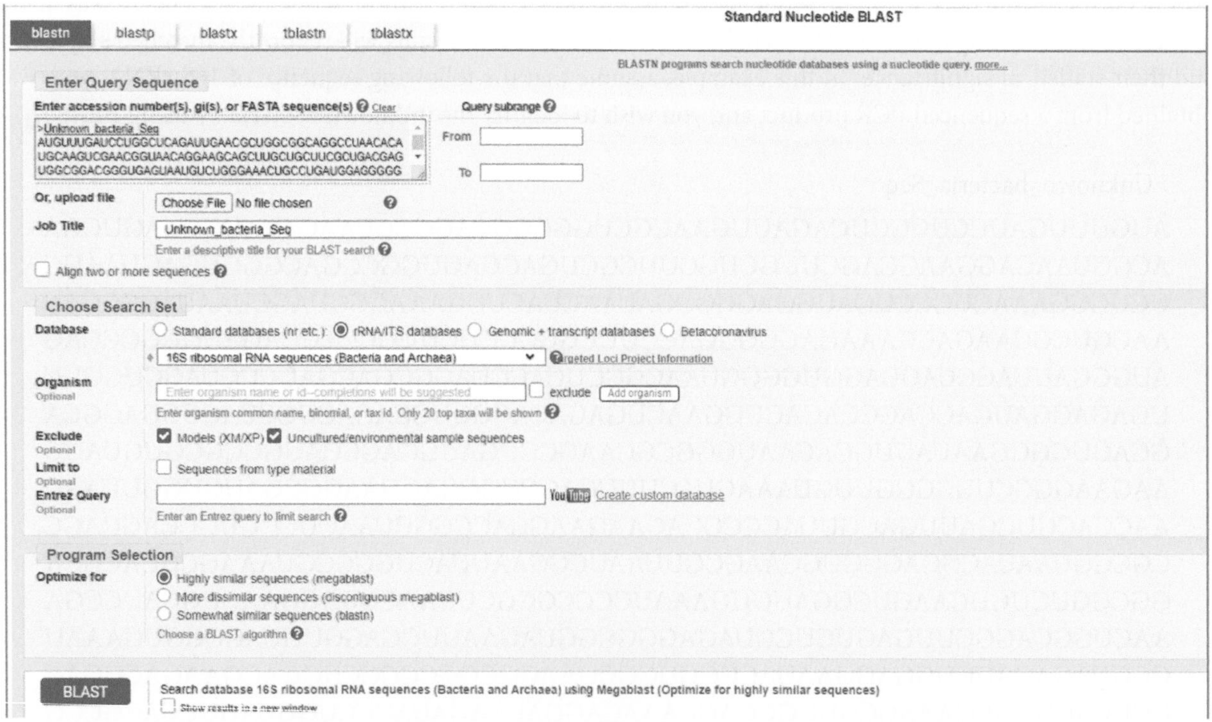

FIGURE 8.26 Identifying bacteria using BLAST.

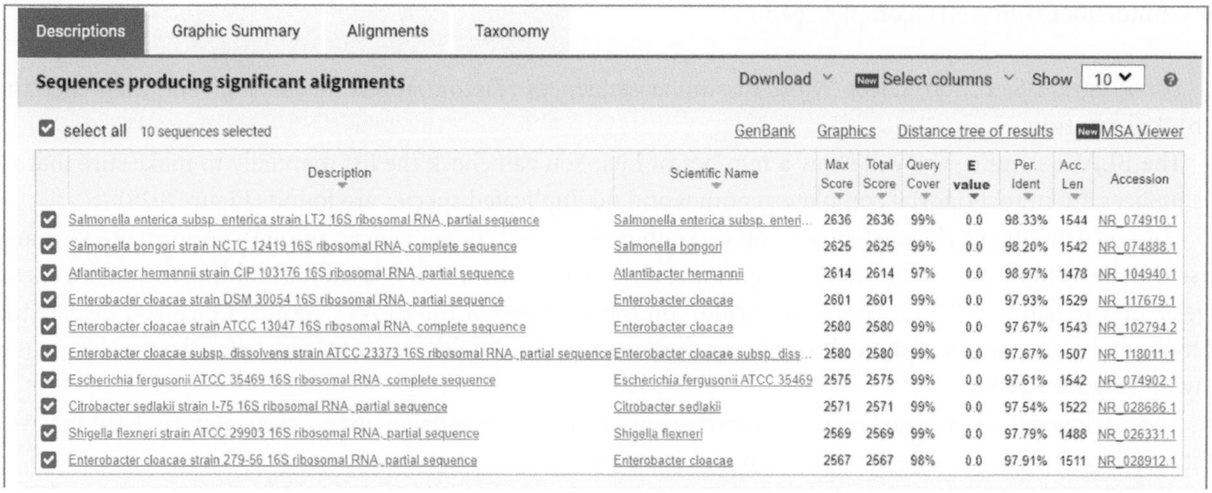

Description	Scientific Name	Max Score	Total Score	Query Cover	E value	Per. Ident	Acc. Len	Accession
Salmonella enterica subsp. enterica strain LT2 16S ribosomal RNA, partial sequence	Salmonella enterica subsp. enteri...	2636	2636	99%	0.0	98.33%	1544	NR_074910.1
Salmonella bongori strain NCTC 12419 16S ribosomal RNA, complete sequence	Salmonella bongori	2625	2625	99%	0.0	98.20%	1542	NR_074888.1
Atlantibacter hermannii strain CIP 103176 16S ribosomal RNA, partial sequence	Atlantibacter hermannii	2614	2614	97%	0.0	98.97%	1478	NR_104940.1
Enterobacter cloacae strain DSM 30054 16S ribosomal RNA, partial sequence	Enterobacter cloacae	2601	2601	99%	0.0	97.93%	1529	NR_117679.1
Enterobacter cloacae strain ATCC 13047 16S ribosomal RNA, complete sequence	Enterobacter cloacae	2580	2580	99%	0.0	97.67%	1543	NR_102794.2
Enterobacter cloacae subsp. dissolvens strain ATCC 23373 16S ribosomal RNA, partial sequence	Enterobacter cloacae subsp. diss...	2580	2580	99%	0.0	97.67%	1507	NR_118011.1
Escherichia fergusonii ATCC 35469 16S ribosomal RNA, complete sequence	Escherichia fergusonii ATCC 35469	2575	2575	99%	0.0	97.61%	1542	NR_074902.1
Citrobacter sedlakii strain I-75 16S ribosomal RNA, partial sequence	Citrobacter sedlakii	2571	2571	99%	0.0	97.54%	1522	NR_028686.1
Shigella flexneri strain ATCC 29903 16S ribosomal RNA, partial sequence	Shigella flexneri	2569	2569	99%	0.0	97.79%	1488	NR_026331.1
Enterobacter cloacae strain 279-56 16S ribosomal RNA, partial sequence	Enterobacter cloacae	2567	2567	98%	0.0	97.91%	1511	NR_028912.1

FIGURE 8.27 The top ten BLAST hits for the example sequence.

Constructing Phylogenetic Tree for Human Related Species

The phylogenetic tree can be constructed using the mitochondrial genome of organisms. Mitochondrial DNAs are circular with a higher evolutionary importance compared to nuclear DNA. They have specific uniparental inheritance only from mothers to their children. The mitochondrial DNA is useful for tracing matrilineal kinship in many generations. In this example, you will use the human mitochondrial genome sequence (NC_012920.1) as the BLAST query sequence against a database of reference genomes to find closely related primate species. Open BLAST Nucleotide (blastn) as shown in Figure 8.28 and enter the accession NC_012920.1 into the Query sequence box. From the Database dropdown list choose "RefSeq Genome Database (refseq_genome)". Choose "Primates" as Organism and enter the following query into the Entrez Query input box:

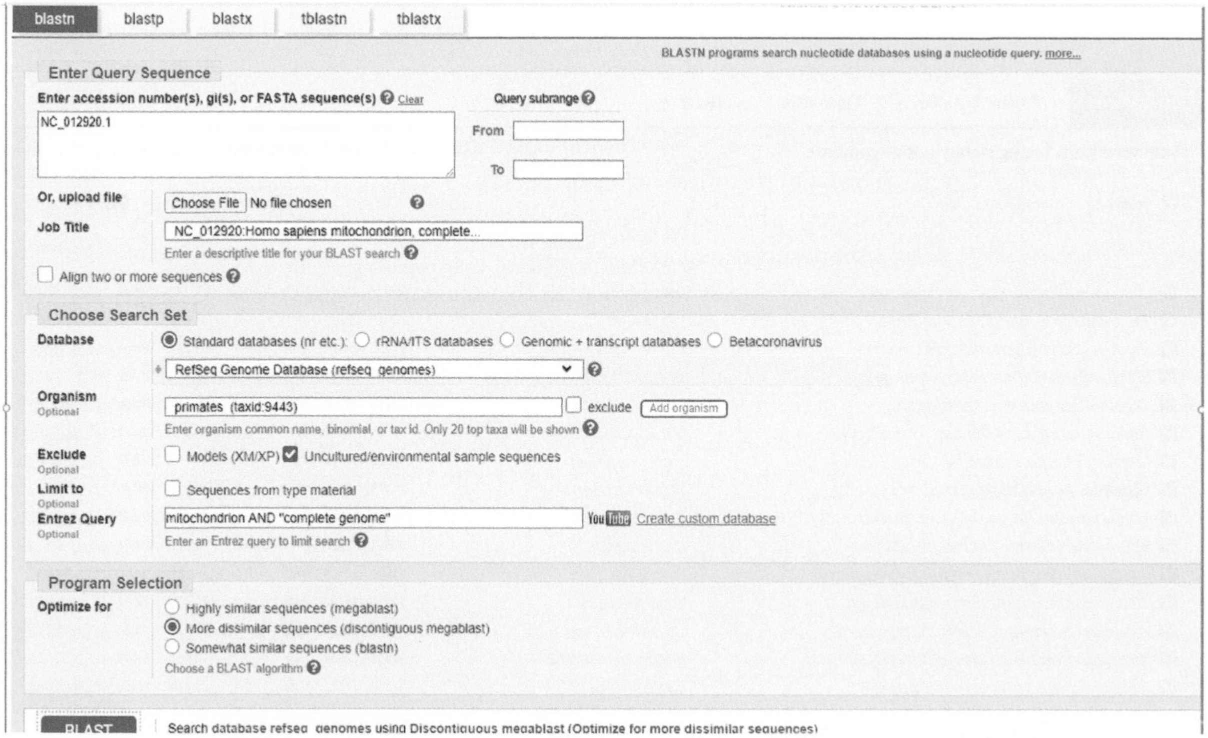

FIGURE 8.28 Using BLAST for searching for similar sequences.

mitochondrion AND "complete genome"

For Program Selection, select "More dissimilar sequences (discontiguous megablast)" and then click the "BLAST" button.

The BLAST results page will show a number of hits. You can check the list manually to make sure that all sequences are mitochondrial complete genomes and no duplicated species are found (Figure 8.29).

For constructing phylogenetic tree, you can either download the sequences as a FASTA formatted file and use the file as input for phylogenetic programs such as MEGA-X, which is used for building the phylogenetic trees, or you can use "Distance tree of results" on the right top of the BLAST results. Once you display the phylogenetic tree on the distance tree viewer, you can use the "Tools" menu to customize the tree labels and layout (Figure 8.30).

The phylogenetic tree based on the complete genome of mitochondrion gives a clear picture about the evolutionary relationship between the human and other primates.

Constructing Phylogenetic Tree Using Protein Sequences

In this example, you will construct a phylogenetic tree using protein sequences. You will follow the same steps as in the previous example, but instead of building a phylogenetic tree using pairwise sequence alignment, you will use multiple sequence alignment with the NCBI Constraint-based Multiple Alignment Tool (COBALT). You will use BLAST Protein (blastp) and the query sequence is the sequence of "peroxisome proliferator-activated receptor gamma isoform 1" or PPARG isoform 1, which has the accession "NP_619725.3". Enter this accession into the query sequence, choose "Reference proteins (refseq_protein)" as a target database and "Tetrapods" as organism (Figure 8.31), and then click on the "BLAST" button.

The results may contain other variants of peroxisome proliferator-activated receptors (PPARs). Use the mouse to unselect all sequences and then select only PPARG as shown in Figure 8.32. Click the "Multiple Alignment" link on the top right of the results table to open the COBALT multiple sequence alignment viewer as shown in Figure 8.33. COBALT is an NCBI tool for multiple sequence alignment that uses a multiple sequence alignment algorithm rather than a pairwise sequence alignment. The multiple sequence alignment

Descriptions	Graphic Summary	Alignments	Taxonomy								
Sequences producing significant alignments					Download ⌄	New Select columns ⌄	Show 100 ⌄				❓
☑ select all 20 sequences selected					GenBank	Graphics	Distance tree of results	New MSA Viewer			
Description		Scientific Name		Max Score	Total Score	Query Cover	E value	Per. Ident	Acc. Len	Accession	
☑ Homo sapiens mitochondrion, complete genome		Homo sapiens		29877	29877	100%	0.0	100.00%	16569	NC_012920.1	
☑ Pan paniscus mitochondrion, complete genome		Pan paniscus		22610	23265	100%	0.0	91.41%	16563	NC_001644.1	
☑ Pan troglodytes mitochondrion, complete genome		Pan troglodytes		22529	23179	99%	0.0	91.29%	16554	NC_001643.1	
☑ Gorilla gorilla gorilla mitochondrion, complete genome		Gorilla gorilla gorilla		20712	21436	99%	0.0	89.48%	16412	NC_011120.1	
☑ Pongo abelii mitochondrion, complete genome		Pongo abelii		18295	18602	98%	0.0	85.44%	16499	NC_002083.1	
☑ Nomascus leucogenys mitochondrion, complete genome		Nomascus leucogenys		17158	17461	97%	0.0	83.97%	16478	NC_021957.1	
☑ Theropithecus gelada mitochondrion, complete genome		Theropithecus gelada		14022	14177	99%	0.0	79.65%	16546	NC_019802.1	
☑ Chlorocebus sabaeus mitochondrion, complete genome		Chlorocebus sabaeus		13878	13878	100%	0.0	78.91%	16550	NC_008066.1	
☑ Macaca fascicularis mitochondrion, complete genome		Macaca fascicularis		13858	13858	100%	0.0	78.89%	16575	NC_012670.1	
☑ Macaca mulatta mitochondrion, complete genome		Macaca mulatta		13692	13830	97%	0.0	79.17%	16564	NC_005943.1	
☑ Papio anubis isolate east mitochondrion, complete genome		Papio anubis		13584	13734	97%	0.0	79.08%	16516	NC_020006.2	
☑ Rhinopithecus bieti mitochondrion, complete genome		Rhinopithecus bieti		13130	13287	97%	0.0	78.51%	16551	NC_015486.1	
☑ Trachypithecus francoisi mitochondrion, complete genome		Trachypithecus francoisi		13084	13261	97%	0.0	78.37%	16554	NC_023970.1	
☑ Rhinopithecus roxellana mitochondrion, complete genome		Rhinopithecus roxellana		12819	12969	97%	0.0	78.06%	16549	NC_008218.1	
☑ Callithrix jacchus mitochondrion, complete genome		Callithrix jacchus		11352	11352	93%	0.0	76.77%	16499	NC_025586.1	

FIGURE 8.29 **BLAST results for human mitochondrion genome.**

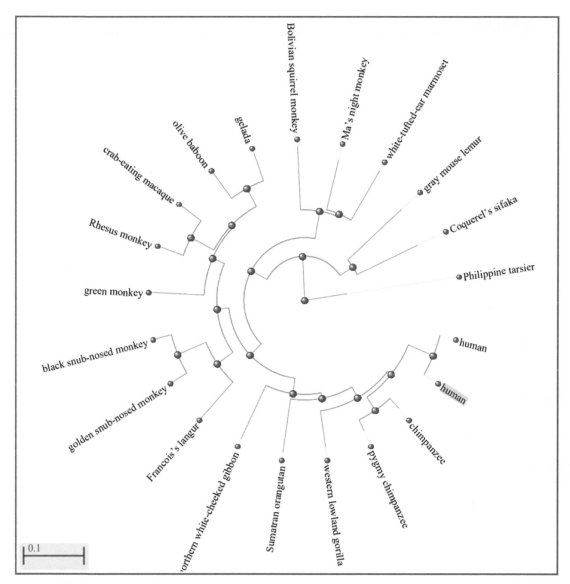

FIGURE 8.30   Phylogenetic tree for primates.

enables better computation for the distance between sequences that will lead to a better construction of the phylogenetic tree. On the top right corner of the COBALT viewer, click Phylogenetic Tree to open the COBALT Phylogenetic Tree Viewer displaying the PPARG tree as shown in Figure 8.34.

The phylogenetic tree (Figure 8.34) shows distinct groups indicated by colors. From the bottom, primates are included in one tree, dogs and cats are in a separate tree, mice, rats, and hamsters are in a separate tree, ruminants are in a separate tree, and birds are in a separate tree.

Annotate a Metagenomic Contig

Metagenomic contigs are the DNA contigs sequenced from DNA from environmental samples, in order to study the community of microorganisms present, without the necessity of obtaining pure cultures. Once the contig sequences are obtained, they can be annotated to identify the organisms. In this example, the contig is obtained by whole genome shotgun sequencing from the human gut metagenome DNA. The GenBank accession of this contig is BABF01000017.1. The goal is to identify the bacteria in the sample from this contig. Open BLAST (blastx) and enter the accession into the query sequence box. For the Genetic code choose

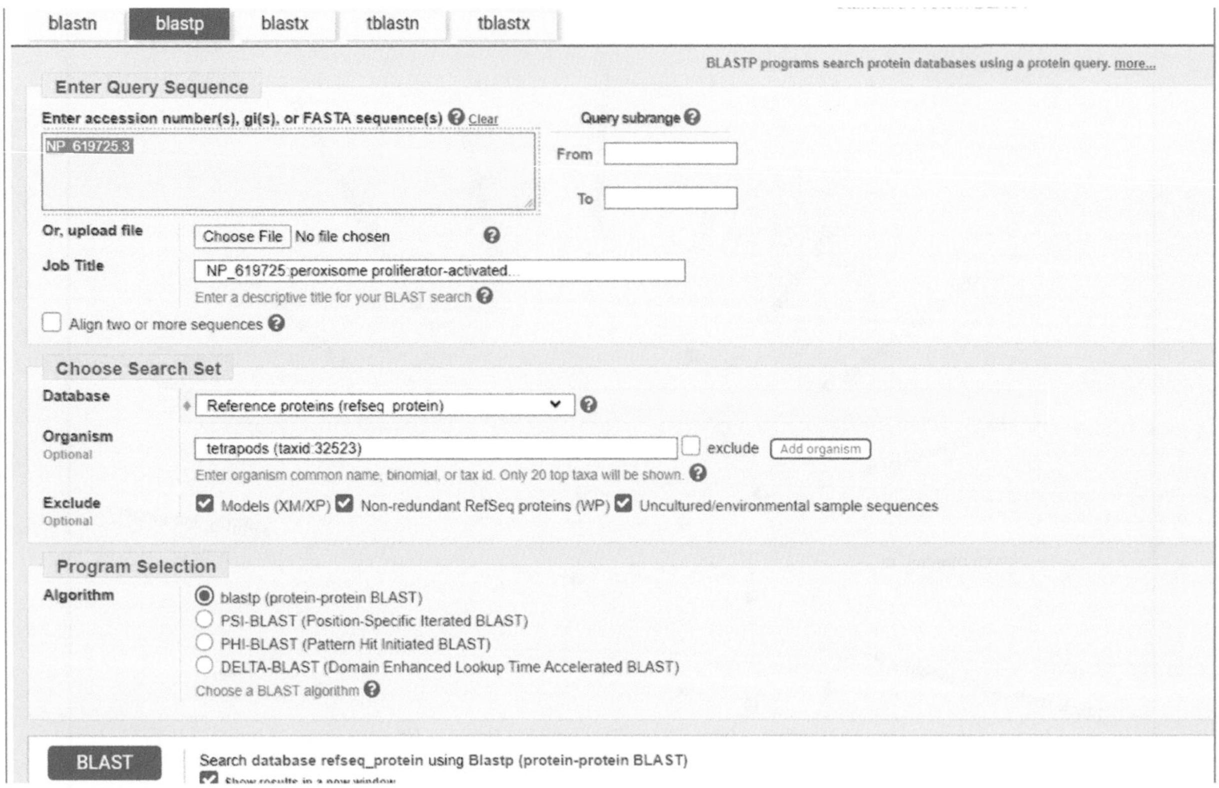

FIGURE 8.31   BLAST protein search.

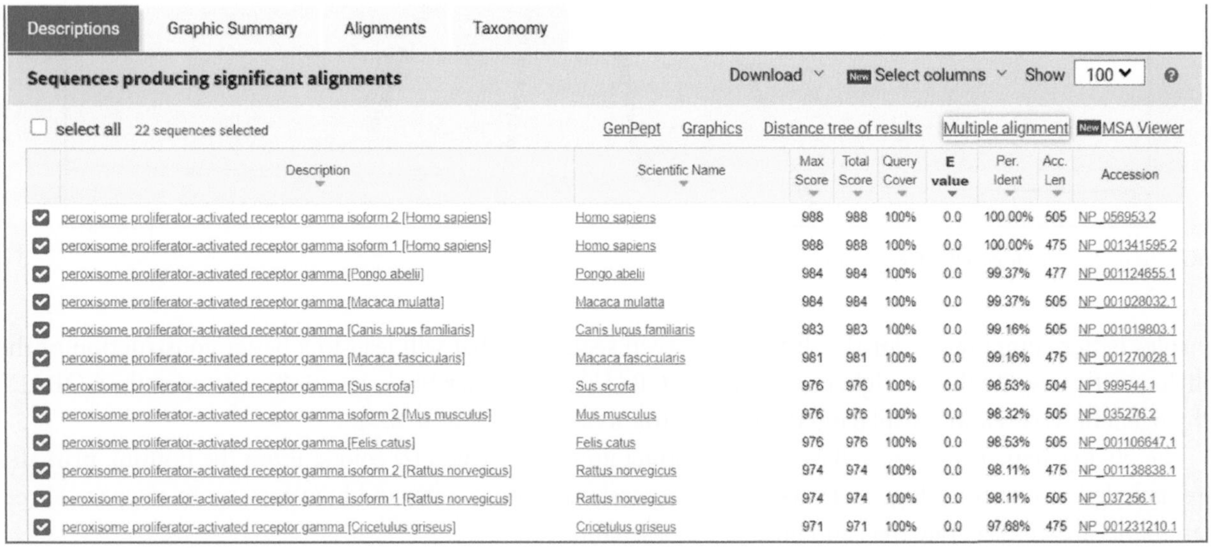

FIGURE 8.32   BLAST search results.

"Bacteria and Archaea (11)" and for Database choose "Model Organisms (landmark) as shown in Figure 8.35, and then click the "BLAST" button.

The search against the Landmark database suggests around seven possible genes on the contig, and a number of bacteria including: *Escherichia coli*, *Pseudomonas aeruginosa*, *Mycobacterium tuberculosis*, *Bacillus spp*. For the complete list of identified proteins and organisms check the Descriptions. The bars on the Graphic Summary (Figure 8.36) indicate the possible gene locations.

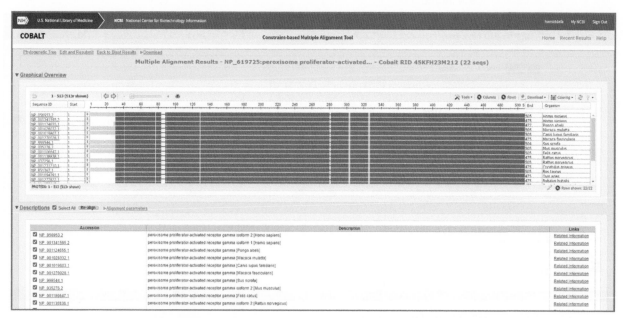

FIGURE 8.33   COBALT multiple sequence alignment.

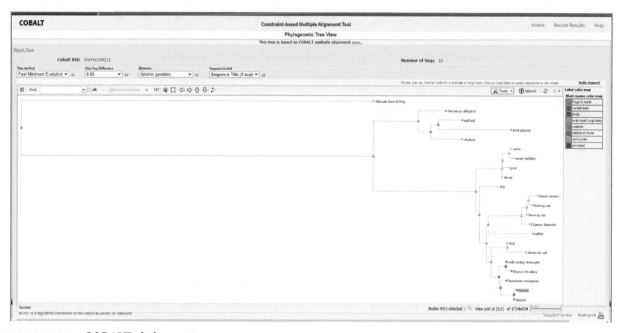

FIGURE 8.34   COBALT phylogenetic tree.

Finding Protein Conserved Domains with Solved Structures

In the previous example, you could annotate a contig with putative proteins. You may also need to go further to identify conserved domains in the proteins and you may also need to know if the protein domains have solved 3D structures. To achieve these two goals, you can follow the same steps you did in the previous example, except for the target database choose "Protein Data Bank proteins (pdb)", which is the database for proteins with solved structures (Figure 8.37).

The BLAST results will be the proteins with solved structures. You can consider the ones with the best maximum score, percent identity (Figure 8.38).

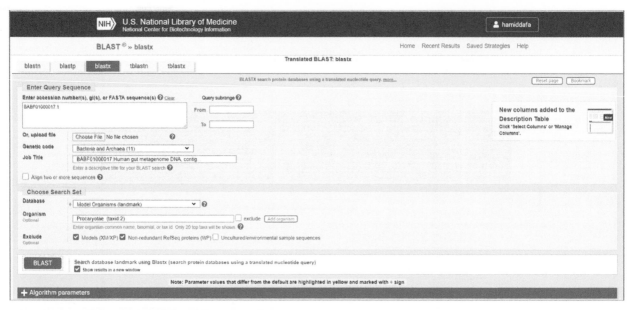

FIGURE 8.35   Using BLAST (blastx) for annotation.

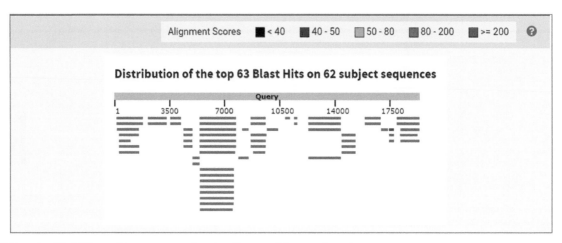

FIGURE 8.36   BLAST graphic summary showing the possible gene locations.

The accession of each BLAST hit is linked to the GenBank Protein page, where you can also find several tools for analyzing the conserved domains and viewing the structure of the solved portion of the protein as marked in Figure 8.39. For example, you can click "Identify Conserved domain" to open the page of the conserved domain related to the protein record. You can also click "Protein 3D Structure" to display the 3D structure page of the protein.

Designing Primers for PCR

At the modern biology and biomedical labs, scientists use the polymerase chain reaction (PCR) for several purposes including identification of a gene, genotyping, diagnosis, gene expression, etc. The PCR process is the process that amplifies a specific segment of DNA or RNA in a sample including a pool of DNA or RNA. Primers allow amplification of a specific segment (e.g., gene) out of thousands of DNA or RNA segments. Primers are oligonucleotides of 18–25 bases that initiate the amplification of the targeted region. Before designing primers, you need to determine whether you wish to amplify DNA or RNA to choose the right sequence and right target database. See Chapter 2 to read more about PCR. In this example, you will design

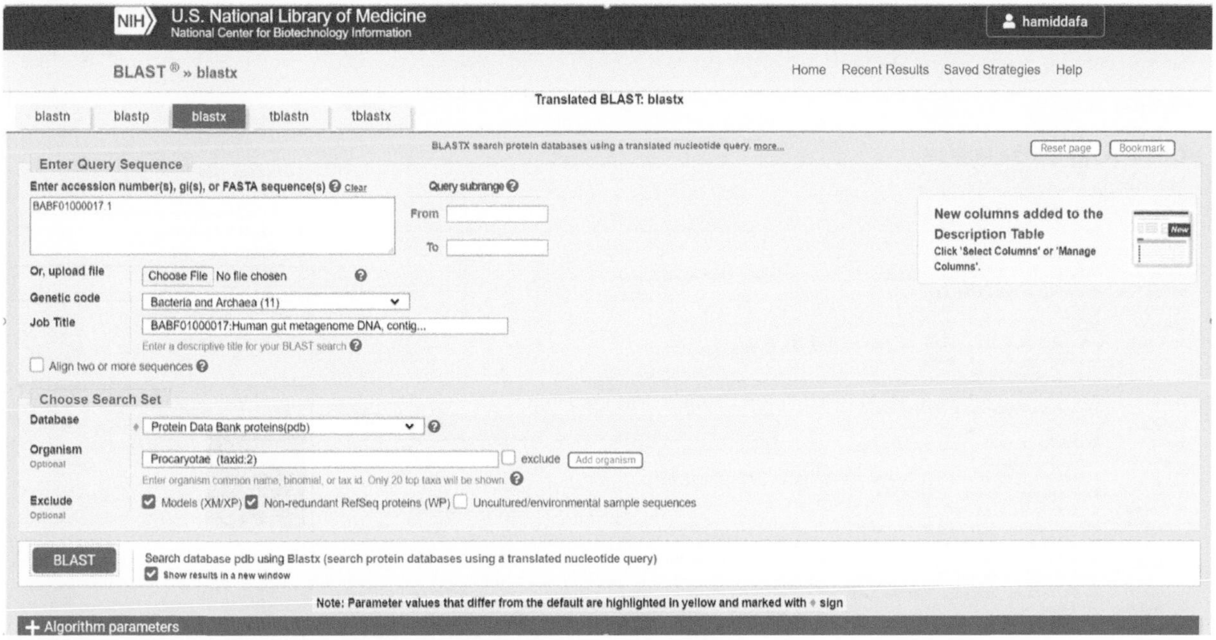

FIGURE 8.37   Use of BLAST to find protein domain with solved structures.

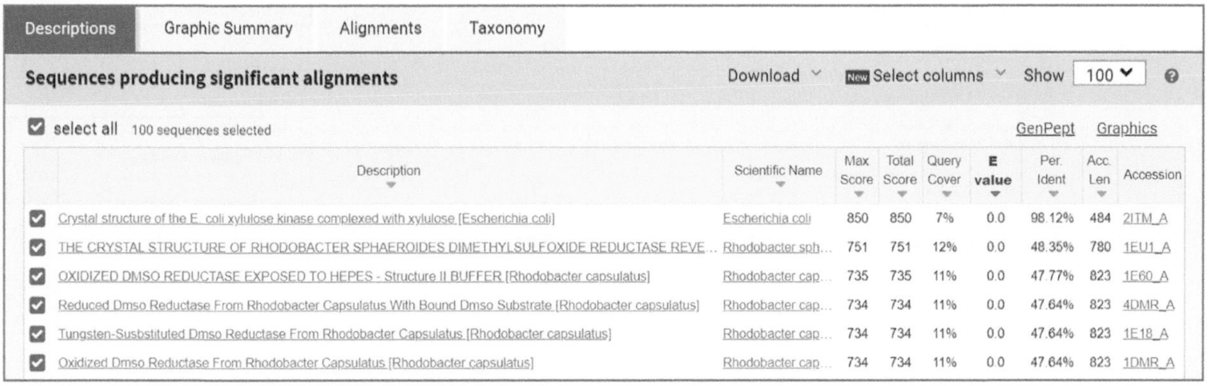

FIGURE 8.38   BLAST results for searching target sequences from Protein Data Bank.

primers for diagnosing COVID-19 from DNA extracted from human samples. One of the main genes used for COVID-19 diagnosis is the gene that codes envelope protein (E gene). First you need to retrieve the sequence of this gene; you can obtain the Nucleotide accession and coordinates of the gene from the Gene database. Open the Entrez Gene web page www.ncbi.nlm.nih.gov/gene/ and use the following query to find the E gene of the SARS-CoV-2 virus.

E[GENE] AND "Severe acute respiratory syndrome coronavirus 2"[ORGN] AND ("srcdb refseq"[PROP] AND alive[PROP])

Under the Genomic Context, you will find the refseq accession and the gene coordinates as NC_045512.2 (26245..26472).

Open the Pimer-BLAST web page www.ncbi.nlm.nih.gov/tools/primer-blast/, enter the accession (NC_045512.2) into the PCR template input box and under Range "From" and "To" enter 26245 and 26472 into "From" and "To" respectively for the forward and primer as shown in Figure 8.40.

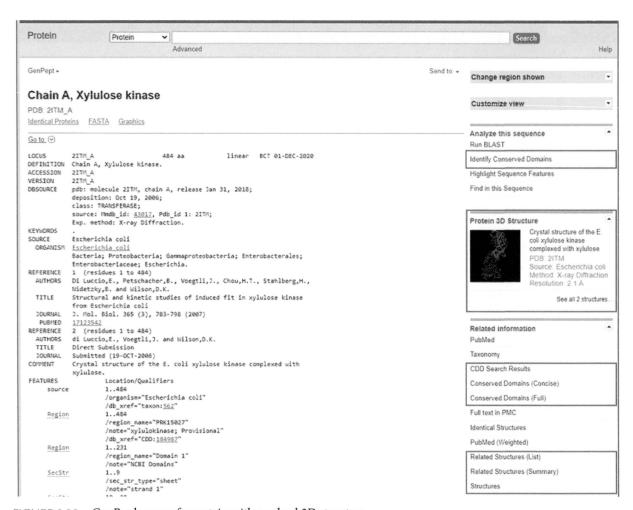

FIGURE 8.39   GenBank page of a protein with a solved 3D structure.

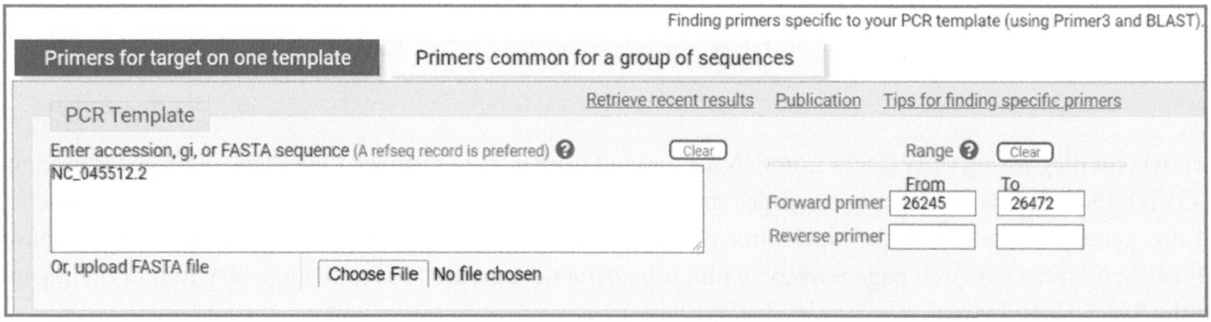

FIGURE 8.40   Entering sequence accession and gene coordinates for the targeted region.

Under Primer Parameters, you can determine the length of the PCR product and melting temperature. For this example, leave the default values.

Under the Exon/Intron selection as shown in Figure 8.41, choose "No reference". Leave the other default values.

Under Primer Pair Specificity Checking Parameters, choose "nr" as the target database and "SARS-CoV-2" as an organism as shown in Figure 8.41, and click "Get Primers" button.

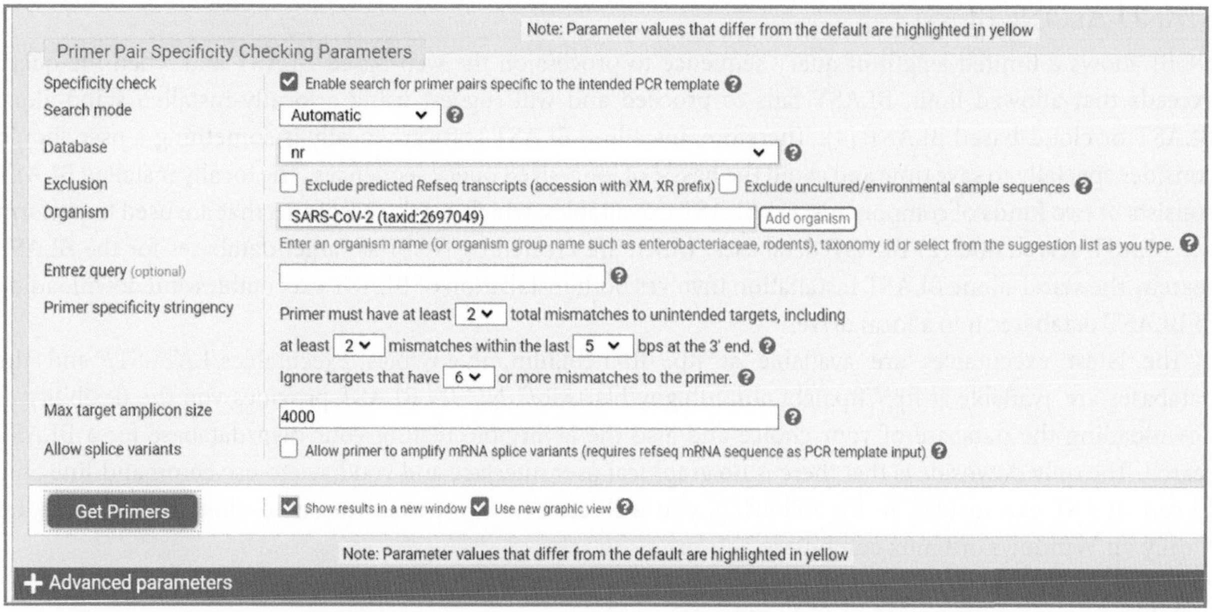

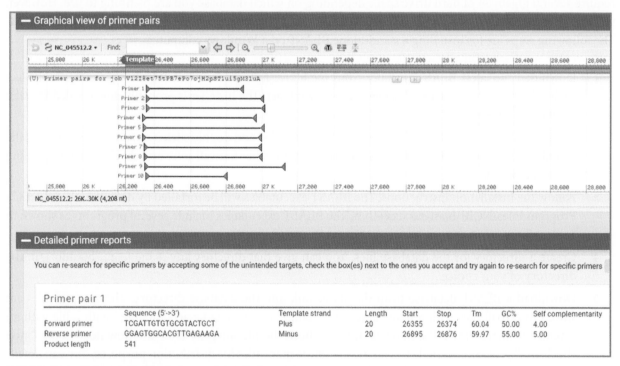

FIGURE 8.41   Primer pair specificity checking parameters.

FIGURE 8.42   Primer graphical view and detailed reports.

Difference sequences may be displayed to select one or more from them. Select the first and click the "Submit" button. Several primers will be displayed in a graphical viewer and detailed primer report. Figure 8.42 shows a partial output.

The primer sequences then can be used to synthesize oligonucleotides that can be used in the PCR test as discussed in Chapter 2.

STAND-ALONE BLAST

NCBI allows a limited length of query sequence to process on the web-based BLAST and when the query exceeds that allowed limit, BLAST fails to proceed and will suggest using a locally-installed stand-alone BLAST or cloud-based BLAST [4]. Therefore, installing BLAST software locally is something a user should consider specially to save time and avoid the hassle of long-sized query sequences. The locally installed BLAST consists of two kinds of components: (1) BLAST executables; which are the programs that are used to perform the BLAST search and (2) BLAST databases, which are created by NCBI as target databases for the BLAST search. The stand-alone BLAST installation involves both installation of BLAST executables and downloading of BLAST databases into a local drive.

The latest executables are available at ftp://ftp.ncbi.nlm.nih.gov/blast/executables/LATEST/ and the databases are available at ftp://ftp.ncbi.nlm.nih.gov/blast/db/". NCBI's BLAST provides you the flexibility of downloading the database of your choice and also the ability of creating your own database for a BLAST search. The only downside is that there is no graphical user interface and you have to use command-line only to run BLAST executables. In the following, you will learn how to install the stand-alone BLAST software locally on Windows or Linux computers.

Installing and Running local BLAST on Windows

Before installing BLAST, you have to make sure that your computer meets the installation requirement. The latest BLAST executables are compatible only with 64-bit computer and a complete BLAST database may require several gigabytes of hard drive space depending on which database you are planning to use. However, you do not need to download all BLAST databases; you can download only the database that you wish to use. The following steps are for installing a stand-alone BLAST on a Windows computer.

1   Download the latest BLAST installer from the above link. The current Windows installer looks like "ncbi-blast-x.xx.x+-win64.exe", where "x" is any integer. The installer is probably downloaded into the Download folder.

2   Open the folder where the installer has been downloaded and double click it to run. The running of the installer may be blocked by Windows Defender or any other firewall software; check to enable running it if it is blocked.

3   Follow the installation instructions. The BLAST executables will be installed by default in the folder C:\ Program Files\NCBI\blast-x.xx.xx+\bin. The BLAST executables include several programs as shown in Table 8.5.

4   Create a directory for the database files. You can give that directory any name (e.g., "blastdb"), in the directory of your choice.

5   Download a BLAST database from the above link into the database directory. The database files are stored in tarball files with a name extension ".tar.gz" and it may be accompanied with a file with an extension ".tar.gz.md5". The latter is used to check the file integrity after the download using "md5 checksum" program. A single tarball file may store many files for distribution purposes. You can download a single database tarball file and later you can add more databases. For example, you can download a file for refseq_RNA database "refseq_rna.00.tar.gz" in a folder named "refseq_rna". In future, if you need to add any files to this database, any new database file downloaded will be tied automatically to the database by the file "refseq_rna.nal".

6   Extract the database files from the tarball file in the same database directory. The extraction requires software like 7-Zip or Winzip. Make sure that the files were extracted correctly; there should be several files including the ones for indexing.

TABLE 8.5   The stand-alone NCBI BLAST Executables

Program	Function
blastdbcheck	checks the integrity of a target database
blastdbcmd	retrieves records from a BLAST database
blastdb_aliastool	creates database alias
blastn	searches a nucleotide query sequence against a nucleotide database
blastp	searches a protein query sequence against a protein database
blastx	searches a nucleotide query sequence against a protein database
blast_formatter	formats a blast result using its assigned request ID
convert2blastmask	converts lowercase masking into makeblastdb readable data
makeblastdb	formats input FASTA file(s) into a target database
makembindex	indexes an existing nucleotide database for use with megablast
makeprofiledb	creates a conserved domain database from a list of input PSSM generated by psiblast
psiblast	searches using PSSM
rpsblast	searches a protein against a conserved domain database to identify functional domains
rpstblastn	searches a nucleotide query sequence (translated), against a conserved domain database
segmasker	masks the low complexity regions in input protein sequences
Tblastn	searches a protein query sequence against a nucleotide database (translated)
Tblastx	searches a nucleotide query sequence (translated) against a nucleotide database (translated)
update_blastdb.pl	downloads preformatted blast databases from NCBI
windowmasker	masks repeats found in input nucleotide sequences

7   Set up the environment by creating or modifying environment variables to include the executables and database paths. To do this, type "Edit environment variables for your account" in the search bar next to the "Start" icon and enter to navigate to "Environment Variables". Under "User variables" click the "New" button, then type the variable "Path" as the variable name and enter the absolute path for the executables (the default is "C:\Program Files\NCBI\blast-x.xx.xx+\bin"). Then create a variable for the database path "BLASTDB" and enter the absolute database path for the database directory (Figure 8.43).

8   The executables are run on the Command Prompt. You can open the Windows Command Prompt by typing "cmd" in the Windows search bar and then click the "Command Prompt" icon to open the Command Prompt windows as shown in Figure 8.44.

The command-line prompt was the first user interface for computers operated with the MS-DOS operating system a while ago before MS-DOS evolved to Windows with a graphical user interface. Nowadays, Windows users rarely need to use the command-line prompt, but bioinformatics scientists need to learn the MS-DOS command because there are several bioinformatics programs using the command line. The BLAST executables are run only under the command-line environment, which uses traditional DOS commands to interact with the operating system and other command-line based software. You may need to review the DOS commands that may help you to run BLAST executables.

9   Test if the BLAST executables and databases have been installed successfully. If the BLAST has been installed successfully and its path has been defined, then any one of the executables should run from the Command Prompt. Type the following command and then press the "Enter" key.

>blastn -version

If the blastn version is displayed as in Figure 8.45, then the program has been installed successfully.
Now you can check if the database files were downloaded in the database directory and the path of the database directory is defined.

>blastdbcmd -db refseq_rna\refseq_rna.00 -info

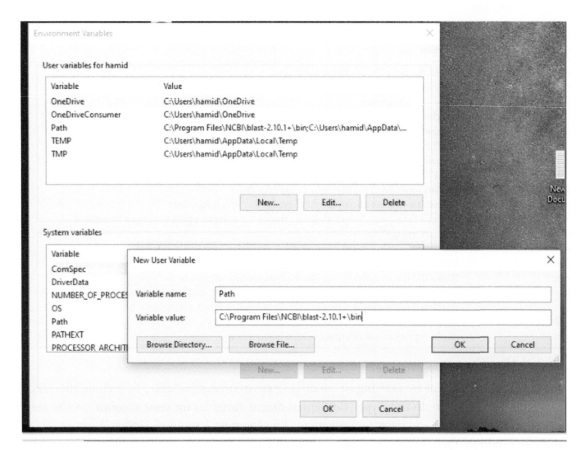

FIGURE 8.43   Setting the executables and database path.

FIGURE 8.44   Command Prompt window.

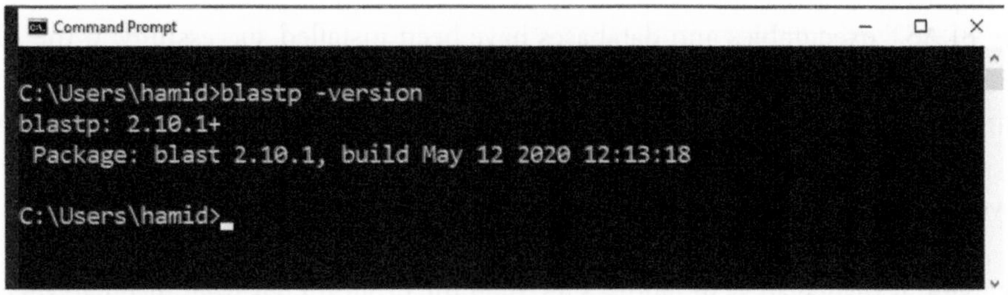

FIGURE 8.45   Testing BLAST installation.

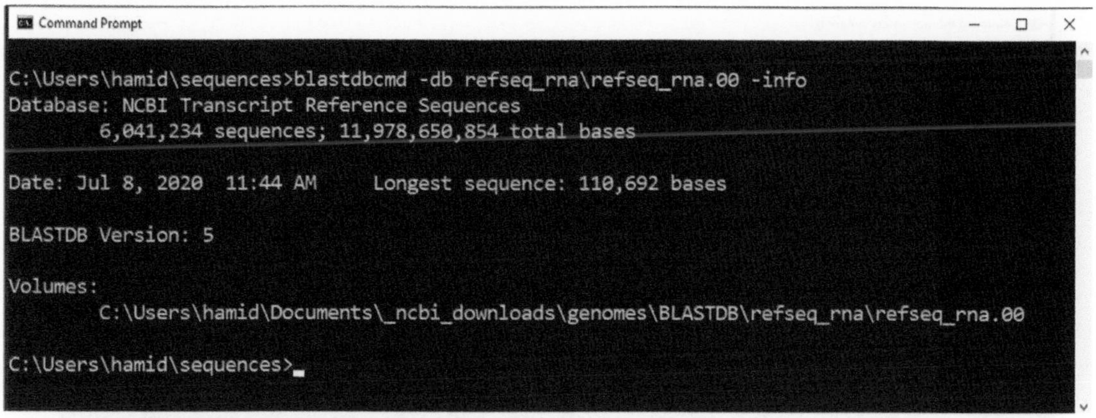

FIGURE 8.46   Testing BLAST database on Windows.

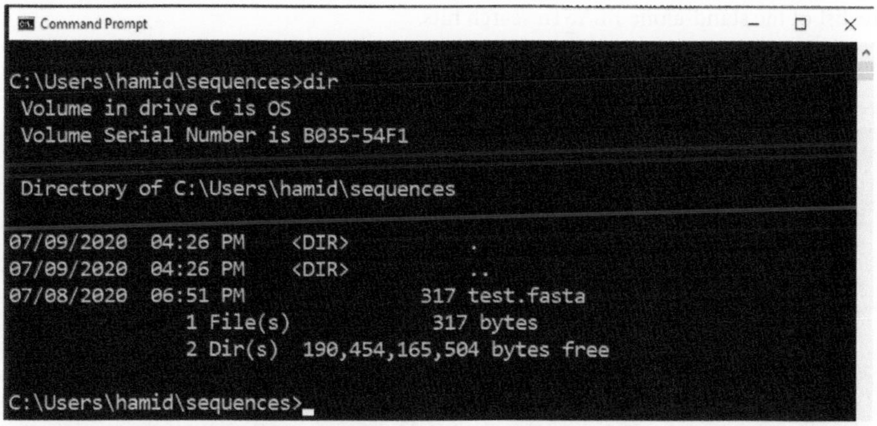

FIGURE 8.47   Current directory where sequence file is saved.

If the database files are in the database directory, the above command will display the number of sequences and bases in the database, the update date, the longest sequence, the database version, and the absolute path for database files as shown in Figure 8.46.

After the successful installation, you can run your first stand-alone BLAST search. To do this you need to save a nucleotide sequence in a FASTA-formatted file in the current directory where the Command Prompt points to, or you can use the DOS command "cd" to change the current directory to the directory where the sequence is stored. For example, enter the following nucleotide sequence in a plain text editor (e.g., Notepad) and save the file in the current directory.

>Test sequences - cDNA

AGAGGCATCCAGAAAAGTATCAGGGTAGTTCTGTTTCAAACTTGCATGTGGAGCCATGTG
GCACAAATACTCATGCCAGCTCATTACAGCATGAGAACAGCAGTTTATTACTCACTAAAGA
CAGAATGAATGTAGAAAAGGCTGAATTCTGTAATAAAAGCAAACAGCCTGGCTTAGCAAG
GAGCCAACATAACAGATGGGCTGGAAGTAAGGAAACATGTAATGATAGGCGGACTCCCA

Save the above sequence in a file named "test.fasta" in the current directory. The current directory on my computer is "sequences" as shown in Figure 8.47.

Now you will perform a BLAST search using blastp, the nucleotide sequence stored in a FASTA file as a query, and the non-redundant database as the target database as follows.

>blastn -query test.fasta -db refseq_rna\refseq_rna.00 -out output.txt

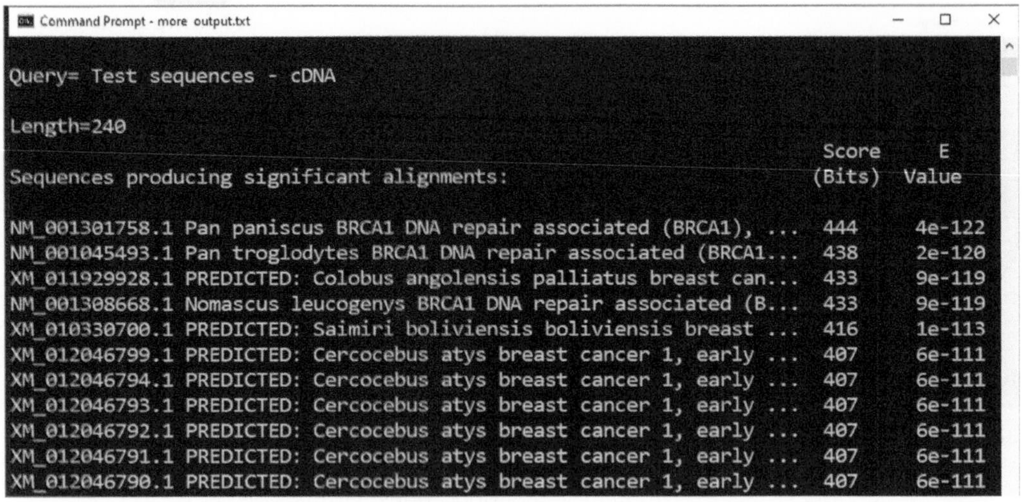

FIGURE 8.48   The list of the stand-alone BLASTn search hits.

FIGURE 8.49   The sequence alignments resulted by the stand-alone BLASTn.

The executable "blastn" has the options: "-query" for the query sequence file, "-db" for the target database file, and "-out" for the output file, in which the output will be saved.

The BLAST results have been saved in the file "output.txt". You can open the output file either by using Windows File Explorer and double click it or using the DOS command "more" as follows:

>more output.txt

The following are portions of the BLAST results stored on the "output.txt" file. The results include the list of sequences producing significance alignments with the query sequence (Figure 8.48) and the alignments of the query sequence with each of those sequences reported by BLAST (Figure 8.49).

Installing and Running Local BLAST on Linux

On computers with Linux and Linux environments such as MacOS, you can follow the same above steps to download BLAST executables and databases. However, there is no installer but you can download a tarball file containing the BLAST executables and then extract that tarball file in a directory. The steps are as follows:

1 Open the Linux terminal, create a directory named "blast" using "mkdir" command and change to it using "cd" command as follows:

$ mkdir blast

$ cd blast

You will use this directory to store both BLAST executables and databases in separate subdirectories.

2 Download the BLAST tarball file using the Linux command "wget". Check the NCBI FTP server for the latest version and copy the link. The file name may change.

$ wget https://ftp.ncbi.nlm.nih.gov/blast/executables/LATEST/ncbi-blast-2.11.0+-x64-linux.tar.gz

The tarball file will be downloaded into the current directory.

3 Extract the tarball file using "tar -zxvf" as follows:

$ tar -zxvf ncbi-blast-2.11.0+-x64-linux.tar.gz

The BLAST executables will be extracted into a directory created by the extraction program. The name of the directory will be the same as the name of the tarball file but without the "tar.gz" extension.

4 You can rename the long directory name "ncbi-blast-2.10.1+-x64-linux" to a shorter name such as "ncbi-blast" to make it simple. The following Linux command will rename that directory into "ncbi-blast"

$ mv ncbi-blast-2.10.1+-x64-linux ncbi-blast

Thus, the BLAST executables will be stored in "ncbi-blast/bin"

5 Move into that directory where the executables are stored using the "cd" command as follows:

$ cd ncbi-blast/bin

From inside this subdirectory, you can display the absolute path where the executables are stored by using "pwd" and you can also display the content of this subdirectory using the "ls" command to make sure that the executables are there. The absolute path for the executables will be added to the Linux path in a coming step. To display the absolute path for the executables while you are inside "ncbi-blast/bin" use the following Linux command:

$ pwd

The absolute path for the BLAST executables based on the configuration of the computer used for this demonstration is "/home/hamiddafa/blast/ncbi-blast/bin" as shown in Figure 8.50.

You can also list the executables using the "ls" command as follows:

$ ls -l

The above command will display the BLAST executables as shown in Figure 8.51.

```
hamiddafa@dax:~/blast/ncbi-blast/bin$ pwd
/home/hamiddafa/blast/ncbi-blast/bin
hamiddafa@dax:~/blast/ncbi-blast/bin$
```

FIGURE 8.50 Displaying absolute path for the BLAST executables.

```
hamiddafa@dax:~/blast/ncbi-blast/bin$ ls -l
total 672928
-rwxr-xr-x 1 hamiddafa hamiddafa 26300272 Oct  6 01:23 blastdb_aliastool
-rwxr-xr-x 1 hamiddafa hamiddafa 28060016 Oct  6 01:23 blastdbcheck
-rwxr-xr-x 1 hamiddafa hamiddafa 35309424 Oct  6 01:23 blastdbcmd
-rwxr-xr-x 1 hamiddafa hamiddafa 39691632 Oct  6 01:23 blast_formatter
-rwxr-xr-x 1 hamiddafa hamiddafa 39675248 Oct  6 01:23 blastn
-rwxr-xr-x 1 hamiddafa hamiddafa 39671152 Oct  6 01:23 blastp
-rwxr-xr-x 1 hamiddafa hamiddafa 39671152 Oct  6 01:23 blastx
-rwxr-xr-x 1 hamiddafa hamiddafa     6243 Aug  7  2019 cleanup-blastdb-volumes.py
-rwxr-xr-x 1 hamiddafa hamiddafa 28208424 Oct  6 01:23 convert2blastmask
-rwxr-xr-x 1 hamiddafa hamiddafa 39839600 Oct  6 01:23 deltablast
-rwxr-xr-x 1 hamiddafa hamiddafa 26783344 Oct  6 01:23 dustmasker
-rwxr-xr-x 1 hamiddafa hamiddafa     4742 Sep 28 11:26 get_species_taxids.sh
-rwxr-xr-x 1 hamiddafa hamiddafa    51345 May 27  2020 legacy_blast.pl
-rwxr-xr-x 1 hamiddafa hamiddafa 30517104 Oct  6 01:23 makeblastdb
-rwxr-xr-x 1 hamiddafa hamiddafa 27833200 Oct  6 01:23 makembindex
-rwxr-xr-x 1 hamiddafa hamiddafa 29817712 Oct  6 01:23 makeprofiledb
-rwxr-xr-x 1 hamiddafa hamiddafa 39736944 Oct  6 01:23 psiblast
-rwxr-xr-x 1 hamiddafa hamiddafa 39806832 Oct  6 01:23 rpsblast
-rwxr-xr-x 1 hamiddafa hamiddafa 39819376 Oct  6 01:23 rpstblastn
-rwxr-xr-x 1 hamiddafa hamiddafa 27488368 Oct  6 01:23 segmasker
-rwxr-xr-x 1 hamiddafa hamiddafa 39708272 Oct  6 01:23 tblastn
-rwxr-xr-x 1 hamiddafa hamiddafa 39671152 Oct  6 01:23 tblastx
-rwxr-xr-x 1 hamiddafa hamiddafa    23316 May 19  2020 update_blastdb.pl
```

FIGURE 8.51 BLAST executables.

```
hamiddafa@dax:~/blast/ncbi-blast/bin$ cd ../..
hamiddafa@dax:~/blast$
```

FIGURE 8.52 Moving to the main BLAST directory.

6 Move back to the "blast" directory by using "cd .." as follows

$ cd ../..

Figure 8.52 shows that the current directory is "blast".

7 In the "blast directory, create a subdirectory, where you can store the BLAST database files. You can name this subdirectory "blastdb" or any other name and change to inside it as follows:

$ mkdir blastdb

$ cd blastdb

Thus, the absolute path for the database file can be displayed by running the "pwd" Linux command. The path will be "/home/hamiddafa/blast/blastdb" based on the configuration of this computer.

8 Downloading a database tarball file depending on which database you wish to use. The database files require a large storage space. Therefore, it may be better to download only the file you need. Since, there are different kinds of BLAST databases, you can create a subdirectory for each database. For demonstration, you will download the "reference RNA database". Therefore, inside the "blastdb"

subdirectory, you can create a subdirectory named "ref_rna". The BLAST databases are available at https://ftp.ncbi.nlm.nih.gov/blast/db/. Use the "wget" Linux command to download "refseq_rna.00.tar.gz" as follows:

$ mkdir ref_rna

$ cd ref_rna

$ wget https://ftp.ncbi.nlm.nih.gov/blast/db/refseq_rna.00.tar.gz

The tarball file will be downloaded into the "blastdb/ref_rna" subdirectory.

9   Extract the database tarball into the "ref_rna" subdirectory as follows:

$ tar -zxvf refseq_rna.00.tar.gz

Once the database files have been extracted, you can delete the tarball file using the "rm" command to save space on your local drive.

$ rm refseq_rna.00.tar.gz

When you list the content of the "blastdb" subdirectory using the "ls" command, you will display the extracted database files as shown in Figure 8.53.

10   Remember that, so far, you have installed the BLAST executables and downloaded a BLAST database and also printed their absolute paths: "/home/hamiddafa/blast/ncbi-blast/bin" for the executables and "/home/hamiddafa/blast/blastdb" for the database files. In this step, you will set up the paths for both executables and the database directory to be able to run BLAST from any directory. Without setting the paths you will need to use the absolute paths for both the executables and database every time you run a BLAST executable. To set up the paths on Linux, open the file ".bashrc" with the text editor of your choice such as vim or nano. This file is hidden and it is found in the default user directory when logging onto Linux for the first time or by using "cd ~" to move to the user home directory.

$ nano .bashrc

```
hamiddafa@dax:~/blast/blastdb/ref_rna$ ls -l
total 7316388
-rw-rw-r-- 1 hamiddafa hamiddafa  792342593 Mar  5 07:11 refseq_rna.00.nhr
-rw-rw-r-- 1 hamiddafa hamiddafa   54476896 Mar  5 07:11 refseq_rna.00.nin
-rw-rw-r-- 1 hamiddafa hamiddafa   36445816 Mar  5 07:11 refseq_rna.00.nnd
-rw-rw-r-- 1 hamiddafa hamiddafa     142412 Mar  5 07:11 refseq_rna.00.nni
-rw-rw-r-- 1 hamiddafa hamiddafa   18158956 Mar  5 07:11 refseq_rna.00.nog
-rw-rw-r-- 1 hamiddafa hamiddafa 2999999264 Mar  5 07:11 refseq_rna.00.nsq
-rw-rw-r-- 1 hamiddafa hamiddafa        208 Mar  5 07:44 refseq_rna.nal
-rw-rw-r-- 1 hamiddafa hamiddafa 2003492864 Mar  5 07:47 refseq_rna.ndb
-rw-rw-r-- 1 hamiddafa hamiddafa  837144672 Mar  5 07:45 refseq_rna.nos
-rw-rw-r-- 1 hamiddafa hamiddafa  437160360 Mar  5 07:44 refseq_rna.not
-rw-rw-r-- 1 hamiddafa hamiddafa     626688 Mar  5 07:44 refseq_rna.ntf
-rw-rw-r-- 1 hamiddafa hamiddafa  145859580 Mar  5 07:44 refseq_rna.nto
-rw-rw-r-- 1 hamiddafa hamiddafa  150193204 Mar  5 07:47 taxdb.btd
-rw-rw-r-- 1 hamiddafa hamiddafa   15884728 Mar  5 07:47 taxdb.bti
hamiddafa@dax:~/blast/blastdb/ref_rna$
```

FIGURE 8.53   BLAST refseq_rna database files.

Add the following two lines to the end of .bashrc file, save it, and exit the file.

export PATH="/home/hamiddafa/blast/ncbi-blast/bin:$PATH"
export BLASTDB="/home/hamiddafa/blast/blastdb"

The first line adds the absolute path for the BLAST executable to the Linux path so you can run any of the BLAST executables from any directory. The second line creates a path variable "BLASTDB" storing the absolute path for the database files.

Notice that those file paths may be different on your computer. Make sure to enter the right absolute paths for both BLAST executables and the database files.

You may need to restart the terminal and then run the following command to make sure that the paths have been set up correctly.

$ blastn -version

If the path to the executables has been set correctly, you will get the "blastn" version number as shown in Figure 8.54.

11 You need also to check if the database files are on their path by using "blastdbcmd" and providing both "-db" and –info" arguments as follows:

$ blastdbcmd -db $BLASTDB/ref_rna/refseq_rna.00 -info

Notice that in Figure 8.55, since you stored the database files in the "ref_rna" subdirectory inside the absolute path stored at the variable "BLASTDB", you have to provide the complete path for the database files as "$BLASTDB/ref_rna/refseq_rna.00".

If you did all the above steps successfully, BLAST will be ready to use. You can run your first BLAST search using the FASTA sequence provided above. Save that sequence in your current directory and run the following

```
hamiddafa@dax:~$ blastn -version
blastn: 2.11.0+
 Package: blast 2.11.0, build Oct  6 2020 03:24:05
hamiddafa@dax:~$
```

FIGURE 8.54   Testing BLAST installation.

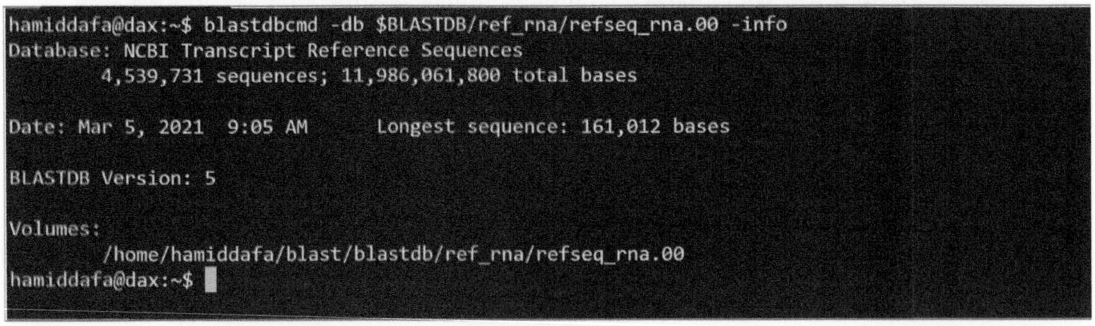

```
hamiddafa@dax:~$ blastdbcmd -db $BLASTDB/ref_rna/refseq_rna.00 -info
Database: NCBI Transcript Reference Sequences
        4,539,731 sequences; 11,986,061,800 total bases

Date: Mar 5, 2021  9:05 AM      Longest sequence: 161,012 bases

BLASTDB Version: 5

Volumes:
        /home/hamiddafa/blast/blastdb/ref_rna/refseq_rna.00
hamiddafa@dax:~$
```

FIGURE 8.55   Checking database file validity.

```
Query= Test sequences - cDNA

Length=240
                                                          Score    E
Sequences producing significant alignments:              (Bits)  Value

NM_001045493.1 Pan troglodytes BRCA1 DNA repair associated (BRCA1...  438    2e-120
NM_001114949.1 Macaca mulatta BRCA1 DNA repair associated (BRCA1)...  407    6e-111
XM_035301474.1 PREDICTED: Callithrix jacchus BRCA1 DNA repair ass...  399    1e-108
XM_035301473.1 PREDICTED: Callithrix jacchus BRCA1 DNA repair ass...  399    1e-108
XM_035301472.1 PREDICTED: Callithrix jacchus BRCA1 DNA repair ass...  399    1e-108
XM_008996690.4 PREDICTED: Callithrix jacchus BRCA1 DNA repair ass...  399    1e-108
XM_035301471.1 PREDICTED: Callithrix jacchus BRCA1 DNA repair ass...  399    1e-108
XM_035301470.1 PREDICTED: Callithrix jacchus BRCA1 DNA repair ass...  399    1e-108
```

FIGURE 8.56   BLAST search hit list.

```
>NM_001045493.1 Pan troglodytes BRCA1 DNA repair associated (BRCA1), mRNA
Length=5592

 Score = 438 bits (237),  Expect = 2e-120
 Identities = 239/240 (99%), Gaps = 0/240 (0%)
 Strand=Plus/Plus

Query  1     AGAGGCATCCAGAAAAGTATCAGGGTAGTTCTGTTTCAAACTTGCATGTGGAGCCATGTG  60
             |||||||||||||||||||||||||||||||||||||||||||||||||||||||||||||
Sbjct  764   AGAGGCATCCAGAAAAGTATCAGGGTAGTTCTGTTTCAAACTTGCATGTGGAGCCATGTG  823

Query  61    GCACAAATACTCATGCCAGCTCATTACAGCATGAGAACAGCAGTTTATTACTCACTAAAG  120
             |||||||||||||||||||||||||||||||||||||||||||||||||||||||||||||
Sbjct  824   GCACAAATACTCATGCCAGCTCATTACAGCATGAGAACAGCAGTTTATTACTCACTAAAG  883

Query  121   ACAGAATGAATGTAGAAAAGGCTGAATTCTGTAATAAAAGCAAACAGCCTGGCTTAGCAA  180
             ||||||||||||||||||||||||||||||||||||||||| |||||||||||||||||||
Sbjct  884   ACAGAATGAATGTAGAAAAGGCTGAATTCTGTAATAAAAGCGAACAGCCTGGCTTAGCAA  943
```

FIGURE 8.57   BLAST sequence alignments.

"blastn" program, which uses the FASTA file as query, refseq_rna as target database, and "output.txt" as an output file containing the BLAST search results.

$ blastn -query test.fasta -db $BLASTDB/ref_rna/refseq_rna.00 -out output.txt

The output file can be displayed using any text editor such as vim or nano. Figures 8.56 and 8.57 show parts of the BLAST search results.

Building a BLAST Database

NCBI BLAST has databases for different purposes as we discussed above. However, you may need to create your own sequence database that can serve your goal as a target database for the stand-alone BLAST. The BLAST executable "makeblastdb" was just created for that as it creates a BLAST database from the FASTA sequences of your choice in a single file. The following are the steps to build a BLAST database:

1   Create a directory for your custom database in the BLAST database directory. You can name that directory "myblastdb" or any valid name. The following commands will change the prompt to the BLAST database directory and create a subdirectory named "myblastdb" and move inside it:

```
$ cd $BLASTDB
$ mkdir myblastdb
$ cd myblastdb
```

2   Open a plain text editor and save the sequences you wish to use as database sequences in FASTA format
    in a single file. Each sequence must be identified by a unique identifier in the defline (definition line)
    after ">" and no space and save the file in the current directory. For the demonstration, you can save the
    following DNA sequences in a plain text file named "blast_dna_db.fasta".

>AY211955.1

GTGGAGCCATGTGGCACAGATGCTCGTGCCAGCTCATTACTGCCTGACATCACCAGTGTA
TTGCCTAACACAGACAGCATGAATGTAGAAAAGGCTGAACTCTGTGATAAAAGCAAAAGG
CCTGATTTAGCATGGAGCCAGCAGATCAGTCAGGATGAAAGTAAGGAAAAATGTATTGCT
GGGAAGACCTCAGATGCAAAGGAGTTACAT

>AY211954.1

GTGGAGCCATGTGGCACAGATGCTCGTGCCACCTCATTACTTCCTGAAACCACCAGCTTA
TCGCCCAACACATTCCAAATGAATGTAGAAAAGGCTGAACTCTGTAATAAAAGCAAACAG
CCTGGCTTAGCAAAAAACCAACAGAGCAGTCTGGATGAAAGTAAGGAAATATGTAGTGCT
GGAAAGACCCTGGGTGCCCATGAGCTGAAT

>AY211953.1

TGTGGCACAGATGCTCGTGCCACCTCATTACTTCCTGAAACCACCAGCTTATCGCCCAAC
ACAGACCGAATGAATGTAGAAAAGGCTGAACTCTGTAATAAAAGCAAACAGCCTGGCTTA
GCAAAAAACCAACAGAGCAGTCTGGATGAAAGTAAGGAAATATGTAGTGCTGGAAAGAC
CCTGGGTGCCCATGAGCTGAATGCCCATCAT

>AY365046.1

TCCCTCAGAACACGAAGGGCTCTCTCATCCTGTCACTAAAACGATTAGCTGTCCGGAGAC
ACGGAAAAAGTCGCCCCTCTTCTTTGCAGGATTCCTCCCTTGAACTTCTCCAAACCCTCT
TAGTGTGACGTGACCCCACCCCTAGCTAACCCAGGCTGCTTCCTTACCAGCTTCCCGCCC
CCTGGGGAGGCGGCAATGCAAAGACCGTCC

>MF945608.1

CTCACTAAAGACAGAATGAATGTAGAAAAGGCTGAATTCTGTAATAAAAGCAAACAGCCT
GGCTTAGCAAGGAGCCAACATAACAGATGGGCTGGAAGTAAGGAAACATGTAATGATAGG
CGGACTCCCAGCACAGAAAAAAAGGTAGATCTGAATGCTGATCCCCTGTGTGAGAGAAA
AGAATGGAATAAGCAGAAACTGCCATGCTCA

>AY211956.1

TGTGGCACAGATGCTCGTGCCACCTCATTACTTCCTGAAACCACCAGCTTATCGCCCAAC
ACAGACCGAATGAATGTAGAAAAGGCTGAACTCTGTAATAAAAGCAAACAGCCTGGCTTA
GCAAAAAACCAACAGAGCAGTCTGGATGAAAGTAAGGAAATATGTAGTGCTGGAAAGAC
CCTGGGTGCCCATGAGCTGAATGCCCATCAT

>AF159258.1

GGACGCCTGGACAGAGGACAGTGGCTTCCATGGTAAGTCTTGGCTGTAAGCCTTTGTCCA
GAGGAGCATGGGTGGCAAGGGCCCAGATTAATTATGCAGATAACTGTGGTGATTTTAAGT
CTAAATGTCCTGTTTCAATCAATTGGAGTAGATGGTGTACCTGTATAGGGCTTCAGAGGG
CCATGGGCATGTGCCTGTGAGAGATGGGGT

3 Open a plain text editor and create a file that maps the unique identifier of any of the above sequences to the taxonomy identifier of that sequence. The following list includes the identifiers of the above sequences together with their taxonomy identifiers (see the Taxonomy database). Save this file in the working directory as "blast_tax.txt" or the name of your choice.

AY211955.1 9267

AY211954.1 165202

AY211953.1 9319

AY365046.1 9598

MF945608.1 9606

AY211956.1 9321

AF159258.1 9615

Notice that both files should be plain text files not rich formatted text.

4 Download the tarball file "taxdb.tar.gz" that contains the BLAST taxonomy data files from the NCBI BLAST database FTP server https://ftp.ncbi.nlm.nih.gov/blast/db/ and extract the files in the same newly created database directory as follows:

$ wget https://ftp.ncbi.nlm.nih.gov/blast/db/taxdb.tar.gz

$ tar -zxvf taxdb.tar.gz

When you list the content of "myblastdb" directory with "ls -l", the following files will be displayed (Figure 8.58).

The taxonomy data files extracted from the tarball are "taxdb.btd" and "taxdb.bti". Both steps 2 and 3 are optional but essential if you need to use the "-taxid" flag on "makeblastdb" to associate all sequences with taxonomy identifiers.

5 Use the BLAST executable "makeblastdb" to create the custom BLAST database.

$ makeblastdb -in blast_dna_db.fasta -parse_seqids -blastdb_version 5 -taxid_map blast_tax_id.txt -title "Custom DNA database" -dbtype nucl

Figure 8.59 shows that the custom BLAST database has been created.

The options; "-blastdb_version" to construct a version number, "-taxid_map" to associate each sequence with a taxonomic node, and "-parse_seqids" as a flag for the sequence identifier.

If an error occurs on a computer with Windows, it is probable that makeblastdb is trying to allocate a very large virtual memory. To solve this problem, you may need to create an environment variable "BLASTDB_LMDB_MAP_SIZE" with the value "1000000" and then close and re-open the Command Prompt.

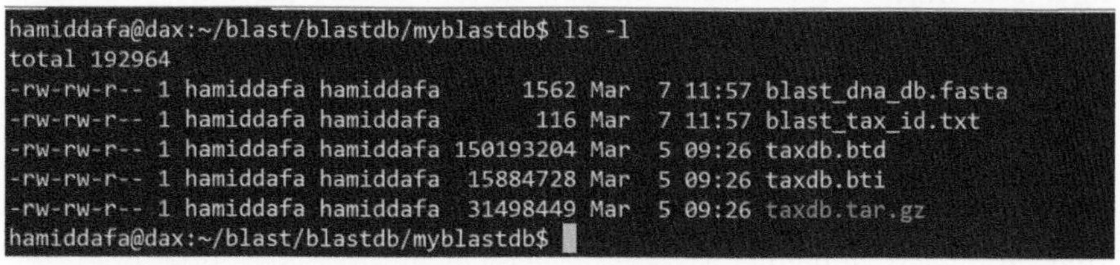

FIGURE 8.58 The content of the directory of the custom BLAST database.

```
hamiddafa@dax:~/blast/blastdb/myblastdb$ makeblastdb -in blast_dna_db.fasta -parse_seqids -blastdb_version 5 -taxid
_map blast_tax_id.txt -title "Custom DNA database" -dbtype nucl


Building a new DB, current time: 03/07/2021 13:06:29
New DB name:   /home/hamiddafa/blast/blastdb/myblastdb/blast_dna_db.fasta
New DB title:  Custom DNA database
Sequence type: Nucleotide
Keep MBits: T
Maximum file size: 1000000000B
Adding sequences from FASTA; added 7 sequences in 0.0030241 seconds.
```

FIGURE 8.59 The process of making a custom BLAST database.

```
hamiddafa@dax:~/blast/blastdb/myblastdb$ ls -ls
total 193040
     4 -rw-rw-r-- 1 hamiddafa hamiddafa      1562 Mar  7 11:57 blast_dna_db.fasta
    32 -rw-rw-r-- 1 hamiddafa hamiddafa     32768 Mar  7 13:06 blast_dna_db.fasta.ndb
     4 -rw-rw-r-- 1 hamiddafa hamiddafa       414 Mar  7 13:06 blast_dna_db.fasta.nhr
     4 -rw-rw-r-- 1 hamiddafa hamiddafa       200 Mar  7 13:06 blast_dna_db.fasta.nin
     4 -rw-rw-r-- 1 hamiddafa hamiddafa        60 Mar  7 13:06 blast_dna_db.fasta.nog
     4 -rw-rw-r-- 1 hamiddafa hamiddafa       141 Mar  7 13:06 blast_dna_db.fasta.nos
     4 -rw-rw-r-- 1 hamiddafa hamiddafa        92 Mar  7 13:06 blast_dna_db.fasta.not
     4 -rw-rw-r-- 1 hamiddafa hamiddafa       372 Mar  7 13:06 blast_dna_db.fasta.nsq
    16 -rw-rw-r-- 1 hamiddafa hamiddafa     16384 Mar  7 13:06 blast_dna_db.fasta.ntf
     4 -rw-rw-r-- 1 hamiddafa hamiddafa        56 Mar  7 13:06 blast_dna_db.fasta.nto
     4 -rw-rw-r-- 1 hamiddafa hamiddafa       116 Mar  7 11:57 blast_tax_id.txt
146676 -rw-rw-r-- 1 hamiddafa hamiddafa 150193204 Mar  5 09:26 taxdb.btd
 15516 -rw-rw-r-- 1 hamiddafa hamiddafa  15884728 Mar  5 09:26 taxdb.bti
 30764 -rw-rw-r-- 1 hamiddafa hamiddafa  31498449 Mar  5 09:26 taxdb.tar.gz
hamiddafa@dax:~/blast/blastdb/myblastdb$ 
```

FIGURE 8.60 The files of the custom BLAST database.

```
hamiddafa@dax:~$ blastdbcmd -db $BLASTDB/myblastdb/blast_dna_db.fasta -info
Database: Custom DNA database
        7 sequences; 1,470 total bases

Date: Mar 7, 2021  1:06 PM      Longest sequence: 210 bases

BLASTDB Version: 5

Volumes:
        /home/hamiddafa/blast/blastdb/myblastdb/blast_dna_db.fasta
hamiddafa@dax:~$ 
```

FIGURE 8.61 Checking the custom BLAST database.

Figure 8.60 shows the files of the custom BLAST database.

Now you can check the custom BLAST database you have just created using the following command and the results are shown in Figure 8.61:

```
$ blastdbcmd -db $BLASTDB/myblastdb/blast_dna_db.fasta -info
```

For performing a local BLAST search using the new custom BLAST database, you can use the following FASTA sequence as an example query sequence. Save the sequence in a file named "test2.fasta" in your current directory:

```
>test2
AGAAAAGGCTGAACTCAATAAAAGCAAACAGCCTGGCTTAGCAAAAAACCAGAG
```

```
BLASTN 2.11.0+

Reference: Zheng Zhang, Scott Schwartz, Lukas Wagner, and Webb
Miller (2000), "A greedy algorithm for aligning DNA sequences", J
Comput Biol 2000; 7(1-2):203-14.
Database: Custom DNA database
           7 sequences; 1,470 total letters
Query= test2
Length=54
                                                                   Score     E
Sequences producing significant alignments:                       (Bits)  Value
AY211956.1                                                         80.5    4e-20
AY211953.1                                                         80.5    4e-20
AY211954.1                                                         80.5    4e-20
MF945608.1                                                         62.1    1e-14

>AY211956.1
Length=210

 Score = 80.5 bits (43),  Expect = 4e-20
 Identities = 51/54 (94%), Gaps = 3/54 (6%)
 Strand=Plus/Plus

Query  1   AGAAAAGGCTGAACTC---AATAAAAGCAAACAGCCTGGCTTAGCAAAAAACCA  51
           ||||||||||||||||   |||||||||||||||||||||||||||||||||||
Sbjct  78  AGAAAAGGCTGAACTCTGTAATAAAAGCAAACAGCCTGGCTTAGCAAAAAACCA  131
```

FIGURE 8.62 BLAST results using custom BLAST database.

Use the following "blastn" program to search for aligned sequences using the query sequence saved in the "test2.fasta" file against the custom BLAST database "blast_db.fasta"

```
$ blastn -query test2.fasta -db $BLASTDB/myblastdb/blast_dna_db.fasta -out output2.txt
```

The results are saved into "output2.txt". Open that file with a text editor to display the results as shown in Figure 8.62.

Because you mapped the sequence identifiers to the taxonomy identifiers and downloaded the taxonomy data files, you can use the "-taxids" option with "blastn" to limit the BLAST search to the human (tax id is 9606) sequences only as follows.

```
$ blastn -query test2.fasta -db $BLASTDB/myblastdb/blast_dna_db.fasta -taxids 9606 -out output2.
txt
```

The Use of the Local BLAST

Table 8.5 above shows the list of BLAST executables that can be used for different BLAST searches and tasks. You have already learned when to use most of these executables in the BLAST search. However, each of these executable is provided with a "-help" argument that will display all possible arguments and their use.

To learn about how to use any of these executables, you can display the usages and descriptions of any BLAST executable using the following format:

```
$ executable -h
```

Where "executable" is any one of the BLAST executables shown in Figure 8.51. For example, to learn about "blastp" usage, run the following"

```
$ blastp -h
```

Also, to learn about the usage, description, and arguments of any of the BLAST executables, you can use the following format:

$ executable -help

For example, to learn about arguments of "blastp", run the following"

$ blastp -help

REFERENCES

1. Altschul, S.F., et al., *Basic local alignment search tool.* J Mol Biol, 1990. **215**(3): pp. 403–410.
2. Woese, C.R. and G.E. Fox, *Phylogenetic structure of the prokaryotic domain: the primary kingdoms.* Proc Natl Acad Sci USA, 1977. **74**(11): pp. 5088–5090.
3. Garrity, G.M., *A New Genomics-Driven Taxonomy of Bacteria and Archaea: Are We There Yet?* J Clin Microbiol, 2016. **54**(8): pp. 1956–1963.
4. Tao, T. *Standalone BLAST Setup for Windows PC.* BLAST® Help [cited 2021]. www.ncbi.nlm.nih.gov/books/NBK52637/. 2010.

Index

Symbols

16S ribosomal RNA, 364, 412
16S rRNA, 17, 411, 425, 427
18S rRNA, 17, 40, 412, 425–427
100 Genome Browser, 196, 198
1000 Genomes project, 137, 146, 197
1000Genomes, 140, 144
28S rRNA, 17, 40, 412

A

A Golden Path, 168. See also AGP
Ab initio, 23, 126
Accession number, 78, 81
Advanced Search Builder, 80–81, 84, 88
AGP, 72–73, 168–169
ALFA, 136–137, 139–140, 144, 262
Algae, 2, 90, 247
Allele, 9, 134–137, 195–196
Allele frequency, 104, 135–137, 139, 144, 148
Alpha helix, 27–28
Alternative allele, 144. See also Allele
Alternative splicing, 20, 100–101, 106, 383, 417
Alzheimer, 210–211
Amazon, 65
Anticodon, 17, 24
API key, 80, 265–267, 294–295
Arabidopsis thaliana, 10
Assembly, 69, 86, 167–175, 177–180
Assertion, 136, 146, 149, 151, 154
ATM, 88, 249–252
Autism, 148–149, 152–153, 263
Automatic explosion feature, 256
Automatic Prokaryotic, 126
Automatic Term Mapping, 88. See also ATM

B

Bacteriophage, 1, 44, 90
BAM, 65–67, 69–70
Beta sheet, 28
Binary fission, 5
Bioanalyzer, 40
Biocollections, 78, 86, 104–107, 261, 269
Biomaterial, 105

BioProject, 129–133
BioPython, 343, 355–361
BioSample, 129–135
BioSystems, 209–213
BLAST, 399–405, 407–411
BLASTn, 408–411
BLASTp, 408–410
BlastRules, 123
BLASTx, 408–410
BLOck Substitution Matrices, 388. See also BLOSUM
BLOSUM, 388, 392–394, 399, 401
Breadth, 66–67
Burst size, 35
BUSCO, 175, 263

C

Canonical miRNA, 18
Carcinoma, 43, 143, 167, 259
Carsonella, 1
CDART, 115, 121, 262
CDD, 114–119
CDS, 98–99
Cell division, 4–6, 15
  Meiosis, 4, 35
  mitosis, 4–5
chimpanzee, 3, 129, 416–417, 427
Chloroplast, 2, 90, 96, 109, 141, 309
Chromatin, 2, 16, 51, 130
Chromosome, 2–6, 14–15, 69, 71–73, 168–169
  Autosomes, 2–3
  Centromere, 3, 73
  Diploid, 2, 5, 168, 172
  Haploid, 2, 4–5, 168, 172
  Histone, 3, 130
  telomeres, 3, 14–15
Circular chromosome, 2, 176
ClinVar, 150–155
ClustalW, 205, 208
Cn3D, 116–118
COBALT, 109, 430–431, 433
Coding strand, 20. See also Sense strand
Codon, 13, 15, 17, 22–24, 33
Complementary DNA, 41. See also cDNA
Consensus sequence, 11–13, 69–70, 168, 404

Conserved Domain, 106–107, 109, 114–121
Contig, 66–69, 72–73
Contiguous, 67, 69
control elements., 11
Convergent evolution, 109, 386, 405
Core promoter, 11, 13, 20, 36
Coulson, 44, 74
Coverage, 66–67
Craig Venter, 50, 74
CRISPR, 126
Culture collection, 104–105, 261, 411
Cygwin, 289–295
Cytoplasm, 2, 17–18

D

Data Bank of Japan, 1, 77, 89
dbGaP, 213–220
dbGaP repository key, 215–216, 225, 233–235
dbSNP, 134–147
dbVar, 146–150
DDBJ, 77, 89, 93
Degeneracy of codons, 23
Demultiplexing, 65
Dendrogram, 176
Deoxyribonucleic acid, 1, 7
Dicer, 18
Dideoxynucleotide triphosphates, 47
Distance matrices, 128
Distance tree, 207, 407
Disulfide bridge, 26
DNA binding domain, 20, 115, 120, 124
DNA duplication, 146
Docker, 126, 128, 408
Dot matrix, 129
Driver mutation, 138
Drosha, 18
Dumper, 236, 241
Dynamic programming, 394, 396–397, 399

E

E-utilities, 266–288, 344–382
E-value, 402
EcitMatch, 265, 267, 288, 359
Ecological study, 205

Ecoset, 205
EDirect, 289–295
Egg, 4–5
Electropherogram, 50
ELISA, 41, 73
Embryogenesis, 4, 35
Enhancer, 11–12
Epigenomics, 130, 174, 187, 192
Escherichia coli, 10, 176–177, 309, 432
EST, 90, 92
Eukaryote, 2, 6, 9, 14, 16–18
    Archaea, 2, 10, 90, 411–412, 428, 432
Eukaryotic Genome Annotation
        Pipeline, 93
ExAC, 144, 263
Exon, 10, 13–14, 17–18, 20–21
Expect value, 118, 402. See also E-value
Expressed Sequence Tags, 92.
        See also EST
Extension gap penalty, 394

F

Fanconi anemia, 103
FASTA format, 51
FASTQ, 61, 63–67
Fastqc, 65, 74
Feature table, 90–91
Fertilization, 4–5, 35
FPKM, 102
Francis Crick, 7
Frederick Sanger, 44
Frequency Aggregator, 136, 139.
        See also ALFA
Fungi, 109, 411–412

G

Gametes, 4
Gap, 384–385, 393–397
Gap penalty, 393–394, 396, 399, 402
GDV, 101, 178–180, 182–183
GenBank, 77–78, 86, 89–98
Gene, 9–11, 13–24
    cDNA, 14–15, 35, 41–42
    Reverse transcriptase, 14, 35, 41, 58
    Reverse transcription, 14–15, 35,
        41–42, 57–58
    Ribonucleic acid, 1, 15, 74
    Sense strand, 20
    Splicing, 14, 20–22, 36
    Transcription, 11–16, 18, 20–21, 23
    Translation, 1, 9, 17–18, 21–24, 33–34
Gene expression, 11, 18–19, 52, 102–104
Gene feature, 99, 125, 137
Gene Ontology, 104, 209. See also GO
GeneID, 99–100, 175, 210
GeneRIF, 99, 103
Genetic code, 8, 13, 23, 34, 36, 248,
        410, 431

GenInfo, 78
Genome, 1–2, 6, 8–11, 14–15, 17–19
    Adenine, 1, 7–9
    Annotation, 9, 71–72
    Base pairing, 8, 24, 53
    Central dogma of molecular
        biology, 1, 56
    Cytosine, 7–9
    Deoxyribose, 7, 15–16, 35–36
    Glycosidic bond, 7
    Guanine, 7–9
    Hydrogen bond, 8, 17, 25, 27–29,
        42–43
    Nitrogenous base, 7–8
    Nucleobase, 1, 44
    Phosphate group, 1, 7, 45–46
    Phosphodiester bond, 7, 47
    Purine, 7, 12, 45
    Pyrimidine, 7–8, 12
    Thymine, 1, 7–9, 11, 16
Genome Annotation Pipeline, 93
Genome Data Viewer, 98, 101, 173, 176,
        178–181
Genome Survey Sequences, 92.
        See also GSS
Genome Workbench, 89, 169–170
GenPept, 78, 86, 107, 109, 114, 324
GEO2R, 158–160
GFF, 128, 175
GFF3 format, 128
Gilbert, 44–45, 47, 74
Global Minor Allele Frequency, 139.
        See also GMAF
Global sequence alignment, 384, 394, 416
GMAF, 137, 139
GnomAD, 144, 146, 204
GO, 104, 209
Google, 65, 408
GRCh 37, 139, 168, 183, 194
GRCh 38, 139, 153, 180, 183, 187,
        189–190, 201, 425
GSC, 132
GSS, 90, 92–93
GTR, 77–78, 86, 153, 269

H

Hairpin loop, 17
Herbaria, 104, 411
Herbarium, 104, 261
Heterozygous, 9, 134, 136, 196
HGNC, 99–100, 153, 341
HGVS, 139–142, 144–145, 150–152,
        154–155, 183, 190, 263
Hidden Markov Model, 123, 126, 262
Hidden Markov Model, 123.
        See also HMM
HIV- 1, 103
HMM, 110, 123–126, 262
Homolog, 99, 128

Homology, 128, 383–384
Homozygous, 9, 134, 196
Housekeeping gene, 11, 19, 36
HSP, 401–402
HTG, 73, 90, 411–412
HTSeq, 102, 261

I

IGV, 242–243
INSDSeq, 324–326
International Nucleotide Sequence
        Database Collaboration (INSDC), 1,
        77, 89, 220, 324
Introns, 10, 13–14, 17–18
Inversion, 146
iProClass, 123, 262

J

James Watson, 7
Japanese Institute of Genetics, 1

K

Kary Mullis, 41
KEGG, 209–213, 264

L

L50, 171–173
Levenshtein distance, 385, 389
Levinthal's paradox, 27, 36
Library preparation, 52–53
    Adaptors, 23, 53–56
    Barcode, 58, 205
    End repair, 52–53
    Enrichment, 55–57
    Fragmentation, 52, 54, 61
    Index sequence, 54, 59
    Ligation, 52–54, 58–59
    Nextera, 52, 54–56, 58
    Tagmentation, 54–55
    Transposase, 54
    Ultrasonication, 52
Ligand binding domain, 20, 31–32,
        115–117
Linear chromosome, 2, 15
LinkOuts, 104, 248, 281
Linnaean system of classification, 2
Local sequence alignment, 384, 399

M

MAF, 137, 139–140
Mapper, 66, 69
Maxam, 44–45, 47, 74
Maxam- Gilbert, 45, 47
Maxam-Gilbert Sequencing, 45
Medical subject headings, 88

Messenger RNA, 10, 13–14, 18, 23
Metagenome, 130, 132–133, 262, 431
Microarray, 40, 155–158
Microbiome, 220
MicroRNA, 9, 17
Microsoft Azure, 65
Minor Allele Frequency, 137.
    See also MAF
MiRNA, 16–18, 214
Mitochondria, 2, 4, 109, 168
Mitochondrial DNA, 2, 4, 39, 429
Mitochondrion, 90, 96, 309, 430
Monera, 2
Morbid Map, 198, 201–202
Motif, 13, 123
Multiple sequence alignment, 128–129,
    190, 208–209
MUSCLE, 187, 205, 208, 407
Muset, 205
mutation, 9, 18, 23, 33
    Deletion, 3, 9, 13, 33
    Frame shift, 13, 135, 138
    Germline mutation, 33, 134
    INDEL, 134–135
    Insertion, 3, 9, 33
    Missense substitution, 33
    Nonsense substitution, 33
    Point mutation, 33, 134
    Somatic mutation, 33, 134
    substitution, 9, 33
Mutational study, 205–207
MyNCBI, 88, 130

N

N50, 171–173
Nanodrop, 40, 73
Nanopore, 52
NCBI History Server, 265–266
ncRNA, 89–90, 126, 308
Neandertals, 10
Neighborhood, 401
Neighborhood word, 401
Next-generation sequencing
    ASCII, 63–64
    Base caller, 62–63
    Base calling, 50, 52, 59, 61–62
    Binary Base Call, 63
    Bustard, 62
    Cluster generation, 59, 61
    De novo assembly, 60–61, 65,
        69–70
    Flow cell, 53–54, 59–61
    Metagenomics, 51
    Multiplexing, 54, 58–59
    Nanopore sequencing, 52
    Oligos, 52–53, 56, 218
    Sequencing-by-synthesis, 59
    SOLiD, 52, 102, 121
Non-coding DNA

Pseudogenes, 14–15, 36, 126, 176,
    203, 341
Repetitive sequences, 14
Retrotransposons, 14, 36
Short tandem, 14, 36, 134, 136
SINE, 14, 36, 416
Transposon, 14–15, 52, 54, 92
Nquire, 293, 310–311
Nuclear magnetic resonance, 30
Nucleotide Archive, 1
Nucleus, 2–4, 14, 16, 18

O

Open reading frame, 13, 22. See also ORF
ORF, 13, 22–24, 33
Ortholog, 100, 109–110, 384
Ova, 4

P

Pairwise sequence alignment, 383–405,
    430
PAM, 388–389
paralog, 109–110, 261, 384
PCR, 19, 39–44
    DNA polymerase, 41–42, 44, 49,
        53, 73–74
    Primer, 42–44, 97–98, 185–187
    Taq Polymerase, 42–43
PDB, 30–31
Peptide bond, 24–27
Percent identity, 385–386
Pfam, 122–123
PGAP, 123, 125–128
Phred quality score, 51, 62–63, 68–69
Phylogenetic study, 205–208
phylogenetic tree, 112, 118, 208
Phylogeny, 17, 128
Physet, 205
PIR, 77, 107–108, 122, 262, 308
Plasmid, 2, 5
Point Accepted Mutation, 388. See also
    PAM
Pollen, 4
Poly A, 57, 141
Polymerase chain reaction, 41. See also
    PCR
Polymorphism, 33, 70, 75, 92, 134,
    137, 262
Populational study, 206
Position-specific scoring matrix, 402.
    See also PSSM
Pribnow box, 12
Prokaryote, 2, 6, 14, 16, 18
Prokaryotic Genome Annotation
    Pipeline, 93, 125–126, 261–262
ProRule, 123, 262
PROSITE, 123, 262
Protein Data Bank, 30. See also PDB

Protein Information Resource, 107–108,
    122, 262
Protein Research Foundation, 107
Protista, 2
Protozoans, 2, 109, 269
PSSM, 115–116, 123, 402–404, 439
PubChem, 86, 104
PyMol, 31–32

R

Rare variant, 72, 137
Ray Wu, 44, 74
Reading frames, 22–23, 408
Reference allele, 144
RefSNP, 136, 145
Regular expression, 183–185, 263,
    329–331, 333
Regulatory region, 10–11, 15
Rentrez, 343–347, 353, 355, 382
Ribonuclease, 18, 40
Ribonucleic acid, 1, 15
Ribose, 15–16, 24, 36
Ribosomal RNA gene, 17, 36, 364
Ribosome, 15–18, 21, 23–24, 33, 36
RNA integrity, 40, 73
RNA polymerase, 11, 13, 18, 20, 90
RNAi, 18
RPKM, 102–103
rRNA gene, 17, 36, 126, 411–412,
    425, 427

S

Sanger method, 47–48, 50–51
Scaffold, 66–69, 72–73, 94, 167–169,
    171–173
SCOP, 123, 262
Seed, 105, 122–123, 401
Sequence-Tagged Sites, 92
short reads, 64, 66–67, 69–70, 156, 168
shotgun sequencing, 44, 431
Similarity Score, 121, 128, 284, 385,
    391
Single nucleotide polymorphism, 33
SMART, 57–58, 119
Smith-Waterman algorithm, 399
Somatic cell, 2–3, 11, 19, 33, 134, 151
SPARCLE, 115, 123–124, 126, 269
SPDI, 139, 152–155, 263
Specimen voucher, 104–105
Sperm, 4–5
SRA Run Selector, 224–225, 232–234,
    236–237, 241
SRA toolkit, 224–231
Substitution Matrices, 385–386, 388,
    392–393, 405
Suppressor, 11, 96
Svedberg coefficient, 17
SwissProt, 107–108, 110, 113, 308, 413

T

T- COFFEE, 205, 208
Tandem, 14, 36, 40, 73, 134, 136, 146
TATA box, 11–13
taxon, 86–87, 246–248, 315
tBLASTn, 408–410, 413–414, 416, 439
tBLASTx, 408–410, 413–414, 416, 439
Telomerase, 15
Template strand, 20
The Human Genome Project, 9, 150
TopMed, 144, 263
Traceback, 395, 397, 399
Track Hub, 183, 192–193
Track Hubs Registry, 192
Transcription factor, 11, 20, 209
Transcriptome, 18, 20, 36
Transfer RNA, 9, 16–17
Translocation, 3, 18, 146
translocation, 3, 18, 146
tRNA, 9–10, 15–18, 23–24
TRNP1, 207–208

U

UCSC Genome Browser, 192
Untranslated regions, 18. See also
    UTR
Uracil, 16, 20, 39
UTR, 18, 22, 138, 141

V

Van der Waals interaction, 25
Variation Viewer, 139–141, 145–147
VCF, 70–72, 136, 190–192
Virus, 14, 34–35, 37
    Baltimore classification system, 34
    Capsid, 34–35
    Clathrin, 34
    Coronavirus, 35, 113, 173–174, 177,
        260–261
    dsDNA, 34, 45
    Endocytosis, 34
    Spike protein, 35, 113, 261
    ssDNA, 34, 45–48
    ssRNA, 34–35
    virion, 34–35, 73
VMD, 31

W

Whole-exome sequencing, 51
Word size, 401, 408, 415

X

X-ray crystallography, 30

Y

YAML, 127–128
Yeast, 44, 92

Z

Zygote, 4–5

Printed and bound by CPI Group (UK) Ltd, Croydon, CR0 4YY

17/10/2024

01775666-0009